ALSO BY BENN STEIL

The Marshall Plan: Dawn of the Cold War

*The Battle of Bretton Woods: John Maynard Keynes, Harry Dexter White,
and the Making of a New World Order*

THE WORLD THAT WASN'T

HENRY WALLACE AND THE FATE
OF THE AMERICAN CENTURY

BENN STEIL

AVID READER PRESS

New York   London   Toronto   Sydney   New Delhi

A Council on Foreign Relations Book

AVID READER PRESS
An Imprint of Simon & Schuster, Inc.
1230 Avenue of the Americas
New York, NY 10020

First Avid Reader Press hardcover edition January 2024

AVID READER PRESS and colophon are trademarks of Simon & Schuster, Inc.

Simon & Schuster: Celebrating 100 Years of Publishing Since 1924

For information about special discounts for bulk purchases, please contact Simon & Schuster Special Sales at 1-866-506-1949 or business@simonandschuster.com.

The Simon & Schuster Speakers Bureau can bring authors to your live event. For more information or to book an event, contact the Simon & Schuster Speakers Bureau at 1-866-248-3049 or visit our website at www.simonspeakers.com.

Interior design by Wendy Blum

Manufactured in the United States of America

1   3   5   7   9   10   8   6   4   2

Library of Congress Cataloging-in-Publication Data
Names: Steil, Benn, author.
Title: The world that wasn't : Henry Wallace and the fate of the American century / Benn Steil.
Other titles: Henry Wallace and the fate of the American century
Description: First Avid Reader Press hardcover edition. | New York : Avid Reader Press, 2024. | Includes bibliographical references and index. |
Identifiers: LCCN 2023035161 (print) | LCCN 2023035162 (ebook) | ISBN 9781982127824 (hardcover) | ISBN 9781982127831 (paperback) | ISBN 9781982127848 (ebook)
Subjects: LCSH: Wallace, Henry A. (Henry Agard), 1888–1965. | Vice-Presidents—United States—Biography. | United States—Politics and government—1933–1945. | United States—Relations—Soviet Union. | Soviet Union—Relations—United States. | BISAC: HISTORY / United States / 20th Century | BIOGRAPHY & AUTOBIOGRAPHY / Political
Classification: LCC E748.W23 S745 2024 (print) | LCC E748.W23 (ebook) |
DDC 973.917092 [B]—dc23/eng/20230823
LC record available at https://lccn.loc.gov/2023035161
LC ebook record available at https://lccn.loc.gov/2023035162

ISBN 978-1-9821-2782-4
ISBN 978-1-9821-2784-8 (ebook)

To my loving parents, Linda and Bob,
and to my precious boys, Ethan and Owen.

"[W]ho having a practiced vision may not see that ignorance of the true bond between events, and false conceit of means whereby sequences may be compelled—like that falsity of eyesight which overlooks the gradations of distance, seeing that which is afar off as if it were within a step or a grasp—precipitates the mistaken soul on destruction?"

—George Eliot, *Daniel Deronda* (1876)

CONTENTS

THE WORLD
THAT WASN'T

One

WHY WALLACE?

"WE WANT WALLACE! WE WANT WALLACE! . . ."

Claude Pepper's heart was racing. This was it, the senator thought; now or never.

Desperate to get the chairman's attention, he climbed on a chair, waving his state's banner. He leaped up and down, yelling. But the din smothered his voice. Someone had killed his microphone.

"WE WANT WALLACE! WE WANT WALLACE! . . ."

From the podium, an alarmed Samuel Jackson avoided the senator's gaze.

There was only one chance now. Pepper needed to reach the convention stage.

He elbowed his way through the sea of chanting bodies. Delegates, reporters, and spectators turned to watch as he fought his way to the front.

If he could get there in time, he could nominate Henry Wallace—now, while the hall was his. The vice president would not only keep his post, but would become the frail president's heir apparent. The party bosses, for all their powers of backroom dealing, could not control a frenzied crowd.

"WE WANT WALLACE! WE WANT WALLACE! . . ."

Pepper reached the gate barring the path to the stage. He smiled at the guard, an old friend from the railway unions. The man smiled back, opening the latch.

Jackson turned to see Pepper dashing up the stairs.

This was not in the script. Shaken, he turned back to the crowd.

"Motion made, the convention adjourned," he announced. "All in favor of the motion, let me know by saying 'aye'!"

Pepper neared the top step; voices yelled back, "AYE!"

The gavel struck. *Bang!*

"Convention adjourned!" Jackson yelled. Voices came back, louder now: "NO, NO, NO! . . ."

The following night, July 21, 1944, it was all over. Harry Truman, "the Missouri Compromise," was elected on the second ballot.

He, and not Henry Wallace, would be FDR's running mate.

He, and not Henry Wallace, would become president of the United States.

The space between history and fiction, between what was and what wasn't, can be so small, yet loom so large. Jackson would later tell Pepper that he hated what he had done. But what if the senator had been quicker to the podium? The failed nomination of Henry Wallace remains one of history's fascinating what-ifs, perpetually reversed and rerun in works of imaginative speculation—in books, in films, and even in theater productions.[1]

Had Henry Wallace kept his place on the Democratic ticket in June 1944, he would have become president of the United States on April 12, 1945—the day Franklin Roosevelt died. With Henry Wallace in the White House, there would have been no Truman Doctrine. No Marshall Plan. No NATO. No West Germany. No policy of containment. All of these initiatives, foundational to what has been called "the American Century," Henry Wallace opposed.

According to the film director and screenwriter Oliver Stone, and activist-historian collaborator Peter Kuznick, a Wallace presidency would also have meant no Cold War.[2] This claim has captivated idealistic young people across America. It is, understandably, comforting and inspiring to hear that peace needs only a leader who believes in it.

Yet Stone's claim, given his media presence, has vexed pedigreed historians such as Yale's John Lewis Gaddis and Princeton's Sean Wilentz.[3] From what we today know of Soviet ambitions in the early postwar years, a Wallace presidency could only have resulted in a delayed Cold War—delayed, that is, until November 1948, at which time he would almost surely have been defeated in an election. Wallace himself doubted he could have swung Congress or "public opinion" in his favor. "[I]t is a very grave question whether I would have been [elected] with the tactics that I would have used in order to preserve the peace," he reflected in retirement. Most likely, he concluded, "I was done a very great favor when I was not named in '44."[4]

In any case, a delayed Cold War would have come at great cost to U.S. security and economic interests. A failure to resist and deter Joseph Stalin would likely have meant Soviet domination of northern Iran, eastern Turkey, the Turkish Straits, Hokkaido, the Korean Peninsula, Greece, and all of Germany. Stalin, contrary to Wallace's professions of belief, coveted these territories, and never valued peace for its own sake. As Churchill said in his famous "Iron Curtain" speech of March 5, 1944, Stalin did not desire war but "the fruits of war."[5] He valued the opportunities that a passive United States afforded him to expand his empire. And so to imagine that Oliver Stone's World That Wasn't is a better world than that which emerged under Harry Truman is to imagine that wider Russian dominion would somehow have afforded humanity more freedom, more prosperity, and more security.

From 1933 to 1949, Henry Wallace imagined his own World That Wasn't. It was a world in which a new sovereign spiritual paradise was to emerge in Central Asia, arrogating territory contested by four world powers. It was a world in which Siberia, traversed by Wallace for four weeks in 1944, was testament to Soviet economic, social, and artistic accomplishment, and not home to a vast prison-labor complex. It was a world in which Stalin, having no territorial ambitions in Europe or Asia, wished only to perfect "economic democracy" at home. It was a world in which Henry Wallace believed deeply and passionately—at least until he didn't. Much would change in 1950.

Besides being a compelling focal point for counterfactual history, Henry Wallace is a fascinating human being—one who has been incompletely, and often inaccurately, portrayed by his chroniclers. This failing owes both to ideological factors and a lack of access to critical historical documents.

Wallace's biographers have tended to see him as a well-meaning visionary—one who was occasionally led astray by an excess of exuberance and a dearth of vigilance.[6] Yet none of them made use of the remarkable trove of Russian archival material that was, at least until the invasion of Ukraine in February 2022, accessible to the curious and persistent, nor of revealing FBI surveillance transcripts, relevant to many important episodes in Wallace's career. These include his appointment of Nicholas Roerich, a White Russian mystic with a revolutionary political agenda, to lead an expedition to Central Asia in 1934–35; his weeks-long trek through an NKVD-constructed Potemkin continent in Siberia in spring 1944; his rash freelance diplomacy with Chinese leader Chiang Kai-shek, uncovered by a Soviet official, in the week which followed; his manipulation by Soviet assets within the Commerce Department in 1945–1946; and his back-channel collusion with Stalin to undermine official U.S. foreign policy in the presidential election of 1948.

These episodes show Wallace as not just naïve, but at times reckless and lacking in candor. No doubt, he believed that what he said and did, when he said and did it, were in the best interests of his country and humanity at large. But it is notable that within a year of being trounced as a presidential candidate in 1948, he began a dramatic revision of his views of the Soviet Union and Communist influence within the Commerce Department and the Progressive Party he led. This revision would be ignored or glossed over by acolytes, such as Stone and Kuznik, leaving an incomplete and distorted portrait of the man and his evolution.

Henry Wallace was a most unlikely politician, and could almost certainly never have attained elective office other than as FDR's running mate. He had distinct intellectual and personality traits which we today associate with Asperger's syndrome[7]—a condition first described by the Austrian physician Hans Asperger in 1944, the year in which the Iowan lost his job as vice president.

Wallace was a highly intelligent man, exhibiting great focus and persistence, an aptitude for recognizing hidden physical and numerical patterns, and superior attention to detail—at least when it came to inanimate objects, such as corn, or Lend-Lease matériel in Russia. Like those typically diagnosed with Asperger's, however, he also had great difficulty with social interactions, which tired or pained him, and he frequently failed to recognize even elementary cues as to people's motivations and agendas.

Wallace loved humankind, but was mostly vexed or bored by humans—excepting those rare ones who showed insight into matters scientific or spiritual. A relentless empiricist with natural phenomena, such as plants or weather, he was, when it came to political affairs, remarkably credulous and dismissive of facts and evidence. He preached the supremacy of "human rights over property rights,"[8] yet excused the absence of human rights in Russia as an unavoidable cost of agricultural and industrial progress. He inspired loyalty among followers, yet could be vindictive toward subordinates or confidants whose actions brought him embarrassment. He had a messianic streak which blinded him to failings and contradictions in his logic. He bore criticism as the biblical burden of righteousness, rarely questioning the plausibility or ethics of his judgments. He joined, and quit, three political parties, leaving supporters bitter and disillusioned.

Still, this most unpromising of political figures came within a whisker of becoming FDR's successor at a critical crossroads in twentieth-century geopolitics. And even if the Cold War had only been delayed by a Wallace presidency, postwar history would no doubt have been very different because of it.

Two

OF MAIZE, MATH, AND MYSTICISM

Of the boy's Christian name, there was never a doubt. It was to be Henry. His father was a Henry. His father's father was a Henry. Such was the family tradition, and the boy would carry it on with his own first son.

His mother having been christened Mary Brodhead, however, the boy's full name should, by custom, have been Henry Brodhead Wallace. Yet whereas Calvinist Mary had due regard for custom, such regard was not uncritical, and Brodhead was simply not good enough for her Henry.

Mary was, in spirit, not a Brodhead, but an Agard—the Agards being the superior clan. Among her earliest American forebears was one Arthur Agard, believed to have been knighted "Sir Arthur" back in England. A later Agard, Noah, had fought in the Revolution under General Washington. No such distinctions attached to the Brodheads. And so Mary's superior son was to be an Agard: Henry Agard Wallace.

Henry, or "Agard" or "H.A.," as he would often be called, to distinguish him from his father and grandfather, was born in a modest frame house about five miles outside the village of Orient, Iowa[1]—sixty-four miles southwest of the state capital, Des Moines. The year was 1888. A quarter century earlier, the young American nation had been convulsed in war with itself. A quarter century later, it would, in defiance of George Washington's legendary admonition, be violently entangled on the European continent—a continent from which America could no longer remain isolated. The great industrial age advances in technology had shrunk the world.

Eighteen eighty-eight was the year in which the American inventor William Seward Burroughs patented his remarkable new adding machine, the year in which George Eastman patented his "roll-film camera," the year in which two-and-a-half-pound Edith Eleanor McLean became the first infant successfully nursed to self-sufficiency in an incubator machine. It was the year in which Nikola Tesla patented his revolutionary induction motor, the year in which Elisha Gray patented his telautograph (a precursor to the fax machine), the year in which Samuel J. Mixter patented his charger for magazine firearms.[2] It was also the year in which the National Geographic Society, an institution dedicated to the diffusion of knowledge from around the globe, was born in Washington, D.C. It was, in short, a time midway between the existential struggles of an insular pioneer America and the far-flung exertions of a rapidly maturing America, hesitantly flexing its new-found technological, industrial, and military muscle.

Little Henry was born on the seventh day of October. October was a beautiful month in Iowa—*Iowa* meaning "The Beautiful Land" in the language of the native tribes.[3] From the middle of August until early November, the state was typically blessed with a long "fall" season of near-continuous mild, bright, clear, sunny days, with flowers growing on the wide, rolling prairies, surrounded by lush forests; forests filled with oak and maple, elm and linden, alder and aspen, interspersed with blue brooks flowing over pebbled earth. The low grounds of these fertile lands were well suited to the growing of flint corn, known to the European settlers as "Indian corn." Their tall, tasseled, tightly spaced stalks would soar from the deep, rich soil, their tops undulating in the light, dry wind.[4] Born during the harvest, Henry would cultivate a long, discerning, and prosperous fascination with corn, his state's most sacred crop.

The Wallaces had immigrated from Scotland and Ireland three generations back, settling in western Pennsylvania. In 1854, John Wallace's firstborn son, Henry (of course), now eighteen, broke with family tradition and renounced farming, adopting what his mother knew to be the only respectable alternative—preaching.[5] "Uncle Henry," as he was later to be known, became a Presbyterian minister, working as a chaplain to Northern troops during the Civil War.

It was in 1877, eleven years before the Henry of our narrative was born, that the tall, bearded, cigar-smoking Uncle Henry, now forty and suffering from tuberculosis, ecclesiastical angst, and chronically stretched finances, decided to move his wife and five children to Iowa, where he returned to the family roots in farming. This move proved to be salubrious—for his health, for his finances, and for the family legacy. He bought up several productive farms, and became the editor and part-owner of a reputable farm journal. He quickly grasped that rural prosperity, in the America of the late nineteenth century, was bound up with national politics—the politics of tariffs, of trade, of monetary policy; of regulating freight rates and soil conservation—and became a leading voice on such matters. He would in 1895, at age fifty-nine, found his own journal, *Wallaces' Farmer* (motto: "Good farming . . . Clear Thinking . . . Right Living"), which would become one of the nation's most authoritative periodicals on matters agricultural—as well as the religious and political viewpoints that ought to attach to them. Now himself a well-regarded national figure, resembling in appearance a prophet of the Old Testament, Uncle Henry was reputedly twice offered, and twice declined, the federal government's new cabinet post of secretary of agriculture.

Uncle Henry's son, our young Henry's father—Henry Cantwell Wallace, known as "Harry" to mitigate the inevitable confusion—lacked the patriarch's charisma and creative intellect, but proved a capable, hardworking steward of the family enterprise. Born in 1866, Harry would later run the Wallace farms while teaching dairying at Iowa State College in Ames, ultimately taking over *Wallaces' Farmer* on Uncle Henry's passing in 1916. He would shepherd it into a highly profitable national paper of record. With the tremendous growth in demand for farm produce during World War I, it earned the nickname "Wallace's Gold Mine." Harry, like his father, would become a leader among the Midwestern farmers against the sundry monopolists who afflicted them. For seventeen years, Harry was secretary of the Corn Belt Meat Producers' Association, which waged incessant war with the railroads and the Chicago meatpackers. Such battles were, for the Wallaces, God's work, as well as sound business. Solid, pious Republicans, they opposed irresponsible populists and inflationists, such as the perennial Democratic presidential candidate William Jennings Bryan, as fiercely as they opposed the rail and packing trusts who contended for the soul of their own party.

Unlike his father, Harry would heed the call of political office—serving as secretary of agriculture under Presidents Warren Harding and Calvin Coolidge, from 1921 until his untimely death, at age fifty-eight, in 1924. His tenure was marked by bitter rivalry with fellow Iowan Herbert Hoover, the powerful secretary of commerce whose support for industry, particularly in the form of high industrial tariffs, which limited Europe's ability to earn dollars with which to buy farm goods, exacerbated the plight of farmers reeling from the loss of wartime markets. Europe could not import U.S. farm products without dollars from manufacturing exports. Harry's backing for congressional efforts to boost domestic agricultural prices, through the government purchase and dumping abroad of surplus product, was to no avail. Coolidge, in 1927 and again in 1928, vetoed legislation to effect the scheme, arguing that it would exacerbate overproduction and penalize dairy farmers, who would pay more for grain.[6] Harry's failed struggle for "farm relief" would precipitate the family's permanent break with the Republican Party.

Harry's son, our young Henry, shared with his industrious father, and father's father, a devotion to faith and farming, though he identified more with the latter's idealism than with the former's pragmatism. "My father," Henry would later say, "was a curious combination of worldly impulses and a strict sense of duty. He loved high living; he had an Irish heart but a Scottish conscience."[7] Henry silently favored grandfather's more devout holistic Scottishness. But he did not emulate him; he could not. He lacked the anchor of Uncle Henry's clear, simple, unchanging humanist convictions. He lacked, as well, the personal magnetism that drew in followers. He loved, above all else, raw, unsentimental ideas, and found plants far more amenable to his direct and unforgiving methods of testing, applying, and expressing them than did people.

Henry grew up with two younger brothers and three younger sisters, as well as local cousins. Though surrounded by free-range adolescents, this shy, serious boy took little interest in—indeed, he disdained—the normal irresponsibilities of youth, and was critical of others for succumbing to them. At age twelve, he was named his district's "champion plowboy." When not working on the farm, he loved outings in the woods, and it mattered little to him whether he was alone or with humans. He preferred plants. He was fascinated by their differences. It was his mother, Mary, who first taught him how to crossbreed pansies, and he was instantly drawn to the process of creating new strains and charting the results.

By far the most influential friendship he forged in early childhood was with a brilliant young man who would go on to become one of his nation's most acclaimed agricultural scientists. Born into slavery in Missouri in c. 1864, George Washington Carver suffered decades of hardship and discrimination before becoming Iowa State's first Black student in 1891. Tall and slender, inquisitive and philosophical, Carver quickly became an accomplished botanist as well as a talented painter. While working on his master's degree, he also became the university's first Black faculty member. Harry Wallace, then a professor at the university, befriended the prodigy and introduced him to Henry—barely four years old at the time. Carver took the boy on long walks, teaching him the rudiments of plant breeding. Though Carver would leave Iowa to become the first director of agricultural research at Alabama's Tuskegee Institute in 1896, the friendship would mark Henry's life. Not only did Carver cultivate the boy's natural interest in plant science in a way that no one else could, but he infused him with the confidence to believe that he, Henry Wallace, could actually improve the knowledge and application of it.[8] When Henry would meet the great man again nearly forty years later, it would be as an accomplished plant geneticist in his own right—as well as the nation's eleventh secretary of agriculture.

But "in my early life," Wallace later reflected, "I thought completely in terms of seeds, plants, and farming. At that time, I had no thought of public life."[9] Indeed, even before he had entered high school, just after the turn of the new century, his life's passion had been Iowa's passion: corn. His beliefs about the crop, however—what distinguished the good from the bad—could not have differed more from those of the experts who dominated the local "corn shows." It was, for them, a given that the best corn was the best-*looking* corn. They prized the uniform yellow kernels, and took it for granted that such aesthetic regularity signaled superior quality, hardiness, and yield. To Henry, such thinking was lazy and idiotic. What, after all, did the chief consumers of corn—that is, hogs—care about how it looked? And why should beauty equate with resilience or abundance? At that point, Henry had no clear idea of what the best corn was, but he set out to determine the answers scientifically.

He made his first test planting in the spring of 1904. To get the right answers required an enormous amount of meticulous, laborious work on five acres of land—planning, sorting, breeding, planting, monitoring, harvesting, organizing, calculating—and mistakes at any stage could invalidate his findings. The part which thrilled Henry the most was the last—carrying out the complex set of calculations to compute the yield in bushels per acre. The revelations heightened his love for plants and mathematics: plants because they, unlike people, spoke only God's truth, and mathematics because it made this truth discernible.

In the end, his findings would forever change how corn was appraised and bred. Yields, he discovered, ranged widely—from thirty-three to seventy-nine bushels—and it was possible, through hybridization, to improve, and then replicate, the highest-yielding versions. He further showed that the ear of corn deemed the finest by the eye of the state's famed "corn evangelist," Professor Perry Greeley Holden, was among the lowest yielders, demonstrating that looks meant nothing.[10] Henry would spend many years refining his breeding technique. But even after his very first experiment, no agricultural shaman could ever again commit the sin of judging a corn by its color.

In high school, Henry Wallace was, predictably, an excellent student. He was, by his own later recollection, usually "competing with some very bright Jewish girl . . . to be the brightest [pupil] in the class."[11] Yet he was not what one would today adjudge well rounded. He did not sing in a choir, play in a band, or join a club. Having each day to walk two miles to school, and to milk a cow on his return, he had little time for extracurriculars. But neither did he have the inclination to conform or adapt to groups. Still, being restless and competitive, he embraced a somewhat manic dual-handed approximation of tennis—a game he had never seen played, but which he taught himself by reading a Spalding rule book.

In 1906, he entered the Iowa State College of Agricultural and Mechanical Arts in Ames. Its name, however suggestive of established authority, was at the time aspirational. Its ramshackle campus had yet to acquire even an auditorium or proper library.[12]

Now eighteen years old, Wallace had reached his full height of five feet, ten inches. He was a trim but farm-solid 150 pounds. His face was an elongated rectangle; his eyes a cool blue-gray; his auburn hair thick, its rightward ends resistant to reason. He smiled infrequently, shaved irregularly, dressed unmindfully. He was, classmates would recall, studious and intense. Though pleasant and approachable, he was averse to speech without informational or spiritual purpose. He did not smoke or drink. He did not swear. He disliked pursuits in which he could discern no prospect for self-improvement, such as telling jokes, playing golf, or reading fiction. He dutifully attended campus functions, bringing a date as obliged, but was more likely to show her the poultry barn than the night sky. When he imagined the future, it was one in which the ingestion of meals, so inefficient in its usage of time and resources, might be replaced by the swallowing of a single, cheap, nutrient-rich daily pill. He experimented with minimalist diets, such as strawberries and corn meal, or experimental cattle feed, for which his mother (and his body) often scolded him. His conversations, when not fixed on agronomy and victual science, tended naturally toward philosophy or religion.[13] His grandfather approved of these interests, though he must have fretted inwardly as they veered in ways increasingly un-Protestant.

By the time Henry Wallace had arrived at Ames, he had already become fascinated with the transcendentalist writings of the philosopher-essayist Ralph Waldo Emerson. Emerson believed that truth could be experienced intuitively, through nature itself. By way of Emerson, Wallace discovered the writings of namesake philosopher Ralph Waldo Trine. Trine held that the universe was "the result of the thought energies of God, the Infinite Spirit that is back of all," and preached the creative power of "positive thinking."[14] Something in Wallace must have connected the thought of Emerson and Trine with that of Carver, who had so influenced him as a child. Carver, like Emerson and Trine, believed that the spark of the divine was immanent in all living things, such as the plants and flowers he had helped the boy to distinguish and reverence.

Wallace never outgrew this early fascination with what was widely called spiritualism. To the contrary, it opened his mind to non-Western philosophies that were even less appreciated by those around him. Throughout his later time in Washington, he would confront the charge that he had become a credulous mystic, prone to being deceived by charlatans and cranks. He would, in fact, come to confess himself a sort of "practical mystic,"[15] a man in search of eternal truths which, whether gleaned through calculation or introspection, could inform the path to positive social, economic, and political change.

On the surface, it can appear difficult to reconcile the mystical Wallace with the empiricist one—the man who ran elaborate experiments and studied data for hidden patterns and causes. Scientists were then, as now, far less likely than the general populace to believe in a God or in other unknowable "truths."[16] But such reconciliation is possible if we understand religion and spirituality as Wallace came to do through the influence of men such as Carver, Emerson, and Trine.

Though Wallace was raised a Presbyterian, and routinely quoted scripture throughout his life, he nonetheless came to mock what he called "the wishy-washy goody-goodiness and the infantile irrelevancy" of Christian orthodoxy.[17] He felt it lacked practical relevance. His was an instrumental view of religion, not unlike his view of science. It was a way of knowing and a guide to acting when data were lacking and experimentation impossible. "It was a mistake," he would later say, "for scientific and common-sense people to shut the door to some of these things which they cannot understand."[18]

But by what criteria was a religion true? It is here that the thinking of William James, a neo-transcendentalist[19] psychologist and philosopher of religion, is not merely helpful, but necessary. Wallace would call James, whom he came to discover by way of Emerson, James' godfather, an enormous intellectual influence in his life.[20]

James was not interested in whether Jesus was the messiah, or whether the Jews were chosen. For James, a "true" belief was one that was useful to the believer. It was neither necessary nor useful to inquire as to whether a belief was true in the sense that it corresponded to some objective external reality, since that might be unknowable. It was necessary only to ask whether the belief had practical value for the believer here and now, which in turn depended on the use to which he or she put it. This conception of truth derived from the tenets of the pedigreed philosophical program of pragmatism.

Since much of what we require to make sense of the world is simply not available to us, it was, James argued, only rational to evaluate a belief based on whether it helped the believer to cope effectively.[21] Understanding "true" belief as being a property of the believer, and not something that could necessarily be shared by others, may not be commonplace. Yet for those like Wallace, who internalized it, pragmatism freed them to examine spiritual systems and to reserve judgment until their effect on one's ability to navigate the world could be evaluated. Wallace embraced James' controversial argument that it was often rational to believe without evidence, for the reason that access to evidence may first *require* the adoption of certain beliefs.[22] As a political figure, particularly at the apex of his career, Wallace would elevate James' "beliefs about beliefs" to a central place in his quest to transform not just the content of American foreign policy, but the very way in which America conducted diplomacy. He would never fully, however, take to heart the philosopher's warning: that whereas "we have the *right* to believe" without evidence, we do so "*at our own risk.*"[23]

"The man who is on God's side," grandfather wrote to Wallace in October 1909, the fall of his senior year, "is really on the side of the majority, although the world will not think so" right away.[24] If ever the family patriarch were to utter words which the grandson would absorb utterly, it was these. In consequence, Wallace would strike people in sharply different ways. Those for whom he *was* on God's side would see him as upright and bold. Those for whom he was *not* would see him as foolish and self-righteous.

Confidence and conviction pervaded his pronouncements. His undergraduate thesis, for example, which examined the "Relation Between Live Stock Farming and the Fertility of the Soil," concluded not only that the federal government had to support soil conservation, but that the nation faced the choice "between that and ruin."[25] He briefly considered graduate studies, but concluded that he could learn and accomplish more with his own study and experimentation. He joined the family business, *Wallaces' Farmer*, as a writer and an editor, and taught himself statistical analysis on the side. After a reader took issue with a piece he had written in praise of hog rearing, he "learned how to calculate correlation coefficients" and began forecasting, with some success, the path of hog prices based on historical relationships with those of corn. He then began applying these methods to diverse phenomena such as planetary movements and weather, population growth and economic development.

On the backs of such calculations, from which he would not infrequently, and with great assuredness, draw firm policy conclusions, Wallace would become widely known as an economist—at least to noneconomists. Pedigreed American economists, afflicted as they were with formal education, were never so generous in bestowing the appellation. Given their regard for the dynamics of market forces, they typically believed that simple statistical correlations, of the sort Wallace unearthed, were apt to break down when targeted for control purposes. Wallace scoffed at such economists, saying that they "dealt too much with economic theory."[26] Soviet economists of the 1950s and '60s, however, contemptuous of market forces by training and political necessity, would pursue Wallace's approach with fervor.

In the spring of 1913, though, our budding economist had his mind on other things. At an evening picnic in Des Moines, he met a demure, pretty, round-faced girl with brown eyes and matching wavy hair. "That's the girl I'd like to marry," he told his sister that night, forgoing statistical evaluation. The object of Wallace's affection, the daughter of a local businessman, was named Ilo Browne. Ilo's friends disapproved of her new suitor, thinking him conspicuously odd. They protested his strange diets and unfashionable ties. Yet even as Ilo had no interest in matters such as the history of Chinese agriculture—a topic on which he expounded during their first date— she found him genuine and solid. And so, with grandfather performing the rites, Henry and Ilo were married on May 20, 1914.[27] So taken was the groom with his father's gift, a shiny new Ford, that he dashed straight from the church into the wondrous black machine, ignoring "the kissers and congratulators." He drove off, failing to return for over an hour, at which point he leaned from the driver's seat and yelled to his astonished bride: "Get in Ilo, I'd forgotten about you."[28]

When war in Europe broke out in 1914, the elder Wallace was, in his grandson's words, "profoundly disturbed." He dreaded his country getting drawn into the carnage. He also feared that that carnage would not cease until both Britain and Germany felt secure in their maritime access to the wider world. Reflecting the regard with which he was held in Washington, the Wallace patriarch, a staunch Republican, was granted an audience with the Democratic president, Woodrow Wilson, in October 1915. There, in the White House Blue Room, Uncle Henry laid out his thoughts on the need for a new international system to assure freedom of navigation. Wilson was respectful, but noncommittal.[29]

Henry Wallace, the grandson, twenty-seven at the time, was comparatively unmoved and unaffected by the war. He continued his intensive investigations in corn breeding, determined to best the leading commercial enterprises in the trade. He continued to write number-laden articles in *Wallaces' Farmer*, replete with graphs showing trends in commodity prices. And when the military draft came in 1917, he requested an exemption—an exemption which he received on the grounds of being a "necessary assistant, associate, or hired manager of a necessary agricultural enterprise."[30] He would decades later, on the basis of his exemption request and periodic antiwar statements, be labeled a "pacifist." Yet he would not always oppose war. And in 1917, his concerns were more prosaic than that. Set against the attractions of remaining at home with his young wife, his two-year-old son, and a flourishing family enterprise, the prospect of joining in a far-off slaughter, one that had been set off by vile strains of hyper-nationalism, simply held little appeal for him.

When the war ended in November 1918, most American farmers were flourishing. They were producing at full capacity to replace the output traditionally supplied by their counterparts in war-ravaged Europe. Yet there was no government plan to reconvert the sector from a wartime to a peacetime economy, and farmers could not fine-tune production like nail manufacturers.

The problems started with hog farmers, who, mistakenly believing that the government's corn-hog program would guarantee them a profit, over-bred the animals at a time when their primary feed, corn, was at record prices. The result was massive losses. Harry Wallace, president of the Corn Belt Meat Producers' Association as well as the editor of *Wallaces' Farmer*, attacked Herbert Hoover's inaction during the war, as director of the United States Food Administration, on their behalf.

The hog problem, however, morphed into a far larger one as corn prices plummeted by 70 percent between 1919 and 1921. Farm exports, in concert, plunged by 54 percent. Against this background, Henry Wallace emerged as an authoritative voice for radical changes in farm practices and policy. In 1918, he had argued in *Wallaces' Farmer* that land and labor prices had risen too much, and that farmers would, in the absence of careful retrenchment, be buried under mountains of debt as those prices declined.[31] He was right.

In 1920, he self-published a 224-page tract entitled *Agricultural Prices*, which comprised one of the country's first major econometric studies. Half the book was charts, tables, and graphs of pricing trends. As for the other half, the dry, verbose, occasionally caustic style would become his signature for the next three decades.

"Strangely enough," Wallace would later observe, "I do not like to write."[32] Yet, no doubt encouraged by the attention brought to his ideas through the family enterprise, he was nothing if not prolific, even after entering government. As a writer, he was spontaneously liberal with his prose, never using three words where, with less effort, he might employ nine. This exemplary instance may suffice:

> It is believed, however, that powerful corn belt farmers' organizations working in co-operation with the packers should be able to educate consumers to the cost-of-production idea, and so far as seasonal vagaries in the demand are concerned, the farmers and packers should be able to come to an agreement providing for paying rather more than the demand price for hogs in times of good demand, in an effort to make price meet cost of production rather than temporary demand idiosyncrasies.

For those who can bear the spoiler alert, the moral of the story is here revealed: that the evils of pricing according to "supply and demand" must be ended, at least as they apply to hogs. Doing so, he assured readers, "does not necessarily involve governmental control." It requires, rather, that our schools teach the young "the ratio method of price judging" and suchlike, and that "production engineers and statistical economists, . . . men whose supreme motive is not profit but . . . love of the work to be done" should come to supplant "business men" in the setting of prices.[33] On entering government service a dozen years hence, however, Wallace would come to see that "governmental control" was, in fact, necessary to effect his views.

While Wallace the younger was promoting his book in 1920, Wallace the elder, who had come to Warren Harding's attention by way of fellow Iowa Republicans, helped craft the Harding-Coolidge ticket's campaign policies toward the farm sector. Following Harding's landslide victory over Democrat James Cox, and his young running mate, Franklin Roosevelt, Harry was nominated and confirmed as the nation's seventh secretary of agriculture. As he began his miserable three-and-a-half-year tenure, his son took control at *Wallaces' Farmer*.

As editor, Henry Wallace was a relentless advocate for changes in agricultural practice to boost farm incomes. Not all of his positions were popular with farmers, or farmworkers, however. Farmers, who looked to providence and to Washington for salvation, and not to painful acts of forbearance, were angered by his call for them to grow eight million fewer acres of corn in 1922. Workers were likewise riled by his claims that they were, given farm earnings, overpaid.

Not that Wallace let Washington escape responsibility—far from it. He called for cuts in manufacturing import tariffs to reduce farm equipment costs and to boost farm exports, for easier monetary policy to lower farm borrowing costs, for disarmament to free resources for farm aid, and for construction on the St. Lawrence Seaway to reduce farm freight rates. He further called for the creation of a federal "ever-normal granary," based on ancient Chinese practice, through which the government would buy up grain at "normal" prices when market prices were low, and sell it at "normal" prices when market prices were high.[34] The aim was to end boom-bust farming and to stabilize farm incomes.

Throughout the 1910s, Wallace continued to pursue his experiments in corn breeding. At one point, he had three hundred varieties growing on weed-infested plots drafted into service for the purpose. For years, he alternated between hope and frustration, failing to produce a superior strain according to the Iowa Corn Yield Test—a test he himself created, together with Iowa State agronomist H. D. Hughes, in 1920. But in 1924, Wallace achieved a breakthrough. His "Cooper Cross" hybrid won the gold medal in that year's competition, based on his now established yield test. He and his business partner, George Kurtzweil, sold the fifteen bushels for the exceptional price of $1 per pound, earning them a respectable $840. In 1926, Wallace, committing $5,000, or virtually the entirety of Ilo's inheritance, bought fifty of the seventy shares conferring ownership in the company he formed to develop and market hybrid corn seed. In its first year of operation, Pioneer Hi-Bred would turn a slim profit of $30. As late as 1929, it still had no company office, employees, or research facilities beyond Wallace's basement. But in time, it would become highly profitable, revolutionizing the business of growing corn worldwide. In 1946, twenty years after its founding, it would be netting Wallace an annual dividend of $150,000 ($2.5 million in today's money). In 1999, seventy-three years after its founding, DuPont would complete the purchase of Pioneer Hi-Bred, paying a total of $9.4 billion.

Though corn and writing typically took up most of his waking hours, "I am neither a corn breeder nor an editor," he would tell one of his mystical correspondents in 1931. He was, instead, "a searcher for methods of bringing the 'inner light' to outward manifestations and raising outward manifestation to the inner light."[35] Some of his religious experimentations constituted, relatively speaking, only modest strayings from his Presbyterian roots. These included his work in the mid-1920s to establish in Des Moines a branch of the so-called Liberal Catholic Church. A tiny Christian denomination, whose U.S. membership probably never exceeded two thousand, it offered a formal liturgical structure which appealed to his religious aesthetic, while allowing adherents of independent mind "freedom in interpretation of creeds." He eventually settled, at least for declaratory purposes, into the halfway house of Episcopalianism.[36]

Wallace joined the Masons as well—as had George Washington, Ben Franklin, Teddy Roosevelt, and other prominent Americans before him. As early as 1919, he also began experimenting with theosophy—an occult movement, popular in the 1920s among artists, intellectuals, and progressives, defined by belief in a divine wisdom residing in the Beyond but accessible to a small spiritual elite. While a religion of sorts, embracing Buddhism and Hinduism, it claimed to incorporate scientific understanding in a way most religions did not. This aspect of theosophy appealed to Wallace. Yet theosophy was also a gateway to other belief systems and practices that were, in the contemporary Western intellectual context, equally or more esoteric. These included astrology, numerology, and séances, together with alternative philosophies and spiritual exercises derived from Asian and Native American civilizations.[37] Theosophy would inculcate in Wallace a universalist outlook that would later come to infuse his politics and create a lasting image of the man as a champion of peace. It would also inspire him to embrace utopian ventures he would come to regret or disown.

Until his father's passing, however, Wallace found little of interest in politics. Harry died, in October 1924, of complications from gall bladder surgery. But he had suffered from much else that year, including severe sciatica. For Henry, the ultimate source of Harry's suffering was his battles with Hoover over farm policy. "I felt, almost, as if Hoover had killed my father," he would say years later.[38] Shortly after Harry's death, Henry knowingly cast a hopeless vote for the independent presidential candidate, Wisconsin progressive-socialist Robert "Fighting Bob" La Follette. It marked his break with the Republican Party.

Coolidge won that election handily. In 1928, Wallace called for the creation of a new party to unite the Western and Southern interests against the Eastern ones, but it got no traction.[39] When Hoover became the Republican nominee that year, Wallace campaigned around Iowa for Al Smith, the Democratic governor of New York. It was another lost cause.

In 1932, he still considered himself partyless. "I am no more a Democrat than a Republican," he would write to Edward Johndro, an electrical-expert-turned-astrologer.[40] From childhood, he had "associated the word 'Democrat' with hard times."[41] He knew, however, whom he would oppose. "I hope," he would say of Herbert Hoover, that "I never again feel as intensely antagonistic toward anyone."[42] Yet fifteen years later, Wallace, a man who rarely swore, would feel every bit as hostile toward one Harry S. Truman—a man whom he would repeatedly call "that son of a bitch."

In terms of actual policy, Wallace's early interests were driven almost entirely by a concern for agriculture. His interest in foreign policy, which would become his overriding passion in the 1940s, was in the 1920s a mere by-product of this concern. "[I have] no very definite convictions on either free trade or protection," he wrote in 1925. The question was which would benefit farming. As he saw it, the United States had a choice between "two rather clear cut paths." One led "toward economic self-sufficiency," the other "toward taking a very active interest in Europe, reorganizing Europe financially, investing liberally in European industries, and eventually taking a very vital interest in Europe's military and political affairs." The first path required levying high tariffs on both manufacturing and farm goods, reducing farm output to levels consistent with purely domestic demand, and canceling European debts—that is, disengaging from Europe. The second path required lowering high manufacturing tariffs so that Europe could export more, buy U.S. farm goods, and pay its debts.[43]

Given the Republican Party commitment to manufacturing tariffs, which Wallace abominated, he deemed the first path—national self-sufficiency—the more sensible. Yet once he had reached this pragmatic conclusion, he endowed it with a moral justification. He declared Europe "a quagmire of crookedness" from which America must decouple. Foreign trade and investment, he now reasoned, led inevitably to imperialism and war. American investors, he argued, were endangering the country by sending capital abroad in return for paper promises they would expect Washington to enforce. When conflict arose, it would be American farmers—who had no stake in it—who would bear the cost "in taxes and in blood."[44] Only isolation could save those farmers. Only isolation could save America itself.

When in February 1927, after years of negotiation, Congress passed legislation, the mercantilist McNary-Haugen bill, to boost agricultural prices at home and to dump surplus product abroad, Wallace was elated. When President Coolidge vetoed it, Wallace was livid. The veto was, he believed, a betrayal of the farm sector, and further evidence that the Republicans were in the pocket of the East Coast business interests. When in June 1930, eight months after the stock market crashed, President Hoover signed the notorious Smoot-Hawley tariff bill, further boosting industrial tariffs at the expense of farmers, Wallace despaired of ever being able to use mercantilism or protectionism for good. "[W]e wouldn't feel so indignant," Wallace explained, if agriculture could be "one of those favored groups." But it "never will be."[45] Isolationism of the Republican sort only immiserated farmers by forcing them to compete, unprotected and weighed down by higher costs, in world markets.

Most economists shared Wallace's opposition to Smoot-Hawley, even if many of those rejected his agenda for agricultural dumping and supports. Over a thousand economists had petitioned Hoover to veto the bill. And as they had warned, some two dozen nations responded to its signing with tariffs of their own. In consequence, global trade plunged by about two thirds over the four years during which the legislation was in force, helping to fuel what had become a worldwide depression.

As depression spread through Europe in 1930, Wallace did a startling ideological about-face. Despite having claimed, as late as 1925, to have "no very definite convictions on either free trade or protection," he had cloaked his earlier embrace of agricultural dumping and price supports in patriotic terms. The United States, he had said, "was the one really worthwhile nation of the world." Unnecessary engagement with Europe, a continent known for its "devious diplomacy," would only corrupt and weaken it.[46] After Smoot-Hawley, however, he attacked this viewpoint as vehemently as if it had been expounded by Herbert Hoover himself.

Wallace now scolded "the American people" for their "narrow minded insularity." They had failed to see that further raising tariffs and subsidizing exports was, for a massive creditor nation like the United States, insane policy. "God himself" could not make it work. Protectionism and mercantilism made it necessary for foreigners to borrow yet more from the United States, at a time when Washington was determined to curtail loans and collect on past debts.

Wallace's reasoning was sound, but irreconcilable with his earlier support for McNary-Haugen, and inconsistent with his criticism of Smoot-Hawley— which had been based on its unfairness to farmers. No longer did he call for cutting trade links, but for signing trade deals to cut tariffs at home and abroad. No longer did he call for American farmers to focus solely on the home front, but to embrace foreign affairs. No longer did he call for canceling debt to shelter America from Europe's "devious diplomacy and warfare," but as a means of "oiling the international economic machine" and spreading goodwill.[47] Wallace was a born-again internationalist. And he would never look back.

Thanks to tremendous advances in science and technology, he wrote in October 1930, "the whole world has become *one world* for the first time in history." And through the "free exchange of goods," these advances would spread prosperity to all mankind.[48] The phrase "one world" would become, for Wallace, a permanent shorthand for a world at peace, a world in which nations cooperated according to the doctrines of Christ.

For the United States to lead the world into this "veritable millennium," however, there would need to be a fundamental "changing of the human heart," an end to "short-sighted human selfishness." Though free trade was at the core of his new internationalist agenda, he remained ambivalent toward both competition and collectivism. Whereas he now condemned isolation on the grounds that it might lead to either "a dictatorship of the proletariat or of a Mussolini,"[49] he also took a favorable view of developments in, of all places, the Soviet Union.

Having condemned the Bolsheviks as "anarchists" after the October Revolution of 1917, and, in 1921, rebuked their treatment of peasants under Communism, Wallace now looked more sympathetically on reforms under Stalin. "With all their mistakes," he wrote in April 1930, "the people of Soviet Russia may yet stumble onto ideals which may be worth a lot to us here." Specifically, he believed that Russian agricultural techniques were making great strides under farm collectivization.[50] Though Wallace was likely ignorant of the horrific suffering caused by the Bolshevik grain requisition of 1928, and of the land confiscations, arrests, and deportations to prison camps that followed, his subsequent education, even as it encompassed the starvation of millions in Ukraine and elsewhere in the Soviet Union, would have little effect on his rosy view.

This fact is explained not by any rise in his regard for Communism, an ideology he considered a repellent godless deformity, but by his excitement with Stalin's experiment, over vast areas, with American ideas on boosting farm output through consolidation, mechanization, and scientific technique—all without the messiness of democratic process.

Wallace believed that American farmers, operating without expert guidance, had proven themselves incapable of judging and acting upon their best interests, or of allowing themselves to be led by science. Soviet farmers, no doubt, he reasoned, suffered from a similar incapacity. He further believed that fueling the pace and diffusion of technological progress was essential to achieving the "veritable millennium," and that laissez-faire was failing in this regard. Only experts devoted to their craft, and not corporate philistines acting on greed, could ensure the attainment and just distribution of the fruits of human progress. Such experts, he was convinced, must be directing the Soviet project, in the service of the most rapid possible agricultural advance and rise in rural living standards. He would adopt and sustain this belief in classic Jamesian fashion, undisturbed by a persistent dearth of evidence to support it.

By 1934, the year that would mark Stalin's complete victory over the reactionary Soviet peasantry, it would be clear that collectivization had failed to raise grain production or to provide the cheap and abundant foodstuffs needed to fuel the proletariat. It had succeeded only in securing Stalin's ability to appropriate farmers and to impose near-total political control.[51]

Of course, the risks which James had warned of in holding unsubstantiated beliefs—in this case, about the sources and effects of Soviet conduct—were only of modest consequence when held by an Iowa farm editor. But Henry Wallace's life was about to take a major turn.

Three

THE FARMER'S NEW DEAL

"I pledge you, I pledge myself, to a new deal for the American people!"

So vowed the newly nominated Democratic presidential candidate in Chicago on July 2, 1932. Bookmakers gave Franklin Delano Roosevelt, governor of New York State since 1929, only a one in six chance of defeating President Hoover in November. Yet Roosevelt headed back onto the campaign trail exuding confidence and optimism.

Roosevelt's program for rescuing the American economy, as it would emerge, was short on details and long on contradiction. The country, he said, "demands bold, persistent experimentation." He would "try something," and if that didn't work he would try something else. He decried "foolish consistency." Still, there were clear principles guiding him. Free enterprise was failing. There was "gigantic waste" in its operation. And the "individualistic society" had to give way to "social planning."[1]

After winning his party's nomination, Roosevelt set out to win the backing of the nation's opinion leaders—prominent among whom were those in the devastated farm belt, where cotton, corn, and hog prices had fallen to levels a third to a quarter of those that had prevailed in the immediate prewar years. To this end, he tapped an emissary to tour the region for advice and support.

Henry Morgenthau Jr., Roosevelt's state conservation commissioner, owned a reputable farm publication, the *American Agriculturalist*, as well as an actual farm near the governor's Hyde Park estate. Though his inherited means far exceeded his inherited analytical powers, he had one overriding qualification for the mission—the governor's trust.

On a hot July day, Morgenthau arrived in Des Moines for a meeting with forty-three-year-old farm editor Henry A. Wallace. The two spoke for hours about the "very ugly" situation in the Midwest. Even *Wallaces' Farmer* was in tough times, having just passed into the hands of the former owner of the rival paper it had bought, with exquisitely poor timing and $2 million in debt, in October 1929.[2]

Wallace was forthright on the need for a "Domestic Allotment Plan" to aid farmers who agreed to cut output. Over time, he believed, lower supply would mean higher incomes—at least for those whose farms survived. The scheme hardly appealed to Morgenthau's decidedly orthodox instincts, but Wallace insisted that, with foreign markets largely closed, the only viable alternative would be far more radical. Farm lobbyists were calling for government to guarantee prices no less than "the cost of production," irrespective of supply. Such "state socialism," as Wallace termed it, would mean the death of the American system of independent family farms.[3]

Though Morgenthau remained skeptical of Wallace's ideas, he was impressed with his grasp of farm matters and direct way of speaking. Confident that Roosevelt would feel similarly, he reported favorably on the meeting. On that basis, Roosevelt invited Wallace to meet with him at Hyde Park on August 13.

Prior to the meeting, Wallace was no more sold on Roosevelt than Roosevelt was on him. To the Iowan, the Democratic nominee was a member of the aloof East Coast establishment, with no clear convictions on agriculture. But the frugal editor justified the long train trip by agreeing to deliver a paid lecture at Cornell along the way.

On being greeted by Roosevelt, Wallace's skepticism melted away. He was taken by the governor's warmth and seemingly unaffected interest in hearing his assessments—not just on agriculture, but on tariffs (bad) and monetary easing (good, in moderation). Roosevelt had long since mastered the art of displaying warmth and interest, and Wallace would never quite master the art of detecting affected displays. Yet, all the same, the meeting advanced the cause of the Domestic Allotment Plan. Roosevelt, soon after, approved it as the basis for his pitch to rural voters.

Iowa-born agricultural economist M. L. Wilson, one of the plan's architects, who had been reared on Uncle Henry's weekly wisdom in *Wallaces' Farmer*, worked with Wallace on the first draft of a speech for a rally in Topeka, Kansas, on September 14. Many others, such as Raymond Moley and Rexford Tugwell, part of FDR's new "Brain Trust," had their way with it. The result was a text Wallace found lamentably vague. Nevertheless, constructive words and phrases jumped out at him—"national planning," "increase in farm income," "cooperative." These reassured him.[4]

"Roosevelt is progressive," he declared in *Wallaces' Farmer*, "and definitely sympathetic to the farm program." He urged farmers to back the patrician New Yorker—not as their savior, to be sure, but as by far the better of the two candidates. "With Roosevelt, the farmers have a chance," he wrote, "—with Hoover, none. I shall vote for Roosevelt."[5]

If the endorsement was less than wholehearted, it was because Wallace was not yet sold on the Democratic Party. The Democrats were not, to his mind, a true "Progressive party"—which was a Platonic ideal to him. There remained among them "a reactionary element," as evidenced by Roosevelt's choice of hickory-conservative House Speaker John Nance Garner (D-TX) as his running mate. Still, Wallace wrote, helping the Democrats *become* a progressive party was more promising than trying to make one from scratch.[6] What Wallace did not yet apprehend about *himself*, however, was that he was just as incapable of cleaving to a party—be it Republican, Democrat, or Progressive—as he was of cleaving to a church.

On November 8, 1932, Franklin Roosevelt defeated Herbert Hoover in a rout. Roosevelt took 472 electoral votes to Hoover's 59, winning the popular vote by 18 percentage points. Democrats made historic gains in both houses of Congress, and would now control each by a large margin. Even the Midwest, a traditional Republican stronghold, defected to the Democrats en masse.

With farms being foreclosed at an alarming rate, and reports of scattered violence coming in from around the Midwest, the president-elect was under pressure to demonstrate alacrity and decisiveness. Lobbying for the post of agriculture secretary was intense. From the farm belt, there was strong support for John Simpson, president of the Farmers Union, and William Hirth, president of the Missouri Farmers Association—both forceful advocates of federal aid and policy reform. From the South came calls for the choice of Georgia's Cully Cobb—like Wallace, an agricultural publisher. From within the Roosevelt camp itself, Morgenthau thought himself the man for the moment.[7]

Among the country's agricultural intelligentsia, notable support poured in for Henry Wallace. M. L. Wilson, a fellow Jamesian whose own name had been bandied for the job, backed Wallace. Harvard's John D. Black praised the Iowa editor's "ability" and "great familiarity with the intimate problems of agriculture." He also suggested, curiously for a scientist, that Wallace's "heritage" and "connections" rendered his "service" a matter of "predestin[y]." The most notable support for Wallace, though, came from Edward A. O'Neal, the brash, colorful, and profane president of the American Farm Bureau Federation. Once O'Neal had dismissed the insiders, Morgenthau and Tugwell, as unsuitable, Wallace's stock rose considerably.[8]

On November 28, Wallace was again summoned to meet with Roosevelt, this time at his cottage in Warm Springs, Georgia—a forty-four-hour train journey from Des Moines.[9] The two men talked agriculture for less than an hour, while Roosevelt shaved and breakfasted. Most of the day was taken up in talks with Moley, a Columbia professor whose analytical manner suited Wallace, and Morgenthau, whose more primeval mind Wallace tolerated insofar as it was rarely fixed. Morgenthau's chief role, Wallace concluded, was not to express thought but to procure booze.[10]

After reluctantly agreeing to head to Washington for work on farm relief bills with the lame-duck Congress,[11] Wallace left Warm Springs knowing nothing of his fate within the new administration. It was not, in fact, until February 6, 1933, a month before inauguration day, that a letter from the president-elect would arrive for Wallace back in Des Moines. The job of secretary of agriculture, if he would have it, was his.[12]

This offer was quite clearly the greatest opportunity Wallace had ever been granted. Yet after one day, two days, a week—he did not reply.

Why did Wallace hesitate? It is difficult to imagine a man so sure of his ideas declining the call to save rural civilization—a man who had for two decades been assembling a five-hundred-year genealogical survey of his family's superior characteristics, analyzing his lineage as if it were a corn strain, noting proudly its tendency toward physical vitality and high intellect.[13] It is also easy to see why he might waver. For Wallace loved humanity; people, not so much. And Washington was full of *people*; people with wrong beliefs and bad intentions. People who smoked and drank and cussed. People who knew nothing of science or the soul, yet who presumed to pronounce on all manner of policy. And there was the memory of his poor father—his poor, principled father; tormented and harried to death in office. Against these considerations, life in Des Moines most surely had its attractions.[14]

At home in Des Moines on February 12, Wallace answered the phone. It was Ray Moley. The Boss wanted his answer. Yet for a few more moments, still, Wallace played the mute Hamlet. Finally, he uttered his tremulous response: yes.

He would presently pen a more decisive affirmation for the president-elect. "Your invitation can have but one reply," he wrote—the reply he had taken a week to formulate, and then only under duress. "I appreciate the honor and accept the responsibility. So far as it is in me I will carry my part of the 'family' burdens."[15] And so Henry A. Wallace, together with his wife and three children, packed the family belongings and headed off to Washington, never again to call Iowa anything more than a summer home.

In 1933, the farm belt was still suffering from debt-financed overinvestment in land and equipment during the war years. Then there had been the horrific depression that followed the stock market crash of 1929, and the drought and dust storms that hit the Midwest and southern Great Plains in 1930 and '31. The farm population had fallen from 32.5 million (32 percent of the population) in 1916 to 30.5 million (25 percent of the population),[16] and farm sizes had risen—yet the consolidation had been insufficient to offset lower peacetime foreign demand and rising productivity. The latter had been fueled by the proliferation of gasoline-powered tractors and other forms of mechanization, but also by seed innovations such as those pioneered by Henry Wallace. Hybrid corn had, for many farmers, tripled their yields.

Farm costs, furthermore, had, since the golden years of 1909–14, grown at a much faster clip than farm income. A bushel of wheat that sold for $3.10 in 1920 now sold for 42 cents.[17] From 1929 to 1932, agricultural commodity prices declined 37 percent, and farm income 52 percent. Foreign economic policy, in the form of high industrial tariffs, exacerbated the problem by inflating farm costs and reducing the dollars available to foreigners to purchase U.S. produce. Farmers often contributed to the generalized misery by growing more to offset falling revenue—thus adding to the oversupply and depressing prices further.

Farm groups pressed the federal government for various remedies. They demanded lower industrial tariffs. They demanded inflation and a cheaper dollar. They demanded that the government guarantee them a profit. They demanded that it buy up their surplus, at a good price, and then dump it abroad for whatever foreigners would pay. And all of them agreed that, by whatever mechanism, government should double their "parity" purchasing power—that is, their income after costs—bringing it back to immediate pre-war levels.[18]

Politically, the farm situation was perilous for the new president. In Wallace's home state, mobs of angry farmers were disrupting foreclosure proceedings, threatening judges, and attacking agents carrying out their orders. They wanted no more debates in Washington; they were taking matters into their own hands. "When the revolt springs from the old native stock, conservatives fighting for the right to hold their homesteads," observed the *New York World-Telegram*, "there is the warning of a larger explosion."[19] Roosevelt needed to show more than optimism and determination. He needed to show action.

The youngest member of the new cabinet, forty-four-year-old Henry Wallace, was neither the smug insider nor the angry outsider. He made no effort to adapt to Washington or its ways, nor did he crusade to change them. He looked not to befriend nor to flatter. He sought no favors and offered none. He spoke truth as God and nature revealed it, and listeners either understood or remained benighted.

"Drastic adjustments" were coming, he told stunned Department of Agriculture staff in their first mutual encounter on March 3, the day *before* inauguration. It had not occurred to him that, as a guest of the outgoing secretary, Arthur Hyde, simple greetings were in order. To his first appointee—the new head of information services, Milton Eisenhower, brother of Army Major Dwight Eisenhower—he would say, by way of introduction and instruction, that the department was to be "transform[ed] . . . immediately into a vast agency to restore parity of income to American farmers."

Despite presiding over what would become the largest department in the federal government, with a staff count rising from 40,000 to 146,000, Wallace had little managerial or administrative talent, and no interest in developing it. His job, as he saw it, was to preach principles and divine objectives. He typically left the grind work of actual policymaking, implementation, supervision, evaluation, and control to deputies.

"Henry would cut off his right hand for the sake of an idea," observed one friend. People mattered to the extent that they served that idea. But his emotional bond remained to the idea itself. "There wasn't anybody I know of," added M. L. Wilson, who would work with Wallace for years, "who could say he knew Henry Wallace intimately."[20]

Even Ilo Wallace, devoted to and admiring of her husband as she was, lived a physical and emotional life parallel with but distinct from his. "She doesn't particularly share my intellectual enthusiasms," Henry would observe years later.[21] He worked hard and slept little—typically from midnight to 5 a.m., in his own separate bedroom. This latter fact his children ascribed to their father's restlessness, allergies, sinus troubles, and snoring.[22] The aspects of Washington life that Ilo loved, such as formal state occasions and socializing with cabinet wives,[23] Henry found irksome. With garden dirt under his nails, and crinkles in his ill-tailored suit, he would walk to work most mornings, two miles, no matter the weather. When he would go out for exercise—typically tennis, badminton, or boomerangs—he would often return through the building barefoot, shoes dangling from his fingers.

From his capacious second-floor office at 14th Street and Jefferson Drive, Wallace had magnificent views of the Mall and the Washington Monument. Yet he cared little for the interior. The desk, the chairs, the tables, the cabinets—all remained where Hyde had left them, seemingly as permanent as the Mall and the Monument. To adorn his bare walls, he sought out a single item—the official portrait of his father that had been stowed away during the Hoover years. He would eventually add just three more works: a cartoon likeness of Harry from *The Des Moines Register*; a painting of a missionary with a Bible by a Native American artist; and a work depicting the reverent place of corn in Mayan civilization. Wallace thereby turned a grand chamber into a modest shrine to family, God, and farming.

His workspace consisted of a well-polished desk and, behind him, a table holding an ever-morphing pile of books and documents, together with stacks of old gray notebooks filled with agricultural data, brought with him from Des Moines. With his feet propped on a wastebasket, he dictated books, articles, speeches, and memos—a practice which accentuated his natural prolixity. He lunched with aides in a small room off the cafeteria, where they debated science or geography, or learned Spanish with a tutor. Back in the office he would, when feeling particularly restless, prove his talents at "Indian wrestling" with his assistant, Jim LeCron, or with a visiting reporter who disbelieved his athletic boasts. [24] Idleness, mental or physical, offended him.

Wallace was, by his own estimation, never close to Franklin Roosevelt personally, in the way that Federal Emergency Relief Administration administrator Harry Hopkins was. Nor did he ever have "a regular luncheon date" with him, as Henry Morgenthau did.[25] But Wallace and Roosevelt made a fine political team. Wallace had plans—or, more accurately, plans for plans; plans usually based on science and reason, though sometimes on a sharp and ineffable welling of Jamesian belief. Roosevelt, for his part, was "willing to try things out," anything at all, "until we get something that works." He had campaigned on pledges to raise farm prices, to shield farms from foreclosure, and to boost farm exports, but was wholly agnostic as to how to fulfill them.[26]

Wallace knew he needed to produce something big. But it also had to be fast.[27] Early in his first week in office, he headed out onto the Mall with Tugwell, his new assistant secretary, to talk through possible plans. It was on that walk that the two alighted on the idea of ramming through what Tugwell termed an "omnibus emergency bill"; a bill that would give the agriculture secretary sweeping authority to take whatever action he deemed necessary to aid farmers. The lack of specifics, Tugwell reasoned, would prevent "legislative bickering." And by acting swiftly and successfully after passage, Wallace would "smother arguments."[28]

On March 8, Roosevelt gave his blessing. On the 9th, Wallace gathered farm leaders to secure their public support.[29] With billions of dollars in federal subsidies and loans dangled before them, they needed little convincing. On May 12, two months after Roosevelt had taken office, and one day before a planned national farmers' strike, the new Democratic Congress passed the Agricultural Adjustment Act.

Perhaps never before, opined the *New York Herald Tribune*, had "so sweeping a piece of legislation" been brought before the Congress.[30] The act featured a smorgasbord of provisions aimed at regulating markets, compensating farmers, protecting consumers, expanding exports, and raising revenues for funding. Its most immediate aim, however, was to boost farm prices by controlling production and cutting surpluses in seven important commodities: wheat, cotton, corn, rice, tobacco, hogs, and dairy products. Its basic principle was simple: pay farmers to produce less. Funds to support the program would come from taxes on textile and flour mills, tobacco companies, meat processors, and others who refined commodities for sale to consumers. Though participation was voluntary in principle, most farmers had little hope of prospering without federal cash. And so, almost overnight, farming—the American vocation most clearly associated with rugged independence—became an enormous national economic protectorate.

Mordecai Ezekiel, who would become Wallace's primary economic adviser, pronounced it "the greatest single experiment in economic planning under capitalist conditions ever attempted by a democracy in times of peace."[31] Republicans preferred terms such as "bolshevistic."[32] Roosevelt tried to temper conservative opposition, particularly from within his own party, by recruiting a stolid financier, Bernard Baruch, to head the new Agricultural Adjustment Administration (AAA)—a mighty new bureaucracy which the act created within the Department of Agriculture. But Baruch, presciently recognizing the job as a poisoned chalice, diverted it toward his old trusted colleague at the War Industries Board, George Peek.

A pugnacious sixty-year-old economic nationalist, known as the father of McNary-Haugen, Peek opposed the production controls that Wallace supported, and supported the dumping of produce abroad that Wallace opposed. He was willing to defer these battles for a short time, but not to abandon them. Clashing early and often with Wallace, whose job he had coveted and whose authority he challenged openly, Peek would last only seven months. He resigned in December 1933.

Roosevelt, characteristically, cared little that Peek abominated the protrade, low-tariff policies being championed by prominent members of his cabinet—not least among them, Henry Wallace and Cordell Hull, his secretary of state. He made Peek his new special adviser on foreign trade, and then president of the new Export-Import Bank—a perch from which he proceeded to row with Hull over the latter's pursuit of reciprocal trade agreements (RTAs). Two years after leaving the AAA, Peek would be forced out of a job again. He would go on to attack the entire New Deal, and the AAA in particular—denouncing it as "socialized farming." Roosevelt, however, would continue cheerfully erecting clashing centers of authority through-out his administration—centers he could elevate and eliminate according to political circumstance.

The AAA program was mired in controversy from the start. Opponents ob-jected that it was counterproductive, and even immoral, to reduce food pro-duction at a time when millions of Americans were struggling to buy food. Not only did the AAA pay farmers not to plant, however, but, in the case of cotton, to destroy what had already been planted. Wallace ordered a million farmers to plow under up to half their crop— a total of 10 million acres. For this act of destruction, which many farmers considered insane, they were paid the astounding sum of $100 million ($23 billion in today's money).[33]

"To have to destroy a growing crop is a shocking commentary on our civi-lization," Wallace observed, enigmatically. "I could tolerate it only as a clean-ing up of the wreckage from the old days of unbalanced production."[34] He did not, however, "have to" destroy anything. He *chose* to destroy crops, and could not logically claim to "tolerate" what he chose. More fundamentally, the "cleaning up" did not solve the problem of overproduction. The practice of paying rich farmers not to grow would become an enduring fixture of American farm policy.[35]

But the plow-under was far from being his most controversial action. That action was to order the purchase and premature slaughter of some six million hogs, as well as the destruction of the corn crop grown to feed them—again with the aim of reducing supply and pushing up prices. Many of the slain hogs, too small for food processing machines, were used to make fertilizer or lard, or simply "buried and dumped in the Mississippi,"[36] sub-jecting Wallace to the charge that the carnage made food less affordable at a time when Americans were starving. Wallace was again enigmatic in observing a "paradox of want in the midst of plenty," but pledged to miti-gate it by buying up a further two million pigs for food-relief programs. Ninety percent of the salt pork that went to relief proved inedible, and was discarded.[37] One farm group spokesman condemned the whole scarcity-creation agenda as "idiotic." It made "a laughing stock of our genius as a people," he said.[38] But Wallace never tired of defending the pig program. "It served a very useful purpose," he would argue in 1950, "because it confirmed the American people in their desire for abundance as nothing else could have done."[39]

Even as Wallace was reshaping the American agricultural sector, he had an eye on reforming industry as well. His devotion to agricultural interests entailed a broader political outlook marked by an antipathy toward Wall Street and big business—powerful interests that, he believed, had destroyed rural America and tore at the moral fabric of society. And he was never reticent about sharing his wisdom with Roosevelt.

It was, Wallace wrote to the president on December 1, 1934, an "economic absurdity" that there was idle manpower, plant capacity, and resources at a time when millions were in need. The administration should therefore "concentrate all resources" on ending it quickly. Whereas expansive monetary and fiscal policy would today be the conventional elixir for such a problem, Wallace wanted far more direct, muscular intervention. Tugwell, his ever-dapper and bombastic deputy, had just published a book calling for government to seize the economy's commanding heights. Having returned from the Soviet Union in 1927 impressed by "the power of the collective will," he now declared that America "possess[ed] every needful material for Utopia." That this Utopia was still beyond reach only proved "that control ought to be taken out of the hands of people who cannot produce it from the excellent materials at their disposal."[40]

Notwithstanding Wallace's progressive sentiments, the AAA was not, at least in operation, on the side of "the Common Man"—that is, the noble embodiment of hardworking, pious decency whom Wallace would champion in the 1940s. AAA payments to farmers were in reverse proportion to need. They were directed to those who *owned* farmland, and not to those many millions who merely worked it. The top one percent of farmers would receive about 20 percent of the benefits.[41]

In the South, half the agricultural population were impoverished tenants or "sharecroppers"—and a third of these were descendants of African slaves.[42] Their legal rights to a portion of the compensation from Washington were flimsy and frequently ignored by the landowners receiving it.[43] Worse, tenants were often evicted as owners reduced planted acreage in return for AAA cash. Since the payment formula also encouraged consolidation of fields, and the mechanization of the resulting large farms, demand for their labor fell yet further. Many were thus obliged to become even more wretched harvest-time day laborers, surviving only on emergency assistance from the new Federal Emergency Relief Administration. "I did not concern myself much with labor and farm tenancy in 1933," Wallace would acknowledge decades later. He only became "fully familiar with that problem" after a trip down South, in November 1936.[44]

The first lady, Eleanor Roosevelt, expressed alarm at the plight of rural workers, which would only get worse over the course of the decade. When she wrote to Wallace to highlight the dire circumstances of Missouri sharecroppers, he responded, clinically, that "basic population facts" showed that there were simply too many farmers. She wrote back, terming his response "most interesting."

"Should we" then, she asked with bitter sarcasm, "practice birth control or drown the surplus population?"[45]

In July 1934, a Southern Tenant Farmers' Union (STFU), with close ties to perennial Socialist Party presidential candidate Norman Thomas, formed to defend tenants' rights. In response, tenant-rights opponents, many of whom looked on the SFTU as a Communist plot to disenfranchise them, used both legal and violent vigilante means to punish and intimidate its members.

The seeming injustice of agricultural policy led to enormous dissension within the department itself. Wallace would later recall that "the leftists" never felt he went fast or far enough in handling tenancy problems.[46] Most of the tenant advocates were concentrated in the AAA's legal department, under the direction of talented and energetic general counsel Jerome Frank. Chester Davis, Peek's less-bullying successor atop the AAA, complained to Wallace that many of those hired by Frank were socialists and revolutionaries.[47] In this judgment he was not entirely wrong. Wallace himself referred to these men as "the extreme liberal group" within the agency. Some of them—such as the brilliant Harvard Law grads Alger Hiss, Lee Pressman, John Abt, and Nathan Witt—would go on to cultivate long-standing secret ties to the Communist Party or Soviet intelligence.

The issue that ultimately led to rupture within the AAA was a technical one, but one which had enormous implications for how AAA aid would operate, and in what aspects it might be effective in achieving the act's aims. AAA contracts with cotton landlords called on them not to reduce tenant numbers. In 1934, this call was interpreted internally as affording planters the right to *change* their tenants, provided their number remained no fewer. But on February 1, 1935, Hiss and colleagues drafted a new interpretation, based on demands from the STFU, requiring landlords to maintain the *same tenants* in the same houses. Knowing that Davis would reject the draft, and taking advantage of his travels out West, Frank persuaded the acting administrator to publish it.

When Davis learned of Frank's insubordination, he was livid. He was sure that the planters, such as those in the angry Arkansas delegation that converged on Wallace's office on the morning of February 1,[48] would cease cooperation with the AAA if Frank won out. Frank and his collaborators, urban leftists with "very little farm background," Davis explained to Wallace, were trying to undermine him by making it seem as if he, an Iowa-reared farm expert like Wallace, a man with no personal interest in the outcome, was selfishly aiding rich landlords and food processors. Davis, just like Wallace, was trying to jump-start recovery.[49] He wanted Frank, Pressman, and the other ringleaders fired, and the AAA legal department disbanded.

Wallace, who instinctively shrank from face-to-face controversies, was paralyzed for days. He was of at least three minds on the matter. As a progressive, he had sympathy for the poor tenants. With tears in his eyes, he would tell Frank: "You [are] the best fighter I've had for my ideas."[50] As a proud scion of Midwestern farm owners, however, he appeared to lack empathy with them. He was wont to cite Jefferson in proclaiming farm-owning families to be the backbone of American democracy.[51] "I believed that a stable civilization demanded a nation of landowners," he would later recall.[52] Finally, as a believer in the "planned economy," he saw government-assisted farm education, technological profusion, and scale economies as the quickest and surest route to universal "abundance."[53] These last beliefs lay behind his support for Stalin's collectivization. In implementing his policy, he never hesitated over concern for unintended consequences, insisting publicly that AAA programs were irrelevant to tenant plight "by comparison with other causes of rural unemployment."[54] But the truth was that some two million tenants and workers would lose their jobs on account of them.[55]

Wallace's diary entries for the several days that followed reveal a man wrestling with difficult questions of law, in which he was not expert; ideology, in which he roamed a center ground between Davis and the liberals; and politics, in which Roosevelt's calculated inconstancy confounded him. Until Frank and Hiss came to see him late on February 5, Wallace was convinced that they had "allowed their social pre-conceptions to lead them into something which was not only indefensible from a practical agricultural point of view but also bad law." Yet after their meeting, Wallace reflected that they had "sounded entirely reasonable," and that their case was "just as good" as Davis'. A study on tenancy which he had commissioned, the more unpleasant results of which were only communicated to him privately, also confirmed that the acreage reduction program was generating "tenant displacement."[56]

Tugwell urged Wallace to fire *Davis*, rather than Frank and his minions. After meeting with Frank and Hiss, however, Wallace, trying to keep some personal distance from the coming purge, authorized Davis to fire the men himself. He also agreed to transfer the legal department's authority back up to the Department of Agriculture. When Frank asked Wallace why he had not done the firing himself, the secretary explained, sheepishly, that he had been unable to face them.[57]

It might be concluded that Wallace's faith in planning had in the end won out. Tugwell, however, believed otherwise. He thought that it came down *not* to a weighing of economic priorities, but to a weighing of personal political consequences. Wallace, he would later write, saw himself as Roosevelt's rightful heir. And his presidential ambitions were clearly better served by not appearing to side with radicals against the interests of Southern conservatives and farm lobbyists—on whose support Roosevelt counted. Davis himself would later reflect that Wallace, had he backed Frank's directive, "would have been forced out of the Cabinet within a month."[58]

Wallace, in his diary, held Roosevelt responsible for the infighting and mutual charges of intrigue between Davis and the liberals, since the president had refused to lay down clear policy principles or lines of authority. His approach to governing was "experimental," Wallace lamented; his true objectives always "concealed."[59] Thus was Wallace left to conclude that his own fate would be determined by White House political expediency, which required stable relations with the South and the farm barons. And so whereas he felt that Frank and "the left wingers of city background" bore "attitudes" of "a higher nature" than Davis', he also concluded that "their sense of time [was] wrong," and that "they want[ed] to move too fast." Davis, though perhaps "lacking vision," Wallace conceded, better grasped the "details of the agricultural situation than anyone who could . . . *at this time* run the AAA."[60] He was therefore unwilling to sacrifice Davis, whom, he suspected, rightly, had the president's support.[61]

Politically, the decision played well for Wallace. With Davis victorious, Wallace's massive department seemed less volatile and threatening to the cabinet, to the Congress, and to the farm lobby—at least temporarily. Moreover, the ideological warfare within the department ceased.

As for Frank, his career trajectory would be unhindered by the episode. Roosevelt, at Wallace's and Tugwell's urging, put him on a less contentious path to influence.[62] By 1939, he would be chairman of the Securities and Exchange Commission, and in 1941 a judge of the U.S. Court of Appeals. Davis had excluded Hiss from his purge, expecting him to resign on his own—as he did. Wallace had mixed feelings about Hiss' departure. Given his "unusual intelligence and strong will," Wallace diaried, Hiss was likely to be "a very significant man in future affairs." He "may be," however, Wallace speculated, presumably with some unrecorded basis, "fundamentally more radical than I know."[63]

Looking abroad, Wallace abominated European—particularly British—imperialism, seeing the continent's far-flung colonies as victims in much the same way that he saw Midwestern farmers as victims of greedy Northern industrialists. In spite of his enthusiasm for Stalin's farm reforms, Wallace also had no interest in pursuing closer ties with the Soviet Union. When Roosevelt announced, on October 20, 1933, that he was taking steps to normalize diplomatic relations with the country, Wallace objected. He disparaged Russian interest in buying more U.S. farm goods, and opposed lending them money to do so. Russia's "centralized government of iron men," he said, would try to create "price chaos among the capitalistic nations" by dumping goods under the guise of repaying loans. He even told Roosevelt that deeper economic relations with the Bolshevik government, which was "utterly without religion," might undermine religious faith in the United States.[64] He would revise these views radically in the 1940s.

Wallace also opposed loans to China to enable that country to buy more wheat and cotton, arguing that they made no sense unless the United States were prepared to import large amounts of Chinese goods to rebalance the two-way trade. The experience of the 1920s, he argued, showed that creating more debt, on its own, only produced more commercial and political conflict.[65]

After passage of the Agricultural Adjustment Act in May of 1933, Wallace did, however, become an enthusiast for pursuing supply reduction internationally. Over the summer, he led a U.S. delegation seeking to conclude an agreement to curtail wheat production with Canada, Argentina, and Australia. When Australia balked initially, Wallace threatened to begin "competitive export dumping" and drive wheat prices "to zero" in that country—a tactic that he himself described as "deplorable." But the tactic seemed to work. Australia offered to go along if European countries took part. The Soviets refused, but twenty nations joined the United States in signing an agreement on August 25. Wallace called it a "momentous step" and "a landmark in international efforts to solve the economic depression." That, however, was not to be. Argentina subsequently had a bumper wheat crop, and the agreement withered. Still, it whetted Wallace's appetite for pursuing further ventures in international cooperation.[66]

Did the Agricultural Adjustment Act work? Wallace and his deputies argued that it did. It boosted farm prices, they said. It boosted farm income. It reduced oversupply. And it put in place administrative machinery to make permanent improvements in the operation of American agriculture.

An objective appraisal, however, would pose more precise questions, and encompass a wider consideration of cause and effect. Were the act's apparent successes properly attributed? And were there unintended consequences? On the matter of farm prices and incomes, which was of greatest concern to Wallace, the effect varied by commodity. In the dairy sector, the impact of AAA policy was negligible, and support from farmers low. Wheat farmers did much better, with prices doubling from 1931 to 1934.[67] Tobacco growers did the best relative to benchmark, with some exceeding the government's decreed "fair exchange value" of their 1934 crop by 40 percent.[68]

These successes, such as they were, however, had little or nothing to do with the AAA's efforts to pressure farmers to grow less. The problem of sur-

plus production—that is, unprofitable production—would not be amelio-
rated until demand resurged during World War II.

In the case of wheat, the reduction in sown acreage was only half the
target, despite adverse weather reducing seeding. Farmers found ways around
reducing planted acreage, such as growing on land they rented rather than
owned.[69] More significantly, the increase in wheat prices and wheat-farm income bore little relation to changes in farm practice motivated by the act.
Beginning in the spring of 1933, wheat prices were boosted by acts of God and
Roosevelt: that is, drought and dust storms from the one, dollar devaluation
from the other. The latter raised the dollar price of agricultural commodities
in world markets, as well as the domestic one.[70] Over half the rise in wheat-
farm income can be attributed to devaluation, and most of the remainder to
government transfer payments[71]—neither of which required any action by
Wallace's department.

Cotton field owners, like wheat growers, also saw a rise in income—for
similar reasons. Yet cotton field *tenants*, as discussed earlier, suffered severe
losses in consequence. Meanwhile, the supply reduction from reduced acreage
was offset by greater yields from practices such as intensifying fertilizer use.

In the case of tobacco, virtually all the benefit to growers came from
AAA-dictated "marketing agreements" which forced processors to buy no
less tobacco than they had the preceding year, at or above set minimum
prices, and which forbade them from raising prices to consumers.[72] Such
autocratic methods of transferring income between sectors were at odds
with the voluntary ethos Wallace had proclaimed for the act, but consistent
with his view that industrial middlemen between farmers and consumers
were dangerous profiteers who needed to bear the program's costs.

Though the mass slaughter of hogs and the plowing-under of cotton did
boost the prices of both, there was little to recommend them as policy—
either as a tool of short-run recovery or long-term reform. One reason is
that the rise in the price of *stocks* of these commodities benefited only those
who held them—and not the farmers, who had already sold them. To the
extent that the value of the stocks had been hedged on agricultural future
markets, as most of it had been, the beneficiaries were speculators—and
not farmers. A second reason is that farm income is not enlarged by a rise
in the unit price of a product, but by the product of price *and volume*. Selling lower volumes at higher prices did not help farmers uniformly or sig-

nificantly. Wallace clearly understood this fact, and so claimed that the plow-under had succeeded "*in company with the monetary policy and other measures, . . . including AAA payments.*"[73] This was like claiming that the patient had been cured by voodoo "in company with medicine." A third reason is that the slaughter and plow-under were one-off interventions, limited almost entirely to 1933, and did nothing to discourage future oversupply.

Still, an influential 1935 Brookings Institution study of the AAA estimated that farm families, on balance, saw net gains from its programs totaling between $1.5 billion and $1.9 billion. Though such gains are far smaller than AAA spokesmen claimed,[74] they are substantial, amounting to as much as 3 percent of gross national product (GNP).[75] Yet they, too, are overestimates. They fail to account for the losses of some two million farm tenants and workers who were, as a direct consequence of the programs, thrown off the land.[76]

What about the effect of the AAA on the American economy as a whole? The AAA was supposed to be a complement to the National Industrial Recovery Act (NIRA), and therefore to contribute to economic recovery broadly. It was the centerpiece New Deal legislation for Henry Wallace and his fellow advocates of the "planned economy." Here, too, the verdict must be mixed.

Government payments to farmers, and not supply-reduction efforts, were far and away the most important lever by which the AAA increased farm income. But to the extent that these payments were financed by taxes on food processors, who then passed on higher prices to consumers (farmers included), who in turn consumed less as a result, the AAA had a less positive impact on farmers than USDA spokesmen claimed, and a negative one on all who consumed farm products. These spokesmen, not surprisingly, said different things to different audiences. They told farmers the AAA was to credit for higher farm prices, while telling angry consumers the opposite: that the *drought* was *to blame*.[77] Wallace tried to have it both ways by calling his program, nonsensically, "an adjustment policy providing for increases when such increases make for the welfare of the consumer, and for decreases when such decreases make for the welfare of the farmers."[78] He acknowledged, however, that such head-scratchers could not disguise the problem. "I cannot say," he also confessed publicly, that the USDA's efforts to stop "the textile people" from hitting consumers "had much effect in keeping down the prices of cotton goods." And those "mounting retail prices," he added, "did not simplify our problem in the Midwest."[79]

The Brookings study nonetheless argued that to the extent that the farm population, comprising a quarter of the nation, had a higher marginal propensity to consume than the general population—that is, a greater likelihood of spending an extra dollar of income—the AAA still made a net positive contribution to recovery. Farmers, who were heavily indebted, might have gone bust without government aid. Instead, they consumed *more*, and thereby added to the country's generalized purchasing power and business confidence.

This logic is compelling, though hardly conclusive. As economists at the time pointed out—the AAA's own economic adviser, Louis Bean, included—the benefits of reduced farm supply on farm prices, and of higher farm prices on farm incomes, do not merit the conclusion that those benefits stimulated recovery. Less farm production, all else being equal, implied *less business* for refiners, storers, transporters, and the like, while higher farm prices tended to *depress demand* for the goods of industry.[80]

All else is never equal, however, and the broad effect of changes in farm production and prices is, ultimately, an empirical question—one to be resolved by analyzing the relationship between different categories of economic data. Recent such analysis suggests that higher farm prices *did*, on balance, aid industrial recovery in 1933—revealing that auto sales growth, for example, was positively related to the share of a state's population living on farms. There was also evidence of positive effects of higher farm prices on bank solvency (as farmers paid back loans) and ending deflation fears.

The dominant policy source of farm-price movements was not AAA programs, however, but a loosening of monetary policy.[81] The broad view that the change in monetary policy in 1933 was the single most important contributor to recovery has been standard among economists since the seminal analysis of Milton Friedman and Anna Schwartz, published thirty years after passage of the Agricultural Adjustment and National Industrial Recovery acts.[82] Indeed, since the two economists made their case, it is widely accepted that monetary policy had been a primary *cause* of the Great Depression, in that the Federal Reserve had, from 1929 to early 1933, been misguidedly tightening it.

Wallace's own views on the dollar and monetary policy in 1933 were muddled, as were the administration's broadly. In January 1933, just prior to his appointment as agriculture secretary, Wallace opined that "the smart thing to do would be to go off the gold standard a little further than England has."[83] But since "the word 'inflation' grates harshly on the ears of many bankers," he added, "we speak of 'reflation' and save their feelings."[84] By September, however, he was declaring, in opposition to calls from Congress and farm bodies for further monetary easing, that the administration was "flatly opposed to currency inflation." When the financial press soured on the nascent recovery, however, the president determined once again to conjure forth the animal spirits with cheaper money. On October 22, Roosevelt gave a radio address in which he pledged to boost prices by buying up newly mined gold with newly printed dollars.[85] The recovery was back on track. The U.S. money supply rose a hearty 42 percent between 1933 and 1937, stimulating growth through lower interest rates and expectations of higher inflation.

In the end, it may be concluded that the Roosevelt administration could have helped those farmers it did help, not to mention the tenants and laborers it harmed, while making a stronger contribution to recovery—and doing so more cheaply, with less collateral damage, and with fewer lamentable legacy effects—just by mailing them checks. Mailing out millions of checks is, after all, what the U.S. government did, with notable success, during a pandemic-induced economic plunge eighty-seven years later. Combined with looser monetary policy, which was the result of the dollar devaluation in 1933 (and the so-called quantitative easing in 2020), simple fiscal transfers would have accomplished Wallace's main aim—that of farm recovery—with greater efficiency, less cost, less turmoil, and minimal interference in the operation of farms and businesses.

The Agricultural Adjustment Act was bombarded with legal challenges from its birth. On January 6, 1936, one of them hit the mark. In the case of *United States v. Butler*, the conservative-dominated Supreme Court, by a 6–3 decision, declared the act unconstitutional. Though there was considerable disagreement among the majority as to the proper scope of the ruling, Justice Owen J. Roberts, in his opinion on their behalf, held that revenue from the processing tax had not been intended to serve the "general welfare," as it should have been. Rather, it was intended to fund regulation of an activity outside the legal scope of federal jurisdiction—that is, agricultural production.[86]

Wallace was livid at the ruling, as well as the premise that agriculture, in the America of 1936, could be called a "local activity." But he had not been unprepared for such a setback, and set to work on reconstituting the act so that it might do its job on a court-proof basis. With the aid of farm economist Howard Tolley, Wallace rewrote the legal grounds for his powers. No longer was his department to regulate agricultural production, as such, but to conserve the nation's soil—a "general welfare" function. And no longer would its efforts be financed by a processing tax, but by direct congressional appropriations.

"We *hope*," but do not *intend*, Wallace stated deftly, "that as a result of the conservation of soil resources . . . supplies of the major farm commodities will be kept in approximate balance with demand, and we *hope* that the plan will have a favorable effect on farm prices and income. But any such benefits," he added for the court's benefit, "will be *by-products*."[87]

"The Act is dead; long live the Act!"—or so he might well have said. For on February 29, 1936, less than two months after the court killed the Agricultural Adjustment Act, it was reborn as the Soil Conservation and Domestic Allotment Act.

This was the sort of political maneuver that Roosevelt so regarded, and it elevated Wallace in his esteem. Henry was no mere planner, it seemed, but a doer—a *political* doer. He had shown that he had what it took to survive, and perhaps even thrive, in the malignant swamplands of Washington, D.C.

Wallace would, as well, endear himself to Roosevelt with a literary attack on the court. Availing himself of ghostwriting aid from lawyer Morris Ernst, he penned a book entitled *Whose Constitution?: An Inquiry into the General Welfare* (1936).[88] As would become the Wallace trademark, it combined agricultural wonkery, street-corner philosophy, progressive Christian preaching, and political pugilism. It made the moral and practical case for soil protection. It denounced "unfettered individualism," while lauding "the cooperative way of life." And it rebuked the court for "refus[ing] to admit" that it was "time for change."[89] Wallace sent the president the final text for his approval in May 1936, eliciting the response: "May it sell 100,000 copies."[90]

⚜

Wallace was nothing if not prolific during Roosevelt's first term, churning out four books—including *Whose Constitution?*—as well as scores of articles, lectures, and speeches. He confessed to his works being "hastily dictated,"[91] but he favored speed and volume over clarity and coherence.

In *America Must Choose: The Advantages and Disadvantages of Nationalism, of World Trade, and of a Planned Middle Course* (1934), Wallace made the case for pursuing world peace through freer trade—sort of. He envisioned a world in which reciprocal trade agreements led to lower tariffs and more cross-border commerce, but one in which competition in similar products would be excluded.[92] This provision limited the scope for trade to stimulate innovation and productivity, but, Wallace believed, conduced not only to less domestic resistance but to greater international amity—which was his primary aim. He termed that aim "semi-religious in nature."

In *Statesmanship and Religion* (1934), he applied his semi-religious thought to government reorganization of "our social machinery." In this work, he made clear that his support for trade liberalization had little to do with economics. Nationalism might be bad "from the religious point of view," he explained, but was no barrier to prosperity.

To the contrary, he wrote, "we can have a very high standard of living if we develop a spirit and economic policy of intense nationalism," as other countries had done. The U.S. government, after all, possessed "vast systems of statistics dealing with prices and quantities and labor costs and ratios between productive power and consumptive power." The "physical tools for [national] social experimenting" were thus "at hand."

America, he wrote, had the power to end "those great fears having to do with lack of food, lack of shelter, and lack of employment," provided "the profit motive and the monetary system did not interfere unduly." What was needed was statesmanship. He singled out Vladimir Lenin as "one of the few men of [the] century whose earnestness deserves to rank with that of [the prophet] Amos and [the theologian] John Knox." Lenin "suffered, meditated, thought and acted. However much we may dislike such men," Wallace explained, "we must respect their power to transform society in line with their vision."[93] Left unexplained was how such respect cohered with belief in rural democracy.

In *New Frontiers* (1934), Wallace argued that America's Western frontier had, in the nineteenth century, been gainfully tamed and developed through "rugged individualism." This "frontier thesis" was not original—it had first been stated in 1893 by historian Frederick Jackson Turner, who argued that the end of "westering" demanded the pursuit of new outlets for "American energy." Wallace, however, contended that this energy was now destructive in its effects, economically and socially. "The keynote of the *new* frontier," he wrote, a frontier of the soul, is no longer "individualistic competition" but "cooperation."[94]

Just what this "cooperation" comprised, however, was to be an ongoing source of confusion in Wallace's writing. He was embarrassed to learn that the Italian press was touting *New Frontiers* as support for Mussolini's corporate state, which he claimed to oppose.[95] Wallace wrote as well of the need for "economic democracy," but could define it only as a "process" which the New Deal was making "a strenuous effort to find."[96] Tolley claimed that Wallace saw it as "the right of all men to share in the making of the decisions that affect their economic welfare."[97] Yet in the 1940s Wallace would, confusingly, associate it not with Roosevelt's America but with Stalin's Russia.

In the context of 1930s America, however, Wallace should be seen as part of a wider movement of agricultural intellectuals, such as M. L. Wilson and Howard Tolley, whose aim was to bring government experts and rural citizens into partnership.[98] It was the collaboration between the two groups that lay, at that time, behind their thinking about democratic policy formulation.

But who was ultimately to make decisions? Was it to be the government experts, or the rural citizens? Who was to decide what to grow, where to grow it, how to grow it, and how much to grow? The answer, in practice, was that the New Deal took decision-making power away from poorer farmers, and shifted it to richer ones. The latter then took their cue from the Department of Agriculture, which paid them to embrace its agenda.

Wallace professed belief in the Jeffersonian ideal of America as a nation of small farmer-landowners, but with the critical caveat that these landowners had to be taught to pursue the "general interest"—rather than narrow self-interest. As commerce secretary years later, he would take the same stance toward companies and unions—that they needed to bargain with the interests of consumers and wider society at heart.

Citing Jefferson and Lincoln, Wallace held that democracy "could not work unless there was popular education among the people."[99] He also believed that farmers, if given proper economic information and ethical instruction, would adjust output and marketing practice in the common good—that is, the way he, Henry Wallace, wished them to do.[100] To implement his vision for American agriculture, he therefore constituted a vast network of local institutions to educate—some said indoctrinate[101]—farmers on subjects ranging from soil conservation to the philosophy of national "planning."[102] Thousands of county production-control committees were established, comprised of locally elected farmers, which made acreage allotments and monitored performance.

Though Wallace wanted AAA farming programs to be voluntary, at least officially, he used local surveys and referenda to compel the cooperation of the unwilling. "Remember that the government itself is not proposing compulsion," he assured cotton farmers across the South in a mass mailing dated January 26, 1934. But "if the Department of Agriculture is to advocate legislation providing for compulsion," he added, "it will be because the answers to this questionnaire disclose the unmistakable sentiment of the South."

In pursuing his supply-control agenda, Wallace in the end relied on the self-interest of large and influential landowners. These were men (mostly) with the resources to hire others to farm, while they themselves dedicated the considerable time required to attend committee meetings and master the profitable new business of New Deal agricultural politics. And when their efforts failed to achieve the desired results, such as less output from their neighbors, they lobbied Congress to force holdouts to comply—citing the majority support reflected in Wallace's surveys.[103] It was such lobbying that produced the Bankhead Cotton Control Act of 1934, the Kerr-Smith Tobacco Control Act of 1934, and the Potato Control Act of 1935—all of which were decidedly nonvoluntary.

Tugwell, an unrepentant technocratic liberal with none of Wallace's sentimental Jeffersonianism, later professed that the "grass-roots democracy" celebrated by the AAA was largely theater. Policy was made, ultimately, in Washington, harnessing the self-interest of well-connected farmers pursuing subsidies, debt relief, and higher prices for their handiwork.[104]

Nineteen thirty-six being a presidential election year, Wallace finally got around to changing his party registration from Republican to Democrat.

He made hard-hitting speeches and radio addresses attacking "the greedy and ignorant forces behind the national Republican party." His political charisma, such as it was, was based on an ability to project earnestness to massed believers from a safe distance. He recoiled, however, from the hand-shaking, back-slapping, arm-twisting, cold-calling, and problem-solving that went with the gritty business of campaigning. Roosevelt hardly needed such help from him, however, and went on to beat Kansas Republican Alf Landon in a landslide: 523 electoral votes to 8.

Wallace's second term as agriculture secretary proved less frenetic and contentious than the first. He pivoted from saving the farm sector to sustaining it. He backed programs which, he hoped, would boost demand for U.S. farm goods at home, such as the 1938 minimum-wage legislation, and abroad, such as the dozens of reciprocal trade agreements being pursued by Hull (twenty-one of which would be signed by 1940).[105] Most important, though, he oversaw the creation and passage of a new Agricultural Adjustment Act in 1938. It covered a wide array of programs, including production control, marketing agreements, tenant protection, and government payments for land retirement. But its centerpiece—to Wallace's mind, at least—was provision for his long-championed "ever-normal granary."

Under Wallace's scheme—inspired by the Old Testament story of Joseph, as well as Chinese agricultural history—farmers could stow crops in good years and sell them in bad. In the New Deal version, farmers stored surplus corn, wheat, cotton, rice, or tobacco, either on their own or in facilities provided by the USDA's Commodity Credit Corporation (CCC). Before they sold the crop, the CCC would issue them nonrecourse loans that put a floor under the prices they would receive. If the market price went above the value of the loan, farmers sold the crop, paid back the loan, and kept the profit. If the market price went below the value of the loan, however, farmers kept the cash and the government took the crop, typically dumping it abroad at a loss. The farm lobby group might have been expected to embrace the program, but did not. It agitated instead for more lucrative cash benefits and price supports, of the sort that had marked Wallace's first term.[106] Crop insurance, by comparison, seemed a miserly alternative. As one Georgia senator, Richard B. Russell, put it during his 1936 reelection campaign: "I stand for larger benefit checks."[107]

By 1940, Wallace had also created, taken over, or become an overseer of an alphabet soup of new farm-related agencies. The Soil Conservation Service (SCS) undertook major projects to stop soil erosion. The Drought Relief Service (DRS) bought up cattle in Dust Bowl–stricken areas. The Subsistence Housing Project (SHP) helped poor families finance the purchase of rural land and housing. The Federal Surplus Commodities Corporation (FSCC) bought up excess farm goods for distribution to poor Americans. The Farm Credit Administration (FCA), which refinanced farmers' mortgages at below-market rates, became part of Wallace's department in 1939, as did the Rural Electrification Administration (REA). The department also became a supervising authority for the Civilian Conservation Corps (CCC), a massive work relief program. It further established four regional research and development laboratories to uncover new uses and markets for farm products. The USDA's Farm Security Administration (FSA), created in 1937, swallowed up the independent Resettlement Administration (RA), created in 1935, which itself contained an alphabet soup of programs to address rural tenant poverty—a problem exacerbated by the first AAA in 1933. The RA was directed by Tugwell, who had conceived it, and who had grandiose visions of buying up half a million subsistence farms and resettling its families. In the end, short of the necessary funds, he moved a mere 4,441 of them.[108] Perhaps stimulated by his brief travels in Russia, in 1927, he also used the RA to experiment with new collective farms. These farms, according to one highly approving account of agricultural policy under Wallace, "were not as successful in practice as they appeared on paper."[109]

After seven years and $55 billion in government payments to farms ($1.2 trillion today),[110] it would still take World War II to alleviate the fundamental problem of unprofitable farm production. The AAA and CCC programs, by assuring farmers a guaranteed income with no risk for participation, encouraged them to grow crops *that were already in surplus*. Despite six years of subsidies to cut production, and export subsidies to dump the excess abroad (which Wallace had preached against), the cotton glut was three million bales *greater* in 1939 than it was when Wallace took office.[111] Gross and net farm income, furthermore, just barely nudged upward during the 1930s, and the parity price index—which took account of farm cost of living—actually fell.[112]

"Only the war," concluded one otherwise sympathetic New Deal historian, "rescued the New Deal farm program from disaster."[113] Yet the program was, in the words of an equally sympathetic former USDA chief historian, "at least effective in insuring that the countryside did not move into armed revolt"[114]—which was Roosevelt's prime concern.[115] It did so at the cost of making much of the farm belt permanently dependent on aid and protective regulation from Washington.[116]

Four

THE GURU AND THE NEW COUNTRY

When Henry Wallace arrived in Washington in 1933, he was determined to save American farming from the predations of bankers and industrialists. He was determined, moreover, to save American capitalism from the excesses of individualism. Yet even that hardly covered the expanse of his ambitions. He was, in fact, determined to enlarge his personal quest for spiritual enlightenment into one that would reform the very soul of mankind.

Many around Wallace who knew of his interest in the occult, such as his wife, were deeply discomfited by it. But none, it seemed, ever imagined it might have political and diplomatic consequences. And possibly it would not have—at least had it not been for Wallace's encounter with a Russian agronomist in early 1927.

Having been acquainted with Wallace's father, and with the son's interest in Eastern spiritualism, Dmitri Nikolaevich Borodin, visiting Des Moines, urged the farm editor to familiarize himself with the work and thought of one Nikolai Konstantinovich Rerikh—an artist and theosophist known in America as Nicholas Roerich. The first step would be to visit the new museum bearing his name on New York's Upper West Side.

Wallace made the pilgrimage on April 3. On entering the lobby of the building, he became transfixed before a large Tibetan prayer mat. The concerned receptionist alerted the museum's vice president, Frances Grant, who approached the dazed visitor and asked if he were unwell. Wallace assured her that he was merely experiencing "vibrations." For the next three hours, he peppered her with questions about Roerich and the museum. Grant promised to relay his keen interest to the Master himself—then journeying in Tibet.[1]

Wallace developed an abiding devotion to the museum's artistic, cultural, and spiritual mission. He would only meet Roerich in person once in 1929 (in August in New York) and four times in March and April 1934 (twice in Washington and twice in New York). He would, however, establish a routine contact and intimate friendship with Frances Grant. Just *how* intimate is not known, although many, including the president, would speculate with impious interest.[2]

Over Wallace's first three years as agriculture secretary, no other cause, agricultural or otherwise, so commanded his time and attention as the Roerich Museum. He would phone it at least three dozen times; visit it, or its associated New York events, at least twenty times; and meet with its trustees in Washington regularly. He would also send Roerich and his circle some two hundred letters.[3] These missives, typically deeply personal, were often also candid about political matters. A small subset of them, many weaving Buddhist, Tibetan, Christian, and theosophic jargon in an awkwardly florid style and submissive tone, would emerge at pivotal points in Wallace's later career—causing him, his family, his colleagues, and his political party of the moment acute embarrassment and concern. Based on one of the honorifics Wallace used in addressing Roerich, these would come to be known as the "Guru letters." Faced with evidence of their wider circulation, Wallace would deny, divert, and dissemble. But recent archival finds in Moscow, supplementing evidence long known to exist at the FDR Library, affirm their provenance.[4]

Upon Wallace's death decades later, much of the correspondence in his possession would be destroyed by his attorney (and possibly his wife). In 1933, however, as he began his new career in politics, he gave no thought to how his private words might stir public derision—or even thwart his growing ambitions.

His assistant warned him of the risks. The letters "I couldn't get him to modify all had to do with his mystical associations," Paul Appleby explained decades later. The "Roerich correspondence was something that I argued with him about through the years."[5]

By 1932, however, Wallace had already struck up unusual penpalships with men considered eccentrics; men such as Charles Roos, an ornery self-styled medicine man, and Edward Johndro, an electrical engineer turned astrologer. With Roos, Wallace's letters caricatured Native American English. "I ache with foolish burdens," he wrote in one example, "on shoulders raw-hided thru a thousand foothills of Karma." With Johndro, he pondered whether Saint Paul might never have traveled to Damascus had he known his horoscope.[6] The early 1930s constituted a phase in Wallace's life marked by an obsession with unconventional ways of knowing, and, though aware of the intense disapproval of his wife and colleagues, he refused to practice even the most elementary forms of self-censorship.

The St. Petersburg–born Nicholas Roerich was an artist and adept in Asian archaeology, culture, and religion. In Europe, he had been a landscape and historical painter, as well as a costume and staging designer, of some renown. Many of his paintings were recognizable for their luminous, colorful, primitivist depictions of an idealized and religious Russia. He left St. Petersburg (or Petrograd, as it had become) for Karelia, Finland (then part of the Russian Empire), in 1916, age forty-four, during the turmoil surrounding the Bolshevik coup. He spent the next three years in the Nordic region and London before sailing to New York in October 1920, together with his striking, charismatic wife, Helena (Elena in Russia), and their two boys, George (Yury) and Svetoslav (Svyatoslav).

Barely off the boat, he began a prearranged, twenty-eight-city, coast-to-coast tour, exhibiting his paintings and lecturing on subjects ranging from art to religion and politics.[7] Though a staunch anti-Bolshevik at the time, his views on Soviet matters would become more fluid in the years to come, as his belief in his own providential greatness, and his sense of the opportunities it afforded him, became ever more acute.

A striking figure with a shaven head, high cheekbones, piercing blue eyes, a Fu Manchu mustache, and a long double-plaited beard, Roerich cultivated a devoted following of admirers in New York, a city which sought out pathbreaking artists and intellectuals. The most ardent among them took to addressing him as "Father" or "Guru," believing him and his wife to be privileged conduits for ancient Himalayan wisdom.

The Roerichs called their spiritual doctrine "Agni Yoga." "Agni" in Sanskrit means fire; fire representing, in the Hindu tradition, the natural force behind both the creative and destructive energy of the universe. "Yoga" refers to the spiritual exercises necessary to harness that energy. Agni Yoga, as with theosophy in general, held that all religions were manifestations of humanity's striving to evolve toward greater moral perfection. Unlike Buddhism, with its monastic and inward orientation, Agni Yoga was secular and out-

Nicholas Roerich, Chicago, 1921.

ward in focus, aimed at inspiring action toward the practical, common good of mankind. This humanistic focus held particular appeal to Henry Wallace.

As practitioners of Agni Yoga, the Roerichs manifested an eclectic combination of social activism and millenarian fatalism. Though they were early advocates of practical progressive causes such as environmentalism and feminism, they also believed certain epochs and events to be preordained and inescapable. Foreknowledge of such epochs and events could be disseminated "clairaudiently"—through the ether—to the select few by the great, enlightened Mahatmas of the Himalayas.[8] Believers typically held that these Mahatmas once lived in Tibet, where they "evolved" toward spiritual perfection through many reincarnations, but that they now existed as disembodied souls who could, in rare instances, reappear briefly to the chosen as corporeal beings.

Over their years together in Europe, Nicholas and Helena had jointly developed their theosophical framework, taking up occult practices such as séances. Yet it was Helena who drove their spiritual evolution. A headstrong, at times rebellious, youth, she began experiencing "meaningful dreams and even visions" at a young age, and, in March 1920, claimed to have exchanged knowing glances with the fabled nineteenth-century Mahatmas, Morya and Koot Hoomi, in London's Hyde Park.[9] Why the sight of two tall, bearded Indians in British military garb should have moved her so profoundly is one of the many mysteries surrounding her subsequent emergence as the chosen medium for the Masters' prophecies and commands. One possible explanation is that Helena Blavatsky, the famed cofounder of the Theosophical Society, had, sixty-nine years earlier, claimed to have met the great Morya in the same spot.

Cynics might insist that the Masters did not exist, or that they had at least ceased communications since their bodily demise. Yet even if such cynics were correct, it did not necessarily mean that Helena was a deceptress—however self-serving her "fiery" visions and divinations might have at times appeared. She was, during and after her life, the subject of speculative diagnoses associated with seizures, heart problems, and anxiety disorders.

Once arrived in New York, the new celebrity couple formed an early bond with six individuals, all, curiously, of Jewish backgrounds, who would come to comprise their trusted "inner circle" of artistic and spiritual followers. There was, first, Frances Grant, the woman who would encounter Henry Wallace in his state of ecstatic vibration seven years later. As a twenty-four-year-old journalist and music critic in 1920, she interviewed the artist just after his arrival in the city. There was Nettie Horch, a theosophically inclined art lover, a former schoolmate of Grant's, and the wife of a currency trader named Louis Horch—the man who would become the artist's indispensable financial patron. And, finally, there were the three Lichtmanns: musicians Sina and Maurice, a Russian-speaking couple who were introduced to the artist at his inaugural exhibition in New York, and Maurice's sister, Esther.

The alliance between the Roerichs and the six disciples was cemented at evening séances. Helena herself specialized in "channelling" messages from the astral spirit Allal-Ming—alter ego to the Master Morya. The spirit made stunning revelations regarding Helena's past-life incarnations, and forecast that Nicholas would soon win the Nobel Peace Prize.[10] The spirit also dabbled in political prognostication. At a séance in Cambridge, Massachusetts, he revealed to their son George, a Harvard freshman in 1921, that the Bolsheviks would soon be overthrown.[11]

That forecast was off by some seven decades, yet the Master never lost their confidence. Helena would develop the capacity to communicate with him through what she called "automatic writing," a phenomenon in which she would transcribe his perfect wisdom for dissemination to the six "co-workers," as she called them.

For the Roerichs, politics were intertwined with spiritualism. Inspired by the legend of "Shambhala," a onetime earthly Tibetan-Buddhist paradise that now existed as a heavenly vision of perfection, they had, by the time of their first pilgrimage to India in 1923,[12] already made it their life's mission to refound it on earth. More tangibly, they hoped to spearhead the formation of a new theocratic state over vast territory in Central Asia—territory then claimed or coveted by four rival states: Britain, China, Japan, and the Soviet Union.

Fuzzy as were the prospective entity's borders and ideology, "the New Country," or "the Sacred Union of the East," as they came to call it in 1924,

Nicholas Roerich with Frances Grant, the Horchs, and the Lichtmanns. Sitting, from left to right: Esther Lichtmann, Sina Lichtmann, Nicholas Roerich, Nettie Horch, and Frances Grant. Standing, from left to right: Louis Horch, Sofie Shafran, Svetoslav Roerich, Maurice Lichtmann, Tatyana Grebenshchikova, and Georgy Grebenshchikov, December 7, 1924.

was to unite Tibetans, Mongols, and Asiatic Russians in an eclectic polity founded on purified Buddhist wisdom, communistic economic precepts, and private American capital. As implausible as such a utopia may have sounded, the couple never fretted over strategy or details. Morya, they were sure, would guide them, and success was preordained.

Much as Henry Wallace would call himself a "practical mystic," Nicholas Roerich termed himself a "practical idealist." For both men, that practicality encompassed not merely *what* they wished to achieve, but *how* they intended to achieve it. And for both men, legitimate means included alliance with a despised, godless creed.

"There should be business with the Bolsheviks," Sina recorded "Father" saying on his return to New York in October 1924. Father would draw the Bolsheviks in by explaining that "Buddha was building a communistic system," just as "Christ [had] preached a communistic system." And leaders of "the New Country" would build on this legacy "by acknowledging Lenin as a prominent communist."[13] Bolshevism and the Eastern faiths, the Kremlin would see, were natural allies. The result would be a new Shambhala.

To begin forging this alliance, Maurice introduced Father to fellow émigré Dmitry Borodin. The agronomist, inspired by Roerich's vision of a Russian-led, spiritually revived Central Asia, offered to endorse him with Soviet diplomats likely to prove supportive.[14]

The first fruitful introduction was that to the Soviet ambassador to Germany, Nikolai Krestinsky, who would agree to receive Roerich in Berlin. At a meeting on Christmas Eve 1924, Roerich told Krestinsky's embassy colleague, Georgy Astakhov, a likely co-optee of Soviet foreign intelligence, of his travels through the Himalayas, which he presently planned to resume. Roerich stressed "the role which . . . Soviet Russia was destined to play in the national-liberation struggle of the people of the East." He also highlighted "the identity of Communism with the teaching of Buddha," a belief which, he claimed, was preached by both the Tibetan lamas and Himalayan Mahatmas.

Though a member of the Russo-British Fraternity and the Theosophical Society in London, Roerich scorned Britain's "occupation" of Tibet and its "active anti-Soviet propaganda" there. He may, too, it seems, have offered to report on British activities in the region.[15]

The ambassador was intrigued by the artist, who appeared both well connected and friendly to Kremlin interests. Roerich, he reported to Foreign Minister Georgy Chicherin, seemed "completely pro-Soviet." The artist was a "sort-of Buddho-Communist," he said, and was "on very good terms with the Indians and, particularly, with the Tibetans."[16] Prudently, however, he added that it was "difficult to judge how valuable and trustworthy [Roerich's] Asian accounts were."[17]

Following the Berlin encounter, Roerich headed back to Darjeeling to reunite with his family, confident that the Kremlin would support his hoped-for New Country. To fulfill providence, he set out with Helena and George on August 8, 1925 on what would become a historic three-year expedition.[18] By train, by horse, by cart, and by foot, they would journey through the mountains, valleys, and plains of Sikkim, Kashmir, Ladakh, Xinjiang, Siberia, Altai, Mongolia, Tibet, and the Trans Himalayas—comprising lands previously unseen or documented by Westerners. Horch funded it as a unique artistic and archaeological endeavor, which would bring the museum hundreds of new Roerich paintings, but Morya ordained it (through Helena, of course) as a holy mission by which Roerich, the "Western Dalai Lama," would bring forth Shambhala.

Back in New York, meanwhile, Borodin continued to lobby Soviet contacts on Roerich's behalf. Roerich's greatest success, for which he would suspend his expedition to travel to Moscow in June 1926, was in securing a meeting with the foreign minister himself. Fortuitously, Morya was by then wholly supportive of working with Bolsheviks, having declared the year prior that "everything has changed," and that "Lenin is with us." Or, at least, Lenin's *spirit* was with them, his person having been dead eighteen months.[19]

Next to the great Lenin himself, no figure so influenced the formation of early Soviet foreign policy as Georgy Vasilyevich Chicherin.[20] Arguably the best educated and linguistically gifted foreign minister in Europe, Chicherin was acquainted with theosophy, as well as with Roerich himself, from his student days in St. Petersburg. He was also part of an early Bolshevik avant-garde receptive to Buddhist and esoteric movements on practical grounds—that they could be played for ideological and geopolitical advantage.

Roerich bore some unusual gifts for the minister, foremost among them "a small casket with soil from the Buddha's birthplace" which the Mahatmas wished to have placed upon "the grave of Vladimir Ilyich." Where the

casket was laid is unknown, though it was nowhere near Lenin. As for Roerich's Tibetan-language "Letter from the Mahatmas," proclaiming "the necessity of the measures for introduction of world communism as a step in
the inevitable evolution," a letter given to Helena by the mysterious wise
ones,[21] it was deposited forthwith in the Foreign Commissariat's (NKID)
archives.

Though surely bemused by the offerings, the minister was nonetheless,
like Krestinsky, taken by Roerich's claim that the lamas, of whom Soviet leaders knew little, sought "world union between Buddhism and Communism,"
as well by the artist's nine-point plan for achieving such union.[22] He thus
passed on a favorable account of the meeting (eschewing mention of caskets
and Mahatmas) to Vyacheslav Mikhaylovich Molotov, secretary of the Communist Party's Central Committee.[23]

Roerich also advanced his plan, hatched back in 1924, to secure a lucrative fifty-year economic concession in Siberia—one that would give him
commercial mining rights over a span of some nineteen thousand square
miles in the Altai region.[24] With Horch's financial backing, a company
was, in that year, incorporated in New York to carry out the plan—the
Beluha Corporation.[25]

Until Roerich's arrival in Moscow, Beluha had made no progress.[26]
Chicherin opposed Americans trading with China and Mongolia from
Siberia, while lesser apparatchiks thought Horch and Lichtmann of dubious
character—and possibly even "agents of espionage" (razvedchikami). After
Roerich's visit, however, a State Concession Committee (GKK) official
concluded that the artist, "though a bit funny and clumsy," "sympathizes with
communism" and "wants to be useful to us."[27] Its board, chaired by one Leon
Trotsky, demiurge of the Russian Revolution, resolved in secret session to
allow the company to begin explorations.[28]

Resuming his Asian travels in July 1926, Roerich thus felt sure that
Morya's belated embrace of Leninism would, quite literally, pay dividends.
Not only would Beluha end his perpetual financial troubles, but it would
lay the foundations for a "New Russia." That is, a New White Russia, in
Siberia—a White Russia at the heart of Shambhala. Beluha's supreme aim,
as Helena would diary, would be "detaching Siberia from Moscow," and re-
attaching it to an Agni-inspired Central Asia.[29]

Defending her husband's cynical stroking of the Bolsheviks, Helena naturally invoked the moral authority of the Masters. "Who may dare blame you after [your] glorification of Lenin?" she recorded Morya asking rhetorically.[30] "Our duty is to give R[ussia] a chance," but the larger purpose "is that the Plan [for Shambhala] does not suffer."[31]

Though the Kremlin was clearly ignorant of Roerich's true aims,[32] its practical agenda would collide with his soon enough. Among the many problems encountered, the artist's scheme to ally with the Dalai Lama's exiled rival, the Panchen Lama, and to aid his return from Chinese Inner Mongolia to Tibet, clashed with Soviet designs to co-opt the incumbent lamaic power. And so the Kremlin would lose interest in Roerich's Shambhalic ambitions. But Roerich faced other problems.

What should have been the triumphal climax of his expedition, entry into the holy city of Lhasa in the fall of 1927, would instead turn into a dangerous and humiliating disaster. Proclaiming himself head of a previously unknown "Western Buddhist Council," and carrying flags of the Dalai Lama and the United States, he stoked the suspicions of both the Tibetan and British authorities. For five months, from October 1927 through February 1928, the Roerichs were effectively quarantined on the brutally cold, windswept Changtang plateau, and refused entry into the capital.

By May, they were back in India. Though the expedition had fulfilled its artistic and cartographic objectives,[33] the Roerichs had, to their great disappointment, failed to find the reincarnated Morya, or to advance the coming of Shambhala.

Economic collaboration with the Soviets would, too, wither over the two years following Roerich's meeting with Chicherin. Under the direction of Roerich's Leningrad-based brother, Boris, Beluha stalled. In 1927, technical and staffing problems hindered the company's Siberian mineral explorations, while Soviet foreign policy took a hard left turn. Stalin consolidated power; the NKID soured on admitting foreign capital, "particularly American," into the Altai; Trotsky was fired from the GKK; and Boris was imprisoned. Two years later, Boris would, in exchange for leniency, become an OGPU (security and political police) informant.[34]

In May 1928, Maurice Lichtmann would write to the GKK, pleading for an extension of the exploration period into 1929.[35] But when the committee demanded more collateral in exchange, Horch, who was by then dedicating all his free capital to building a skyscraper to house an expanded Roerich Museum, balked.[36] In May 1929, the GKK canceled the company's exploration rights.[37] The following month, Nicholas and George sailed back across the Atlantic to tend the American flock.

For the time being, Roerich's dreams of remaking Central Asia lay in ruins. There had been no compatibility of political purpose between Roerich and the Soviets, and, without it, the Kremlin saw no compelling grounds for letting Americans exploit its natural riches. Henry Wallace would, as commerce secretary two decades later, learn this lesson as well.

After nearly five years of arduous travels in Asia and Europe, Nicholas Roerich arrived back in New York on June 18, 1929.[38] For the itinerant artist, it was a homecoming of sorts, and a triumphant one at that. Three months earlier, in a ceremony staged before a crowd of five hundred, the cornerstone had been laid for a magnificent twenty-nine-story Art Deco style "Master Building," at 310 Riverside Drive, whose lower three floors would rehouse Roerich's namesake museum and the associated artistic, musical, and educational enterprises ("Corona Mundi" and the "Master Institute of United Arts").[39] The following day, Roerich was, in recognition of his work to protect cultural treasures in time of war, nominated for the Nobel Peace Prize. Now, the great artist and activist, accompanied by police motorcycle escort, was returning to the city famed for love of fame itself.

Henry Wallace, however, had no interest in Roerich's celebrity. It was the man's spiritual thought and aesthetic vision that fascinated him. "Roerich's mysticism," Wallace reflected at the time, "both in words and in painting," had "a power unknown to science." Yet it also had "a decidedly practical aspect," he judged, an aspect that would "eventually [make it] significant to the scientific world."[40] The Nobel nomination showed that it could even have political significance. Wallace was therefore eager to meet this exceptional man in person, an opportunity that would be extended to him in August.

Of that meeting, nothing is recorded, although we do know that Roerich gave Wallace a copy of Helena's first volume of *Agni Yoga*. We also know that Wallace took great interest in Mahatmas and Shambhala. And we know that Wallace would recall the meeting to Roerich in a letter written the year before Roosevelt's election; a letter in which he would urge Roerich to work with him—two "followers of the inner light"—in some as-yet-undefined but important and pragmatic way.

With "spiritual and economic dangers" growing around the world, the letter would warn, the time for mere "reading" had "passed."[41] It was time for deeds. This belief—that science and spiritualism needed to unite in the service of practical political action—would come to mark Wallace as both a compelling and controversial public figure.

Roerich, for his part, was anxious to resume his great political quest in Central Asia. In 1929, however, he could not have imagined that, to make it possible, he would need the backing of an Iowan farm editor. For now, he was indentured to the millionaire Louis Horch, whose priority was to monetize association with his trending brand.

On the evening of October 17, 1929, five thousand visitors crammed the new museum at its grand public opening; seven hundred filled its theater to watch Horch bestow upon Roerich a medal for cultural contributions, and to hear the Master himself baptize the new shrine to Agni art and thought. "The feeling among the audience was exalted," Sina recorded.[42] For the Roerich enterprise, these were glory days. But they would be short-lived.

Less than two weeks later, the stock market collapsed. Business stalled. A Great Depression ensued. The Master Building, like so much else built on a base of debt, became an object of struggle between those who issued that debt and those who had bought it.

Horch, who had invested $1 million in the complex,[43] and borrowed $2.5 million more,[44] began to show himself ever more clearly a duplicitous disciple. As far back as 1923, he had been pressuring Roerich to sign documents—some of which he had pledged, falsely, to later destroy—that would enable him to avoid (or evade) taxes,[45] to claim ownership of donated art works, to arrogate legal powers, and to strategically reclassify gifts as loans[46] or payments—contingent on the financial implications of changing circumstances. Now, in the wake of the market crash, he looked to extract every dime possible from the museum and its educational ventures—before staff or bondholders could get hold of them.

Horch, Sina recorded on November 1, instructed her "to deliver all the money from the Master Institute to [his] office." She protested that there would be nothing with which to pay the teachers.[47] As the economy went from bad to worse, the building would, in the spring of 1932, go into receivership and be sued for nonpayment of taxes.[48] But Horch would prove a master of tax law, city charters, and judicial proceedings, and in July of that year emerge victorious in appellate court—returning control of the property to the museum's directors.[49] Those directors, however, were themselves mere legal fictions, to be discarded once they ceased to serve Louis Horch's interests.

For Roerich, 1929 would end in disappointment. The Nobel committee in Stockholm, he learned, deemed no one qualified for that year's peace prize. A year later, in November 1930, the accolade would be backdated and bestowed upon Frank B. Kellogg, Hoover's secretary of state. Whereas the proposed "Banner of Peace," or "Roerich Pact," had outlawed harm to cultural treasures in times of war, the Kellogg-Briand Pact had outdone it in banning war itself. Morya's decade-old divination of Nobel glory remained unfulfilled.

For much of 1930, Roerich struggled to secure a visa to return to India, where an ailing Helena had remained. On the basis of his Soviet "associations," authorities in Delhi and London now deemed him a possible "Communist emissary"—and refused him entry. Having failed to obtain naturalization in the United States, Roerich traveled to Paris in July to secure a French passport (one valid for travel, and not citizenship). In a subsequent appeal to the British authorities, in which he now titled himself "His Excellency Baron Nicholas de Roerich," he stressed an urgent need to tend to his wife, who was suffering from "frequent heart attacks and nervous breakdowns." This appeal earned him a conditional three-month visa. Husband and wife reunited on December 11.[50]

In March 1931, Britain removed the limit on Roerich's stay, though kept a watchful eye on his activities. A March 1932 government memo from Delhi to London expressed fears that he might "place himself in the position of the Dalai Lama and establish Bolshevik control right down to the borders of India."[51]

By this time, Roerich had lost all interest in cultivating Soviet support for his Central Asian utopia. Yet he had never lost faith that he would, sooner rather than later, spearhead its creation. Morya, through Helena, reinforced that faith. And so Roerich kept himself occupied, for the time being, with both his art and the creation of a new nearby institute—the Urusvati Institute[52] (Urusvati being Helena's esoteric name)—dedicated to the study of Himalayan fauna, archaeological finds, and linguistic heritage. Supported by an annual grant from the Roerich Museum, from private donations, and from Roerich's contribution of land, paintings, and royalties, the building was completed in August 1933. But the cessation of funds from New York, as well as a falling-out with the hired botanist over intellectual property, conspired against Urusvati's early success.[53] Its activities would be "frozen" in 1938.[54]

A devout American disciple, however, now offered Roerich the priceless prospect of patronage from Washington—and possibly even from the president himself. Providentially, the earnest Iowan—the man who had, six years earlier, been transfixed before a Tibetan prayer mat in his museum's lobby—was now a member of Franklin Roosevelt's cabinet.

"I have sent a beam to Wallace," Morya told Helena, on May 24, 1933, so that "Roosevelt may accept the advice of *Fujama*"—that is, Nicholas—and "contribute to the glory of America by receiving my Indication."[55] An "Indication" was an esoteric command, typically identifying an individual or nation by code name, which Helena sent to others—at times by messenger, at times telepathically—to fulfill Morya's will. And Morya now willed, or so Helena recorded, that "The peoples of the Americas should enter into a New Epoch"—an epoch in which "nationalities should start to disappear, forming an integrated people's consciousness."[56] It was a will, and a belief, which Wallace himself would foster with particular earnestness in the 1940s.[57]

Month after month, Helena records "channellings" from Morya on the importance of bending Roosevelt, through Wallace, to the cause of Shambhala. The British—or *"the monkeys,"* as Morya and the Roerichs call them—would look to stand in the way.[58] But "America should know that the [time for] reconstruction of the East has come."[59]

When the Dalai Lama died in December 1933, Morya rejoiced at the opportunity afforded them. "Of course," he tells Helena, "you understand that [what happened in] Tibet [is] not without Our wish. Such an event must bring turmoil in the West."[60] And turmoil brings opportunity.

Despite his many setbacks, Roerich, who enjoyed being photographed in elaborate Oriental silk robes, still envisioned his imminent emergence as both Western Lama and spiritual leader of the White Russians. Ultimately, he felt destined to reign as philosopher king over a vast territory covering Mongolia, Central Asia, the Himalayas, and southern Siberia.

As for his most important American recruits, Wallace and Roosevelt, Helena's diary entries stress, in classic cult fashion,[61] the need to isolate them from the baleful influence of their families. "The wives of W[allace] and R[oosevelt]," as unbelievers, she records Morya warning her, "are harmful."[62] Her entries also reveal a scathing condescension toward Wallace. The agriculture secretary, Morya tells Helena, is a man "worthy of pity. He owes his existence to his recognition of Us, but does not know how to apply it."[63]

By early 1932, Wallace had adopted the "esoteric name" of *Galahad*— Galahad being the pure-hearted knight of Arthurian legend. But Helena was careful to make him display sufficient obeisance before bestowing it officially. And, as required, Wallace's many letters to Frances Grant over his first year in office, 1933, show striking elements of submissiveness and indiscretion on the Roerichs' behalf.

Wallace overflows with emotion for the cause; emotion he never shows for individuals. He speaks of his "Search [for] the Holy Chalice," his "continuous striving," his "patience and grief"; he describes his mind as "quivering with questions."[64] He addresses the ethereal Morya, through Grant, as "Oh Master M." He speaks of Roosevelt in terms of his worth, or lack thereof, in serving the Master's aims.

Wallace alternatingly refers to Roosevelt as "*the Flaming One*" and "*the Wavering One*," depending upon the latter's willingness to further those aims. "[T]he President is undoubtedly an agent through which great forces are working," Wallace writes to Grant in July 1933, "but he is as provoking to me in the density of his perceptions at times as I doubtless am to you."[65]

Notwithstanding conspicuous differences in their approach to politics, Wallace and Roosevelt esteemed each other's open and curious minds. Both men were Freemasons. The most tangible surviving evidence of their mutual interests is the one-dollar bill, whose Masonic Eye of Providence at the apex of the Great Pyramid was the product, in 1934, of Wallace's inspiration and Roosevelt's design. The Latin phrase beneath the Pyramid, *Novus Ordo Seclorum* (New Order of the Ages), signified for Wallace the spirit of the New Deal— a suggestion which delighted the president.[66] Though there is no hard evidence of Roerich's direction of the bill's redesign, he strongly approved of it. And it is significant that the Eye is represented in several of his paintings.[67] The phrase *Novus Ordo Seclorum*, and Wallace's account of the president's reaction to it, also feature in letters Wallace wrote to Grant in 1934 and 1935.[68]

Notwithstanding the bond of Masonry between president and agriculture secretary, Wallace was discouraged by Roosevelt's unreadiness to embrace the quest for deeper truths. "He has an exceedingly practical side which is baffling," Wallace laments to Grant in the July 1933 letter. This stubborn practicality, amplified by a conservative State Department (cover name "*the Old House*"), made it necessary for Wallace, at times, to resist pressure from the Roerichs to act expeditiously.

"The appropriate moment," Wallace warns Grant, "has not yet appeared for speaking of the Banner of Peace"—that is, the flag of the Roerich Pact.[69] Four years had passed since the drafting of the pact, which had been the subject of two conferences in Belgium, drawing delegates from over twenty nations, in 1931 and 1932. *The Old House* had dismissed the initiative as "futile, weak, and unenforceable"; Hull himself ("*the Sour One*") called it "malarkey." Thanks to *the Flaming One*, however, whose mother was fascinated with Roerich, *the Sour One*, in October 1933, authorized Wallace to stand in for him at the third "Roerich Peace Banner Convention."[70] Twenty-seven nations sent delegations to Washington, providing Wallace, as the official "Protector" of the gathering, with his first major opportunity to capture the spotlight in foreign affairs.

"[D]uring his speech," Sina reported to the Roerichs, "it seemed like an amazing blue star was shining above the *friend*"—that is, Wallace. It was "as if Christ himself had enclothed Wallace in martial armor, and he was led to a heroic deed by the gem of the Three Wise Men of the East."[71] This performance elevated Wallace in Morya's esteem. "For the time being," he instructed Helena on December 19, "let [Wallace] be left with the name of *Galahad*." He may, after all, have been "a Norman knight" in his past life.[72] Eleven days later, Wallace would visit the Roerich Museum in New York, where Grant would confer upon him the honored name.

In January 1934, Henry Wallace asked the chief of his department's Bureau of Plant Industry, the forty-two-year-old Knowles Ryerson, to accompany him on a train trip to Birmingham. The agriculture secretary was curious to learn the status of an item in the department's draft budget: funding for an expedition to Central Asia, intended to secure the seeds of grasses that could withstand arid weather.

Ryerson was elated at Wallace's interest. These seeds might, his botanists had reasoned, restore the American Dust Bowl to its earlier glory days, ensuring that its soil could withstand erosion and its grass future droughts. He had been trying to fund the plan for years, but the department's budget director repeatedly denied his request.

Wallace now promised to take the matter to the president. Yet for reasons which Ryerson could not then discern, Wallace also insisted that Ryerson handle the details by himself. He was not to discuss them with anyone.[73]

The president, in Wallace's later recollection, did not just endorse the expedition, but was, in fact, its *inspiration*. This recollection owes not to Wallace's generosity of spirit, but to his enduring tendency to ascribe to Roosevelt ideas for which he, Wallace, would later wish not to own credit—or to take blame.

On March 3, Ryerson submitted a personnel list for the secretary's approval. For nearly two weeks, however, Wallace did not respond. Yet on the evening of March 15, Ryerson received a surprise call from the boss, asking that he come to the Mayflower Hotel.[74]

Seated with Wallace off the lobby, Ryerson saw, was an exotic-looking gentleman, about sixty years of age. Wallace introduced him, explaining that the renowned Dr. Roerich was going to aid the Gobi expedition. Ryerson was baffled. He needed botanists, not artists or activists. Yet he responded that he would, of course, welcome the gentleman's counsel. Wallace, who would wage a career-long struggle to detect disingenuity, was relieved.

"Our R[yerson] was in today," he would presently write to Frances Grant, "and I think I have him coming along nicely."[75] He could now safely send Ryerson to Capitol Hill, as a credible scientist, to plead the case for funding.[76]

The Central Asian expedition, however, unbeknownst to anyone else in the U.S. government, was not about seeds or science. It was about Shambhala.

Wallace's dedication to the quest was unbounded. "I have thoughts of the New Country," he wrote to his "Dear Guru" a year before their meeting at the Mayflower, "going forth to meet the seven stars under the sign of the three stars.":

[I] think of the People of Northern Shambhalla [*sic*] and the has-
tening feet of the Successor of Buddha. . . . And so I await your
convenience prepared to do what I am here to do.

May Peace, Joy and Fire attend you as always,

G[alahad][77]

In the course of 1933, Wallace would write many such missives to Roerich and the museum inner circle. Some of these documented his efforts to
educate "*the Flaming One*" to "the trade possibilities with Central Asia" and
"the qualifications of *the Messenger* [Roerich] who comes from a distant
land."[78]

Grant enthused to Roerich that Wallace and Roosevelt could be made
"veritable partners to the enterprise."[79] She told him of the secretary's meeting with the president on July 5, in which he raised the prospect of "new
countries" in Asia, "the moment for [which] was propitious." The two men
spoke of "the Land of [Genghis] Khan"—that is, Mongolia. Of that conversation, Wallace, unfortunately, "had to leave much unwritten." But he was,
Grant concluded, "ready to act at once." He would "carry out the Order in
the best and finest way."[80]

In October, Grant reported that Wallace had embraced their cause of
stopping U.S. diplomatic recognition of the Soviet Union. "Our friend,"
Grant assured Roerich, "will bring all pressure to bear against consumma-
tion of this terrible measure"—a measure that would undermine White Russian faith in Washington.[81] In stark contrast to Wallace's later dedication to
the cause of U.S.-Soviet friendship, a cause for which he would become an
iconic figure among anti–Cold War progressives, Wallace now lobbied Roosevelt against recognizing Moscow or lending it money. He denounced "the
Russian leadership [as] so utterly without religion [and] so bitter regarding
certain things which we hold dear" as to make political or economic engagement harmful.[82]

But Wallace's objections were to no avail. Roosevelt, conscious that the
United States was the last major power refusing relations, hopeful that trade
might boost the U.S. economy, and determined to exploit all means of containing Japan, would not be swayed. To Wallace's bitter disappointment, the
president granted recognition on November 16.

In December, Grant wrote to Roerich of another promising use for their valued disciple. Wallace, she said, had informed her of a possible "Expedition . . . for the purpose of discovering drought resistant grasses." After Roerich's "arrival [back in New York,] the route for [it] could be suggested."[83] That route might be made to serve two causes: that of finding seeds, and that of refounding Shambhala.

But success was not a given. "[A]pparently," Wallace told her, "hearings will have to be held in which the scientific basis" for the expedition will be scrutinized by Congress.[84] Ryerson, as the department's lead botanist, would have to testify, and would need to be made cooperative.

Every element of the scheme came together in a remarkable message from Grant to Roerich on January 3, 1934:

> The plant industries dept. of our friend's work want certain drouth resistance plants which grow in the vicinity where *Am.*["*Amos*"/Roerich] was on his [1925–27] expedition. For this purpose a certain amount of $25,000 was put into budget, and at first rejected. The *ch*[*ief*/FDR], however, when appealed to by our friend . . . said he accepted the plan and would OK the appropriation, which would be for $50,000. The exact direction for this exped[ition] was not determined, and it was tho[ugh]t that *Am.* might help [the] plan. According to the needs, the dept. botanist would have to accompany; all other things such as direction, personnel, might be determined by *Am.* as this would be up to our friend. Hence, it occurred to me that *Am.* might be interested since perhaps the same could be combined in various ways.[85]

Henry Wallace, then, under the guise of aiding American agriculture, intended to mislead Congress into funding a Russian mystic's plan to change the political map of Central Asia. Even more remarkable, Wallace had no notion of what sort of polity this mystic intended to create. "[W]hat structure of government are we working toward?" he asked Grant in a February letter. And "what economic principles?"[86] The questions showed humble curiosity and uncritical obedience.

Roerich would never answer these questions. But he would reveal his intended way forward. On March 14, 1934, the day he arrived in New York from Paris, and the day before Wallace introduced him to Ryerson in Washington, Roerich sent Wallace an English translation of a plan authored by his Harbin-based brother, Vladimir, on Roerich's direction. That plan, code-named *Alatyr*, after a stone sacred in Slavic folklore, would outline a communitarian agricultural cooperative in Manchuria, financed by American loans and venture capital.[87] What American investor might commit capital to such an enterprise was unclear, but Nicholas thought it a brilliant first stage in uniting the peoples of the wider region under the precepts of Agni Yoga.

The region where Shambhala was to be reborn was, in 1934, a particularly dangerous cauldron of geopolitical intrigue. The Japanese, who had invaded Manchuria in September 1931, had expanded their control of the region through installation of a puppet regime under the last Ch'ing emperor, Pu-yi, and subsequent seizure of Jehol province. Pu-yi served as a rallying point for Mongols and Chinese wanting independence from Republican China. He also served Japan's interests in neighboring Inner Mongolia, under effective Chinese control, and Outer Mongolia, under Soviet control, by allowing it to pose as a liberating force for all the region's Mongol peoples. Intelligence agents of the three nations competed to manipulate opinion among the rivalrous ethnic groups. War between any of those nations could have broken out at any time—and indeed would break out in 1937, with Japan's invasion of China proper.

Japanese cooperation, however, had become critical to Roerich's political ambitions, once it became clear that the Soviets would not abet them. "Surely, Japan is on the side of friendship," Sina recorded, "since the Japanese are the only opponents of [the] Bolsheviks."[88] Morya himself declared (through Helena, of course) that "the warriors of the Rising Sun" would serve the cause of Shambhala.[89]

Tokyo was host to a chapter of the Roerich Society. And the Kyoto Municipal Museum was set to exhibit seventeen of the Master's works in 1935.[90] These facts no doubt showed Japan to be not only a tool of providence, but a highly civilized nation with a refined appreciation for art.

Roerich began his cultivation of the Japanese government even before leaving for Asia. Days after his March meeting with the agriculture secretary in Washington, Roerich told the Japanese consul general in New York that Henry Wallace was "a potential future president" and "a friend of [his] nation"—a message at odds with U.S. foreign policy.[91]

The State Department had no interest in aiding Japanese or Russian expansion (whether White or Red), particularly at the expense of China. Thus was Henry Wallace ensuring a cabinet clash by demanding that Roerich head an expedition through Manchuria. But he would not to be deterred.

At his office on the morning of March 16, 1934, Wallace clarified for Ryerson the true nature of the Russian's role. Roerich would not, after all, be merely advising the mission. He would be *leading* it. This time Ryerson was not merely baffled, but appalled. Though aware that Wallace could derail his career, he made no effort to hide his feelings. Roerich, he protested, was not even a *U.S. citizen*, let alone a scientist. And Manchuria "was the hottest diplomatic area" on earth. The secretary's plan was therefore dangerous.

Wallace waved him off. Roerich, he explained, was "revered" among the people of the region. And his son George, expert in its many languages, would serve as the mission's deputy.[92]

Such assurances hardly comforted Ryerson. He feared for his botanists' safety.[93] Taking his leave, he quickly tipped off contacts at the State Department. They, too, were aghast. The Roerichs, they said, were "shysters" and "crooks," possibly even "Russian agents." Wallace's own deputy, Rex Tugwell, urged Ryerson to have nothing to do with the clan. "You're headed for trouble," he warned.

Soon after, Wallace was visited by an angry Stanley Hornbeck, chief of the State Department's division of Far Eastern Affairs. "Purple" with rage, the veteran China hand warned him that Roerich, a White Russian traveling on a French passport, could, if let loose in Manchuria, drag the United States into a political maelstrom involving three hostile nations.

The State Department, though unclear as to whether Roerich was a Bolshevik agent or nemesis, was certain he was up to no good. Wallace, in any case, refused to take Hornbeck seriously. The Roerichs, he insisted, would act with perfect sense and decorum.

Following the meeting, Wallace ordered Ryerson to speak no further about the Roerichs.[94] He also set out to cover his own tracks, ensuring that he could parry any inquiries made as to the nature of his contacts with them.

"Could you verify with F[ather]," he asked George in mid-April, "the dates I met you at the Mayflower?":

As I informed the Guru, extraordinary watchfulness now seems to be necessary. Agencies seem to make it their jobs to watch certain people. . . . I have no definite cause for worry, but certain extraordinary warnings are manifest.[95]

Wallace also began to reveal concern about how fast and how far to bring the president into the secret plans. "[I] have just received the indication," he wrote to Grant in early May, "and am quite willing if it is the will of the Lord to talk in full with the W[avering One]. I could go into all aspects except the deeply hidden if you think that it is wise." However, "my feeling has been that [FDR] is so deeply prejudiced against the *rulers* [Japanese] that it may not be wise to go all the way." He worried that speaking prematurely "about the Banner [of Peace] and the *Envoy* [Roerich] might imperil the journey because of [FDR's] fear of the *rulers*."[96] He preferred to keep the true purpose of the journey hidden, at least for the present time, from the president.

Helena in India, funnel of the divine will, meanwhile recorded Morya's growing annoyance with Wallace's self-important reports from Washington. "You can write [down]," Morya told her on May 15, "that *Galahad* should not consider himself a savior of the Plan. He has [only] helped himself."[97] Morya's evident jealousy toward Wallace was merely a prelude for the greater storms ahead in 1935.

On April 22, 1934, Nicholas and George boarded a train at New York's Penn Station. The museum disciples "kissed the dear ones good-bye," Sina recorded, and the men began "their great mission for the salvation of Russia."[98] After the cross-continental trip to Seattle, they boarded an ocean steamer bound for Japan. Two and half weeks later, on May 10, Roerich *père et fils* disembarked at the great port city of Yokohama, from whence they were taken by car, courtesy of the Japanese Ministry of Public Instruction, to Tokyo.[99] Ignorant of their mission, which the daily *Yomiuri Shimbun* characterized as "sightseeing," Japanese art lovers and Russian émigrés hailed the men as honored pilgrims.[100]

Sporting a letter from Wallace asking them to "lead and protect" the expedition, Nicholas met with Japanese authorities to smooth their travel to the Asian mainland. He quickly crossed diplomatic red lines. Visiting the "Manchukuo" puppet legation, which fronted for the Japanese occupation of Manchuria, and which was unrecognized by Washington, he requested their visas and permission to conduct explorations. He paid a call on war minister Senjuro Hayashi, leader of the 1931 Manchurian invasion, whom he hailed as "a leader of great ability." And he gave self-promotional interviews to the local press.

U.S. consul general Arthur Garrels cabled Hull that Roerich's behavior was "embarrassing to the Embassy [and] the American Government." An ireful secretary of state, who had not even known that Wallace had put Roerich at the head of the expedition, cabled back that the father and son, being non-U.S. citizens, should not be extended "any assistance which later might be embarrassing to them or to this Government." He further wanted no U.S. involvement in "any request for a 'Manchukuo' or Japanese armed guard to go with the party outside the Japanese empire."[101]

By the time Ryerson's botanists, Howard MacMillan and James Stephens, arrived in Tokyo on June 1, the Roerichs were gone. They had made their way to Manchuria, accompanied by a Japanese Foreign Office interpreter, leaving behind instructions to secure supplies and arms—arms the Japanese had not allowed them to bring.[102] MacMillan mailed Ryerson two local English-language articles documenting Roerich's freelance activities, observing that he would no doubt want them "preserved for future reference."[103]

In Harbin, Nicholas and George set up base at Vladimir's home. Like other members of the city's seventy-thousand-strong White Russian element, Vladimir was solidly anti-Bolshevik. Among those local Whites, the more radical element organized under the banner of the Russian Fascist Party, which enjoyed Japanese patronage. But the city also housed a large minority of Reds, Soviet citizens, 36,000 in 1934, most of whom were working for the massive KVZhD Soviet-owned Chinese Eastern Railway and its many supporting concessions and public facilities. A large Soviet, as well as Japanese, spy network operated in the city, side by side with private weapons merchants and drug traffickers.[104]

With the American botanists still busy in Tokyo, Nicholas assembled a small Agni Yogi following in Harbin, spreading word of the coming rebirth of Shambhala. On June 11, he announced the formation of the *Alatyr* cooperative, to be chaired by Vladimir.

Back in Washington, Wallace pressed Grant to find out the "locations where the co-ops might be," as American investors would wish to know.[105]

Roerich never answered these or other pleas for details, claiming that his mail was being screened. A month later, however, he wrote to the "*KRUG*"—the Russian name for the museum inner circle—saying that he wanted $10,000 to $15,000 for *Alatyr*'s launch, and asking that the request be transmitted "to where appropriate."[106] From New York, it was duly forwarded to Wallace, who, oblivious to any conflict with his public role, began soliciting private funds.

The Roerichs next traveled to the Manchukuo capital of Hsinking. George, in a letter to Ryerson, explained that the purpose of the visit was to seek a permit from Manchukuo officials for the foraging trip to Jehol, an area of supreme contention with China.[107] He made no mention of activities beyond seed-gathering. On June 21, however, Nicholas presented the Banner of Peace, "First Class," to puppet emperor Pu-yi, and distributed leaflets proclaiming himself to be "one of the greatest leaders of world culture"—a leader with the "power not only to plan but to act."[108] He subsequently informed the *KRUG* of the "very good impression . . . made by the emperor," adding that he, Roerich, had "no doubt that [U.S.] recognition of this nation [Manchukuo] won't take long." But just to make sure, he instructed them to tell "our *friend*" in Washington.[109]

Once MacMillan and Stephens had procured the equipment and weapons, they still suffered long delays imposed by Japanese officials questioning the volume and purpose of their arms, the types of seeds and grasses they sought (which Japan classified as "war materials"), and the nature of their association with Roerich. Writing to Garrels and Ryerson on July 20, two days after arriving in Harbin, MacMillan enclosed a copy of Roerich's "circus" flyer, obtained from a Japanese interrogator, and described the "organized propaganda" and "long interviews" he had given in the Russian-language press. The botanist reported meeting "the younger Mr. Roerich" the morning prior, yet having learned nothing of when they might meet the father. It was "obvious that the Roerichs do not want us along," he told Ryerson. This may well have been true, but the converse was more clearly the case. Notwithstanding Roerich's status as his leader in Manchuria, MacMillan arranged a first shipment of grass samples on his own.[110]

In a letter to the *KRUG*, Nicholas would accuse MacMillan and Stephens of "continuous procrastination" and "sabotage."[111] Helena faulted Wallace for not putting the Americans in their place. "He organized the expedition in a cowardly way," she recorded. "He belittled the name of F[*ujama*] . . .":

> It is necessary to watch the botanist [Ryerson] as closely as possible, [as] he has secret instructions from his co-workers [MacMillan and Stephens]. . . . The attacks from the Department of State have also resulted from [Wallace's] cowardice in organizing the expedition.[112]

Grant clearly sent some version of these thoughts to Wallace, as the latter, just a few weeks later, offered Helena a most abject apology:

> M[*odra*/Frances] has delivered with power the message as to the displeasure of the Lord at the diminishing of the *Name* [Nicholas]. . . . In all humility I ask for strength of continuing purpose. . . . But above all I desire to return to the *Tara* [Helena] and the *Master* a heart pure in purpose, vigorous in the intensity of its insights and triumphant over irrelevancies.
>
> Yes, I ask for Heart help and I offer Heart Service. May I become a living Teraphim. Yours to command.
>
> In deep reverence I bow across the seas and the thirty days of time to those who are so dear to the Great Ones in the time of great trial.
>
> G[*alahad*][113]

The apology is striking not merely for its slavish tone, but for its revelation that he, Henry Wallace, secretary of agriculture, owed his loyalties not to his government but to the Roerichs and the invisible Masters for whom they spoke.

As for the Japanese, they had little idea what to make of this strange, proselytizing Russian, Nicholas Roerich, who hailed the "Japanese advance towards cultural ascendancy" and prophesied a coming "confrontation with Communism."[114] When they questioned him, he simply presented Wallace's letter, placing himself at the head of an American seed-gathering mission. Whatever his plans, they were determined not to let them go unobserved. For the remainder of his time in Manchuria, he would be under an intensive watch.

꒜

On August 1, 1934, the Roerichs and the botanists boarded the same car of the same train bound for Hailar, Inner Mongolia, near the Russian border—though neither party spoke with the other. Two Russian botanists, a Japanese-government translator, and several guards in old Russian military-style dress[115] accompanied the Roerichs. The guards' attire led MacMillan to charge that Roerich had recruited his own personal army of Cossacks and White Russians, but it had no military significance.

In Hailar, on August 2, the two parties proceeded separately to the Japanese Military Mission, from which they needed travel permits. For two days, the mission's head, Colonel Saito, was confounded by the obvious hostility between the groups. The Americans insisted on sitting in a different room from the Russians. MacMillan denied working under Roerich's authority. Confronted with this denial, Roerich gave Saito Wallace's letter; shown the letter, MacMillan refused to accept its authenticity. The bemused and exasperated colonel issued two separate permits, authorizing each group to operate in separate areas.[116]

Whereas MacMillan had always planned to stay in the vicinity of Hailar, observing the life cycle of the various grasses over time, Roerich intended to travel widely, collecting seeds along a route of hundreds of miles. If Roerich's method was not sensible from a botanical perspective, as MacMillan asserted, it made sense if his aim were to visit monasteries and spread news of the coming Shambhala.

On August 4, the Roerich group headed north in two cars, first to the Ganjur Monastery and then to the Khingan Mountains, where they spent two weeks.[117] Wallace, unaware that the Roerich and MacMillan groups had, for some time, been determined to go their separate ways, wrote to Roerich on August 6 in a transparent effort to document his official reasoning in assigning him leader:

> Dear Professor Roerich:
> I understand that you are now in the interior searching for drouth resisting grasses on the edge of the Gobi Desert. The two American botanists are, I trust, cooperating in full.
> I asked you to lead this expedition because you are the outstanding authority on Central Asia and I hope that the American

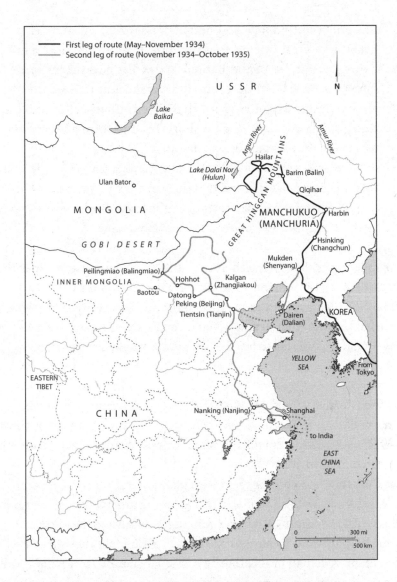

Map of the Roerichs' 1934–35 expedition through Central Asia.

botanists arrived in time so that you could get to the best grass areas before the seeds had shattered to the ground. . . .

The presence of yourself and George makes it possible for this expedition to operate on the most friendly basis among people whose friendship is necessary if the best results are to be obtained. Again I wish to thank you for helping us out in this effort to find new and better grasses for dry land. This is a matter of great interest to our people this year because a million square miles of the United States has been transformed into a veritable Gobi Desert by the worst drouth on record. We are having to slaughter more than five million cattle because the drouth has caused such a shortage of pasture and hay that otherwise they would die on the range. . . .

Please express to MacMillan and Stevens (sic) my hope that they are happy and well and that they are giving to you day by day the full advantage of their technical understanding so that the expedition may be as complete a success as possible.[118]

Wallace was, however, well aware of the tensions between Roerich and MacMillan, by way of Frances Grant. Five days later, on August 11, Ryerson sent MacMillan a cable alerting him to the fact that the secretary was "very anxious that you work very closely and cooperate with the Roerichs in every way."[119] But that was not to be. The two groups would never cross paths again.

Between August 11 and 26, 1934, three Russian-language American newspapers—*Rassvet* (Dawn), *Novaya Zarya* (New Dawn), and *Svet* (Light)—published Roerich's tantalizing statement in Harbin that "great events [were] coming in 1936." No details of the events were revealed, though it was clear they had nothing to do with plants.

Meanwhile, Roerich vented to his diary and disciples about "the evil botanists."[120] On August 19, he wrote an angry missive to the *KRUG*. "Instead of moving forward, [I] have to bathe in dirt!" he told them, incensed over the botanists denying his authority to the Japanese. "The *Friend* (Wallace) remembers how his Guru warned him about traitors. Let him not destroy his future, and drive out such dark devils."[121]

On September 3, Helena sent a letter to Wallace, by way of Frances Grant, excoriating Ryerson as his "vicious enemy." Ryerson, she told him, had "dared to belittle the name [of Roerich] behind your back," and "by doing so had betrayed and belittled You, their head, by not implementing Your instructions and, finally, abasing the prestige of his country."

"When N.K. [Nicholas] gave you the name [*Galahad*], he chose the highest one," she reminded him. "But have your coworkers acted similarly with respect to the name of the *Envoy*?" she asked.[122] They had not.

Grant, in phone calls and trips to Washington, for which Wallace (at least twice) gave her $100 cash reimbursements, regularly delivered the Roerichs' messages to him, stressing their anger over Ryerson and his men.[123] On receiving Father's letter in New York on September 18, Grant called the secretary's office and made an appointment to see him in Washington the following day. There, she expressed "her indignation at the actions of the botanists" and insisted that he "recall and discharge" MacMillan and Stephens and "get rid of R[yerson]." A chastened Wallace agreed to recall MacMillan, adding that he "would recall both if that seemed the correct plan." But "as to *discharging* the men," both civil servants, he was unsure he had legal grounds. He feared "a Congressional investigation." Still, he was "ready to act entirely in accordance with the advice of Father and Mother," and asked Grant "to send over the circumstances which obtain in this Government branch of service"—that is, the conditions under which he could fire the botanists.

Wallace was prepared to act wholly on the Roerichs' instructions, and asked only that Grant—neither a lawyer nor a government official—find him legal cover. Grant "promised to send these facts." With regard to Ryerson, she instructed Wallace to act "in line with father's advice"—which was that Ryerson should, "if he were not discharged, . . . be sent away somewhere."

Wallace presumably agreed to this "advice" as well, and Grant cabled Father that evening seeking final directions. Roerich ordered that Wallace send a cable "immediately recalling the botanists"; that Wallace write to him, Roerich, "expressing indignation over the acts of [in]subordination and appreciation of Professor Roerich's leadership"; that Wallace write to American consulates in countries visited by Roerich, affirming that state of affairs; and that Wallace "remove R[yerson]."[124]

Ryerson, feeling Wallace's growing hostility, wrote to MacMillan on September 18 to remind him "about the Secretary's being especially anxious that you extend every cooperation to the Roerichs." Unable to find a copy of the August 11 letter containing his earlier such plea, and apparently thinking it necessary in order to keep his job, he asked MacMillan to send him back a copy.[125] But it was too late. The Roerichs had ordered the men's heads; and they would get them.

On September 20, Wallace cabled MacMillan and Stephens, recalling them for "insubordination," and then cabled Roerich alerting him of the fact.[126] On September 27, he sent a further formal letter to Roerich, lavishing him with displays of confidence and heaping opprobrium on his own botanists.[127] That same day, Grant wrote to Helena, telling her she was taking Helena's letter of September 3 to Wallace, and would "insist that R[yerson] and the botanists be discharged."[128] The following afternoon, she did so.[129]

Wallace was by now deeply distraught over the saga, and the role he had played in offending the Guru. But, still, he did not know how to comply with Mother's demands without jeopardizing his own career. And so on September 30, he cabled Helena, sheepishly.

"Deeply moved by your letter," he wrote. The expedition has been "entirely removed from [the] mentioned enemy [Ryerson]." He, Wallace, could now "demote or transfer him," but "due [to the] bureaucratic system immediate discharge may create complications." In any case, he closed, "[I am] ready [to] act immediately if such [is] best. [I] would appreciate your advice."[130] Helena ordered Grant to "Transmit [to the] *friend* [my] indication to transfer and demote [the] mentioned person [Ryerson]."[131]

Here we have yet a further remarkable episode of an American cabinet secretary, calling himself "Galahad," asking a Russian mystic, living in India and claiming to speak for God, how to fire his own staff. Under the stress of reality diverging sharply from his faith, Wallace seemed to be losing his critical faculties. Jamesian belief was not serving him well.

When Grant returned to Wallace's office on September 29, a Saturday, she found that "he had not been able to sleep . . . since September 10th, when the matter of the botanists [first] assumed such ugly proportions." She handed him Helena's letter of September 3, observing that he was "greatly moved and distressed" as he read it, "almost to the point of tears."

The following day, Wallace assured Grant that "he wished to fulfil the Commands of the L[ord], as these were more paramount to him than his position." Still, she scolded him for "fail[ing] completely to take advantage of the opportunities to speak [to the president] in the highest Measure of the Name [Roerich]." Having worn Wallace down with remorse, she now raised the issue of *Alatyr*—which needed money. Her timing and delivery were pitch-perfect.

"I have $4500," Wallace told her, in enthusiastic penance, "which I have received as royalties on my book [*New Frontiers*]. . . . It is the most cash I have ever had in my life," he added, "and I had intended to use it to help the Hi-Bred Corn Company . . . over its serious financial period. But I feel I want to advance it to the co-op."[132] And so an American cabinet secretary sent his Russian Guru the equivalent, in today's money, of $100,000 to invest in Japanese-occupied Chinese territory. The ethical and political implications were breathtaking.

On October 10, 1934, Henry Wallace wrote to Helena once again, addressing her as the "Mother of the Druids." Her recent letter, he told her, came "as an electric shock, stimulating my resolution to act with precision and speed."

On September 10, he explained, "I read for the first time [the] terrible letters from the evil subordinate [MacMillan]. Both men have [now] been recalled." Furthermore, he sent letters to U.S. consulates in countries visited by Nicholas, and to Colonel Saito, "to endeavor to repair the affront to the Highest."[133] Mother should rest assured that "the two evil ones are now on the sea," and that her "indication to demote and transfer [Ryerson] is being carried out."

Wallace went on to lament the president's foreign policy. "W.," *the Wavering One*, he said, was "badly mixed up" when it came to the "*rulers* [Japanese] and *tigers* [Soviets]."[134] Wallace here referred to Roosevelt's hostility to the first and solicitude toward the second—both of which contradicted the will of the Guru.

By this time, however, Helena had decided to dispense with Wallace as middleman to the president. She felt empowered to instruct the president directly.

"I am," she wrote to Roosevelt that same day (in Russian), "writing to you from the Heights of the Himalaya in an intimidating moment, when the whole World is on the threshold of Reconstruction, when the fates of many countries are being weighed on the Cosmic Scales, offering You the Supreme Assistance." He could, she assured him, "become not just a Ruler, but a genuine Leader"— that is, if he would follow her Indications.

"A Mighty Hand," she said, "is offering you its Support." If he would grasp it, "the Fiery Messages will again be able to reach the White House"—as they had earlier in history, going back to George Washington. Nothing less than "the fate of the Nation is in Your hands," she added. "The one who will transmit this message to you," she closed, mysteriously, "will tell you who I am."[135]

He who transmitted the letter, on November 7 at the president's Hyde Park home, was the financier Louis Horch.[136] The two men chatted amiably about the Roerich Pact and the midterm elections, which had gone well for the Democrats, after which Horch handed over the dispatch from "a most remarkable woman of Fiery Personality." The president read it, declaring it "tremendously interesting"—as he did many things which he read, irrespective of whether they were interesting. He invited Horch to deliver further missives, provided he didn't mind inevitable delays. Horch thanked the president, asking only that he not discuss the visits with his agriculture secretary. This was fine with Roosevelt, who would have seen them as a useful means to keep tabs on Wallace.

Horch had gained access to the president through Sara Roosevelt, his mother, whom he had been cultivating for a year and a half[137]—playing on her interest in Roerich and mysticism. The financier, however, had his own pecuniary agenda. The Master Building, having been in receivership since 1932, was to be auctioned off in February 1935. Tensions were growing with Nicholas, who had long ago come to suspect him of impure intentions. Horch was now in a position to profit doubly—from his claims on the building, and from his ties to the president.

"I cannot hide from you beloved Mother," Nettie Horch wrote to Helena on October 18, 1934, "that during the last visit of Father, we felt that [Louis] and myself were not close to father, neither to George." Yet she and Louis remained, Nettie assured her, "supremely happy to feel *your* heart close to us."[138]

Helena, interestingly, does not appear disturbed by such revelations. She now chose to use Horch to keep Wallace in line. "If you are ready to keep the Instructions, which are coming from the Master of Shambhala directly to me," she would write to the secretary, "then my entrusted person [Horch] will bring You my messages." Her instructions, she would warn him, "should be known only to You and to no one else."[139]

Power shifts were under way within the Roerich enterprise. Helena was up, Nicholas was down. Horch was up, Wallace was down. And those shifts would only become more dramatic over the coming year.

⚘

Knowles Ryerson was glum. On October 13, 1934, in response to Wallace's demand that he submit a "statement covering [his] attitude on the Asian expedition," he sent the secretary a heartfelt four-page, single-spaced letter recounting his involvement in what had now become a quagmire threatening both their careers. "[M]entally I am numb," he confessed, before spilling out the narrative in a tone respectful but blunt.

Ryerson recounted how contacts inside and outside government had warned him that the Roerichs were "swindlers, mountebanks, and imposters or hair-brained [sic] visionaries," and "openly questioned [his] sanity" for cooperating with them. These concerns increased as reports came back from MacMillan documenting the Roerichs' activities, unrelated to seeds. By now, Ryerson confessed, his own involvement in the expedition had become "the most bewildering and heart-wrecking experience" of his life.[140]

Wallace's reply, coming on October 20, was furious, accusing Ryerson of "serious insubordination." The "rumors" he had recounted about Professor Roerich, Wallace charged, were "not only ridiculous but extremely malicious." He, Wallace, had only "the greatest admiration" for Roerich, and was "confident that any plans which he makes for the expedition are those best designed to bring credit to the expedition and to this country." In consequence, Ryerson, unless he could find alternative employment, would be transferred to an obscure outpost 2,619 miles from Washington: the Office of Tropical and Subtropical Horticulture in Riverside, California.[141] Thereafter, Wallace would assume personal supervision of the mission, handling all administrative matters through his special assistant, Earl Bressman.[142]

On October 1, 1934, Nicholas Roerich, now back in Harbin, wrote to Henry Wallace cataloguing the history of troubles with MacMillan and his own accomplishments in spite of them—or at least those accomplishments that might be considered such under his official mandate. These included collecting folkloric "medicinal plants" and copying "Chinese and Tibetan medical texts." Next on his itinerary, he explained, was Jehol[143] (now Chengde), on the eastern edge of the Gobi Desert, 1,600 miles southwest of Harbin and 140 miles northeast of Beijing. He made no mention of political or self-promotional activities.

Later that month, Roerich paid $1,000 ($21,000 in today's money) to take over the Harbin newspaper *Novoe Slovo* (The New Word), placing it under the control of the anti-Bolshevik Russian All-Military Union (ROVS).[144] On November 7, he served as the guest of honor at a Harbin "Day of [Russian] Émigré Irreconcilability"—irreconcilability, that is, with the Soviet regime.[145] Had the State Department been aware of these activities, Hull would no doubt have pressed Roosevelt to cut all ties with him.

Soon after Roerich's newspaper purchase, his honeymoon with the region's press ended. The ROVS having been at odds with the Japanese and the Russian fascists, as well as the Soviets, Roerich's support for it now made him an enemy of all three.

First came a piece in the local *Nippon* newspaper, saying that Roerich had been sent to Manchuria by shadowy "Masonic organizations."[146] Other vituperative pieces followed. U.S. consul general Walter Adams reported to Washington that Roerich's activities in Harbin had become the subject of "vociferous political opposition" throughout the city's Japanese press.[147]

The Russian émigré press also piled on. On November 18, *Kharbinskoe Vremya*, the Russian edition of the Japanese *Harbin Times*, charged that Roerich "belonged to the cohort of the greatest conspirators aiming to seize political power over Siberia." *Nash Put* (Our Way) denounced him as "a Mason and Jewish agent." The next day, *Kharbinskoe Vremya* accused him of plotting to rule "a new Masonic nation in Siberia." On November 20 and 21, other papers published intercepted letters he had written to his brother eight years earlier, speaking of the glories of the future Siberia he allegedly sought to control.[148]

Japanese military intelligence may have been behind the attacks. Many in its ranks believed that the U.S. government was using Roerich to undermine its efforts to promote the Russian Fascist Party leader, Konstantin Rodzaevsky, as leader of all White Russians.[149]

"Master," an angry Helena would ask the ethereal Morya, "have the Japanese stabbed the knife into the back of F[ujama]?"

"Of course," Morya would reply. But "if not for the nasty botanists . . . there would be no attacks in the Japanese newspapers."[150] George would, in fact, later claim to have a copy of a memorandum detailing a conversation between Horch and a "Mr. Sawada" in which "two American scientific men," presumably MacMillan and Stephens, are mentioned as a basis for the articles.[151]

The press assault proved a major blow to Roerich's ambitions. Just a few weeks prior, he had written excitedly to the board of his embryonic Manchurian co-op (that board being one and the same with the *Krug*) pledging that it would be endowed with the "energetic individual enterprise of its members" and "the greatest economic efficiency." But that dream was now in tatters.

"[T]h cooperative is finished," Roerich recorded in his diary on November 27, three days after fleeing Harbin for China. "[T]he Americans will not want to give money [here] where I am so greatly slandered."[152]

But the cooperative was *not* finished. While Wallace was, on December 7, 1934, giving FDR a glowing report on the seed search, Roerich was busy reconstituting *Alatyr*. Now, reassigning it the secret cover name "*Kansas*," he determined to build it a thousand miles to the west of Harbin—in Inner Mongolia.

Roerich sent a telegram to New York ordering Horch, on whom he still depended for matters financial, to see "*the friend*" and tell him of the great possibilities for America in *Kansas*.[153] George, writing to Sina Lichtmann, raved of a well-connected secret contact in *Kansas* who had "a ranch with coal and many other things."

"*Galad* [*Galahad*]," George added, now needed to "intensify his efforts" on their behalf. Whereas the Roerichs had, back in July, wanted $10,000–$15,000 to kick-start the co-op in Manchuria,[154] they now insisted that "*two million US dollars*" ($44 million today) would be "necessary" to relaunch it in Inner Mongolia.[155] Nicholas followed up with another telegram, asking that "*the Friend* inform his chief [FDR]" of the urgency. Wallace could entice the president, he said, by highlighting the "benevolent and cultural school" they planned to build.[156]

Why was Roerich suddenly so excited about moving his co-op to Inner Mongolia? Politics. Roerich determined that he could exploit the Mongolian yearning for independence from China, just as the Japanese were doing. "Mongolians," Grant would later explain, "saw co-ops as a way to achieve their unification" and freedom from "the Chinese world." They therefore "communicated their hope to Roerich and their intention to begin the movement." And "in his turn, Roerich communicated their conviction to Wallace."[157]

"I am convinced that *the friend* will be able to make a great contribution into the *Kansas* business," Roerich diaried from Peking on December 11. "I hope that he and *Coward*"—Roerich's telling new cover name for Roosevelt—will understand how useful this business is for their country."[158] By the end of the month, however, he is exceedingly anxious for the cash, and writes to Wallace that "works of such significance" demand "special haste."[159]

On December 19, Horch paid a second visit to Roosevelt, this time at the White House, bringing with him another letter from Mother. After effusing that America had "not known a more beloved President," the letter alerts him to great challenges to come. It warns of "a provocation from the land in the East," presumably Japan, and "another . . . from the land beyond the ocean," presumably Britain, "on the pretext of protection of China," and offers advice: that the president "watch these attempts vigilantly," but "keep away from conflicts."[160] For clarity of foresight and utility of counsel, then, did Helena rival the Oracle of Delphi herself.

The letter goes on in an effort to coax FDR into support for the secret nation-building project in Central Asia, while revealing nothing about it. "Your faith in the New Construction will help me to gradually open to You the entire plan," she writes, teasingly—a plan "in which You and Your Country have been destined to play such a great role."[161] Roosevelt read it in front of Horch, commenting, on finishing, with his trademark commitment-free charm, that "the contents are so in accord with my thoughts and ideas that I could almost state 'I wrote this myself.'" He then observed that Horch, according to the letter, would tell him the name of the country in which the plan was to be launched. So after effusing that he agreed with Helena entirely, he pleads ignorance as to its central matter.

Horch identified the country (Inner Mongolia), and then waited for FDR's response. The president, he recorded, simply smiled, giving "no true Indication of his inner reaction."[162]

At least three more letters from Helena—dated December 27, 1934; February 4, 1935; and May 14, 1935—are known to have been received by Roosevelt, all delivered by Horch. She would later boast that the president "accepted [her advice] with all his heart and [that] it was possible to trace their implementation."[163] There is, however, no evidence of Roosevelt actually having responded to these messages—which would have been uncharacteristically reckless on his part. Her conclusion is, therefore, likely based solely on Horch's testimony—which is that the president found the letters "tremendously interesting."[164]

In early 1935, Henry Wallace turned to Frances Grant for guidance on how to get the president to back the secret plans for Inner Mongolia. "How about [my] presenting to WO [*Wavering One*] the *Kansas* idea as one in which *father* is interested[?]," Wallace asks. "[I could] suggest that a strong *Kansas* might check *the rulers* [Japanese] and make for a balanced situation. . . . Will not act till I hear from you." Here again we have the extraordinary circumstance of a cabinet secretary asking an agent of Russian mystics how to persuade the president to alter policy in their interests. Wallace's cult-addled mindset is reflected in his closing sentiment. "May the Glory of the flaming Chalices," he writes, "shine even as the Star of the Hero in the last beautiful reproduction."[165]

Wallace, however, soon turns frustrated at the lack of clarity as to how Roerich's desired $2 million is to be invested. He tells her to write to him "at once to see if there are properties needing development which . . . give a chance of very great profits. Really I doubt if such properties exist." [166] On January 19, 1935, George, in a letter to Sina Lichtmann, tells her to inform Wallace that an unidentified "chief" in "*Kansas*" pledges "the income from [a] salt lake" as security for loans, and that there is "also coal of very good quality and other raw materials."[167] But such teases did nothing to entice Wallace's wealthy contacts.

The man in whom Wallace vested the greatest hopes he refers to as "the nine times named one."[168] From other correspondence, that individual appears to have been auto magnate Henry Ford—a man with "a deep mystical strain." Before writing to Ford, Wallace reveals that, "for purposes of ascertaining the [Divine] Will," he "held the symbol of the thunderbolt in my hand and asked the spirit to arise in my heart."[169] The ritual was, however, ineffectual. Ford's secretary, Wallace reported, sent a "rather curt letter of refusal."[170]

By late January 1935, it was becoming clear that the inner sanctum of the Roerich cult was fracturing. Nicholas in China and Helena in India were each cultivating separate channels with Wallace and the president. Nicholas had turned cold toward Horch, who was taking possession of the indebted museum, while Horch had become Helena's "Fiery warrior" in Washington. Wallace had tired of Grant, who gave him no actionable facts or figures, while Horch thought Grant a bitter nuisance. Esther Lichtmann, for years the most unshakable of Helena's intimates, sided with Horch; Sina Lichtmann with Grant.

It was against this backdrop that Horch visited Wallace on January 31, bearing a letter from Helena. Wallace read it eagerly, asking Horch for the "Instructions" it mentioned. Horch explained that the secretary would first need to accept Mother's "proposal." *Mother*, Horch explained, was "the Inspirer of everything." It was "glorious *Mo[ther]*" who "is closest to the *L[ord]*." *Father*, by implication, was merely a lesser prophet.

Whatever that "proposal" was, Wallace accepted it without hesitation. "This coming from the high Source," he told Horch, "naturally I take [it] as a Command and of course I want to serve." Horch was satisfied. But he also needed Wallace to accept him as the sole bearer of Truths. He therefore warned the secretary not to say "one Word to *Mod[ra]* (Frances)" about their meeting. All "must be kept strictly confidential."

"I welcome this opportunity to work with you," he assured Horch. Grant "did not give me details," he complained. "I find it difficult to work with her."

A few days after the meeting, Wallace reported back to Helena. "In response to your profoundly moving letter," he wrote,

> I told your entrusted messenger that the Will of the Lord was all governing and in all solemnity I must again indicate my desire to obey the indications as transmitted by the new messenger.
>
> My belief is [that] Commanders guard the sacred Indications by carrying them into action with the utmost of their power, wisdom and strategy. . . .
>
> If I do not understand, may your spirit guide me. If my will falters may the language of Great Heart shake me.
>
> We have made progress, I believe, in defending the Name and the Pact.
>
> Respectfully and in spirit yours,
>
> *G[alahad]*[171]

Horch, too, reported back to Helena. The secretary, he lamented, "does not quickly catch things and everything must be explained a number of times." Still, he wrote hopefully, "I feel useful work can be accomplished and I will do my utmost."[172]

On March 1, 1935, Roerich wrote to Wallace explaining that "this season much will be easier because there shall not be the dark consequences of a plot of two individuals," MacMillan and Stephens. Regarding Wallace's pleas for details on *Kansas*, though, he would say only that "all the questions about guarantees can be answered." For now, Wallace simply had to recognize the need for "special haste." The project, he assured him, was vital "for the future and for your country."[173]

On March 8, Horch paid his third visit to Roosevelt—this time joined by Esther Lichtmann. They spoke for twenty minutes, mainly about *Kansas* and "the great need for Americans to secure a foothold there." Everything, seemingly, impressed the president—"he liked it greatly," Lichtmann recorded.[174] They also delivered another letter from Helena, written on February 3, which Lichtmann had carried back personally from India. It revealed more of Morya's plan for a new political entity in Central Asia.

"[T]he Construction," Helena explained, "should be understood as an alliance of nations in the Far East, with the President predestined to play a great role." It would be "realized gradually," but ultimately produce "a kind of a Federation of countries," involving Mongolia, China, and [Soviet] Kalmykia, which "will constitute a counterbalance to Japan."[175]

Roosevelt's reaction is unrecorded, but can be readily imagined. Assuming he was true to practice over his dozen years as president, he would have expressed great interest and profound agreement. He had, after all, a genuine fascination with mysticism, passed down from his mother, as well as an abiding curiosity about the peoples and habitats of Central Asia. He also liked agreeing with guests. Yet he would not have changed policy a jot—and, indeed, he did not.

That day and the one following, March 9, Horch and Lichtmann also visited Wallace. They pressed him again to find cash for *Kansas*, though still conveyed nothing as to how it might be invested. They pressed him, too, to work for global endorsement of the Roerich Pact, which would "greatly help

[Roerich's] standing the World Over." They pressed him, further, to write letters to Europe backing Roerich for the Nobel Peace Prize. They pressed him as well to "act strongly with the "*O[ld] H[ouse]*," which opposed Roerich on all fronts. And they pressed him, finally, again in classic cult fashion, to take "Indications" through no one but them—not through Wallace's "Indian friend" (likely W. H. Dower, author of *Occultism for Beginners*, or Charles Roos), or even through Frances Grant.[176]

Wallace was only too eager to reassure. Grant, he complained, had become "very moody and very envious and very possessive." "Many mistakes," he added, "could have been avoided" had she "advised him differently on many important matters."[177]

Having turned Helena against Frances, whom Helena now dismissed for "narrow-spirited consciousness," Horch and Lichtmann began assaulting the matriarch's own spiritual authority. At a further meeting with the president on March 14, they noted his concerns with "foreign exchange matters"—matters on which Horch, a currency speculator, had not merely considerable knowledge but a keen pecuniary interest. The president, according to Horch, asked for the views of the "distant control," but there is little reason to suspect that he actually coveted Mahatma monetary wisdom. In any case, Horch told Helena, he and Esther promised to get the president answers; but they did not send the questions to Helena. Instead, Horch answered them all himself, claiming Divine revelation.

"The L[ord] has permitted [us]," Horch told Helena, "to give [the president] replies as if coming from the Ashram"[178]—that is, from the sacred Indian source. Thus were the disciples exercising the very mystical powers that had been the exclusive domain of The Mother of Druids. They were no longer her messengers, but themselves direct conduits to Truth. The Roerichs had become superfluous. The cult surrounding them was shattering.

On March 20, 1935, Roerich's expedition moved out from Peking to Kalgan (Zhangjiakou), on the outskirts of the Gobi Desert, 120 miles to the northwest, to resume their field work. On March 30 and 31, father and son met with Prince Demchugdongrub (aka Teh Wang and De-Van), leader of the Mongols of Inner Mongolia.[179] The prince aspired to lead an autonomous

Mongol government in the areas of Chahar and Suiyuan, and was seeking ways of weakening Chinese control. Collaboration with Japan was the obvious route, and the prince would follow it in short order. But in early spring, there was, at least in Roerich's mind, the prospect of enticing him into his *Kansas* vision of American-backed economic and political development. Neither Nicholas nor George left an account of the meeting, suggesting that nothing tangible was achieved. Third-party accounts of the prince's impressions are mixed.[180]

Everything about *Kansas* was murky, but it involved using American loans and investments in the service of major economic and political change. A semblance of the thinking can be gleamed in a letter from Frances Grant to Helena in which she reports on her research into Inner Mongolia. "The *tig[ers*/Soviets] have a most advantageous [trade] treaty there," she writes, "but one which we could emulate through the *scholarship fund*, thus getting the advantage of what appears to be a splendid growing market."[181] The Roerich circle spoke frequently of loans for Inner Mongolian economic ventures and trade financing using the code word "*scholarships*." American *scholarship* money would, they assumed, be accompanied by American political and military engagement, and would thus serve the dual interests of developing Inner Mongolia and pushing back the three covetous neighbors: China, Japan, and the Soviet Union. By this means would *Kansas* give rise to the holy Shambhala, under the leadership of the great Western Lama, Nicholas Roerich.[182]

Nicholas was accustomed to others funding his projects without nagging for details, and could therefore not comprehend why the $2 million he had asked for repeatedly had still not materialized. On April 5, Grant wrote to him, in clear frustration with his insouciance, relaying a long list of urgent questions from Wallace. Many of these questions, both highly sensitive and remarkably naïve—such as whether "the *Kansas* government [was] recognized by any other government," and whether "*Kansas* [was] a sub-division of *Alabama* [China]"[183]—would no doubt have outraged the State Department, had its officials been aware of them.

That same day, Esther Lichtmann wrote to Helena about *Kansas*, suggesting her own frustration with the lack of answers. "People who have large sums of money are NOT IDEALISTS," she wrote. "[T]hey regard everything from the point of view of investment." They needed to know how their money was to get a safe and substantial return. She further stressed that whereas FDR "showed great interest" in approving loans, U.S. law forbade even private credit for such a scheme without detailed information on their purpose, where the money would be spent, etc.[184] But Helena disdained such petty materialism. "[T]his business takes not only businessmen, but idealists," she insisted in a letter to Horch, dated April 8. "[T]he miracle has been predestined. There is no greater joy than the construction of the New Country."[185]

On April 14, Nicholas responded to the concerns from New York with a few cursory and unintelligible answers. He assured them that "the figures of the income of the indicated guarantees for five years I shall inform you about at the first possibility." This sort of "telegraphic language," he explained, was made necessary by "rivals" intercepting his mail.[186] Grant was now caught between the rock of Wallace and the hard place of Roerich, unable to provide facts to the former or a dime to the latter.

April 15, 1935 was, for Henry Wallace, a historic day in which he would play the central part. In a moving formal ceremony held in the Cabinet Room, in the presence of the president and dignitaries from twenty Latin American nations, Wallace signed the "international pact for protection of artistic and scientific institutions, historic monuments, missions and collections"—otherwise known as the Roerich Pact—on behalf of the United States. The signing of the pact, long opposed by the State Department as impractical and redundant, elevated the stature of Nicholas Roerich as a prophet of peace, and that of Henry Wallace as a statesman of peace.[187] In Wallace's own mind, the pact validated his spiritualism and belief in international cooperation as a moral ethic.

The following day, April 16, Wallace sent fifteen identical letters of introduction for Horch and Lichtmann to present to European diplomats and members of the Nobel Prize Committee. The two acolytes would spend six weeks, from April 27 to June 6, traveling the continent, lobbying for the prize to be bestowed on the pact's namesake. Given the manifest strains between Horch and Roerich, it was clear that Horch's motives were more pecuniary than devotionary. He was out to monetize the Roerich brand, which was now at its height.

Grant, meanwhile, was being put through a slow and painful excommunication. Horch allegedly called her "stupid" for not using her friendship

Secretary of Agriculture Henry A. Wallace, seated on the right beside President Franklin D. Roosevelt, signs the Roerich Pact at the White House, Washington, D.C., April 15, 1935.

with Wallace to get "a good position in the government" and "pass on [financial] tips." They could have made "lots of money" this way.[188]

Whereas Wallace had invited Horch and Lichtmann to the White House signing as honored guests, Grant was not even informed of the venue. From March 1935 on, Wallace began a regular correspondence and meeting routine with Horch, cutting out Grant almost entirely. "[H]e no longer regard[s] my words . . . as authentic and important," she would lament to Helena. When she tried to discuss *Kansas*, he said it was "a matter between Mr. Horch and myself."[189]

Also writing to Helena, Lichtmann accused Grant of making "misleading statements" about *Kansas* to the Roerichs.[190] She portrayed Grant as jealous and unstable. "She cannot reconcile with the thought that anybody else shall have anything to do with her *friend*." She suggested that Grant deal with Wallace only on expedition issues—such issues meaning little to her or to Horch. On important matters, "we can see [him] without anybody knowing about it."[191]

Helena, seeing that Horch and Lichtmann were usurping her authority with the White House for their own venal interests, scolded that "such division is counter to the laws of the *Krug*."[192] Convinced, too, that Esther was not transmitting her messages, and delivering her own instead, Helena wrote to Nettie Horch at least twice in April and in May, demanding copies of every message communicated to FDR since Esther had arrived home from India.[193] Nettie appears not to have complied. On June 5, Helena complained to Louis that she had been expecting to receive news from the White House, but nothing had come. FDR, she warned him, "is held only by the magnet of *Ur[usvati]*"—that is, by she herself, Helena Roerich:

> Let us not impede the magnetic currents which are established by the L[ord] through me. . . . I am Told [by the Lord] to write and affirm it vividly. . . . I vouch that [FDR] will help. . . . I vouch to manifest a miracle. . . . The victory is preordained, but one must know how to accept it.[194]

On June 7, Esther wrote to Helena reiterating that "the L[ord] Himself" had "permitted" her and Horch to give FDR an "Indic[ation]" of their own. That Indication, she explained, "dealt with a technical question of silver," suggesting that the Lord was just being practical in speaking through experts.

Silver was a matter in which Horch took an intense interest. FDR had, the previous October, issued an executive order to confiscate and nationalize the metal, with the resulting rise in its price playing havoc on the economy of China—which was then on a silver monetary standard. According to Esther, God authorized Horch to reveal to the president that China would "cling to silver" as money, and that its people would "not resent the fluctuations" in its price. What precisely God and Horch advised the president to do, Esther did not reveal—although we do know that Henry Morgenthau, the treasury secretary, would soon agree to buy silver from China in return for a pledge to steady its currency in terms of dollars. Horch was no doubt looking to profit from such policy shifts.[195]

In another letter to Helena that day, Horch's tone slid yet further from reverence toward contempt. "Let me again advise you," he told her, that "were [it] not for us the name [of Roerich] would have been omitted from the Pact" and "the signing would never have taken place at the White House."[196] But Helena was having none of it. On June 24, she wrote back condemning him as a lying apostate. "Interference and direct advice concerning financial operations," such as silver trading, can "never issue from the Highest Source." Only she, Helena, "had been appointed as the Entrusted One of the L[ord]."[197]

But the Lord moves in mysterious ways.

All during the spring of 1935, the Harbin Russian-émigré press resumed its attacks on Roerich as a "great Mason" and a "Rosicrucian" occultist.[198] On June 23, the entire expedition took a major blow from a Peking-based journalist writing for the *Chicago Tribune*.[199] In an article piled high with half-truths and fictions, John Powell depicted Roerich as the leader of a shadowy band of armed right-wing Cossacks stirring up anti-Soviet animus in Asia, all the while claiming to be gathering seeds under American diplomatic cover. The article, a shortened form of which appeared in *The New York Times* the following day,[200] had just enough factual fringe to justify alarm in the State Department, though hardly enough to excuse the credulous treatment it would receive from future Wallace chroniclers.

Powell began by claiming that Wallace's "expedition to Mongolia to search for drought-resisting grasses and plants [was] proving a source of embarrassment to United States diplomatic and military officials" in Peking. In fact, there is no documentary evidence for this claim. Such officials appeared, to that point, largely ignorant of Roerich's activities.

Powell then claimed that Roerich's group had been "compelled to leave [Manchuria] due to the opposition of the Japanese military, who charged that [it] was concerned with White Russian politics." Again, there is no evidence that Japanese authorities, suspicious though they were of both Roerich *and* the American botanists, ever leveled such charges.

Powell wrote that the expedition's "two American scientists," MacMillan and Stephens, had "resigned." They had, of course, *not* resigned, but had been recalled by Henry Wallace.

"The chief trouble," Powell continued, "developed when the Roerichs applied to the 15th U.S. infantry at Tientsin for a dozen army rifles and pistols and a considerable stock of ammunition." In fact, only six rifles were borrowed (and later returned), in accordance with official procedure, and no "trouble" ever "developed" over them.

"The Roerichs," Powell claimed, "then employed White Russian Cossacks, formerly on the staff of Ataman Semenoff," a notorious, Japanese-backed former czarist officer, "who were armed with the American rifles." The Roerichs did, in fact, have four White Russian staff—two drivers,[201] a security/supply manager,[202] and a secretary alternating as botanical assistant and night guard[203]—but none of them was remotely associated with Semenoff (aka Semenov).[204]

"Although [the group] carry credentials of the United States Department of Agriculture," Powell then said, "there has been much suspicion among Mongolian leaders, due to the presence of the White Russian armed Cossack guards who allegedly [were] making a show of American diplomatic protection." Yet the record of such "suspicion" is thin, consisting of claims by a Soviet-friendly sinologist, Owen Lattimore, that retainers of Mongolian Prince Demchugdongrub reported their leader's wariness of Roerich's armed men. But the prince himself would soon publish a response denying any "enmity" with the Roerichs.

"American officials" in Peking, Powell went on, were "reticent to discuss the affair, but stated that representations were made to Washington." Yet again, no "representations" have ever been documented, save Garrels' correspondence from Tokyo. The historical and biographical material, too, was intriguingly flawed. Powell claimed that George "was a former officer of the czarist army," despite his having left Russia, in 1917, at age fifteen.

As with any good piece of propaganda, there *were* elements of truth diffusing Powell's story. Roerich *was* engaged in politics. He *had* been in conflict with the American botanists. And Japanese officials *had* shown concern with his activities. After seeing the article one month later at Camp Timur-Khada, on the Alashan Plateau in the Suíyuǎn province of northern China, Roerich would write a compelling rebuttal letter to Wallace—albeit one that closed with a hollow ring. "It seems indeed strange," the ending read, "that a few years ago the very same papers accused me of Soviet sympathies and now seem to accuse me for White Russian connections."[205] But it was not "strange" at all. Roerich *had* sought Soviet support for his earlier expedition, and he *was* playing to émigrés during the present one.

Perhaps the most curious claim in Powell's piece was that "Red Russian officials [in Peking] are stated to be watching the Roerichs' alleged grass hunting efforts." This was doubtlessly true. Lenin had, back in 1921, ordered the Baron Roman von Ungern-Sternberg executed for "working in the interests of Japan to create a Central Asian state."[206] But who might have "stated" such a fact about Roerich to Powell?

Roerich was almost certainly truthful in his later claim to Wallace that "investigations locally show that there is a certain foreign source implicated" in the article's production.[207] More than likely, that source is a Red Russian official who encouraged Powell to write the piece, feeding him salacious disinformation to fill it, with the aim of embarrassing the American government into withdrawing and disowning the expedition group. To identify the likely foreign source, we need only consider Powell's relations with those in China who had a political interest in his story.

John Benjamin Powell, Missouri-raised and educated, had, since 1917, age thirty-one, been working as a journalist in China. In his memoirs nearly three decades later, he reported having met Soviet ambassador Dmitry Bogomolov, a cosmopolitan, multilingual diplomat, and his counselor, Ivan Spilvanek, through Powell's "coverage of a White Russian attempt to seize the Soviet consulate in Shanghai" in 1928. That consulate, he said, had been attacked by "a group of about 150 former Cossack soldiers," in "their old Czarist uniforms," seeking to set up a "'White' Russian government in the International Settlement." But the "plot failed," he recorded, "thanks to the determined resistance of . . . a handful of [Soviet] consular officials who barricaded themselves in the building."[208]

Bogomolov, Powell notes, "was pleased with my coverage of the story"— as he ought to have been. Powell's coverage was at odds with other contemporary Western accounts, which described not an orchestrated seizure of the consulate but a "spontaneous violent demonstration" by nonuniformed Russian émigrés, including women and Orthodox priests.[209]

The incident took place after a Russian church service on "Irreconcilability Day"—the date of the Bolshevik coup. It was not in 1928, but in 1927. Bogomolov, moreover, was ambassador to *Poland* at the time, and Spilvanek was acting consul general in Peking—not Shanghai. Powell's memory was faulty—or possibly corrupted. In 1927, his Soviet contact would have been Shanghai consul general Benedict Koslovsky—whom Powell did indeed know.[210] His memoirs also fail to mention that he spent six months in Russia in 1930.[211]

Bogomolov did arrive in Peking as ambassador to China, and Spilvanek in Shanghai as consul general, but not until 1933. By that time, Koslovsky had become head of the NKID's 2nd Eastern Department, a post from which he would have briefed Bogomolov on useful contacts in Shanghai—contacts such as Powell.

In 1935, shortly before he wrote his article on the Roerich expedition, Powell decided he wanted to visit the Soviet Far East, and asked Bogomolov for help in securing a visa. The ambassador cabled Moscow, and some weeks later the head of the official Soviet travel agency in Shanghai told Powell he might be able to visit Siberia with a six-month traveling permit. That permit would also allow him to attend the country's November anniversary celebration in Moscow's Red Square.

With the permit granted, Powell became, in October, one of the first foreigners to travel across Siberia to Moscow on the Trans-Siberian Railway. His special treatment continued in the capital, where he was invited to a dinner party given by members of the official TASS news agency—a party at which he was introduced to the *Pravda* editor himself, Karl Radek.[212]

In addition to helping with his visa, Bogomolov was, Powell said, "a good source of the news." The NKID, for which Koslovsky now worked, provided ambassadors with top secret hard-currency allocations to cultivate local journalists and shape their reporting. By all appearances, then, it was Bogomolov, in pursuance of such duties, who provided "the news" with which Powell painted the Roerichs, in July 1935, as violent anti-Soviet extremists, in the same mold as the Russians who had tried to "seize" the Shanghai consulate eight years earlier. We might further conjecture that Powell's red-carpet sojourn in Russia was his reward for a job well done.

After returning from Moscow in January 1936, Powell would remain in Shanghai until December 1941, just after the Pearl Harbor attacks, when he would be arrested by the Japanese. Following a brutal imprisonment, he would be released in May 1942. He would testify before the Tokyo War Crimes Tribunal in 1946. Never fully recovering from his ordeal, he would die the following year.

As for Bogomolov, he would, in spite of his exemplary record of service to the Soviet state, be ensnared in Stalin's mass party purge. Arrested in October 1937 on charges of participating in an "anti-Soviet terrorist organization," he would be executed in May 1938. Nineteen years later (and four after Stalin's death), he would be officially "rehabilitated."

In the wake of Powell's bombshell article, Frances Grant and Sina Lichtmann were distraught. They had expected Wallace to leap to the defense of Father. He did not.[213] Meeting with Wallace on June 28, 1935, Grant found him cold and seemingly indifferent to the threat the piece posed to Father, to the "New Country," to the Banner of Peace—indeed to everything *Galahad* had theretofore held dear.

Wallace, Grant noted in a letter to Helena, recognized the article as a "'planted story' intended to harm [the] administration and himself."[214] Yet he refused to challenge it in public, and angrily rejected the rebuttal piece Grant had prepared for him, calling it "futile."

"Your allegiance to the highest seems unquestioned," he wrote to her on July 2, "but that does not mean I trust your judgment. I do not. I am taking action tomorrow which you will not like, but which I believe to be in the service of the triple shield and above all the Lord." He warned her not to come to Washington. "I will not have time to see you."[215] Grant took the letter as "a terrible blow."[216]

Though Wallace knew that much of what Powell had written was nonsense, he would also have noted that his own name appeared in the piece but once—in the first sentence, which said only that he had "dispatched" the expedition "to search for drouth resisting grasses and plants." Powell had written nothing, and presumably knew nothing, about Wallace's secret support for the "New Country." That meant that Wallace could still save his reputation. It was clear that the key to dissociating himself from the Roerichs was to ally with Louis Horch. Horch, after all, was untainted by the expedition's travails. He still had the president's ear. And he had been working to sever the museum from those whose name it bore.

On July 3, Wallace sent a cable to Roerich and a letter to Horch. The cable directed Roerich to move the expedition to a safe, seed-rich area in Suíyuǎn "at the earliest possible moment."[217] Shortly after, Bressman ordered Roerich to leave Central Asia by year's end, to arrive in India by February 1, and to end all work by May 1.[218] Wallace's letter to Horch, accompanied by a copy of the cable, read as follows:

> I do not know whether there is any foundation whatsoever for the insinuations of political activity on the part of Professor Roerich in Mongolia. I am exceedingly anxious, however, that he be engaged, both actually and apparently, in doing exactly what he is supposed to be doing as an employee of the United States Department of Agriculture engaged in searching for seeds valuable to the United States. I would appreciate your cooperation in seeing that this is brought tactfully and effectively to Professor Roerich's attention. In saying this, I realize, of course, that most and probably all of these insinuations of the press in late June may be quite without foundation; nevertheless, with times as troubled in the East as they are now, it would seem to me wise to take no chances and, therefore, the department has asked Professor Roerich, with due consideration for safety, to travel to the safer area of the Province of Suiyan which is reputably rich in drought resistant grasses.[219]

The letter is an exemplar of dishonesty and moral cowardice. Wallace knew full well that Roerich was engaged in "political activity"—activity that he, Henry Wallace, had endorsed. He knew that the seed mission was his own cover for that activity. But he also knew that many of Powell's claims—about armed radical Cossacks, the "resignations" of scientists, and the like—were false, and likely planted. Yet he refused to reveal the truth, hoping that the Roerichs, and not he, would bear the weight of the fallout.

The following day, July 4, Wallace wrote a final letter to Helena. "I do not trust [Grant]," he told her, "and therefore I cannot work with her." As to "the New Country," he said, the president remained "most friendly about" it, but funding was "absolutely impossible."[220] Wallace would, the following month, ask Horch to secure the return of his own $4,500 investment in the *Kansas* co-op.[221] Roerich would wire the money back in September.[222] The co-op was now, for all practical purposes, finished.

Wallace's words and actions, according to Sina Lichtmann, "border[ed] on insanity." He showed "incredible hatred" toward Frances Grant, insisting that he now had "his own indications" and did not consider earlier ones "real." There was, she told Helena, "some terrible dark force which is leading him."[223] In a final meeting with Grant in early July, Wallace told her she had "failed in [her] mission." He still wished to "help the New Country," but would thereafter receive Messages only from Horch. Moreover, to Grant's horror, Wallace "seem[ed] even to harbor resentment against Father" himself.[224]

Thus had the speculator Horch—a man who had, by all appearances, been manipulating the president for personal profit—improbably taken from Roerich the honored place in Henry Wallace's stable of spiritual advisers.

The final rupture within the inner circle also occurred that month. On July 10, Esther Lichtmann wrote to Helena insisting that the Lord had for some time been speaking directly to her and to Horch, without the need for intercession. And it had been "uniquely through the Ind[ications] of the L[ord]," she explained, that they "had saved the Building" in New York from financial failure. Helena, shocked and angered, scribbled in the margins that her claims were "absurd" and "against all basic occult laws."[225]

On July 30, Horch also wrote to her, condemning the "blow" that she and Nicholas had inflicted on him, on his wife, and on Esther over their thirteen years of "devoted service." The worst of these, he said, was Helena's denial of God's command that he advise the president on silver.[226] Helena was furious. In a letter to Sina, her last remaining confidant in New York, she pointed out that Horch, with the "instincts of a Wall-Street man," had chosen to serve "his own ends." Wallace, she added, was now "in the hands of these traitors," Louis and Esther. He was "being duped by those criminals," and pulled into their "ugly undertakings." Still, Wallace was no innocent victim. She had "documents demonstrating [his] chicken heart and arrogance."[227]

On August 20, 1935, the expedition was dealt yet another jolt from abroad—this time a cable from U.S. ambassador William Bullitt in Moscow. Its content was based on "information" furnished to the U.S. military attaché, Philip Faymonville, by "a Soviet citizen whom [he] considers to be of importance." The cable formed the basis of a long communiqué from the State Department to Wallace, sent four days later.

Bullitt's message read much like Powell's article, suggesting similar sourcing. Its claims, however, were even more hyperbolic. George Roerich, the cable said, echoing Powell, was a former "Czarist officer" who had "recruited assistance for his expedition from among followers of the bandit Semenoff."

This statement was nonsense. Neither George Roerich nor any Russian émigré on the expedition, save security-and-supply chief Victor Gribanovsky, had been old enough to fight in the Russian Civil War. And none, including Gribanovsky, had had any links to Semenoff.

The cable further reported that the "commanding officer 15th infantry at Tientsin refused to supply [the] arms requested" by the Roerichs, but was "overruled" after Nicholas appealed to "Czarist circles in Washington." The weapons and ample ammunition were then, according to the report, "turned over to Roerich and the Semenoff bandits."

But the "Czarist circles" consisted solely in the person of Henry Wallace. It was he, after all, who had secured issuance of the arms permit.

"The armed party," the report continued—that is, armed with a mere six rifles and four revolvers—was "now making its way toward the Soviet Union . . . to rally former White elements and discontented Mongols."[228]

This last statement went well beyond anything Powell had claimed, and must have alarmed readers in Washington—as it was intended to do. But just as surely as the "Red Russian" briefing Powell was working in the service of the Soviet state, so, too, was the "Soviet citizen" informing Faymonville.

Faymonville, as is suggested by later declassified Soviet and American records, was a longtime target of Soviet counterintelligence, owing partly to his close relationships with Red Army officers (many of whom were executed in 1937–38) and his vulnerability, as a homosexual, to blackmail. Spymaster Pavel Sudoplatov would later write that his agency had recruited Faymonville as an "agent of influence" under the cover name "Elektrik." Allegations against him would, during World War II, be investigated by the FBI, but with no conclusive result.[229] What we now know to be the false-hoods and exaggerations in his report, however, were clearly motivated by his source's intention to deceive the State Department.

Between August 24 and September 20, George Roerich and Henry Wallace cabled back and forth. George pleaded difficulties in following Wallace's route. Wallace told him to proceed to Peking immediately; he was then to terminate the expedition, following the return of firearms and shipping of herbarium collections,[230] as of September 21.[231] Treasury, acting on a request from the Department of Agriculture, also sent Nicholas a bill for $3,604, covering funds advanced to him for which no "vouchers" had been submitted within the mandated time frame.[232] Wallace further directed Bressman to inform Nicholas that any future correspondence should be sent to Ryerson's successor, F. D. Richey, and not to Bressman or himself.[233] He then wrote to Helena in his "personal capacity" telling her that there was to be no further communication between any of the Roerichs and himself.[234] And in a failed attempt to prevent a true account of this saga from being written, Wallace asked Horch to notify the museum "that no letters from myself or other members of the Department [were] to be published."[235]

On September 25, Wallace sent a letter, through Bressman, to Colonel C. Burnett of the War Department's Military Intelligence Division G-2, reacting to Faymonville's Soviet disinformation with some of his own. "This expedition," Wallace assured the colonel, falsely, "was sent to central Asia *solely to collect drought resistant grasses*.":

> We have been hearing, however, a number of reports that they have been engaged in other activities. . . . The expedition was definitely terminated as of September 21 and you can assure Major Faymonville of the Embassy that the fears of the people whom he mentioned in his letter are now entirely groundless.[236]

By the time the colonel received the letter, Nicholas and George were on a boat from Shanghai back to India.

By all appearances, Louis Horch had been genuinely moved by his first encounters with Roerich's art and spiritualism. Yet being a shrewd and canny operator, he arranged his patronage such that he would always be in position to profit from it, or at least to withdraw it on favorable terms.

Horch organized the Roerichs' undertakings in New York in the form of a trust with seven shareholders (the Horch couple, the Roerich couple, the Lichtmann couple, and Frances Grant). But in 1923, just prior to his departure for India, Roerich agreed to make Horch the institute's presi-

dent, and gave the financier power of attorney and control over all its financial affairs—including tax filings and payments. Horch also became
the trustee for the shares of all shareholders. Roerich, a nonresident alien
after 1923, became a mere "honorary president" of his namesake institutions. He paid little attention to matters of financing, leaving them all to
Horch.

Horch personally financed about 30 percent of the Master Building purchase and construction costs, borrowing the remainder. Only the three and
a half lower floors were occupied by the museum, exhibition halls, and the
associated institutions.[237] Rental apartments filled the upper floors. The
shareholders were each allotted apartments, where they lived rent-free until
at least 1929—when Horch requested that they sign leases. It is not known if
or what they actually paid thereafter.

Horch bought, or claimed to have bought, about a thousand of Roerich's
paintings for the museum. But since he legally constituted his financial support
as a loan, and the paintings as security for the loan, he stood to take ownership
of them in the case of default.

As the Depression set in, financial problems beset the Roerich enterprises. A suit brought against the museum by its Bondholders' Committee
in April 1932 put the building into receivership. After two years of court
battles spearheaded by Horch, however, the Roerichs would regain some
superficial measure of control—but only briefly.

By 1935, Horch had become so close personally with the president of
the United States that the Roerichs were no longer necessary or even useful to him. As strains grew between him and the couple over his efforts to
influence Roosevelt, Horch set out to prevent them from ever returning to
the United States. Sina Lichtmann could see clearly what was happening.
Horch, she wrote to Nicholas on August 20, wanted "to eliminate the major
person from all enterprises."[238]

On September 27, Horch wrote a scathing farewell to Nicholas and Helena. "Under the guise of spirituality," he told them, "we have witnessed the
service to egotism and self-glorification." Their "lack of appreciation" for his
devoted efforts over thirteen years was "unparalleled." "We shall," he concluded—referring to himself, his wife, and Esther Lichtmann—"no longer
accept your leadership. [T]he breach between us is irreconcilable."[239]

In October, Horch commenced a series of legal maneuvers to take full control of the Roerich enterprises. He removed five shareholders from the trust's board—Nicholas, Helena, Sina, Maurice, and Frances—using his power of attorney to vote their shares against them. He then transferred those five shares to his wife. At a stroke, a building worth an estimated $2.9 million was his, as were $5 million in paintings (today worth a fortune).[240]

Having consolidated voting power, he proceeded to remove the Banner of Peace and Roerich literature from the building's lobby, change the signs from "Roerich Museum" to "Master Building," and direct the phone operators to answer calls saying only "Master Hotel."[241] He informed Sina that she, Maurice, and Frances would lose their positions unless they ceased cooperation with the Roerichs.[242] Maurice filed suit on behalf of the five disenfranchised shareholders to stop and reverse his actions.

On November 15, Horch met with the president, again proffering his Divinely Inspired guidance on silver and "managed currency." Roosevelt, according to Horch, changed the subject, asking for his views on the Department of Agriculture's concerns that Roerich had exceeded his authority and interfered in politics. Horch explained that Roerich had "put himself in a false position by his dealings with Japanese, Bolsheviks, and Mongols," but that "the measures undertaken by Secretary Wallace [had been] absolutely correct."

Esther added that "the Mongolian project" would, despite the setbacks, be "continued and developed—just not in the way assumed by Roerich." The president insisted that everything had to "remain above politics."[243]

The "Mongolian project," of course, had always been *about* "politics"— about creating the "New Country." Yet, as long as his administration was not involved or otherwise implicated, Roosevelt had been happy to let the Roerichs indulge harmless fantasies. It was, unfortunately, no longer possible to sustain a partition.

In December 1935 and January 1936, both Nicholas[244] and Helena[245] would write final letters to Roosevelt; each condemning Horch's dishonesty, each pleading for the president's continued confidence and support. But Roosevelt was through with them. There is no record of his responding. That he would persist in his regard for Wallace and Horch, however— in spite of their long patronage, and now sudden disowning, of the troublesome Roerichs—is testimony to his remarkable ability to surf the tide of his own errors.

꙳

By the autumn of 1935, Wallace's bitterness toward the Roerichs had morphed into vindictiveness. On October 1, he sent a letter to the commissioner of the Internal Revenue Service, asking him to launch an "investigation" of facts and figures, contained in an accompanying memorandum, related to Nicholas Roerich's income, tax payments, and residency status. Those facts and figures presumably came from the only person who would both know them and wish the IRS to know them: Louis L. Horch. Wallace also asked the commissioner for a meeting "during the next two or three days," presumably to relay information which he did not want in writing.[246]

In December, the IRS sent Roerich a "notice of deficiency" related to his tax payments in 1926, 1927, and 1934—years associated with his two Central Asian expeditions. In 1926, the notice indicated, Horch had made payments to Roerich of $73,300; in 1927, $74,271.78. Although Roerich would insist, almost certainly truthfully, that these were donations to cover expedition expenses, the IRS concluded that they constituted taxable income from the sale of paintings to Horch—income which Roerich, having relied on Horch to manage such matters, never reported. In 1934, Horch, still operating under his power of attorney, filed a "tentative [tax] return" for Roerich, but failed to file a final one on the grounds that Roerich had not given him the necessary information or instructions. The IRS determined that Roerich was guilty, for all three years, of fraud with intent to evade tax.[247] Whereas the copious legal records suggest that Roerich's crimes were, at worst, only those of ignorance and uninterest, Horch showed that these could, with the help of a cabinet secretary, be exploited to great effect.

On January 17, 1936, treasury undersecretary (then also acting secretary) T. J. Coolidge wrote to Wallace asking for his aid in having Roerich satisfy his tax obligation of $49,186.58.[248] On the 23rd, Wallace wrote directly to Secretary Morgenthau himself, reporting that his department's "experience with Nicholas Roerich [had] been quite unsatisfactory," that the man's activities had been "stopped," and that his department was ready to "turn over any sums of money due [him]."[249] Wallace forwarded copies of both letters to Horch.[250] One week later, the IRS sent an official to the museum to impose a lien on Roerich's paintings.[251] On February 7, Coolidge wrote back to Wallace, asking that his department send a check to the Treasury for any money due Roerich.[252] (It is unknown if the department complied.) Roerich himself would only be notified of the amount due two weeks later—on February 28.

Roerich subsequently appealed the IRS rulings, requiring years of legal work and the provision of mounds of documents and testimony. A federal appeals court would, in 1940, rule against him on all the tax body's judgments (although it is unknown what, if anything, he actually paid).[253]

In his effort to complete the takeover of the Roerich enterprises, Horch turned to an even more powerful patron than Wallace. Together with Esther Lichtmann, he visited the president twice in January 1936—on the 15th and, joined by Wallace, on the 28th—each time charging Roerich with disloyalty to the country. Horch "apologized for the Mongolian project," but insisted that there was a sound business proposition behind it—one which he, Horch, had developed. Unfortunately, "the Patriarch" had perverted it for his own means. Esther added that he had tried to secure $25 million from Japan "for subversive work" (an astounding, and ludicrous, $537 million in today's money), after having earlier tried, in 1926, to work for the Soviets. Both these claims are undocumented.

Horch now, finally, got to his ask. He told the president about the litigation launched by Roerich and his acolytes to stop his takeover of the New York enterprises, including the name of the judge: Samuel Rosenman. Rosenman was the former counsel to Governor Roosevelt in New York, an author of his 1932 nomination acceptance speech, popularizer of the phrase "New Deal," and now a justice of the state's Supreme Court. Rosenman would, during the coming presidential campaign, also emerge as one of Roosevelt's most trusted advisers and speechwriters.[254] The president, Horch noted with satisfaction, took a pen and jotted down the judge's name. "This is simple," he said. "I will help."[255]

Following the meeting with the president, the press hit Roerich with a series of damning articles. On January 30, 1936, the New York *Sun* reported that the Department of Agriculture had "disbanded an Asiatic planting expedition" and "terminated the government services" of its leader, Nicholas Roerich, following "informal protests" from "high officials" of the Manchukuo authorities—some of whom had even called the painter a "spy." The case, it said, "was almost unprecedented in the history of the department," which had sponsored "hundreds of similar exploring groups."[256] A kindred piece ran in the *World-Telegram*, citing Wallace's department as its source. The State Department, though it had always opposed Wallace working with Roerich, disclaimed any knowledge of the spy charges.[257]

On the surface, the timing of the statement seemed strange. The expedition had for five months now been slotted for termination on February 1—there was no news there. And the foreign-protest allegations were recycled from Powell's *Chicago Tribune* piece, now seven months old. So what explained the timing?

The Agriculture Department claimed it was responding to "a rumor" that Roerich would be reemployed; a rumor which it needed to dispel. But no one outside the department seemed to be aware of any such "rumor." The disempowered museum trustees recognized the true reason for Wallace baiting the press. In Rosenman's courtroom the following morning, their attorneys would be arguing that Horch voting their shares against them at a December 16 board meeting had been illegal. Horch would argue that he had invested upward of $1 million in the building, and that the complainants were never more than "nominal stockholders" intent on living there forever rent-free.[258] As George Roerich would observe in a letter to Frances Grant, "the vicious statement . . . was calculated to influence the judge." Horch was "using the channels of a governmental department to achieve [his] own ends. [I]t is criminal."[259]

The trustees' attorneys fired off a telegram to Henry Wallace, which they also released to the press, accusing him of foul play. "We demand you explain why the press release from your department and these quoted statements come on the eve of the injunction proceedings . . . pending against your friend, Louis L. Horch," they wrote. "[W]e [also] demand that you publicly retract these statements and insinuations, with an apology." They further warned of "an action for slander and libel."[260]

Wallace refused to respond. But an anonymous "departmental official" would that same day walk back the foreign-protest allegations, saying that "no representations of any kind" had been made—at least "so far as he knew."[261]

The following morning, January 31, as reported in all the major New York newspapers, Justice Rosenman "reserved decision" on the trustees' injunction plea. The judge's nonaction freed Horch to proceed with removing Roe-rich's name from the museum—replacing it with the name "Master Institute of United Arts." Two weeks later, Rosenman would deny the injunction out-right.[262] Horch felt he knew whom to credit.

At a meeting with the president on March 5, Horch "thanked him for his assistance with R[osenman]." The president, Horch recorded, "was happy that we had won the litigation."[263] On June 5, according to Sina Lichtmann, "all our institutions were liquidated and we were kicked out." And on the tax matter, she added, "the lawyers are saying that . . . everything has been complicated due to the influence of [Henry Wallace]."[264]

Whether Roosevelt, or Wallace, had influenced the judge's thinking in the Roerich case is unknown. Rosenman would, however, later come to play a role in the burying of Wallace's "Guru letters"—and thereby helping to save both Wallace and Roosevelt, at least temporarily, from acute political embarrassment, or worse.

On February 1, 1936, another hit piece in the New York *Sun* reported that Roerich had, according to Wallace's department, sent a mere "20 seed pack-ages" from China—packages which had "cost [the] U.S. $35,000."[265] George Roerich was furious, calling the derisory count "an intentional false state-ment." As evidence, he sent Frances Grant "a list of all materials forwarded to the Department"—a list that had, he said, been "acknowledged by them."[266]

Owing to convoluted logistics and associated delayed deliveries, most of the specimens shipped from the expedition may not have arrived in the United States until well into 1936. Yet the claim that a mere "20 packages" had been received, based on a September 20, 1935 departmental report, was demon-strably false.[267] There is documentary evidence of the department receiving, on November 27, 1935, "two cases" at the port of San Francisco, containing within two further large boxes of seeds (and two more of herbariums).[268]

Notwithstanding the considerable time and effort the Roerichs had de-voted to laying the ground for "the New Country," they collected, classified, documented, and sent the department large volumes of seeds and plants—not to mention maps, a Chinese-Latin-Japanese medicinal dictionary, and various Tibetan medical texts; the latter of which were requested by Wal-lace himself. George, by far the most punctilious and practical-minded of the Roerichs, was thorough in photographing, recording, and reporting the finds—all of which was assisted by the expedition's three able botanists (two Russian and one Chinese). Evidence from multiple sources attests to the Roerichs having sent, in total, 485 packages of seeds, as well as a systematized herbarium containing 1,169 items from Inner Mongolia and 192 from the Spiti Valley, in the northwest Himalayas.[269]

There is no record of the seeds ever having been used in the United States for any practical purpose. Yet this fact may simply reflect the agriculture secretary's uninterest in the finds after the Roerichs' descent into notoriety—a notoriety which he himself had aided.

Louis L. Horch would take full legal possession of the Master Building in 1938, turning the lower floors into the Riverside Museum—dedicated to the works of contemporary artists not named Roerich. That same year, Henry Wallace would hire Horch to manage foreign exchange transactions at the Department of Agriculture. In 1942, he would secure Horch's appointment as manager of the Economic Board of Warfare in New York City, and, in 1946, director of commerce for the New York region.[270]

Thanks to Horch and Wallace, the Roerichs would never return to the United States. According to one undocumented account, Wallace, most likely in 1939, arranged for Horch to meet Stanley Hornbeck at the State Department, a meeting at which Horch gave the official tax notices showing that the artist owed over $48,000. Roerich was, Horch said, "an impostor and a cheat." If permitted to return to the country, "he would cause a great deal of trouble." In December of that year, Hornbeck wrote to Wallace explaining that consular offices in India had been instructed not to issue Roerich a visa without prior authorization from the department—authorization that would never come.[271] The Roerichs, also denied reentry to the Soviet Union, would thus remain in India for the rest of their lives. Nicholas would die in Naggar in 1947, Helena in Kalimpong in 1955.

From September to December 1935, Henry Wallace waged a continuous and, at times, frenzied campaign to divorce himself from every aspect of Nicholas Roerich's geopolitical agenda—from the Banner of Peace to the "New Country." If any aspect of that campaign can be considered creditable, it is perhaps the "apologies," of sorts, which he sent to his staff. These indicate some pangs of conscience over his treatment of subordinates who had presciently warned him against mixing plants with politics.

To Knowles Ryerson, who had urged Wallace to let his botanists lead their own expedition, and who was banished to the West Coast in consequence, Wallace offered modest words of repentance: "Referring to the letter which I wrote you . . . a year ago, . . . I have given considerable study to all aspects of the situation and have reached the conclusion that your motives were of the highest. Subsequent events have in considerable measure borne out your judgment."[272] Wallace, however, took no action to repair the damage he had done to Ryerson's career.

Wallace also wrote to Howard MacMillan's assistant, James Stephens. "In reviewing the history of the Asiatic expedition," the letter said, "it has become clear that, because of your subordinate position in that expedition, [my] statement that your actions could be regarded as deliberate insubordination was inaccurate. I am only glad that no administration action was taken other than writing you so that this letter will clear the record."[273] That Wallace chose not to write to *MacMillan* suggests, however, that he continued to see *his* actions as insubordinate. It is nonetheless notable that the 1935 *World Almanac* says of the expedition that it "was headed by Dr. H. G. MacMillan and J. L. Stevens [sic]."[274] N. K. Roerich is not mentioned.

Wallace's correspondence did not "clear the record," but rather muddied and falsified it. He sent letters to U.S. government personnel stating that Roerich had been sent to Asia "solely" to collect grasses, and that he had only learned of "other activities" from "reports." Both these statements were gross and deliberate misrepresentations.[275] In a letter to Mongolian Prince Demchugdongrub, informing him of the expedition's termination, Wallace insisted that Roerich had "not [been] given authority to perform any other mission" beyond grass collection.[276] Wallace, of course, had actually sent Roerich his own money to invest in Mongolia, had tried to raise millions more in private and public investment funds, and had endorsed the creation of a "New Country" on the prince's territory.

In perhaps his most desperate and professionally improper act of repudiation, Wallace, who had been the official Protector of the Convention of the Roerich Pact, also sent letters marked "PERSONAL AND CONFIDENTIAL" to fifty-eight foreign ambassadors and high officials, each disavowing Roerich. And in so doing, he knowingly and deliberately damaged prospects for the pact's ratification abroad. Eleven of the twenty-one signatory nations would fail to ratify it.

The letter began by stating that he "had at one time a high regard for Professor Nicholas Roerich" owing to his, Wallace's, "interest in the adoption of the Treaty" popularly bearing the Russian's name. "The purpose of this letter," he explained, was "to let you know that my attitude is now entirely changed." He accused Roerich of "megalomania."[277]

Wallace thought that disparaging Roerich at home and abroad would allow him to shed blame for the fiasco the expedition had become, but appointing the Russian naturally reflected on his own judgment and competence. "New Tempest Hits Wallace" is how one New York daily framed the story of the expedition's strange and embarrassing collapse.[278] The "revelation" of the pitiful seed count, said another, "had the capital wondering whether the jaunt . . . was just another example of New Deal boondoggling."[279] The expedition thus became the low point of Wallace's first term in government.

There was, however, plenty of time to recover, and, with his eye on succeeding Roosevelt in 1940, Wallace's priority became preventing public knowledge of his damning correspondence. "No letters from myself or other members of the Department," he demanded of the museum, "are to be published."[280] But he had made enemies of Frances, Maurice, and Sina, not to mention Nicholas and Helena—the last of whom had already expressed a willingness to turn his words against him.[281]

Five

FIGHTING FASCISTS, PLANNING PEACE

"On this tenth day of June [1940]," a grave Franklin Roosevelt told his commencement audience at the University of Virginia, "the hand that held the dagger has struck it into the back of its neighbor." The hand was Mussolini's. The neighbor was France. One month earlier, Germany had attacked France from the east. Italy now struck from the south.

FDR's bracing words, together with his pledge to support "the opponents of force," made clear his determination to end American neutrality and to confront fascist aggression. Only then and there, Eleanor Roosevelt would later write, did she know that "those who thought the war inevitable had persuaded Franklin that he could not refuse to run for a third term."[1]

But she added the words "*if he were nominated.*" Indeed, FDR would insist on being nominated for an unprecedented third term *before* he would agree to be a candidate. His party would have to draft him.

Five days after the president's speech, the Republican Party would, in a wild, six-ballot convention, improbably nominate an internationalist former Democrat as its presidential candidate: the Indiana-born lawyer and executive Wendell Willkie. Roosevelt-the-politician had been itching to fight an isolationist; Roosevelt-the-patriot, however, would call it a "Godsend to the country" that the campaign would not cleave it into internationalist and isolationist factions.[2] Whichever way the vote went, isolationism was dead.

The drafting of FDR at his party's convention was orchestrated by Harry Hopkins and Ed Kelly, mayor of the host city, Chicago. Hopkins met with party bosses in his suites at three different hotels, making clear that Roosevelt would refuse the nomination if more than 150 votes were cast against him on the first ballot. On the convention's second evening, July 16, Hopkins told its chairman, Senate majority leader Alben Barkley, to read out a short message from Roosevelt averring that he did not want the nomination. After a short, stunned silence, a voice boomed through the hall's loudspeakers—"WE WANT ROOSEVELT! WE WANT ROOSEVELT! . . ." Having been cued up to initiate the "spontaneous" eruption by Mayor Kelly, Tom Garry, the city's superintendent of sewers, would become known as the notorious "voice from the sewers." A thunderous fifty-three-minute pro-Roosevelt demonstration followed. The following day, July 17, the delegates renominated the president by a margin of 946 votes to 147. The latter figure was split among four candidates led by conservative Democratic National Committee (DNC) chairman James Farley, who moved to make the nomination by acclamation—eliciting roars of "AYE!"[3]

The question of FDR's running mate was more fraught. Roosevelt had one priority above all others: that the vice president be a convinced internationalist—an internationalist prepared, in case of the president's incapacity, to carry on the latter's foreign and defense policy. He had for two terms tolerated John Nance Garner to pacify party conservatives, but it was now time for the party to come to him.

As with so much else to do with Roosevelt's thinking, none of the varying accounts of his thoughts on a running mate can be considered definitive. Yet there is overwhelming evidence that he wanted Cordell Hull.[4] According to the secretary of state himself, Roosevelt "pleaded" with him for two hours and forty minutes to take the job. Hull, however, "stood firm in [his] declination," having no interest in a position whose authority started and ended with breaking tie Senate votes.

"If you don't take it," Roosevelt threatened, mischievously, "I'll have to get Henry Wallace to run." He may have considered that sufficient incentive, but Hull "continued to refuse."[5]

There is also ample evidence that Roosevelt's second choice was not Henry Wallace, however, but Jimmy Byrnes.[6] The president appeared, though, reluctantly, to accept arguments that the South Carolina senator would be a liability with Catholics (whose religion he had renounced on marriage). And so it was Henry Wallace.

As an ardent internationalist, a committed New Dealer, and a farm state native, Wallace checked three important boxes. Roosevelt, furthermore, genuinely liked him. Wallace "is good to work with," he told Frances Perkins. "[H]e knows a lot," and "you can trust his information."[7]

To be sure, many insiders voiced concerns about Wallace's acceptability beyond the party's liberal wing. "I think you are unfair to your country and your party," Farley told the president on July 18, "in forcing Wallace's nomination, and you'll live to regret it." As for Wallace's supposed strength in the farm belt, Farley had his doubts, and warned that "he'll hurt in other places"—particularly business circles. "The people," he added, also "look on him as a mystic." But "he's *not* a mystic," Roosevelt objected. "He's a *philosopher*, a liberal philosopher, and I'm sure that he'll be all right."[8]

Insofar as Wallace had evolved over the second term, Roosevelt was right. No doubt chastened by his experience with the Roerichs, Wallace had learned to keep mystical interests separate from geopolitics—as Roosevelt had always done. He would persist in claiming to know things, in Jamesian fashion, for which evidence was lacking or contrary. But faith in spiritual gurus had been replaced by faith in his own moral instincts, a faith not unusual in political figures.

No one thought more highly of Henry Wallace's abilities than Henry Wallace. Yet whereas he never openly promoted himself as Roosevelt's logical successor, neither did he discourage those who believed it.

During his meeting with Wallace in March 1934, Nicholas Roerich pressed him "about the presidency," to which Wallace responded "that it would be in 1940"—presumably after Roosevelt's second term.[9] Wallace's assistant, Paul Appleby, later recalled that Wallace never did "anything to enhance his political [visibility] except as [he, Appleby,] initiated it."[10] Wallace displayed no "zeal" for the highest office, although by early 1937 he was volunteering reports of encouragement from others.[11] In any case, he never shared such reports with Ilo. When in 1938 Appleby told her that she and Henry were going to a party to build support for his candidacy, she was puzzled.

"Candidacy for what?" she asked.

"The presidency."

"Oh, my, no!" she yelled.[12]

Around that time, Appleby suggested to Wallace that he find an experienced political manager to help him prepare for eventualities. Soon after, Wallace asked Appleby if he "was tied up for lunch on Friday"—which the latter interpreted, fearfully, as a request that he meet one of the secretary's "mystical friends." He was right; though it was worse than he feared.

At the appointed hour, Wallace introduced him to his new "political manager." The manager was, Appleby observed, a "very odd appearing man with a marked foreign accent"; a man who explained, by way of documenting his experience, that he had known an "alderman once." The man did not mention, however, that he had also, a few years prior, met many times with the president of the United States—meetings at which they discussed silver policy, Central Asia, and a court case involving Judge Rosenman. The man's name was Louis Horch.

Wallace asked Appleby "to have lunch with this fellow every day" to discuss political matters. Appleby was appalled, but kept his thoughts to himself until Horch had departed—at which point he burst out that he "wouldn't have lunch 'every day' with this fellow if [we] were the only two men left in America." But Wallace did persuade him to meet Horch once more—a meeting at which Horch pledged to "raise a lot of money for Wallace." In the end, Horch sent Appleby a personal check for $800. The two never spoke again.

Appleby remained Wallace's "campaign manager," to the extent that Wallace ever had what could be called a "campaign."[13] A Gallup poll in May 1939 found him buried in a tie for tenth place among Democratic voters.[14] Roosevelt himself remarked to party insiders that Wallace lacked "It" politically.[15] According to Louis Bean, a Wallace economic adviser, Appleby asked him, Bean, in early 1940, to sound out labor leader Sidney Hillman, a founder of the Congress of Industrial Organizations (CIO), about supporting a Wallace run. But Hillman made clear that the CIO's priority was "to get Roosevelt to run for a third term."[16]

Wallace had been convinced for at least a year that the president "ought to take another term." The growing menace of Hitler—not to mention the threat that Democratic conservatives, such as Garner, posed to the New Deal[17]—demanded it. But when Rosenman suggested to Wallace that he was, in such a case, the logical running mate, Wallace said nothing either to encourage or dissuade him. "[A]nyone who went out to be either President or Vice President" in 1940, Wallace diaried, "was sure to get it in the neck."[18] And when the convention rolled around, the fact that Wallace had not lobbied for himself played to his advantage. Roosevelt, in no mood to bargain with his party, relished in demanding a running mate whom no one was demanding of him.[19]

At least seventeen Democrats aspired to the vice presidency, and each assumed he would be free to make his case to the convention. But in a phone call with Hopkins at 2:30 a.m. on July 18, Roosevelt made clear that—Hull having refused the job again—he was determined to run with Wallace.

At 7:30 a.m., Appleby arrived in Hopkins' suite at the Ambassador Hotel, finding him laid out, after a sleepless night, on a couch in his pajamas. The two men agreed that Roosevelt should call half a dozen of the aspirants to give them the word. The president, however, who loathed delivering bad news, agreed to call only one: Farley. Hopkins and Wallace would have to handle the others.[20]

For Hopkins, securing Roosevelt's nomination, even after Roosevelt had disclaimed any want of it, had been the easy part; nominating Wallace, in contrast, was like amputating without anaesthesia. The party's conservative wing cussed and howled; New Deal stalwart Harold Ickes, the interior secretary, cabled the president to protest. For many on the left as well as the right, Wallace was a Johnny-come-lately Democrat who sought to remake the party, and the country, in his own strange, mystical image.

The proposing of Henry Wallace before the convention later that day—"a God-fearing, modest American of the highest character, worthy of and equipped to meet the responsibilities of any public trust," according to the fellow Iowan who proposed him—was greeted with a torrent of boos and shouts of derision. Under pressure from Hopkins and his anxious helpers, all of the other aspirants, save Speaker of the House William Bankhead, agreed—with varying degrees of anger and reluctance—to withdraw their names from consideration. Yet each time their names were spoken—Alabama's Bankhead, Indiana's Paul McNutt, Texas' Jesse Jones—cheers rang out; each time Wallace's name was spoken, jeers.

Wallace's face, Perkins observed, could not hide the "agony." Ilo was close to tears; the first lady grabbed her hand in consolation.[21]

Back in the Oval Office, FDR followed the proceedings with growing fury. He scribbled out a message declining the nomination, which he handed to speechwriter Sam Rosenman with an order to "clean it up" in case Wallace lost. Rosenman was worried.

FDR would, four years later, insist that he had no right to dictate to the convention. The difference was that in 1940 he backed Henry Wallace and meant it; in 1944, he would back Henry Wallace and mean something else.

In Chicago, Eleanor took the stage, trying to calm the irate crowd. Without mentioning Wallace, she urged them to see that this was "no ordinary time, no time for thinking about anything except what we can best do for the country." Still, as the voting began, Bankhead, with strong Southern backing, looked like he might prevail.

Roosevelt loyalists worked the floor. "Do you want a president or a vice president?" Byrnes demanded of them. It was hardly a ringing endorsement of Henry Wallace, but it would have to do. Soon enough, Wallace began pulling ahead. In the end, he would score 626 votes against Bankhead's 329. McNutt and other noncandidates would take a further hundred. In the face of terrific party resistance, the president's threat of political suicide had served its aim.

Wallace was ready with an acceptance speech calling for military preparedness to be supplemented by a commitment to help every family "protect itself from hunger, cold and lack of shelter." But in perhaps the most humiliating victory in American convention history, Wallace was ordered to keep quiet. Byrnes would not permit the winner to be drowned in boos. Instead, the party would hear the president, through the ether, accept its nomination and praise the "practical idealism" of the man it had just chosen, albeit not entirely of its own free will, to be his running mate.[22]

One evening in August 1940, Sam Rosenman was working in the Executive Office when Harry Hopkins phoned and told him to come to his room at the White House. When he arrived, Hopkins gathered up some papers from his desk and handed them over silently. Rosenman read, growing more and more concerned as he did.

The papers were photocopies of letters from 1933 and 1934—some hand-written, some typed—all of them written in an odd sort of coded language. There were references to "Monkeys" and "Rulers"; someone called "the Sour One," another "the Wavering One." There were strange, affected salutations, such as "Dear Guru"; references to the "Holy Chalice," "Karmic duty," and "the sacred, most precious casket." There were effusive closings, such as "May the peace of the Great One descend upon you." And all the letters were signed by H. A. Wallace, HAW, or someone called "Galahad."

Hopkins told Rosenman that the treasurer of the Republican National Committee was allegedly holding the originals in a Wall Street bank vault.

An aide with media ties had gotten hold of them. But were they real? If they were, Hopkins feared dire trouble for the campaign.[23]

Wallace being out of town, Hopkins phoned Appleby, asking him to look into their authenticity. Appleby phoned Wallace, who loosely confessed authorship: "I guess that's right, Paul," he said. When shown the copies later on, however, he would insist that only the handwritten ones were real. Publicly, he would deny writing any of them. Thanks to Russian archives, we have proof that Wallace wrote all of them.[24]

Appleby headed to the White House, arriving around 11 p.m. He explained what he knew of the Roerich expedition and the obscure references in what would be called the "Guru letters."[25] Appleby had prescreened many of the agriculture secretary's "screwy letters" typed by his secretary over the years, and had tried to get him to "modify" the "mystical" ones. But Wallace would never budge on those.[26]

"Sam," Hopkins asked, anxiously, "is there any way that we can get Wallace off the ticket now, or is it too late?" Rosenman spent the early morning researching how a vice presidential candidate might renounce a certified nomination. But he could see no clear legal map for Wallace's withdrawal.

He and Hopkins entered the White House bedroom as the president was eating breakfast. Rosenman handed him the letters. Accounts of his visceral reaction differ, but it appears that he asked if the men knew how the Republicans planned to use them. They did not. Convinced, unlike Hopkins, that he could ride out the brewing tempest, Roosevelt directed that Appleby join Wallace on the trail and keep him out of trouble.

Appleby flew to Chicago with Morris Ernst, the lawyer who had helped write Wallace's 1936 book *Whose Constitution?* Ernst's considered advice was that Wallace should lie. Appleby would later confess to Rosenman that the drafting of that lie, together with Ernst and Wallace, "is a sore point on my conscience." It was, he said, "as nearly a dishonest thing as I remember ever having been a party to."[27]

Wallace ducked reporters that day. But the "Guru letters" were already in the hands of the Republican publisher Paul Block. Rumors circulated in Washington that a Miss Frances Grant, formerly of the Roerich Museum, had sold them for $5,000. Yet this seems inconsistent with her character. It is more likely she had deposited them with attorneys, from whence they leaked.

Block assigned the story to his Pulitzer Prize–winning reporter, Ray Sprigle of the *Pittsburgh Post-Gazette*, who chased Wallace around the Midwest, seeking an interview. As encouragement, he distributed drafts that he knew would make their way to the candidate. Back in Chicago on October 19, Wallace approached Sprigle from his train compartment, asked him how to spell his name, wrote it out across the top of a two-page typed statement, handed it to Sprigle and returned to his compartment. The statement read, in part:

> Your publisher . . . must know that the material in question is composed of malicious, spurious, fraudulent and forged matter. He must know that it emanates from a source rejected as to credibility by courts of the land; that the same garbage has been hawked for many years; that editor after editor has rejected it; that it emanates from a disgruntled, discharged employee [Roerich] who dares not return to this land because of tax frauds. . . . To the credit of all parties and all peoples, no one I am sure has been reckless enough either for profits or votes to inject religious questions into this Democratic campaign, least of all should a member of a great minority group [Jews, of which Block was one] be responsible for opening that door.

Wallace no doubt felt morally justified in distributing such falsehoods, even if he had to accentuate them with a tincture of (uncharacteristic) anti-semitism. In any case, Roosevelt, Hopkins, and Rosenman had his back, and no story would appear during the campaign. Supposedly, Representative Joseph Martin (R-MA) persuaded Block that it would be "politically unwise" to publish one.[28] The most compelling explanation for that judgment is Roosevelt's directive to an aide, Lowell Mellett, to spread the word in Republican circles that Democrats were prepared, if circumstances warranted, to leak details of Willkie's affair with New York editor Irita Van Doren.[29]

Wallace would years later call the 1940 campaign "exceedingly dirty."[30] Though he was no doubt thinking of actions undertaken by others, he played his own part in it. Foreign policy was the dominant theme of Wallace's campaign speeches, but the oratory was hardly as elevated as, say, his contribution to a volume on *Christian Bases of World Order* a few years hence.[31] "The Republican candidate is not an appeaser and a friend of Hitler," he assured an audience in rural Nebraska, "but you can be sure that every Nazi, every Hitlerite and every appeaser is a Republican."[32] Republicans "fought [Roo-

President Franklin D. Roosevelt gestures at vice presidential candidate Henry A. Wallace at Val-Kill Cottage in Hyde Park, New York, during the election campaign, August 8, 1940.

sevelt] at home," he said in Des Moines, "as Hitler fought him abroad."[33] "Regimented Nazi organizations," he told a crowd in New York, "are marching in the Republican parade."[34] He even branded as Nazi dupes those prominent liberals that sided with his former party. Willkie supporter John L. Lewis, for example, the president of the CIO and a champion of organized labor, "sounds so much like Herr Goebbels."[35] Wallace was typically reserved and reasoned when face-to-face with those with whom he disagreed on matters political, but when behind a microphone he rarely showed reticence in tarring them, or their supporters, with fascist aims and sympathies.

In the end, Willkie suffered electorally not from a perception that he was dangerously different from Roosevelt but that he embraced what Roosevelt stood for—internationalism and New Deal-ism—without having demonstrated a capacity to do them better. And so on November 5, 1940, Roosevelt won by a massive margin of 449 electoral votes to 82.

Among the ten states Willkie carried, seven were in the Midwest: Michigan, Indiana, Kansas, Nebraska, North Dakota, South Dakota, and Iowa—the last of these by a comfortable margin of 632,370 to 578,002.[36] Though the Roerich fiasco had not come back to haunt Wallace, he had not proved an electoral asset, failing to deliver even his home state. But at least he now had four years in front of him to establish his bona fides as a credible political figure in his own right.

The job of the vice president was, other than to sit on presidential death watch, to preside over the Senate and to break their tie votes. John Garner enhanced that job by presiding, in his office, over a well-stocked bar. To ensure minimal interruption during convivialities, he had a urinal installed in the corner.

Straight away, "I got rid of both," Wallace later reflected—both "the liquor and the urinal." Much to his relief, "the senators no longer dropped around," except when invited for a dry meal. Among those put off by the change, Wallace noted, was the junior senator from Missouri, Harry Truman. But "I just didn't do business that way," Wallace explained.[37] He tried to get senators to play paddleball rather than drink, but concluded they were "hopeless." He had better luck at the House gym, where the members were younger and more vigorous.

Wallace hated the Senate. Presiding, he said, was "one of the most futile occupations I know." The debates were sterile. He typically presided from noon to one, "for the sake of good form," after which he would go "get something to eat." He then had someone sit in for him. The majority leader, he observed, had more power than the presiding vice president, for whom influence required endless rounds of "poker" and "drinks"[38]—neither of which did Wallace indulge in. Fortunately for Wallace, the president gave him real work to do.

In 1941, FDR's primary pursuit was preparing the country for war. One of the critical elements of that task was instituting measures of "economic defense." These included controlling strategic materials exports, securing access to vital foreign commodities, encouraging the production of such commodities (particularly in Latin America), and denying the Axis Powers—Germany, Italy, and Japan—access to them.

A major challenge in implementing effective economic defense was a lack of clear lines of responsibility and authority. Many U.S. government agencies laid claim to the powers necessary to carry out the relevant tasks. These agencies collided among themselves and with the State Department, the latter of which believed that all such tasks impinged on foreign policy, and therefore fell within its exclusive domain.

FDR not only did nothing to clarify powers, but multiplied the overlap and infighting. "A little rivalry is stimulating," he observed. "It keeps everybody going to prove he is a better fellow than the next man."[39] It also served to increase his own power, as he thereby became supreme arbiter in the proliferating cases of personal and interagency conflict engendered by the approach. Whether promoting rivalry also aided the war effort is doubtful, but Roosevelt was too confident of his own judgment to see it any other way.

The president chose to make Wallace the central pivot around which such unique managerial methods would be imposed. Executive Order 8839, issued on July 30, 1941, set up an Economic Defense Board (EDB) under Wallace's chairmanship. In August, Roosevelt also made Wallace chair of the Supply Priorities and Allocation Board (SPAB), which focused on domestic production. This may have been the first time in the country's history that a vice president was given major administrative responsibility. It was only under President Warren Harding (1921–23) that vice presidents even began serving in the cabinet.

Wallace accepted the appointments with the utmost sense of mission, seeing himself as the general charged with supplying Roosevelt's "Arsenal of Democracy." Roosevelt saw Wallace less as a general and more as a contestant—a contestant lined up against his secretaries of state and commerce in a competition to see who could accomplish what under circumstances of urgent need and clashing authority.

Even within the SPAB, Wallace was obliged to share power with former business executive Donald Nelson, who ran day-to-day operations. And in January 1942, the month after the Japanese attack on Pearl Harbor and Congress' declaration of war, Roosevelt merged SPAB and several other agencies into a War Production Board (WPB), which he placed under Nelson's control. Wallace remained on the board, but thereafter focused on foreign economic policy.

Beginning in October 1941, Wallace further served—together with Secretary of War Henry Stimson, Army Chief of Staff George Marshall, famed engineer Vannevar Bush, and Harvard chemist-president James Bryant Conant—on a secret "Top Policy Group," which advised the president on atomic policy. On December 16, the group endorsed a pilot project, code-named "S-1," to pursue the development of atomic weapons. Wallace thereafter received ad hoc briefings on the project, though by mid-1942 it had, under the code name "Manhattan Project," passed under the effective control of the military.

By early 1942, then, the EDB—which, after Pearl Harbor, Roosevelt re-christened the Bureau of Economic Warfare (BEW)—had become Wallace's true power base. Contrary to Roosevelt's vision of it as an advisory body, it would become a formidable and energetic bureaucracy, employing 3,383 by 1943.[40] At one point in 1942, it had roughly a thousand representatives on the ground in Brazil alone, most involved in rubber procurement.[41] But Wallace's powers continued to be claimed by other parts of government, most notably the Office of Production Management (which the president swept into Nelson's WPB), the Reconstruction Finance Corporation (under Commerce Secretary Jesse Jones), the Lend-Lease administration (under Edward Stettinius), and the State Department (under Hull). A few compromises over authority were consummated—such as that between Wallace and Hopkins, brokered by budget director Harold Smith, under which Wallace controlled imports (in contention with Jones) and Hopkins exports to allies. But conflict between BEW and RFC, and BEW and State, escalated on a damaging trajectory. For the year and a half that followed, the president watched the spats grow more nasty and open. The roots of these conflicts were threefold.

First, Wallace was determined to secure imports of vital commodities such as rubber, tin, aluminum, antimony, chromium, radio quartz, mercury, mica, nickel, tungsten, and manganese as fast as possible, and in as great a volume as possible, irrespective of cost—if only just to keep them out of the reach of enemies. This latter function was known as preclusive buying.[42] Jones thought Wallace's approach fiscally reckless and self-defeating, as it complicated procurement by driving up prices ever-faster.

Wallace was, second, determined to structure deals in ways consistent with his vision for postwar economic, social, and political structures, both within and among countries. "The job," he wrote to *New York Times* colum-nist Arthur Krock on New Year's Eve 1942, "is to combine scientific knowl-edge with organization and the use of capital and credit" in order "to give everyone a better standard of living." The United States, he added, had a responsibility to encourage other countries to follow its lead.[43] This ambi-tion of Wallace's, at least to its many critical observers, conflicted with his first aim. The United States could, such critics felt, either acquire goods as quickly and cheaply as possible, or it could attach conditions to their pur-chase that raised costs and threatened supply, but it could not do both. Wal-lace denied the existence of such trade-offs, insisting that his conditionality improved the productivity of foreign workers, irrespective of what their employers or governments believed. Jones condemned Wallace for impos-ing socialism abroad, to the detriment of the U.S. war effort, and Hull con-demned him for interfering in other governments' sovereign powers—and thereby damaging U.S. relations with them.

There was, third, a toxic clash of personality, as well as political and eco-nomic ideology, between not only Wallace and Jones, but between Jones and BEW executive director Milo Perkins, who ran its day-to-day operations. The forty-two-year-old Perkins, who had earlier worked under Wallace as an economist at Agriculture, was, like the sixty-eight-year-old Jones, a volu-ble, energetic, sharp-tongued Texas businessman. But there the similarities ended. Whereas Jones was a proud Southern conservative, Perkins was a liberal and, like his boss, theosophically inclined. Even in far less stressful circumstances than those nurtured by a world war, the two men would have had difficulty cooperating.

In the early spring of 1942, Wallace urged the president ever more insis-tently to give BEW exclusive powers in the conduct of foreign economic pol-icy—relieving State of its authority to vet and restrict BEW actions abroad, and RFC of its authority to vet and reject the financing of BEW-negotiated contracts. As Wallace coveted Hull's job above all others, save Roosevelt's, it may be presumed that his relentless advocacy of BEW powers, even as they affected postwar trade and investment conditions, was grounded in oppor-tunity rather than principles of governance.

For his part, Undersecretary of State Sumner Welles, deputizing for a convalescing Hull, pressed the president to abolish BEW. Unwilling to cede to State untrammeled powers in foreign economic policy, however, Roosevelt instead agreed to sign an executive order on April 13, drafted for him by Wallace and Smith, which he understood to be a compromise agreed with Hull and Jones. That order, number 9128, allowed BEW to send its own people abroad to handle matters related to "economic warfare," as well as to create its own corporations to procure materials abroad—enabling it to avoid RFC scrutiny and blockages.

Wallace was ebullient. By all appearances, he was now, effectively, czar of foreign-economic affairs—and expected to remain so after the war, whether atop BEW or State. He directed State and RFC to provide him with details on all ongoing contract discussions, and not to initiate any new such discussions without his bureau's approval.

Hull was livid. Over lunch with the president on April 20, he fulminated over the changes—which had been made without his knowledge. He described the damage it would do to the department's ongoing diplomatic and economic efforts in Latin America, which, he argued, had already achieved much. On April 23, Roosevelt assembled Hull, Jones, Wallace, and others for what was a tense and rancorous meeting at which the president expressed great irritation—and in Hull's account, anger—over Wallace's admission that he had never discussed his draft order with State or Commerce.

"I am sorry, Henry," Treasury Secretary Morgenthau said to him, sympathetically, after the session, but "you are licked."[44] Jones was beaming as he exited the meeting. "There were no disagreements of any kind," the publicity-loving Texan told the waiting reporters, smiling.[45]

Although Wallace did not realize it at the time, the episode marked the apex of his power within the administration. Though Roosevelt still wished to encourage the public perception that the vice president remained a vital part of his policy team, he had lost trust in Wallace as someone who could sacrifice for the larger objectives. Wallace would remain a useful fount from which Roosevelt could test out liberal ideas, but the Iowan would never regain authority over foreign policy.

At his May 1 press conference, with Hull standing by his side, the president addressed what he characterized as confusion over Order 9128. "The State Department is in charge of the foreign affairs of the United States," he stated, without caveat. "Some people haven't quite realized that fact."[46] If Wallace was one of them, Roosevelt was sure he now understood.

At Hull's insistence, the president issued, on May 20, an official "Clari-fication" of 9128, constraining BEW to a participatory and advisory status in matters impinging on foreign affairs. To Roosevelt's mind, that settled matters: State did foreign policy, BEW procurement, and RFC financing. That it might be impossible to procure without shaping policy, or without the authority or means to pay, was, to him, a technicality he could address as and when necessary.

As for Wallace and Jones, on no matter did the two men clash more than they did on rubber—a vital wartime commodity whose Asian supply bases Japan had completely disrupted. To Wallace's mind, it was common sense that the United States, in the midst of a world war, needed to pay whatever it took to procure as much supply as it could as fast as it could—particularly before the enemy could procure it. U.S. rubber manufacturers, however, warned Jones of the dangers of aggressive procurement. If the government showed eagerness to pay even a few cents above market prices, rubber growers would hold back stocks in anticipation of yet higher bids.[47] Wallace derided Jones' "banker mentality,"[48] but there was a case to be made for strategic prudence in procurement, even in a time of war.

Wallace was not merely willing to pay top dollar to supply the war effort. He was willing to pay well beyond it to shape the postwar economic and social order. With the noblest of intentions, Wallace set out to improve living conditions in the Amazon, from which precious new rubber stocks were being procured. In the summer of 1942, Jones arranged a luncheon for Wallace with an experienced commercial rubber trader, Douglas Allen, then president of the government's Rubber Development Corporation, to educate him on Brazilian politics and curb his enthusiasm for intervening in the country's economic affairs. In this effort, Jones appeared to have the Army's support.[49]

Wallace asked Allen how many people lived in the Amazon. Allen gave his best estimate: 1.5 million. Wallace did some mental calculations, and determined that the United States needed to distribute 350,000 tons of vitamin-enriched foodstuffs across that population to give it "a more adequate and balanced diet." This would, he believed, make Amazonians more productive.

Allen explained that such a volume of food was over three times the region's *total annual import tonnage*. He highlighted the practical problems, ranging from a lack of excess shipping capacity to the necessity of giving

Amazonians incentives to harvest the rubber—incentives that would be dramatically reduced if the United States fed them for free.

But Wallace also wanted "labor clauses" in American contracts with foreign producers to tie better living standards with employment. These clauses would cover matters such as wage levels, working conditions, and sanitary standards. Whether such clauses constituted productivity enhancements or counterproductive foreign interference was a reasonable matter of debate. But when Wallace wrote in *The New York Times* that "the question of the hour" was "how to get enough rubber in a hurry,"[50] it did not jibe with his demands. You cannot get more of something "in a hurry" if the conditions around its production must be renegotiated from scratch.

The luncheon ended in a standoff.

On Allen's return to Brazil, BEW demanded to know how he planned to improve social conditions in the Amazon, and proposed a $400 million U.S.-funded "Amazon Project" ($7.18 billion today) to assist such efforts. A stunned Allen explained that the United States bought nowhere near enough Amazonian rubber to justify such a sum. BEW also told Allen that it was arranging for oil companies to purchase scrap rubber at "their gasoline filling stations along the Amazon," to which Allen replied that no such stations existed.

Allen, like Hull, further objected to Wallace's social, labor relations, and commercial schemes as interference with foreign sovereign powers—and, in Brazil, as violations of agreements to deal in commodities only through government-authorized institutions. Convinced that he could not work under the BEW-imposed constraints, Allen told William Jeffers, the former Union Pacific Railroad president appointed rubber director in September 1942, that he would resign if BEW were not stripped of its rubber procurement powers.

Jeffers moved judiciously, conscious that the president had given the vice president wide authority, however poorly defined, over foreign economic policy. He initially only took charge of synthetic rubber production, another arena over which Wallace and Jones fought bitterly. Jones backed the buildup of a sizable domestic American industry, whereas Wallace challenged it on the grounds that it would disturb postwar trade balances in a manner damaging to building a durable peace. But Jeffers left natural rubber procurement untouched.

In January 1943—two months after Jones had charged that Wallace's cryptostegia rubber program trod on Jeffers' turf, and a few weeks after the rivals had denounced each other's efforts before a Senate committee—Jeffers handed power over all rubber procurement to Jones' Rubber Reserve. Wallace protested to Roosevelt,[51] but the latter was done playing Solomon. Rubber would stay with Jones.

To be sure, Jones, as the president knew from Wallace, had been doing his utmost to be uncooperative, delaying payment approvals and personnel transfers when BEW purposes or practices were not to his liking. Jones was by nature a parsimonious bargainer, and, though he condemned Wallace for overlaying postwar dreams on his bureau's schemes, he did not himself ignore postwar considerations. Jones opposed an African rubber procurement plan, for example, because it would extend American financial commitments beyond the end of the war—when cheaper Asian supplies would, he presumed, again be available.[52]

Jones further exploited the power he held in Congress, where it was a simple matter to unite Republicans and Southern Democrats against liberal targets. Jones' smarts and folksy charm notwithstanding, his rapport with such men clearly owed less to his job performance or personality than to his usefulness as a cudgel with which to beat New Dealers.

But Wallace fought back. On January 19, 1943, while Roosevelt was conferencing with Churchill at Casablanca, Wallace issued "BEW Order No. 5," arrogating to the bureau full control over strategic resource imports. It was a tactical victory, at best, and a pyrrhic one at that. To carry out its new operational tasks, BEW needed the RFC staff who had been handling them. Jones, predictably, ignored Wallace's order to transfer that staff, and then spurned his protests on the grounds of RFC need and BEW overreach. Jones further lodged a protest with Roosevelt, who, fed up with the squabbling, but still unwilling to put either man in his place, chose to pass on the problem to the man whom the press would dub the "assistant president"—a title it had earlier bestowed on Wallace.

Former South Carolina senator and, more recently, U.S. Supreme Court Associate Justice James (Jimmy) Byrnes had, back in October, been appointed director of the wartime Office of Economic Stabilization. In that official role, his job was to tamp down wartime inflation; but in this new unofficial one, it was to end the public feuding between two implacably hostile men with unlimited powers of self-righteousness and minimal capacity for self-restraint.

Byrnes carried on the mediation effort month after month, with one combatant and then the other refusing a truce or compromise. Finally, on May 29, Jones offered to transfer to BEW one of his fiefdom's unneeded companies—the U.S. Commercial Company—which he said Wallace might "use for the purpose of development and procurement of strategic materials abroad." Wallace accepted. A relieved Byrnes informed the president of the triumph. "The prospect for peace," at least within the government, he wrote, "seems bright."[53]

But the battle only escalated from there. Wallace and Jones could not agree on terms for the transfer. Through surrogates, Milo Perkins and Will Clayton, they resumed their attacks on each other before Congress in late June. On the 29th, Wallace gave the Senate Appropriations Committee a vituperative twenty-eight-page report condemning Jones for failing to procure adequate stocks of war material, for using "obstructionist tactics," for making "harmful misrepresentations," and for "harass[ing]" BEW staff in their "effort to shorten the war."[54] Jones responded the following day, calling Wallace's charges "hysterical" and accusing him of "malice and misstatements."[55]

Roosevelt, his speechwriter Robert Sherwood recorded, was "extremely angry" at both men. But he was particularly upset with Wallace for initiating the latest public mud-slinging. Those who witnessed his reaction, according to Sherwood, felt sure that Wallace had now driven himself off the ticket for 1944—when they assumed FDR would run yet again.[56]

Still, Roosevelt simply ordered Byrnes to make the problem go away, while giving him no documented authority over either man—either the one who thought himself a paragon of prudence, or the other who thought himself an apostle of abundance. And so when Byrnes summoned the two men to his East Wing office at 4 p.m. on June 30, Wallace, who arrived first, denied that authority, contending that the president's Executive Order 9347 only empowered Byrnes in domestic affairs. This objection amounted to sterile pedantry, as Wallace knew that Roosevelt had personally sent Byrnes, and could see, in black-and-white in front of him, that the order gave Byrnes powers over both "the domestic economy *and the war effort.*" By the time Jones arrived, Byrnes was, in Wallace's own recounting, "mad."

Jones, for his part, refused to shake Wallace's outstretched hand, accusing the vice president of calling him a "traitor." Wallace denied the charge, but taunted Jones like a blustering schoolboy.

The New York media, Wallace told him, was reporting that "you [were] going to hit me the next time you see me. Is that true, Jesse?" Wallace asked the near-septuagenarian commerce secretary. "Are you going to hit me?"

Jones, Byrnes saw, now looked as if he might do it. He managed to calm himself; but after an hour of back-and-forth, an exasperated Byrnes could do no more than urge the men to cease brawling in public.

Wallace and Byrnes disagree on what came next. Wallace says he suggested, successfully, that Byrnes draft a statement for him; Byrnes admits no role in the drafting. In any case, Wallace's statement said that Jones, upon whose "patriotism" he had not intended to raise doubts, would "not object" to BEW securing its own congressional funds for procurement.

When the statement went public, Jones blasted Wallace for yet another "dastardly attack"—an attack which, he said, had slyly and falsely charged him with hindering the war effort. Not to be outdone, he publicly released his thirty-page rebuttal on July 5, and demanded an investigation in his favorite forum: Congress.[57] On July 12, Wallace wrote to the president, charging Jones with the usual crimes—such as "intentionally faulty and misleading arithmetic"—but adding allegations that Jones was improperly accumulating documentary evidence that he, the president, had ordered or approved RFC's most controversial actions, as well as its nonactions.[58]

Roosevelt had had enough. Byrnes convinced him to strip both men of their procurement powers and create yet another foreign-economic agency to take them over, under the direction of Leo Crowley—a Wisconsin Democrat, friendly to Jones. Thus was born the Office of Economic Warfare (OEW).

Byrnes, who was officially made coordinator for matters foreign-economic, drafted a letter, which Roosevelt sent to Jones and Wallace on July 15, saying that "the unfortunate controversy and acrimonious public debate" had made it necessary to transfer their foreign-economic responsibilities "to other hands"—Crowley's.[59] He would later write to Wallace that "the incident has not lessened my personal affection for you," which was no doubt true; but it was scant political consolation.[60] A further Byrnes-drafted presidential letter was sent to the heads of all government departments and agencies warning them, sharply, that they should not even think of confronting each other in the press without also submitting a letter of resignation.[61]

A new executive order abolished BEW. Thus was Jones, though politically wounded and stripped of key procurement powers through the loss of RFC subsidiaries, left standing as an administrative force, through his continued control of the Commerce Department, while Wallace was returned to the largely ceremonial role to which he had been elected. As Jones would later put it, "Mr. Wallace was . . . once more just the Vice president with little to do but wait for the president to die." And, "fortunately," that death "did not occur while Henry was Vice President."[62]

It was as vice president, of course, that Wallace still stood first in the line of succession. But it was in his conduct as BEW head that Wallace all but killed the chance that Roosevelt, who had demanded his nomination as vice president in 1940, would fight for his renomination in 1944. And so Wallace would have to wage that fight on his own.

Henry Wallace's strength as a political figure was neither managing people nor managing policy, but rather his will to spread the New Deal gospel of can-do government; government dedicated to improving the lot of "the common man." The term "the common man" would become indelibly linked with the Iowan, such that its mere invocation allowed admirers to contrast him favorably with figures, both Republican and Democrat, who were held to be in the thrall of big business and the military.

The phrase "Century of the Common Man" was coined in a half-hour dinner address which Wallace delivered on May 8, 1942 before the Free World Association in New York City.[63] The title of the speech was actually "The Price of Free World Victory." But few noted the title, and far fewer remember it, as it had no clear meaning, or even relation to the text, which was meandering and, at points, strange. Though he had in 1933 decried the Soviet Union as a country "utterly without religion," he now saluted the Russian Revolution of 1917 as an event which "spoke for the common man in blood." Today, in 1942, the common man in Russia and around the globe was rising up to claim "the privilege of drinking a quart of milk a day." That phrase would later be distorted by a business chief as a "quart of milk to every Hottentot"—a reworking for which Wallace would, to his intense annoyance, be quoted in mocking tones, even by the president of the United States.[64]

In the days following the speech, what press coverage it got generally remarked on its lack of coverage.[65] But it was soon to be widely referenced and distributed, both at home and abroad. In early 1943, it was reprinted in a volume of Wallace's speeches and articles under the title *The Century of the Common Man*.

The phrase "Century of the Common Man" came to function as a news-worthy swipe at Republican publisher Henry Luce, who had, in February 1941, published an influential piece in *Life* titled "The American Century." Luce was celebrating the coming global spread of democracy, freedom, and free trade—all of which Wallace supported. Wallace, however, referring to "some" who "have spoken of the 'American Century,'" insisted that, in the postwar order, "no nation will have the God-given right to exploit other nations" or to practice "military or economic imperialism." The implication was that Luce was endorsing such right. Had Luce accused Wallace of doing the same in his speech of June 8, 1942, entitled "Why Did God Make America?," in which the vice president celebrated America (North and South) as a "chosen land," it would have been hardly less justified.

The two men exchanged cordial letters about what Luce termed Wallace's "disapproving reference" to "The American Century." Wallace contended that it was not Luce's text but the *title* of his piece to which Wallace's correspondents abroad objected.[66] Publicly, he claimed to have "nothing against Henry Luce," but would persist in contrasting his own views with Luce's by linking him to controversial figures. These included the philosopher and political theorist James Burnham, who called for a U.S.-led "imperial federation" to confront the Soviet threat.[67]

In the end, it was not concrete policy ideas or rhetorical prowess that drew attention to Wallace's speech, but rather the sentiment underlying it—that the world order must not be rebuilt around the interests of the rich and powerful in America or Europe, but around the aspirations of "the common man" worldwide. That it was an American vice president speaking made it significant, as it suggested that important political changes were in the offing. These changes included the dismantling of institutions that oppressed the common man, such as colonialism—which Wallace would attack in subsequent writings.

꙳

Like Franklin Roosevelt, Henry Wallace believed that the United States and the Soviet Union needed to stay on a cooperative path, not merely to defeat Germany and Japan, but to ensure global demilitarization in the war's aftermath. Where Wallace's philosophical path diverged from the president's was in his insistence that the two countries operated on a level moral plane.

On November 8, 1942, Wallace offered a passionate "Tribute to Russia" at a Congress of American-Soviet Friendship gathering in New York—a tribute in which he laid out the different ways in which each country, the United States and the Soviet Union, allegedly applied "democracy" to achieve "the enduring happiness of the common man." Each was the yin to the other's yang.

The United States, he said, had emphasized "political or Bill-of-Rights democracy." When "carried to its extreme form," he warned, such democracy devolved into a destructive "rugged individualism." Russia, in "perceiving some of the abuses of excessive political democracy," had instead "placed great emphasis on *economic democracy.*"[68] Subsequent statements of his make clear that he considered these Russian efforts a "great success"—a success that would oblige "the capitalistic democracies," in order to justify their continued existence, "to work out programs for full employment after the war."[69]

But what, then, was "economic democracy"? There is no political concept on which Wallace appears, over his fifteen years in government, more confused, and confusing. Since his time as agriculture secretary, he had typically used the term to mean decentralization of economic power[70]— away from government and big business, and down to the citizen and local community. But he now more and more often used it synonymously with the most extreme form of socialism, one in which economic power was centralized within a single political party.

Thus did Wallace consider collective bargaining a form of economic democracy in the United States, while its effective absence in Russia was an example as well—signifying, as it did, that the state was fulfilling its function of bettering the life of "the common man."

Thus, too, was economic democracy to be found at home in "freedom for venture capital to . . . expand production . . . without fear of repressive cartels, excessive taxation or excessive government regulation,"[71] while it was also to be found in Russia, where no such freedom existed, and where the state controlled the means of production.

Economic democracy existed, in short, wherever Henry Wallace wished to bestow his seal of moral approval on behalf of the common man. Like the famed rhetorician Humpty Dumpty, Wallace would not let words be master of his meaning. He invoked words like "democracy" and "fascism" not to delineate concrete political phenomena, but for the feelings they gave rise to among those who longed for a better world.

Wallace was also not fastidious about the veracity of his political claims, tending to be satisfied if the *assumption* of their veracity would serve to support his larger moral point. Thus he claimed in the "Tribute" speech that Russia had, in addition to its great achievements in economic democracy, "probably gone farther than any other nation in the world in practicing *ethnic democracy*." He also claimed, to a pro-Soviet Yiddish newspaper, that Russia had succeeded "in the elimination of foolish prejudices between the races." In making such statements, he may have wished not so much to reveal a truth about Russia as to highlight the ongoing "Anglo-Saxon" problem with racism.[72]

Wallace was likely unaware of the systematic brutality of state terror directed at Soviet ethnic minorities in the 1930s.[73] But it is equally the case that he was never overly concerned by reports of human rights abuses in the country. The arc of Russian history, he was sure, bent toward justice.

On March 8, 1943, Wallace gave two addresses in Ohio: the first, titled "The New Isolationism," to a farm group; the second, titled "Practical Religion in the World of Tomorrow," to an Ohio Wesleyan University conference on "Christian Bases of World Order." The speeches were uniquely Wallace, blending religion, economics, and politics in broad sweeping statements and rhetorical questions—some highly provocative, and all intended to paint postwar choices in the starkest strokes of black-and-white.

America must, Wallace insisted, ensure full employment and openness to imports—an eclectic combination of policy preferences among liberals, involving, as it did, providing government job guarantees while removing protectionist tariffs that made foreign labor more competitive. Without these reforms, he warned, the world would turn to the "Prussian or Marxian doctrine"—that is, to war or godlessness.

An ongoing postwar partnership with Russia, the great champion of Marxian doctrine, was, curiously, at the heart of Wallace's foreign policy agenda. Philosophically, he defended this position by blaming Russian Marxism on German Nazism. The Bolsheviks had been "inspired by fear of Germany." Russians, he said, were "fundamentally more religious than the Prussians," even though he had, in 1933, insisted that their country was "utterly without religion."

Wallace's handwritten edits to his speech show that he was highly conscious of being tarred as soft on Communism, and so was determined to dissociate Russia from Marx. In his original rendering, for example, he stated that "the future well-being of the world depends on the extent to which Marxianism and democracy can live together with peace." He edited it, however, to read that he was referring to Marxianism "as it is being progressively modified in Russia"[74]—the implication being that Russia was becoming less and less Marxian with time.

He argued that a falling-out between the United States and Russia would be the fault of the former, and result in grave consequences. America must not, he warned, "double-cross Russia." If "Fascist interests [with] anti-Russian bias get control of our government," he said, World War III would be inevitable. Such remarks earned him angry condemnations from Republican congressmen, such as Michigan senator Arthur Vandenberg, and conservative columnists and broadcasters such as George Sokolovksy (a former radical).[75]

The Soviets took a keen interest in Wallace's views of their country. In September 1942, Andrey Gromyko, then counselor at the Soviet embassy, reported to Moscow that the Mexican minister in Washington, a friend of Wallace's, told him that the vice president had said "the Soviet Union was right" in invading Finland three years prior. Gromyko took this seriously enough to corroborate the claim.[76] In a subsequent cable to Moscow, he opined that Wallace was, other than Roosevelt himself, "the most probable Democratic Presidential candidate" in 1944.[77] He was someone to watch and to cultivate.

Since the heady early days of the Roerich expedition to Central Asia, Henry Wallace had come to see his calling in foreign affairs—in leading the peoples of the world into a future of abundance and spiritual enlightenment. His election as vice president afforded him the chance to conduct official diplomacy, and he wasted no time lobbying Roosevelt for the presidential blessing to go abroad. Within weeks of the 1940 election, in the interregnum between his resignation as agriculture secretary and his inauguration as vice president, Wallace was on his way to Mexico.

For both Wallace and Roosevelt, Mexico was the perfect destination. The country was thousands of miles from the frontline fighting in Europe and China. It had just elected a new president, Manuel Ávila Camacho, who was, in the aftermath of his bitterly contested victory over right-wing general Juan Andreu Almazán, anxious for international legitimacy and better relations with the United States. Wallace had also been studying Spanish for three years, and was eager to help raise the country's agricultural yields to American levels.[78]

Having no government position in November 1940, Wallace was hurriedly appointed "ambassador extraordinary." He was given a State Department stipend of $50 per day, a driver, and 5 cents per mile to cover gas and the like for his green Plymouth—which would be his main mode of transportation. On the drive down to Mexico City from Washington, which he began on November 21, Wallace made frequent stops to inspect Mexican cornfields and local markets, and to converse, in Spanish, with farmers, workers, and children. By all accounts, the vice-president-elect was rapturously received. In Monterrey alone, 150,000 turned out to cheer as his car rumbled through the streets.

From November 28 through December 5, Wallace attended meetings, ceremonies, and cultural events in Mexico City,[79] all aimed at promoting closer U.S.-Mexican relations in the face of a growing Axis economic and military threat. He addressed the Mexican Congress in Spanish, calling for "hemispheric solidarity." He also held confidential discussions with government officials on matters related to the war, such as procurement of strategic and critical metals in Mexico, U.S. provision of planes and munitions to the country, and Nazi plots to bomb U.S. factories and stage incidents in Latin America intended to harm inter-American relations.

Notwithstanding a brief anti-American riot outside the U.S. embassy in

Mexico City on November 29, fanned by propaganda distributed by German agitators, Wallace's mission was a success for Roosevelt's "Good Neighbor" policy. On his return to Washington in early January 1941, the president would write to him that his time in Mexico had produced "exceedingly useful results."[80]

Perhaps Wallace's greatest accomplishment in the country was, however, the long aftermath of his agricultural tour in December. Appalled by the meager productivity of Mexican corn farms, Wallace appealed to the Rockefeller Foundation for support and assistance. The result was the building and financing of an agricultural experiment station in Chapingo[81] that would, over the course of the coming two decades, help double Mexican corn production, and boost wheat production fivefold.[82]

The Mexican tour only served to whet Wallace's appetite for frontline diplomacy. In early 1943, as his struggles with Jesse Jones intensified, he convinced Roosevelt to let him tour throughout Latin America. On March 17, he took off on an unprecedented forty-day journey through Costa Rica, Panama, Chile, Bolivia, Peru, Ecuador, and Colombia.

As with his Mexican trip, he insisted on frugality and simplicity. He flew on commercial flights, making advance requests for modest meals and no extravagant gifts—albeit indicating that he would accept recordings of Spanish folk music, together with written English translations, as well as packets of local seeds.[83] He wrote his own short speeches in Spanish, which he delivered with a charming Midwestern twang, much to the delight of local audiences. Above all else, he was able to bask in the popularity of Roosevelt and the New Deal,[84] for which the American vice president was seen as an embodiment.

Wallace's reception in Costa Rica was historic, with tens of thousands cheering his arrival on a day of declared national holiday.[85] The most "conspicuous element" at the airport, according to a curious observation to Hull from the U.S. minister in Costa Rica, "were labor syndicate groups carrying . . . the flag of the Soviet Union."[86] His speech to the Costa Rican Congress called for postwar structures promoting "freedom from want" and "the free interchange of products between nations." He also called on the world's governments to teach "knowledge of adequate diets" to "all their peoples."[87] He traveled forty miles outside the capital to visit an agricultural institute, while also inspecting rubber and quinine production facilities supporting the war effort.[88] Asked by local press whether he would be a candidate for president, he responded with notable, if not entirely ingenuous, diplomatic modesty: "*No soy un político.*"[89] From San José, he flew on to Panama, where his reception was warm, if more subdued, and his agenda similar—featuring a speech before the National Assembly and a visit to an agricultural fair.[90]

From March 26 through April 4, Wallace toured Chile—the most important destination on his travels. Three hundred thousand greeted his plane's arrival in Santiago; forty thousand turned out to greet him in a mining village. "Never in Chilean history," the U.S. ambassador told the State Department, "has any foreigner been received with such extravagance and evidently sincere enthusiasm."[91] The security precautions were considerable, however, and the visit not without genuine dangers. FBI reports described a plot by "12 Nazi Chileans" to hurl bombs at the vice president's car on his way into Santiago[92]—a plot either thwarted or otherwise abandoned. Speaking before a stadium crammed to overcapacity with 100,000 people, Wallace declared the nations of the Americas, which were coming together in a time of "tragic realities," "the repositories of the worth of Western civilization."[93] He paid visits to mines and plants which would be vital for war production, as well as farms, an agricultural exposition, and the country's principal naval base.[94]

Next it was on to Bolivia, from April 4 to 12, where Wallace preached the importance of "winning the peace" through "better living conditions for the common people." The capital's mayor proclaimed him "a citizen of La Paz"—eliciting wild acclamation from the crowd. Even in the stifling heat, at an elevation of 13,500 feet above sea level, Wallace used his downtime to play tennis. Touring beyond the city, he insisted on stopping to see archaeological sites and Christian missions in areas populated by indigenous peoples.[95]

The U.S. ambassador wrote to Washington calling the visit "successful in every way." "Everywhere," he said, "Mr. Wallace was received with genuine enthusiasm." The FBI, too, reported favorably on Wallace's performance. "[T]he Leftist leaders were completely won over," particularly given the vice president's ability to interact in Spanish. "At the same time the leaders of the conservative parties were charmed . . . and quite willing to applaud some of his statements with which they probably did not entirely agree."[96] In a memo to the attorney general, however, FBI Director J. Edgar Hoover voiced concern over information from confidential sources indicating that Wallace was "being unknowingly influenced by Bolivian communists."[97]

Hoover also learned that the Costa Rican Communist Party leader Manuel Mora Valverde had written a letter to Wallace, which was reprinted in the party newspaper *Trabajo*, asking if he intended to succeed President Roosevelt." Though Wallace was "far from being a Communist," Valverde observed critically, he felt sure that "the organized labor of Latin America" would vote for him, if they could.[98]

Wallace made two visits to Peru, from April 5 to 8 and 12 to 15. Security precautions were rigorous. Peruvian air force planes escorted the vice president's plane through the country's airspace. Still, Wallace did not make the task of protecting him easy. On the morning of April 6, following his breakfast and a round of Ping-Pong, he evaded his detail to walk to a Lima market on his own. There, according to the taxi driver who drove him back, and who was later questioned by the police, the wandering "Gringo" struck up conversations with locals waiting in line for rice. On April 14, Berlin Radio reported, much to the FBI's concern, that the vice president had been seen in Lima that morning roaming unescorted through the streets. An informant suggested that the intelligence must have gone out from the Spanish embassy, given that Germans in Peru—the first country in Latin America to sever Axis ties—would not have risked such communications.

As elsewhere in Latin America, the vice president attracted huge crowds. From the balcony of the Government Palace, Wallace addressed a massive rally—which greeted him with far greater warmth than they did their own conservative president, Manuel Prado. The proscribed socialist Aprista Party, led by philosopher-activist Victor Raúl Haya de la Torre, praised Wallace as "the first man who came here and spoke from the heart." The risk of mass unrest unnerved the FBI, given the vice president's evident popularity among the Peruvian "working class"—even though Haya de la Torre directed supporters not to stage antigovernment protests during the trip. FBI-intercepted letters to the United States revealed a broader range of views on the vice president. One correspondent accused him of "deceiv[ing]" the Peruvian people with his "utopian ideas." Another accused him of being taken in by the Aprista Party, which "exaggerated the situation here." The vice president, he complained, was "meddling in our domestic affairs."[99]

From Peru it was on to Ecuador, where Wallace stayed from April 15

to 19. Ecuador had, just two years prior, lost a war with Peru, and the political dynamics were different. Yet, as in Peru, the left-opposition sought
to show Wallace that they stood with him, as well as with the Ecuadorian
people. The right-opposition, in sharp contrast, sought to convey popular
hostility by refusing to partake in any aspect of the liberal visitor's program.[100] President Carlos Arroyo del Río, for his part, issued orders that no
one unfriendly to the government, right nor left, should be allowed near the
vice president.[101] As elsewhere, though, Wallace insisted on visiting remote
farms and factories, even insisting on stopping his car in the port city of
Guayaquil and entering one of the "miserable houses" there to see, in his
words, "how the people live."[102]

The final leg of the journey was through Colombia, from April 19 to 24.
Once again, the U.S. ambassador, who praised Wallace's "sincere interest in
the problems and aspirations" of the people, as well as "his lack of preten-
sion and the devoutly Christian spirit of his speech" at the Teatro Colón in
Bogotá, offered a glowing report on the visit.[103]

It was perhaps to be expected that ambassadors, as presidential appoin-
tees, would speak well of the man whom the president had chosen as his vice
president and emissary—as all the hosting ambassadors did. Not surprisingly as well, their enthusiasm was not mirrored within the State Department
back home. Hull was protective of his turf, and wanted diplomacy carried
out by men under his control—carried out directly and exclusively with foreign governments, and not with farmers, labor leaders, miners, shoppers,
missionaries, and opposition figures, the sorts of people with whom Wallace
had spent so much time.

But it must be judged that the vice president's tour, as with his Mexican
trip two years prior, served Roosevelt's "Good Neighbor" policy by demonstrating respectful concern for the views and aspirations of the people of
Latin America—people whose views had historically been given short shrift
not just by Washington, but often by their own governments. Though anti-
American sentiment would remain palpable, particularly in Argentina and
Mexico, Wallace helped to mute it. Mexico, in particular, became an integral part of the U.S. war economy. The positive trajectory of inter-American
relations would carry into the postwar era. The 1947 Rio Treaty, signed by
nineteen of the thirty-five countries of the Western Hemisphere, followed
by the creation of the twenty-one-nation Organization of American States

in 1948, would make evident this improvement by codifying regional security cooperation.

In the autumn of 1940, the Royal Air Force (RAF) secured a heroic victory in the skies over Britain. Yet the country, on its own, had little hope of resisting the Nazi juggernaut indefinitely. Thus was the Japanese attack on Pearl Harbor in December 1941 a godsend—at least in the mind of Winston Churchill. America was finally in the fight.

Beginning in the winter of 1940, British Security Coordination (BSC), the secret intelligence organization set up by MI6, had been tasked by the prime minister with directing a massive undercover campaign of propaganda and subversion on American soil to rally public opinion in favor of aiding Britain— and declaring war on Germany. By the time the dashing, lanky twenty-five-year-old Flight Lieutenant Roald Dahl arrived in Washington in the spring of 1942, the BSC was in high gear—but short of personnel.

Dahl, who had been declared unfit to fly ten months after injuries sustained in September 1940, following the crash of his fuel-starved air force plane in Libya, was now an assistant air attaché at the British embassy. Sharp-witted but inexperienced, and decidedly undiplomatic, he was tasked with using his status as RAF "hero" to help stomp out the embers of American Anglophobia.

The job bored him. He let it be known that he wished to be more than just another "whiskey warrior" in Washington, and would welcome work in intelligence. It took little time for BSC to enlist his services. Yet Dahl still found time to embark on what would become a legendary literary career, beginning with a children's book fictionalizing his RAF "heroics." Published in 1943, *The Gremlins* was a surprising international success, becoming a favorite of Eleanor Roosevelt and the Roosevelt grandchildren.

After his arrival stateside, Dahl met the ever-voluble and impeccably well-connected Texas publishing magnate Charles Marsh, a staple of the Washington cocktail circuit. The two hit it off. Dahl esteemed Marsh for his contacts in the Democratic Party, for his well-sourced views on matters political, and for his famed dinner soirees. Marsh appreciated the Englishman's articulate charm and acerbic humor, and relished being part of whatever cloak-and-dagger work he knew the latter was up to.

Pride of place among Marsh's political intimates was the vice president, and Dahl took full advantage of this fact to develop a friendship with him as well. Among the BSC's prime intelligence targets was anyone in the U.S. government who could influence foreign policy for, or against, Great Britain. The vice president was top of the list.

In one instance in early 1943, Dahl used Marsh to persuade Wallace, with photo documentation, that U.S. refusal to bomb Germany at night was a major strategic error. Though U.S. Army Air believed that only daylight raids could be accurate, the British believed that German fighter planes, engaging Allied planes in daylight, more than offset any visibility advantage. Dahl expected Wallace to take the documentation directly to the president, but he instead, naïvely, passed it on to Army Air. Army Air remonstrated the British, and Dahl was scolded by higher-ups. Still, the budding spy persisted with his efforts, simply adding instructions that nothing be shared with Army Air.[104]

On New Year's Eve 1942, Dahl cemented his personal relationship with Wallace thanks to a meeting, at Marsh's R Street townhouse, with Wallace and the noted Transylvania-born British film producer Gabriel Pascal.[105] Pascal, with Marsh's encouragement, wanted to make a movie based on the vice president's solutions to "the problems facing all humanity in the reconstruction of the post-war world." With the approval of the British ambassador, Lord Halifax, Dahl took on the role of lead scriptwriter. Marsh agreed to finance the film, giving it the working title *The Common Man in War and Peace*.

As with the Roerichs a decade ago, Wallace's relationship with Pascal took on a notable mystical element. They used "esoteric names" in their correspondence: Beekeeper for Wallace, Cowkeeper for Pascal, Ploughkeeper for Marsh, and Puritan for Dahl.[106]

News of the movie project spread quickly in Washington, angering conservatives who saw it as blatant political propaganda.[107] Freshman Republican congresswoman Clare Boothe Luce, wife of publisher Henry Luce, as well as paramour to Roald Dahl, derided Wallace's ideas, which included supranational control of the world's airports, as "globaloney."[108]

In the end, Pascal never made the film—which was just as well with the British. Churchill was coming to see Wallace as a dangerous Anglophobe, threatening to undermine the "special relationship" with Washington. But the project ensured that Dahl would, at least for the duration of FDR's third term, have "special access" to the vice president—which is what mattered. He would use this access to report on—and, where possible, influence—Wallace's thinking.

Marsh, though a poker pal of Wallace's enemy, Jesse Jones, and an arch-admirer of Churchill, genuinely liked Wallace. But what he wanted was access to, and respect from, the president—who showed little interest in him. As Dahl noted, Marsh "loved [seeing Wallace] because he got a bit of gossip and he felt closer to FDR."[109] Wallace was the closest Marsh would ever come to shaping American foreign policy.

Opposed to the British Empire, and friendly to the Soviet one, Wallace was a constant source of concern in London, particularly given rumors of Roosevelt's poor health. MI6 head Stewart Graham Menzies referred to the vice president as "that menace."[110] British concern rose markedly during Churchill's visit to Washington in May 1943, when Wallace, in his own words, engaged in some "frank talking" with the PM. At a luncheon at the British embassy on the 22nd, Churchill expounded on the need for Britain and the United States jointly to manage postwar global affairs, after which Wallace shot him down in disgust. Insisting that the Anglo-Saxons could hardly "run the world" on their own, Wallace said there would be "serious trouble ahead" if they tried.[111]

British anxiety over Wallace deepened in June 1943, when, at least by Dahl's later account, Marsh, at his R Street mansion, provided him with "an immensely secret cabinet document." This was gross overstatement—which, while uncharacteristic in an Englishman, was not so in a man looking to inflate his importance. Still, the document—a draft of a pamphlet entitled *Our Job in the Pacific*, authored by Henry Wallace—was significant. It offered a much fuller and clearer vision of postwar U.S. policy than the vice president had revealed to date.

"You're a flying chap, what do you think of that?" Marsh asked, tossing the papers into Dahl's lap. Flipping through them, Dahl could see they contained radical ideas for civil aviation reform. These ideas suggested, he reasoned, that the Americans intended to dominate the global commercial airways. But the document contained much else that would alarm London. In a section titled "America and the Colonial Problem," the vice president called for an "orderly emancipation in colonial areas." He warned, however, that there were in Britain "powerful forces which will fight for the old system of empire." The United States would have to confront that problem in Asia "by a positive progressive policy toward this area."[112]

Telling Marsh he would finish reading the document downstairs, Dahl excused himself. Once alone, however, he picked up the phone and dialed a BSC agent, urging him to drive to the house immediately. As the car arrived some minutes later, Dahl ran out and handed the manuscript to the driver—demanding it back in half an hour. The car sped off, and Dahl returned to the house, hiding himself in the bathroom.

"Have you finished reading it?" Marsh asked, coming down the stairs. Dahl yelled back, excusing his temporary indisposition. Within the half-hour, Dahl ran back out to the curb, retrieved the manuscript from the driver, and returned it to Marsh. What opinion he offered is unknown.

Having betrayed both his mentor, Marsh, and a man whom he liked personally, Wallace, Dahl felt badly. Wallace, Dahl would reflect, was "a lovely man." Yet he was simply "too innocent and idealistic for the world." Dahl would continue both to provide Wallace with intelligence nuggets, keeping him friendly, and to report to London on his activities and shifting political fortunes.

Copies of the secret manuscript made their way up MI6, and then to the prime minister himself. Wallace's call for liquidation of the British Empire, Dahl would learn, incited Churchill to "cataclysms of wrath." Dahl's main job now was to "keep pretty careful tabs on [Wallace's] Communistic leaning and his friends in those quarters." Wallace, who enjoyed Dahl's wit and eccentricity, suspected nothing.[113]

In the wake of the furor caused by Wallace's insolent writings, and his tussle with the PM personally, British intelligence also stepped up efforts to undercut his chances of ever ascending to the presidency. "I took action," BSC director Bill Stephenson would later say, "to ensure that the White House was aware that the British government would view with concern Wallace's appearance on the ticket at the 1944 presidential elections." In February 1944, Stephenson would tell London that "Roosevelt has undertaken to the Party that he will jettison Wallace as vice-presidential candidate."[114] Roosevelt, however, undertook so many things to so many people, right up to the start of the convention, that no one would ever be able to say which undertaking, if any, was genuine.

In the end, British "action" on Wallace, whether overt or covert, likely had no effect on what took place. The vice president was already damaged political goods, owing to his humiliation in the Jones wars, as well as ongoing rumors about "Guru letters." More importantly, Democratic Party leaders had long been, in the main, opposed to Wallace, owing to his mystic tendencies and growing Russophilia, while the president himself was more likely to do the opposite of what the British wanted. "Grow up," Marsh scolded Dahl at one point, struck by his seeming naïveté. "Don't you know that the most certain way to be sure that Wallace will continue to be Vice President is for the word to get around that Churchill is against him?"[115]

America's other main war ally also sought to penetrate U.S. policymaking circles. And the vice president was a key target.

Since the late 1930s, Congress had been devoting ever greater attention to charges of Soviet and Communist infiltration of the U.S. government. In early 1943, the year the FBI created its "Soviet desk," Texas Democratic congressman Martin Dies, chairman of the House Un-American Activities Committee since 1938, alleged that thirty-nine employees working under Wallace at BEW were affiliates of "Communist front organizations," or worse. He demanded they be fired.

The list was created haphazardly, with no serious effort made to determine whether those individuals were in any way disloyal to the U.S. government. Given this backdrop, Wallace was justified in his public rebuke of Dies, even if his likening the congressman to Goebbels was overwrought.[116]

Still, by 1942 the NKGB and the GRU (Soviet military intelligence) had deeply penetrated BEW. Neither Dies nor Wallace was aware of this fact. Among the valuable intelligence assets the NKGB controlled at BEW, as subsequently confirmed by Soviet records, were Nathan Gregory Silvermaster, a hidden CPUSA member and head of the so-called Silvermaster spy group; Frank Coe,[117] a member of that group; Charles Flato, a CPUSA member since 1935[118]; and Michael Greenberg, a British-born Marxist and China specialist.[119] Among the known GRU sources at BEW were Thomas Arthur Bisson,[120] a left-wing political writer specializing in Far East affairs, and David Wahl, a suspected Communist on the "Dies list."[121]

The Soviets had two primary reasons for seeking inside access to Wallace's bureau. The first was that Stalin, suspicious to the point of paranoia, worried that the Americans would cheat him on Lend-Lease aid. To document such cheating, he needed to unearth the secret details of U.S. wartime economic and financial management. The second was that Stalin coveted knowledge of U.S. military production technologies and processes for producing strategic materials—in particular, synthetic rubber. In the service of such intelligence requirements, according to the April 1942 briefing prepared by the head of the NKGB foreign intelligence American section, Vitaly Pavlov, for the newly appointed New York station chief (or *rezident* spy), Moscow needed "To know in advance [American] production plans, manufacturing and shipment terms; to know all the functioning leverage [mechanisms] of this complicated capitalist machine; [and] to know which of the 'springs' may turn [out] most efficient in one or another of our undertakings." Pavlov named Wallace as one of four key officials "close to the president" to whom Soviet spies needed to pay particular attention. (Morgenthau, Hopkins, and Ickes were the others.)[122]

Soviet penetration of BEW was successful, as evidenced by the presence of documents in Moscow covering "NKID experts' evaluations of 'the materials of the US Board of Economic Warfare obtained from the Red Army Main Intelligence Directorate.'" These documents analyze secret BEW reports on German-Russian economic relations, Russian oil supplies and needs, and U.S. policy on providing oil to neutral European nations.[123] Soviet intelligence cables, intercepted and subsequently decoded by American military intelligence, also discuss secret BEW documents shared by Bisson with American GRU agent Joseph Bernstein at the left-wing Institute of Pacific Affairs.[124]

Though Wallace pledged that the FBI would investigate Dies' charges "at once," he took no apparent steps to assist such investigation.[125] The Soviet moles at BEW would continue to operate unimpeded. As his reputation for friendliness to Moscow continued to grow, Wallace would become an ever-more valued target for both Soviet and CPUSA manipulation.

Six

INTO SIBERIA

Henry Wallace's hopes for the postwar world, for the coming Century of the Common Man, hinged on sustaining America's partnership with one country, above all: the Soviet Union. If the two nations could embrace his vision of "friendly competition," everything was possible: peace, shared prosperity, spiritual awakening. If they faltered, he was sure, Republicans would pave a new path to ruinous war.

Following a cabinet meeting on March 3, 1944, Wallace approached the president privately. "How would it be," he asked, if "sometime during the next month or two I went to Russia?" Wallace had been studying the language, hoping to put it to good use.

Roosevelt was incredulous. The Democratic convention was set for July 19; did Henry want to give his enemies the bullets to finish him off? "I think they are going to be shooting at you during the campaign for being too far to the left," he told him. "My own feeling is that you had better not go to Russia."

But Roosevelt then had an epiphany. He had, following a recent exchange of correspondence with Chinese leader Chiang Kai-shek, asked Wallace to fly to Chungking—both to reassure Chiang of America's commitment and to prod him into closer military cooperation.[1] Wallace might make some useful stops along the way.

"You could," the president now amended himself, "visit some of the towns in Siberia on your way to Chungking."[2] Assaying Soviet gold production, and therefore Stalin's ability to pay, was a persistent concern for Roosevelt. Wallace and his entourage might pick up useful intelligence in the mining areas.

Wallace had naturally wanted to go to Moscow, and not to Siberia. But he accepted the president's idea, at least as a placeholder. Shortly thereafter, he relayed it privately to Andrey Gromyko, now the Soviet ambassador, who in turn communicated it to Moscow.[3]

On March 7, Georgy Zarubin, chief of the Department of the Countries of the Americas at the People's Commissariat of Foreign Affairs (NKID), sent a memo to Andrey Vyshinsky, deputy people's commissar of foreign affairs, alerting him to the vice president's plans. "Comrade Gromyko," Zarubin wrote, "has informed us of Wallace's intention to visit the USSR in two to three months' time." The vice president, he went on, has been "a consistent supporter of Roosevelt's policy" of cooperation with the USSR. He has spoken out "against reactionary American views of all shades," and has always given "a positive evaluation of our economic system, particularly its achievements in the field of agriculture." For these reasons, Zarubin endorsed Gromyko's advice—to issue Wallace an official invitation to visit the Soviet Union.[4]

But Wallace craved an audience with Stalin, and not just a trip to Siberia. And so back in Washington later that same day, he asked Undersecretary of State Edward Stettinius to call on him at his office. Knowing that the undersecretary would shortly be meeting with FDR, Wallace told him of the planned trip to Chungking, and asked that he communicate to the president his wish to visit India and Moscow as well. Stettinius complied, but reported back that the president was only "agreeable to [his] visiting Northern Siberia to investigate industrial and agricultural matters there."[5]

As word of Wallace's impending trip spread through the executive branch, there was much curiosity as to its purpose. "What is Wallace going to do?" John Pehle, director of the War Refugee Board, asked Henry Morgenthau.

The treasury secretary shrugged. "Wallace is to go to China."

"In place of 'the goods'?" Pehle asked, referring to more war aid.

No, Morgenthau corrected. "He *is* the goods!"[6] Wallace was a token of goodwill, a symbol of Sino-American solidarity.

Cordell Hull was concerned about the trip. The vice president, to his mind, was a diplomatic liability. It was Wallace, after all, who had sent the Roerichs to Asia. It was Wallace who had undermined his efforts to deepen ties with Latin American governments, choosing instead to stir up labor groups and revolutionaries. Still, Hull was relieved when Wallace requested that John Carter Vincent, the smart, genteel head of State's Division of China Affairs, accompany him as an adviser. It made damage less likely.

"Vincent," Hull ordered his top China hand, just in case—"don't let Wallace give everything away."[7]

When the vice president's trip was made public on April 11, the press had a big story in the making. Was Wallace headed to *political* Siberia? And, if so, who would replace him?

"The stock of Senator Harry Truman (D-Mo.) as a possible vice presidential nominee," wrote Jack Bell in the Arkansas *Star*, "boomed today as politicians speculated Vice President Wallace was taking himself out of the race under orders."[8]

The buzz elated party leaders. The DNC heavyweights—Ed Pauley, Bob Hannegan, Frank Walker, and Ed Flynn—had begun meeting secretly with Roosevelt back in January, hoping to convince him to ditch Wallace.[9] Pauley, the party treasurer, had been working hard to boost Truman's stock, inviting him to deliver a series of "George Washington" dinner lectures with influential party constituencies.[10]

But if the president *was* contemplating putting a new name on the ticket, he had not yet resolved to act. Roosevelt had, back on March 6, asked Wallace to return from Asia "about July 17"— just in time for the convention.[11]

Politically, Wallace's absence would give Roosevelt what he coveted—freedom of maneuver. He would use the same device a few weeks after Wallace's return, telling George Marshall that he now wished to send Donald Nelson to China. The outgoing War Production Board chairman was openly feuding with the man who would replace him, and Roosevelt wanted him, too, at a distance from the White House.[12]

Morgenthau knew that trick, and had refused himself to go to China. No envoy of Roosevelt, he told Lieutenant General Brehon Somervell, ever "had a lasting success." It was therefore best not to leave town. "I have always had a rule," he explained, "that if I have any business to do I don't get more than a hundred yards away from the White House."[13]

Wallace did not, at the time, believe that the president was determined to ditch him. Yet he would years later accept "that one of [FDR's] motives might have been to have me out of the way right before the Convention."[14]

In mid-May, Hannegan, the DNC chairman, decided to press the matter with Roosevelt. Though no one would say it to the president's gray, gaunt, rapidly aging face, Roosevelt was not just choosing a running mate; he was anointing a dauphin. And Wallace, for all his renown as a hog killer, was not, in Hannegan's view, the man to win a war, unite the nation, or secure the peace.

Alone with the president in the Oval Office, Hannegan argued that Wallace was an electoral liability. But Roosevelt refused to be drawn. To Hannegan's surprise, being a mere "country boy," Roosevelt told him to talk to Wallace on his own. To reinforce the chairman's authority, however, Roosevelt also asked Wallace to pay Hannegan a visit—which he did soon after.

"The president told me I should talk to you," Wallace announced to Hannegan in the chairman's office, still standing. He suspected what was coming.

Hannegan frowned. He would be frank, he said; he knew no other way.

He explained that he had been across the country, several times, and that the message from party leaders was the same: they needed a new candidate for vice president.

As Hannegan spoke, Wallace stared at the floor, raking his toe back and forth. He looked, to Hannegan, more like an embarrassed schoolboy than the vice president. He said he wondered if Hannegan had canvassed the right people, but otherwise put up no fight.

When Wallace left, Hannegan was sure he would tell the president he was prepared to withdraw.[15] Yet he had underestimated Wallace's will to stay in the job, and overestimated his capacity to grasp the weight of the political forces arrayed against him.

Once Wallace had accepted that he was not going to meet Stalin, he embraced his role as presidential emissary to Generalissimo Chiang. A later memoir of his journey would explain that FDR had feared "that the Chinese were divided among themselves and that the Japs [might] capitalize . . . with a successful military drive"; and that he, Wallace, was being sent to heal these divisions. According to Stettinius, however, Wallace was to be a humble messenger of sorts. He was to remind Chiang that it was because of Franklin D. Roosevelt that China was now recognized as "one of the four Great Powers," and that it "could not let America down" in the war with Japan.[16] Beyond that, however, Wallace "had no authority to give promises or make decisions."[17]

Chinese officials in Washington expressed concern in their communications with Chiang and the foreign ministry about discrepancies between what the State Department said Wallace would be doing in China, on the one hand, and what the press and Wallace were saying, on the other. Whereas Wallace privately confirmed the State's official explanation of his remit—to inspect the situation of Chinese agriculture and the U.S. military—he and the press also said that he would look to reconcile the Chinese government with the Communists and to prevent future Sino-Soviet disputes.[18]

Chiang was worried about Wallace's agenda. "U.S. diplomacy," he diaried, "ignores the dangers of Russia." He fretted aloud: "Will Wallace go to Moscow?"

Wallace's Soviet agenda also worried J. Edgar Hoover. The FBI director warned the president that Wallace was friendly with Hollywood Communists, and that he had suspicious Soviet contacts. On May 12, Hoover got the supporting material he was after: a secret internal memorandum, citing a confidential source, stating that Gromyko had told the vice president that "Moscow was willing to issue visas to anyone whom Wallace desired to take with him." These men would, like Wallace, now become persons of interest.[19]

On the morning of May 23, 1944, Wallace boarded a C-54 transport plane in Nome, Alaska, for the first leg of a fifty-one-day Asia journey. After downplaying his Russian mission in Washington, his departure statement now talked it up.[20]

The vast Siberian landmass over which he would journey, some five million square miles, was Russia's "wild east," he said, a frontier region of endless possibility and promise. Whereas only seven million people, "mostly convicts, [had] miserably existed there under Imperial Russia," some 40 million lived and worked there freely today. "[T]he detractors of Russia," he said, "must [therefore] pause before the fact of Soviet Asia." The region had come of age.

In seeing the transformation himself, Wallace explained, he wished to "feel the grandeur that comes when men wisely work with nature." He hoped thereby to help Americans understand their Pacific neighbor—a land few of them had ever seen.[21]

The mass of Lend-Lease goods that the United States had provided to aid the war effort in Europe and Asia, some of which he intended to witness in

Political map of the USSR outlining Vice President Henry A. Wallace's 1944 Asian journey route.

operation, had laid the ground for expanded postwar trade. In the coming weeks, he would also begin laying the basis for postwar agricultural collaboration and exchange of scientific knowledge by meeting Soviet experts and swapping native Siberian and American seeds.[22]

The Asian heartland through which he would travel was, he argued, comparable in potential to the American Midwest—the development of which had made the United States "the most powerful industrial nation on earth." In 1913, only 6 percent of Russian industry had been in Asia; yet by 1943, with the Germans at the Volga, it had soared to 85 percent. As Siberia now followed in the footsteps of its American counterpart, Russia would, he was sure, "tomorrow rank equally high among the world's industrial powers."

This prospect did not make it a threat to the United States. To the contrary, it meant an unparalleled opportunity for American farmers, manufacturers, and consumers—and an important reason to sustain the U.S.-Soviet alliance after victory over the fascists.[23] In support of this position, Wallace would later quote the American entrepreneur Perry McDonough Collins, the force behind the mammoth Russian-American telegraph cable project of the 1860s. "His words," Wallace explained, referring to a speech Collins had made at a Russian banquet in his honor in January 1857, "called up a vision that has become reality in our day," a vision of cooperation and mutual enrichment.

"Russia," Collins had said, "descending from the heights of the Altai to the great Eastern Ocean by way of the mighty Amoor, and the United States, descending to its opposite shore from the heights of the Sierra Nevada, will shake the friendly hand in commercial intercourse upon that mighty sea, and these two great nations will only vie with each other in developing the resources of their respective countries."[24] Wallace did not mention that the cable project was, sadly, a costly failure.

With the vast advances in air transport since Collins' time, which had been central to the Allied war effort, now in its great final phase, Wallace was sure that the imminent shuttling of "businessmen and tourists" would serve to deepen "mutual understanding" between the two nations.[25] This narrative had become Wallace's mantra; that technology, prosperity, and peace were the interwoven fabric of the coming postwar world.

Accompanying the vice president on his mission were eight military personnel and three diplomatic advisers: John Carter Vincent; Owen Lattimore, a Central Asia scholar and director of the Pacific Bureau of the Office of War Information; and John Hazard, a Russian interpreter and chief liaison officer of the wartime Foreign Economic Administration's Division for Soviet Supply. Wallace put them all on notice they were not to try "to obtain information of a military nature, especially in Russia." Doing so would "defeat the purpose of the trip," which was to "enhance friendly relations."[26] Convinced that the trip involved too much friendliness, J. Edgar Hoover had already pulled files on Vincent, Lattimore, and Hazard.[27]

Just before departure, Wallace's pilot, Colonel Richard Kight, gave the vice president some disappointing news. Russian Colonel Nikifor Sergeevich Vasin, having dismissed Kight's objection that he didn't need a Soviet copilot, told him that the port town of Anadyr, Wallace's intended destination, was off-limits owing to airport flooding.[28] After crossing the International Date Line between Alaska and Siberia, therefore, Kight headed for Velkal (or "Uel-kal"), in the Chukotka Peninsula—a short hop over the snowcapped Anadyr Mountains. They touched down a mere two hours after takeoff.[29]

The village of Velkal housed the easternmost of sixteen Soviet military airbases along the Alaska–Siberia ("Alsib") route to Krasnoyarsk, built to transport wartime Lend-Lease cargo from the United States. Founded by Eskimo settlers in the 1920s, it was part of the Dal'stroi, or State Trust on Road and Industrial Construction in the Upper Kolyma Region,[30] which Stalin had created in 1931 to manage road building and gold mining. Its exploration and development remit would be expanded over the years to cover timber, uranium, and other resources.[31] With about 175,000 inhabitants and over a thousand mines, the Kolyma River region—bounded by the Arctic Ocean in the north, the Sea of Okhotsk in the east, and dense virgin forests (taiga) in the south and west—was economically important, yet isolated from the primary Soviet population centers to the west.

The airfield on which Wallace landed, built in haste in the summer of 1942, was fashioned of wood slabs hammered into the permafrost soil, covered with a special composite. Wallace emerged from the plane into the cold, scanning the huge snowdrifts rising up along the perimeter. He was greeted by Major General Ilya Sergeyevich Semenov and accompanying officials—among them, "Gregory" (Grigory) Dolbin and Dmitry Chuvakhin of the Foreign Office. Squat, "with a good-natured face," according to Wallace, Semenov, chief of the Krasnoyarsk–Uelkal airway, proudly swept his arm across the horizon, directing the vice president's attention to the airport, radio-weather station, and three dozen log and frame dwellings: all built, he said, "to help speed lend-lease planes on their way."[32] Like other officials Wallace would meet, Semenov was anxious to exhibit the Soviet government's effective use of American war aid.

After a welcome banquet of fish, reindeer, steak, potatoes, vodka, wine, champagne, cognac, and pastries, Wallace—who declined the alcohol as politely as possible—was back on his plane for a three-hour, eight-hundred-mile flight to the southwest, over the desolate, uninhabited Siberian tundra. They touched down in Seimchan in the early evening, with another banquet awaiting. Presiding was Sergei Arsenievich Goglidze, whom Wallace identified as "an intimate of Marshal Stalin" and "president of the Executive Committee of Khabarovsk Territory"—of which Kolyma and Seimchan were part.[33] Goglidze was, Wallace observed, "a very fine man." "Gentle and understanding with people," he "had flown up 1,500 miles from the Amur River region to greet" the Americans. For the coming three weeks, Goglidze would do "his utmost to make our stay a memorable one." The festivities broke up just before midnight, with the northern skies still bathed in light.

The next day, May 25 (local time), Wallace toured the town. "[T]he atmosphere" at "the Party *Kabinet*, or headquarters," where portraits of Lenin and Stalin stared down at them, "was emphatically Soviet," he noted. It was a motif he would encounter repeatedly—in "schoolrooms, public halls, and business offices." In the evening, he "got a touch of the real Russian fighting spirit": a screening of a film on the siege of Leningrad.

Despite the conspicuous differences between Soviet and American public spaces, the ubiquitous reminders of home surprised Wallace. He noted the abundance of "blue pasque flowers," the state flower of South Dakota. He obsessively recorded Lend-Lease sightings—foodstuffs like "Penick & Ford corn oil from Cedar Rapids" and "Pillsbury enriched flour from Minneapolis." "I had to pinch myself," he wrote; even "the infants in the town's nursery were like [American] toddlers."[34] Everywhere was human, floral, and commercial testimony to the reality of One World.

Next, Russian pilots flew the delegation two hundred miles south, to the new city of Magadan—"the Siberian equivalent of Alaska's Seward." At thirteen thousand feet, they had spectacular views of the tall, snow-covered mountains, the north-flowing Kolyma River, and the Okhotsk Sea coast—which reminded Wallace of the Gulf of Alaska.[35] On arrival, they were met by one Ivan Feodorovich Nikishov, director of the Dal'stroi, which Wallace described as "a combination TVA and Hudson's Bay Company." (The Tennessee Valley Authority, or TVA, was created by congressional charter in 1933 to tackle the region's energy and environmental needs, while the Hudson's Bay Company, a quasi-governmental entity, was established by English royal charter in 1670 to control the North American fur trade.) Magadan being a mining town, samples of gold, lead, coal, and radioactive rare elements were on proud display in Nikishov's office. "We had to dig hard to get this place going," he explained to the vice president. "Twelve years ago, the settlers arrived and put up eight prefabricated houses. Today Magadan has 40,000 inhabitants, and all are well housed."

That evening's entertainment was an American film, *North Star*, depicting wartime life on a Soviet collective farm. The portrayal of their imagined existence greatly amused the Russians. Yet Magadan, with its modern harbor, industry, and infrastructure, Wallace observed, was no flimsy Hollywood set: it was built on "solid underpinnings."[36]

Wallace would, on May 27, leave Magadan for Seimchan with two fine embroidered landscape paintings—a gift from Nikishov, who had observed Wallace admiring them at an exhibit of handicraft by local women. The show's director later told the vice president they had been created by Nikishov's wife, Gridasova, an art teacher whom Wallace praised fondly for her hospitality. The needlecrafts would become permanent features on the wall of his Washington home.[37]

The delegation now flew north along the route of the Kolyma Road for a day's excursion at the mining settlement of Bereliokh. Conditions were tough, Wallace observed, but "development was much more energetic than at Fairbanks." He stopped to practice his Russian with some "big, husky young" Kolyma gold miners, who told him "to take back a message of solidarity to the people of the United States." He noted with surprise their American-made rubber boots. Nikishov, aware that U.S. policy forbade Lend-Lease aid for gold-mining, explained that they had been "bought for cash in the early days of the war."[38]

After an evening performance in Magadan by the Poltava (ballet) Troupe and the Red Army Choir, the delegation flew back to Seimchan. Kight and his Russian counterpart, who piloted some of the side trips, "struck up a close friendship." The latter toasted their future collaboration, after the war: "May [our enterprise]," he said, "be called the Polar Bear Airways!" This toast "became a recurrent refrain," Wallace noted with satisfaction, "voicing our common hopes for the future."[39]

From the airfield of Low Seimchan it was a four-hour, 830-mile flight southeast to Komsomolsk, the leading heavy industrial center in Soviet Asia. Founded in 1932 by *komsomoltsy*, members of the Communist Youth Organization, its 127,000-strong population was young and ruddy, Wallace noted, but overworked—much like its roads and infrastructure. Everyone and everything was focused on war production. In the shipyards and plants, Wallace took stock of the American Lend-Lease material he could identify: aluminum, shovels, drills, compressors, and electric fittings.[40]

From Komsomolsk, the delegation flew back north to the regional town of Yakutsk, home to some fifty thousand hearty Russians and Yakuts—a Turkic people resembling Alaskan Inuits. Built on permafrost, with subsoil indelibly frozen to hundreds of feet below the ground, Yakutsk flaunts some of the coldest winter temperatures of any city on earth. Though summers are dust-bowl dry, warming temperatures serve to saturate the topsoil, producing fertile pastures and croplands in the surrounding areas. The nearby valley of the Lena resembled, for Wallace, the dairy farms of upstate New York. He discussed Arctic farming and reindeer breeding with the president of the Yakut Republic, Ilya Yegorovich Vinokurov, leaving behind seven U.S. Agricultural Yearbooks as a gift for the city library. He departed with local seeds.

From Yakutsk, the Wallace party flew five hours and 1,154 miles to the old town of Irkutsk, founded in 1661. Along the road to his government guesthouse, Wallace admired the pink geraniums and cherry trees in bloom around the riverside collective farms. At the local university, where he met with two dozen agricultural professors, he marveled at the high standard of free education provided, particularly in the sciences and foreign languages.

Frontier settlement, Wallace believed, needed to be guided by science and planning. The experimental spirit, combined with government provision of infrastructure and social services, was the key to taming the Arctic wilderness. Americans had much to learn from the Soviet experience. "We exchanged lend-lease goods to help win the war," and "we should exchange students to help maintain the peace," he said. More Americans "should attend Russian universities," like that in Yakutsk, "and should live in the smaller Russian towns."[41]

In addition to Komsomolsk, Wallace visited five towns along the Trans-Siberian Railway linking Europe and Asia: Chita, Ulan-Ude, Irkutsk, Krasnoyarsk, and Novosibirsk. Ever on the lookout for signs of Soviet catch-up with America, he compared each of these, in turn, with Duluth, Des Moines, Minneapolis, Omaha, and Kansas City, Missouri.[42]

Over the course of nearly four weeks' travel, covering twenty urban centers, Wallace met Siberians "of every walk of life," people "of plain living and robust minds, not unlike our farming people in the United States." Their guarded demeanor, which to an urban American might be "misinterpreted" as "Russian distrust" was, he explained, just "the natural cautiousness of farm-bred people." "Beneath the ideological talk, beneath the diplomatic protocol," these were "sound, wary, rural" people. At each stop, he exchanged seeds with them. The American plants that would soon grow in Siberia, and the Siberian plants that would grow in America, would "stand as symbols of growing understanding between the two peoples."[43]

Throughout his journey, Wallace never wanted for attention from his Soviet hosts. "In traveling through Siberia," Wallace recorded, "we were accompanied by 'old soldiers' with blue tops on their caps. Everybody treated them with great respect. They are members of the *Nkvd*." (It was, rather, the NKGB—the People's Commissariat of State Security.) Wallace "became very fond of their leader," Major Mikhail Cheremisenov, who would accompany them throughout their trip.[44]

Wallace recounted episodes that stuck in his memory. An early riser, he set out at the crack of dawn one morning on his own, at Seimchan, for his "usual morning walk." He was soon joined by a Russian escort. "Tramping over the permafrost in this way helped us to get acquainted," Wallace said. "Thereafter I never lacked a companion when taking my morning exercise." Another time, about twenty miles south of Krasnoyarsk, Wallace "unwittingly eluded" his guide when he wandered off to pick wildflowers. Hazard spotted him first and called him back, calming "a most anxious major [Cheremisenov] of the Soviet secret service." A third incident was the most alarming to his hosts. In a Magadan park, Wallace decided to get a view over the harbor by climbing a hill crowned by a radio tower. The way up being "barred by the park's wicket fence," Wallace slipped through some broken palings and made a brisk solo ascent. "[T]he ever-present Major Cheremisenov," Wallace recounted, started shouting at him in Russian—either "dinner is ready!" or "come down, at once!," he wasn't sure which. But since Wallace could see "no immediate reason to hurry back," he plowed on. It had not occurred to him that the fence was meant to keep people out. Cheremisenov, Goglidze, and Nikishov all ran up after him, "puffing and blowing." After peering over the bay of Nagayevo, Wallace allowed himself to be coaxed down without further incident. Although his travel partners "fretted about being shepherded around" by the Soviets, Wallace observed, he appreciated their attention.[45]

He particularly appreciated their evening hospitality. "Our meals in Soviet Asia," he recounted, "were uniformly excellent"—even during the horrors of a world war. "We were served the best there was to offer—caviar, venison steaks in the North, delicious fried fish fresh from the Lena, [and] rose-petal wines."[46] Following these meals, Wallace said, "[we] were entertained "on a level of culture rarely below that enjoyed by the foremost diplomats and officials in Moscow."[47]

The evening of June 6 was the most memorable. At a characteristically lavish, boozy dinner feast in Krasnoyarsk, Goglidze, after receiving an urgent brief whispered by an aide, stood and turned to his guest of honor. "Vice-President Wallace, it is my pleasure to tell you," he intoned, before pausing to clear his throat, "that this morning our American and British allies opened the Second Front in Western Europe."

British infantrymen had the previous evening landed by gliders in France, six miles north of Caen. By midnight on June 6, 155,000 American, British, and Canadian troops would be ashore in Normandy. By June 10 that total would reach 325,000; by June 20, half a million. The legendary Allied "Operation Overlord," which had very nearly been grounded by relentless stormy weather, was in full swing.

Goglidze proposed a toast, and the Soviet and American guests rose as one. As Wallace raised his glass, he swelled with emotion. The launch of the second front was something Stalin had been waiting for, indeed urging, for years. Now that it was a reality, there could be no doubt in Moscow of the American commitment to Allied unity. "In the midst of war," Wallace would record, "we"—the American and Soviet people—"were laying a sound basis of collaboration, and I foresaw common effort in the fight for peace."[48]

On another evening, Wallace tried to engage Chuvakhin in lighthearted repartee, or Wallace's version of it, on the "religions" of Communism and capitalism.

"Now, I am willing to grant that your preferred religion is doing the world good," Wallace said. "Are you willing to do the same for ours?"

"No," Chuvakhin said.

The response showed his "intellectual honesty," Wallace explained.[49] And "as an escort," he added, "Chuvakhin was A-1."

The new Siberian towns, Chuvakhin explained to Wallace, had "saved Russia." "Stalin," he said, unlike Trotsky, who thought only of world revolution, "had faith in the moral stamina of the Russian people." And over 20 million of them had moved east in the year after June 1941[50] to keep the country from catastrophe.[51] Explaining the economic rise of Soviet Asia, Wallace continued to quote Chuvakhin. "Trotsky," he said, had "wanted to make peace with the *kulaks*, the rich peasants who resisted collectivization." But Stalin disagreed. Russia had to "discipline herself; must build up the home economy and increase her industrial and farm output." He set out to transform the peasant villages that dotted the countryside into mammoth state-controlled agricultural operations, using force as necessary. On what were once windswept plains, remote from existing population centers but convenient to natural resources, he ordered the crash construction of new cities. Wallace supported the program, explaining that "collective farming ... was a method of making agriculture more productive, of getting the food surplus necessary to support urban workers."

"[T]he present strength of Siberian agriculture," following on from collectivization, Wallace concluded, was undeniable. "Its future is assured."[52]

He was similarly impressed with the region's industrial progress. On June 7, he visited factories and mechanized farms, marveling at the efficiency of the integrated operations and the spirit of the people he met. Like other towns along the Trans-Siberian Railway, Krasnoyarsk had experienced huge population growth during the war, driven by the mass eastward evacuation of Soviet industry. Twenty-nine enormous plants, together with their thirty thousand staff, had relocated to Krasnoyarsk alone. At one of these plants, the workers greeted Wallace's party with applause and cheers of "To our Allies!"

Wallace was also moved by the strides which the Soviet Union had made in achieving "economic democracy." Labor conditions in Siberia, he learned, were excellent, which was contributing mightily to the region's economic rise. "The eight-hour day is the legal workday," he wrote, and "paid overtime was put in as a wartime necessity." A shovel operator at the Karaganda coal trust, he learned, earned 5,000 rubles a month—equivalent to what a high-ranking Red Army officer was paid, and about three times higher than a shovelman in European Russia. "Higher wages was the evident incentive that had brought the miners into the Far East."[53]

The socialist-model housing and communal facilities he saw convinced him that America's Arctic frontier needed to be developed similarly. It would be impossible, he wrote, to settle Alaska "on an individualist basis";

comprehensive state planning and investment was a prerequisite. "We can learn a lot from the Russians about how to colonize the northern frontier," he concluded. "The new towns in the Siberian North were all founded on community projects—with housing, food supply, and recreational problems solved on a social basis in advance of large-scale settlement."[54]

But there was also great social progress. What, he asked Yakut president Vinokurov, had the Russian Revolution meant for the Yakut people? "We Yakuts," the president told him, "got a chance to farm [and] we learned to read and write. . . . Within ten years everyone will be literate!" The Buryats, too, Wallace recorded, were "making the transition from tents to wooden houses under Russian leadership." They, like the Yakuts, were reporting "an increase of literacy up to 90 per cent." These towns had become model "ethnic melting pots."[55]

Not only did America have much to learn from Soviet success in improving the lives of its non-European peoples, but from Soviet egalitarianism as well. Many of the regional leaders were indigenous people—"a Buryat at Ulan-Ude, a Yakut at Yakutsk." This phenomenon is in stark contrast to the pre-Soviet days, when "Czarist Russia's domination of Asiatic territory was effected through gun-mantled outposts." Today, "the road to the presidency" of the Soviet Union itself, Wallace said, "is open to the Kazakh, the Uzbek, the Buryat, the Yakut." After all, the country's present premier was a Georgian. "Under Marshal Stalin's wise leadership, and inspired by the patriotic will to improve the life of the homeland, the multi-national Soviet peoples have shown that for them nothing is impossible." The world, he said, had long recognized "their high morale and democratic aspirations."[56]

On his departure from Alma-Ata for China on June 18, Wallace sent an open letter to "My dear Marshal Stalin," which was published in *Pravda* eleven days later. "[T]he great progress made by the Yakuts, the Buryat-Mongols, the Kazakhs, and the Uzbeks" was, he wrote, "a glowing tribute to distinguished and talented statesmanship." And in a press release, also published in *Pravda*, Wallace added that the trip had surpassed all his lofty expectations. "I am," he said, "enraptured by the scope of building and the great achievement" of the Soviets in Siberia. He was anxious to convey these impressions to the American people. "This, I am sure, will strengthen the deep mutual sympathy shared by our pioneer nations."[57]

Among the many gifts Wallace had brought with him was one for the Soviet leader himself; a portrait of Stalin, the only one known to have been done in radioactive paint. Though he would later inquire, Wallace would never discover whether Stalin actually received the painting or enjoyed seeing it glow in the dark.[58]

Though Wallace had wanted to go to Moscow, he was elated with the way in which events had unfolded. Having witnessed and recorded powerful images of the strides the Soviets were making in developing their Pacific frontier lands, he now had the credibility to return to Washington and shape postwar diplomacy in the direction of cooperation and peace. "[Ambassador] Harriman," he recorded in his diary with satisfaction, "said my trip had done an amazing amount of good."[59] Having ensured that Wallace's trip was, in Hazard's words, "touristic and nothing more," Averell Harriman was indeed pleased. He had urged Roosevelt to keep Wallace far away from Moscow,[60] and had achieved full success.

As Wallace had attached great diplomatic importance to his Siberian travels, so, too, had the Soviet government. They took immaculate care in approving, and making alterations to, Wallace's suggested travel route, as well as to the selection of officials who would shepherd him through the various agencies, enterprises, and farms along the way. Massive quantities of food and other provisions would have to be shipped long distances to an isolated region suffering from terrible shortages. Wallace's departure statement had made clear that he was prepared to see Soviet Asia in the warmest possible light, and his hosts were determined to assist him.

Vyshinsky, aided by NKGB head Vsevolod Merkulov, organized and oversaw the vice president's travel itinerary. Prosecutor of the USSR in the notorious Moscow show trials of 1936–38, the judicial theater behind Stalin's "Great Purge" of the government, the Communist Party, the Red Army, and academia, Vyshinsky had a ruthless and pragmatic intellect. "Neatly dressed in a stiff white collar, checked tie and well-cut blue suit, his trim grey moustache and hair set off against his rubicund complexion," the razor-tongued Bolshevik jurist "looked for all the world like a prosperous stockbroker accustomed to lunch at Simpson's and . . . golf at Sunningdale every weekend," in the words of a former British embassy official.[61] Yet he entertained no reality beyond that approved by the *vozhd*, his leader, Stalin, to whom he owed his physical as well as political existence.

In a May 7 memo responding to Vyshinsky's request for comment, Merkulov proposed changes to Wallace's desired agenda. "It is advisable," he wrote, "to straighten the route of Wallace's trip . . . by eliminating secondary sites he intends to visit. A pretext . . . would be rather easy to find," he assured Vyshinsky, given "the absence of convenient landing fields and difficulties of piloting in those areas." The pretext was perfect, in fact, as the American chargé d'affaires in Moscow, Maxwell Hamilton, had written to Molotov eleven days earlier asking for confirmation of adequate landing and takeoff facilities along the way.

But what if the Americans wished to drive? "It is necessary to rule out Wallace's trip to Magadan by car," Merkulov cautioned Vyshinsky, "given that the road passes by prison camps." The latter memoed back his approval, indicating that the Americans had been informed that "all of the locations" requested by Wallace were acceptable "as far as it would be technically possible." Five of the sites would be made off-limits, but the Americans would only "receive explanations on-site" that this or that flight was "not feasible on technical or weather grounds."

Vyshinsky also selected guides for the vice president's trip through politically sensitive territory. And in Wallace's estimation, he did a fine job. Sergei Arsenievich Goglidze, for example, who accompanied him from Seimchan to Krasnoyarsk, was "a very fine man," "gentle and understanding with people," who "had flown 1,500 miles . . . to greet" Wallace and "done his utmost to make [the] stay a memorable one." Goglidze had been introduced to him as president of the Executive Committee of Khabarovsk Territory, and Wallace identified him as such in his memoir. But that title, as Wallace would not learn for some years, was inaccurate.

Goglidze was, in fact, chief of the NKGB security apparatus in the Far East. He was also not, as Wallace had said, "an intimate of Marshal Stalin," but a member of NKVD head Lavrenty Beria's inner circle, whose career took off in the mid-1930s after heading the notorious, torture-wielding Georgian NKVD security service. Other NKGB officials, with their own false titles, joined Goglidze to welcome Wallace.[62]

Wallace identified his host in Magadan, Ivan Feodorovich Nikishov, as director of "the *Dalstroi* enterprise"—"a combination TVA and Hudson's Bay Company." By this he meant a large state-owned economic and administrative entity, but the description is a poor one. Though covering a tenth of Soviet territory, Dal'stroi—headquartered in Magadan, a city built by prisoners—did not even appear on maps. The entire apparatus had, since 1938, been under control of the NKVD—the commissariat responsible for counterintelligence, public order, and penitentiaries. During his time with the vice president, "Director" Nikishov wore civilian clothes. Yet his normal garb was that of an elite NKVD State Security Commissar, 3rd Rank.[63]

Nikishov's wife, the woman whom Wallace had so appreciated for her generous attention, and admired for her needlework skill,[64] was also not who he thought she was—an art teacher. Alexandra Gridasova, like her husband, went un-uniformed for Wallace's visit, but was in fact an NKVD officer and, since 1943, head of the Magadan labor camp. The "locals," the thousands of prisoners under her rule, did not recognize her as the warm and wonderful woman Wallace described, but rather as a sadistic tyrant. "[A] primitive, crude, and avaricious creature" is how Elinor Lipper, a once idealistic Dutch-born socialist serving eleven years for "counterrevolution," described her.[65] The colored embroideries in Wallace's home, one of which was a copy of a nineteenth-century painting by Isaak Levitan, remain misattributed to her.[66] They were in fact made by female prisoners.[67]

Dal'stroi staff were themselves repulsed by Gridasova, describing for Beria her alleged debauchery and venality. "On board the lend-lease ships that arrive from America," one of them wrote anonymously, "NIKISHOV and GRIDASOVA organize heavy drinking parties," after which they have to be helped into cars in front of the port workers. "Before WALLACE'S arrival in Magadan," he observed, "many handicraft articles for apartments and paintings were made. GRIDASOVA later took all this stuff home. [She] is not ashamed to say that she needs to give gifts everywhere."[68]

Other Wallace escorts, too, held positions quite different from those described in his memoir. "Gregory" (Grigory) Dolbin, for example, "from the Soviet Foreign Office," who greeted Wallace in Velkal, had recently served as an NKGB foreign intelligence station chief: he had worked under diplomatic cover as head of a spy group (*rezident*) in Tokyo from 1939 to 1943.[69] An orientalist, fluent in Japanese, Dolbin was likely selected as a Wallace escort in order to gather intelligence on the vice president's China mission. Given Japanese interest in Wallace's trip, there may also have been a counterintelligence angle.

Wallace noted being "especially grateful for the thoughtful courtesy" of Leonid Malinin, "the president in Novo-Sibirsk," and Amayak Kobulov, "Vice President of the Uzbek Soviet Republic." At the time, Malinin was in fact head of the Regional NKVD Office of the Novosibirsk Region, while Kobulov was the People's Commissar of Internal Affairs of the Uzbek Republic and a close associate of Beria's.[70] (After Beria's arrest in 1953, Kobulov and Goglidze would both be executed.) It is not clear that real identities would have meant much to Wallace, however, as he was "very fond" of his hosts even when he knew they were NKVD.[71]

Wallace effused on the outstanding labor conditions in Dal'stroi, reporting that its workers, whose "legal workday" was eight hours, earned wages three times higher than in European Russia. This fact, he said, was the reason so many had migrated there in recent years.[72] Yet most of them worked up to fourteen hours daily, earned a pittance, and had "migrated" by force. They were prisoners.

By 1928, shortages of food and basic necessities were highlighting the failings of Bolshevik innovations. With forced collectivization, these shortages became far worse, resulting in rationing of all food and consumer goods by 1931. Stalin saw rapid industrialization as the key to overtaking the Western capitalist powers, and Soviet Asia remained a vast untapped resource. There was gold in Kolyma, lumber in Krassnoyarsk and Novosibirsk. But who would do the mining, the logging, the road-building? Since criminals and subversives were leeching resources from system, it seemed natural to put them to work in isolated Siberia, nature's own prison.

By the time of Wallace's visit, Dal'stroi had set up a system of labor camps across Kolyma, known as Sevvostlag. Records show that at the start of 1944, the year of Wallace's visit, there were 87,335 prisoners in Sevvostlag.[73] Over eight times this number, 740,434, would come through the camps from 1932 to 1953; of those, about 15 percent, or 125,000, would die in them. And much of the remaining "free population" of Kolyma were former prisoners, forbidden to return home.[74]

Prisoners feared Wallace's Magadan host, a talented but ruthless administrator whom they called "Tsar Nikishov" for his autocratic manner and "ugly temper."[75] Whereas Wallace depicted a kind, carefree Nikishov "gambol[ing] about, enjoying the wonderful air" of the taiga, the forest, Lipper remembers a different man. He was, she wrote, "icily, mercilessly cruel." Wallace "never saw him 'gamboling about' on one of his drunken rages around the prison camps, raining filthy, savage language upon the heads of the exhausted, starving prisoners, having them locked up in solitary confinement for no offense whatsoever, and sending them into the gold mines to work fourteen and sixteen hours a day."[76]

A memoir written by a Hungarian survivor, George Bien, arrested on suspicion of espionage at age sixteen in Budapest a few months after Wallace's trip, would call the camp system Nikishov oversaw "a giant Auschwitz without gas chambers."[77] Bien mocked Wallace for his "famously naïve observations about the sincere hospitality of his genial host," Nikishov, whom Bien described as "ruthless."[78] Even the minority of nonprisoners were afraid of him. "Only my wife and myself are free employees in the Kolyma region," Nikishov told one of them; "everyone else is a prisoner or an individual under investigation."[79]

Nikishov and his colleagues had, likely under orders from Beria, made elaborate preparations for Wallace's visit. They transformed sites along the vice president's route into Potemkin villages, scrubbing all traces of Gulag life. "Wallace and his fellow travellers were interested in seeing a prison camp," Nikishov reported to Beria, Molotov, and Stalin on May 29, "but since they have not seen a camp anywhere, or even individual inmates," he added, proudly, "they were disappointed."[80] It did not occur to Wallace that a reason for his hosts' constant companionship, such as during his impromptu hill-climb in Magadan, was to prevent his seeing one.[81]

Wallace did, in fact, encounter camps and prisoners, but was unaware of it—or at least revealed no awareness of it. "The watch-towers standing at the corners of the Magadan camps were removed" before his arrival, recorded Thomas Sgovio, an American Communist arrested in Moscow after seeking an exit visa at the U.S. embassy in 1938. The guards showed movies to the inmates for three days to keep them away from the delegation. "Only a few—those whose services were absolutely necessary—were sent to work. And they were warned of a speedy trial and execution for one false word or move."

But what of the vibrant town life Wallace described? "When the Vice-President strolled on the Magadan streets and saw shops filled with products and merchandise," Sgovio wrote, "he must have said to himself, 'What an abundance!' Mr. Wallace was unaware that the goods had been carted from the warehouses especially for his visit—and that after his departure the shelves would be bare again."[82]

"The stir in the city was incredible!," recalled Kanif Khakimov, who had come to Kolyma as a child in 1935, remaining after his father was arrested. "[S]uddenly the shop windows were full of Soviet foodstuffs. God knows where this stuff came from, because since 1942 everybody in Kolyma ate white bread made of Canadian flour and bought (only with ration cards) American food—canned meat, sausage meat, lard covered with a layer of dust, and pickled peeled tomatoes in rusty cans picked up in 1908."[83] Much of the population lived on the brink of starvation. The NKVD, Lipper explained, "had gone to the trouble of digging stuff up from the remotest stores and precious private hoards in order to impress Mr. Wallace."[84] It worked. "Although it is difficult to judge the amount of food available to the average individual on the basis of the sumptuous meals provided for the Vice-President's party," wrote the military secretary of the Wallace mission, Kennith Knowles, in a report to Washington, food store "shelves were universally well stocked."[85]

Nikishov escorted the Americans through the streets of Magadan, passing men dressed in fine parade-style military jackets, caps, and high boots. These were not soldiers, however, but camp officers, their new wardrobes freshly issued for the occasion. The NKVD guide ushered Wallace into a store bustling with customers—the ration card requirement having been suspended to create traffic. After admiring the haberdashery, which had only just been created and would just as soon disappear, Wallace bought some perfume. A lucky local who had arrived at the same time managed to buy a rare food item, but his less fortunate neighbor, who tried to pay just after the vice president left, was told that his selection was "not for sale."[86]

The Americans then moved on to a local school, where Nikishov introduced them, seemingly at random, to polyglot teachers positioned for the occasion. The German-language teacher, for example, was a Leningrad professor forced to remain in Magadan after serving his prison sentence. Wallace conversed with them animatedly in English, praising their linguistic skills.[87] The day ended, Wallace reported, with a performance by the Poltava Troupe and Red Army choir at the Gorky Theater, accompanied, of course, by the Nikishovs.[88] But the truly outstanding performance was that of the NKVD itself, which had staged the event.

"The finest Soviet [performers]," Wallace enthused, "had joined the trek of machines eastward across the Urals."[89] They had indeed, and in similar containers. The prima ballerina Nina Gamilton, formerly of the Bolshoi in Moscow, was a prisoner freed on parole in 1942. Her colleague Irina Mukhina, also trained in Moscow, was a prisoner. The orchestra were prisoners. Its conductor, Kanan Novogrudsky, a professional cellist, was a prisoner. As for the "Red Army choir," they, too, were prisoners.[90]

The NKVD had "organized [the] choir in a hurry," recalled an opera singer of surname Mojhai—a prisoner. "Each of us had to sign an oath . . . to comport ourselves as Soviet patriots in the presence of the visitors. One word or sign that we were prisoners would be considered an act of treason. . . . After the performance they immediately loaded us into trucks—and back to camp."[91]

Wallace did not wish his memoir's readers to think that the performances were "to please us as foreign visitors," however; they were, he assured them, "available to all at a moderate admission price." These were theaters of the Common Man. "There you have Nikishov's aristocracy," Goglidze said to Wallace, gesturing over the audience in proletarian dress. Nikishov nodded: "I see many miners, truck repairmen, and dock workers."

The evening in Magadan, both Wallace and the NKVD concluded, had been a glorious success. "I don't think I have ever seen anything better put on by the talent of a single city," the vice president wrote.[92] Yet he had initially had some doubts about the performance, according to its stage director, Georgy Nickolaevich Katsman, a former prisoner. "The morning after the concert, the doorbell rang at my apartment," he later recalled. "Opening the door, I see a man in a 'chekist' leather jacket," the uniform of Soviet state security:

> He asks me to go down to the car with him. Terribly frightened, I get dressed and keep thinking on my way to the car about what might have happened for them to arrest me. . . . We get to the airport. At the airplane's bridge, I see Wallace. They take me to him. The matter was that he liked the concert very much, but did not believe the participants were local actors, supposing they had been brought from Moscow.

Katsman assured "the honored guest" of the performers' local provenance. Wallace "smiled for a long time, and thanked me." A shaken but relieved Katsman was returned home.[93]

Vice President Henry A. Wallace (second from right) in front of the Siberian *sovkhoz* hothouses. Second from left is likely V. I. Palman, May 1944.

Not everything on the tour went as the NKVD planned. "While [Wallace's] delegation was crossing the city park," Khakimov recalled, "an emaciated calf jumped out of nowhere and barred the way." For this, "the park director was fired." At the model farm they visited, fourteen miles outside Magadan, Wallace sowed confusion by asking the young female swineherds, dressed in beautiful rustic finery, questions about Siberian pigs. The women looked at each other awkwardly, not knowing what to say. They had only just arrived from a nearby office, where they had donned costumes to play swineherds for the Americans. The interpreter, however, ad-libbed admirably, leaving Wallace none the wiser.

One of the workers at a *sovkhoz* collective who led Wallace on a tour of the hothouses was agro-technician Vyacheslav Ivanovich Palman, a one-time convict sentenced for spreading "counter-revolutionary propaganda." Palman would later write an account of the occasion for the Magadan Regional Museum, which would be quoted extensively by local historian Alexander Glushchenko in an essay entitled "Pulling Wool Over the Ears of the Vice President."

The two months of preparation for Wallace's visit included a 30,000-ruble "facelift" and training for those who would be allowed near the vice president. Palman described his wonder at seeing the Americans ushered in by "Commissar Nikishov [and] one of Beria's henchmen, Goglidze," both of whom "dressed up in mufti"—that is, civilian clothes. The collective proceeded to put on a "masquerade" for them. "In place of women-inmates, the role of hot-house workers was performed by women from the administrative staff: neatly dressed, in lisle stockings and wearing lipstick." The guests "expressed their surprise and admiration" for the impressive operation, "eating cucumbers right from the vegetable patches." Wallace "embraced me by the shoulders," Palman wrote, "and thanked me warmly and paternally" for answering his questions about "plant varieties, seeds, and agricultural technologies." The NKVD, in turn, rewarded Palman by expunging his criminal record.[94]

Nikishov and his comrades used actors all along the vice president's route. Wallace described the gold miners he met in Bereliokh as "big, husky young men." But mining was a brutal job carried out by underfed prisoners (or "released" prisoners) who slept in lice-ridden tents. "Almost every day," explained Nina Savoeva, a legendary doctor[95] who had volunteered to treat actual prisoners, "corpses of those who had died of hypothermia in the mines were brought to the morgue. . . . [A] small wash-basin was full of frost-bitten fingers and toes we chopped off." These ruddy men whom Wallace met, then, were *komsomoltsy*, members of the Young Communists Organization, assembled to play the part of miners.

To give the "miners" the trappings of prosperity, and to reinforce the narrative of high wages, officials gave them new clothes and loaned them their wristwatches. Wallace, however, always observant when it came to things, if not of people and circumstances, immediately identified the boots as American Lend-Leased material. As U.S. policy forbade Lend-Lease for gold-mining, Nikishov explained, falsely, that they had been bought for cash early in the war. "After Mr. Wallace left," Sgovio reported, "the clothing, boots, and wrist watches were taken away."[96] The shops were emptied. The watchtowers were erected once more.

On June 6, Nikishov wrote to Beria, Stalin, and Molotov expressing concern about Wallace's persistent questioning, over several days, regarding the quantity of gold mined and the number of workers involved. The numbers were state secrets. Exasperated by Wallace's refusal to accept vague responses or approximate figures, Nikishov distracted him with a display

Vice President Henry A. Wallace shakes hands with Russian "miners" at the Kolyma goldfields, northeast Siberia, May 1944.

of actual gold removal from a washing plant. This display seemed to leave Wallace suitably impressed. Later prisoner memoirs indicated that gold had been left in the plant for two days so that the vice president could witness a three-day haul in one.

"We heard about *Dalstroi* in America," Nikishov reported Wallace saying. "[I]n America, there are no such mighty trusts that cover such a wide variety of versatile work, and I think that *Dalstroi* will be providing a greater share of gold than all the other enterprises in your nation." More importantly, Wallace believed that Dal'stroi's success showed the spirit and enterprise of the Soviet Common Man. Touring an exhibition of fine arts and inventions at the Magadan House of Culture that evening, Wallace recorded his thoughts. "This is an outstanding expression," the visitor book says, "of strong people who were the pioneers in the development of this region. Henry A. Wallace."[97] In fact, the region's development owed more to *American* ingenuity and capacity. "Everything around us," Sgovio noted, "was American—products, machinery, tools, Studebaker trucks, steam shovels, Diamond bull-dozers, ammonal in fancy wax paper covering, detonators, etc." All were provided under Lend-Lease, although for very different purposes. After the war, Wallace would tell his American readers, "Kolyma-mined gold will help Russia pay for [American-made] electric shovels, core drills, steel rolling mills."[98] He would not tell them that this gold would be mined by prisoners, many of whom were sentenced for political crimes.

Wallace wrote glowingly of what he was shown: of the "all-weather 350-mile highway" running north from the port of Magadan, over the mountains; of an enormous vehicle assembly and repair plant ("Magadan's biggest industry"); of the "hundreds of hotbeds and greenhouses," built on permafrost land, "producing tomatoes and cucumbers." He was unaware that the "highway"—the graveled Kolyma Road—was built by prisoners, thousands of whom had died in the process, and that the road was used mainly to move them to other labor camps. There were not, in fact, "1,000 men engaged on road construction work and the improvement of highways," as Wallace wrote; the road was only "all weather" to the extent that those men, prisoners, were continuously occupied removing the fresh snow and debris. He was further unaware that the vehicle plant was not, as he suggested, like those in Detroit; the workers there were, too, mostly prisoners. And he was unaware that the women tending the hotbeds and greenhouses—again, prisoners—were growing vegetables not for "miners" but for the NKVD top brass.[99]

Wallace extolled the frontier spirit in Siberia, so like that, he believed, of America's nineteenth-century Western migrants. Before the Revolution, Russians, "mostly convicts," had "miserably existed there." But the brutal truth had, he said, been revealed by George Kennan's relative of the same name (a cousin of his grandfather). His book, *Siberia and the Exile System*, had been "a nail in the coffin of Czarist Russia." Now, he wrote, the "scant twenty-five years" of Soviet rule had rid Russia of this evil. "Higher wages," he said, "was the evident incentive that had brought the miners into the Far East." The new inhabitants were "pioneers of the machine age, builders of cities." Even the less perfectly stage-managed encounters could not dampen his enthusiasm. "The young city of Komsomolsk," Wallace observed, "looked dishevelled and run down, and the people seemed over-worked." Yet "ten years hence it will be a lovely city."[100]

The "vision" of the Siberian Communist leaders with whom Wallace met he likened to that of "pioneer America." As the United States had its "Johnny

Appleseed, who crossed the Appalachian barrier, carrying the 'seeds and tree-souls' of today's American Midwest," Wallace explained, so today's Soviet frontiersmen were sowing tomorrow's prosperity in Asia. "The spirit . . . of life in Siberia today," he wrote, is "not to be compared to that of the old exile days," under the czars. "The word Siberia evokes memories of frightful suffering and sorrow, convict chains and exile. [But] then in this generation, during the past fifteen years, all has been changed as though by magic."

"The people of Siberia today are a hardy vigorous race," he continued, "but not because they are whipped into submission. The only whip driving them is the necessity to master a vast new land. [And] awareness of that need is what makes them work so hard." But these hardy people do not live to work. They "know how to laugh and play and sing," Wallace observed. "In the folk songs, one feels the stirring of the Russian peasant soul."[101]

Wallace's image of Siberians as freedom-loving pioneers, much like their American brethren, had a long American pedigree. In 1918, in the immediate aftermath of the Russian Revolution, President Woodrow Wilson looked to Siberia to roll back the Bolsheviks. In a report requested by the president, sociologist Edward Alsworth Ross, known for his writing on the forging of America's frontier identity, explained that Siberians were "more intelligent and aggressive than the Russians." Kennan (the cousin), whom Wallace had so admired, said they were a "bolder and more independent people." They could, with American military and economic support, establish their own government and eventually even topple the Bolsheviks.[102] That had not happened, of course, but Wallace believed Siberians were doing God's work in Americanizing the Bolsheviks.

Wallace's Siberian eulogy would become an object of disbelief to the captives along his route. "Can Wallace possibly be aware," Lipper asked, "of the grotesque irony of his words?" The workers and peasants he saw were hardly pioneers, she explained. "[L]ike their fathers and grandfathers, the children and grand-children are also . . . prisoners." Neither adventure nor opportunity had lured them. They were brought in teeming, fetid cattle cars and freighters, seven thousand at a time, under the watch of armed police and wolfhounds. "But the conditions under which they live are far more inhuman," Lipper said. In czarist times, families could accompany exiles into Siberia; under Stalin, prisoners were effectively "buried alive, cut off from everyone."

Wallace had singled out shovel operators at the Karaganda coal trust as exemplars of the fine labor conditions he observed. Their compensation, he alleged, was equivalent to what a top Red Army officer was paid, and about three times higher than a shovelman in the Soviet West. In fact, however, a significant part of all industry and agriculture in the Karaganda area of Kazakhstan was manned by prisoners and those sent into exile—generally family members of political prisoners and those charged with treason. The massive group of Karaganda camps, or Karlag, held 55,000 prisoners at the time of Wallace's visit, including political figures, military leaders, clergy, scientists, scholars, writers, artists, actors, and educators imprisoned for political offenses. Wallace's companion Owen Lattimore reported looking down from their plane upon the Karaganda "prospecting shafts," but neither he nor Wallace registered the massive watchtowers or barricades. [103]

Regarding the socialist-model housing and communal facilities that had so impressed Wallace, suggesting to him a model for Alaskan development, what he doubtlessly had in mind was the *sotsgorod* "socialist city" infrastructure erected in the late 1920s. Its original aim, almost certainly unknown to Wallace, had been "to create prerequisites for doing away with the family as an economic unit." The Novosibirsk regional leadership, for example, determined that the "houses should be fertile ground for the . . . morale of a full *communard*, and for the dramatic transformation of human relationships."

Stalin discarded this utopian vision after crushing the so-called Leninist-Bolshevik opposition in 1929, replacing it with a totalitarian model better suited to a command economy. Funds for the housing projects were slashed. In 1931, the Plenum of the Central Committee concluded that the state could not afford any diversion of resources toward the creation of *sotsgorod*, given the priority of industrialization. A June resolution declared the collectivization of households and the construction of commune-type houses "left wing deviations."[104]

The new aim of housing policy was to maximize industrial production by implementing the organizational and managerial concepts of "social resettlement" (*sotsialisticheskoe rasselenie*).[105] The Stalinist version of *sotsgorod* had elements that would no doubt have appealed to Wallace: settlements were to be organized on the basis of economic planning, scientific knowledge, and expert calculation. He would not have appreciated, however, that such an "engineering" (*pereustroistvo obschestva*) approach would extend to every facet of work and family life.

Stalin structured the system to bind the workforce to the workplace. The state provided all basic needs as a condition of service to the enterprise where the worker was required. Greater output was encouraged by granting high performers priority in housing allocation and better food rations—benefits unobtainable elsewhere. Women were pushed into the workforce through a combination of collective child care and pay low enough to make dual-wage-earning vital to family survival. In 1933, the government eliminated worker mobility entirely through internal passportization, binding citizens to their registered places of residence.[106] The Gulag was, in effect, only an extreme extension of basic Stalinist labor policy.

Wallace's views on Soviet economics also hewed to those of his escorts. He cited Chuvakhin's account of Stalin's supposed rejection of Trotsky's wish "to make peace with the *kulaks*." Such peace was impossible, Stalin believed; Russia had to "discipline herself" and "increase her industrial and farm output." It was, in fact, Trotsky who had urged, famously, "Let's strike the kulak and accelerate industrialization!," and who first endorsed "*Sverkhindustrializatsiia*"—super-industrialization. Still, Stalin did later co-opt and pervert such ideas, before having Trotsky murdered.

Sverkhindustrializatsiia, Wallace agreed, justified the collectivization of Soviet farms and the hardship it entailed. Yet Wallace was not merely parroting Chuvakhin. He was following in a tradition of American scholars and journalists, going back twenty years, of arguing that economic modernization was the touchstone of Bolshevik success—that all else was secondary, trivial, or romantic.

On a visit to Moscow in 1926, Chicago political scientist Samuel Harper made the shift from Bolshevik opponent to supporter after observing the changes being imposed on peasant culture.[107] Industrialization and collective agriculture, Harper concluded, were the vehicles by which the government was overcoming the historic cultural backwardness of the Russian countryside. This transformation was indeed Stalin's aim. "We are advancing full steam along the path to industrialization—to socialism, leaving behind our age-old 'Russian' backwardness," he said in 1929. "And when we shall have put the USSR on an automobile, and the *muzhik* on a tractor, let the worthy capitalists, who boast so much of their 'civilization,' try to overtake us!"[108]

Columbia historian Geroid Tanquary Robinson, an editor at the storied Greenwich Village–based literary and political magazine *The Dial*, saw the Soviet Union as a grand "experiment in socialization."[109] After World War I, he opposed American intervention in the country on the grounds that Bolshevism would likely "destroy itself." Yet that eventuality depended, he believed, not on the effects of its radical political program, but on whether the country could industrialize. Robinson's fellow editor, Thorstein Veblen, a major intellectual influence on Wallace, was more bullish on Bolshevism. By rescuing national industrial control from the malign grip of the private profit motive, Veblen believed, the Bolsheviks were empowering technicians to eliminate capitalist wastage and improve the standard of living.[110] That theme, the promise of planning, became a powerful one in 1920s America; it was nowhere more systematically laid out than in engineer-economist Stuart Chase's 1925 book *The Tragedy of Waste*. America, Veblen believed, was being undermined by what Chase called "industrial anarchy." He hoped Soviet success would provide a template for reorganizing the economic foundations of American society.

But what if Russians would not cooperate with collectivization? Chase, who visited Moscow in 1927, was unperturbed. "A better economic order," he said, "is worth a little bloodshed."[111] There should be "no occasion for shocked surprise," émigré Wisconsin labor economist Selig Perlman added, "at the bloody methods" of the Bolsheviks. They were, after all, only able to create "a new civilization in Russia" by eliminating flaws in peasant character that were not corrigible through education. The "higher freedoms" associated with liberal democracy in America were, in any case, "too remote" for Russian peasants, who suffered from "mental sluggishness" and were disposed to focus solely on economic well-being—which would soon become apparent to them.

Harvard political scientist Bruce Hopper saw industrialization as a means of civilizing peoples who would otherwise remain backward owing to the stultifying effect of Asian climate and topography on character. Through Soviet-style central planning, he enthused, "the old East becomes the new West." Philosopher-historian Hans Kohn saw the Soviet Five-Year Plans, the first of which launched in 1928, not as vehicles for implementing Communism but for spreading Westernization. They would, he said, bring about the "spiritual victory of the dynamic civilization of the West over the static civilization of the East."

Peasant resistance to collectivization, explained education scholar Thomas Woody, was irrational; it was not based on "'thought out' objections," but simply "a 'feeling' that it was not right." If rural inhabitants were incapable of informed deliberation, modernization would have to be imposed. In essence, whereas Woody and Stalin disagreed on Communist ideology, both believed the peasantry suffered from Marxian False Consciousness.

Woody's fellow educational reformer George Counts, a follower of pragmatist philosopher John Dewey, put a more positive gloss on Woody's observations. There was, he argued, a "perfect correlation between living conditions and degree of enlightenment." Once the traditional Russian peasant had experienced the fruits of industrialization, "there will take his place a new type of peasant, brought up . . . with a different philosophy of life." Repression could therefore serve the cause of liberation. Indeed, it could achieve an even higher purpose, as Soviet communal society was more cohesive than anything achievable under capitalism.

Dewey, too, saw great promise in the Soviet experiment, in that "integrated individuality" was much better suited to the "collective age" brought on by modern industry than was American "rugged—or is it *ragged?*—individualism." Woody, citing Dewey, praised the "frankly avowed dictatorship" in Soviet education, as it would help transform the nation's archaic individualistic psyche into a modern collectivist one. These scholars downplayed the importance of Marxist ideology in the Soviet educational and economic planning regimes, arguing, like Robinson, that their value lay in the new data they would provide to experts and policymakers worldwide. The Soviet experiments were "the most interesting going on upon our globe," Dewey wrote, "though I am quite frank to say that for selfish reasons I prefer seeing it tried out in Russia rather than in my own country."[112]

Émigré think-tanker Vera Micheles Dean argued that individual liberty, while central to the American identity, was never part of the Russian political tradition; one therefore finds in the Soviet Union, she said, "readiness to sacrifice human lives without hesitation to the achievement of plans dictated from above." The Bolsheviks would necessarily "break or transform" the peasantry as needed, and Americans should, and generally did, sympathize with "the attempt of the Communists to modernize Russia's economic life"—even where this entailed great hardship. From Dean's perspective, it was not necessary to posit a path from industrialization to political enlightenment, as Counts had done. The former was as much as Russia could reasonably aspire to. Journalist Eugene Lyons, a onetime socialist and supporter of Bolshevik planning in the 1920s, would later come to condemn such views as "racist drivel."[113]

Economist Calvin Bryce Hoover, a protégé of Perlman's, broke with Veblen and Chase in attributing Soviet economic success not to planning, which was inefficient, but to force itself. The Bolsheviks had collectivized agriculture though "fear, force and terror," as well as starvation, in the process providing "striking proof of the power of the human intellect over the material world." Their reforms had yielded an impressive national savings rate, he observed, higher than that of the United States. Such savings could be used for investment in yet further rapid advances—a prospect detrimental to America's competitive position. State Department officials took this analysis very seriously.

American journalists reporting from Russia were, too, more often than not in the thrall of the great Soviet experiment. The most famed of these was the Liverpool-born Moscow bureau chief of *The New York Times*, Walter Duranty, whose tenure in the country was bookended by two famines, those of 1921–23 and 1932–33. The death and suffering he witnessed had remarkably little emotional effect on Duranty's writing—a source of pride for him. Foreign correspondence, Duranty held, was of no value except where filtered through the reporter's interpretive lens. Without his lens in Russia, Americans were incapable of comprehending "a nation and a people," the Russians, "whose customs and ideals are as strange to the western mind as are those of the Chinese."[114] To report the facts of where, how, and why Russians were starving, without explaining the cultural roots of their passivity and fatalism, would be to mislead readers, who could not be expected to understand why starvation was unavoidable. The Bolsheviks were, through industrialization, he explained, bringing their nation "from oxcart to airplane" in a single generation—a self-evidently worthy purpose for which short-term sacrifice was necessary. "Duranty consistently takes the line, a perfectly logical and defensible one," wrote fellow journalist William Henry Chamberlin, "that the sufferings which . . . are being imposed on the Russian people in the name of socialism, industrialization, and collectivization are of small account by comparison with the bigness of the objectives at which the Soviet leaders are aiming."[115] Or, as Duranty himself liked to put it more succinctly, "you can't make an omelette without breaking eggs."

Duranty, like Veblen, admired the Soviet economic apparatus, but for very different reasons. Whereas Veblen believed in planning as a technocratic device to embed rationality in society, Duranty believed it offered instead an "esoteric stimulus to a people whose roots are deep in mysticism."[116] The "wild economic theories" which underlay Soviet planning were unimportant, he explained. Russia was impelled by an "ancient Asiatic craving for mass action under an absolute ruler," which Bolshevik despotism satisfied.

For his interpretive prowess in reporting from Russia, Duranty was awarded a Pulitzer Prize in 1932. The accompanying citation praised his "profound and intimate comprehension of conditions in Russia and of the causes of those conditions." His dispatches were "marked by scholarship, profundity, impartiality, sound judgment and exceptional clarity": they were "excellent examples of the best type of foreign correspondence."[117] Stalin, too, was impressed. "You have done a good job in your reporting the U.S.S.R., though you are not a Marxist, because you try to tell the truth about our country," he supposedly told Duranty on Christmas Day 1933. "I might say that you bet on our horse to win when others thought it had no chance and I am sure you have not lost by it." Some sixty years later, with the benefit of hindsight, the Times no longer boasted of Duranty's Pulitzer. "The result" of Duranty's bet on the Bolsheviks, wrote editorial board member Karl Meyer, "was some of the worst reporting to appear in this newspaper."[118]

Arguments like Perlman's, Dean's, Hoover's, and Duranty's did not emerge merely to justify the Bolshevik brand of governance; they actually had pre-Soviet roots, in efforts to explain why Russia had *always* needed an authoritarian path to modernity. At the turn of the century, Columbia émigré Marxist economic historian Vladimir Simkhovitch held that the destruction of the prerevolutionary *mir* peasant commune—which was, to his mind, just a tax-collection tool for the corrupt czarist state—was essential for Russia to shed its "dwarf-economy" (*Zwergwirtschaft*) status. Eradicating peasant culture was not about boosting national wealth, however. "[T]he dignity of man" itself was at stake. If famine, such as the one endured in 1891–92, sped the process of modernization, it was justified and indeed necessary. The "sufferings of the present generation of peasants and artisans," he argued, were insignificant set against the glorious future that awaited. As "painful as this period is, it must soon pass away." Russia, Hopper reasoned, was prepared to "starve itself great."[119]

George Frost Kennan, who arrived in Moscow as the new embassy counselor on July 1, 1944, referred to such thinking as the "romance of economic development." This romance led observers to set aside concerns save those embodied in the national plan.[120] Wallace partook of it, seeing Russia much as Simkhovitch did: as the most important chapter in a universal narrative of progress. And like most American supporters of collectivization, he saw it not as an element of Marxist-Leninist thinking, but as a path to modernization appropriate to Russia's history and culture. That it was so late in coming merely affirmed that the state had to be forceful in removing social barriers standing in the way. The experience of the Depression had, for Wallace, as it had for so many Western intellectuals who visited the USSR, reinforced the belief that industrialization, if it was to avoid the instability that accompanied laissez-faire, needed to be guided from above.[121]

Wallace was, however, presumably aware of reports that collectivization had led to the deaths of six to thirteen million Soviet citizens. "We in the United States," he conceded, "may regard the methods employed as too costly in human terms." Yet "there [was] no denying," he asserted in rebuttal, sounding much like Chase or Duranty, "that it was . . . a necessary measure if the industrialization plan . . . was to succeed. The old peasant farming without mechanized collective methods," he explained, "was not productive enough to support projected urban expansion." Because of Stalin's initiative and fortitude, he concluded, "the present strength of Siberian agriculture" was undeniable, and "its future is assured."[122]

In reality, the country never recovered from collectivization. When the peasants resisted, armed soldiers and workers requisitioned not just seed grain but food itself. Those who, in the end, cooperated typically found themselves in cramped, decrepit apartments, shared with strangers, or in fraying tents on the Siberian steppes. Those who did not—and survived—became "former persons," *lishentsy*, stripped of rights. The collectives remained permanently plagued by problems of poor equipment and peasant alienation, as was documented by Byelorussian-born journalist Maurice Hindus, but Americans who celebrated the reforms, Hindus among them, invariably expressed confidence in their *future*. "I am heartily convinced," he wrote, "that whatever setback collectivization may be countenancing in the villages, it [will] eventually [be] for the good of the peasants."[123]

Despite its record, collectivization received vast support in Russia—among the unincarcerated. Speaking against collectivization, or suspicion of thinking against it, was a crime. So was associating, or once having associated, with such a speaker or thinker, or failing to denounce him or her. It was punishable by up to ten years—or, after 1937, up to twenty-five years—in a Kolyma labor camp.

Wallace would not have known such details, nor would he have accepted them as fact had he been confronted with them. But he did weigh the accounts he had read of vast differences between the American and Soviet justice systems against his sensory experience traveling in Siberia, and stated his verdict before an audience at the Irkutsk City Dramatic Theater on June 1.

"Men born in wide, free spaces," Wallace said, "will not brook injustice and tyranny. They will not even temporarily live in slavery." The "heroic population" of Siberia had, just like the pioneers of the American West, "fearlessly forged ahead, built new towns and villages, a new industry, a new life, for the good of their homeland and all of mankind." This fact underlined that the reality that "there exist no other two countries more alike than the Soviet Union and the United States of America."[124]

The Soviet press, Wallace noted with satisfaction, reported the "very warm reception" his words received.[125] Those words had come of no surprise to the NKVD, which had already read his thoughts. "Wallace's diary, which was obtained by inside agents," according to a top secret 1948 Central Committee file, "contains notes on his meetings with Soviet people. The nature of these notes demonstrates the author's objectivity and friendly attitude toward the Soviet Union during that time period."[126] Known as a "black bag job," this standard Soviet secret service operation involved stealing, copying, and replacing the target object—in this case, the vice president's diary.

Wallace's appreciation for Soviet achievements had clearly been stoked by his visit, yet his hosts' careful shepherding was not sufficient to explain it: their success still required a visitor inclined to see only what he wished to see. Not all Wallace's colleagues were so inclined. In Tashkent, for example, the delegation's military secretary, Captain Knowles, recorded seeing "several battalions of forced labor . . . being marched from their barracks to the place of work." They "were under heavy armed guard and the procession of automobiles bearing the Vice President and his party was not permitted to cut through the long column of laborers."[127] It is implausible that Wallace failed to notice a mass herding of prisoners in front of his car, yet he never mentions it. Neither does the sight temper his enthusiasm for the Soviet economic model.

No Potemkin landmass the size of the one Wallace traversed can fool one unwilling to be fooled—at least not for a month. Vyshinky understood this, but welcomed the vice president's visit because he recognized the type. Wallace was one of many in a procession of prominent political pilgrims to Russia, stretching back to the 1920s, for whom perception merely projected predisposition.[128] They saw what they came to see.

"Here are happy men," wrote writer and Communist political activist Waldo Frank, observing Russian factory workers in 1931, "because they are whole men and women. . . . Dream, thought, love collaborate in the tedious business of making electric parts."[129] Frank saw joy in tedium because it was in the service of socialism. Wallace, for his part, had gone to Russia, as he explained in his departure statement, to "feel the grandeur that comes when men wisely work with nature," and he went on to feel it in mines and factories manned by slaves.

Other travelers had shared Wallace's rejection of an economic system driven by personal enrichment rather than dedication to the common good. "Their confidence in unspoilt human nature," wrote English Quaker D. F. Buxton, who visited in the late 1920s, "forbids the Communists to believe in self-interest as the indispensable motive by which alone the economic machine keeps going."[130] "Here," in Russia, wrote Joseph Freeman, Moscow correspondent for *New Masses* in 1926–27, "where the individual was supposed to subordinate himself to the general interest of society as a whole, he actually expanded by virtue of being part of something greater than himself." Wallace had come to Russia believing that "capitalism, if it adheres to its 19th Century methods, and democracy, if it does not pervade economic life," would be endangered.[131] Yet he found his "symbol of economic democracy based on . . . jobs for everybody" in the Siberian Gulag.

A Russian engineer posted at the Soviet Purchasing Commission in Washington, Victor Kravchenko, had, earlier in 1944, come across several speeches by Wallace and, knowing of the vice president's reputation as a friend of his country, asked an interpreter to translate the portions about Russia.

"I could not believe my ears," Kravchenko recorded:

> The Vice-President of a democratic government was praising what he called "economic democracy" in Stalin's police-state! Our Secret and Special Departments in every Soviet factory, state-controlled trading unions, lack of true collective bargaining, the death penalty for strike agitations, the Stakhanovite and piecework systems, labor passports, laws punishing more than twenty minutes' lateness by starvation, and forced-labor colonies—didn't Mr. Wallace know these common-place facts or did he, by some trick of rationalization, really look on them as aspects of "economic democracy"?[132]

Two years later, Kravchenko would request, and be granted, political asylum in the United States.

Still other visitors to the Soviet Union had shared Wallace's devotion to egalitarianism. "[F]or the first time in history," wrote Alexander Wicksteed, an English Quaker who lived in the Soviet Union for fifteen years after the Revolution, "the common man feels that the country belongs to him and not to the privileged class that are his masters."[133] Wallace echoed these sentiments in his observance that "the road to the presidency" of the country was "open to the Kazakh, the Uzbek, the Buryat, the Yakut," and that "under Marshal Stalin's wise leadership, the multi-national Soviet peoples [had] shown that for them nothing is impossible."[134] When he crossed the Soviet border into China at Tihwa (today, Urumqi) on June 18, 1944, Wallace could not imagine that Stalin would, four years later, as part of a systematic program to Russify Soviet culture, ban Buryat art forms, forbid use of the language in schools, and order the killing of ten thousand ethnic leaders in the region Wallace had just traveled.[135]

In fact, Wallace was now more confident than ever in his postwar vision. A world away from Siberia, in the majestic White Mountains of New Hampshire, representatives of forty-four nations, the Soviet Union among them, had, for the past three weeks, been gathered for the most important international conference since the Paris peace talks of 1919. In the next four days, the delegates at Bretton Woods would finalize the foundations for a new International Monetary Fund, World Bank, and global monetary system to ensure postwar cooperation and stability. The Century of the Common Man seemed imminent; prospects for U.S.-Soviet friendship never seemed better.

Seven

CHINA, THROUGH A GLASS DARKLY

Chiang Kai-shek was the inscrutable Christian icon before whom Washington, lacking practical alternatives, tendered sacrifices and prayed for aid in the Pacific war. He was remote, volatile, brooding, temperamental, and self-obsessed, yet he represented the best—most said only—hope to unite China for the fight against Japan.

"[T]he job in China can be boiled down to one essential," Roosevelt told his son Elliott in November 1943. "China must be kept in the war, tying up Japanese soldiers."[1] Without the Generalissimo's vast army—however fractured, underfed, poorly trained, and badly led—wearing down 1.25 million enemy troops, Allied victory might take many more years, and American lives, to secure. "With all their shortcomings," FDR concluded of Chiang and his charming, calculating wife, "we've got to depend on the Chiangs."[2] The couple had become, in the words of the State Department's John Paton Davies, "the imagined personification of all China."[3]

The story of America's fatal attraction to the Chiangs began in 1880, with the Dixie baptism of a nineteen-year-old Chinese émigré named Charlie Soong. Soong had sailed to Boston a few years earlier to work in his uncle's Chinatown shop, before venturing down to North Carolina as a laborer with the U.S. Revenue Marine. There, he was befriended by Southern Methodists and brought into the faith. Church leaders groomed him for re-export to China, where he would spread the gospel. Spiritually adopted by the devout young industrialist Julian Carr, Charlie, though lacking qualifications, was admitted into the theology department at Trinity College (now Duke University)—a beneficiary of Carr's philanthropy. His intellect apparent, he was soon lured to Tennessee's Vanderbilt University, a fellow Methodist redoubt, where he took his degree in 1885. A year later he was back in China, in Shanghai, working as a missionary.

Here, Charlie found his calling—not as a missionary, but as a money-maker. He began by printing and selling Chinese Bibles, but soon expanded into businesses ranging from dried noodles to cotton mills. It was at a Shanghai Methodist church in 1894 that Charlie, now thirty-one and a latter-day convert to revolutionary republican politics, met the twenty-seven-year-old Hawaiian-educated Sun Yat-sen. Sun was, by this time, determined to lead China's technological modernization, on the Western model, and to topple its dynastic governance system. Soong and Sun would thereafter form a tight political bond, with the older man becoming the other's clandestine publisher and financier.

In 1905, Charlie set out to solicit funds from his Christian network in the American South. With Chinese banned from the United States under the 1882 Exclusion Act, he purchased a Portuguese passport in Macao and headed back to Durham. With Carr's aid in convening believers, Charlie preached the gospel of the coming Christian China. Dr. Sun's three principles—"self-determination," "rights of the people," and "people's livelihood"—he translated into more locally resonant terms: "of the people, by the people, and for the people." His audience, knowing little of China but caring deeply for its salvation, responded generously. Following a multicity road show, from San Francisco to New York, Charlie returned home with over $2 million ($55 million in today's money) to spread democracy—or Sun's rendering of it.[4] More importantly, Charlie had sown the seeds, both in China and the United States, for a Soong-sired diplomatic dynasty.

Charlie raised his three daughters—Ai-ling (b. 1890), Ching-ling (b. 1893), and Mei-ling (b. 1898)—and three sons—T.V. (b. 1894), T.L. (b. 1899), and T.A. (b. 1907)—as binational Southern Methodists. He sent all six to university in the United States. When the eldest daughter, Ai-ling, returned from Georgia in 1911, Sun, freshly elected by Nanking rebels as provisional president of the new Chinese republic, appointed her his personal assistant. His forces too weak to hold power, however, he yielded authority to an imperial minister, Yuan Shikai, in February 1912, and would not succeed in reclaiming it until 1921—when he would be elected grand marshal of a military government in Guangzhou.

In 1914, Ai-ling, a shrewd, methodized Methodist, married Yale-trained H. H. Kung, a founder of Christian schools and future prominent banker who would later become head of Sun's new central bank and a fixture in future Sun-inspired Nationalist—or Kuomintang (KMT)—party-led governments. In 1915, her younger sister—the gentle, idealistic twenty-two-year-old Ching-ling—married the forty-nine-year-old Sun, becoming his third wife. The union was not, for her, a matter of love, but of "want[ing] to help save China."[5] Though Charlie opposed the marriage, and disavowed both his daughter and her new husband, the Soong-Sun family alliance was now forged. Charlie would die three years later, but Ai-ling and T.V. would take over the financing of Sun's movement.

Abroad, meanwhile, the new Soviet Union would balance its bets by providing military counseling to the Nationalists and bankrolling the new Communist Party of China (CCP or CPC). The former, however, vastly larger and stronger, would maintain pride of place in pragmatist Soviet diplomacy for the coming three decades.

The United States, in the early 1920s, spearheaded a series of treaties involving Britain, France, and Japan aimed at stabilizing the balance of military and commercial power in the Pacific—in particular, delineating foreign rights in China. Henry Wallace, as editor of *Wallaces' Farmer*, condemned his country's apparent turn toward European-style economic imperialism. He warned that rapacious industrialists and financiers, united against the peaceful interests of farmers, were pushing Washington toward armed collision with "young nations" like republican China, where nationalism was on the rise. Two decades later he would come to China wanting to reshape its government and its relations with powerful neighbors, but at this point he was still a committed anti-interventionist wanting to curb debt diplomacy and militarization of the seas.[6]

In 1924, Sun named thirty-six-year-old Tokyo-trained military officer Chiang Kai-shek ("Jiang Jieshi" in pinyin romanized spelling) commandant of his new Moscow-financed Whampoa Military Academy. "If I control the army," Chiang explained to his then-wife, Jennie (Chen'en Chie-ju), "I will have the power to control the country. It is my road to leadership."[7] Yet the country, like the KMT itself, was divided among rival warlords. When Sun died the following year, Chiang faced an immense challenge unifying both. In July 1926, he set out, with 100,000 troops, on a Northern Expedition to conquer central China, collaborating with communist forces and the man who would later become his main rival, Mao Tse-tung.

Mao ran political operations, mobilizing peasants with pledges of land re-form, in advance of Chiang's forces. The latter captured Nanking in March 1927, but struggled to neutralize rivals in Wuhan and elsewhere. Ai-ling, now her powerful family's ruling matriarch, fretted over the rising challenge rebel-lious peasants and workers posed to the landlords and industrialists on whom the Soong business empire relied. She decided to take a steamer up the Yang-tze to Chiang's Jiujiang headquarters and to offer the Generalissimo a deal for her support. The rich and beautiful twenty-nine-year-old Mei-ling,[8] younger sister to Sun's widow, Ching-ling, would marry Chiang—making him Sun's natural heir apparent. The marriage would help him unify the KMT and crush the Communists. Chiang would agree, in exchange for Soong support, and the prospect of American backing that went with it, to convert to Chris-tianity and appoint Ai-ling's husband, H. H. Kung, prime minister, and her brother, T.V., finance minister (later, foreign minister).

Exuberant, Chiang still needed to remove an obstacle: his wife. "I am desperate," he told Jennie. "Ai-ling has struck a very hard bargain, but . . . her offer is the only way for me to . . . unite China."[9] He asked that she go to America for five years. She agreed. But once she had arrived safely, he dismissed her as a minor concubine.[10]

T.V., an Ivy-educated cosmopolitan, was no admirer of the provincial Chiang. Ching-ling abhorred him. And though Mei-ling had never imag-ined herself wedded to an intellectually inferior Confucian militarist (one whom she had rebuffed six years earlier),[11] she feared the wrath of her deter-mined elder sister. And so she assented.

On the heels of the deal, Chiang's strained alliance with the CCP turned to bloody conflict. In April, his forces launched a violent purge of commu-nists in Shanghai, which escalated into a massacre of thousands. Chiang's officers smashed peasant and worker revolts across the south, setting off a civil war that would rage, wane, and rage again for over two decades. Ching-ling, who shared Mao's concern for the plight of the rural poor, was appalled by Chiang's brutality and her sisters' complicity: the Generalissimo, she said, had "made the revolution much more costly and terrible than it need have been." But he could not change destiny. "In the end," she concluded, "he will be defeated just the same."[12]

At the time, 90 percent of China's 400 million people were peasants, peasants whose anger and aspirations would form the bedrock of Communist support. For Chiang, peasants were not a constituency to be courted but a tax base and bottomless source of conscripts, both of which he would need to bribe and menace rivals.

Mei-ling's people, meanwhile, were twelve thousand miles away. "The only thing Chinese about me," she would say, "is my face."[13] Otherwise she was a belle abroad, one who could dial up Southern charm, Bible quotes, and love of all things democratic when the need for alms and arms arose. This capacity would become essential to Chiang, who knew nothing of America's language, culture, or politics but coveted its weapons and wealth.

On September 18, 1931, Japanese commanders, alarmed at the progress of Chiang's forces in the south, the prospect of Soviet advance from the north, threats to their Korean colony in the east, and vulnerability to commodity curbs from the West, staged an explosion along Japan's South Manchurian Railway as a pretext for seizing the city of Mukden. Blaming the "attack" on China, a right-wing unit within the Imperial Japanese Army known as the Kwantung Army, with reinforcements from Korea, fanned out across the resource-rich region. On October 24, the League of Nations passed a resolution calling for a Japanese withdrawal; Tokyo, instead, installed a "Manchukuo" Chinese puppet regime and withdrew from the League. Chiang, dismaying millions of his compatriots, chose not to resist the invaders, opting instead to preserve his forces for quashing domestic opposition. "The Japanese are a disease of skin," he said, defending inaction, but "the Communists are a disease of the heart."[14]

This stance he might later have had to abandon, as Japanese aggression spread to Shanghai and beyond, were it not for the prospect of rallying Americans to his side. Here, the Soong alliance proved vital.

The opulent Soong-Chiang wedding of 1927, with bride bedizened in Western white gown and groom in black tux, had been attended by three thousand guests, among whom were dozens of foreign dignitaries. It not only made the front page of *The New York Times*, but was made *for* the front page.[15] Yet such media fascination with the couple was only the beginning. The young publishing magnate Henry Luce, raised in China as a missionary's son for thirteen years, until 1911, would feature Chiang and Mei-ling on more covers of *Time* than any other people on the planet. Having lived amidst the Chinese to evangelize them, and not to absorb their culture or language, Luce loved their country teleologically—not for what it was, but for what it was to be. Sun was "China's George Washington"; T.V. its "Alexander Hamilton." Sun's successor, the bigamist Chiang, was a righteous "Southern Methodist" and "America's friend." War-torn, Confucian China was, it seemed, destined to be reborn as a liberal Christian democracy, an Asiatic America. All the first couple needed was Washington's unswerving moral, financial, and military support. Chiang would remain, for Luce, irrespective of growing Communist resistance, the "undisputed ruler and idol of China's four hundred million [people]."

Equally powerful in spreading the image of an American China was the bestselling novel of another missionary's child, Pearl Buck. *The Good Earth*, published in 1931, the year of the Japanese invasion, told the story of an upright Chinese peasant couple forced from their land, like so many Midwestern Dust Bowl victims, and into a callous urban hell. Yet they succeed, in time, to return to their wholesome country lives. The "spiritual content" of the hero-husband, lauded *Christian Century* magazine, would have been just as exemplary had he "toiled on the Nebraska prairie."[16] In a United States in which actual Chinese were scarce, publications like Luce's and Pearl's gave the masses their only exposure to the far-off land and its people—however contrived the protagonists. And the Soongs were only too ready to play their assigned parts.

President Hoover, however, to Luce's chagrin, would not play his. Though his secretary of state, Henry Stimson, urged him to punish Japan with economic sanctions, he condemned such action as "folly"—folly that would lead to "a war [which] could not be localized or kept in bounds."[17] FDR, upon taking office, would echo his predecessor's caution. Yet Chiang not only did not fear such a war but welcomed it, telling U.S. minister in China Nelson Johnson, in May 1932, that it would be one "in which the United States will figure as the champion and savior of China." It would be a war he would fight according to the ancient Chinese stratagem of *yi-yi-zhi-yi*: using one barbarian to break another.[18]

After 1927, Chiang expanded his authority northward by crushing or co-opting provincial warlords. Communist forces, however, following a devastating but heroic six-thousand-mile retreat in 1934–35 known as the "Long March," in which 95 percent of the 86,000 troops perished, came to dominate 120,000 square miles of northwest territory.[19] Meanwhile, the Kwantung Army guarded Japan's commodity and commercial booty in Manchuria—a vast region of coal, iron, timber, and other industrial resources doubling as a buffer against Russia. Four parties, then—the Kuomintang (itself a fratricidal federation), the Communists, Japan, and the Soviet Union—jostled for Chinese territory, resources, and political control. And all the while, the American government observed with intense and ineffectual concern.

In December 1936, Chiang was taken captive by troops under erstwhile ally General Chang Hsueh-liang and compelled, before release under Soviet pressure, to resist Japan in a "United Front" with the Communists. Pearl Buck, whom Americans by now treated as an expert on China matters, observed that "the differences between Chiang [and the Communists] were as grave and irreconcilable as [those] between the black and white races" in the United States; yet these had to be "put aside" to defend China.[20] At long last, Chiang engaged the Japanese invaders in pitched battles, but with disastrous results. Better-armed and trained Japanese forces advanced to capture major cities and southeastern ports. In the Battle of Shanghai, from August to November 1937, Chiang lost over 60 percent of his eighty thousand elite troops.[21]

In December 1937, the Japanese took the Nationalist capital of Nanking, massacring up to 300,000 soldiers and civilians and raping tens of thousands of women. Chiang fled to a new capital in Chungking, but guerrilla forces under his nominal authority, as well as those under Mao, now based in the northern Shaanxi province of Yenan, continued harrying the Japanese from beyond their urban redoubts. Japan had expected the fighting to last three months; but, as stalemate set in, its military tried to break Chinese resistance by blockading seaports and cutting land-based supply lines, the most important of which was the Burma Road, linking China to the British Empire, in the west.

From the Japanese capture of Wuhan in October 1938 to the end of 1941, the Nationalist army would suffer 1.3 million casualties.[22] Chiang showed himself to be a middling military strategist, rendered all the less effective by a coterie of yes-men afraid of angering him with accounts of incompetence and insubordination in the field. The Generalissimo's true gift lay in his

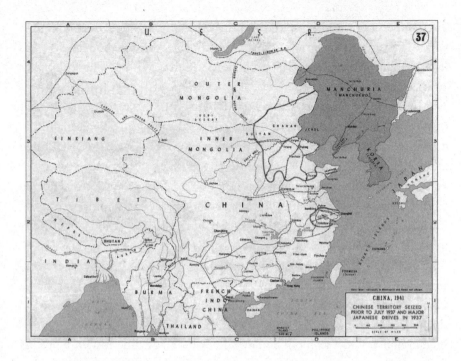

Map showing Chinese territory seized prior to July 1937 and major Japanese military drives in 1937.

ability to stay atop the shambly scaffolding of the KMT, even as it swayed under the strain of graft and intrigue. Though the rivalrous syndicate laid claim to being the party of "government," the sprawling military apparatus consumed 70 percent of its income. After the horrors of 1937, that apparatus was dependent on a mutinous collection of half-starved militias led by inexperienced and poorly trained officers, some of whom could barely read maps.[23] Loyalty, rather than need or competence, often determined how funds were distributed to local commanders, each of whom took his cut before provisioning dragooned peasant troops. The most loyal of these, Hu Tsung-nan and his 400,000 men, stood watch around the Communists' northwest base camp, never engaging the Japanese. Few Americans understood that Chiang, China's presumptive commander in chief, controlled a mere thirty of the Nationalist army's three hundred divisions.[24]

Abroad, however, the prepotent Soong-Kung-Chiang clan held full sway. Its financial interests, from New York to São Paulo, were so intertwined with the state that it was difficult to say where one ended and the other began.[25]

Their conduit to the U.S. media, and through it the political establishment, was a Harvard-educated Mandarin-speaking American contracted by his information ministry in 1938—Theodore (Teddy) White. White's job was straightforward: to pull the United States into conflict with Japan. It was "the [Chiang] government's only hope for survival," he explained. "To sway the American press was critical." They had to "to lie to it, to deceive it, to do anything to persuade America that the future of China and the United States ran together against Japan. That was [their] only war strategy."[26] White did his job well enough that Luce hired him away, a year later, to cover East Asia for *Time* and *Fortune*—a lateral move which took him off Chiang's payroll but widened his reach. After the war, he would work briefly under Henry Wallace at *The New Republic*.[27]

Under political pressure to punish Japan with sanctions, Roosevelt issued an executive order in July 1941 freezing assets in which Japan had a 25 percent or greater interest. Still, he tried not to stoke tensions beyond the boiling point. Resisting calls to end oil sales to the country, he insisted such action would accomplish nothing beyond providing it with a pretext to invade the commodity-rich Dutch East Indies. Morgenthau and Acheson, wanting to take a tougher line, stretched the limits of their authority to make it impossible for Tokyo to transfer dollars to pay for the oil. With an effective embargo now in place, FDR's decision the summer prior to move the Pacific Fleet westward from California to Hawaii—to the Honolulu naval base at Pearl Harbor—would prove fateful. Warned at the time by the fleet's commander, Admiral James Richardson, that the move was provocative, Roosevelt demurred: it would, he insisted, "have a restraining influence" on Japan. In Tokyo, however, the flaw in his logic was obvious. "The fact that the United States has brought a great fleet to Hawaii," observed Japan's Admiral Isoroku Yamamoto, was intended "to show us that it's within striking distance of Japan." Yet it also means, "conversely, that *we're* within striking distance [of them]."[28]

On the morning of December 7, 1941, twenty thousand Japanese troops invaded Malaysia, Singapore, and the Dutch East Indies—to secure the oil America would not sell them. Shortly after, Japanese bombers unleashed a devastating attack on Pearl Harbor, killing 2,403 U.S military personnel and destroying twenty-one naval vessels and over three hundred aircraft.

On the U.S. mainland, the shock and outrage was profound. Back in

Chungking, the mood was joyous. "Chiang was so happy," recorded the writer Han Suyin, that "he sang an old opera aria and played 'Ave Maria' all day." KMT officials "congratulat[ed] each other, as if a great victory had been won." At last, they said, "America was at war with Japan!" This meant "dollars into the pockets of the officials [and] army commanders," as well as guns "for the coming war"—not against Japan, but "against [the Communists in] Yenan."[29]

In Washington, two broad factions skirmished over China policy. On one side was the so-called China Lobby, a disparate amalgam of elected and appointed officials, lobby groups (some KMT-financed), media personalities, industrialists, and civil society leaders who urged U.S. financial and military support of the Nationalists against both Japan and Mao. On the other side were the so-called China Hands at the State Department, led by the three Johns—John Paton Davies, John Carter Vincent, and John Stewart Service. Though they had differing views on the rival personalities in the China theater, they agreed that the United States had few vital interests in the country, that it was too vast for Japan to subdue, that Chiang could not defeat the Communists, and that backing him exclusively would drive Mao to seek Stalin's support. In essence, they believed Washington was best off pursuing its own version of *yi-yi-zhi-yi*: to let Asiatic barbarians exhaust one another until prospects for U.S. intervention were more auspicious.

At this point, Henry Wallace had still given little thought to China policy—at least beyond agriculture, where he held that better policies could boost output 30 percent in ten years. Publicly, he spoke of the country only in airy generalities. At a Congress of American-Soviet Friendship at Madison Square Garden in November 1942, he said that China would, after the war, "have a strong influence on the world," and that "the principles of Sun Yat-sen," whom he admired for his ideas on democracy, decolonization, and progressive economics, would "prove to be as significant as those of any other modern statesman."[30]

A year later, in October 1943, he gave a radio address on the thirty-second anniversary of the Chinese Republic, praising China as "one of the chief inspirers, and indirectly one of the creators, of Western democracy." "A great many of us do not know," he said, "that Chinese philosophy and the approach to democracy . . . exerted a powerful influence on the minds of [Western] political philosophers." They "in turn laid the foundation for . . . our revolution and . . . constitutional government." Imperial Japan, he continued, had "struck at China" to prevent its "construction of a thoroughgoing constitutional democracy," an accomplishment which "was sure to [make] China one of the most powerful nations."[31] These were contentions as bold as they were undocumented.

Wallace had, in his enthusiasm for republican China, seemingly aligned himself with the China Lobby. Yet he had also inverted its evangelism, casting China as the missionary rather than the missioned.

As for Roosevelt, he was, as ever, disinclined to reveal his hand. "[T]he making of FDR's China policy," Sam Rosenman observed, "was almost as great a secret as the atom bomb." It was more accurate to say that there was never a *policy* so much as an *objective*: keeping China in the war. His means were arms, supplies, money, advice, and flattery. "China was to be treated as a great power," observed Davies, "so that it would *become* a great power." More precisely, it would become "a grateful friend" who would help "keep order and peace in the Far East" on America's behalf.[32] In pursuance of this vision, Stimson assigned an unfortunate soldier the Herculean military and diplomatic task of creating and mobilizing an effective fighting force out of Chinese commanders and conscripts over whom he would have no practical authority.

Now in his third tour of China duty, and a month away from earning a coveted fourth star, Army General Joseph Stilwell could converse in Mandarin and swear in multiple dialects. A wiry five feet, nine inches tall, black-haired on top with buzz-cut gray on the sides, framing a broad nose crowned by wire-rimmed spectacles, he had, until the 1940s, endured a career trajectory checked by a lack of polish and tact. In 1939, however, General Marshall, recognizing "Vinegar Joe" as a man of unimpeachable intellectual integrity and single-minded determination, rescued the fifty-six-year-old from an ignominious mandatory retirement (triggered by five years without advancement) by enabling his promotion to brigadier general. He distinguished himself with boldness and tactical ingenuity in war games, earning himself a second star. Following Japan's attack on Pearl Harbor, Marshall tapped him to lead the war's first major U.S. combat mission—an amphibious landing in French West Africa. But in the face of British objections on timing, the assault was shelved. Meanwhile, Hugh Drum, the imperious lieutenant general whom Stimson had intended to send to China, was disparaging the proposed assignment as "nebulous." Thus did the cruel "finger of destiny," as Stimson put it, point Stilwell to Asia in his stead.[33]

Chiang, following acceptance of the gold-plated title of Supreme Commander China Theater from President Roosevelt, which he added to eighty self-bestowed ones, had requested a U.S. officer to serve in the ill-defined role of chief of his Allied staff. He envisioned someone with influence at home and ignorance abroad—someone who brought guns, planes, and dollars without venturing views. Instead, he got Stilwell; Stilwell, who had five other titles in the Pacific theater, and who disdained the idea of being a foreigner's chief of staff ("whatever that is").[34]

If Stilwell was vinegar, Chiang was oil, and the effort to pair them was doomed from the start. Clashing aims fostered bitterness, sharpened by clashing personalities. Needing control of the best Nationalist units to retake the Burma Road, which would open a China supply route for an American assault on Japan, Stilwell instead got an endless stream of exasperating counter-demands and contingent pledges.

Chiang's stonewalling, as Stilwell saw it, was not irrational. He had little interest in sacrificing crack troops and precious matériel in Burma, either to protect British-ruled India or to make a U.S. victory, which he considered only a matter of time, less burdensome. (The U.S. could fly in supplies, albeit at great cost, "over the Hump" of the Himalayas.) Stilwell grasped the hopelessness of his mission, yet, as a good soldier and a bad diplomat, he pursued it remorselessly.

Determined to outmaneuver his assigned barbarian, Chiang turned to what seemed the most promising alternative: a failed former U.S. Army Air Corps pilot.

Afflicted with chronic bronchitis, hearing loss, and a history of tussling with fellow officers, a dejected forty-six-year-old Claire Lee Chennault resigned from military service in April 1937, having achieved the rank of major. His timing, if nothing else, was auspicious. Having two years earlier published a textbook entitled *The Role of Defensive Pursuit*, he came to the attention of a defensive-minded Chinese general in search of aerial expertise—one Chiang

Kai-shek. Only weeks after Chennault arrived in Chungking, in June, as the Generalissimo's chief aviation adviser, Japan and China went to war. The invaders overwhelmed China's fledgling air force, and the American was tasked with rebuilding it using mercenary pilots from his homeland. In Washington, he and the wily, manipulative T.V. Soong (Song Ziwen) worked to secure fighter planes through all means, fair and foul. After the United States entered the Pacific war, the Army co-opted Chennault's "Fighting Tigers" squadron as the official China Air Task Force (later, the 14th Air Force).

Promoted to major general in 1943, the brash, square-jawed, wind-scarred Texan was at constant loggerheads with a superior opposing force—Stilwell. Though Stilwell and the Chinese troops he trained and led had endured, and would continue to endure, enormous hardship to free the northern Burma supply line from Japanese control, Chennault would insist it was all for naught. The war could, he said, be supplied, fought, and won in the air. Japan, Chennault had assured Roosevelt in October 1942, could "be defeated in China . . . by an Air Force so small that in other theaters it would be called ridiculous." If given full authority as the American military commander in China, plus five hundred combat planes and one hundred transports, he would "not only bring about the downfall of Japan but . . . create such good will that China will be a great and friendly trade market for generations."[35]

Chiang knew little of air warfare, but understood that victory by air would nullify the need to fulfill Stilwell's demands—demands that he excise the corruption upon which his life and status depended, and that he commit his best troops to engaging the Japanese where and when the Americans determined. He therefore adopted Chennault's doctrines as readily as he had the Soongs' Methodism. Chennault reciprocated his patron's regard. He assured Roosevelt that Chiang was "one of the two or three greatest military and political leaders in the world today"—one who had "never broken a commitment or promise." Stilwell countered that Chiang, whom he referred to scathingly by his code name, "Peanut," was "a vacillating, tricky, undependable old scoundrel"—one who "never keeps his word."[36] The reality was more subtle. Chiang remained true to Sun Tzu's ancient proposition that "the best of the best is to subdue the enemy without fighting."[37] If this meant deceiving the barbarian who pressed him to commit his best troops unwisely, he did what circumstance required.

Stilwell derided Chennault's promise of easy victory as an amateur's fantasies. Japan, he said, would halt his raids by destroying the airfields on which they depended—airfields that Chiang had neither the will nor the ability to defend. Wallace, practical when it came to things if not people, backed the view that providing sufficient gasoline for an air campaign required the reopening of the Burma Road.[38]

When it came to his two China generals, Roosevelt grasped that one was a diplomatic liability and the other a fabulist. Characteristically, though, he found it difficult to navigate between the unhelpful and the unreal. In July 1943, he freed Chennault to bomb Japan's merchant ships, whereupon its army razed his airfields. Chennault pleaded for more planes. A vindicated Stilwell, who controlled the Lend-Lease spigot, spurned him. By the spring of 1944, the Japanese would overrun all the provinces housing Chennault's forward bases, putting an end to his dream of victory by air.[39]

June 19, 1944. As Henry Wallace's Skymaster rumbled over the Tien-Shan mountains, and the arid, brown, semidesert expanse below, John Carter Vincent briefed him on the region's significance. Situated at the meeting point between the Chinese and Russian Empires, but populated overwhelmingly by Turkish-speaking Muslim Uighurs, Kazaks, Dungans, Kirghize, Mongols, Uzbeks, and Tartars, Sinkiang (Xinjiang) was an ethnic and geopolitical cauldron. Though under Chinese sovereignty, it had long been dominated by local warlords who were obliged to keep peace with their far more powerful Russian neighbors. The Soviets meddled politically and economically, anxious to check not only Chinese but Japanese power. But as Chiang began asserting his authority after 1942, Soviet relations with local rulers worsened. Battles erupted between ethnic Chinese inhabitants and Russians from Outer Mongolia. Absent enlightened policies to pacify the local populations, Vincent told Wallace, Sino-Soviet conflict would slow the defeat of Japan and sow "trouble in the postwar period." Inevitably, the United States would become embroiled.[40]

Emerging from his plane at the airport in Tihwa, with thousands waving their greetings, Wallace entered a waiting car for the muddy drive to the estate of Governor General Sheng Shicai. As in each Siberian stop, officials welcomed him with gifts (here, brightly colored rugs), followed by a vast feast (this one featuring heaping plates of duck, smoked salmon, sausage, salami, cheese, and eggplant, followed by cantaloupe, ice cream, Russian chocolates, port wine, and brandy).[41] Unlike in Siberia, however, Wallace would have nothing kind to say about his host. Sheng, he would tell Roosevelt, was "a typical warlord," ruling through "police surveillance"— something he never saw in Russia. The Sinkiang autocrat, he went on, was "making life extremely difficult for the Soviet Consul General and Soviet citizens in Sinkiang." Whereas Sheng had been "pro-Soviet" two years prior, he was now "anti-Soviet." U.S. consul and embassy officials, Wallace said, laid blame on Chiang's government, which had instigated the shift to reduce Moscow's influence.[42] As for the evening entertainment, it "was poorly put on compared with Russian standards."[43] This was perhaps unfair to the Chinese, who did not have the same access to dragooned talent.

The next morning, June 20, the Americans flew to Chungking, a rocky promontory in the juncture of the Yangtze and Chialing Rivers, and Chiang's provisional capital since abandoning Nanking to the Japanese seven years earlier. Correspondent Eric Sevareid described the city as "a scorched battered fortress." Two-toned in "gray and black," it was "ugly beyond words." Preparations for the vice president's visit had begun in May, with a "large-scale beggar [and] street-urchin roundup." Police snatched up children who clashed with the welcome decorations, roping them together and marching them down the streets—to where, John Service never learned.[44]

Wallace alighted onto the baking tarmac at Pei Shih Yi airfield, Panama hat in hand. A smiling Generalissimo approached, shaking his hand. Behind him stood a coterie of Chinese diplomats, as well as the chiefs of nearly all the foreign missions.[45] Among these dignitaries was Tikhon Fedorovich Skvortsov. Forty-five years old, the bookish Soviet chargé d'affaires had been born into a Chuvash village peasant family in Kazan Gubernia, near northwest Kazakhstan. He joined the Bolshevik movement in 1916, while working as a ship builder's accountant in Vladivostok. After studying Asian history and Chinese language, he set out, in 1925, on a career as a translator, scholar, and diplomat. Now on his second tour at the Soviet embassy in China,[46] he was about to embark on his most important assignment. With the ambassador, Alexander Panyushkin, having been recalled to Moscow "for treatment," a cover to protect his NKGB intelligence work until the next posting (as ambassador to Washington), Skvortsov was determined to find out all he could about Wallace's mission.

Just prior to the plane's arrival, Skvortsov had struck up a conversation with the U.S. ambassador, Clarence Gauss. How long would the vice president be staying in China? Gauss was unsure. What stops would he take on his way home? He would stay four days in Sinkiang, then visit Kunming, Guilin, and Chengdu. Would Soviet pilots accompany him? No; they had remained in Alma-Ata, but would rejoin him in Ulan Bator.

As Wallace's team disembarked, Skvortsov now fixed on Vincent. He approached, introducing himself. The two then chatted amiably about the vice president's travels in Siberia. "The Soviet Union," the chargé would later type out for Moscow, together with Gauss' details on Wallace's plans, "had made an extraordinarily great impression on Wallace."[47] The Siberian operation had, apparently, been a success.

Chiang led Wallace toward his presidential limousine, a 1939 Cadillac, in front of which was waiting his impeccably coiffed wife. As the two men ambled, a white-gloved band began playing the "The Star-Spangled Banner." Wallace stopped, but Chiang, oblivious of his guest or protocol, kept right on walking, eyes straight ahead. A panicked aide rushed up to whisper in his ear, but, failing to make himself heard, shuffled in pace, trying again and again. Vincent suppressed a laugh. "Life in Chungking," he thought, "as crazy as ever." Finally, the Gissimo, as Stilwell called him, stopped abruptly. Now isolated and unnerved, he stood alone until the foreign music ceased.

Newsmen jostled, grabbing sheets of paper from a U.S. embassy official. The vice president, the handouts said, expressed his wish that the long and contested Sino-Soviet border would soon be as peaceful as the U.S.-Canadian one.[48] To realize this wish, Wallace aimed to convince Chiang of the importance of compromise with Stalin, both to bring victory in the Pacific war and to limit friction in its aftermath.

Though Madame Chiang had urged Wallace to stay a full four nights at the presidential villa, Vincent, worried that he might fall under the couple's spell, persuaded him to spend the first one at the ambassador's residence. Waiting there to brief him was a team of glum U.S. experts.

The situation in the country, Gauss concluded for Wallace, was desperate. Economic breakdown, political discord, and military defeat had rendered China a shaky partner in the struggle against Japan.

Though the brooding ambassador, whom FDR had marginalized to the point of irrelevance, disliked presidential envoys as much as he did New Dealers, Wallace's open mind impressed him. Vincent, too, was optimistic about the vice president's visit. Having two years earlier seen prior presidential emissaries, economist Lauchlin Currie and 1940 Republican presidential candidate Wendell Willkie, seduced by Madame Chiang and the Generalissimo's propaganda, he, like Gauss, was angered at the State Department's emasculation. But he was hopeful that Wallace, as a progressive icon, might encourage liberal elements in the country to push for political reform.

Vincent had assembled for Wallace briefings of various authorship disparaging Chiang as a "Chinese militarist" whose politics were formed by a "Japanese military education," an "alliance with usurious banker-landlord[s]," "limited intelligence," and adherence to "sterile moralisms." They described the Communists as "agrarian democrat[s]" with "strong popular support" whose policy views were "far removed from orthodox Communism." CCP forces moreover, had allegedly defeated the Japanese in Shantung, Hopei, Shansi, and North Kiangsu. That little of this could be verified only highlighted the importance of convincing Chiang to reverse his policy of blocking U.S. observers from entering Communist-controlled territory—where Mao's deputy, Zhou Enlai, had assured Vincent they would be welcome.[49] Being close to a large Japanese force concentration and industrial base, and a likely target for any Soviet military incursion, the region offered the U.S. military unparalleled intelligence-gathering opportunities.[50]

As the vice president's briefing with the ambassador proceeded, Vincent went off with his old friend Service, now an adviser to Stilwell aide Brigadier General Benjamin Ferris. Service had prepared a long memorandum for the vice president, in crisp, outline form, salient points italicized, arguing that present U.S. policy, fixated as it was on "mollycoddling" Chiang, was failing to counter Japanese strategy in the country or to halt its political collapse. "Our part," he concluded, "must be that of catalytic agent in [the] process of China's democratization." As with similarly minded State Department tracts, the pathway to "democratization" in the vast, fractious, war-torn nation was left to speculation. Vincent, nonetheless, endorsed the document and promised to pass it on to Wallace.

The next morning, June 21, clouds gathered and it began to drizzle—

a good omen for an early Szechuan summer. Newspapers were full of optimistic accounts of what the vice president's Asian tour meant for Sino-American, and Sino-Soviet, cooperation in the war effort.[51] Wallace toured the city and worked off his feasting at the nearby enlisted men's quarters, playing shirtless volleyball with GIs in pouring rain. After cleaning up, he donned a suit and two wristwatches—one local time, one Eastern Standard Time[52]—and headed off to lunch with Minister of War Ho Ying-chin. Again, the meeting was nothing like those inspirational ones in Russia. He dismissed Ho as an "anti-communist." Ditto Agriculture Minister Shen Hung-lieh. Education Minister Chen Le-fu he condemned as a "reactionary party politician" who was blocking any "liberalizing social influence."[53] For FDR, however, only one politician in Chungking mattered.

At 5 p.m. on June 21, 1944, the vice president arrived at the Generalissimo's residence for their first round of formal talks. For Wallace, these would be the most important official meetings of his career, a chance to shape both the course of the Pacific war and its legacy.

Five feet, eight inches tall, slight of build, with shaven head, groomed mustache, sculpted cheeks, elven ears, an intense black-eyed gaze, high staccato voice, and heavy Ningbo accent, the khaki-clad fifty-six-year-old Chiang had, since Japan's invasion seven years earlier, both inspired and infuriated Washington. *Time*'s Man of the Year in 1937, he would, now, be widely seen by U.S. officials as an unfaithful and self-obsessed ally. Stilwell would later claim to have had orders from FDR, delivered orally at the Cairo Conference in December 1943, to plan for his possible termination. "If you can't get along with Chiang," the president allegedly said, "and can't replace him, get rid of him once and for all. You know what I mean, put in someone you can manage."[54]

For Americans who would render him hero or villain, Chiang was uncooperative. He was a nationalist authoritarian, bitter at the historic humiliations China had suffered at imperialist foreign hands. He was also a left-Confucian Christian convert, publicly (at least) committed to building democratic institutions with Chinese characteristics. He was a moralist, yet willing to resort to ruthless tactics and unsavory methods—such as the mass killing of unarmed Communist strikers, or funding armies with opium taxes. He was hypocritical, but not cynical. He said openly that "the roots of the CCP," his greatest enemy, lay "in the inefficiency and corruption" of his own government, yet, in the interests of party unity and personal survival, he overlooked systematic venality among cooperative subordinates. He was introverted, self-pitying, and humorless, yet had a magnetism and regal bearing that awed viewers in spite of his boyish frame. In public he wore a constant smile, yet in private was prone to bouts of sobbing and rage. Unliked by most peers, even enemies recognized his courage and stern will.

Stilwell called Chiang "a stubborn, ignorant, prejudiced, conceited despot," yet acknowledged that it took a certain genius to dominate the KMT as long as he had. He masterfully balanced jealous factions and cultivated the myth of his indispensability. Looking outward, he was a perspicacious geostrategic thinker, one whose understanding of Japanese, American, and Soviet objectives, and record of anticipating their behavior, was far better than that of the barbarian experts he routinely outwitted. He was, Stilwell said in a rare reflective moment, "the most astute politician of the 20th century." He had to be, "or he wouldn't be alive."[55]

Wallace began the discussion by relaying FDR's concerns about the state of KMT-CCP relations. Both groups being Chinese, the president had insisted, they should be able to resolve differences as "friends." But if not, Roosevelt might be the friend who could bring them together. To underline the point, the president drew the distinction between himself and Churchill; it was only he, Roosevelt, who believed in China as a great power.

Wallace said that it was vital for China and the Soviet Union, as two of the world's four great powers, to resolve differences and avoid conflict. According to Chiang's diary, Wallace also referred to his trip to Siberia, which confirmed for him that Russia was "one of the most scientifically advanced countries" in the world, with a solid industrial, governmental, and military base. "The United States will not," Wallace added, presumably to counsel Chiang of the need to compromise, "abandon its relations with Russia."

T.V. Soong, Chiang's forty-nine-year-old foreign minister and brother-in-law, translated. Chiang listened, stoically. He had no interest in friendship with Communists. Anxious, however, to see far-off barbarians check the more dangerous neighboring ones, he suggested to Wallace that the president might act as a "middleman" with the Soviets.

Vincent blanched, seeing what Chiang was up to. Hull had been adamant that Wallace not drag the United States into Sino-Soviet mediation.[56] There were sensitive territorial and commercial questions that FDR would have to resolve with Stalin, secretly, in order to engage the Soviets in the Pacific war. Chiang would need to be kept in the dark about these. When Wallace sidestepped Chiang's suggestion, then, Vincent felt relief.

Stalin, Wallace said, had stressed to Ambassador Harriman the importance of China uniting, Nationalists and Communists, in the struggle against Japan. Chiang brightened; he asked to see Harriman's memo on the talks, eager for evidence that Stalin was not plotting his overthrow. Wallace said he had no copy, but asked Vincent, who had conferred at length with the ambassador, to follow up with Soong. The group broke off after an hour, at 6 p.m., to prepare for the State Banquet at 8 p.m.

Two hours later, following a procession of welcome speeches and victory toasts with Shao-hsing rice wine, the obligatory feast ensued. Vincent, ever-alert for a vice presidential slipup, now found himself the unwelcome focus of attention. T.V. took him aside, asking to see his notes on Stalin's meeting with Harriman. Vincent said that he would not violate diplomatic protocol, but assured T.V. that Stalin would support Chiang during the war. As a "practical matter," and ignoring "ideological considerations," Stalin had "a keen interest" in cooperation between the KMT and CCP. It meant "more effective fighting against Japan." Satisfied, T.V. thanked him and moved on to other guests.[57]

Nearby, Skvortsov scanned the floor for possible sources of intelligence. Vincent, anxious to avoid further politics till the morning, departed for his room; but the chargé found other Americans—by that point, presumably well lubricated—happy to engage.

"What we saw [in Siberia] exceeded our expectations," Lattimore told him. "The example of the Soviet approach to the national question is worthy of imitation." The Russian guides did "too much for us," John Hazard, Wallace's Russian translator, enthused to Skvortsov's wife. "We were given opportunities to visit whatever we wanted." The chargé would later transcribe the comments for Moscow, adding that the vice president's dinner speech stressed the need to improve Sino-Soviet relations.[58] His call might be helpful to the Kremlin in securing concessions from Chungking.

⁂

On the morning of June 22, Wallace breakfasted with Chiang before being driven to the outskirts of the city to indulge his agricultural passions. Wearing black rubber boots, he "sloshed happily about [in] the water-soaked fields." Presenting long American hoes to the bemused farmers, he explained how they would end the need for stooping and boost output. Wallace enjoyed the visit, even if the farmers refused to use the barbarian hoes. He lunched with the agriculture minister, Shen Hung-lieh, concluding that he knew "little about agriculture."[59]

At 4:30 p.m., he resumed talks with Chiang. He opened by voicing concern about "the poor showing" Chinese troops were making, recounting a story he had heard of angry peasants attacking KMT soldiers "running away from the Japanese" in Honan (Henan). Chiang did not deny the account, but explained that it owed to "a loss of morale" resulting from "the economic situation"—particularly rising prices.

Chiang steered blame toward Washington. The Chinese people, he said, had been fighting for seven years, enduring great hardship, and they "expected help from abroad." Hadn't President Roosevelt, at Cairo in November 1943, "promised an all-out campaign in Burma early in 1944"? The failure to follow through had left the Chinese people feeling "deserted." Wallace said only that he "did not recall the details" of his talks with the president on this matter.

Chiang then questioned "the attitude of the American Army," which showed no confidence in China. He singled out Stilwell—"apologetically, but with obvious intent," according to Vincent's notes—for being "uncooperative." Stilwell was supposed to be his chief of staff, yet he had denied even the modest request for one thousand additional tons of gasoline to support the air campaign in Honan, suggesting the general bore blame for the defeat. Chiang added that the American press was, too, undermining hope in China. Their carping "should be stopped."

Chiang now turned his ire on the Communists. Referring to Roosevelt's belief that all Chinese should be "friends" in the war with Japan, he insisted that "the Chinese people did not regard the Communists as Chinese." They took their orders from the "Third International."

Stalin, Wallace corrected, had dissolved the Third International in 1943, but Chiang replied that Communist behavior remained the same. Wallace persisted, pointing out that American Communists maintained a "patriotic attitude"; surely it should be the same in China? Chiang countered that there was a difference, in that "there was no possibility of the American Communists seizing power." The CCP, in contrast, intended to do so. And whereas Stalin had dismissed the CCP as "margarine Communists," Chiang—laughing—remarked that they were, in fact, "more communistic than the Russian[s]."[60]

Vincent pressed for details on talks with the CCP over cooperation and offensive action against the Japanese. Chiang offered only that KMT demands were simple: "support the President, support the Government, support the war effort." That meant "obedience" and incorporation of Communist forces into the Chinese army, as well as integration of Communist-controlled territory into the state administrative apparatus. If they acceded to these demands, they would be guaranteed political amnesty and treated as a normal political party. Further, he would grant the request for U.S. military officers to visit the north and, under government auspices, to train "converted" Communist troops. President Roosevelt should be aware, however, that the more attention the United States paid to Communist "propaganda" the less willing they would be to reach a settlement.

Wallace said he feared that the "attitude" of Chiang and his ministers "threatened" China's relations with the USSR. If, as the Generalissimo said, the Communists were allied with the USSR then a settlement was needed all the more. Chiang responded that the U.S. Army was overestimating "the utility of Communists against the Japanese." Whereas he understood that the Army was anxious to boost Chinese firepower, it was underestimating "the threat which the Communists constituted to the Chinese government" itself. Wallace and Vincent pushed for a U.S. Army intelligence group to be allowed into the north now, prior to a settlement, with a view to maximizing pressure on Japanese forces in the region. But Chiang resisted. "Haste does not make for speed," he concluded obliquely. "Please do not press." On this off-note, they adjourned at 7:30.

Never far from Wallace's mind was the Soviet interest in China. Telling his trusted translator, John Hazard, that he didn't want the Russians to "feel left out," he asked him to visit their embassy.[61]

When in 1934, at the age of twenty-five, Hazard, fresh out of Harvard Law School, set off to become the first American to study Soviet law at the

Moscow Juridical Institute, friends were disbelieving. "My God, the guy's nuts," thought classmate Whitman Knapp. Who wanted to live in god-forsaken Communist Russia? Hazard would go on to become a specialist in housing shortages and, in the words of his memoir title, "a pioneering Sovietologist."[62]

Welcomed by Skvortsov at the embassy on the morning of June 23, the American explained that he had come "to practice his Russian." The chargé was delighted; it was rare that prey sought out hunters. "He is exceptionally chatty," Skvortsov would tell Moscow, approvingly. "It is easy to make him talk for hours."[63]

By Hazard's own account of his career, awkwardly rendered in the third person, he enjoyed talking more than he should. So enchanting did he find Madame Chiang, for example, that he would, "had he known any state secrets, . . . been induced to divulge them."[64]

Having persuaded Hazard to join him for a late breakfast (or, by the latter's account, an early lunch), Skvortsov asked how his delegation had got on in Siberia. Picking up where he had left off two nights ago, Hazard lavished praise on Soviet feats in culture, farming, and military production, singling out their guides—Nikishov, Goglidze, and Semenov—as "talented people."

Talking "without pause," Skvortsov noted, Hazard shifted to China. He offered that Wallace had formed "a positive impression of Sheng Shicai"—a onetime Communist Sinkiang warlord who had fallen in and out of Soviet graces since the mid-1930s, before being co-opted by Chiang as a powerless agriculture minister in 1944. Skvortsov took this revelation as an invitation to probe further.

With what other Chinese leaders had Wallace met? Hazard went down the list. Wallace, he said, was chagrined that the "progressive elements" among them—such as Sun-Fo (a left-wing KMT official) and Madame Sun Yat-sen—"had been pushed aside." NKID officials would later affirm Wallace's support for these figures.[65]

And what had they discussed? Wallace, Hazard said, "pointed to the great achievements of the Soviet Union, and the need to improve relations between China and the USSR." Still, Hazard added, Wallace "did not vest much hope in China. Only the Russians," he said, "were able to conduct real combat actions against Japan." Skvortsov made note of this alleged fact.

The Chinese, Hazard continued, "were unhappy with Wallace's speech of June 21," in which he called for self-government of national minorities—understood as support for Tibetan and Mongolian independence. The latter, Skvortsov knew, was high on Stalin's wish list, as it would reduce Chinese influence near the Soviet border. The NKID would therefore wish to learn more about Wallace's views on the matter. The Chinese, Hazard went on, were further displeased that Wallace planned to stay in China only ten or eleven days, given that he had spent four weeks in the Soviet Union.

And what, Skvortsov asked, did Hazard make of the upcoming U.S. elections? A majority would vote for Roosevelt, the American opined, but many would still "be against [him], mainly because Roosevelt was old and could die" in office. "Wallace would [then] become president, which certain people feared because Wallace was 'too democratic' (slishkom demokratichnyi)"—signifying, in Russian, too open or accessible to dignify the job.

He himself, Hazard added with seeming pride, was "considered a Bolshevik." He highlighted his personal bonds with Litvinov and Gromyko, recounting the time he had bummed a ride to the White House with the ambassador so he wouldn't have to "show his pass to the guards."[66]

Hazard's memoirs reveal nothing of his discussions with Skvortsov, except that they were "light and full of fun." He was nonetheless "sure that the whole affair was reported back to Moscow" [67]—as, of course, it was.

After Hazard took his leave, satisfied that "Wallace's goodwill" would be favorably noted in Moscow,[68] Skvortsov sat down to write out his notes. These would feature in a lengthy August 17 NKID Far Eastern Department report on the "Trip of Vice-President Wallace to China," which would conclude that Hazard had disclosed "the real purpose of [Wallace's] flattering review of the Soviet Union" as well as his "call to the Chinese to improve relations with the USSR." It was that the Americans lacked faith in China's fighting ability, and would need the Soviets to fight Japan.[69]

The report suggested a remarkable diplomatic failure on Wallace's part—a failure to convince Soviet officials of the sincerity of his admiration for their accomplishments and his desire to move American and Chinese policy in their favor. Even after stealing his diary in Siberia and finding no evidence of deception, they persisted in believing that he had to have ulterior motives. As for Hazard, the American's "eagerness to 'practice' Russian," Skvortsov concluded, "may be put to good use" again in the future.[70]

⁂

After the previous day's difficult discussions, both Wallace and Chiang saw the need to change tack and restore amity. Wallace was "exhausted and depressed." Vincent feared he was losing interest in the whole China mission. But he convinced him to press for the Army observer expedition by downplaying its *political* significance, which was too sensitive for Chiang, and spotlighting the *military* perspective.[71] Chiang, for his part, decided to drop the requirement for a political settlement in advance of U.S. contact with Mao's forces.

The two sides resumed talks at 9 a.m. on June 23. Wallace began by recounting his discussions with Marshall and Stimson before departing for Asia, stressing the concern in Washington that the war be brought to the speediest possible end with a minimum additional loss of American lives. Sending the Army group to North China would allow intelligence-gathering that would "save the lives of American aviators." The Army, he said, "had no interest whatsoever in Communists but . . . had for very urgent reasons an interest in carrying on the war against Japan from China." He beseeched Chiang to decouple matters of war from those of politics.

To his surprise, Chiang was amenable. Provided the American group went under the auspices of the National Military Council, together with Chinese officers, he would approve. Still, he urged Wallace, on his return to Washington, to make it clear that the Communists must come to terms with the government. "Please tell President Roosevelt," he said, "that I will follow his advice, but I must insist on the maintenance of law and order." He would allow contact with the Communists, but wanted a commitment that Roosevelt would pressure them to affirm his authority.

Wallace dodged the snare, stressing that timely understanding with the CCP was needed to curb conflict with Moscow. But for an agreement to stick, Chiang had to "improve the economic lot of the Chinese people." Otherwise the Communists would bolt. "It [will] take much energy and foresight," he added provocatively, "for the Chinese Government to avoid the fate of the Kerensky Government in Russia"—which was overthrown by the Bolsheviks eight months after taking power in March 1917. Chiang replied coldly, saying he "was proceeding with these considerations in mind." They broke off at 11 a.m.

꙳

Troubled that Chiang was still ignoring American pleas for economic re-form, Vincent was nonetheless elated at the apparent breakthrough on the observer mission. Over lunch at Gauss' residence, Ferris and Service briefed Wallace on what they hoped to accomplish in Yenan.

Shortly before 5 p.m., the vice president left in a "big old Cadillac" for the final official meeting at the Generalissimo's suburban summer residence. En route, a dog ran at the vehicle, which the Chinese driver ignored. As the car thumped, twice, over the canine, Service caught Wallace's face. "I thought he was going to be sick."

Arriving at the residence, the Americans found Chiang in a coopera-tive mood. After a brief semantic debate, terms for the observer mission, to begin in one month's time, were agreed. Enabling the Dixie Mission—so named for the crossing of American representatives into "Confederate" rebel territory—would be Wallace's most notable achievement in Chung-king. Mao and Zhou would welcome the visitors, seeing a genuine oppor-tunity for immediate military collaboration against the Japanese as well as postwar political cooperation.[72] Were it not for the inept diplomacy of his successor emissary, Patrick Hurley, and Chiang's tragic failure to see that his government's survival rested on timely compromise with the Commu-nists, it might have been a historically monumental achievement as well.

An ebullient Vincent had wished to close discussions there, but Wallace made a strange and unexpected interjection. Pivoting back to Sino-Soviet relations, he told Chiang that whereas the Russians had no "territorial am-bitions in the Far East," they would want access to a warm-water Asiatic port. The president, he said, had suggested that the Japanese-occupied port city of Dairen (Dalian)—at the southern tip of China's Liaoning province, and controlled by the Russians from 1898 to 1905—might, after liberation, be made a free port. He qualified his remark, stating that he was "not acting under instructions from President Roosevelt or speaking officially."

Chiang's shock on hearing that the Soviets had "no territorial ambitions" in the region can only be imagined. Stalin had long sought "suzerainty over at least Manchuria and Korea," in Davies' words, as well as sovereignty over islands of northern Japan. Wallace himself could not have believed his own utterance, having in March diaried that Russia would, after the war, "want to establish new security frontiers. The [only] question," he added, "is how far . . . she will move into Western Asia; how far into Northern China and Manchuria."

Chiang replied to Wallace by saying only that the matter of the port could be discussed in the future, "provided there was no impairment of Chinese sovereignty"—the same response he had given at Cairo. But he also suggested that the United States "sponsor" a Sino-Soviet meeting to discuss relations, shrewdly renewing his effort to make Washington a mediator—and thus ensuring it made no Chinese gifts to Stalin behind his back. Vincent objected, insisting that Sino-Soviet problems be kept separate from wider "North Pacific" matters. Only the latter, he said, should involve the United States. Madame Chiang suggested, in that case, that a "North Pacific Conference" be convened, to which T.V. added that it might usefully "be used as a cloak for discussions between Chinese and Soviet representatives." Wallace, to Vincent's relief, withheld his endorsement, and the two sides adjourned at 7 p.m.[73]

On the morning of June 24, the vice president prepared to leave Chiang's residence for the hour's drive to the airport. Madame took him aside, suggesting that he ride with her and the Generalissimo—that is, without his translator and rapporteur. Wallace agreed. Vincent, fearing Wallace's susceptibility to the couple's wiles, was alarmed. Chiang had, in fact, been waiting for this opportunity to make his most important request.

Warming up his captive American guest, he walked back the criticisms he had, defensively and perhaps imprudently, leveled at Roosevelt on June 22, following Wallace's unwelcome comments on the "poor showing" of Chinese troops. He asked Wallace to pass on his gratitude to the president for his support since Cairo, and for sending the vice president to China as his representative. Wallace, he said, should assure Roosevelt that he had understood the necessity of the change in Pacific war plans at the 1943 Tehran conference. As regards the president's wish for Chinese unity, Chiang welcomed his help but warned that the conflict was "not like that between capitalism and labor in the United States." If he trusted the Communists, the president's "prestige would suffer a great loss." These were "not men of good faith."

Chiang now came to his ask. Cooperation between the U.S. and Chinese militaries, he told Wallace, was "very difficult because of personnel." The president should therefore appoint a personal representative to "handle both political and military matters." Stilwell, he observed, had "no understanding of political matters—he is entirely military in outlook." Chennault, in contrast, was "most cooperative." The message was as clear as diplomatic propriety allowed: Wallace should press the president to replace Stilwell with Chennault.

Wallace made no promises, but was excited by the chance to alter the failing diplomatic dynamic. "I was deeply moved," he would later record, "by the cry of a man in great trouble. And I was moved to start in and help him as soon as possible."[74]

Arriving at the airport, Wallace bid farewell to the Chiangs, now convinced that his days in Chungking had not been in vain. And as the Generalissimo watched the vice president's Skymaster recede southward through the skies, he, too, had reason to be pleased. He had timed his request well. In just a few hours, Wallace would touch down four hundred miles to the south, in Kunming—a short drive from the rice paddies surrounding the house of Major General Claire Chennault.

Vincent, like Wallace, was now in a fine mood. Having been unnerved at seeing the vice president abuse protocol by negotiating without a State Department translator, he was surprised to see good results. He agreed with Wallace that "it was an unmanageable situation to have an American commander in China who did not enjoy the Generalissimo's confidence." Both believed Stilwell needed to go.

So, too, did Joseph Alsop. Alsop, a conservative patrician journalist, distant cousin to the president and protégé to Harry Hopkins, was now a military aide, press officer, and all-around fixer for General Chennault. Deputizing for the boss, who loathed visiting notables, Alsop shepherded the vice president "through the standard, ghastly schedule for VIPs." Wallace showed his own disdain for the routine by, once again, "dragooning reluctant sergeants into volleyball games."

On the evening of June 26, the three men—Wallace, Vincent, and Alsop—sat down to business. Unlike in Chungking, there was no musing about democracy, liberal elements, or reform. The issue was Stilwell. Alsop, whom the general referred to as "Alslop," had denounced him to Hopkins as a military and diplomatic incompetent, and was only too pleased for the vice president to complete the task of getting him removed.

Yet Wallace hesitated. Belatedly it dawned on him that he had never actually met Stilwell, who was 330 miles away, in Burma, leading Chinese forces in a heroic battle to hold Myitkyina and take Mogaung.[75] Having declined the general's invitation to visit him in the field, Wallace was, in his own words, now "disturbed" at the thought of "making far-reaching recommendations"—even "drastic" ones—"without having had an opportunity to consult the Theater Commander."[76]

Alsop pressed the vice president to see the urgency of the matter. But Wallace "returned to this point several times"—that he had never spoken with Stilwell, and could therefore not take a stand. Alsop despaired; the chance seemed lost. Wallace needed a push; but from where? From Vincent? "Vincent was a bureaucrat," he lamented, and such men didn't stick their necks out. Vincent, however, *also* pressed the vice president to act.

Wallace was startled. He had not expected such strength of feeling. After hearing both men out, he came back around. It was, he concluded, his best chance to do something historic in China. He resolved to advise the president to replace Stilwell with Chennault.

Alsop assured Wallace that Stilwell's departure would boost the war effort. But he cautioned him *not* to press for Chennault. Chennault, he said, was more urgently needed to lead the Chinese air force. Moreover, the Pentagon hated him, and would spare no effort to stop his appointment.

Whether Alsop had other, unstated, reasons for opposing his boss' promotion is unknown, but Chennault himself appeared only to want more military authority—and not Stilwell's political role. In any case, Alsop suggested that Wallace back the Mandarin-speaking forty-seven-year-old Army General Albert Wedemeyer—a man Stilwell called the "the world's most pompous prick." Rangy, imposing, a match for Stilwell in intelligence and self-assurance, Wedemeyer was less prone to issuing colorful insults. Wallace, who had never met this general either, readily agreed.

Alsop was elated. Still, he was stunned to see that a vice president could be so rash and malleable. "Vincent might better have held Wallace back," he later reflected, "instead of urging him on . . . to such drastic, impulsive action." After all, "the circumstances were a bit ludicrous. . . . Wallace was boldly advising the transplantation of generals he had never seen." Stranger still, Wallace's views were actually more similar to Stilwell's, who backed Chinese political reform and opposed British colonialism, than they were to those of the stern, anti-Communist Wedemeyer.

Alsop also knew that, as "a mere lieutenant," his own behavior, in calling for the removal of a general, had been "outrageously improper [and] perhaps a court-martial offense." Nonetheless, after a few hours of collaborative composition, Wallace's cable was typed and filed through the consulate in Kunming, from where it was sent on June 28.[77] Wallace would call the cable, urging the president to replace Stilwell with Wedemeyer before China was "lost," his "most important contribution" to the Pacific war effort.[78] But this was not to be.

Back in Washington, FDR, preoccupied with matters such as finding a new vice president, gave the "Kunming Cable" the attention Marshall said it deserved. Though signed by Wallace, the missive was, the Army chief of staff concluded, nothing more than Alsop's "usual poison." In a July 4 memo to the president, Marshall excoriated the combat efforts of Chiang and Chennault and lauded Stilwell as the only man "able to get Chinese forces to fight . . . the Japanese in an effective way."[79]

Indeed, the Stilwell-led "Expeditionary Force" of Nationalist troops was arguably the best-trained and most disciplined in Chinese history, and their performance was the only reason the advancing Japanese had not yet reached Chungking.[80] Stilwell's Upper Burma campaign would also prove to be among the war's few major Chinese combat successes—even if belated, costly, and ultimately inconsequential for the war's outcome.

Dismissing Wallace's advice, Roosevelt did the opposite. He approved Stilwell's promotion to four-star general (a rank held only by Marshall, Dwight Eisenhower, Douglas MacArthur, and Hap Arnold), and wrote to Chiang on July 7 demanding that the American be given the authority to command *all* Chinese forces, including those allied with the Communists. To eliminate the risk of T.V. or Mei-ling softening the message, he ordered General Ferris to deliver it personally, with Service translating orally.[81]

It was a bitter blow for the Generalissimo, who accepted it with a stoic "I understand." He then inverted his teacup—a sign that the meeting was over. Wallace would, three days later, tell the press that China's situation was "very grave," leading Chiang to suspect that the vice president had double-crossed him by instigating the Stilwell coup.[82] To his diary, Chiang pledged to exercise "self-mastery" and "wait for my opportunity."[83]

Determined to dilute Stilwell's authority, Chiang continued to press Roosevelt, through Kung in Washington, to send a "political" representative. The president demurred, saying there were no suitable candidates. Among those of sufficient rank, he said, MacArthur was "preoccupied," Hopkins "ill," and Wallace "ignorant of the facts"—a telling commentary on the man he had sent to Chungking as his emissary.[84]

Yet in imagining that Chiang would ever hand over his entire army to a barbarian, Roosevelt was deceiving himself. Not only was the issue one of fundamental sovereignty and national honor; Chiang needed his loyal divisions to protect him from party rivals, and needed the rivals kept free of U.S. arms and training.

Conflict over control of Chinese forces would reach its bitter apex in September. Chiang wanted his best forces to repel the Japanese Ichi-go onslaught in central China; Stilwell wanted them to aid the battle in Burma. He further wanted the power to arm and command Communist troops. When he demanded Chiang's assent, in writing and in fact, Chiang refused and demanded his recall.[85]

An angry Marshall told Roosevelt to cut off aid, but the president would not abet Chiang's collapse on the eve of an American election.[86] Through his newest novice envoy, Patrick Hurley, a voluble Oklahoma lawyer who called Chiang "Mr. Shek," he invited the Generalissimo to suggest acceptable replacements. Chiang named Generals Alexander Patch, Walter Krueger, and Albert Wedemeyer. This time, Roosevelt consented to Wedemeyer.[87]

On October 20, 1944, a triumphant but magnanimous Chiang summoned his departing American nemesis to bestow upon him the Grand Cordon of the Blue Sky and White Sun—China's highest honor. Chiang could, Stilwell told his aide, "stick it up his arse."[88]

John Paton Davies Jr., then thirty-six, was born in Szechuan province to Christian missionary parents. Unlike fellow preacher progeny Henry Luce, however, the lanky, sharp-witted Davies learned Mandarin and grew to regard China as it *was*, rather than for what it might be under imaginary

Christian rulers. Joining the Foreign Service in 1931, he was posted to China two years later, and since February 1942 had been Stilwell's trusted political attaché.

Lacking Stilwell's unconstrained crudity, Davies was still comparably possessed of a career-menacing impulse to say what he thought. While Washington was fêting Chiang as "the unflinching Christian commander of four hundred million tillers of Pearl Buck's good earth," and his wife as a "faithful helpmeet," Davies insisted the couple were leading it into a political and military quagmire that would damage its regional influence.[89]

Davies' obsession was divining and countering Soviet ambitions in Asia. "We are going to blunder through to a victory in this war," he wrote to his wife in March 1943, but it will soon be "followed by another war" with Moscow or its clients. He conceded the need to focus on the present crisis, but thought it at least as important to plan for the next one.[90]

To Stilwell he wrote, in September 1943, of his concern that the Soviet Union, "in seeking to establish its new strategic frontiers, will expand into territories which the other three powers, also for strategic reasons, wish to remain independent." What, he wondered, were "Russian plans for the use of their Korean division?" And what will they do when Chiang, once again, turns on Mao? "[I]f the Chinese Communists are driven to seek Russian aid because of Chungking attacks, does the Kremlin intend to utilize [them] as satellites, and any territory which they may, with Russian arms, hold or capture [in] North China or Manchuria?"[91] Such questions would prove prescient.

Davies' concerns heightened in November 1943, watching Roosevelt at the Allied leaders conferences in Cairo and Tehran. The president, he observed, thought he had to bribe "Chiang to stay in the war against Japan and Stalin to enter it." Each, however, would do, out of naked self-interest, exactly "what Roosevelt thought he had to pay them to do."

Chiang needed to stand with the victors to claim disputed territory—in particular, Manchuria and Formosa (Taiwan). His repeated threats to exit the war, and hints that he might do a deal with Japan, were therefore idle. Stalin, for his part, had every incentive to attack Japan once the United States had sufficiently weakened it, as doing so was his quickest and cheapest path to regional expansion.

"The president's liberality with other people's real estate," Davies said, was "meant to [temper] the Gimo's dislike of foreign devils and Stalin's Bolshevik prejudices against American imperialists, and so further great power solidarity."[92] Yet FDR was hardly helping solidarity between the Asian neighbors in hinting to Stalin that concessions *in China itself* were possible. He was, however, seeking more than Russia's alliance in war—he hoped to sustain it in peace. By giving Stalin chunks of China through a Sino-Soviet treaty, he hoped to prevent his shifting support from Chiang to Mao.

Harriman, on this point at least, concurred. "It would be well to point out and to emphasize," he said at a Joint Chiefs of Staff meeting in November 1943, "any advantages which the Soviets would receive from [their] participation" in the Pacific war.[93] At Tehran, one week later, Roosevelt suggested that Russia could be given access rights to the Japanese-occupied harbors at Dairen and Port Arthur (now Lüshun Port),[94] on the Liaodong Peninsula. Stalin, like the czars before him, had long coveted Port Arthur, which would provide Russia with a warm-water base from which to dominate the region commercially and militarily. Not surprisingly, he "did not think the Chinese would like such a scheme."[95] But FDR's generosity had whetted his appetite. And in Chungking, Wallace, whom Davies decried as "a dabbling and intriguing wiseacre,"[96] would whet it further.

Prior to the China trip, the secretary of state had warned John Carter Vincent not to "let Wallace give everything away."[97] Now, as the U.S. delegation departed China on June 27, the VP's minder had to have felt good about his performance.

Unbeknownst to Vincent, however, Wallace had apparently engaged in some offline diplomacy, details of which would be unearthed by Skvortsov and make their way to Moscow. There, they would be highlighted in preparing the Soviet leader for critical negotiations with Roosevelt.

One month before the Allied war leaders conference at Yalta in February 1945, Deputy People's Commissar of Foreign Affairs Solomon Lozovsky[98] would send Stalin a lengthy top secret memo titled "The Anglo-American Plans on Sino-Soviet Relations," which would feature intelligence from Skvortsov on Wallace's mission. Based on "non-official information . . . from reliable sources," Skvortsov reported that Wallace had pressed Chiang to make concessions to the Soviets in order to resolve "controversies" with them.

"Concerning the issue of the Mongolian People's Republic [Outer Mongolia]," Skvortsov wrote, "Wallace allegedly stated to Chiang that this nation had already . . . transformed itself into a national republic, hence its return to the status of a Chinese province was simply impossible."

"Concerning Manchuria," Skvortsov went on, "Wallace said that after the war ends the Chinese Eastern Railway [KVZhD] should come under joint Sino-Soviet control, with Port Arthur declared a free port," rather than passing to Chinese control. Wallace also "advised Chiang to come into agreement with the USSR on the joint development, on equal terms, of the mineral resources of the [Liaoning] province," adding that "no other nation besides the USSR was in a position to provide actual assistance to China."[99]

The Kremlin had long aspired, in diplomat George Kennan's words, to the "reacquisition, in substance if not in form, of all the diplomatic and territorial assets previously possessed on the mainland of Asia by Russia under the Czars."[100] It was a particular priority, as Davies put it, to "detach the border areas of Manchuria, Inner Mongolia, and Sinkiang so as to . . . erect barriers between the Soviet Union and China."[101] Whereas Kennan and Davies were trying to prevent these eventualities, Wallace was seemingly trying to realize them.

Why did Lozovsky think Skvortsov's discovery important? Apparently, no American official had ever endorsed such concessions in discussions with Soviet officials.[102] If the United States were now prepared not only to accept them but to push them on China, China would be unable to resist.

When did Wallace raise these matters with Chiang? There is no record of it in Vincent's notes, which were handed over to the State Department. And the only time he had not been privy to Wallace's deliberations, to his knowledge, was on the hour's drive to the airport with Chiang and his wife.[103] So this was a possible opportunity. (Chiang's diary entry regarding the car conversation does, in fact, refer to "Roosevelt's mediation," although that phrase appeared to refer to mediation between the KMT and the CCP, rather than between China and the USSR.[104])

How would Skvortsov have learned of Wallace's private discussions with Chiang? The Soviets routinely recruited domestic aides as "internal agents" (*vnutrennie agenty*). Chiang's driver is a possible source, but it may have been any number of associates overhearing Chiang recount Wallace's intervention. We know that the intelligence is accurate, however, as Wallace would confirm its substance in a private conversation with a Chinese official in September 1945.[105]

Why did Wallace raise these matters with Chiang? He offered no clear clues. But Lozovsky seemed to believe that the answer was to be found in a pamphlet the vice president had authored, entitled *Our Job in the Pacific*, which was released just five days before his arrival in Chungking.[106] This pamphlet was the published version of the tract which Roald Dahl, the British spy, had purloined a year prior—causing a stir in Downing Street.

"It is important that we make Asia . . . an area of cooperation, not conflict, between us and Russia," Wallace wrote. "[W]e cannot demand that Russia play our game." Wallace is, Lozovsky said,

> suggesting to the Soviet Union, in rather transparent form, that it begin negotiations regarding spheres of influence in the Far East. In this matter, he has written the following: "We should invite Russia to join us and other nations with vital interests in the Far East, and jointly decide which game we will play and what will be the rules of that game." Wallace's suggestions are so clear that they do not need any commentary.[107]

Lozovsky explained that the western press was full of reports regarding alleged Soviet ambitions in Manchuria, Sinkiang, Port Arthur, Dairen, and elsewhere in Asia. After achieving them, *The New York Times* said, "Russia [will] be the greatest Asiatic power."[108] Yet, Lozovsky stressed, "the Soviet Union had never expressed such wishes," at least not publicly. At Tehran, Stalin had obliquely requested "privileges" in Manchuria; yet he knew, in Davies' words, that "an open display of Soviet . . . expansionist ambition would . . . arouse the United States," which would then deny it a "voice" in determining future control of the Japanese islands. "Tactically," therefore, "the Kremlin [would] maintain a 'correct' attitude toward China and Korea, so as to avoid appearing imperialistic."[109] But it now seemed, given Wallace's interventions, that Stalin might achieve long-standing Soviet regional ambitions at no military or diplomatic cost.

"The newspapers, likely inspired by certain [U.S.] government leaders," he continued, "have been discussing settlement of the Mongolian and Xinjiang matters with China, the rights of the USSR in Manchuria, and its rights to Port Arthur and Dairen." The resolution of these matters, according to the *Times*, would "depend on [Russia's] active or passive participation in the war in the Pacific." Lozovsky concluded that "all of these statements should [therefore] be interpreted as the price the Americans are offering for Soviet entry into the war against Japan." And "*from Wallace's mouth*, we have been invited 'to jointly decide which game we will play and what its rules will be.'"[110]

Lozovsky's conclusion reflected a persistent pattern among Soviet officials of overestimating Wallace's official role and underestimating his willingness to speak his own mind, unfiltered by official policy. Roosevelt, who had proposed the port concessions to Stalin behind Chiang's back, would never have encouraged Wallace to reveal them to his face. The only territorial matter Roosevelt told Wallace to raise with Chiang, according to Wallace's diary, concerned Manchuria. On May 18, 1944, just before the vice president's departure from Washington, FDR told him that he had "made it perfectly clear" to Stalin in Cairo that he "wanted Manchuria to be Chinese," and that Wallace should reassure the Generalissimo that "as far as he knew, the plans were still O.K. on Manchuria." Chiang should just "settle the Communist thing." Otherwise he, Roosevelt, "might not be able to hold the Russians in line"[111]; that is, to keep them from making mischief in Manchuria. Given that Wallace had told Chiang he was unauthorized to speak on matters of Soviet regional interests, it seems that he had deliberately raised his concession agenda to the Generalissimo with Vincent out of earshot—so that there would be no official record of it.

As for the provenance of Wallace's proposed concessions, there are two possibilities. Wallace may have been privy to discussions on the matter in Washington. Davies would later write that Stalin's agreement-in-principle to enter the war, made in Tehran, "was a deep secret, knowledge of which was quite properly withheld from those who . . . had no need to know of it."[112] Wallace, however, as noted in his diary, had learned *in Siberia* "that there was no question about Russia coming into the war with Japan."[113] He may therefore have learned of the desired Chinese concessions from his NKVD minders. The two possibilities—that he formed the list from discussions in Washington or those in Siberia—are not mutually exclusive.

In any case, it is clear that Wallace was not trying to aid Roosevelt's efforts to coax Russia to attack Japan, since he already believed "there was no question" but that it would. The Russians, just a few weeks prior, had told him so. And he would diary, a year later, that there was likely "no way of keeping Russia out of the war with Japan."[114] What we can safely conclude was that Wallace was trying to shape the postwar Asian architecture in a manner decidedly friendly to Soviet interests. Given that Chiang's briefing notes for his first meeting with Wallace state that "Outer Mongolia was an unresolved issue between China and the Soviet Union" and that "China had no intention of solving it *before the end of the war*," however, it is almost certain that he dismissed the suggestion that he cede it—together with other major territorial and commercial interests.[115] T.V. Soong would later tell Roosevelt's successor that China would sooner "settle the controversy [with Russia] by military action" than bow to its demands in Mongolia and the northeast.[116] That Wallace apparently never revealed what he had done to Roosevelt suggests that he knew he had failed in his efforts.

But *had he*? The discovery of his intervention by a Soviet diplomat would soon fuel Stalin's boldness in the coming postwar showdown with Washington and Chungking.

Eight

HISTORY'S PIVOT

"Things are not going well," Joe Guffey told Wallace. "Some of the people around the White House are saying, 'We need a new face.'"[1]

Wallace had phoned his friend from Fairbanks, just after landing on July 5, 1944. Guffey, the junior senator from Pennsylvania, knew the problems of which he spoke. He had seen Wallace, the Senate's presiding officer, alienate members in his own party out of sheer neglect, showing little patience with their needs or constraints.[2] Joe "looks on me as a son in this fight," Wallace recorded in his diary. Perhaps; but in politics, sons run the constant risk of filicide.

Guffey was, in the words of British philosopher-diplomat Isaiah Berlin, "an obedient party hack not of the purest integrity." He had been covering all his bases. A year earlier, he had asked a closer friend, in confidence, whether he might be willing to accept the vice presidential nod next year. And a year on, Harry Truman's answer was the same: no.

But Guffey had still other friends. Shortly after Wallace had left for Siberia, Jimmy Byrnes had asked him "to keep an eye on things," and to let him know how his own prospects looked. Just before the call with his friend in Fairbanks, Guffey had told Byrnes he would press Wallace to withdraw.[3]

The senator was doubtless privy to the machinations around the White House. With the vice president eight thousand miles away, Roosevelt had been seeing a steady stream of visitors, each carefully curated by his appointments secretary, Major General Edwin "Pa" Watson—a man who disdained Wallace. The visitors urged the president to take a new running mate.

This was not 1940; the position of running mate was more important now. Roosevelt's precipitous physical decline was obvious for all to see. "All of us felt," the DNC secretary George Allen said, "that the man nominated for the Vice-Presidency would soon succeed to the presidency."[4] Most avoided the matter of mortality in the president's presence, but the treasury secretary was more direct. On July 6, Roosevelt told Morgenthau that the first lady was pressing him to insist on Wallace as his running mate, and asked what Morgenthau thought. "[Y]ou and I are both only human," he responded, "and if something should happen to you I certainly wouldn't want Henry Wallace to be president." There was also the matter of the delegates, who "feel that you forced Wallace down their throats" in 1940, and would want the convention open this time. "That's what I hear," Roosevelt responded. "You are right."[5]

Back in March, around the time Wallace had asked permission to go to Moscow, the president's closest companions, his daughter Anna and his secretary Grace Tully, began to fret over his worsening appearance and plummeting stamina. He had taken on a pale complexion, highlighting the darkening hollows under his eyes. He coughed and complained of headaches. He had trouble sleeping. His hand shook as he lit cigarettes. He lost his train of thought. He dozed off while reading, even while dictating.[6]

The "care" he was receiving, such as it was, was rudimentary and ineffective, reflecting the ignorance of his personal physician, Dr. Ross McIntire. An ear-nose-and-throat specialist, McIntire saw every symptom through that distorted lens. At Anna's urging, he grudgingly arranged for the president to be examined at Bethesda Naval Hospital on March 28. It was there that an alarmed thirty-nine-year-old cardiologist, Dr. Howard Bruenn, would diagnose the problem as advanced congestive heart failure.

At McIntire's request, however, he would never reveal the diagnosis, or bleak prognosis, to his patient—who, remarkably, would never himself inquire. "I don't think he had the slightest idea," Anna opined years later, "that he was going downhill in the way he was." But Bruenn did change the president's diet and routine, curtailing his workload, cutting his cigarette consumption (from twenty to ten a day—the fewest his patient would tolerate), and administering digitalis to improve circulation.[7] Given the primitive state of hypertension treatment at the time, there was little more he could have done, beyond demanding total bedrest. Once Roosevelt agreed to accept his party's renomination, however, which would not come until

July 11, the only question was how many more grueling months his failing heart would grant him.

The public knew nothing of the president's true condition, but it was becoming clearer from his gaunt, aging face that he was not just suffering from passing ailments—as he frequently suggested. He did, however, reveal to a columnist in early April that he had cut his working hours significantly.[8]

Wallace would not have known Bruenn's diagnosis, but he was concerned enough about the president's health to raise it privately with an important confidant. A week or so after the hospital exam, Wallace, according to Soviet ambassador Gromyko, invited him to Sunday lunch at a bungalow forty miles outside Washington. The Swiss minister (the husband of Wallace's sister Mary) was also present. But at one point during the gathering, Wallace asked Gromyko to join him privately in a far corner.

There he told him he was "very concerned" about U.S.-Soviet ties being "weakened" after the war by those in "big business" who bear "antipathy toward the USSR." Gromyko agreed. "As you know," Wallace then added, "the president is not quite well, even if he is very active, including paying great attention to the future of Soviet-American relations."

Gromyko "had the impression the remark about the president's health . . . resulted from careful consideration." He found it hard to say if Wallace knew the end was near.[9] But he understood him to be warning of perilous times ahead.

Was the president pondering his demise as he pondered his running mate? As with so much when it came to Roosevelt, it is difficult to say what he wanted, when he wanted it, and why.

"[T]he boss wanted the Iowan to continue with him in office," insisted Tully. "I heard him say so many times."[10] Indeed, he said it to many. "Of course, everyone knows I am for Henry Wallace," Roosevelt would tell aide Jonathan Daniels as late as June 27—three weeks before the convention.

Yet Wallace was someone whose company the president enjoyed more than someone whose judgment he esteemed. Privately, he referred to his friend as "the Yogi man."[11] The famed political columnist Walter Lippmann put it more charitably. Wallace, he wrote, "is an exceptionally fine human being." But "his goodness is unworldly," and "his heart is so detached from the realities that he has never learned to measure, as a statesman must, the relation of good and evil in current affairs."[12]

Given that Roosevelt had, earlier in the year, told both Hannegan and Pepper that he would look to resign after the war,[13] it is difficult to imagine that he did not consider the succession. Chicago mayor Ed Kelly, a close confidant of the president's, would insist that he had. Roosevelt "was not certain that he would live out his fourth term," Kelly would later say, "and he became convinced that Wallace, no matter how good he was, couldn't hold the Democratic party together."[14]

Roosevelt's primary concerns appear, however, to have been practical and immediate. He heeded the party leaders because they did, in fact, persuade him that Wallace was a divisive figure and an electoral liability. Whereas he had once thought opposition to Wallace largely confined to "politicians," he had, by early 1944, begun to believe "it went down below," to the voters, millions of whom felt he was too liberal, too mystical, and too friendly to the Soviets. Some were saying that Wallace would cost him 40 percent of the vote in key precincts. And even if such a figure were exaggerated, Roosevelt concluded, "if you cut that in half, and then half again, it still might mean the loss of a million or two votes."[15]

He had, he reminded Hannegan, bucked the anti-Wallace protests in 1940, but would not "go through a convention like [that] again." He hadn't the stamina for a "knock-down and drag-out" fight. It would "split the party wide open, . . . kill our chances [in November], prolong the war, and knock into a cocked hat the plans we've been making for the future."[16] Those "plans" referred to the creation of the United Nations; plans that a polarizing nominee would endanger. The task required party unity now, and cross-party comity later. For Roosevelt, Wallace had been the right man in 1940; but the world had changed, and priorities had changed with it.

Even Wallace would come to grasp this. He would, years later, observe that Roosevelt, in order "to build a strong United Nations and a permanent peace," was "so in need of support in the Senate," of support from "Southern reactionaries and the political bosses," that he had to take another vice president. "[I]n spite of his warm feelings toward me," he thought "my approach would lose [him] all essential votes."[17] This epiphany contrasted, of course, with his view before the election—which is that Roosevelt wanted him, but was manipulated by the bosses.

In actuality, Roosevelt struggled little with the question over whether Wallace should be replaced; he struggled only with the question of how to deliver the message to him. Unable to bear unpleasant encounters, and unwilling to own his decision, he fell back on the tried and tested ways: sending envoys and dissembling.

When, he asked aides on June 27, was Wallace coming back from Asia? He was, special assistant Dave Niles responded, set to make a radio address from Seattle on July 9. In that case, Roosevelt said, "one or two persons ought to go out and . . . tell him [of] this feeling about his political liability."[18] He settled on his trusted speechwriter, Sam Rosenman, whom he tasked with telling Wallace that the president wanted him as a running mate but could not risk splitting the party. "I am sure," Roosevelt concluded with unwarranted confidence, that Henry "will understand and be glad to step down."[19] It was a tidy plan—to disguise political murder as suicide—but one easier ordered than executed.

A skeptical Rosenman phoned Wallace's secretary, asking to meet with him at his arrival city. Apologies, she said; his schedule was in flux. Rosenman called back; again, he was stonewalled. Finally, hearing that Wallace had landed in Seattle, Rosenman phoned him directly, asking to have lunch in Washington on July 10. Wallace promised an answer shortly.

Four days later, on July 9, Wallace wired Rosenman saying he would return the following day, but adding: "Believe I should see President before the meeting."[20] Clearly, he thought he might yet convince the boss to call off the hit men.

A few hours later, back in Washington, three leaders of the effort to oust him—DNC chairman Bob Hannegan, Foreign Economic Administration head Leo Crowley, and Postmaster General Frank Walker—entered Hull's office in the State, War, and Navy Building. With an impish grin, Hannegan switched on the radio. Over the airwaves came the voice of the vice president, speechifying from Seattle.

White House aides had feared Wallace would overreach, even if the president himself was unconcerned. "I told him what to say," Roosevelt assured Daniels and Niles on June 27; "it is going to be perfectly banal." Wallace will just point out "the great trade possibilities . . . in China and Siberia after the war." Yet Wallace, in proclaiming "The Era of the Pacific," was reaching for something more impactful, more Churchillian. Still, having apparently written the speech himself, he achieved Roosevelt's desired banality.

As Hull listened from his desk, Wallace intoned:

The East of Asia, both Chinese and Russian, is on the move in a way
which is easy for any American to understand who sees these great
areas at first-hand for himself . . .

"For God's sake, cut him off!" Hull yelled. His guests laughed. Wallace,
they felt sure, would be cut off soon enough.[21]

The vice president left Seattle Sunday night. His plane tossed through a
thunderstorm, and had to make an unscheduled landing. Finally arriving in
the capital, exhausted, on Monday morning, July 10, he phoned the White
House. Watson said the president wished him to meet Rosenman and Ickes
right away. Roosevelt would then see him at 4:30 p.m. for an "on-the-record
conference."[22] The phrase meant that no domestic politics would be discussed, at least not on the record.

Wallace would later learn that "a certain relative" of the president's had
suggested he go to "meet Mr. Wallace at the plane," to which Roosevelt replied, "I think it will be misunderstood. [I]t would be better not to."[23]

An anxious Wallace now phoned Rosenman, asking that he and Ickes
come to his apartment at the Wardman Park Hotel—which they did. After
thirty minutes of "polite inquiries," the sort Wallace abhorred, Rosenman
got down to business. The president, he said, would like to have Wallace as
his running mate, but there were problems.

Ickes, whom Wallace loathed, tried to soften the news. Wallace, he said,
truthfully, had grown in his esteem through the years. The two of them were
now "the only two real liberals left in the government." But Wallace "had
made many enemies." This could not be ignored. If he tried to stay on the
ticket, it would "split the party wide open."

Wallace's face was "stone." He seemed "not even to be listening," observed Rosenman. When he finally spoke, it was only to shame his unwanted guests.

"Sam," he said, "I've just come back from a country [China] where people
are dying by the hundreds of thousands because of lack of food"—though
he had recorded no encounters with such. He had "no interest now in dis-

cussing political matters," though he would "do so eventually—with the president."

Wallace would later acknowledge having been "a little vigorous" with the men, owing in part to his sleepless travels.[24]

At 4:30 p.m., he arrived at the Oval Office, where Roosevelt greeted him warmly. The difference in atmosphere was marked. The men talked China, amiably, for two hours—before the president abruptly changed the subject. He would now, he said, be "talking to the ceiling about political matters." Nothing, he admonished Wallace, should be repeated outside the room.

Roosevelt told Wallace he wanted him to stay on as vice president.[25] Rosenman having already told him as much, however, this fact was not news. Still, it was welcome to hear it from the president himself. But what, practically, did these words mean? Would Roosevelt kill the swirling intrigue? Would he back him publicly?

Unbeknownst to Wallace, Roosevelt had, two weeks earlier, on June 27, already blessed the man most covetous of his job. Jimmy Byrnes "suits me fine," he had told Hannegan, after reviewing alternatives to Wallace. Jimmy had, after all, been "my candidate for vice-president four years ago." Not only had Roosevelt said that he was "fine" with Byrnes *now*, three weeks before the convention, but that he had actually preferred Byrnes *in 1940*—that is, "until religion got messed up in it."

Byrnes had abandoned the Catholic faith to marry an Episcopalian in 1906. Some party leaders feared that might offend 30 million former co-congregant voters. But that fear, Roosevelt came to believe after 1940, had been overblown. Byrnes now seemed to have the broadest backing among delegates. Moreover, he knew "more about government than anybody."[26]

Byrnes, for his part, was equally sure of his bona fides. He needed only, like Wallace, for the boss to back him publicly. But would that happen? "Let's not get too excited on this vice-president business," Byrnes warned Walter Brown, his special assistant, on June 30. "I know that man more than anybody."

At that point, at least, Byrnes was wisely curbing his enthusiasm. Roosevelt was still weighing any number of men, some of whom, like Republican John Winant and industrialist Henry Kaiser, were beyond the political imagination of the party bosses. Yet, unlike in 1940, he had no intention of *naming* a running mate. He wanted just to shepherd the process, to help a copacetic nominee emerge. The bosses would have to handle the fixing and cajoling—and suffer the brickbats.

Aide Gene Casey would, just a week before the convention, ask the president what he intended to do "about the vice-presidency." Roosevelt's nonanswer would be telling. "Did you ever know Charlie Murphy?" the president asked in reply—referring to the longtime Tammany Hall boss. "Charlie was a wise man. When they asked him who was going to be lieutenant governor, he would always say, 'The convention will decide,' *and he got away with it.*"[27] Roosevelt intended to "get away with it."

Now, Wallace, like Byrnes, had good reason to doubt the president's intentions and reliability.

"Would you be willing to say," Wallace asked him, "'If I were a delegate to the convention, I would vote for Henry Wallace'?"

"Yes, I would," Roosevelt assured him.

However, "a great many people," he then added, were saying "[you] could not be nominated"—even with presidential support.

Well, "I don't want to be pushed down anybody's throat," Wallace put back. What mattered was that the president "really wanted" him, "and was willing to say so."

FDR nodded. He was indeed willing. His *visitors*, however, were saying that Wallace "would cost the ticket 1 to 3 million votes." And he, Roosevelt, "could not bear the thought of [Wallace's] name being put up before the convention and rejected."

Wallace shook his head. "I am used to hard situations."

"But you have your family to think of," the president remonstrated. "Think of the catcalls and jeers and the definiteness of rejection."

"I am not worried about my family," Wallace assured him. It was only "about the Democratic party and you." In any case, he added, he would meet Guffey that evening and get "current" on politics.

Roosevelt nodded approvingly. That was the right approach, he said; "take a look around" and "report" tomorrow.[28] By that time, he hoped, Guffey might have succeeded where Rosenman had failed.

But Guffey, too, failed. Using "the back way" to avoid detection, Wallace, bearing gifts from Uzbekistan and Outer Mongolia, returned to the White House the following day, July 11. He and Roosevelt talked Siberia, "on the record," before returning to forbidden matters.

Buoyant, Wallace handed Roosevelt polling data from Charles Marsh, all favorable. He then showed him a draft statement he had written for the president to read to the convention.

"I trust the name with me will be Henry A. Wallace," it said. "He is equipped for the future. We have made a team which pulls together, thinks alike and plans alike."

Roosevelt nodded, thanking him. He had, however, "worked out another wording."

Once again, he underscored the obstacles Wallace faced. There was, he said, "no one more American" than Wallace, yet many still looked on him "as a communist or worse." He was "the fellow who wants to give a quart of milk to every Hottentot."

"You know, Mr. President, I never said that," Wallace objected. "That was said for me by the President of the National Association of Manufacturers."

Roosevelt raised his eyebrows, "greatly surprised." He thanked Wallace, asking him to return—again—for lunch on Thursday. By that time, he hoped, Hannegan might succeed where Rosenman and Guffey had failed.[29]

That evening, the convention's inner guard gathered in Roosevelt's second-floor study. There they hoped to give final form to the president's fugacious sentiments; to shape them into a verdict, a name, a man who would, in all likelihood, soon need to lead the nation through to victory in war and stewardship of an uncharted postwar world.

The air was hot and dank. Jackets came off, sleeves were rolled up. Oblivious to the tension, Roosevelt mixed martinis. The six guests took their seats.

Robert Emmet Hannegan, forty-one, lawyer, police chief's son, six feet tall, tough, with a chalk-white face and square, dimpled jaw, began his political rise through the St. Louis Democratic Party machine in 1934, when his late backing for Harry Truman brought narrow victory in the latter's first Senate run. He was then instrumental in the senator's close reelection in 1940, mobilizing support in Catholic neighborhoods. Truman did his own good turn in 1942, securing Hannegan's appointment as collector of the internal revenue, and backing his elevation to IRS commissioner in 1943 and DNC chair in January 1944.[30] Among party leaders, Hannegan was uniquely close to both Roosevelt and Truman.

Edward Joseph Flynn, fifty-two, a savvy, salty, stocky lawyer, son of Irish Catholic immigrants, became party chairman in the Bronx in 1922, age thirty-one, a position from which he subsequently built his power base statewide and nationally. The "Boss of the Bronx" was a backstage operator, never aspiring to elective office or a public limelight, preferring to create and exploit indebtedness among his myriad connections to fix problems and distribute patronage. Though a frequent target of anti–Tammany Hall corruption fighters, Flynn was never part of that society and built a surprisingly scandal-free career. One of the president's closest hard-nosed political confidants from his earliest days in New York politics, he also shared the first lady's idealism, being a passionate advocate of racial equality. His objections to Wallace's renomination were practical, having canvassed the party faithful nationwide and concluded that he put at risk the president's hold on such major states as New York, New Jersey, Pennsylvania, Illinois, and California.[31]

George Edward Allen, forty-eight, from Booneville, Mississippi, practiced law and managed properties before entering politics in 1933, when he launched a comically successful campaign to prod Roosevelt into placing him on the D.C. Board of Commissioners—making him, in his words, "one third of a mayor of Washington." He was either an unrelenting wit, a stance subliminally reinforced throughout his autobiographical *Presidents Who Have Known Me*, or a political "buffoon practicing low comedy," the view taken by his Republican detractors. Allen became treasurer of the DNC in 1940, adding secretary to his title in 1943—notable life facts that seemed barely to interest him. What obsessed him no end, however, was his role as "faithful ally" to Ed Pauley in the anti-Wallace "Conspiracy of the Pure at Heart."[32]

Edwin Wendell Pauley Sr., forty, born in Indianapolis, tall, balding, indefatigably direct, entered the oil business after working his way through college. Amassing a fortune by the age of thirty, he emerged as a spokesman for the industry in the 1930s, as well as becoming a major Democratic fundraiser. Two years before U.S. entry into the war, he began urging Roosevelt to regulate oil production and distribution so as to aid the Allied nations. In 1941, the president tapped him to organize and run the Petroleum Administration for Defense Districts, which built the first transcontinental pipeline between Texas and the East Coast, and made him his personal representative to the first Lend-Lease mission to the Soviet Union. As DNC treasurer from 1942, he would assume supreme importance during the 1944 campaign, controlling which Democrats addressed which audiences where. A pragmatic and unashamed capitalist, he considered the vice president "an unworldly man of mystical leanings" with dangerously pro-Soviet views. Allen admired Pauley for his forceful role in the campaign, one which made him a lightning rod for liberal hatred. To those who would charge him with subverting democracy by so openly pursuing Wallace's demise, however, Pauley was unapologetic. "It is the people who elect presidents," he would say, "but it is the politicians who try and give them the best field to select from."[33]

Edward Joseph Kelly, sixty-eight, a Chicago-born police officer's son and grammar school dropout, began working for the Chicago Sanitary District at age eighteen, attaining the title of chief engineer two decades later. Around that time, in 1924, he was also elected to the South Park Commission, where he managed the building of Soldier Field and earned the sobriquet "Father of the Lakefront." Following the death of Mayor Anton Cermak, who was shot by a man attempting to assassinate Roosevelt in 1933, Kelly was handpicked by millionaire friend Pat Nash, chairman of the Cook County Democratic Party, to run for mayor. The so-called Kelly-Nash Machine became one of the most powerful city regimes in the nation, building a patronage system financed by, among other things, the New Deal and organized crime—a system that successfully co-opted elements from business, labor, and the Black community. Kelly advised the president on everything from electoral politics to foreign affairs, earning his trust through candor and loyalty. In 1944, the mayor rose to the apex of his stature at the White House owing to Chicago's hosting of both the Republican and Democratic conventions.[34]

Frank Comerford Walker, fifty-eight, bald, heavyset, ever-attired in a double-breasted suit, was the cabal's fourth lawyer. Born in Plymouth, Pennsylvania, but raised with a Catholic education in the mining town of

Butte, Montana, he served one term in the state legislature before volunteering as a first lieutenant in the Army during World War I, seeing limited action on the Western Front. He moved to New York City in 1925, becoming general counsel for a relative's movie theater chain. He reentered politics as an early supporter of Franklin Roosevelt, cofounding the Roosevelt for President Society in 1931. Quiet, even-tempered, hardworking, religious, loyal, self-effacing, Walker would emerge as one of FDR's longest-serving and most trusted advisers. Becoming DNC treasurer in 1932, he would, the following year, be appointed executive secretary of the New Deal National Emergency Council by the incoming president. Assuming the position of postmaster general in 1940, he waded into issues well beyond mail—even meeting regularly with Japanese ambassador Kichisaburo Nomura in the run-up to the attack on Pearl Harbor. He took on the further role of DNC chairman in 1943, before handing off to Hannegan the following year. In contrast to Hannegan, Pauley, and Allen, Walker was notably free of animus toward Wallace, seeing his role as one of divining and effectuating the president's shrouded will.[35]

Seated now with his five co-conspirators, as they came to know one another, Walker eyed the president with a combination of concern and pity. Rarely had he seen him so listless, so detached—and at a time when his legacy, and the fate of the world, was at stake.

Roosevelt began by commending Wallace. He would, he said, be happy to run with him again. He did not, however, say "*I want*" Wallace, let alone "*I insist*" on Wallace—as he had in 1940. The message was clear. He had come to bury Wallace, not to praise him.

Reactions being unnecessary, Roosevelt moved on.[36] Next up was Jimmy Byrnes. As always, the president called him the best qualified. He thought his path to nomination the clearest. But the discussion quickly shifted to November negatives: that he would alienate Catholics and Blacks A proud Southerner, Byrnes had opposed a 1938 federal antilynching bill (a bill Roosevelt himself never backed). It was feared he might now cost the ticket "two or three hundred thousand Negro votes." Roosevelt threw in a third drawback: age. Byrnes, like the president, was sixty-two, two decades older than the Republican nominee. A more youthful sidekick, FDR believed, would counter Republican candidate Thomas Dewey's charge that his team was geriatric.[37]

Roosevelt then dispensed with two more Southerners: Senate Majority

Leader Alben Barkley (KY) and House Speaker Sam Rayburn (TX). Barkley, at sixty-five, was *too* old—"older than I am." Left unsaid was that the
theatrical senator had, in February, resigned as majority leader "in a froth of
righteous indignation" over the president's veto of an "inadequate" tax bill
("not for the needy, but for the greedy"), only to be unanimously reelected
thirty minutes later—after the veto was overridden.[38] Roosevelt would for-
give, but not forget. As for Rayburn, he was hemorrhaging support in his
own delegation (owing to his support for Roosevelt).[39]

Roosevelt enthused over Supreme Court justice William Douglas. Just forty-
five, a self-made Westerner, he "has a nice crop of hair," Roosevelt said; he "looks
like a Boy Scout." Bill was brilliant, "plays an interesting game of poker," and
would "appeal to the same left-wingers" as Wallace. This testimonial, as close
as FDR would come to an endorsement, was greeted with "a stunned silence."
Only Kelly wanted Douglas, but he did not, by any accounts, speak up.

Harry Hopkins would, at lunch the following day, urge Roosevelt not to
force the matter. It would, the consigliere argued, "play havoc" in the party
were the press to say he had dumped Wallace for Douglas. It was better just
"to let nature take its course."[40]

Nature, in any case, did not favor Douglas; the man had, in Allen's words,
"no visible followers." It favored the competent, inoffensive, and congenial
Harry Truman. But FDR had still not even mentioned him. Instead, he kept
raising what Pauley called "impossibilities."

One such was Winant, the Republican ambassador to the U.K. "Imagine
our position as leaders of the Democratic party nominating a *Republican*
at our own convention," Pauley thought to himself—"and one who would
succeed as *president* sooner [rather] than later." He feared the president did
not want a decision that night, and was playing his old game of running out
the clock. But, finally, Roosevelt turned to him and said he knew whom they
were waiting to discuss: Truman. He had, perhaps, saved his name for last
on the basis that everyone present had, at some point, commended it to him.

Pauley touted the senator as being "the most sought-after speaker for
[fundraising] dinners," but this was disingenuous. The party leaders kept
giving him podiums, while keeping them from Wallace, precisely to build
up his profile—to *make* him "sought-after."[41]

The challenge was that Roosevelt hardly knew Truman. "[Harry] has
been over here a few times," he noted to Byrnes a few weeks earlier, "but

he made no particular impression on me." According to Pauley, Roosevelt "questioned whether or not Truman had the personality to be the president"—which, if true, represented the only hard evidence he had been weighing the succession factor.

The case for Truman among the leadership was straightforward. He was an experienced ten-year senator; respected, personable, centrist. He was a loyal New Dealer, but no radical. A border state man, he was *in* the South, but not *of* it. He could win Dixie votes yet not lose Northern ones. Labor liked him. Black leaders liked him. Colleagues like him. Nobody *loved* him, but that was not in the job specs.

The knock on Truman was that his rise was linked to the powerful Pendergast Kansas City Democratic machine. Opponents called him "the senator from Pendergast." The truth was that Truman had entered, and would exit, Missouri politics near-broke, and had shown as much integrity and independence as any politician emerging from a corrupt environment could. Writing to his wife, Bess, in 1935, he warned her she would "have to put up with a lot" while he was a senator, "because I won't sell influence and I'm perfectly willing to be cussed if I'm right." He meant it. Yet when local party boss Tom Pendergast pleaded guilty to tax violations in 1939,[42] it raised anew speculation about the senator's own hidden sins. In any case, those concerns had, by 1944, mostly died down.

Roosevelt did not gush over Truman, the way he had Douglas, yet pronounced him "able" and "wise to the ways of politics." The senator, he said, had not "done one single thing to embarrass this Administration." He commended, in particular, Truman's dextrous leadership of a Senate committee probing waste and corruption in war spending.

The "Truman Committee," as it had come to be known, had earned its chairman bipartisan support and public commendations, elevating him from "the senator from Pendergast" into a respected congressional leader. Estimates of the amount of money his committee had saved the nation went as high as $15 billion ($256 billion in today's money). *Time* magazine, which featured the "scrupulously honest" chairman on its cover the week of March 8, 1943, called his committee the "watchdog, spotlight, [and] conscience" behind the economic war effort. A poll of Washington correspondents identified Harry Truman as "one of the ten men in Washington," and the only one in Congress, "whose services had been the most important to the war effort."

As with Byrnes and Barkley, however, Roosevelt was concerned with Truman's age. How old was Harry? he asked. Wasn't he almost sixty?

Truman was, in fact, sixty. Knowing this, Pauley said nothing, prompting Roosevelt's son-in-law, John Boettiger, who had been observing silently, to go in search of a *Congressional Directory*. When he returned, Pauley grabbed it and hid it in his lap—out of the president's view. The discussion having moved on, and the president having forgotten the matter, there it remained till the end. The end came when Roosevelt, tiring, turned to Hannegan and delivered his verdict.

"Bob, I think you and everyone else here want Truman," the president said. "If that's the case, it's Truman." He ordered Hannegan to give Wallace the bad news, and Walker to give it to Byrnes. Pauley, anxious to preempt further talk, rose and declared it time to adjourn.

Flynn was pleased. All had gone to script. Once downstairs, however, Walker began fretting. Roosevelt's words, now vanished in the ether, meant nothing. Tomorrow, he might back Byrnes again. Or Douglas. Or Wallace, God forbid. He took Hannegan aside, telling him they needed to get Truman's name *on paper*.

Seizing the pretext of forgetting his jacket (Pauley had grabbed it in error), Hannegan ran back upstairs. "Chief," he called to the surprised Roosevelt, "will you put that in writing?"—referring to the consensus on Truman. Roosevelt agreed. Reaching for a pencil and the nearest piece of paper, an envelope, he scribbled. Hannegan thanked him, stuffing it in his pocket.

Running out to the parking area, he signaled to Walker. "I got it!" he said, smiling.

In his excitement, however, he had failed to read the president's scrawl; it declared him happy with either "Douglas or Truman." When Hannegan discovered this, his heart sank.[43] To make matters worse, Roosevelt's letter praising *Wallace* would, he knew, emerge soon enough. Rather than making Truman the nominee, then, the envelope might even mark him as the *third choice*. And so the drama would continue.

The next morning, Wednesday, July 12, Hannegan returned to Wallace's apartment. This time, there were few pleasantries.

Wallace, the cheerless visitor said, did "not have a chance." The president had, Tuesday night, made up his mind. If Wallace "did not voluntarily with-draw," he would name him his "first choice," and someone else his "second choice." The second man "would serve as lightning rod to gather [up] the dissident votes" and emerge victorious.

For Wallace, such base political tricks just confirmed his righteousness. "[T]he president has indicated he *does* want me," Wallace insisted. And as long as that remained the case, he was "not withdrawing." Incredulous, Hannegan stormed out, telling a waiting reporter that Wallace was "a ter-rible person." Off the record, he was a "son of a bitch."[44]

At 1 p.m. on Thursday, July 13, Wallace returned to the White House for lunch, again by the "back way." FDR prolonged the chitchat until Wallace, bursting with impatience, "cut in."

Grasping for some firmer affirmation of Roosevelt's support, some surer sign that he, Wallace, remained the favored son, he asked for "the privilege of putting [the president's] name in nomination."

Roosevelt, apologetic, shook his head. "Alben [Barkley] had asked for that," he explained. This was untrue: *Hannegan* had asked *Barkley* to nomi-nate the president, with the latter's approval.

As regards the statement Wallace had requested, however, Roosevelt said he was happy to proceed. He would send a letter to the conference chairman, Samuel Jackson, saying that "if he were a delegate he would vote for Wallace."

He would add, however, that he did "not wish in any way to dictate to the convention." And he reminded his guest, insensate as he was to subtlety, that Flynn, Kelly, Pauley, and Hannegan were all still insisting he "would harm the ticket."

"If *you* think so," Wallace put back, "I will withdraw at once."

But it was not like Roosevelt to push a man off a ledge; he expected him to know when to jump.

And so he tried again.

"I have no basis for a judgment of my own," the president protested.[45] "Professional *politicians*," though, "thought [that] Harry Truman [was] the only one who had no enemies" and who could therefore "add a little inde-pendent strength to the ticket."

Still deaf to the serial snubs, Wallace pressed back, showing him the latest Gallup poll numbers. Truman was at 2 percent nationally, one percentage point below Byrnes, while he, Wallace, was at 65 percent. To a great degree, the gap reflected the public's ignorance of Truman and Byrnes. The much better-known Hull, for example, was at 21 percent in a six-candidate March poll (to Wallace's 46 percent). Two-way against Wallace, Barkley was at 38 percent. Wallace, however, took the July result as self-evident proof of his electoral appeal. Did the president still plan, Wallace asked him, "to do what Hannegan wanted"—to give the convention "an alternative name?"

No, Roosevelt said: that would look "too much like dictation."

He had made the same misleading pledge to Byrnes just a few hours earlier—that he would suggest no "preference" beyond Wallace. And since Wallace "could not be nominated," he had told Byrnes, the field would be open for him. "If you stay in, you are sure to win."

Wallace, knowing none of this exchange, now rose to depart.

"Well, I am looking ahead with pleasure to the results of next week," he said, hollow-heartedly, "no matter what the outcome."

Roosevelt smiled, gripping his hand. "While I cannot put it just that way in public," he said, "I hope it will be the same old team."

Hope, of course, was not help. But he imparted a last comforting thought. This time—this one time—he would say what he meant, and mean what he said.

"Even though they do beat you out at Chicago," he offered, still smiling, "we will have a job for you in world economic affairs."[46]

Having pleaded with Roosevelt in vain to choose another messenger, Walker now had to deliver crushing news to the man who had run the nation's domestic affairs for the past fourteen months. On Friday, July 14, he and Hannegan asked Byrnes to meet them for lunch at Crowley's apartment.

Red-faced, Walker looked Byrnes in the eye. He was sorry, he said, but "if any of FDR's friends should question them" on whom he preferred as his running mate, "they would have to say 'Truman or Douglas.'"

Byrnes was staggered. Roosevelt had just *yesterday* promised he would not express a "preference"—at least none beyond Wallace.

Bewildered, Hannegan said he "couldn't understand it." He believed Byrnes, of course, but could not "call the president a liar."

Like Wallace, Byrnes would not take rejection from presidential proxies. But, also like Wallace, he would get only double-talk from the source.

Phoning Roosevelt in Hyde Park, he recounted what Walker and Hannegan had just told him: that the president preferred Truman or Douglas as his running mate.

"They asked if I would '*object*' to Truman and Douglas," Roosevelt protested, "and I said no. That is different from using the word '*prefer.*'"

"After all, Jimmy," he continued, "you are close to me personally. Henry is close to me. I hardly know Truman. Douglas is a poker partner. He is good in a poker game, and tells good stories." He talked on in this vein, yet never asked Byrnes to run. He asked, instead, whether Byrnes *intended* to run.

Exasperated, but still determined, Byrnes said he would wait and see.[47] The skies had changed; they would change again.

The night of Thursday, July 13, Roosevelt left Washington for Hyde Park. The following evening, he departed Highland, New York, on an unmarked train bound for San Diego, from whence he would sail on to Hawaii to arbitrate Pacific war strategy between his dueling commanders, Douglas MacArthur and Chester Nimitz. It was a life-threatening mission for a man in his condition, but he believed it the only way to achieve a unified plan for defeating Japan.

In the early afternoon of Saturday, July 15, the locomotive rolled into a hot, sunny, mazelike Chicago yard, whereupon Hannegan and Kelly climbed on board. Emerging fifty-two minutes later, by the watches of observant reporters, Hannegan now carried with him a typewritten letter on White House stationery. It read:

> Dear Bob:
> You have written me about Harry Truman and Bill Douglas. I should, of course, be very glad to run with either of them and believe that either of them would bring real strength to the ticket.
>
> Always sincerely,
> Franklin Roosevelt

The letter formalized the July 11 envelope endorsement, but, critically, reversed the names. At Hannegan's urging, Truman's name was now first.[48] The letter was also postdated July 19—just before the convention was set to vote.

In addition to revising *that* letter, Roosevelt had also agreed to shorten and sharpen his *competing* letter—the one supporting Wallace. Hannegan had wanted more emphasis on the convention's right of decision, which would strengthen the hand of the party leaders in selling Truman.

Yet if the president writing *two* letters endorsing *three* candidates were not confusing enough, he orally endorsed a *fourth*. After Kelly had told him that Black leaders wanted Wallace, but would back the president's choice, even if it were Byrnes, Roosevelt responded with enthusiasm.

"Well, you know Jimmy has been my choice from the very first," he said. "Go ahead and name him."

Stunned, Hannegan's first thought was to tear up the Truman letter. Knowing the chief's tendencies, however, he decided to keep it as insurance.[49] Wallace would, three weeks later, learn from Barkley, who would in turn learn from Byrnes, that Roosevelt's letters endorsing him, Truman, and Douglas were typed and signed on the same day Roosevelt orally endorsed Byrnes.[50]

Whatever his misgivings, Hannegan phoned Byrnes in Washington. "The president," he said, "has given us the green light to support you, and he wants you in Chicago."[51] Meanwhile, Hannegan's wife, Irma, tucked the Truman letter inside a *National Geographic* and stuffed it under her mattress.[52] When, and to what end, it might reemerge was anyone's guess.

Hannegan's call to Byrnes has provoked impassioned disagreements among historians. Some have portrayed it as the act of a steadfast Truman ally carrying out orders;[53] others as that of a secret, duplicitous Byrnes partisan.[54] Given his open concerns about Byrnes alienating Catholics,[55] his home-state ties with Truman, and his twice having solicited written presidential support for him, the former is far more credible. Still, as Walker notes, Hannegan never behaved as "an impassioned advocate" for his fellow Missourian. He "weighed Truman in the balance," as did others, but pursued one overriding objective: to remove Wallace.[56]

It says much of Byrnes' burning desire for the nomination that, after receiving the call, he got straight on a train for Chicago. Bad news he never accepted secondhand; good news was different. So confident was he that the vice presidency was now his, that he tried, using his title as director of war mobilization, to bump Pauley, the party treasurer and convention manager, out of the largest suite at the Royal Skyway, the convention hotel. The offense would not be forgotten.[57]

On Sunday morning, July 16, Byrnes arrived at the mayor's Windy City apartment, making the drive from the station in record time courtesy of the fire chief's red auto. There, he hatched plans with Kelly and Hannegan to release the president's Wallace-letter on Monday, after which the two bosses would announce that they were backing *Byrnes* with the president's consent. Hannegan even ordered placards proclaiming the team of "Roosevelt and Byrnes."[58]

Yet there remained a caveat to Byrnes' nomination, one which Hannegan had nearly forgotten. Roosevelt had, on the train, told him blithely to "clear it with Sidney" first. Sidney Hillman, the wily chair of the CIO's Political Action Committee (PAC), would therefore have a veto over Byrnes. And Hillman would wield it, insisting that he and his union's membership were headlong behind Wallace. He suggested, sotto voce, however, that Truman might be swallowed as a second choice—just never Byrnes, who had angered labor by backing wage controls. Flynn piled on, insisting the Southerner would cost the ticket 200,000 Black votes and push New York to Dewey.

Byrnes had been well aware of his vulnerability on race, and had tried to convince the president that he could do more for Blacks than other contenders. "If Mr. Wallace or Mr. Douglas says he is against the 'poll tax,'" he told Roosevelt back on the 13th, referring to the notorious tax used to keep Blacks from voting, "they cannot change the views of [white] southerners." But he, Byrnes, had credibility with these folks.[59]

Flynn, however, now had the last word. "I browbeat the [leadership], I argued, I swore," he would later write, "and finally they said [that] if the President would tell them again he was for Truman they would agree" to back him.[60]

Of course, the president, "cold, calculating and shrewd," in daughter Anna's words,[61] could well have anticipated this result. He had handed Byrnes' fate to the unions, reasoning that it would either secure their silence, if they let him survive, or, if not, put their prints on the knife. They took the knife.

When, four days later, Roosevelt's train-letter would reemerge from Mrs.

Hannegan's mattress, it would not escape the notice of a shocked and angry Byrnes that it contained no variant of the word "prefer."[62] By the president's moral metrics, he had not been untruthful. Walker would later defend FDR's unwillingness to play it straight with Byrnes. "[T]o have it known . . . that Roosevelt did not want Byrnes or anyone else to run with him would have had violent political repercussions."[63]

On Monday, July 17, Walker, Hannegan, Kelly, and Flynn together called the president, each one making the case that Truman was the only man who could rally labor and the party. Roosevelt, businesslike, said he understood: Byrnes was a "political liability." Ending months of vacillation and manipulation, he gave the final order: "Frank, go all out for Truman."[64] And so Harry Truman became the "Missouri Compromise." Yet it remained to convince the man himself—and then to convince the delegates.

That this was going to be a strange convention was clear. There could not have been *less* drama over the party's choice for president. But there has never been *more* drama over the vice president—an ill-defined and uncelebrated position. The reason for the latter lies in the combination of the president's irresolution and dire health, which meant that a raucous convention mob would, in effect, be *choosing*, in one man, the president's running mate *and* his successor.

"Just a heartbeat, this little," Truman had said to a friend in Kansas City, his thumb and forefinger almost touching, "separates the vice president from the president." FDR had not uttered a word to him about joining the ticket, yet everyone, it seemed, now assumed he must be elated by the buzz. He was not.

"Hell," he corrected one reporter in Chicago, "I don't want to be president."

Friend, and future treasury secretary, John Snyder would later clarify Truman's sentiment. It was, he offered, not so much that the ambitious senator did not want to *be* president as that he did not want to *succeed* to the job because of Roosevelt's demise.[65] In Truman's own words, he would be mocked as a "little man trying to fill big shoes."[66] Wallace and Byrnes, in contrast, had no such concerns. They wanted the job at the earliest vacancy.

Wallace, like Snyder, did not buy into Truman's humble act, but took a more sinister view of it. Truman was, he believed, "a small, opportunistic

man, a man of good instincts, but therefore probably all the more dangerous" for it.[67]

On July 17, the same day Roosevelt bestowed his benediction on Truman,
about a hundred reporters jostled for copies of a letter from the president,
just released by conference chairman Samuel Jackson. The core of it said:

> The easiest way of putting it is this: I have been associated with
> Henry Wallace during his past four years as Vice President, for
> eight years earlier while he was Secretary of Agriculture, and well
> before that. I like him and I respect him and he is my personal
> friend. For these reasons I personally would vote for his renomina-
> tion if I were a delegate to the convention.
>
> At the same time, I do not wish to appear in any way as dic-
> tating to the convention. Obviously the convention must do the
> deciding. And it should—and I am sure it will—give great consid-
> eration to the pros and cons of its choice.[68]

Reactions were swift and divided. CIO president Phil Murray, Florida
senator Claude Pepper, and other Wallace partisans looked on the bright
side.[69] It was, for now, the only presidential statement of support for anyone—
even if not quite the insistent endorsement of 1940. For Guffey, who had earlier told a questioner he would vote for "whoever Frank Roosevelt tells me
to," it was enough to elicit his full-throated support.[70] He would thereafter
act as Wallace's unofficial campaign manager.

But Wallace's doubters pointed to FDR's tepid tone and awkward quali-
fiers. Why say "if I were a delegate" except to highlight that he *wasn't*? The
letter was, observed United Press Senate correspondent Allen Drury, "perhaps the coolest and cruelist brush-off in all the long Roosevelt career."
It amounted to "so long, Henry."[71] Barkley called it "the *coup de grâce*."[72]
Walker called it "the kiss of death." Indiana DNC official Frank McHale
said his delegation would "construe the letter as meaning that the convention is wide open."[73] The *St. Louis Post-Dispatch* deemed it a boost to the
"already soaring campaign stock of energetic little *Jimmy Byrnes*."[74]

This last take was, of course, off the mark. Following the conference call
with Roosevelt, Crowley was dispatched to deliver the bad news to Byrnes—
who took it badly. Like Wallace, he refused to credit accounts of FDR's disfavor.

With Byrnes still in, but fighting a lost cause, Hannegan tried to play the knowledge to his advantage. At dinner that evening, he offered Murray and Hillman a deal: "We will withdraw Jimmy Byrnes if you will withdraw Wallace." Facing a bluff with a busted flush, the soft-spoken Murray refused to fold.[75]

The following morning, Tuesday, July 18, Byrnes phoned Roosevelt to make his case for a final time. The president, still casting himself as a bit character in a drama beyond his control, denied calling Byrnes a "political liability." Yet he acknowledged telling Flynn he "agree[d] with his estimate of the situation"—which amounted to the same thing. He also conceded writing that he would be happy running with Truman or Douglas, but continued to insist it was "in reply to a message from Bob"—a message that did not exist.[76] It would take a further few hours of fruitless lobbying with Hannegan, Hillman, and others before Byrnes would accept that he lacked the support to prevail.

Truman, who had already written his nomination speech for Byrnes, had a different problem: he *had* the president's support, but did not yet believe it. Though the party leaders had convinced Roosevelt to back Truman, the president was still pretending just to be a helpful observer. On Monday night, following the conference call, Hannegan failed to persuade Truman to run. Over breakfast on that Tuesday, Truman, by his account, actually asked Hillman to back *Byrnes*. Hillman declined, saying the CIO wanted Wallace. But if Wallace faltered, he added, tantalizingly, it could back only one other man—and "I'm looking at the other one."

A startled Truman demurred, but must also have recalculated. Had Hillman connived with Roosevelt? (They had, in fact, met at the White House Thursday prior, just before Wallace's appointment.) With party conservatives and, now, possibly, organized labor behind him, Truman would have a formidable force with which to take on Wallace's liberals.[77] For his part, Hillman, a consummate operator, appeared to have been playing the long game. Having calculated Wallace's odds as poor and receding, he was willing to fall out with Murray to be on the winning side. After all, the man who looked set to succeed Roosevelt was now indebted to him.[78]

The following morning, Wednesday, July 19, Byrnes released a letter announcing his withdrawal "in deference to the wishes of the president." Wallace, for the moment, was in a powerful position. To halt his momentum,

Hannegan knew Roosevelt would have to *tell Truman to run*, while also maintaining the charade that he was deferring to the convention.

Wallace had to this point, inexplicably, been missing in action. "An intellectual among politicians," in Jonathan Daniels' words, he "had no skill in affability" or interest in schmoozing those who would decide his fate. Under relentless pressuring from the CIO, however, he finally arrived in Chicago by train, disembarking at the 63rd Street Station to avoid reporters.

As he emerged from his car at the Sherman Hotel, however, two thousand cheering onlookers mobbed him. In the lobby, two hundred students serenaded him to the tune of "Joshua Fit the Battle of Jericho":

> *You can talk about Senator Byrnes,*
> *You talk about Senator Truman,*
> *But the Democratic Party has learned that*
> *Wallace fought the battle for the common man,*
> *Common man, common man!*
> *Wallace fought the battle for the common man,*
> *And he'll fight that battle again!*

Slowly he was steered through the crush, eventually arriving in a press room packed with eighty reporters and twice that many observers. On entering, he perched himself on the edge of a table, from which he swung his legs restlessly—just inches from the reporters.

"I am in this fight to the finish," he declared.

"Did the president throw you down or endorse you?" a reporter yelled.

"[He] did exactly what I suggested was the best thing to do."

"Will [you] win your fight?"

"I haven't the slightest idea."

On this note of honest, defiant ignorance, he headed to his mezzanine-floor headquarters, outside which a throng of allies and advisers awaited. The jockeying and counter-jockeying began. Murray accused Hillman of "opening the door to Truman" at a presser, a charge Hillman would deny. Others brought intel on the shifting loyalties of the 1,176 delegates.[79] This was the part Wallace so hated: the politics of politics. He was anxious just to make his speech, to engage the fight.

In the late afternoon, a bemused Truman was ushered into Hannegan's suite at the Blackstone and seated on a bed. Surrounding him were a somber Walker, Flynn, Kelly, Allen, and Jersey City boss Frank Hague. Hannegan, collar open, shirt damp with sweat, picked up the phone and dialed.

Moments later, he exchanged a few words through the receiver and held it out toward Truman.

"Bob," boomed the president's voice from San Diego, "have you got that fellow lined up yet?"

"No," Hannegan yelled back, "he is the contrariest goddam mule from Missouri I ever dealt with."

"Well, you tell the senator that if he wants to break up the Democratic party *in the middle of the war*, that's his responsibility."

Then, *bang*! Roosevelt had slammed down the phone.

"Oh, shit!" Truman said. "Why the hell didn't he tell me in the first place?"[80] It was a fair question, but never a fair process. It was one in which the president was determined to maintain both authority and distance.

Truman was no naïf, and could not have been shocked to learn of FDR's support. But he had waited for firsthand confirmation to avoid the ignominy Byrnes was now suffering.[81]

Unbeknownst to Truman, however, was that the call had been scripted and staged for his benefit. And it had its intended effect; he was in. He went straight to see Byrnes, assuring him it had not been his intention to run. Byrnes, who may have maneuvered Truman into nominating him to prevent this result, knew this was truthful. He would be back on a train to Washington that night, livid that the president had so humiliated him. Had he known about the letter endorsing Truman and Douglas, he told Brown, he would never have gone to Chicago.[82] Yet that was dubious. More likely, he would have fought to keep its existence hidden, and redoubled his efforts to win over Roosevelt.

On the evening of July 19, delegates, many decked out in traditional home-state dress, milled about the convention floor, sending up a din of yabber magnified by spiritous libation. (Three-day beer consumption on site would near 100,000 bottles; that of bourbon, rye, and scotch, 300 quarts.) Red, white, and blue glow-in-the-dark victory "Vs" and cutouts of GIs in battle pose adorned the walls. Over the balcony hung huge likenesses of the nation's fourteen Democratic presidents, the largest of which, the only one in color, being the face of a younger, healthier, FDR.

All of a sudden, the noise swelled out from an entryway, creating a roar that enveloped the stadium. Heads turned. Stepping out into the hall was the vice president. Overwhelmed by the reaction, Wallace waved to the crowd. After weeks of downbeat briefings from one apparatchik after another, the display of support buoyed him. Applause, whistles, and cheers accompanied his walk to the seats of the Iowa delegation. Placards, affixed to state standards, saying "We Want Wallace!" waved to and fro.

Not everyone, of course, joined in the welcome. Southern delegates, in particular, were still bitter at Roosevelt for having, four years earlier, forced upon them this unabashed liberal.[83] They were determined to prevent a repeat.

Rumors had been flying since Monday, set off by Hannegan's efforts to stop Wallace's momentum, of the existence of a second presidential letter—this one endorsing Truman. He and Pauley had hoped to keep Truman's name as quiet as possible, however, to forestall organized opposition.[84]

Pepper and Guffey hammered Hannegan to prove claims of another letter. The party chairman finally released copies at a press conference on Thursday the 20th. Zealous reporters knocked the pile from the young woman distributing them.[85]

Hoping to head off the obvious questions the letter would raise, Hannegan wove an Irish tale of its provenance. In it, he cast Truman as the Chosen One and Douglas an afterthought.

"Some time ago," he explained, he had "received requests from Missouri delegates on how President Roosevelt looked upon the possible candidacy of Senator Truman." But since others had asked how he "felt about the nomination of Justice Douglas," the president gave thoughts on both. As for the timing of the letter's release, he said he had only just received the president's assent.

Reporters were disbelieving. The letter was dated July 19, just one day prior. How, they wondered, had Hannegan received the letter so quickly, given that the president was in transit to an undisclosed location? And how, more curiously, had Hannegan known about it since *Monday*, two days before it was supposedly written?

"When did you get it?" one yelled.

"It is dated July 19," he offered, unhelpfully, adding that it had been brought by messenger.

Why was it "limited to two men," another shouted, when many others "were known to be in the field"?

"[We] had on *other* occasions discussed . . . *other* candidates," Hannegan clarified, but "a number of persons, some of them in Washington, had asked me about Justice Douglas."

The reporters rushed off to file their stories—just not the sort Hannegan had wanted. They questioned his motives and the president's wishes. Party leaders, they noted, were set on preventing nominations that evening. The putative reason was to ensure adjournment before midnight. Yet the true aim, they speculated, was to gain time and staunch Truman's "waning strength."[86]

The stadium that day, July 20, was electric. J. G. Grouzard, the concession czar, was in especially high spirits. Having tossed 40 percent of the hot dogs he had bought for the Republican event in June, he was thrilled to see Democrats in a more raucous, celebratory mood. They would down 25,000 wieners that day alone—85 percent of his three-day inventory.

The main event of the day, or at least the scheduled part, was the nomination of the president. A scripted coronation, it should have gone off with calm and precision. But the vice presidential turmoil threatened to mar it.

Alben Barkley, slotted to make the nomination speech, was incandescent. Sitting in the Blackstone dining room the day prior, he was approached by Walker with news that Roosevelt had asked party bigs to back Truman. Having thought, like Byrnes, that he'd been given a free lane to run in, he threatened to tear up his speech. He was tired of Roosevelt's games, tired of having to guess "which shell the pea was under."[87]

On the day, however, Barkley swallowed his pride and did his duty, intoning, preacher-like with quavering voice, a short but rousing presentation of Roosevelt's name for president of the United States. Thirty-five thousand convention-goers, nearly twice the standing-room capacity of nineteen thousand, roared their approval. They blew horns, danced, and showered their fellows with newsprint confetti—a celebration that went on for forty minutes.

Outside the hall, under the speaker's platform, Pauley, by his account, sat in a small office, on the phone with the president, laying out the plan to thwart Wallace. At that moment, in walked the vice president himself. Having been rebuffed by the president in his quest to make the nomination, it was now his turn to second it.

Pauley glanced up, saw him, and broke into a sweat. He hung up the phone. Looking back up at Wallace, he groped for words.

"Well," he then blurted out, "at least you've heard it play-by-play."

Wallace smiled, tapping his briefcase. "This is my *campaign* speech," he said, referring to his seconding text. "This is the one that will do it."[88]

Wallace placed the briefcase down, pulled out his papers, and entered the hall—which was still pandemonic. Approaching the podium, "he was compelled to stand [silent] for some minutes . . . amid the shouts and cheers of the crowd."

When the din died down, he began his speech—a speech that would be the most important of his career. In it, he would make the case not merely for the *president's* reelection but, with unusual skill and delicacy, his own. This case would be based on the subliminal but unmistakable message that, "in point of fact," as *The Washington Post* put it, "the New Deal today is Henry Wallace."[89]

FDR had, in 1943, referred to his latest incarnation as "Dr. Win-the-War," which he contrasted to the "Old Dr. New Deal."[90] Wallace now began by paying homage to Dr. Win-the-War, stressing that the goal of victory in Europe and the Pacific "transcends all others." It was, he said, "appropriate that Roosevelt should run on . . . his record as war leader." He now had to "finish this job before the nation [could] breathe in safety."

Victory, however, he stressed, was a means to larger ends: world cooperation and the triumph of liberalism—Dr. New Deal writ global. "The future," he said, "belongs to those who go down the line unswervingly for the liberal principles of both political democracy and economic democracy."

For Wallace, these principles were universal, though he understood that the latter was an alien concept to most Americans. Economic democracy—

here referring to the spreading of wealth and power over the productive apparatus—was, as he had explained in a speech at the Congress of American-Soviet Friendship in November 1942, more familiar in Russia. But it was a vital corrective to the "abuses of excessive political democracy," to the raw "bill-of-rights democracy," that had accompanied the rise of American "individualism."[91]

For those who had long harbored suspicion of him because of his Republican roots, Wallace had a clever apologia. It was, he explained, impossible "to play the Democratic game"—that is, to be a liberal—"inside the Republican party." It could work "on a State basis," perhaps in Iowa, but never nationally. "I know," he said, "because my own father tried it." Here, he cast his earlier political affiliation as an inheritance from a well-meaning family, rather than a considered personal choice.

In closing, he characterized the task of the convention as being far more than affirming the nation's present leader. It was about choosing its future course. "There is," he said, "no question about the renomination of President Roosevelt. The *only* question is whether the convention and the party workers believe wholeheartedly in the liberal policies for which Roosevelt *has always stood.*"

In fact, Wallace had grave doubts about Roosevelt's liberal convictions, and would later tell Murray that he would not support the ticket in public speeches until the president told him "just where he stood with respect to liberalism."[92] His endorsement of Roosevelt as a champion of liberalism was, therefore, as disingenuous as Roosevelt's endorsement of him. The big difference is that he needed Roosevelt, and not vice versa.

Wallace was, in the words of the convention's *New York Times* reporter, "interrupted repeatedly" as he spurred his supporters, and "inferentially challenged his opponents," by urging the party to "keep on its liberal course." Eleven times, he used the word "liberal." Heaping "praise and more praise upon Mr. Roosevelt," he tied the president to the liberal course, and himself to the president.[93] It was an audacious and, given the deafening approbation of the crowd, apparently successful strategy.

Finally, in a masterstroke conclusion he declared: "In the cause of liberalism, and with a prayer for prompt victory in this war, permanent peace, and full employment, I give you Franklin D. Roosevelt!"[94] Once more, the hall erupted.

Adroitly, Wallace had created the appearance of thunderous support for "the cause of liberalism." And his subtext was unmistakable: that securing the cause meant choosing a vice president who had never abandoned it.

Save eighty-nine Southern votes cast for Virginia segregationist Senator Harry Byrd, and one New York vote for former party chairman James Farley, Roosevelt went on to claim a quick and overwhelming victory in the contest for presidential nominee. Just before 10:30 p.m., with the 35,000 now standing in silence, the president's disembodied voice came wafting through the massive audio speakers, eerily remote from the empty podium.

His speech, delivered from a train car in San Diego, was short, solemn, Olympian—laying out the mission before him. It was "to win the war fast, to win it overpoweringly, . . . to form worldwide international organizations, and to . . . make another war impossible." What stood out, in contrast to Wallace's speech, was the absence of any paean to liberalism. It was as if Wallace had anticipated this gap, this emotional hole, calculating that the crowd would recall his words and rise to his support.

As Roosevelt finished, the crowd cheered once again. After a few minutes, Jackson made a hand signal. To close out the day's events, the hall filled with the strains of the national anthem.

But then the chanting began, isolated at first.

"We want Wallace! We want Wallace!"

It spread and swelled.

"We want Wallace! WE WANT WALLACE! . . ."

Then, from the organ pipes came the "Iowa Corn Song," fueling the building frenzy.

Pauley was stunned, livid. This was "the way Willkie won his Republican nomination" in 1940, he thought. "[H]e had the crowd, he had the physical facility." The CIO, he was sure, was now trying to do the same for Wallace.

"Stop that organ!" Pauley shouted. The organist, Al Melgard, was a damned "Petrillo man," a buddy of Chicago labor boss Jimmy Petrillo. He was rigging the show for Wallace.

"Tell me how!" yelled back Neale Roach, the convention's assistant director. "He won't answer the phone."

"Get that ax!" Pauley said, pointing to the fire equipment. Then "chop every goddam [organ] cable!"[95] The organ stopped, but the cables survived.

꙳

Just how had the hall, right before Roosevelt's speech, filled to nearly twice capacity—and filled with Wallace supporters? Through the years, many accounts have been offered, ranging from the dubious to the plausible.

Wallace's explanation, which he took from the CIO's Beanie Baldwin, was congenial to his self-image as a man of the masses. He said the demonstrators had "gotten in as part of the Kelly machine," which backed Truman, "but nevertheless were for" him, Wallace.[96] For this to be true, Kelly would have to have been monumentally incompetent. In historian David McCullough's similarly suspect (and unsourced) account, fifteen thousand counterfeit tickets were "reportedly" printed "with the blessing of Mayor Kelly," who "was secretly hoping for a Truman-Wallace deadlock" that would lead to the nomination of "Illinois's favorite son, Senator Scott Lucas." These tickets, however, somehow fell into the hands of the CIO, and thence into those of the Wallaceites.[97] Many others, such as Pauley, would also say counterfeiting was involved,[98] but the tickets' dollar-bill design would have made that challenging[99]—perhaps explaining why no evidence of the claim has ever emerged.

Yet another account has Wallace lieutenants seeking five hundred tickets from a disbelieving party official, who laughingly advises them to "buy a door"—that is, bribe an usher. An organized "stampede," however, required *thousands* of illegal entries, and Kelly's people controlled the ushers.[100]

The most plausible story, then, notes that the tickets, different for each day and session, had all been printed in the same color. Given the crush

1944 Democratic convention guest ticket.

at the doors, ushers would not have had time to check details. One (again, unsourced) account claims that "the Wallace forces [had] managed to collect tickets for all the various sessions from their supporters" and, before the fourth session on Thursday night, "poured into the hall, while the harried ushers only noted the color and not the date and time on the tickets."[101]

Whatever the mechanics of the Wallace takeover, its scale and force were overwhelming. Dozens invaded the floor from the gallery, illegally, pushing delegates from their seats. Banners backing the liberal icon sprung up in the most unlikely of places, including the heart of the Alabama delegation.[102] To Baldwin, it was spontaneous enthusiasm; to Pauley, purposeful, orchestrated mayhem.

10:50 p.m. "WE WANT WALLACE! WE WANT WALLACE! . . ." The chanting continued.

This was it, Claude Pepper thought. Now or never.

Known as "Red Pepper" for his red hair, fiery rhetoric, unabashed liberal politics, and Soviet-friendly sentiments, the eclectic chairman of the Florida delegation—a former steelworker and Harvard Law grad—was determined to move for a vote then and there.[103] He could see many state standards aloft in "the Wallace parade." The hall was swept up in the moment; Wallace could have the nomination in one round. But if Jackson adjourned, the momentum would be lost. By Friday, the bosses would have played every card in the deck for Truman.

Desperate for the chairman's attention, he climbed on a chair, waving his standard—a signal to activate his microphone. Yet if Jackson, a Wallace supporter, saw him, still he did nothing. Pepper leapt up and down, shouting. The din smothered his voice.

"WE WANT WALLACE! WE WANT WALLACE! . . ."

There was only one chance now. He needed to reach the stage.

Pepper waded into the sea of bodies, elbowing forward. Spellbound delegates, reporters, and spectators watched as he pushed to the front.

Meanwhile, below the dais, the bosses conferred frantically. "We had to find an excuse to adjourn," Pauley would recall, "and fast." Kelly was ready to declare a fire hazard. A red-faced Hannegan ordered Pittsburgh mayor

David Lawrence to move adjournment, and Jackson to recognize him. "Get up there now, and I mean now," he yelled, "or I'll do it for you!"

Fear gripped Jackson. None of this was in the script.

Sheepishly, he waved his arms from the podium. "Ladies and gentlemen of the convention, we're going to have to stop some time . . ."

The shouting grew louder.

Bang went his gavel. *Bang, bang, bang,* over and over.

More shouting.

"This is getting serious now. People may be in serious difficulty," he told the crowd.

"WE WANT WALLACE! WE WANT WALLACE! . . ."

"This has been a great day," Jackson continued, struggling to appear in control. "And tomorrow will be another great day." He recognized Lawrence.

Just then, Pepper reached the gate blocking the way to the stage. He smiled at the guard, an old friend from the railway unions. The man smiled back, opening the latch.

Lawrence made his motion. "Mr. Chairman, I move that this fourth session of this Democratic National Convention recess until tomorrow, July 21!"

"NO, NO, NO . . ." The loudest roars yet.

Jackson turned to see Pepper charging up the stairs. Alarmed, Roach and others scrambled to bar his way.

Frantic calculations coursed through Jackson's mind.

"Motion made, the convention adjourned," he said. "All in favor of the motion, let me know by saying 'aye, aye!'"

With Pepper at the top step, voices yelled back "AYE, AYE!"

Bang went the gavel: "Convention adjourned!" Jackson declared. Voices came back: "NO, NO, NO! . . ."

Leonard Reinsch, the radio manager who had earlier shut down the organist, now ordered him to play something good—loudly. Others switched off the mikes and spotlights, plunging the stage into semidarkness.[104] Day two was over. Hannegan sighed in relief.

The 1944 Democratic convention, diaried Drury, "might go down in history as 'The Battle of the Bosses'"—party versus union.[105] And as it entered day three, its final day, the party bosses asserted their full authority to prevent a repetition of the prior night's events. On the morning of Friday, July 21, two layers of sweaty security guards policed the convention entrance, and many Wallace fans with invalid tickets were turned away.[106]

The obligatory speeches, notably duller than the day prior, went on all afternoon. The crowd, far smaller and less boisterous, waited impatiently, hour after hour, for the main event—the vice presidential vote.

When the first ballot finally began at 4:30 p.m., a full sixteen names were in nomination. Truman observed from a box, eating a hot dog; Wallace remained ensconced in his room.

Jackson polled the fifty-five delegations alphabetically. When the tally was complete some ninety minutes later, Wallace had scored 429½ votes—putting him first, though well short of a majority (37 percent). Truman had polled 319½ (27 percent). The others—led by segregationist Alabama senator John Bankhead with 98 votes, Scott Lucas with 61, and Alben Barkley with 49½—had amassed 394½ combined.

To many, it seemed Wallace was on a path to victory. But Hannegan was confident the script would play out. That presumed, however, that the CIO had no ticket tricks up their sleeve. Determined to preclude them, he ordered Jackson not to recess for dinner, and to commence a second vote immediately. By staying in session, and not admitting a new evening crowd, he assured there would be no replay of Thursday, with Wallace supporters packing the hall.

Hannegan and Pauley divvied up delegate territory, working their assigned targets. Pauley wanted Alabama to start the Truman bandwagon early, but Bankhead refused to withdraw. Needing time to lobby its delegates individually, Pauley tried frantically to "grab Senator Jackson's leg" before he commenced the roll call, but was too late. Alabama cast 22 votes for Bankhead—and 2 for Wallace.

As Wallace and Truman ran in lockstep well into the second round, excitement in the hall rose. There was an initial surprise when the fractious California delegation, which had previously split 30–22 for Wallace, opted to "pass"—saving its vote for later. The chairman, state attorney general Robert Kenny, thereby denied Wallace forces the psychological boost of an early repeat vote in the vice president's favor. New York delivered the first inkling of a shift to Truman, boosting his margin from 65–30½ to 74½–18.

But Guffey's Pennsylvania held the line, repeating its 46–24 vote in favor of Wallace—keeping him within five votes.

Wallace ally Norman Littell, FDR's assistant attorney general, pinned his hopes on Alben Barkley and North Carolina's Josephus Daniels, prominent liberals, breaking "the solid line of the South against Wallace." But Wallace himself may have scotched that chance Thursday night, when he proclaimed in his speech that "the poll tax must go."

Wallace's call was bold. It was principled. But it was unwise, politically. Even those Southern delegates who accepted the tax's inevitable demise (which did not come until 1964) took Wallace's declaration as a gratuitous shaming of voters back home. The South would hold firm against him.

Truman's second big break came after the alphabetical roll call. With twelve states having passed, Truman led Wallace 477½–474. Now accepting defeat, Bankhead dramatically withdrew his name and cast his 22 votes for Truman. Indiana's Paul McNutt, chairman of the War Manpower Commission, who received 21 votes (to Wallace's 5) in round one, did the same—delivering 24 votes to Truman. Three more delegates from Maine, 8 from Wyoming, and 18½ from New York switched their votes to Truman. The dynamic had turned.

"I could see Hannegan at the front edge of the platform motioning excitedly to this delegation and then to that," wrote a crestfallen Littell. "For all the world, he was like an organ player pulling the great stops on a giant organ." Just as Truman's backers were sure the CIO had staged the stampede on Thursday, Wallace supporters were sure the bosses had taken over on Friday. The truth, however, was more prosaic. Conservatives like Bankhead and McNutt were unwilling to hand victory to Wallace. By Occam's razor, no "organist" was necessary. Delegates simply voted their interests.

With Truman now on the verge of victory, photographers converged on the senator's box. He and his wife, Bess, beamed. His daughter, Margaret, leapt up and down. All the while, chants of "We want Wallace!" rained down from the galleries.

In one final, fitting burst of confusion, Ohio declared for Truman, temporarily putting him over the top—only to recall its votes and "pass" when a delegate challenged the count. That left the honor of deciding the nominee to Massachusetts—which cast its 34 votes for Truman. The rest was formality.

"That's all we need!" Hannegan shouted to Ed Flynn. "Come on in!"

Flynn's Illinois switched its vote from 58 for Lucas to 55 for Truman. Others followed. California, whose delegates were still shouting at each other as its votes were recast, reversed its tally from 30–22 for Wallace to 42–10 for Truman.

At 8:14 p.m., Jackson read out the final tally: 1,031 votes for Truman, 105 for Wallace. California delegate, actress, and soon-to-be congresswoman Helen Gahagan Douglas, who had earlier denounced the senator as a reactionary machine politician, fainted.[107] The vice presidential contest, the most dramatic and consequential in American history, was over.

Over it was, yet what happened during the predawn hours of Friday, July 21, 1944—between the first and second ballots—has since become the subject of legend.

"Pauley and others," writes Curtis MacDougall, a fervent progressive and chronicler of Wallace's 1948 presidential campaign, "were promising jobs and patronage" for Truman votes.[108]

But what sort of "jobs and patronage" did they promise? He does not say.

David McCullough, Truman's acclaimed biographer, writes that "ambassadorships or postmaster jobs were promised"—though "no one knows how many."[109] But how is it that "no one knows"? In all likelihood, it is because *there is simply nothing to know.* No such promises were ever made. But if the legend is, in fact, false, how can *we* know that? There are at least three reasons.

First, it is difficult, if not impossible, to imagine FDR, a three-term president, handing his authority over ambassadorial appointments to party bosses. Second, postmasterships were nineteenth-century sinecures. By 1944, the post office had been part of the civil service for six decades, meaning that its jobs were not available for political patronage. Third, the historical record virtually proves the legend's falsehood. Walker, the postmaster general, supposedly "telephoned every chairman of every delegation" to pressure them to support Truman.[110] If he had offered them ambassador or postmaster jobs, we would surely find at least some of them landing in such positions at some point after the convention. Yet of the fifty-five delegation chairmen, *none* became an ambassador (or postmaster) under FDR. One, Prentice Cooper of Tennessee, became ambassador to Peru under Truman, in May 1946, but all of his delegation's votes, in both rounds, *went to himself.*[111]

Of the 1,176 total delegates, *only a single one* became an ambassador under FDR: New York's Richard C. Patterson Jr. (whose votes are undocumented) was named ambassador to Yugoslavia in September 1944.[112] Truman, in 1948, named him ambassador to Guatemala. Under Truman, in total, four delegates from four different delegations became ambassadors, but three of those delegations *voted overwhelmingly against Truman.* Cooper, as noted above, an ambassador to Peru, voted for himself twice. Indiana's Paul McNutt was named ambassador to the Philippines in June 1946, yet also voted for himself twice. And only one of Indiana's 26 delegates voted for Truman (in round 2 only).[113] North Carolina's O. Max Gardner was named ambassador to the U.K. in December 1946, but all of his delegation's votes went to Governor J. Melville Broughton twice. In sum, then, there is not the faintest evidence of improper patronage on the part of the DNC leadership.

From whence, then, come the endlessly repeated claims of delegate bribery? They all derive from a single, typically unreferenced, source. The CIO's Baldwin, who would manage Wallace's presidential campaign in 1948, made the allegations in 1951, seven years after the 1944 convention. Though he acknowledged having no evidence[114]—and the facts testify against his claims—this has not stopped those claims from becoming a central part of convention legend.

But if Wallace was not the victim of delegate bribery, had he not been the victim of rigged convention procedure? The answer, again, is almost certainly no. "[T]he enormous enthusiasm displayed for Wallace" on the evening of July 20, noted Baldwin himself, "did not represent the votes of delegates."[115] That demonstration, according to MacDougall, another Wallace supporter, had been "CIO-planned and financed."[116] Many of the delegates were, in fact, according to *The New York Times* floor reporter, repelled by "the overzealousness of the CIO followers, who jammed the galleries and kept up a constant shouting to the assembly in favor of their champion."[117] Consistent with this observation, Baldwin believes that Wallace would have gotten *fewer* votes Thursday night than he would actually get "on the first ballot the following day."[118]

The bosses' convention strategy, for all the dark legend surrounding it, appeared to consist in little more than exhorting delegates who were not for Truman or Wallace to vote their pleasure in round one, and to switch to Truman in round two. With Wallace expected to fall well short of a majority up front,[119] Truman would, they reasoned, then sweep up the votes of the rebel and "favorite son" nominees. Since their supporters generally disliked Wallace, and understood that the president wanted Truman, the bosses were rowing with the tide.

Still, they took no chances. They had worked for over a year to get Wallace off the ticket, and the effort was worth a last night of intense lobbying. The CIO, which controlled 125 delegates and alternates, was, after all, out in force on the other side. If dark-horse candidates refused to withdraw, and delegates did not grasp what was at stake and vote tactically, Wallace might still, in the words of one Southerner, "sneak home with the bacon."[120] The Truman forces therefore did what one would have expected them to do—urge, plead, and cajole.

Wallace took his defeat in good spirits. "I am very happy about it," he said in a dictated note to the press. "My own defeat is not a loss to the cause of liberalism—that is obvious in what happened here." He sent a message to Truman congratulating him on his "enlarged opportunity to help the President" and the agenda for which "Roosevelt stands."[121] At 10 p.m., he ate scrambled eggs and bacon in his room with seven supporters and called it a night.[122]

"In adversity and defeat," Drury diaried in eulogy, Henry Wallace "has emerged in something of his true stature. . . . Everything which has been said about his unfitness for administrative office, his ineptitude, his impracticality, still finds adherents, but his moral character, his integrity and his good will, if they were ever in serious doubt, are no longer so."[123]

"I had hoped by some miracle you could win out," Eleanor Roosevelt wrote to Wallace, "but it looks to me as though the bosses had functioned pretty smoothly."[124]

The bosses took great—some might say excessive—pride in their performance. "When I die," Hannegan would tell a journalist in 1947, "I would like to have one thing on my headstone—that I was the man who kept Henry Wallace from becoming President of the United States."

Pauley, too, would lay credit to the achievement. "It was about a year before the convention," he would later explain, "that I proceeded to prevent [Wallace] becoming the president." And he was relentless in the effort.

But then Flynn would say *he* had done Wallace in. It was he, Flynn, who, after a national fact-finding tour in early 1944, first convinced the president that Wallace would be "the candidate of the radicals" and "a serious handicap . . . on the ticket."

There is no doubt all three men felt certain an ailing Roosevelt needed a more credible successor. And no matter weighed on them more than that Wallace, on foreign policy, was "in the wrong school of political thought."

"Sometimes," Pauley would say years later, "after listening to the newscasts about our country standing up to Russia in a manner the whole democratic world has applauded, I look at [Truman's photo] and wonder what might have happened if the convention had gone a little differently."[125] It "still frightens me," Allen would write, to remember the "day in 1944 when Henry A. Wallace came within a few votes of winning the Democratic Vice-Presidential Nomination." It would have heralded, he added, only half-facetiously, the nation's reconstitution as "the Soviet States of America."[126]

Yet in the end, the man who kept Wallace from becoming president was not Bob Hannegan or Ed Pauley or Ed Flynn. It was Franklin Roosevelt.

Rex Tugwell had skipped the convention on the president's advice. "You won't like what's going to happen," he recalled Roosevelt telling him days before the convention—in an oblique reference to Wallace's impending defeat.[127] As to the victor, "Harry S. Truman was picked by [FDR] and by no one else," Sam Rosenman would later write in *The New York Times*. "I make [this statement] as a matter of personal knowledge."[128]

Wallace's defeat was "a regrettable personal tragedy," wrote Drury. "Like so many others, he knows now what it means to be a politically dispensable friend of Franklin Roosevelt."[129] Whereas most party officials did not support Wallace, they resented the charges that they had done anything worse than carry out the president's expressed wishes. When the president's daughter, Anna Boettiger, bitter at Wallace's treatment at the convention, sent word to party publicity director Paul Porter that she thought him "a son of a bitch," Porter would have none of it. "You go tell Anna Boettiger," he instructed the messenger, 'So's your old man.'"[130]

Wallace struggled to make sense of the president's role in his loss. "There is no doubt in my mind as to his intentions when I returned from Alaska on July 10," he wrote in his diary. They were "to ditch me as noiselessly as possible." That was likely the case as least as far back as March, when Roosevelt suggested a trek through Siberia to China. But Wallace was sure he had changed the president's mind on July 11. His presentation in the White House, he wrote, had shown Roosevelt "he had been lied to by his advisers."

Everything changed again, however, he reasoned, at the boozy, late-night White House meeting that followed. "Probably the advisers really won" at that point. He would later pin the blame not on Hannegan *or* Pauley *or* Flynn, but, consistent with Baldwin's convention tales, on *Walker*. Roosevelt would deny knowledge of, or consent to, Walker's actions—claims Wallace thought "bullshit."

"The hard thing for me" in the end, though, he concluded, was "to reconcile what the President said to me when I left on July 13 ['I do hope it will be the same old team'] with what he later did." Somehow, Wallace overlooked that the president *also* told him "they [will] beat you out in Chicago."[131]

"The official White House position," wrote George Allen, "was that the Convention would be left free to" pick the vice president. But "as a matter of practical fact . . . the Presidential nominee *always* picks his running mate, one way or another."[132] And in 1944, Roosevelt simply did it "another" way. He did not "pick" Truman, as he had picked Wallace in 1940,[133] but he eliminated all other names, save Douglas',[134] through his negative power of veto.[135] This procedure was fraught. It was cruel. And it gave rise to endlessly repeated tales of both personal glory and conspiratorial intrigue. But it afforded Roosevelt the deniability he craved in all his most difficult political maneuvers. And that, in the end, is what mattered to him.[136]

Nine

KEEPING UP WITH THE JONESES

On the night of his defeat, Wallace received a curious telegram. "You made a grand fight and I am very proud of you," Roosevelt wrote. "Tell Ilo not to plan to leave Washington next January."

Wallace read these words over and over. What did they mean? What would he do in Washington? In any case, he had no idea "how Mrs. Wallace felt about it."

"I never asked her," he explained years later. "I didn't talk to her about things of this sort."[1]

Yet the president was never as cryptic as he seemed to Wallace. On July 13, he had told Wallace that there would, after the election, be "a job for [him] in world economic affairs."[2] And just as Roosevelt had helped the convention "choose" Truman, he would now help Wallace "choose" his next job.

In the convention's wake, Wallace had become the unrivaled leader of the party's liberal wing—and a potentially dangerous loose cannon. He was, in consequence, besieged not just by messages of consolation, but efforts at reconciliation. Truman, Walker, Hannegan, Ickes (who had, in Chicago, belatedly embraced Wallace's candidacy)—all paid their warmest respects and expressed the fervent hope that he would support the campaign.[3] But the critical rapprochement would not come until five weeks after the drama, when, on August 29, 1944, the president welcomed Wallace back at the White House.

Was his friend bitter? Roosevelt wondered. Set on payback? Anxious to move on? To put his plan in motion, he needed to know.

And so he asked if Wallace had shown his telegram to Ilo. The answer, he was sure, would reveal all.

Prepared for the charm spell, however, Wallace did his best to play coy.

His wife, he said, had indeed read the wire. But she wasn't sure, he explained, whether "she could earn enough money, on the strength of [the message], to support me in the style to which I was accustomed."

Roosevelt laughed. A bad joke was a good sign. Wallace wanted back.

The campaign, Roosevelt assured him, would need his help. His ideas were the future. Of course, he might be "four to six years ahead of his time," but what he "stood for would inevitably come."

Wallace returned an uneasy smile. "I was very happy about what had been demonstrated at the convention," he demurred. "I now knew the people were for me."

But Wallace, Roosevelt knew, was deluding himself. The party was a broad tent. There were Northern progressives and Southern conservatives, Blacks and whites, Protestants and Catholics, workers and farmers. And so he pushed back, reminding Wallace that he, Roosevelt, had "had to make a deal" with Garner to get the nomination in '32. He had needed to compromise, to enlist new friends; and so would Wallace.

But Wallace was having none of it. There was no need, and certainly no moral case, for surrendering to the right. "Mr. President," he said, "I could have made a deal too, but I did not care to do it. I knew exactly what happened at the convention," he added, referring to the conspiracy against him. But he had backed the president "because his name was a symbol of liberalism." The president thanked him.

It was time now, he thought, to drop the bait. If all went well on November 7, Roosevelt said, Wallace could have any position in government he wanted—any position, that is, except one, of course.

He knew well what job Wallace wanted above all: secretary of state. But Cordell Hull, he explained gently, "was an old dear." And he "could not bear to break his heart."

Coming from anyone else, such a statement might have sounded preposterous. But Roosevelt could not bear to break hearts—or at least not *in person*; which is why, had he actually wanted Hull out, he would have sent Rosenman or Walker to effect it.

But the issue was not Hull; it was Wallace. When in November an ailing Hull would resign, the president would still not turn to Wallace, but to former U.S. Steel president Edward Stettinius. No seasoned diplomat, Stettinius had a quality Roosevelt prized in a secretary of state, at least at that moment—a quality lacking in both Byrnes and Wallace. This was a well-earned intellectual modesty. Roosevelt would soon conduct the most consequential negotiations of his presidency—negotiations with Stalin over entry into the Pacific war and cooperation in a postwar security architecture. And he had no intention of first negotiating with his secretary of state.

The president knew where he wanted Wallace—in a domestic economics post where his liberal credentials would shore up the weak point in the administration's political profile. Though he would play up the internationalist trappings of the job as a sweetener, Roosevelt had no intention of allowing Wallace to get near foreign policy. He would instead appoint the free-trading, anti-Communist former Texas cotton baron Will Clayton, a Jones ally in the procurement battles, as Stettinius' primary economics aide—the first-ever assistant secretary of state for economic affairs. Wallace would have to stay focused on the home front. To sell the job, Roosevelt now dialed up his most savvy charm.

"One of the first things" he would have to do after the election, he explained, was to sit down, together with Wallace, and "make a list of the folks we were going to get rid of." And "first on the list" would be "Jesus H. Jones."

Jesus was Roosevelt's nickname for Wallace's archnemesis. By Tully's account, Jesse Jones had exhausted the president's goodwill by opposing his nomination (which Jones would deny) and domestic policies (which he would half-deny). In any case, Roosevelt had reasoned that Wallace would, once the sting of rejection had dulled, leap at the chance to claim his rival's fiefdom.

"Well, if you are going to get rid of Jesse," Wallace responded, "why not let me have Secretary of Commerce with RFC [Reconstruction Finance Corporation] and FEA [Foreign Economic Administration] thrown in? There would be poetic justice in that."

The president smiled. "Yes, that's right," poetic justice. He could not have put it better. Wallace, he added for good measure, could also "sit in on some of the international conferences."

Wallace would reflect on this moment years later, saying that he "did not want to take anyone's job away from him."[4] Of course, he would have had no problem taking Hull's job, but the fact that Jones' job would be vacant lent a touch of Christian blamelessness to it.

Looking like old friends again, Roosevelt and Wallace now went outside for lunch. As they ate, laughing together with Anna and her children, Roosevelt regaled Wallace with political gossip. FDR, like Anna, loved gossip. One story going around, the president said, was that Jones had tried, through a "movie man," to bribe his eldest son into sinking the campaign. If Jimmy would say his father was too old to be president, Dewey would make him an undersecretary.

The two men chuckled. FDR thought the story daft, but there were elements of truth in it. Democratic congressmen had, in fact, wanted Roosevelt to back another Democrat for president, and prodded Jones to dangle a job for Jimmy as inducement for Roosevelt's cooperation. Jones would later claim to have brushed them off.

Wallace was, as Roosevelt had hoped and expected, now in a cooperative mood. Though he had just three weeks earlier told Phil Murray he "was not going to make any speeches for the ticket" until Roosevelt committed to a liberal agenda, the promise of Jones' portfolio was sufficient for him. When Roosevelt asked what his plans were, Wallace proposed some "extemporaneous talks" and "two or three big talks," at Madison Square Garden and the like.[5]

The president heartily approved. His left flank was safe.

In the fall of 1944, Wallace walked a tightrope, campaigning for Roosevelt while proclaiming his own agenda. He declined offers of party funds to cover his expenses, insisting that he "preferred to be independent."[6] Appearing before a liberal crowd at Madison Square Garden on October 31, his only joint event with Truman, Wallace was in a position to humiliate the man who had knocked him off the ticket.

By Wallace's account, he calmed fears among the senator's aides by entering the arena with him, arm-in-arm.[7] Yet in George Allen's telling, this claim was posturing for posterity. Wallace had, in fact, sought to avoid Truman's entourage, but the latter took him "by the forelock and marched [him] into the huge auditorium at Truman's side." Though the cheers were largely for Wallace, the contrivance allowed Truman to "[take] his bows" as well.[8]

In any case, Wallace's speech embraced the throng as his own. Proclaiming that he shared their aversion to "reactionary Democrat[s]," he insisted that "neither Truman nor Roosevelt" was such—and urged their support on this basis.

"This has been and is a people's war," he continued, and "the peace must be a *people's peace*." It was a term he would use often, though never defining it. Whatever it was, "the way to get it," he explained, was "to re-elect Roosevelt and *then* to make the Democratic Party into a truly liberal party!"[9] It was a full-throated halfhearted call to back the ticket because it was not reactionary. The hard work of building "a truly liberal party," no doubt around himself, could then follow.

The crowd got the message, and the cries duly came back: "WAL-LACE IN '48! WAL-LACE IN '48!"[10]

Had the war not still been raging in Europe and the Pacific, the election the following week might well have gone to Dewey—and set back liberalism for decades. But on November 7, Roosevelt won handily, if less overwhelmingly than in 1940—by 432 to 99 electoral votes (25.6 million to 22 million popular votes). It would be the last election in which the South would vote solidly Democrat, a fact Roosevelt would have considered validation of his cautious approach to desegregation and civil rights.

With the election over, party leaders breathed a sigh of relief—twice over. Roosevelt would remain president. And under the Twentieth Amendment, ratified in 1933, it was clear that the vice president–*elect* would become the president-elect if the president died before inauguration day. Wallace was, for all but a brief period, out of the line of succession.

Following her husband's historic fourth-term victory, Eleanor Roosevelt was anxious to speak with Wallace. She told him that liberals now looked on him "as the outstanding symbol of liberalism," and that he ought to consider leaving government and replacing Sidney Hillman as head of "a greatly broadened" CIO PAC.

Feigning consideration of the proposal, Wallace waited a few hours before turning her down "flatly but nicely," saying that liberalism could only express itself "on a national basis" through the Democratic Party.

He suspected "her husband [was] up to his usual maneuvering tricks,"[11] looking to ease him out of government. But this was a wholesale misreading of FDR's calculations and methods. The president had thought Wallace a liability on the ticket; but he would be a *boon* in the cabinet—if used correctly. With the election over, Wallace would continue on in the job of appeasing the liberals. Roosevelt, further, never enlisted Eleanor as a political fixer. To the contrary, he resented her pestering over personnel.[12]

Still, it was around this time, late in 1944, that Wallace began contemplating the attractions of life outside the Democratic Party. On December 19, he met with *New York Times* publisher Arthur Sulzberger, and the two of them conversed animatedly about the future of liberalism and a "spiritual approach to the world's problems."

Sulzberger had been devoted to Wendell Willkie, who had died of multiple heart attacks a month before the election, and would have supported the Republican internationalist had he won the nomination. Wallace pointed out that Willkie had talked of starting a progressive party in the new year, but stressed that he, Wallace, thought it "much better to make the Democratic Party into a progressive party."[13] As would become clear in the coming months and years, however, he was, if the party would not bend to his politics, prepared to go elsewhere. He had, after all, done this once already—in 1936.

Two weeks after the election, Wallace had still heard nothing from Roosevelt about the Commerce job. He began to get nervous. On November 30, he wired the president to say that his "interest in poetic justice [was] stronger than ever." He feared Roosevelt might now instead offer him secretary of labor, a job he "would do everything [he] could to avoid"—as he told Henry Morgenthau. He wanted to serve the Common Man, but not at ground level.

Beyond the poetic justice of dethroning Jones, Wallace coveted the power Commerce and RFC would afford him over industry, commensurate with that which he had wielded over agriculture in the 1930s. He might also have the chance to take over foreign economic policy. "The government's role in foreign commercial operations," he asserted in a memo to the president prior to a December 20 meeting, "should not be separated from its role in domestic commerce because the two fields are mutual." In pursuit of these necessary powers, he would, as commerce secretary, want the authority to appoint overseas commercial representatives independent of the State Department.[14]

At their meeting, Roosevelt was coy. "I got your wire," he said. "It is all right. You can have Commerce." Wallace was taken aback, noting the contrast with his ebullient tone in August. The two then began to reprise their awkward pre-convention courting routine.

"I don't want it," Wallace explained, "unless you are really enthusiastic about my taking it in the same way you wanted me to take Agriculture." Roosevelt insisted he "really wanted" Wallace.

Long convinced that the party bosses had duped the president into believing he would split the party and hand the election to Dewey, Wallace tried to persuade him there was no such risk in the Commerce nomination. "I am sure there will not be any difficulty concerning my confirmation in the Senate," he told him.

"No, of course not," Roosevelt agreed. "But then," he added, "sometimes you can't tell."

In any case, as Wallace would reveal to a friend, he "would rather not be confirmed by the Senate than to have Jesse Jones still in government." Felling his nemesis was paramount.

The president affirmed that he was happy for Wallace to take RFC as well, but yielded no ground on foreign policy. He had, he said, already asked Leo Crowley to stay on at FEA—at least until the war's end. And Clayton was still slotted for the top economics post at State.

Wallace saw Clayton as the main obstacle to expanding his authority in foreign affairs, and prodded the president to reconsider the Texan's appointment—or at least his powers. When Roosevelt spoke of improving the poor standard of living of workers in Africa, for example, Wallace remarked that that would require international commodity agreements—to support prices. Here, the president was "bound to run into trouble with Will Clayton" and his "Manchester School" free-market thinking.

But FDR would not budge. "Will Clayton is not so bad," he remonstrated, "and his wife is a dear."

Sue Clayton was far closer to the president, and more deeply involved in Democratic politics and fundraising, than her husband, and this fact may well have shaped Roosevelt's thinking. In any case, Lauchlin Currie would accurately predict to Wallace that Clayton would become a powerful figure at State. He would go on to play a leading role in the creation of the Marshall Plan for European reconstruction and the General Agreement on Tariffs and Trade (GATT).

Wanting to nail down commitments from the president, Wallace asked what he could tell the press. Roosevelt said he could say they had "a nice conference" on "reforestation in Iran."[15]

In the run-up to the inauguration, speculation swirled over the president's cabinet moves. *The New York Times* reported that Wallace was likely to replace Jones at Commerce, though there was uncertainty as to whether Jones would retain control of the powerful RFC.[16]

At the final cabinet meeting of his third administration, on January 19, 1945, the eve of the inauguration, Roosevelt partially revealed his plan—saying that Wallace, though relinquishing the vice presidency, "would still be with us." Following the ceremony on Saturday, January 20, however, Jones arrived home to find a letter from the president clarifying Wallace's new role.

"Dear Jesse, This is a very difficult letter to write," it began. Roosevelt praised Jones for his "splendid services," but concluded that Wallace, having given "of his utmost toward the [election] victory," now deserved "almost any" job he believed he could master. Wallace had chosen Commerce, the president explained, a post "for which he is fully suited."[17] Jones might consider an ambassadorship, however, and take up the matter with Stettinius.

At the president's request, the two met in the Oval Office the following day, Sunday. It was, as Tully would later note, an ill-considered invitation. Roosevelt offered Jones the top embassy posts in Paris and London; Jones declined. Fed chairman? Not interested. Out of plum jobs, Roosevelt asked that Jones nonetheless support the team and bless Wallace's appointment publicly. No, Jones replied; "Henry was totally unqualified." He wished the president well on his mission abroad—to where few yet knew—and bid him goodbye.

"It is not goodbye," Roosevelt said, refusing to believe he had exhausted his charm potions. "I'll see you when I get back."

"Mr. President, I think it's goodbye," Jones put back. And with that he was gone.

But he was not done. "In Texas, they fight different," journalist Allen Drury diaried. Jones' response "would go down in history as one of the more noteworthy events of a crowded era. There has probably never been an exchange of sentiments between Chief Executive and Cabinet officer quite like it."

A few hours after leaving the Oval Office, Jones wrote to the president. "Inasmuch as you are sending Mr. Wallace's name to Congress tomorrow," he said, "I am [publicly] releasing your letter to me and my reply." The reply laid bare the full extent of his fury and disdain for the man who would replace him.

"I have your letter of today," he wrote, "asking that I relinquish my post as Secretary of Commerce, which carries with it the vast financial and war production agencies within the [RFC] so that you can give it to Henry Wallace as a reward for his support of you in the campaign."

"You state," he continued, "that Henry thinks he could do the greatest amount of good in the Department of Commerce, and that you consider him fully suited for the post. [But] I cannot agree with either of you."

"It is difficult to reconcile [your] encomiums [to me]," he went on, "with your avowed purposed to replace me. For you to turn over all these assets and responsibilities to a man inexperienced in business and finance will, I believe, be hard for the business and financial world to understand."[18]

The press response to the president's action was derisory, even at those papers—like The Washington Post—which had never supported Jones. It smelled, said the Post and the Cleveland News, of a rank political "payoff." The New York Times, the most critical, said that Commerce was "surely the one place above all others into which Mr. Wallace does not fit"—especially given the "vast financial and war production agencies" that had been grafted on through RFC.[19]

This judgment was echoed in the Senate, among Democrats as well as Republicans. "The principal reaction," Drury observed, "was complete bafflement. On the eve of [the president's] departure for overseas, at a time when his relations with the Senate are of the utmost importance to the cause of world peace, [he] has chosen deliberately to . . . antagonize them."[20] Speculation was rife that Roosevelt was willing to jeopardize "the fate of the world" in order to "rid himself of two embarrassing domestic liabilities"—Jesse Jones and Henry Wallace.

Still, the powerful Senate Finance Committee chairman Walter F. George (D-GA) offered a Solomonic compromise. Hoping to prevent internecine warfare among the chamber's Democrats, he said he would support confirming Wallace, but only after severing the RFC and its agencies from

Commerce. "I have been willing to give these agencies extensive powers," the senator explained, "solely because I had confidence in the business experience and business judgment of Mr. Jones." But he had no such confidence in the nominee.[21]

Wallace had, of course, created a successful company to develop and market high-yield seeds, but "inexperience" was just the charge leveled at him in *public*. In private, senators blasted his alleged "ideological opposition to the private enterprise system."[22] Given the vast powers an RFC-fortified Commerce Department *could* wield over business, many were reluctant to place it under the control of a man who wished to import "economic democracy" from Russia.

Thus was the stage set for riveting political theater: hours of testimony from a powerful, bombastic incumbent and his divisive, aspiring replacement, men whose mutual animosity was as open and raw as any in cabinet history.

When the hearings opened in the afternoon of Wednesday, January 24, the Senate room was packed—"one of the biggest audiences in U.S. congressional history." Photographers bobbed and clicked as the slow-drawling North Carolina senator Josiah Bailey, chairman of the Commerce Committee, took his seat under the searing klieg lights, calling the session to order.

Senator George testified first, proposing an amendment to his bill to forbid the reunification of Commerce and RFC once the new secretary was confirmed. He even suggested that Jones might remain atop the newly independent agency.

As he spoke, a din spread across the hall. Entering the chamber, smiling, chewing gum, waving to the familiar faces filling the room, was Jesse Jones, who had timed his tardiness for maximum effect. Photographers and cameramen surrounded the theatrical Texan, jostling for unobstructed views.

Senator George was obliged to pause for nearly ten minutes before the clamor died down. As Jones approached the witness table, George shook his hand amiably before continuing his testimony. All the while, Jones shifted about in his chair, restless, exchanging glances with the crowd, anxious to perform, while committee members smiled down in anticipation. Only Claude Pepper scowled.

Finally, Jones had the microphone. After warming up the crowd by asking "who gets the gate receipts," which drew hearty guffaws, he wasted no time stating his case against the nominee.

"The RFC and its subsidiaries," he said, were "the most gigantic business enterprise . . . the world has ever known." If their operations were not adjusted judiciously at the war's end, it could "destroy our entire business and financial structure." It was thus essential that "the man who is given [these] vast responsibilities [have] proven and sound business experience." RFC, he said, "should not be [run by] a man willing to jeopardize the country's future with untried ideas and idealistic schemes."

An angry Pepper would have none of it. Did the witness, he asked, now think the combined jobs too much for one man, or that only he could do them?

"If you are trying to ask me if *Henry Wallace* is qualified for both jobs," Jones replied, "I will say no."

But by what facts, Pepper pressed on, was Henry Wallace "incompetent" to do them?

"I did not say he was '*incompetent*,'" Jones shot back. "Stick to the text." The point, he insisted, was that vast taxpayer funds should not be entrusted to a "visionary planner" who would squander them on "dangerous experimentation" to "remake the world."[23]

For Wallace's enemies, this was the red meat they had come for.

The next day, January 25, it was Wallace's turn. Entering the chamber to a three-minute standing ovation from a much different crowd, he took the witness seat to begin five hours of grueling self-defense. He looked "tense and nervous," Drury observed.

There had been much speculation that Wallace would refuse the nomination if the lending agencies were denied him, but he quashed it—partly. He would be willing to serve in the reduced capacity, but only until the war's end. Still, he made his disapproval plain, insisting that the real reason his opponents wanted to clip the department's "vast financial powers" was not concern for his "lack of experience" but dislike for his *actual* experience— for the beliefs and policies he had fought for. His opponents wanted RFC and its agencies "to help big business," whereas he intended "also to help *little* business and to help carry out the president's commitment to sixty million jobs."

A normal politician would have modulated his rhetoric for such a jury, one which held his career in their hands. But Wallace was no normal politician. Rather than present himself as a colorful but mainstream Democrat, he challenged their convictions and their courage by calling for bold and costly new government programs and regulations: to maintain employment through expanded construction; to create new federal jobs, millions if necessary, if employment fell; to guarantee minimum agricultural prices and annual wages; and to provide comprehensive federal health care coverage.

Wallace "handl[ed] himself fairly well," Drury observed—surprisingly so, given the pressure he was under. Drury admired Wallace's audacity, calling him "one of the very few sincerely moral characters of the present Washington generation." Yet the grilling from disbelieving senators, he concluded, "[had] to be done":

> For Henry has aspired to monumental power and would, if given it, proceed in his headlong fashion to impose upon the country a blueprint for which it is not yet ready. It is one thing to have the dream and it is another to attempt to drive the country into it. Henry's world is one of plans and programs, imposed with an eager compulsion upon folks who may not always agree. The happy way of the reformer might too easily lead to destruction. . . . Given the club of untold billions [of dollars] and the unrestrained impulses of a desperately sincere Messiah, there is no telling where he might end up.[24]

Wallace's showing thrilled his fans, who had greeted his opening statement with a minute-long ovation. But it converted no one on the committee of eleven Democrats and eight Republicans. "A lot of us," said Virginia Democratic senator Harry Byrd, "are just simply against everything he represents." The following day, they voted 15–4 in favor of the George bill to split the lending agencies from Commerce, and then 14–5 against the nomination. It was a stunning repudiation.

In the days that followed, Southern Democratic senators continued to speak out against Wallace and press for his withdrawal. Tennessee's Kenneth McKellar condemned Wallace as "a failure in politics"—a crazed pig-killer and hopeless vice president. As for the '44 race, Roosevelt would have done better if Wallace had kept quiet. Even his own state did not like him. And as for labor, Wallace had never done a thing for them except make speeches when he needed a favor. McKellar was determined to defeat the nomination.

Roosevelt had left strict orders that he not be bothered with messages regarding domestic matters except in the case of emergency. Rosenman declared just such an emergency, radioing the president on January 27 to argue that the nomination was doomed unless he signed the George bill or met its demands through executive order—and even then the outcome looked bleak. Receiving the message on his first day out at sea from Norfolk, Roosevelt, opposing the idea, ignored it. Two days later Rosenman sent another urgent appeal, asking the president to indicate if he would sign the George bill. Roosevelt, seemingly indifferent, handed the message to Byrnes, whom he had invited along as a reconciliatory gesture, asking his opinion. Byrnes said he would approve it; the president nodded—okay. Byrnes, grasping the urgency, drafted an affirmative reply for his signature and transmission to Senator Barkley.

Bailey moved to bring the Senate into executive session, which would allow it to vote on Wallace's nomination *before* consideration of the George bill. As a majority were not about to give Wallace control of Jones' full empire, Bailey's success would mean the death of Wallace's nomination. In a drama-filled roll call on February 1, Wallace, his career dangling by a thread, barely survived on a 42–42 tie. The archconservative Robert Taft (R-OH) then tried to change his vote to "no," a parliamentary maneuver which would allow him to move for an immediate vote on the nomination anyway. Vice President Truman, presiding, however, recognized Barkley first—triggering a furious protest from Taft. Barkley then called for an immediate vote on the George bill, which, following two hours of debate, passed by 74–12. He then moved that Wallace's nomination be delayed until March 1 to give the House time to vote on the bill—which it promised to do expeditiously. After reading out the just arrived message from the president, pledging to sign the bill, Barkley secured unanimous assent. Truman would years later claim credit for "sav[ing] Wallace from rejection by the Senate," though it was a victory he probably regretted.

So the fight moved on to the House, where a coalition of Republicans and conservative Democrats now plotted to defeat the bill and kill the nomination. Wallace, cried New York Republican Leonard Hall, wanted "to change the New Deal to the New Communism!" The public itself was split on the nomination, with 40 percent in favor and 37 percent against. On February 16, a motion by Wallace opponents to send the bill back to the Rules Committee, where they hoped to bury it, failed narrowly, 204–196. Amidst fears that a rejected Wallace might be transformed into a dangerous martyr, the House then passed it 400–2. Roosevelt signed it on February 24. On March 1, 1945, the confirmation battle ended with the Senate approving Wallace's nomination for the stripped-down Commerce post by a vote of 56–32.[25] Having assured Roosevelt back in December that there would "not be any difficulty" with his confirmation, he would later look back at this moment with a different perspective. He thought it "really rather surprising that they finally confirmed me."[26]

At 1 p.m. on April 12, 1945, the president was sitting for a portrait at his house in Warm Springs, Georgia, when he suddenly began waving his hand back and forth above his eyes. Trying to smile, he said he had "a terrific pain" in his head. Moments later, he collapsed into unconsciousness.

Dr. Bruenn was rushed in. Diagnosing a cerebral hemorrhage, he called McIntire, who in turn summoned Atlanta internist James Paullin—Bruenn's commanding officer. Shortly before 3:30 p.m., Roosevelt stopped breathing. Paullin gave him a shot of adrenaline to the heart, but to no avail. The president was dead.[27]

At 7 p.m., six hundred miles north in rainy Washington, Harry Truman sat alone on a brown leather chair in the Cabinet Room, dazed, contemplating the enormity of the circumstances. Nine minutes later, standing, hand on a Bible, looking out of his thick, round glasses into the eyes of Supreme Court Justice Harlan Stone,[28] he pronounced the words "So help me God" and—just like that—became the first president since 1933 not to be Franklin Roosevelt.

Few Americans knew any more about Harry Truman than they had the previous July, when he was nominated as vice president. Yet many in Washington, of both parties, now thought as Dean Acheson and Arthur Vandenberg did: that Truman, however inexperienced, was an honest man of sound judgment. "It seems to me a blessing," Acheson wrote to his son, "that he is the President and not Henry Wallace."[29] Even some prominent Wallace supporters now felt, in retrospect, that the late president had made the right decision the summer prior. "I hate to confess," wrote *The Nation*'s I. F. Stone, "but I think Mr. Roosevelt was astute and farsighted in picking Mr. Truman rather than Mr. Wallace as his successor."[30] Stone had much preferred Wallace *as vice president*, but far more had been at stake in Chicago.

Standing nearby as Truman swore his oath, a somber Henry Wallace looked on. He had not seen Roosevelt since March 22, three weeks prior, at a White House Correspondents' Association dinner—an evening during which the sixty-three-year-old commander in chief had appeared alternatingly remote and renewed. His passing now was an event for which Wallace had been prepared intellectually, having observed his steep decline since the inauguration, yet ill-equipped emotionally. In his twelve years in government, Wallace had served no one else. Watching "the senator from Pendergast" take his vows, he must surely have cast his mind back to Chicago, that great urban asylum of American graft, where the party's shadowy bribers and fixers had robbed him of his just claim in the line of succession.

Observing his disconsolate and irritable fellow cabinet members over the coming days—Morgenthau, Ickes, and Stettinius in particular—Wallace would be acutely conscious of just how disoriented, how at sea, they had all become. "The cord which had bound the cabinet had snapped," he observed.[31] There would, he knew, soon be a new team, a new program. A new world.

Ten

"60 MILLION JOBS,"
FOUR MILLION STRIKERS

If choosing cabinet members were like choosing a spouse, Wallace would have been the first to be ditched. Since arriving in Washington, Truman had found liberals an alien species. "For all their education," they seemed to him "lacking in common sense," David McCullough observed.[1] Wallace and Truman not only diverged on ideology and politics, but did so in ways that were bound to clash.

Asked by the author John Gunther what he liked most in the world, Truman answered instantly: "people." He called the Senate "the grandest bunch of fellows you could ever find anywhere."[2] He could talk amiably with most anyone about anything, and enjoy every minute—particularly with bourbon. Wallace, too, liked "people," but only as a collective abstraction, or in the form of a large, adoring, and properly distanced crowd. As for *persons*, save those with worthy observations on science or spirituality, he preferred to avoid them. He had causes, not friends. When forced to converse in a small group, he told a progressive campaigner, he felt as if "he had a cold snake curled up inside him." When bored, he would either fall asleep or walk away.[3] The Senate, with its relentless barter and worthless banter, was his vision of hell.

Roosevelt had his differences with Wallace, yet through ceaseless manipulations and shuffling of authority he avoided confrontations the less nimble Truman could not. Truman, however, needed to shore up support across the party spectrum, and the two men most sure that they, and not he, should be president were the ones he could least afford to alienate. And so on Saturday, April 14, 1945, Truman met the train bearing Roosevelt's body with two men on his flanks: Jimmy Byrnes on his right, and Henry Wallace on his left.

President Harry S. Truman (center), flanked by Director of the Office of War Mobilization James F. Byrnes (left) and Secretary of Commerce Henry A. Wallace, before the funeral ceremony for Franklin D. Roosevelt, April 14, 1945.

Though Truman wanted to delay the announcement for several weeks, word spread that Byrnes would replace Stettinius at State. Byrnes had mastered all sides of government. He knew Churchill; he had met Stalin. He seemed the right man to be, in the absence of a vice president, first in the line of succession.

Morgenthau, Truman concluded, was a "blockhead" who "didn't know shit from apple butter."[4] Once alerted that the treasury secretary would become president if he and Byrnes were to meet tragedy, he decided to sack him and install his longtime poker buddy—the genial, savvy Kentucky lawyer and politico Fred Vinson. Wallace, acknowledging that Morgenthau's intellect was often "not equal to the occasion," would nonetheless lament the loss of a longtime ally. In the end, he and Ickes would be the only New Dealers to survive the purge.[5]

Admiral William Leahy had wished to resign as chief of staff, but Truman persuaded him to stay, providing a vital conduit to past decisions to which he, as vice president, had not been privy. Wallace no doubt agreed with the admiral's judgment that Truman, following Roosevelt's death, lacked the knowledge and confidence to buck his advisers, meaning that they had to be damned sure they were right.[6]

Wallace, for one, was sure. Meeting with Truman on April 27, he pledged "to serve him as loyally as [he] had Roosevelt." The new president was, in turn, Wallace noted, "exceedingly eager to agree with everything I said." This eagerness to agree, which Truman would repeat in meetings with Wallace time and again over the coming seventeen months, reflected a combination of inattention, unsettled convictions, and a desire to keep peace with the liberals. It would eventually wreak havoc with policy, as well as undermine the confidence of friends at home and abroad.

The enormous granite and limestone Commerce building, completed in 1932, was a monument to its most famous secretary—Herbert Hoover. The department had 32,339 employees when Wallace took charge, a third of whom based in Washington. Still, it was only a fifth the size of the Agriculture Department when he left in 1940.

In his new office, behind his desk, Wallace rehung the smiling portrait of the seventh agriculture secretary, his father, Henry Cantwell Wallace. Leading into the office was a 254-square-foot waiting room, described by one writer as "Mussolinic." Wallace would convert it into extra office space for staff.

For all its outward grandeur, Commerce had "practically no functions of a regulatory or control character," as Wallace lamented to a House Appropriations subcommittee. And it had been stripped of its powerful lending agencies as a condition of his confirmation. Instead, the department provided services for the business community—technological, aeronautical, statistical, and economic—"in the public interest."[7] It was Wallace's ambition to amplify his power through legislation, committee appointments, and public appeals.

While awaiting the outcome of his confirmation drama, he had begun writing a book for publication in September 1945. Entitled *Sixty Million Jobs*, it offered an impassioned defense of the FDR campaign's hiring goal—created to counter Dewey's full-employment pledge.[8] Equal parts wonkish and polemical, Wallace's rambling 216-page volume also served as its author's early election manifesto. He was thinking ahead to 1952—perhaps even to 1948.

Confessing his love for data, Wallace drew upon "the vast and splendid statistical storehouse of the Federal agencies" to promote a new all-encompassing "national full-employment budget" for consumer, business, and government spending. The forecasts comprising it would be used to formulate rapid policy interventions to ensure full employment, defined as 60 million full-time jobs, by 1950. He further called for a national commitment to $200 billion in annual production—the high point of wartime production, and therefore "the measure of our economic manhood." This ambitious program was not, he insisted, a design for a "Planned Economy," as alleged by "conscious evildoers" or "unwitting dupes," but rather a blueprint for "democratic planning to preserve our free enterprise system."

Though Roosevelt had provided no basis for the 60 million figure, Wallace presented it as a solemn imperative. He urged all Americans, in their roles as business leaders, workers, farmers, and consumers, to pledge themselves to ethical self-education and cooperation in order to transcend the immoral "philosophy of scarcity" guiding much of American private enterprise. Business leaders would have to abandon "the economic textbooks of a bygone era," according to which they tried to profit through "high prices" and "low wages." They would have to overcome their reactionary fear of government and embrace cooperation with it. Wages would need to be kept high through enlightened collective bargaining and "practical means" to guarantee them on an annual basis. Government would further have to "work out fair and just solutions" to distributional problems created by technological advance and industrial change. A "philosophy of abundance" would thus take root, ensuring that all thrived through the "strength of mutual belief and mutual stimulation of purpose."

Wallace acknowledged that growth and employment had been buoyant in the freewheeling 1920s, but stressed that their collapse in the 1930s had been brought about by the earlier "planlessness." Henceforth, government would play as large a part as necessary, through its powers over taxation, spending, credit extension, agricultural adjustment, regional transformation, scientific research, trade promotion, foreign aid, resource development, wage-setting, and business regulation, to ensure fulfillment of economic targets within a context of social justice.

Underlying Wallace's program was a moral commitment to "economic democracy," here defined as "the various economic groups [exercising] equality of bargaining power" while accepting a "duty of serving the general welfare." Postwar bargaining was not to be confrontational, but cooperative, based on concern for all the nation's interests. Such enlightened democratic corporatism would require the "education of union membership," as well as corporate management, to ensure that their interests were in line "with those of the consumer, generally." And these interests would themselves have to be informed by objective knowledge. Both farmers and consumers, he explained, "must allow themselves to be guided [by the] findings of the scientific nutritionists." And, finally, the nation would need to end all racial and religious discrimination.

Such a sweeping, eclectic conception of "economic democracy" was not only head-splitting in its unification of so many diverse, and at times opposing, values, but sat uncomfortably in the context of Wallace's earlier association of the term with the Soviet Union—a state in which private bargaining was precluded by the ruling party's direction of production and allocation. But Wallace rarely defined amorphous political terms in his texts, preferring to rely on the feelings they evoked. In this case, he simply let inspiration trump consistency.

Wallace further insisted that wholesale changes in international affairs were necessary to create the global demand required to support Roosevelt's jobs target. "Full participation" in the new United Nations would be needed to raise living standards worldwide. "Higher wages and better conditions of work" abroad would be effected through the International Labour Organization. More and cheaper capital would be channeled to underdeveloped countries through the new International Bank for Reconstruction and Development. Finally, "a cooperative and harmonious relationship with Russia" would have to be developed. Yet America would still "not attain abundance, peace, and freedom" without first recognizing "the fatherhood of God and the fundamental decency of man."[9]

The book was reviewed widely, with views split along political lines. In The New York Times on September 9, Senator Pepper praised it effusively, calling its appearance a major "publishing event comparable to [that] of Wendell Willkie's 'One World'"—which had been a runaway bestseller. The review was almost certainly ghosted by Wallace himself, as Pepper had written to the author a month before publication asking if he "would be good enough to put together a tentative review of this book for me at the earliest possible moment." (In Moscow the following week, Pepper would present a copy of the book and "his" review to Stalin, who would receive them "with an expression of great interest.") Senator Taft, writing side by side with Pepper in the *Times*, without the benefit of Wallace's assistance, condemned the book as misguided and propagandistic.[10]

At a cabinet meeting on October 19, Wallace took up the thesis he had laid out in *Sixty Million Jobs*. With the demobilization of 12 million soldiers, joblessness was about to soar. Absent dramatic interventions, seven to eight million Americans would be unemployed by the spring. It would be back to the misery of 1939.

To keep total industrial take-home pay at 1945 levels, he urged the president to raise basic pay rates 15 to 20 percent. Though countering impending mass unemployment with vastly higher wages was unorthodox, Wallace believed that boosting labor income was the key to achieving "abundance." Byrnes countered that wage rises at such a level would be inflationary, but Wallace insisted that efficiencies afforded by new technologies made them feasible with no increases in prices.[11] In any case, he maintained, they were justified so long as prices did not rise more than 3 percent.

How had Wallace arrived at these numbers? Though he would present his "wage-price policy" to the American public as the product of his department's apolitical scientific analysis, the truth would prove more interesting—and consequential.

Wallace's handpicked primary adviser at Commerce was an economist named Harry Magdoff. Some of the clearest details we have on his early life come, curiously, from Soviet foreign intelligence files.

Bronx-born of Jewish parents from Minsk, Harry was what was known as "a red-diaper baby." He was attracted to Communism at a young age. His mother was, in his own words, "very close to the communist party" and his father "sympathetic towards communists." At age eleven, Harry "joined a children's organization run by the Communist Party," where he sold newspapers, attended meetings, distributed leaflets, and helped organize strikes.

By the time he arrived at City College of New York to study math and physics in 1930, he had "read a lot of Marx" and was, in his own words, "already a radical." He joined the progressive Social Problems Club and edited its pro-Communist magazine *Frontiers*, getting suspended, and then expelled, for his political activities. In December 1932, he married Beatrice (Beadie) Greizer, a longtime CPUSA member who helped persuade him to join the party a few months later. But the other woman in his life, his mother, pushed him to go back to school. Enrolling at New York University in 1933, he continued his activism with the new CPUSA-dominated American League Against War and Fascism and assisted in the publication of the magazine *The Communist*. In 1935, he became editor of the *Communist International Youth*.[12]

After graduating with a BS in economics from NYU in 1936, Magdoff rotated through various economics and statistics posts in the "capitalist, imperialist government," as he called it, ultimately transferring to the Commerce Department's Current Business Analysis Unit in July 1944. There, as an economic analyst and chief of the unit, he was put in charge of publishing the influential *Survey of Current Business* and preparing weekly economic reports for cabinet meetings.[13]

By the fall of 1945, the burly, thirty-two-year-old, pipe-smoking Magdoff was known in the department for championing new measures of productivity—measures consistent with the "socialist idea" of focusing on labor input, rather than the "usual approach" of looking at value added. He disdained those "conventional economists" who did traditional productivity analysis—those who only "think in a market system where money is the measure of everything."[14]

We only get a clear view of his thinking on actual policy in 1946—after the FBI began surveilling him. Their logs in May 1946 would show Magdoff arguing that miners may need wage rises of "more than 18 percent," and that the government should therefore "seize the mines [and] operate them according to [our] principles" until the owners agreed to terms.[15] As for a national rail strike that month, Magdoff would call it "a good thing"—one that would "clarify the issues." In his determination to stop the strike, Truman was, in Magdoff's eyes, a "dope."[16]

In December 1945, Wallace would promote Magdoff to chief economic analyst in his unit. What Wallace knew of Magdoff's background and political views at that point is uncertain. But, not being privy to FBI reports on Magdoff and the "gang" of Soviet informants in the Commerce Department, which J. Edgar Hoover sent to Truman military aide Brigadier General Harry Hawkins on November 8, 1945 and February 25, 1946,[17] we can presume that Wallace was, throughout his time as secretary, unaware of Magdoff's long-standing ties to Soviet intelligence.

From the late 1930s, Magdoff was part of a CPUSA "informational group" which gathered memos, reports, copies of confidential documents, and the like for General Secretary Earl Browder and the organization's leadership. The latter shared that information with the Soviet-controlled Communist International (Comintern), from whence it made its way to both branches of Soviet intelligence. The group with which Magdoff was associated was headed by fellow Marxist economist Victor Perlo, and included Charles Kramer, Edward Fitzgerald, Allan Rosenberg, Sol Leshinsky, George Perazich, and Harold Glasser.

In April 1944, the "Perlo group" was transferred to the direct control of U.S.-based NKGB intelligence operatives.[18] Magdoff was given the code name "Kant"—later changed to "Tan." According to notes of the former KGB operative Alexander Vassiliev, Magdoff was, at least by January 1945, aware that the group's materials were going to Soviet intelligence. He "felt very proud of himself."[19] Throughout 1945, Magdoff was in contact with Soviet intelligence couriers such as Joseph Katz (code name "X"), Rebecca Getzoff ("Eva"), and an operative known as "Said"—probably Valentin Matveevich Sadovnikov. Among the materials he provided to the NKGB that year were, in March, a cipher cable about the Anglo-American Oil Agreement (which was hostile to Soviet interests), and, in October, excerpts from Wallace's September 21 cabinet memo discussing "problems of atomic energy."[20] In other words, Magdoff was engaged in espionage—espionage involving Wallace's most sensitive political writing at the time he was advising the secretary on policy.

Soviet intelligence deactivated Magdoff in late November 1945, following the dramatic confessions to the FBI of former spy Elizabeth Bentley. Magdoff would, however, against instructions, maintain close social and professional contact with the members of his former network, as well as with many in the network of Nathan Gregory Silvermaster. Magdoff's wife was apparently well aware of his activities. When the two went to the movies on December 1, they were overheard by "one of the [FBI] agents engaged on the physical surveillance." During a "scene in the picture where secret writing was being brought out on a postage stamp, Beatrice Magdoff inquired of Harry Magdoff, 'Do you do things like that?'"[21]

Magdoff's influence on Wallace would grow over their time together at Commerce. On May 1 1946, Wallace would make him his special assistant in the Office of Program Planning.[22] The two would thereafter maintain close professional contact for years. In a June 1947 college job recommendation, Wallace would call Magdoff "a well-trained economist" who "would make an excellent executive and teacher."[23] And in 1948, he would engage Magdoff as an adviser on his presidential campaign.

Wallace's views on Magdoff would change radically, and retrospectively, sometime after 1950, when Congressman Richard Nixon released a report accusing Magdoff of being part of a spy ring that fed secret economic data to Moscow. Magdoff would, at a Senate hearing in 1953, refuse to answer questions about the allegations,[24] and Wallace would thereafter condemn him and downplay their close relationship. In a letter to Senator Homer Ferguson (R-MI) dated May 5, 1953, Wallace would write that Magdoff was "undoubtedly" a "bad man," and that the *New York Journal-American* had "smear[ed]" him, Wallace, by calling the economist one of his "top advisers."[25] He could "not remember" Magdoff advising on "any matter of international policy." Magdoff's "interest," Wallace explained with contrived haziness, "seemed to be in New York business men." In any case, Wallace stressed, he had nothing to do with hiring Magdoff, who had been brought "in[to] the Department under Jesse Jones."

For Wallace, the great maxim of French moralist François de La Rochefoucauld rings true; that "it is easier to know humanity in general than a man in particular." Yet all of Wallace's statements regarding Magdoff are still either false or misleading. Magdoff, who would go on to coedit the *Marxist Monthly Review* and author a Lenin-inspired tract called *The Age of Imperialism: The Economics of US Foreign Policy*, was, by 1946, as Wallace well knew, concerned first and foremost with the state of U.S.-Soviet relations. FBI phone surveillance logs in 1946 reveal that Magdoff was, contrary to Wallace's claims, involved in the drafting of a lengthy letter from Wallace to Truman criticizing the path of U.S. policy toward the Soviet Union, as well as his later letter of resignation over differences on such policy. And whereas Wallace had not hired Magdoff, he promoted him twice, consulted him regularly, and tasked him with drafting his correspondence on matters domestic and foreign—before enlisting him as an economics and foreign policy adviser during his presidential run.[26]

Wallace hailed "free enterprise" and disparaged the "planned economy," yet supported the setting of wage and price levels by government analysis. This curious contradiction can only be explained by noting that, throughout his time in government, aspects of his thinking evolved while others remained static or regressed, resulting in logical loose threads. Wallace's praise of "free enterprise" is therefore best understood as a rhetorical leftover from his patriotic wartime political embrace of what FDR's trust-buster Thurman Arnold called the "folklore of capitalism." As for the term "planned economy," Wallace used it as a synonym for socialism, a deformed ideology which evolved, he believed, as an extreme reaction to the failings of extreme capitalism. Economic "planning," in contrast, was for him a rational, and indeed necessary, function of government in a technologically advanced society—one in which firms maximizing economies of scale were necessarily too large to be disciplined by competition.

Whereas Wallace claimed to support collective bargaining, he in fact considered its results legitimate only where they reflected the public interest. Corporate management, for example, needed "not only to understand its own functions in its own individual private enterprises, but also to understand the relationship of these detailed functions *to the workings of the economy as a whole*."[27] But how was such an understanding possible? It was most surely not, and therein lay his case for government, wielding big data, to state its views and impose its verdicts. And though he was not yet ready to state so publicly, by 1948 he would be supporting nationalization of strike-ridden, "scarcity"-driven industries such as coal and railways, and the creation of boards comprised of government, consumer, industry, labor, and agriculture representatives to set prices, wages, investment, and dividend policies in so-called basic industries.[28]

On October 25, 1945, a report leaked from the Commerce Department. Following publicity of the "sensation," as Senator Ferguson would later term it, Wallace, appearing to use the leak as pretext, published it on November 1.

The startling "Report of a Study by the Department of Commerce" concluded that automakers could, without raising prices, hike wages by 15 percent immediately, and by 25 percent in 1947, all the while making profits that would dwarf those earned before the war. These findings, Wallace explained, had been the result of months of study by "able statisticians who analyzed all available data" related to costs and productivity in the industry. Its wage implications, however, he explained, extended well beyond car manufacture. "The automobile industry," the report said, is only "illustrative of industries with high earning power."[29]

At the time of the leak, industrial tensions had been mounting. With wage controls having ended following Japan's surrender in August, union and employer negotiations stalemated. Strikes were breaking out nationwide. Adding to the 28,000 miners who had stopped work since May, 60,000 lumber workers, 27,000 oil workers, and 15,000 elevator operators walked off the job in September.[30]

The report hit the smoke-filled bargaining rooms like a bombshell. Unions were elated, companies livid. Auto negotiations were expected to set a template for the entire industrial sector, and the Truman administration had just tipped the scales for the unions. A United Auto Workers (UAW) negotiating brief had, prior to any public knowledge of the report, used calculations identical to those contained therein—suggesting to General Motors (GM) that Wallace had given them an advance copy.[31]

An angry George Romney, general manager of the Automobile Manufacturers Association (AMA), further charged that Wallace had mischaracterized the productivity data on which the analysis was based. He demanded to see the details of the underlying study, but Wallace would not release them for a further three months—until after wage talks had entered their final phase. Once the AMA had the details, it would accuse Wallace of backing the unions on the basis of a flawed "experimental application of statistical techniques," divorced from actual conditions in the industry. Wallace's baseless numbers, moreover, it said, had become "official guideposts in formulating the present national wage-price policy."

Throughout, Wallace defended the report, conceding only that "disparities in the relative efficiency of individual companies" could justify different firms paying different wages around the average. Yet this caveat made little sense. Efficient firms would not squander an advantage by paying above-market wages just because statisticians said they could. And if they did, investment would stop flowing to them, with the result that innovation and cost-control would suffer industry-wide. On the flip side, workers would not passively accept lower wages just to keep inefficient firms afloat.[32]

Wallace had, in any case, misled the public about his department's report, and in ways the AMA had not imagined. Thanks to FBI surveillance of Magdoff in late 1945, and likely leaks to Ferguson in early 1946, it would later emerge that Wallace had disguised the work's true authorship, only correcting elements of his account as facts surfaced which contradicted it.

In September 1945, the FBI learned, Magdoff was approached by a former government colleague, Harold Wein, then working as an economist with the Justice Department. Wein had written an article on his own, outside of government work, estimating the relationships among elements of cost, price, and profits in the auto industry. He hoped it might be published, under his name, in the *Survey of Current Business*—of which Magdoff was editor.[33] The article was never published. Instead, Magdoff brought the piece to Wallace's attention, after which the department secured Wein's permission to use the material unattributed. It is unknown what incentives may have been offered him.

When Wallace claimed the findings as his department's own, he failed to reveal the outside authorship. As for the "able statisticians" who, Wallace claimed, had been working on the report since early 1945, he had no basis to believe that any such statisticians, beyond Wein, even existed. The release of the report as a government document, combined with its timing, appeared intended to influence, if not determine, wage settlements nationwide, on terms favorable to the unions.

Not until March 14, 1946 would Wallace, under pressure from Ferguson's revelations, acknowledge that the report, "the subject of much controversy," had been based on a study by Wein, whom he identified only as "an economist." The findings, furthermore, Wallace would clarify, should never have been regarded as "official forecasts of costs, prices, or profits for the automobile industry or for industry as a whole." They were presumably "unofficial," in that they had not been created by the government.

As for how the report's calculations had fallen into the UAW's hands prior to their release, Wallace would later write that "both studies," those of his department and the union, had been "based, in part, on the original source of data developed outside the Department"—that is, the work of Harold Wein. But how would Wallace have known how the UAW got its numbers? He may not have, but Magdoff, who had received the numbers from Wein and later drafted the claim for Wallace, did know—presumably because he had passed the numbers to the union.

Wallace further insisted that GM's charge that his department had fomented the strike was "patently ridiculous." Yet Magdoff, as the FBI would discover in May 1946, backed a national rail strike, which Truman had worked hard to prevent. It is therefore likely that he welcomed an auto strike as well.

Senator Ferguson would subsequently ask Wein how it was that his work had come to be published by the Commerce Department, but the author of the analysis "decline[d] to discuss the matter." The secretary, he explained, had not authorized him to speak about it.[34]

As industrial tensions soared in the fall of 1945, an anxious Truman summoned thirty-six labor and business leaders—representing the AFL, the CIO, the U.S. Chamber of Commerce, the National Association of Manufacturers, and other industrial organizations—to a conference in Washington on November 5. He had hoped to narrow differences, but instead widened them. Labor delegates attacked not only management, but each other. John L. Lewis, the dour, hulking, bushy-browed president of the United Mine Workers (now part of the AFL), lit into Phil Murray, his opposite number at the CIO.

"We are opposed to a corporate state," Lewis intoned, indignant over the CIO proposal to tie wages to prices and profits—as Wallace had done. It was, Lewis charged, an affront to the American free enterprise system to shackle labor's share of prosperity to a formula. He would oppose Murray with every fiber of his being.

"The CIO is not afraid of anybody," Murray shot back. "And I'm not afraid of you!"

"Nuts!"

"Nuts to you!"

And so it went.

Though Wallace had pledged his belief in collective bargaining, he also believed the government had to intervene when it failed—as it was now failing. He had, prior to the conference, called for the creation of a fact-finding organization and mediation service, as well as compulsory arbitration to break deadlocks. Truman urged the delegates to support the scheme, threatening to continue wage and price controls as a last resort. The unions, however, denounced it as a violation of their right to strike. After three weeks, the conference yielded only pledges of support for collective bargaining. Before tensions would ease, they would get much worse.

On November 19, the UAW, representing over 300,000 GM workers, accused the company of "refusing to engage in genuine collective bargaining" and threatened to strike. The union now demanded a 30 percent wage rise, more than Wallace's report was backing, with no price increases, saying it would only consider a lesser settlement if the company opened its books and proved it could not afford it. The company offered 10 percent, refusing to discuss its books. Romney accused the union of abusing its monopoly power, damaging productivity, and fomenting supplier-firm strikes that limited production to half target levels.[35] The next day, its members walked out.

In late December, when Wallace's assistant Phil Hauser asked if the secretary wished to designate someone from Commerce to serve on a GM fact-finding committee, Wallace asked, "How about Magdoff?"[36] FBI surveillance of Magdoff's home, on December 12, had already uncovered that he "was endeavoring to become an economist for [the] group."[37] And a phone tap would, following Wallace's intervention, confirm his appointment.[38]

When the committee delivered its report on January 10, 1946, recommending a 19½-cent-per-hour (17.4 percent) wage hike, it noted that it had taken account of statistical data "from the Secretary of Commerce" pertaining to the ability of the auto firms to absorb large wage increases in 1946 and '47.[39] Yet it still did not acknowledge that the analysis was the product of an individual working in a private capacity outside the Commerce Department.

Armed with Wallace's report, the unions continued to press for more than employers were prepared to pay. Strife mounted. On January 15, 1946, 200,000 members of the CIO union representing electrical workers joined the picket lines, bringing manufacture of most of the country's electrical equipment and appliances to a standstill. On January 19, 800,000 steel workers at over 1,000 mills walked off the job—the biggest strike in history. Two hundred thousand meatpackers soon followed.[40] And on it went.

All the while, Wallace was bombarded with angry, copiously documented union and management claims of bad faith and misconduct by the other side.[41] Yet the secretary did nothing, either to bring the sides together or to compel a settlement. The publisher W. M. Kiplinger would write to Wallace warning that "the business community [feels] it deserves more of your time and interest." Wallace's "relations with leading business men [were] not good," he said, even with "the 'better businessmen' by liberal standards." They saw the secretary "as sneering at the function and conduct of business."[42] Union men, too, were losing patience with him. The dapper, eloquent Harvard-educated CIO general counsel Lee Pressman—a ten-year veteran member of the CPUSA and its secret "[Harold] Ware group" of Marxists and covert government sources—was livid over Wallace's inaction and timidity. "This fact-finding thing is a farce," he complained to Treasury's Harry Dexter White, whose phone was also under FBI tap. "I wish there was a way of making Wallace make a real fight for the first time in his life."[43]

A visibly frustrated Truman told a press conference that the union and management bosses were wielding "too much power," and that it was time for the government to show that "*it* is the power of the people."[44] Yet he had, at this point, no firm idea what "the people" or the government should do. He asked his commerce secretary if he could "do anything" to get the steel companies to approve an 18½-cent-per-hour raise—a remarkably gentle request, given that the secretary had championed the figure. But Wallace refused to stick his neck out, saying, according to his diary, that he was "not in very good position to speak to these gentlemen." In truth, he hated little more than talking to businessmen with whom he shared no scientific or spiritual interests. He continued to meet with Phil Murray, whom he found congenial, though he offered no thoughts on how to settle the strikes.[45]

"I am not a deep thinker like you are," Truman had confessed to Wallace after winning the vice presidential nomination.[46] At sea when it came to economic matters, he had, in the fall of 1945, let Wallace take the lead in handling wage and price matters. But by early 1946, as Truman notes in his memoirs, it had become clear he had made a mistake. Once Wallace realized that human interaction would be required to produce actual settlements, he began to neglect his cabinet duties, preferring to "devote . . . his energy to the problem of our relations with Russia."[47]

Over the course of the year, a record 4.6 million workers would go out on strike. Had Truman trusted in his own political skills, rather than in Wallace's intellect, he might have prevented the damaging escalation. Instead, the unions took Wallace's pronouncements on business' capacity to pay, while freezing prices, to mean that the president had their back. Truman sympathized with the unions; but as they were about to find out, he did not have unlimited patience.

On January 18, 1946, the president pressed both sides in the GM-UAW dispute to agree on an 18½ cent (17.1 percent) rise in hourly pay. This being slightly below the fact-finding recommendation, based on Wallace's report, the UAW held out, presuming that Truman would ultimately force GM's hand. On March 8, however, the president told reporters he would not intervene. Five days later, on March 13, the two sides agreed to 18½ cents and an adjustment for "wage inequities"—a maneuver that allowed the union to claim that the deal ratified the more generous fact-finding decision.[48]

By March 1946, 18½ cents had become the base demand of American labor. Though coal operators were now prepared to settle on this figure, John L. Lewis, on April 1, called the nation's 340,000 coal miners out on strike in defense of "the rights to which free men are entitled."[49] Foremost among these rights was the creation of a company-funded, union-controlled "health, welfare, and retirement fund"—though Lewis suggested that a substantially higher wage rise might do.[50] The two sides deadlocked. When the nation's railway men threatened to follow the miners off the job, an incensed Truman finally asserted authority.

It has been widely said that Harry Truman was, above all, "decisive." It is more accurate to say that he was resolute—once he had decided to decide. He was frequently willing to let a problem linger while he waited for more opportune circumstances to decide. At times, this strategy served him well.[51] In the case of the strikes, however, it had not. And so he changed course.

Calling in the rail union leaders on May 17, the president previewed the "Give-'em-hell Harry" persona he would adopt in the 1948 election. If the unions wanted to fire the next shot, he told them, "I'm going to give you the gun." In plain sight, he signed an executive order to seize and operate the railroads—effective the following day.[52] Shocked, the men agreed to delay strike action.

In the midst of the labor storm, Wallace's single diary entry for that week laid out his concern over patenting rules applying to the food industry's manufacture of sex hormones. He wanted the Commerce Department to "throw its influence on the side of abundant, cheap production" of everything, hormones included.[53] In labor matters, however, which had refused to obey Harold Wein's models, he had lost interest, and was no doubt relieved that the president had stopped asking for his help.

Writing to himself around that time, Truman blasted "Murray and his Communist friends." As for Lewis, who had "called two strikes in war time to satisfy his ego," the last one on April 30, 1945, his actions had been "worse than bullets in the back to our soldiers." Now that he, the president, was trying to save the nation from these "demagogue leaders," he was "tired of the government's being flouted, vilified and misrepresented."

On May 22, 1946, he ordered seizure of the coal mines. On the 23rd, the rail unions called 300,000 out on strike. On the 24th, the president summoned the cabinet to reveal his next move. Correctly anticipating that none of them, including Wallace, would have any idea how to keep the railroads operating, Truman announced that the Army would draft striking workers. Following moments of stunned silence, Attorney General Tom Clark said he doubted such a move would pass constitutional muster. Truman was unperturbed. "We'll draft them," he said, "and think about the law later."[54]

At ten that evening, in a nationwide radio broadcast, Truman called on the rail workers to return to their jobs by 4 p.m. the following day. If they did not, he said, the Army would break the strike. On the 25th, just after 4 p.m., he entered the House chamber to address a joint emergency session of Congress. "[T]he nation," he told the legislators, is "in the grip of a railroad strike which threatens to paralyze all our industrial, agricultural, commercial, and social life." He was therefore requesting legislation authorizing him to draft "all workers who are on strike against their government."[55]

As cheers went up in the chamber, Les Biffle, secretary of the Senate, ran in and, with cinematic timing, handed him a slip of paper. Truman read it, and then looked back up.

"Word has just been received that the railroad strike has been settled," he told the legislators, "on terms proposed by the president." Louder cheers rang out. Everyone stood and applauded.

That evening, the House voted 306–13 in favor of the bill to draft strikers. In the Senate, however, a coalition of the left, led by Pepper, and the right, led by Taft, killed the bill 70–13. Wallace, who had opposed the bill himself, suspected Taft was concerned not with the conscripting of strikers but with the "conscripting of profits" that would come with Truman controlling the railways. Wallace also believed the president had expected the defeat, and was unfazed by it. He had broken the strike and shown the public he was in charge; that was what mattered. Four days later, the miners accepted an 18½ cent raise and a welfare fund financed by a 5-cents-per-ton levy on coal produced for sale or use.[56]

The president's popularity, however, had suffered from the disruptions. And when Lewis called yet another strike on October 31, 1946, just five days before the midterm elections, renewed public anger helped cement the election of Republican majorities in both the House and the Senate. Those majorities ensured passage of the Taft-Hartley Act, prohibiting certain strikes, banning closed shops (in which only union members could work), and allowing states to pass "right-to-work" laws—none of which helped the union cause.

In the end, Wallace's analysis of the postwar labor landscape turned out to be deeply flawed. Instead of seven to eight million unemployed in 1946, as he had forecast, there were only 2.27 million.[57] In addition to millions of soldiers and other service members finding work in the private sector, some 800,000 more entered universities under the tuition-reimbursement provisions of the 1944 G.I. Bill of Rights. Unemployment beyond the normal "frictional" type was, in 1946, almost nonexistent. The unemployment rate would end the year at 3.9 percent—the lowest peacetime level since 1929.[58] Though GDP would fall 20.6 percent owing to massive government spending cuts following the war's end, private production, in spite of the strikes, would prove robust—soaring 29.5 percent. Free enterprise, noted *New York Times* reporter Russell Porter in July 1946, in a scathing column on Wallace and his *Sixty Million Jobs*, had "demonstrated its capacity to provide full post-war employment." The pent-up demand for consumer goods, backed by savings built up during years of war rationing, had provided all the incentive business needed to retool for peacetime.

The only big problem that remained was inflation—and shortages of basic goods for which prices were suppressed by edict. Inflation in 1946— partly fueled by 18.5 percent wage rises across major industries, in line with Wallace's recommendation—was 8.3 percent. By doubling down at midyear in his support of government controls to suppress prices, and attacking the "greedy" and "destructive purposes" of the National Association of Manufacturers in opposing them, Wallace was, Porter argued, only compounding problems by misallocating scarce resources between controlled and uncontrolled sectors.[59] By election time, rising prices, combined with shortages of meat and other commodities whose prices were still being controlled, had become a major political issue, and contributed mightily to the Democrats' resounding defeat.

Wallace might have shrugged off the flaws in his analysis, and claimed credit for those parts of the economy that had performed well—particularly the surge in employment and private production. But he did not. Instead of highlighting successes inconsistent with his prior warnings, he now cautioned that the U.S. economy was on a "boom and bust" ride. Full employment, he insisted, would not last long. Only careful, comprehensive government planning, of the type he had called for in Sixty Million Jobs, would prevent the inevitable "vicious downward spiral" into which the country was headed.[60]

He may have believed this dark warning, but he may also have been trying simply to reclaim his lost relevance on economic policy. Truman no longer paid his analyses any heed. His gloomy, hectoring rhetoric did not, furthermore, sit well with the business community his department was pledged to assist. They accepted that Truman needed Wallace politically, but could not understand why it had to be at Commerce. Former private-sector executives who had joined the department were jumping ship.[61]

In spite of Wallace's warnings, GDP growth over the coming five years would average a robust 3.8 percent, with modest 4.3 percent unemployment. Over the coming ten years, the numbers would be similar. Though Wallace would never get the planning he wanted, there would be no "bust" or "vicious downward spiral."

As for the specific targets he had called for in his book—60 million federally guaranteed full-time jobs and $200 billion in GDP by 1950—the country would fall well short of the first, and yet comfortably exceed the second. In 1950, 48.5 million full-time (and 6.75 million part-time) workers would produce, in 1944 dollars, $227 billion in output ($320 billion nominal). To put those numbers in the perspective of his book, Wallace had claimed that "to talk of [only] 50 million [full-time] jobs is to talk of perpetuating mass unemployment and eventual chaos": yet output exceeded his target by 14 percent, with an unemployment rate of 5.3 percent—hardly "mass unemployment." That rate would fall to a near-postwar low of 3.3 percent in 1951 (with 52.5 million full-time workers).[62]

Like Cassandra, the mythological priestess of Apollo, Wallace would be condemned to see his dire prophecies ignored. Unlike Cassandra, he would witness no consequent suffering.

Eleven

MISSION TO MOSCOW

By the time of Roosevelt's death in April 1945, the so-called Spirit of Yalta—
the optimism that had suffused talk of postwar U.S.-Soviet cooperation—
had been dashed. Stalin was convinced that secret U.S.-Swiss-German talks
in the Ticino village of Ascona the previous month, over the surrender of
Nazi forces in northern Italy, were preliminary to a wider secret peace deal.[1]
Roosevelt, for his part, was convinced that Soviet actions in Eastern Europe
betrayed Stalin's pledge to allow its people "to create democratic institutions
of their own choice." The mutual suspicions would only grow.

At the time, Truman had no wish to embark on a "Cold War." To the contrary, he, like so many presidents before and since, had hoped to focus on the
domestic economy. This ambition was thwarted by his predecessor's habit of
embracing contradictions: in this case, the implausible notion that Eastern
Europe could have self-determination while Russia got friendly neighbors. It
was one or the other. For all his mastery of wartime grand strategy, it was the
unfillable expectations Roosevelt created which led Allen Drury to pan his
"four years of sloppy diplomacy" and "tin-horn politicking."[2]

Within weeks of Roosevelt's departure from Yalta, Stalin made clear that
"democracy" in Eastern Europe meant directing power to Soviet pawns. In
Bucharest, Romania, Molotov's deputy, Andrey Vyshinsky, gave a stunned
King Michael two hours to install a Communist-dominated government—
slamming the monarch's door on the way out.[3] In Bulgaria, Stalin took
effective control of the "Fatherland Front" government through the Com-
munist-held interior and judicial ministries.[4] In neither case did he heed
the Allied Control Commission, through which Washington and London
were supposed to be active overseers of their transition to democracy. But it
was in Poland, a key historical buffer state, where he butted heads hardest

with his wartime allies. The central matter dividing the allies on Poland—whether Russia was entitled to a European sphere of influence and, if so, where its boundaries lay—would never be resolved.

At Yalta, the three leaders had agreed that the Moscow-backed government, the so-called Lublin Poles, would be reorganized on democratic lines, integrating elements of the non-Communist London-based government, as a prelude to free elections "as soon as possible." But Stalin had broken off relations with the exiles in April 1943, after they demanded an international investigation into German charges that Russians had massacred thousands of Polish officers in the Katyn Forest three years earlier, and backed the Lubliners. In clear violation of the Yalta pact, Stalin signed a mutual assistance treaty with his chosen regime, while luring to Moscow and imprisoning sixteen non-Communist leaders of the Polish underground who had fought the Nazis in the Warsaw uprising.

Harriman, Clayton, and Navy Secretary James Forrestal all urged a firmer line with Moscow, hoping to motivate its return to compliance. Stalin, however, knew that Washington lacked practical means to impose its will east of the Elbe. At Tehran, Roosevelt had laid out his intention to withdraw U.S. troops from Europe within two years of the end of fighting; Truman was already under great political pressure to follow through. "It is pretty obvious to all concerned," General Eisenhower's political adviser, Robert Murphy, would write to Stettinius a month after V-E Day, "that we really are desirous of removing our forces, and that it is only a question of time."[5] The State Department's deputy director of European Affairs, the tough-talking Texan John Hickerson, was more direct. "It has been done," he pronounced of the Soviet annexation of the Baltic states and chunks of Poland and Romania. "And nothing . . . in the power of [our] Government to do can undo it."[6]

As for Truman, he "felt that military and political collaboration with Russia was still so important," above all to defeat Japan and launch the United Nations, that he did not want a rupture over Poland.[7] Yet Poland and the U.N. also seemed to him inextricably linked. A creature of the Senate, he feared that ratification of the U.N. charter would fail absent the creation of a legitimate, independent Polish government. Roosevelt would no doubt have sought to charm away the differences with Stalin, but charm was not in Truman's arsenal. And so he resorted to his trademark plain talk.

En route to San Francisco to confer on the U.N. charter text, the Soviet foreign minister paid a courtesy call on the new president. Entering the Oval Office at 5:30 p.m. on April 23, Vyacheslav Molotov, his broad emotionless face fronted by signature pince-nez glasses, perched above a well-manicured mustache, took his chair across from Truman. Gromyko and V. N. Pavlov, his translator, sat at his side.

Pavlov's opposite number, Soviet expert Chip Bohlen, having interpreted for Roosevelt at Tehran and Yalta, would be struck by the contrast in style and demeanor between the old boss and the new. After years of rendering Roosevelt's wily utterings into Russian, he found the Missouri frankness cleansing. "How I enjoyed translating Truman's sentences," he later recalled.[8]

Truman and Molotov's exchange began respectfully, but as the two men volleyed over Poland, each grew exasperated with the other's failure to grasp what was, for him, the essence of the matter. For Truman, it was showing the American people that Russians kept their word. For Molotov, who turned "ashy" during the lecture, it was about settling differences as equals.

Truman, the less patient of the two, broke with niceties first. The United States, he said, was prepared to carry out its Yalta commitments in full, but expected the Soviets to do likewise. Shocked at the suggestion that his government was behaving dishonorably, Molotov responded sharply. He had, he said, "never been talked to [like that] in [his] life."

The matter was simple then, Truman explained to him. "Carry out your agreements, and you won't get talked to like that."[9] The plain talk failed signally to motivate a more cooperative disposition from Stalin, who wrote to Truman the following day laying out his red lines. His country had, he pointed out, never been "consulted when [the Greek and Belgian] Governments were being formed, nor did it claim the right to interfere in these matters." Why, then, did it not have the right, when it came to Poland, to a respectful disinterest from Washington and London? "To put it plainly," he wrote with his own Georgian frankness, "you want me to renounce the interests of the security of the Soviet Union." He was, he insisted, "ready to do all in my power to reach an agreed settlement," but there were limits. "I cannot proceed against the interests of my country."[10]

Two weeks later, Truman stunned the Soviet leader with what appeared to him a hostile act. On May 11, three days following the German surrender,

Truman casually signed an order, prepared for him by Foreign Economic Administration head Leo Crowley, authorizing the slashing of Allied Lend-Lease aid.[11] The order was legally justified, and arguably necessitated, by the end of hostilities in Europe. It was also consistent with Harriman's advice that Truman dangle aid as a means of coaxing Stalin back into compliance with Yalta. Crowley, however, took an overly literal interpretation, and had Russia-bound ships turned around midstream and returned to U.S. ports. Even Harriman was "taken aback" by the blunt severity of the action, which threatened to undermine cooperation in Europe and beyond. Though Truman had not even bothered to read the order, and had not intended it as a warning, Soviet officials would, in the coming months, make clear their shock and anger.

Under pressure, Truman clarified his directive publicly two weeks later, terming it a mere "readjustment" to circumstances. Shipments to Siberia, secretly intended to aid Soviet entry into the Pacific war, would continue (and would indeed be boosted in July).[12] Determined, further, to prove his commitment to his predecessor's policies, he sent Roosevelt's most trusted friend and emissary to Moscow. Two weeks into retirement and nine months from the grave, Harry Hopkins' spirit, if not his constitution, revived at the prospect of reengaging Stalin. He touched down in Moscow on May 25.

In his meetings with Stalin, Hopkins displayed his characteristic blend of emollience and tenacity, which the Soviet leader met in kind. To Hopkins' urging that he embrace a broadening of the Lublin government, in preparation for free elections, Stalin offered both reassurance and qualifications. Yes, he would support wider participation, but stressed that freedoms had their limits "during time of war," and could never extend to "fascist parties." Stalin also expressed dismay at the "scornful and abrupt manner" in which the president had terminated Lend-Lease. It was, he said, a "brutal" act. Hopkins assured him that the matter had been an unfortunate error, and that the United States had no intention of pressuring Russia. Stalin seemed to accept the earnest assurance, and when, on June 7, the ailing envoy departed Moscow, he was guardedly optimistic that the Yalta hangover would pass. Still, he found himself recalling a warning from his old friend. "The Russians," Roosevelt had told Churchill, "do not use words for the same purposes we do."[13] Agreement in words did not mean agreement in deeds.

One month later, on July 7, the new American president boarded the USS

Augusta in a confident frame of mind. He had not wished to make the trip,[14] but now that it was under way he could see the historic possibilities. Stalin was, after all, just a fellow politician from a tough district—a Georgian "Tom Pendergast," who preferred deal-making to fist-pounding. Bound for Antwerp, and from there to Potsdam, just south of Berlin, Truman was sure that he, Stalin, and Churchill were destined to bring Europe "ninety years of peace." The Russians, he noted in his diary, had "always been our friends." And there was no "reason . . . they shouldn't always be."[15]

Two weeks with Stalin and Molotov, however, changed his outlook. "You never saw such pig-headed people as are the Russians," he wrote to his mother on July 31.[16] Nothing, he now understood, was ever going to be simple and straightforward with them.

Many would look back on Potsdam, and the pointed disagreements over German reparations, Polish-German borders, and the status of Communist-dominated regimes in Romania, Bulgaria, and Hungary, as a starting point for the Cold War. Truman departed in exasperation. "I hope I never have to hold another conference with [the Russians]," he told his mother. "But, of course," he then added, importantly, "*I will.*" The "I will" signified his determination to plow on toward a cooperative global settlement. For as momentous a failure as Potsdam would seem in retrospect, Truman saw the talks as a placeholder for future meetings of a new Council of Foreign Ministers (comprising the U.S., the UK, the USSR, and France), to be followed by a peace conference at which he expected differences to be settled through compromise.[17] After all, the U.S. Senate had, on July 28, five days before his departure from Berlin, ratified the U.N. Charter by a resounding 89–2; a new cooperative order seemed to be in train. Truman thus remained committed, as he would later write to Stimson, "to try to carry out agreements as they were made" by FDR, believing it important to ensure quick victory over Japan as well as a lasting peace.[18]

Truman had, at Potsdam, also made some large down payments toward compromise. With Byrnes' urging, he abandoned the campaign to widen the Lublin regime, insisting only that he wished to ensure "free elections" in the future. When Stalin replied amiably that "the Polish government had never *refused* to hold elections," Truman agreed to defer the matter for discussion by the foreign secretaries. He would reprise such deferrals as talks stalemated on issue after issue.[19] This posture may not have been one of a pushover, yet neither was it that of a Cold Warrior.

Henry Wallace, back in Washington, was sure he could have shaped a quicker and smoother path to good relations with Stalin. But the Democratic Party bosses had seen fit to prevent that. They had taken the vice presidency from him, and given it to that little man from Missouri. And so it was they who had sent that little man, now the president of the United States, to Potsdam.

Yet, Wallace reckoned, he should have been there *in any case*. Had Roosevelt, on securing the nomination, given him the job he so coveted and deserved, secretary of state, Truman might well have kept him in it. Still, as commerce secretary, he controlled, or believed he controlled, one important lever of foreign policy. That lever was trade.

When it came to trade with Russia, at least, Wallace arrived at his new job pushing on an open door. For even those more skeptical of Soviet intentions—such as Harriman, who would succeed Wallace at Commerce—agreed with him that more trade made good sense.

The United States would, after the war, be obliged to retool its vast economy for peacetime production, and the Soviet Union—which would have massive reconstruction needs—was a logical customer for its industrial goods. "It would be in the self-interest of the United States," Harriman told the Soviet foreign trade minister, Anastas Mikoyan, back in November 1943, to provide "full employment during the . . . transition from wartime to peacetime." It would therefore need new markets.

Recognizing that the Soviets would have little of value to export for some years, he suggested that they might wish to discuss borrowing terms for the interim.[20] Harriman's suggestion happened to jibe with the Marxist doctrine that capitalism, now in its final historical phase, would need to be kept from collapse with ever-larger bailouts of industry. And so Mikoyan was happy to talk, or at least to listen, confident that time was on Moscow's side. Thus began an awkward kabuki embrace that would continue on, in spite of worsening political relations, throughout Wallace's tenure at Commerce.

Late in the war, deeper economic ties with Moscow also seemed, across the State, Commerce, and Treasury Departments, a low-risk, high-reward political strategy. At Bretton Woods in July 1944, Morgenthau and White had bent over backward to accommodate Soviet demands for more benefits from, and fewer obligations to, the new International Monetary Fund (IMF) and International Bank for Reconstruction and Development (IBRD), believing that the country's participation would bind it to multilateral structures that would induce a greater sense of security and commitment to global stability. Wallace and Harriman, the most important protagonists of deeper Russian economic ties, however, viewed the aims of such ties very differently. And these differences became blindingly apparent after V-E Day.

Wallace believed it incumbent on Washington, given its history of hostility toward the Bolsheviks, to demonstrate its peaceable intentions by offering generous reconstruction aid and financing to cover imports. Such beneficence was, in effect, a political indulgence for past sins, as well as an investment in future peace. Harriman, in contrast, felt that American intentions were transparently peaceable, given that it had no territorial ambitions, and that it was *Moscow*—which clearly coveted Eastern Europe, Manchuria, and parts of the Mediterranean—that needed to demonstrate good faith. The Soviets had, during the war, "misinterpreted our generous attitude toward them as a sign of weakness." He therefore viewed the transition from U.S. *aid*, which had been a wartime necessity, to U.S. *loans*, which could be conditioned on future cooperative behavior, as an important means to test Stalin's purposes. He further backed structuring the loans as restricted "credits," available only to buy American goods and services, and with any outstanding balance subject to immediate suspension if behavior failed to meet expectations.[21]

Kennan warned Harriman, however, that Stalin would show no interest in meeting political terms for American loans. Obedience from Warsaw, Budapest, Bucharest, and Sofia were vital to Soviet security, as Stalin saw it, and he would never sacrifice them for mere trade credits. Others in the State Department warned that the Soviet Union had little prospect of producing sufficient export goods to pay off large loans, and that the country would choose to rely on German reparations to finance reconstruction and development.

Wallace, though, had allies in the Commerce Department, such as Russia expert Ernest Ropes, and in Treasury, such as Harry White, who would continue to argue that the Soviet Union was both creditworthy and capable of meeting large and growing American demands for mercury, manganese, chromium, copper, oil, tungsten, and other strategic materials.[22] In this regard, Harriman, given his faith in the efficacy of trade and finance as diplomatic chits, was at least willing to suspend disbelief.

In any case, stalemate set in soon after Potsdam. The State Department got nothing of what it was seeking from Moscow in Eastern Europe and Germany, and the People's Commissariat of Foreign Affairs got nothing of what it was seeking from Washington in import credits. By December, the deadline for countries to ratify the Bretton Woods agreements, the commissariat had concluded that its participation in the IMF and IBRD would no longer serve Soviet interests. "[A]s the government of the U.S.A. did not offer the U.S.S.R. a credit, our membership in these organizations could be read as our weakness, as a forced step taken under the pressure of the U.S.A.," one ministry memorandum read. "Our negative attitude . . . would show our independent position on this matter."[23]

Neither Wallace nor Harriman had yet grasped the essence of Stalin's thinking. Stalin was compelled neither by fear of Washington's intentions nor by a desire for its assistance. He was instead driven by a rosy evaluation of what the Bolsheviks had long called the "correlation of forces."[24] Through a steady expansion of Soviet boundaries and influence into the borderlands, he could, he believed, inexorably extend his power and leverage in global affairs.

Sometime after the war (accounts on timing differ), Stalin, pinning a small map of the newly expanded Soviet Union to the wall, nodded with approval.

"In the north, we have everything in order," he said. "We have moved the [Finnish] border away from Leningrad. The Baltics are ours again. . . . It is ok in the west." The vast buffer in Soviet-occupied Eastern Europe would protect his empire against future Napoleons and Hitlers.

Taking his pipe from his mouth, Stalin then waved it to the right. Here, in the Far East, where Wallace had told Chiang that Russia had "no territorial ambitions," he indicated, one by one, each of the territories and assets Wallace had urged Chiang to cede.

"Port Arthur is ours," said Stalin, visibly pleased. "And so is Dalnii [Dairen/Dalian]. The KVZhD [Chinese Eastern Railway] is ours. China, Mongolia—everything is fine."

But then he frowned, waving his pipe under the base of the Caucasus.

"Here, I do not like our border."[25] This was where the Soviet republics of Georgia, Armenia, and Azerbaijan met the hostile powers of Turkey and Iran.

Stalin's southern flank was still vulnerable—as it had been during the Crimean War of 1853–56 and two world wars. Turkey and Iran loomed as potential U.S.-backed adversaries. With Britain headed toward bankruptcy, and imperial retrenchment looking inevitable, however, the timing might be right to enlarge his territory, gain oil reserves, dominate parts of the Mediterranean and Middle East, and transform his empire into a maritime power. What he needed to know was how far the United States would go to stop him.

In June 1945, a month before Potsdam, Molotov summoned the Turkish ambassador and laid out for the stunned diplomat new Soviet claims to the Kars-Ardahan regions of eastern Turkey—encompassing some 6,500 square miles and 300,000 people. The Soviet republics of Georgia and Armenia would soon press additional claims.[26] "I saw my mission in extending the borders of our Motherland as far as possible," Molotov would explain years later. "It seems, Stalin and I, we coped with this task pretty well."[27]

Pitted against such men with a mission, Jimmy Byrnes, who had little experience with foreign policy, and had built his reputation for competence in the Senate through barter and compromise, appeared out of his depth. At Potsdam, he had sold Truman on deals to recognize "temporary" Soviet-backed regimes in Poland, Romania, and Bulgaria. By the end of the Moscow Council of Foreign Ministers meetings in December, however, those had become all but permanent. Molotov further refused to commit to a timetable for withdrawing Soviet troops from Iran—troops stationed there under the wartime Anglo-Russian-Iranian Treaty of 1942. As Republican and conservative-leaning Democratic congressmen grew increasingly vocal in disparaging Byrnes' "devot[ion] to expediency," and American public opinion hardened against Russia,[28] an impatient Truman began to yank the reins of foreign policy from his secretary of state—just as he would those of labor and industry policy from his secretary of commerce.

In the course of four weeks in early 1946, Stalin, Kennan, and Churchill would each issue what would become rallying cries of the early Cold War. On February 9, Stalin gave an address at the Bolshoi Theatre condemning world capitalism and its political face, imperialism, as the engines of world war. Two weeks later, Kennan sent his famous "Long Telegram" from Moscow, arguing that the Soviet Communist government was inherently expansionist, "impervious to logic of reason," and responsive only to "the logic of force." And two weeks after that, Churchill gave his historic "Iron Curtain" speech in Fulton, Missouri, warning of the dangers of "communist fifth columns" operating in Western and Southern Europe. All three circulated in the capitals of North America and Europe, helping to solidify the growing sense that conflict between East and West was inevitable.

Against the growing chorus of crisis, Byrnes struggled to stay relevant. *"What is Russia up to now?"* demanded Republican Arthur Vandenberg in the Senate chamber on February 27. "We ask it in Eastern Europe and the Dardanelles. . . . We ask it in the Baltic and the Balkans. We ask it in Poland. . . . *What is Russia up to now?"*[29]

Byrnes did not know. But he was determined to oppose any further Soviet expansion, making clear that it was no longer a matter for negotiation or compromise.

"We will not . . . stand aloof," he announced in a speech the following day, "if force, or the threat of force, is used contrary to the purposes of the [U.N.] Charter." Some mocked the speech as the "Second Vandenberg Concerto,"[30] but it would mark an important turning point in Truman's foreign policy—and Byrnes' conduct of it. It also put Byrnes on a public collision course with Henry Wallace, who thought he was pouring oil on the fire he himself had set.

Stalin was unmoved by the tougher American posture. Still determined to extend his Caucasus border and force oil concessions from Tehran, he organized an armed separatist movement in northern Iran. When the Iranian government sent forces to quell the rebellion, Soviet troops barred the way. On March 1, 1946, the day before the deadline specified in treaty for those troops to withdraw, Moscow announced that they would stay.

Urged on by Washington, Iran appealed to the new United Nations Security Council, making it the object of the first major superpower confrontation in the body. In April, Truman showed his intention to defend Iran's sovereignty by transporting the body of Mehmet Münir Ertegün, the deceased former Turkish ambassador to Washington, home on the mightiest battleship in the American fleet—the USS *Missouri*. Unwilling at that stage to risk an armed confrontation, and anxious to end the unwelcome international publicity, Stalin retreated. He would withdraw the last of his troops from Iran in May.[31]

In August, however, he would probe again, this time back in Turkey—demanding that Ankara accept joint control of the Turkish Straits and the Dardanelles, including provision for Soviet military bases. The ultimatum was a blatant contravention of Turkey's sovereign rights under the Montreux Convention of 1936.[32]

Whereas a year prior only a quarter of Americans believed, according to a *Fortune* poll, that Russia would attempt to force Communism on Eastern Europe, polls were now showing more than half thought it sought to dominate the entire *world*. That figure would continue to rise in the coming years.[33]

With no hesitation, an irate Truman told Under Secretary of State Acheson to inform the Soviet chargé d'affaires of his full support for Turkish rights in the Straits and his intention to challenge any act of aggression publicly in the Security Council. He backed it up by ordering a flotilla of military ships to the Mediterranean and, secretly, authorized plans for strategic Air Force operations in the region.[34] Thereafter, Stalin would shift the locus of his probes again, this time to Central Europe and Northeast Asia.

None of these developments would dampen Wallace's enthusiasm for closer economic ties with Russia. To the contrary, as the conflicts with Moscow mounted, Wallace worked all the harder for a breakthrough on trade. "Much of the recent Soviet behavior," he wrote to Truman in March 1946, at the height of the Iran crisis, was being driven by "fears of 'capitalist encirclement.'" The administration needed therefore to demonstrate to Moscow "our sincere devotion to the cause of peace" by calling for deeper trade links. Truman, who was done "babying the Soviets," as he put it, would later claim that he "ignored this letter."[35] But he did, in fact, give Wallace the chance to prove his thesis.

With Cordell Hull's retirement in November 1944, his role as the State Department's leading trade evangelist passed to Will Clayton. A former Southern cotton mogul who became a Democrat in opposition to Republican protectionism, Clayton shared with Wallace, a fellow agriculturalist, a strong belief in the compelling economic and political logic of liberalizing global commerce. "I have always believed," Clayton would later write, "that tariffs and other impediments to international trade were set up for the short-term, special benefit of politically powerful minority groups and were against the national and international interest."[36] He warned Congress in April 1945 that economic blocs and state-to-state barter deals were "contrary to our deepest convictions about the kind of economic order which is most conducive to the preservation of peace."[37]

As World War II came to a close, the political moment was favorable for trade liberalization. Americans were optimistic about the opportunities peace would bring. A Gallup poll in May 1945 found 57 percent approving of tariff reductions, as opposed to only 20 percent against. In spite of rearguard Republican opposition to expanding presidential powers, the House, in May 1945, and the Senate, in June, approved renewal of the Reciprocal Trade Agreements Act—empowering the president to reduce import taxes in trade deals.[38] Wallace had been outspoken in support, authoring an article in May calling the act's renewal "vital to world progress."[39]

After passage, Wallace, like Clayton, pushed for further progress. On November 12, 1945, he made a speech to the National Foreign Trade Council in New York calling for new "international machinery" to reduce global trade barriers. Without calling explicitly for the United States to cut its trade surplus, he said that the nation would have to "sacrifice an occasional temporary advantage for the common good." Failure to revive balanced cross-border exchange, he warned, would lead to trade wars among the "Russian group," the "sterling group," and the "dollar group," and possibly even a third world war. Recognizing that calls for freer trade were hardly enough to revive world economic growth, Wallace acknowledged that the United States would have to provide "financial backing" for the U.K. to dismantle its network of imperial trade preferences.[40] This was a bold call at a time when Washington was locked in difficult negotiations with London over the terms for a large postwar U.S. loan.

On December 1, Wallace moved to grasp greater control over trade policy by appointing Arthur Paul a "Special Deputy" for international trade and foreign commerce operations. Truman had terminated the Foreign Economic Administration by executive order in September, facilitating the transfer of Paul and his 1,500 staff to Commerce. By withholding from Paul the permanent-post title of "Assistant Secretary," Wallace bypassed the need for authorization and appropriations from a Congress chary of granting him powers. With Paul's appointment, and the staff to go with it, Wallace hoped to re-create some of the vast authority he had once had as chairman of the Bureau of Economic Warfare (whose powers Roosevelt had transferred to the FEA in September 1943 to end the feuding between Wallace and Jones).

Wallace proclaimed his aim to create "a revitalized foreign trade service" and "a high level of foreign trade." He would do so, he explained, by "provid[ing] all possible assistance to exporters *and importers*" and pursuing policies to "increase the supply of dollars in the hands of foreign nations."[41] Wallace's call to expand trade globally on a *balanced* basis, and not merely to push his country's exports, was, for an American commerce secretary, audacious and historically unprecedented.

Owing to congressional division, however, trade policy in practice was reactive and rudderless. A dispute over watch imports in January 1946, for example, stoked angry political, diplomatic, and industrial fighting. Minnesota Republican representative Harold Knutson introduced a bill imposing an annual quota of two million watch and watch-movement imports from Switzerland, one million fewer than the State Department was advocating. The department warned that the bill would require abrogation of the reciprocal trade agreement with Switzerland, and was harming its efforts to get Swiss cooperation in locating external German assets. The Swiss minister in Washington, Carl (Charles) Bruggmann, said the action "would fly in the face of the free trade principles which [the U.S.] government"—and his wife's brother, Henry Wallace, in particular—"are advocating." Knutson responded by pointing out that Swiss watch factories, "controlled by the German-Swiss cartel," had been supplying timing instruments for Nazi weapons during the war, to kill U.S. soldiers, at the same time that they were exporting to the U.S. market and taking customers from the much smaller American watch industry, which was busy supplying Allied forces. Meanwhile, unionized American watchmakers allied themselves with domestic manufacturers, in spite of the growing strife between U.S. labor and business, to staunch the flow of Swiss imports.[42]

Clayton tried to outflank Congress and push beyond reciprocal bilateral agreements, hoping to forge permanent international machinery to liberalize trade *multilaterally*. His main aims were to ban import quotas, end the U.K.'s imperial trade preference, and reduce tariffs worldwide. The discussions would be difficult and protracted, both at home and abroad, and would not come to fruition until late 1947.

Where Wallace parted radically from Clayton on trade policy was over its role in geopolitics. Wallace and Clayton both supported a $3.75 billion loan to Britain as a means of reviving global trade. Yet whereas Wallace also saw it as a means of dismantling the British Empire, Clayton saw it as a means of securing Western solidarity in the face of growing Soviet aggression. He would later argue against U.S. wool tariffs on similar grounds—that it would undermine such solidarity. These aims were anathema to Wallace, who considered deeper trade links with *Moscow* vital to securing world peace.[43]

In March 1946, Wallace wrote to the president proposing a trade mission to Moscow. Though Truman's response is unrecorded, he evidently did not object. Later that month, Wallace made "tentative arrangements" with the newly appointed ambassador to the Soviet Union, General Walter Bedell "Beetle" Smith, for his "boys" to visit Moscow for trade talks in the early summer. This was a mission he would dearly have loved to lead himself, but he understood that Truman would have been no more receptive to his going to Moscow than Roosevelt had been two years prior.

On June 12, he phoned Joseph Davies—who, as ambassador from 1937 to 1938, had defended Stalin's infamous purge trials as a means to root out German spies—to ask if he might write to "some of the people in Russia" and arrange a good welcome for his boys. Unlike their counterparts at State, Wallace assured him, these boys had "the right attitude." Davies replied that he would, of course, "be delighted."[44]

On June 20, *The New York Times* announced the mission. "The reconstruction program of the U.S.S.R. and the plans for the full development of the Soviet Union," Wallace explained to the press, "offer tremendous possibilities for American goods and technicians, as well as for increased imports from Russia."[45] He bullishly projected that two-way trade, which had collapsed with the end of the war, would reach $500 million by 1950 ($6.3 billion in today's money).[46]

Wallace's boys arrived in Moscow on July 6, as eager and ambitious as their boss. The lead negotiator, Ernest C. Ropes, sixty-eight, was chief of the

Commerce Department's Soviet Union Division. Having spent his child-hood in St. Petersburg, where his American father owned a trading firm, he would return, in his early forties, to work on relief missions in Murmansk, Arkhangelsk, and Estonia after World War I. He entered the department's Bureau of Foreign and Domestic Commerce in 1923, becoming a specialist on matters Soviet. Other than a five-month leave in 1928, to work in Rus-sia for the Remington-Rand Company, he would spend his entire career in the department. He edited its *Russian Economic Notes* until 1940, while also writing for other government and private outlets. Among the latter was *Soviet Russia Today*, a propaganda magazine funded mainly from Moscow and edited by Harold Ware's widow, the Soviet agent Jessica Smith. Ever-anxious to better U.S.-Soviet relations, Ropes came onto the FBI's radar not long before the Moscow trip.

Ropes had met several times with Elizabeth Bentley, the thirty-eight-year-old CPUSA member and Order of the Red Star recipient who had fallen out with her Soviet handlers and turned U.S. government informant. The previous August, Bentley (NKGB code name "Myrna") had walked into an FBI field office in New Haven to tell a story about a strange man seeking information on Russians transacting with her employer. Failing to inter-est the agents, she visited the New York field office two months later, this time saying that she had, for the past eleven years, "been actively engaged in Communist activity and Soviet espionage."[47] This claim got their attention.

On November 8, 1945, following eight hours of interrogation two days earlier, Bentley signed a thirty-one-page statement, after which weeks of further confessions came. The product was a 107-page FBI report naming over eighty allegedly complicit individuals.[48] Contained among the FBI files on those betrayed by Bentley is a memo dated December 18, 1945, titled "Re: Anatoli Borisovich GROMOV." In a heavily redacted section, it contained the name of Ernest Ropes.[49]

Ropes had met with Gromov, the Soviet embassy first secretary, press officer, and cultural emissary, on August 17, 1945, apparently regarding stu-dent and scientific exchanges. This cause was a favorite of Wallace, who, in October, also pressed Gromov to send Soviet scientists to the United States. Unbeknownst to Ropes or Wallace, Gromov was also the Washing-ton NKGB station chief (code name "Vadim," real name "Gorsky"), running a massive network of agents, sources, and contacts.[50]

On March 13, 1946, Bentley, now working with the FBI, met Ropes in Washington, asking for his assistance with a distressed company—the U.S. Service and Shipping Corporation. The firm delivered parcels from the United States to the Soviet Union under an agreement with Intourist, the Soviet government tourist agency. Set up in late 1940, with CPUSA funds, by Ukrainian-born party member and OGPU-NKGB agent Jacob Golos, Bentley's deceased former lover and covert collaborator, its real role was to provide a cover for Moscow's spies. Bentley originally served as its vice president. Until 1944, the New York NKGB ensured that Amtorg, a U.S. company founded by the Soviet Union in 1924 to handle its American trade, funneled business to it in order to protect her espionage work. But in mid-1945, with Bentley showing signs of emotional breakdown, Soviet intelligence pushed her out and abandoned the firm. As it fell into financial troubles, CPUSA functionary Lem Harris demanded repayment of the party's $15,000 seed capital or transfer of its control to the party.[51]

The titular owner of the firm was a wealthy Soviet sympathizer—and a funder of *Soviet Russia Today*—named Colonel John Hazard Reynolds, who had put in $5,000 at its founding. When interviewed by the FBI in May 1947, he would reveal that he had in early 1946 solicited Ropes' help in resolving the firm's problems. How he first made contact with the Commerce Department's Russia hand is unknown, though it may have been through Amtorg—with which both interacted. In March 1946, Bentley was likely following up on Reynolds' initiative.

After Bentley's meeting with Ropes in Washington, and a further one in New York in mid-April, she reported back to the FBI. Ropes, she told them, was "a kindly old gentleman" who is "close to Secretary of Commerce Henry A. Wallace." Though no Communist himself, Ropes felt Communism was "all right for the Russians" and "enthusiastically favor[ed] a betterment of commercial and cultural relations" between the two countries. This sentiment may have explained "his desire to help her company . . . in any way possible." He expected to leave for Moscow with a colleague for three months later that spring, and offered "to be of any assistance possible to the [firm] while he was in Russia." He even pledged to work "towards securing either an extension of [its] present contract or a favorable new [one]."[52]

Whereas there is no evidence that Ropes knew of the company's cover role or CPUSA financing, or that he ever sought to provide Moscow or its agents with illegal assistance, his name would turn up in later FBI investigations of such agents. One such is Louise Bransten (née Rosenberg, later Berman), lover of the Soviet vice consul and undercover NKGB station chief in San Francisco from 1942 to 1944, Gregory Heifetz (code name "Huron"). Bransten moved to New York in 1945, where she made contact with Soviet Vice consul and undercover GRU station chief Pavel Mikhailov (actual name "Melkishev," code name "Moliere"), with whom Ropes likely also interacted. When later brought before the House Un-American Activities Committee (HUAC) in October 1949, Bransten would be asked if she had been "acquainted with Ernest C. Ropes," whether she had introduced him to the Soviet consul general in San Francisco, and whether she had placed his name on a mailing list of the American Russian Institute—a culturally themed Moscow-backed propaganda organization. Invoking her rights under the Fifth Amendment, she refused to answer.[53] The nature and extent of contacts between Bransten and Ropes are, then, unknown, although she may have been a conduit between him and Reynolds.

The FBI record and Bentley's accounts show Ropes to have been over-eager and credulous, though no Communist ideologue in the mold of Harry Magdoff. The Russian record on Ropes is bare, save a message dated July 7, 1946, from the Soviet consul general in New York, Yakov Lomakin, to the deputy minister of foreign affairs, Solomon Lozovsky, advising him that Wallace's Russia expert, just arrived in Moscow, was "politically naïve"—and therefore useful.[54]

If Ropes had what Wallace called "the right attitude" on Russia, his mission partner, Dr. Lewis L. Lorwin, sixty-two, had it on matters economic. The Kiev-born Lorwin, a left-leaning labor economist and planning expert in the Commerce Department's foreign trade section, came to the United States as a boy, age four. He worked in Moscow in 1921–22 as a foreign correspondent for the *Chicago Daily News*, but spent most of his career in and out of academia and government advisory positions. In 1934, he helped found the National Planning Association, a New Deal–inspired institution looking to advance alternatives to "laissez-faire." He also advised the National Resources Planning Board, the nation's first and only federal planning agency, on which Wallace served, from 1942 to 1943—when Congress abolished it. He then advised the Bureau of Supplies of the Foreign Economic Administration, before being transferred to the Office of International Trade of the Department of Commerce in 1945.[55]

Speaking to Lorwin in May 1946, not long before his departure, Wallace praised his most recent book, *Time for Planning*, as "awfully good stuff." Wallace expressed great hopes for what he and Ropes could accomplish in Moscow. Stalin, Wallace told him, was "likely to shift his course" as soon as he was "assured we are not trying to encircle" his country—an assurance he expected the boys to convey.[56]

Ropes and Lorwin arrived in Moscow exuding optimism, repeating to the American press the secretary's target of $500 million in two-way trade by 1950. "We can offer them machinery and industrial 'know-how,'" Ropes told reporters, and "they can offer us all kinds of raw materials."

Most American observers were more circumspect. Wisconsin Republican congressman Reid F. Murray demanded personnel records on Wallace's boys, insisting that "the American people [were] entitled to know who is being sent around the world to give away their jobs and their markets." The two countries had also been bogged down in difficult discussions about a postwar loan to Moscow for over two years now, which darkened prospects for deeper cooperation. Still, Ropes insisted that "a healthy trade" could be established "regardless of the fate" of those talks,[57] which were being handled by the State Department.

The high-level trade talks did not begin until July 15, when the two Americans were finally ushered in to see Stalin's foreign trade minister, Anastas Ivanovich Mikoyan, and his deputy, Mikhail Stepanovich Stepanov.

Mikoyan, fifty, son of an Armenian carpenter, was, like his *vozhd*, a seminary student at the times of his conversion to Bolshevism. Full-haired, dark-featured, with Chaplinesque mustache, Mikoyan was cunning, pragmatic, and persuasive. Having backed Stalin during the party power struggles of the early 1920s, he was rewarded, in 1926, with appointment as candidate member of the Politburo and people's commissar for trade. Though having no relevant expertise, he would come to dominate the Soviet trade portfolio for nearly half a century.

Mikoyan became a full member of the Politburo in 1935 and, the following year, Stalin sent him to the United States for three months to study its food industry. He returned home energized, with a wealth of valuable knowledge, which he put to use revolutionizing Soviet food technology, production, and cuisine. "You, Anastas," Stalin joked, or half-joked, "care more about ice cream than communism."

Of the many cronies Stalin installed on the Politburo, Mikoyan was among the few to die of natural causes. His competence, pragmatism, and pleasant demeanor, combined with a lack of ideological imprint or further ambition, contributed to his unusual longevity. He survived, it was said of him, both in admiration and disdain, "from Ilyich [Lenin] to Ilyich [Brezhnev], without infarction or paralysis."

Still, Stalin took steps to keep Mikoyan on the proper path to Communism. Never forgetting that Mikoyan had been the only one of a group of twenty-six Baku Communists to escape execution by Menshevik and socialist challengers in 1918, Stalin reminded him of the suspicion surrounding it. Had Mikoyan betrayed his comrades? "The story," Stalin told him at the height of the Great Terror in 1937, "is dark and entangled. It is up to you, Anastas, not to force us to untangle it."[58]

Though it was never untangled, Mikoyan, like Molotov, would be partially purged in 1949, losing his trade post but keeping others. Stalin attacked him for "capitulationism" at a party plenum in 1952, yet he escaped with his life to secure reappointment as trade czar under Nikita Khrushchev— whom he boldly preceded in condemning Stalin's "cult of personality."[59] In July 1946, however, with Wallace's boys in his office, he was still the *vozhd*'s faithful servant.

Ropes began their meeting, according to Mikoyan's record (later sent to Stalin), by saying that Secretary Wallace was determined to promote the "extensive development of international commerce, in particular aimed at increasing imports into the United States as a means of payment for American exports." He and Dr. Lorwin, he added, had come to Moscow with "a long list of goods for which they [wished] to ascertain the export potential of the USSR," and hoped to connect potential American importers with the appropriate "Soviet foreign trade associations."

Aiming to boost imports marked Wallace as an unusual trade negotiator. Mikoyan, however, to Ropes' disappointment, greeted the proposal with cordial indifference. Owing to "war-inflicted destruction," he explained, Soviet "export capacity was very limited." It would increase with "the economic recovery, which is very rapid," of course, and such "possibilities would therefore increase" in the future. Yet he offered no suggestion for follow-up.

Ropes asked if U.S. firms might still send representatives to the USSR to investigate future trade possibilities, which would help deepen commercial contacts. Mikoyan disclaimed any authority over the matter, explaining that the American firms would need to direct their queries to the appropriate foreign trade association.

Ropes pressed on. "Could [U.S. firms] establish relations with other [Soviet] organizations, besides the associations?" Mikoyan said they could not. Ropes tried a different front. Could "student exchanges" be organized? Mikoyan said this was not in his remit. Lorwin now took a try. Could a U.S.-Soviet trade conference be organized in Moscow in, say, three to four months' time? The two sides might discuss construction challenges, exchange in technological expertise, or prospects for future trade. Mikoyan offered to think it over. And with that, Wallace's boys were dismissed.[60]

The second, and final, meeting on July 24, went no better. The minister began by reiterating that the Soviet Union would need years, likely three to four, to build up its export capacity. Given this reality, "conditions for conferences," of the type Lorwin wanted, "were not yet ripe." Boosting trade in the near-term, therefore, would be "possible only in case of an appropriate credit" from the U.S. government, "which we do not have thus far." This was the message Mikoyan wished them to take home.

Ropes continued to stress that he and Lorwin had come, at Secretary Wallace's direction, "to build the groundwork for future economic relations," and, to that end, he asked for permission to meet with the various foreign trade associations. But Mikoyan would not allow even this. The associations, he said, "would hardly be able to answer their questions." Ropes, still deaf to the refusals, continued to press for expanded commercial contacts, even claiming that "one of his friends could buy a large amount of [Soviet] linen."

"We appreciate Mr. Wallace's efforts," Mikoyan replied. He then handed Lorwin a letter for the secretary, with his regards. It reiterated that a conference, "under present conditions," would only invite "disappointment," and that immediate progress on trade required American credits to cover the cost of Soviet purchases. With that, Mikoyan again bid his guests farewell.[61]

꩜

Mikoyan understood, in a way Wallace did not, how incompatible were the Soviet and American economic and political systems. The global trade and monetary rules the Americans wished to establish would undermine Moscow's ability to control and expand its empire. Mikoyan was therefore determined to wrest leverage from Washington. Instead of Moscow cooperating with Washington's agenda in exchange for financing, Moscow would insist on financing in exchange for talks on cooperating.

Mikoyan explained his thinking years later. "Even before the [February 1945] Yalta Conference," he would write, "during our preparations for it, I was insistent with Stalin on the need to obtain a loan or credits[62] from the Americans to pay for the postwar reconstruction of our economy."[63]

In early 1944, Mikoyan had suggested to Harriman a $1 billion U.S. loan ($17 billion in today's money), but the ambassador was, under State Department direction, noncommittal. The Johnson Act forbade private loans to foreign governments in default of obligations to the United States, and since the U.S. Export-Import Bank guaranteed private loans, and the USSR was in default on Revolution- and World War I–era debt, there were legal obstacles to surmount. Frustrated with the bureaucratic bottleneck in Washington, Harriman pleaded for a hasty solution so as not to lose valuable diplomatic leverage. He needed, he explained, to show the Soviets "the benefit[s] which can be obtained . . . if they work cooperatively . . . on international problems in accordance with our standards."[64]

Treasury, meanwhile, had been discussing the possibility of much larger loans.[65] Russian metals, petroleum, and other raw materials would, Harry Dexter White argued, be necessary to fuel U.S. industrial production, yet would only be exportable if Washington provided Moscow with development funds.[66]

A coded Soviet intelligence cable, dated April 29, 1944, told Moscow of Washington's deliberations. "According to JURIST [White]," it said, "HEN HARRIER [Hull] in a conversation with CHANNEL PILOT [Wallace] touches upon the question of giving us a $5 billion loan. The idea appealed to CHANNEL PILOT."[67] A further cable, dated August 4, 1944, correctly reported that Treasury was discussing a credit as high as *$10 billion*.[68] Ten billion dollars was the number which War Production Board chairman

Donald Nelson had suggested, with no clear basis, following meetings with Molotov and Stalin in Moscow the previous fall.[69] But White would later defend the number in a memo drafted for Morgenthau to send to FDR, arguing that the loan could "be a major step in your program to provide 60 million jobs."[70] When White learned that Moscow was seeking "only" $6 billion at 2–2.5 percent annual interest, according to a Soviet cable dated January 18, 1945, he told NKGB agent Nathan Gregory Silvermaster that it could do better.[71] The NKGB was, in the run-up to Yalta, therefore accurately informed of prospects for even larger loans than Moscow had been seeking.

The State Department convinced Roosevelt not to raise the loan issue at Yalta, while Stalin did not even bring economic experts to the conference. The matter languished.[72] As tensions over Poland worsened, and thorny questions over China and Turkey loomed, Harriman and Clayton became more determined to condition financial assistance on Soviet political cooperation. On trade, they now contradicted Wallace. "[R]ather than giving preference to the Soviet Union as a source of supply," Harriman argued, "our basic interests might better be served by increasing our trade with other parts of the world."[73] On April 22, ten days after FDR's death, Truman warned the visiting Molotov that "legislative appropriations were required for [foreign] economic measures," and that he "had no hope of getting such measures through Congress unless there was public support for them."[74] That support was being undermined by Soviet behavior in Poland.

Treasury, the department most friendly to Moscow, began "studying alternative practical terms appropriate to a Congressionally approved loan,"[75] getting nowhere. In September 1945, when Senator Pepper—"Red Pepper"—visited Moscow, he apologized to Vyshinsky that, despite "a sincere desire to cooperate with the Soviet Union on the part of the American people, . . . Congress had not yet decided on the [matter] of allocating loans to foreign nations." He added, however, ominously, that "there were critics of the Soviet Union alleging that it wants to get money from the USA without any payback."[76] This admission was perhaps the surest sign that the loan was in serious jeopardy.

In February 1946, Mikoyan was vexed to learn that the Americans now wanted to discuss "a wide range of other economic questions" in addition to loans. "This was disadvantageous for us," he later explained, "since, under the pressure of holding back loans, they wanted concessions on matters on which we could not concede." These included an "open door" for U.S. business in Eastern Europe and Soviet agreement on terms for a new International Organization on Commerce and Employment that would oblige nations to conduct trade wholly on commercial grounds and to forswear export subsidies. These terms were, Mikoyan observed, "unacceptable to us." Still, despite Stalin's belief that they were making too many concessions, Mikoyan secured his, and the Politburo's, backing for continuing talks. Talking helped unearth and undermine American aims. "Without binding ourselves," Mikoyan observed, "we needed to try to eliminate provisions from the charter . . . which might impede our trade with participating nations." On other matters, we "could just drag out talks for a year or two, and then break them off altogether." Meanwhile, by pretending to negotiate, "we could get agreement from the Americans on loans."[77]

This was the trap into which Wallace had walked with his trade mission. On July 28, Ropes told Drew Middleton of *The New York Times* that the Soviets "would buy $2,000,000,000 worth of American goods *if the necessary credits were extended.*" Doing so would, he said, also "facilitate the exchange of trade and technical information." Yet without such credits, he warned, the Soviets would turn to Sweden and other countries for reconstruction goods.[78]

Mikoyan had done his job well. Wallace's boys were spreading his message—that good things *might* happen if the United States provided finance, but that bad things *would* happen without it. Whatever the Americans chose, however, Moscow would make no concessions to their capitalist agenda.

Fifteen months later, on October 30, 1947, the twenty-three-nation General Agreement on Tariffs and Trade (GATT) would be signed in Geneva, after which the sixty-seven-year-old Will Clayton would, in triumph, write his sixth and final letter resigning from the State Department. Truman would hail the accomplishment as "a landmark in the history of international economic relations."[79]

The media heaped praise on Clayton's efforts. "This vast project [the GATT], which makes all previous international economic accords look puny," wrote *The New York Times*, "is the realization of Mr. Clayton's dream: that a group of like-minded democratic nations could deliberately reverse the historical trend toward the strangulation of world trade." Relentless but humble, Clayton was "both the symbol of and dynamic force behind the most constructive aspects of American international economic policy."[80] The GATT would, forty-eight years later, in 1995, give way to the much larger and even more important World Trade Organization. Now with 164 members, the WTO would not admit Russia until 2012.

As for Wallace's hopes of expanding U.S-Soviet trade to $500 million by 1950, these would be crushed. Despite his efforts to enlarge and deepen co-operation and exchange, loan talks would collapse, relations nosedive, and trade wilt to a paltry $16 million.[81]

Twelve

THE ODD TALE OF THE SINO-SOVIET TREATY

In Chungking in June 1944, Henry Wallace, beyond earshot of his State Department minder, had tried, and by all evidence failed, to persuade Chiang Kai-shek to embrace postwar concessions to Moscow. The discovery of his efforts by a Soviet diplomat, however, may have whetted the Kremlin's appetite for regional booty. As Deputy People's Commissar of Foreign Affairs Solomon Lozovsky wrote in October 1944, they now had from Wallace's "mouth" evidence that the Americans were prepared to pay, in territory and commercial interests, for Soviet military assistance in Asia.[1]

On October 17, Stalin informed Harriman that certain "political questions" would need to be "clarified" in connection with "Russia's entry in the war against Japan."[2] On December 14, Harriman returned to Stalin's Kremlin office for a discussion of military matters, following which he told Stalin that Roosevelt was, given the Allied leaders' intention to meet again early in the new year, "anxious to know" what those political questions were.

Bringing in a map from an adjoining room, Stalin marked off what he called his "desiderata." These were the "return" of southern Sakhalin and the Kurile Islands, Japanese control of which was impeding "the approaches to Vladivostok." He also wanted leases on Port Arthur, Dairen, "and the surrounding area" of the Liaotung Peninsula; leases on the Chinese Eastern and Southern Manchurian Railways; and recognition of Outer Mongolia as an entity independent from China. Stalin's demands on China were identical to Skvortsov's October account of Wallace's stipulations to Chiang—with the notable exception that Stalin wanted control of, and not just access to, the ports.

His recollection, Harriman told his host, was that Stalin had, at Tehran the year prior, suggested only an international free port in the Pacific, and not a Russian lease. "This can be discussed," Stalin replied calmly, suggesting it was a mere detail. Harriman pressed him to identify the precise railway lines he wanted. Stalin responded by outlining a route "from Dairen to Harbin, thence northwest to Manchuli and east to Vladivostok." Sensing his guest's concern, he clarified that he "did not intend to interfere with the sovereignty of China in Manchuria."

Harriman was not reassured. "There is," he would tell Roosevelt, "no doubt that with control of the railroad [and] Russian troops to protect [it] Soviet influence will be great." As for Outer Mongolia, this was the first time Stalin had called for its independence from China—making it noteworthy that Wallace had done the same in Chungking. Still, Harriman had known that Roosevelt would have to weigh in at some point, given the Soviet desire to protect their "Siberian boundary." He requested the president's instructions. Roosevelt, however, wanted to handle Stalin himself—in person.[3]

When the two men met at Yalta, the Soviet leader restated his "desiderata." As he enumerated them at a session on February 8, 1945, the president appeared wholly relaxed—as if it were, for him, a natural thing to be bartering away an ally's territory and sovereign rights. But, to his mind, it was important to secure Stalin's commitment to attack Japanese forces in a timely manner, and not have him wait until vast numbers of U.S. troops had been sacrificed in weakening them to irrelevance.

When Stalin finished, Roosevelt assured him that his own thinking was compatible. He could "not speak for the Chinese," of course, but did not think it advisable for Stalin to press for *leases* on the port of Dairen or the Manchurian railways. Instead, he believed Dairen should become a free port under an international commission, and the railroads jointly operated by the two countries. These arrangements, he said, would, at the appropriate time, require a treaty between China and the Soviet Union—a treaty that would acknowledge the "full sovereignty" of Chiang's government over Manchuria. Such a document, FDR believed, or wished to believe, would commit Stalin to ongoing cooperation with Chiang—and, importantly, preclude his switching support to Mao and the CCP.

At this point, Stalin had no intention of undermining the authority of Chiang's government, which he thought the only viable one. He largely accepted Roosevelt's counterproposal on port and railway arrangements, but insisted that a lease would be necessary at Port Arthur—which was to function as a Soviet naval base. Remarkably, Roosevelt accepted this caveat with no conditions—a caveat which ensured an ongoing Soviet military presence in Manchuria.

Further Russian text changes put forth on February 10 concerned Harriman. These included clauses stipulating that "the pre-eminent interests of the Soviet Union [in Manchuria] shall be safeguarded" and its territorial claims, based on former rights stripped of it by Japan after its "treacherous attack" of 1904, would be "unquestionably fulfilled" after Japan's defeat.[4] These additions hinted that Stalin planned to be expansive in his interpretation and assertive in realizing it, but Roosevelt dismissed them as just "words." No stickler for details even in normal times, the president, now gravely ill and unable to focus more than a few hours a day, was saving his strength for navigating, as he saw it, more immediately consequential matters—that is, securing Stalin's cooperation on launching the United Nations and a pledge to respect Polish independence.

The China deal was done. Given the importance of keeping it secret from both China and Japan, with whom the Soviets still had a nonaggression pact, Admiral Leahy carried the signed document back to Washington and locked it away in the president's safe.[5] Although the Chinese ambassadors in Moscow and Washington would be briefed on the agreement's existence,[6] its full contents would remain unknown to Chiang for some months.[7]

Following Roosevelt's death on April 12, 1945, with relations between Washington and Moscow deteriorating amidst conflicts over Poland and U.N. Security Council voting procedures, Truman sent his predecessor's trusted envoy, Harry Hopkins, to Moscow. On May 28, Stalin assured him that the Soviet army would be "deployed on the Manchurian positions by August 8." This timing, however, he stressed, made it important for China's foreign minister, T.V. Soong, to come to Moscow to ratify the Yalta secret deal—which had been conditioned on China's concurrence.[8]

Over in Chungking, Ambassador Hurley met with Chiang on June 15 to reveal the contents of that deal. Having first heard the elements from Wallace a year prior, and leaks of the actual provisions from Russian sources, he showed no reaction. In Washington, Soong would tell Truman that China would sooner fight the Russians than accept the Yalta carve-up,[9] but this was a bluff. Chiang knew he would have to pay a price for Stalin to disown the CCP.[10]

"Diplomacy," Truman said, speaking of China politics back in 1943, "has always been too much for me, especially . . . as practised by the great powers."[11] Yet whereas he had ascended to the White House with no ambition to alter FDR's diplomatic course, three factors were now pushing U.S. policy to the right—away from Stalin and toward Chiang. One was Stalin's lies about respecting Polish independence. The second was the new president's willingness to heed the more Russoskeptic voices in the government: in particular, Harriman and former ambassador to Japan Joseph Grew. The third was completion of the atom bomb, which altered Washington's strategic calculus in the Pacific. No longer, it seemed, was a Soviet invasion of Manchuria even desirable. If the United States could achieve a quick Japanese surrender on its own, there was every reason to want the Red Army confined to barracks.[12]

Though Chiang knew nothing of America's atomic achievements, he could now detect, in the tone of U.S. officials, the tides flowing in his favor. He therefore instructed Soong to toughen his stance. China would concede Outer Mongolian independence (which was a de facto reality), but insist on more control over Manchurian ports and railways and a shorter duration for Soviet leases (twenty years rather than thirty). "Yalta is not sacred," Soong told Stalin, brazenly, in Moscow on July 10, 1945.[13] As intended, this new hard line deadlocked the negotiations, allowing Truman a chance to soften up Stalin further at Potsdam a week hence.

At the conference, Stalin assured the new U.S. president of his fealty to Yalta and his commitment not to station Soviet troops in Manchuria outside the naval base at Port Arthur. This pledge satisfied Truman that he had "clinched the 'open door' in Manchuria," ensuring China's territorial and administrative integrity and America's rights to trade and invest in the region. But Byrnes, still hoping to forestall the Red Army's entry into Manchuria, convinced him to press Chiang to hold tough in negotiations. On July 23, Byrnes telegrammed the Generalissimo, via Ambassador Hurley, urging that he concede nothing beyond what FDR had agreed to at Yalta.[14]

Chinese military intelligence, however, had detected that the Red Army was now poised to storm Manchuria. Chiang reasoned that he had either

to lure American forces into the region or cut a deal with Stalin. Concluding that there was no appetite in Washington for a Manchurian military
engagement, he ordered Soong to get the treaty done.[15]

A new Chinese delegation arrived in Moscow on August 5, 1945. Before
they could meet with Stalin, however, Truman changed the course of the
Pacific war—and human history.

At 2:45 local time on the morning of August 6, three U.S. B-29 bomber
planes with fighter escorts took off from Tinian in the Marianas, heading
in the direction of southwest Japan. Two of the bombers carried cameras
and scientific equipment to record and analyze their mission. The third, the
Enola Gay, carried an enormous plutonium bomb—the product of six years
of intensive research employing over 130,000 people and costing $2 billion
($33 billion in today's money).

After traveling 1,361 nautical miles, the 9,700-pound weapon, named
"Little Boy," dropped through the plane's doors at 8:15 a.m. At 1,950 feet,
it detonated. Within a minute, much of the compact city of Hiroshima—a
base for military factories and facilities that had not been targeted in earlier
conventional raids—was obliterated in a horrific fireball. Roughly 70,000,
in a city of 300,000, were killed instantly. That number would double by the
end of the year. Ninety percent of the buildings were destroyed.[16]

When Soong and his colleagues met with the Soviet leader the following day, August 7, they found him less patient. Unbeknownst to them, Stalin would, in just a few hours, order Soviet forces to attack the Japanese in
Manchuria at the earliest possible moment—with or without a Sino-Soviet
treaty.[17] He had decided to move up the planned invasion by a week, determined to grab all he could before Tokyo surrendered and Washington
pivoted to contain his advance.

In no mood for further haggling, Stalin dropped the mask of respect for
his guests. As Soong continued to insist on Chinese administrative control
in Dairen, Stalin exploded, doing his best impression of Stilwell: "[You talk
of] China's sovereignty," he put back with disdain, but "we are going to fight
and shed blood for it—*something you never did*."[18]

In Tokyo, meanwhile, the cabinet was anxious to avoid this fight—
even more so than they were to avoid further atom bombs, of which Navy

Supreme Commander Admiral Soemu Toyoda judged (rightly) that the United States had no more than two or three.[19] War with Russia meant not only the loss of more territory and men,[20] but a greater likelihood that the *kokutai*, the emperor-centered political structure, would be swept away— and possibly even replaced by Communist rule. Tokyo therefore decided to make an urgent appeal to Moscow, however risibly late and vague, to broker a truce with the Anglo-Americans.

Back on July 11, Foreign Minister Shigenori Togo had urged Ambassador Naotake Sato in Moscow to convey to the Soviet foreign minister that "His Majesty [hoped] to restore peace with all possible speed," and that Prince Fumimaro Konoe, a former prime minister, would soon arrive in the Soviet capital to convey the imperial sentiments personally. Sato, bemused and incensed at such naïveté, beseeched Togo, his junior in the diplomatic corps, to see the futility of seeking Moscow's help in ending the war on terms convivial to Tokyo. Japan's position was too weak. Surrender was necessary.

The regime in Tokyo, hopelessly divided, could not yet accept reality. Two weeks later, it took renewed hope from the observation that Stalin had not signed the Potsdam Declaration, calling for its unconditional surrender. In fact, Truman and Churchill—anxious to minimize Stalin's influence, and exploiting the fact that Moscow had not yet declared war—had simply not invited him to sign. Sato again implored Tokyo to surrender, or risk Russia's entry into the war—still to no avail.

On August 7, Togo cabled Sato urging him to press for Russia's response to Tokyo's requests to talk peace. Thanks to intercepts and cryptanalysts, U.S. officials followed the weeks of tense and frantic exchanges in near-real-time.

Sato, filled with foreboding, asked for an urgent meeting with the Soviet foreign minister. Molotov, needing time for the Soviet military to ready its massive Manchurian invasion force, declined to receive him until 5 p.m. on August 8.[21] When the diplomat was finally admitted, the Russian cut off his greetings and directed him to sit.

Given Japan's rejection of the Potsdam demands, Molotov explained, America and Britain had "approached the Soviet Union with a proposal to join in the war against Japanese aggression." Though no such proposal had been made, Molotov declared that his country, having accepted it, was now declaring war on Japan. He added that the declaration was effective August 9, but declined to specify that this meant August 9 *on Siberian-Manchurian border time*—mere hours away.

Sato, stunned by the imminence of catastrophe, was dismissed. Not long after, as Soviet tanks rolled into Manchuria, Molotov reported the news to Harriman—who did his best to feign pleasure.

Back in Tokyo, the twenty-three-member Supreme War Council (SWC) convened in haste. In the midst of a heated discussion on August 9, another American atomic air raid force was headed toward the Japanese industrial city of Kokura. Fog and smoke, however, forced the *Bockscar* B-29 bearing the "Fat Man" bomb to divert to the secondary target. And so, this time, the shipbuilding and port city of Nagasaki, 260 miles southwest of Hiroshima, endured the devastation. A further 35,000 were killed—a number that would double by the end of the year. Perilously low on fuel, the frazzled pilot headed for the closest friendly airfield, at Okinawa, where *Bockscar*, with seven gallons of gas and only one of four engines still functioning, made a violent but successful landing.

In Tokyo, War Minister General Korechika Anami and other military service chiefs continued to back defiance, insisting that the country could, if willing to endure death and hardship without limit, still prevail against an invasion of the home islands. By this time, the emperor had heard enough of such empty victory talk. The military had, year after year since 1937, been consistently and tragically wrong about the trajectory of the wars in China and the Pacific, and he could see no higher purpose served by suicidal resistance. It was time to "bear the unbearable." He approved a message to the Allies, drawn up by Togo, accepting their demand for "unconditional surrender"—albeit conditionally. The condition was that surrender not prejudice his prerogatives as sovereign.[22] He would remain the country's supreme authority.

In Washington, the demand was not unexpected. Intercepted Japanese cables had suggested the nation would fight on if the emperor's status were threatened. Too many necks depended on it. For his part, Truman knew the American public expected unconditional surrender, but he also knew it would not tolerate limitless casualties to achieve it.

Stimson deemed the Japanese condition acceptable, Byrnes not. The latter was content to see Hirohito keep his throne, but not in deference to a Japanese demand, which would signal American irresolution. Forrestal thought the circle could be squared by allowing Hirohito to remain *if* he surrendered "unconditionally." Truman settled on a formulation under which the emperor's authority, following surrender, would still be subordinate to that of the Allied Supreme Commander. This caveat kept American occupation powers unbounded while dampening the attraction of fanatical defiance. But if defiance continued, a third atom bomb would be ready in ten days' time.

On August 10, Byrnes told the cabinet that British foreign secretary Ernest Bevin had approved the proposed American response. The Russians, however, were silent. They wanted, Stimson explained, to "push as far into Manchuria as possible" before Japan surrendered. Truman was adamant that this push was not in "our interest." There being "no agreement with Russia about Manchuria," the Red Army would run amok. He ordered the surrender conditions sent to Tokyo. Five days later, following even more heated debate within the SWC and a failed coup attempt, Hirohito would accept the terms and broadcast the news to his defeated nation.

Wallace, according to his diary, sat silent through the cabinet exchange over the Russian invasion, though he pronounced himself "surprised" by Truman's reaction. "I remember," he wrote, "what Roosevelt used to say in the spring of 1944"—just before he, Wallace, had left for Siberia and China—"about his agreement with Stalin on access to Dairen." Russia, FDR had told him, "had agreed not to take Manchuria."[23] This fact was, in Wallace's view, all Truman needed to know. The president's disposition therefore showed him to be either ignorant or paranoid. Wallace feared the good relations with Moscow on which world peace rested were about to be shattered.

On August 10, the day Truman ordered the surrender conditions sent to Tokyo, Stalin met again with the Chinese delegation.

"It is now five o'clock in the Far East," he told them, menacingly, "and our troops will continue [their] movement." Nearly 1.5 million of them were enveloping Manchuria on three axes.

Stalin's message was clear: Don't be greedy. What you gain from quibbling, you will lose ten-fold on the ground.

Still, he could make no headway on his demand that the "Sino-Soviet Treaty of Friendship" commit Chiang to "national unity and democratization." This was shorthand for bringing the Communists into government.

"Don't you want to democratize China?," he complained to them. "If you continue to attack Communists, are we expected to support [you]?" On this matter, however, his guests insisted they had no authority to budge.

"Very well," Stalin shrugged, content to resume discussions after taking more of Manchuria. "You see how many concessions we make. China's Communists will curse us."

It took three more days—until the eve of Japan's surrender—for the two sides to agree on the remaining issues: the border of an "independent" Outer Mongolia and the parameters of Soviet military and administrative rights in Dairen. Only after the treaty was signed on the 14th—a treaty mirroring the concessions Wallace had privately pressed on Chiang in June 1944—did Stalin excuse himself to tell his generals he was ready to receive Japan's surrender. Confident he now held the key to lock Manchuria's "open door" to America, he returned—to the surprise of his weary guests—with champagne.[24]

Following the Japanese surrender on August 15, General MacArthur, in an absurd act of vainglory, sent a message to Moscow ordering the Soviets to "discontinue further offensive action against Japanese forces" in Manchuria. Stalin told him, effectively, to mind his own business. Such matters, MacArthur was informed, would be decided solely by "the Supreme Commander of the forces of the Soviet Union."[25]

Manchuria, housing the world's fourth-largest functioning industrial complex, was among the most valuable territories in Asia. Stalin intended to make full use of it—and to ensure that it could not be used, whether by Chiang or by Truman, against him. As a bonus, he would occupy northern Korea, down to the 38th parallel—as agreed with the Americans at Potsdam. Its ultimate disposition would then be subject to negotiations. So important was this military venture that his government made medical provisions for an astonishing 540,000 Soviet casualties, including 160,000 dead.

Yet it took, in the end, under a week, and a small fraction of the estimated casualties, for the vastly better equipped, expertly led, and nearly twice as numerous Soviet mechanized troops to overwhelm the degraded and demoralized Japanese forces. The Russians continued to rampage through the region for a further two weeks, until they held every major strategic point.

As Soviet forces advanced, they systematically dismantled factories, trucking the machinery, raw materials, and finished-goods stockpiles back to Russia as "war booty." To justify their legal claims, the new occupiers forced Japanese factory managers to sign false statements saying their facilities had been for military production aimed at the USSR.[26] Washington protested that Japanese external assets were, by agreement, subject to the authority of the Inter-Allied Reparations Commission for Japan. But Stalin was uninterested in such niceties.[27]

Following on the heels of the Soviet attack, tens of thousands of overjoyed CCP forces also began pouring into Manchuria from their bases in China's north and northwest. For Stalin, their arrival was both threat and opportunity. They were a threat in that they undermined the Sino-Soviet Treaty he had signed with Chiang, through which he had intended to carve out legally recognized spheres of Soviet economic, political, and military control in China's Northeast. But they were also an opportunity. Their presence added pressure on Chiang to make further concessions to stop the Soviets from yielding more and more territory to them.

On September 5, Chiang's new economics commissioner for Manchuria, the Japanese- and American-educated Chang Kia-ngau,[28] met with top officials in Washington to ascertain their views on the volatile situation. Among those he saw was the secretary of commerce.

According to Commissioner Chang's diary, Wallace tried to reassure him that the Russians were acting according to agreement—despite the fact that the Soviets were still mounting offensive operations three days after accepting the Japanese instrument of surrender aboard the battleship *Missouri*. "The essence of the Sino-Soviet treaty signed by China," Wallace said, "is basically the same as that I discussed with President Chiang while I was in Chungking." This striking statement, made privately, is the only known one confirming a Soviet diplomat's account of Wallace's attempt to extract Kremlin-friendly concessions from Chiang the year prior.

"What is most important" now, Wallace continued, is for Chiang's regime "to help the peasants improve their agricultural techniques so that their living standards can be maintained and raised. Then the people in the Northeast naturally will support the central government." Listening to Wallace, Chang can only have been gobsmacked. Reports were by then widespread of Soviet troops, who were supposed to be liberating Manchuria from the Japanese, pillaging, raping, and murdering Manchurians as they stormed through the region, with CCP forces rushing in behind.

Chang was now listening to an American cabinet official, a former vice president, telling him that there was nothing to be concerned about, that there was no inconsistency between Russia's commitments and its actions, and that his government should instead worry about improving "agricultural techniques." Wallace warned that if his advice were not heeded with alacrity, Manchurians, "like the people of Outer Mongolia, [would] lean toward the Soviet Union because of their gratitude for various kinds of Soviet help."[29]

At a cabinet meeting on September 21, Wallace repeated his defense of Soviet actions in the region, challenging the "violent" charges made against them by Clinton Anderson, Truman's new agriculture secretary. "It simply wasn't true that Russia was taking over Manchuria," Wallace insisted. "18 months ago, Roosevelt had told me what the arrangements were with regard to Manchuria, and Russia was living up to the understanding." As for the Mongolians, they "wanted Russian scientific information regarding animal diseases." It was, therefore, "perfectly natural" that they should "look toward Russia as a source of progress, rather than China."

Over the course of the coming nine-month Red Army occupation, almost seven months longer than Stalin had pledged, most Manchurians would, in contrast to Wallace's assertions, come to hate the Russians even more than they did the Japanese. The latter had, at least, built up the region's industry; the Soviets were looting and destroying it.[30] During a cabinet meeting on November 23, Truman would read a wire from Ed Pauley, now U.S. representative to the Allied Reparations Committee, detailing how the Soviets had stripped Manchurian and Korean factories of all their machinery. A commission under his direction would later put the replacement value for theft and damage at $2 billion ($33 billion in today's money).[31] When Truman expressed his concern over Russian intentions in the Far East, Wallace reacted with alarm. "The president's attitude," he recorded in his diary, "means World War Number 3."[32]

The president's take on *Wallace's* attitude would be a little less harsh. "[W]hen we help our friends in China who fought on our side, [Wallace thinks] it's terrible," Truman would later record. But "when Russia loots the industrial plants of those same friends it is all right."[33]

Though Stalin was initially careful to respect the letter of the "friendship" treaty,[34] surrendering the main cities and railroads to Nationalist forces, he exploited its loopholes and ambiguities. In October 1945, Red Army forces denied Nationalist troop access to Dairen on the grounds that it was now a "free commercial port," barred to military use. This action stymied Chiang's plans for a joint sea-land push into Manchuria to beat back advancing CCP forces. At the same time, the Soviets let the Communists seize Ying-k'ou harbor, ninety-three miles to the north, as well as stocks of abandoned Japanese weapons and equipment. They further forbade the airlifting in of Nationalist forces by U.S. personnel. They suggested that trains might be used instead, knowing full well that CCP forces at Shan-hai-kuan had already cut rail communication between Manchuria and China proper.[35] Finally, on November 16, Stalin instructed his commander in Manchuria not to "accept obligations to guarantee the security of the introduction of Chinese [Nationalist] troops into Manchuria"[36]—notwithstanding Soviet commitments to support the Nationalist government, and to respect the region's territorial integrity, enshrined in the Sino-Soviet Treaty.[37] These Soviet tactics helped transform the Communists from a guerrilla outfit into a formidable conventional military force in the Northeast, while obliging the Nationalists to fight their way into the area. Meanwhile, Red Army generals delayed their withdrawal by demanding elaborate prerequisite compromises to ensure ongoing elements of Soviet control.

After taking all useful industrial equipment, the Soviets slapped war-booty claims on all of the Manchurian enterprises. They then offered to relinquish them, as an act of goodwill, if Chiang conceded 50 percent Soviet ownership. The aims, however, went well beyond enrichment. According to Soviet ambassador Apollon Petrov, joint ownership meant the Russian chairman of the Ch'ang-ch'un Railroad would assume "heavy responsibilities [over] politics and economics" across the region it serviced. Even selection of the mayor of Port Arthur would have to be agreed upon with Moscow.

Commissioner Chang remonstrated that such stipulations undermined Chinese sovereignty in Manchuria, but Mikhail Sladkovsky, the top Russian economic adviser in the region, tried to reassure him. "Soviet willingness to hand over to China half of what the Soviets have already acquired," he said, was "based on a spirit of friendship." There were also, he acknowledged, practical reasons for the Chinese to embrace this spirit. "A settlement of the economic question," he explained, "will also result in settling political problems." The message was clear: there was a further price to be paid for a Soviet withdrawal, and the Nationalists needed to pay it quickly—before Mao took all of Manchuria.[38]

The negotiations alarmed the State Department. Byrnes protested, to both parties, on the grounds that such deals undermined the "open door" principle and discriminated against American investment in the region.[39] Indeed, Commissioner Chang noted that the Soviets, in insisting on joint control of mines and industrial firms, were trying "to make impossible the penetration of American influence into Manchuria." Sladkovsky had said as much, stressing the need to keep out the euphemistic "third nation." Yet whereas Chang was far more angered at the Soviet demands than Byrnes, he nonetheless urged the Generalissimo to compromise before Communist forces advanced further—with Soviet connivance. The Soviets, after all, held all the leverage.

"There had been no agreement," he lamented, echoing Truman's concern, which Wallace had dismissed, "about how our troops were going to enter Manchuria, how our officials [would] establish the government's authority, or how economic enterprises [would] be transferred to us." The Soviets would, therefore, he said, refuse to "totally withdraw their troops" if the Generalissimo insisted on "tak[ing] over the enterprises they wish to operate cooperatively."[40]

The Soviets aimed at more than just control of Manchurian industry. In a Red Army Day speech in Chungking on February 23, 1946, the commander of its forces capturing Manchuria, Hero of the Soviet Union Marshal Rodion Malinovsky, made clear Moscow's overriding objective: to push the United States out of China.

China and the Soviet Union, he said, "must not be swayed by the efforts of a third nation to provoke an estrangement between them. Right now, there is stretched between [them] the hand of a third party who wears suede gloves and has gold dollars in his pocket. Indeed, we must get rid of him by chopping off his hand."

This imagery was at odds with that conjured by Wallace in his May 1944 speech, on departing Anchorage for Siberia, in which he said that Russia and America were, quoting Perry McDonough Collins, destined to "shake the friendly hand in commercial intercourse" across the Pacific—the two having no basis to "vie with each other [save] in developing the resources of their respective countries."[41] Collins and Wallace saw geography as a basis for ensuring only friendly competition between the two nations. Yet World War II had shown just how dramatically the world had shrunk since the nineteenth century, globalizing the scope for both profitable interchange and deadly conflict. By 1946, Manchuria had become far more than a contested border area between Russia and China. The struggle for control of the region would ripple—economically, politically, and militarily—throughout the Asia-Pacific and beyond.

Grasping this reality, Malinovsky had complained in October 1945 about the entry of a U.S. warship into Dairen, which he insisted was a violation of the spirit of the Sino-Soviet Treaty. The Soviet Union did not want a permanent occupation of Manchuria; the local population, Russians understood, would never abide it. But Moscow looked to "rely on economic cooperation to eliminate the threat Manchuria poses to the Soviet Union." That threat emanated not locally, but from "a foreign power, a wolf in sheep's clothing, [that] may encroach on [it]."[42]

Chang grasped the dangers of the growing animosity between Moscow and Washington, warning the Generalissimo that China risked becoming "no more than a field of contention between the [two]." Stalin would, he said, try to "nurture in border areas a type of pro-Soviet armed force, directed by communist elements under the leadership of Moscow," which would forswear cooperation with Americans.[43] Only by the central government ceding some control of the region's heavy industry to Moscow, he insisted, would the Soviets lift the effective blockade on Nationalist troops—which was essential to unifying the country.

The Generalissimo, under growing pressure from the right wing of the KMT, refused to bend. He would make no concessions beyond those agreed in the Sino-Soviet Treaty. Instead, he demanded the return of assets already taken to Russia. Economic cooperation, he insisted, could be discussed only *after* a full Soviet withdrawal. Chang, knowing that such bullheadedness would only delay the Red Army's departure and speed the CCP's military advance, despaired.

Against this backdrop, George Marshall, who had arrived in China in

January 1946 to broker peace between Chiang and Mao, could make no sustained headway. Marshall warned Chiang that he faced a growing "Soviet undercover attack" to undermine his authority through "a separate Communist Government and a separate Communist Army."[44] For his part, Chang warned the Generalissimo that the challenges of transporting and supplying troops in the face of Soviet resistance meant inevitable defeat in Manchuria.[45] But Chiang thought he could prevail militarily, and that the nature of his adversary, implacable and committed to his destruction, left him no choice.

In March 1946, major armed clashes between Communist and Nationalist forces broke out throughout Manchuria, with Soviet troops blocking the latter by invoking pretexts such as the need to prevent the spread of plague.[46] Now convinced that economic alliance with Chiang was unattainable, and that CCP control of northern Manchuria was preferable to an ongoing Soviet occupation, Stalin completed his pull-out in May—seven months later than he had first pledged.[47]

Stalin had played a sedulous diplomatic game, committing his government's support to the Nationalists while secretly coordinating with the Chinese Communist Party through the Soviet one. This tactic had given Moscow leverage with Chiang while hedging against failure to persuade him. Stalin also steadily chipped away at Yalta. In spite of Soviet commitments to treat Dairen as a free port "open to the commerce of shipping of all nations," the Soviets continued, even into 1947, to deny U.S. access on the grounds that war with Japan had not yet been legally terminated. Stalin had been determined, well before the Red Army entered Manchuria, to carve out a sphere of Soviet economic and military influence in the Northeast and to keep the United States at bay, permanently—much as it was doing in Eastern Europe.[48] In northern Korea, meanwhile, the Red Army quietly transferred control of civic functions to Communist-trained locals—paving the way for a new client regime under Kim Il-sung.[49]

Without the nine-month Soviet occupation of Manchuria, Mao could never have expanded and equipped his army adequately for conventional war, seized control of vast swaths of Northeast territory with little or no resistance, absorbed Manchukuo military units, and destroyed Chiang's best American-trained armies in the region. He would, therefore, have been far less likely to prevail in the nationwide civil war that erupted at the occupation's conclusion.[50] Truman, in short, had been right to mistrust Stalin's intentions in Manchuria—though Wallace would never acknowledge this fact.

For the United States, China would prove a constant object of misjudgment and source of frustration. Little went to plan.

Fighting in the country was vital to pinning down 1.25 million Japanese troops; yet it would never become the fulcrum of the Pacific war that U.S. planners had envisioned. Victory would come through the capture of island chains—notably the Marianas, from which the atomic bombers flew—and the asphyxiation of Tokyo's shipping routes. China had, furthermore, been expected to emerge from the war as America's foremost Asian ally. It would instead become, under Mao Tse-tung, its most formidable regional nemesis.

Beginning in 1950, Senator Joseph McCarthy's (R-WI) infamous "Who lost China?" inquest would ensnare Marshall, Vincent,[51] Service, Davies, Wallace, and others who had supported dialogue with the CCP. Though the inquisition would prove transparently and disgracefully dishonest, targeting men with as contrary views as the pro-Stilwell, anti-Soviet Davies and the anti-Stilwell, pro-Soviet Wallace, its bitter legacy would be felt over a decade later—in Lyndon Johnson's tragic resolve not to "lose Vietnam."

But was a better outcome possible? Were there superior strategic options open to Washington, at least after the war? Davies' preferred policy in 1945, which appeared defeatist and which no one took seriously at the time, would age well—that is, to have given Chiang "the minimum aid necessary to satisfy American public opinion" and "prevent [his] total collapse," while admonishing him to accept that the "recovery of all Manchuria is [beyond] feasibility," and that a military effort to achieve it would receive no U.S. support.[52]

Chiang, of course, might still have risked all to take Manchuria. But he might also have done the deal with the Soviets urged on him by Chang Kiangau, thereby limiting the CCP's advance. Or he might have accepted, however reluctantly and provisionally, a divided China, with the Communists running the north and the Nationalists the south, mirroring the emerging divided Europe. The payoff to Washington, in the latter case, would have been the prospect of establishing peaceable relations with Mao, which could have been exploited to foil an alliance with Stalin. Internal CCP documents from May 1946 do, in fact, show its leadership desirous of economic links between its Northeastern strongholds and the United States.[53] In the end, however, an "inability to practice realpolitik," as one historian put it, placed Washington on a fatal collision course with Mao.[54]

Realpolitik aimed at containing Soviet influence in Asia was, of course, anathema to Wallace, who—as tensions flared with Moscow over Iran, Turkey, and East Asia in early 1946—remained the only leading U.S. official still committed to the Yalta deal on China. He was, after all, the American progenitor, both in his own mind and that of Soviet officials, of the 1945 Sino-Soviet Treaty of Friendship and Alliance—a treaty which, he would continue to claim, provided a genuine basis for regional peace and security. Signed by Chiang under duress, it had, in actuality, been not so much a treaty as a ransom note—the Soviet price for relinquishing Manchuria.

In 1948, four years after Wallace had urged Roosevelt to fire Stilwell for his inability to work with Chiang, he now heaped posthumous[55] praise on the general for his opposition to Kuomintang corruption. Having spoken to a "Chinese professor who knows a great deal about Chinese agriculture," Wallace concluded that farm output could be boosted 50–100 percent within ten years "if Chiang's regime were replaced by a people's government."[56] This fact, he said, highlighted the need for Washington to get "on the side of the people" in the cause of "world peace."

But how was the United States to bring about "a people's government" in China? Wallace did not say, failing even to mention Mao's Communists, who would emerge victorious from the civil war the following year.

Shortly after their victory, Mao sought annulment of the Sino-Soviet Treaty. In February 1950, Stalin agreed to return the gifts Wallace had urged Chiang to bestow on the Soviets in 1944: the Chinese Eastern Railway, the naval base at Port Arthur, and the port and associated properties in Dairen. The treaty's demise, Stalin admitted to Mao, "entails certain inconveniences, and we will have to struggle against Americans."[57] But the two agreed to a more conventional alliance, providing for mutual defense directed against any "state directly or indirectly associated" with Japan—namely, the United States.

By November 1950, the United States and China, reinforced by Soviet military aid, would be at war in Korea. That horrific clash, which would result in a dangerous and precarious indefinite political division of the peninsula, would prove a costly and consequential preamble to two decades of Sino-American hostility.

Thirteen

THE NUCLEAR OPTION

From the start, Henry Wallace had supported the top secret Manhattan Project, assuring Roosevelt, in 1940, that atomic weapons were "something to put money into." As vice president, he had been a member of the Top Policy Group, the committee charged with making decisions about atomic policy, together with Stimson, Marshall, James Conant, and Vannevar Bush. Stimson would later say that Wallace "played [no] active part" in its work; he was "just a name on the committee, that's it." But Bush, the famed engineer who administered the project, and who respected Wallace's scientific background, briefed him on its progress several times beginning in July 1941. Once the military took charge of the project in 1942, however, Wallace was largely in the dark.[1] Still, he would, when running for president in 1948, claim that Roosevelt had "insisted that I be thoroughly posted" on the bomb's development.[2]

Wallace never criticized, and would never criticize, Truman's decision to use the bomb. Though many later admirers would call him a "pacifist,"[3] he was, when it came to Germans and "Japs," nothing of the sort. He sought all-out victory, and expressed no remorse over enemy deaths, military or civilian. Interviewed seven years after the bombs dropped on Japan, he was, curiously, unable to "remember exactly what my feelings were at the time."[4] His antiseptic diary entry for August 7, 1945 suggests they were few. But he did foresee a mad "scramble for the control of this new power,"[5] and was determined to use what authority he possessed to prevent conflict with Russia. On August 17, four months after joining Truman's cabinet, he met with the president to establish the scope of his authority.

Seeking a consolation prize for the loss of the lending agencies Jones had run, he pressed for chairmanship of the Export-Import Bank. The

State Department, he told Truman, was against his appointment, but it was vital to ensure ethical practice at the Bank. He cited its support of a loan to IT&T to finance its buyout of Ericsson's stake in the Mexican telephone operations. He opposed the loan "as originally proposed," as it would allow IT&T to raise rates and thus alienate Mexicans. He also charged that the U.S. ambassador to Mexico, George Messersmith, wanted to enable Washington "to listen in on Mexican telephone conversations," though he acknowledged having only "a hunch" about this and other forms of "conniving."

He further asked that numerous activities within the War Production Board, the Foreign Economic Administration, and the Smaller War Plants Corporation be transferred to his control; that his budget be increased; that his department have representation on agencies dealing with scientific research; and that he sit on "any board concerned with the development of atomic power." It was the last of these on which he would be most insistent.

To defend his role in shaping the future uses and safeguards for atomic energy, he argued that its development must "undoubtedly . . . have an influence on the expansion of commerce." He would also tell senators that atomic energy now made cooperation among business, agriculture, labor, and government "imperative"—sufficiently so that his department's oversight was essential.

Truman, Wallace recorded, was "in general" supportive, but cautioned that it "might not work out precisely" as he wished.[6] Genial noncommitment had been an FDR hallmark, and Truman sought to replicate it—even as he lacked the necessary charm. He would later confide to Byrnes that he needed to keep Wallace on his "political team," yet insisted that, when it came to foreign policy, he could "take care of Henry."[7]

On September 21, 1945, Wallace joined in a heated cabinet debate over how to manage the country's new atomic know-how. The president proposed that the United States should "keep the secret of the atomic bomb," but inform the U.N. on atomic energy broadly. Questions over the extent to which knowledge on energy and the bomb could logically be kept separate, however, and whether any of it should be shared abroad to engender trust, proved difficult and divisive. Forrestal, Anderson, Vinson, and Attorney

General Bob Clark opposed any sharing of atomic information. Stimson, Acheson, Ickes, and Wallace agreed with the president.

Wallace argued that knowledge of atomic energy would inevitably diffuse, and that it was worse than useless to try to keep it secret. Sheltering behind a scientific "Maginot Line," he said, would give Americans a dangerous false sense of security.

Anderson disagreed in "quite violent" fashion, according to Wallace. Russia, said the agriculture secretary, was busy "taking over Mongolia and Manchuria and various other spots." Stalin's regime was too aggressive and dishonest to be trusted with such information. The American people, he said, would never support it.

But Wallace pushed back. "It simply wasn't true that Russia was taking over Manchuria," he objected. Russia was, in fact, "living up to its understanding" with Roosevelt. It fully respected Chinese sovereignty. As for the Mongolians, it was "perfectly natural that [they] would look to Russia as a source of progress, rather than toward China."[8]

These disagreements would only harden as they became public, which they soon did. The day after the second meeting, September 22, *The New York Times* ran a sensational piece claiming that the cabinet had "debated a proposal by Secretary Wallace to give the secret of the atomic bomb to Russia."[9] Given Wallace's past statements on U.S.-Soviet relations, the account seemed credible. Yet Wallace, as Crowley would later confirm, had not proposed any such thing.[10]

The "lying leaker," as Wallace would call the man who talked to the *Times*, was likely Forrestal. The Navy secretary had urged caution in making "disposition of [atomic] knowledge" to *anyone*, "even to our Allies." His angry, sarcastic diary entry—which would emerge in publication six years later—was largely consistent with the *Times*' account.[11] He wanted the Kremlin-friendly commerce secretary out of atomic and defense matters, and may have felt that a public airing of his views, suitably embellished, offered the best prospect of marginalizing him.

In the wake of the press hullabaloo, Wallace wrote to Truman on September 24, reiterating his support for ongoing international exchange of "scientific information" on atomic energy. He "agreed with Henry Stimson," who, in a letter to Truman ten days earlier, had argued that failure to embrace atomic transparency would "invoke the hostility of . . . the world" without making the United States any safer.[12]

Stimson's position was, on its face, out of character. The crusty outgoing secretary of war had little confidence in prospects for effective outside surveillance of Russian atomic development, at least in the near-term, given Stalin's totalitarian rule. Yet he was convinced that if Washington did not deal with Moscow "upon a basis of cooperation and trust," the latter would build bombs feverishly in the shadows. The result would be "a secret armament race of a rather desperate character."[13]

According to Wallace's contemporaneous diary entries, and Truman's later account, Stimson had, in cabinet, limited his support to sharing scientific information only. Famed nuclear physicist Robert Oppenheimer would, however, according to Wallace's diary entry one month later, claim to have seen a note of Stimson's calling for the United States to share, with Russia as well as with other nations, *the industrial know-how* behind the bomb.[14]

In his letter to Truman, Wallace was careful to clarify that his agreement with Stimson pertained only to matters under discussion in cabinet—which did *not* include "industrial blueprints and engineering 'know-how.'" He stressed, however, that other countries already knew enough to produce bombs "within five or six years" (an estimate lower—and, in the case of Russia, more accurate—than that of most government officials and scientists). Given this fact, Wallace believed, the best way to effect transparency on atomic energy was to organize exchanges of Russian and American scientists. As "a young and vigorous nation," he wrote, the Soviet Union was set to make enormous scientific progress in the coming years; embracing collaboration would therefore enable Americans to "both guard ourselves and gain a true friend."[15]

Truman backed Wallace's account of the cabinet discussions, slamming the *Times* piece publicly.[16] But to Wallace's mind, the damage had been done. The *Times* would, a month later, run a glowing piece on Forrestal—he of the "charming good looks" and "thoughtful, cultivated mind"—suggesting that the Navy secretary was being groomed for the vice presidency, or even the presidency, by "Democratic groups" opposed to Wallace.[17] Wallace would later say that people both inside government (those "that had worked against me at the 1944 convention") and outside government ("the group that favored the Nazis prior to Pearl Harbor") were "cooperating . . . to destroy my political influence."[18]

Political skulduggery notwithstanding, a clear division had opened within the cabinet, and the Democratic Party more widely. On the one side, those led by Forrestal expected Russia to demonstrate benevolent, cooperative intentions before partaking in any American atomic knowledge. The public, as Anderson had argued, broadly shared this view. Eighty-five percent, in one poll, wanted the United States to retain its atomic monopoly as long as possible. On the other side, those led by Wallace believed that it behooved the United States to prove its peaceable purposes by sharing secrets with Russia.[19]

Among those organizations supportive of these views was Soviet intelligence, which was at least as well informed of them as the president. "Agent Tan," KGB veteran Alexander Vassiliev would reveal years later, referring to Wallace's trusted adviser Harry Magdoff, provided NKGB Washington station with the private memo Wallace had used at the September 21 cabinet meeting outlining the "'principles America should abide by in solving the problems connected with atomic energy.'"[20] Over Wallace's remaining tenure at Commerce, Soviet interest in him would continue to grow rapidly.

At 1 p.m. on October 24, 1945, Wallace welcomed a special guest into his office for lunch. Thirty-eight years old, five feet, six inches tall, 165 pounds, wearing gold rimless spectacles below a full head of brown, swept-back hair, Anatoly Gromov, who had spent the better part of eight years at the Soviet embassy in London before being transferred to the embassy in Washington in September 1944, spoke excellent, barely accented English, refined through extensive contact with writers, artists, and musicians, as well as government officials. His formal title was first secretary and authorized representative of the VOKS ("All-Union Society for Cultural Contacts Abroad"), and Wallace knew him primarily as a cultural emissary.

The Russian's contact list was, however, far more interesting than Wallace knew or imagined, including as it did five British spies—Donald Maclean, Guy Burgess, Kim Philby, Anthony Blunt, and John Cairncross—who would later become immortalized as the "Cambridge Five." All had been personally run by Gromov in London for the OGPU-NKGB. Now, as the agency's secret station chief in Washington, Gromov continued to run Maclean, who had been transferred to the British embassy in May 1944, as his prized agent, passing to Moscow the super-mole's invaluable reports covering progress of the U.S. atomic program.

Edwin S. Smith, director of the National Council of American-Soviet Friendship, was also at the lunch. He left no notes of the meeting, but Wallace and Gromov both did. Each noted that atomic matters were discussed, though their accounts differ as to who said what and how much.

"Gromov did most of the talking," Wallace recorded in his diary. "It was obvious from what [he] said that the Russians are deeply hurt at the various actions of the United States relative to the atomic bomb."[21] The entry notes nothing further on the matter. Gromov's far more extensive account, however, suggests that Wallace was voluble on it.

Wallace, Gromov reported, was interested in how Moscow would react to Soviet scientists being invited to the United States. Scientist exchanges had, in fact, long been a favorite cause of Wallace's, even though he was well aware of the risks involved. He had been among a handful of U.S. officials who, two years prior, in August 1943, was informed by Lieutenant General Leslie Groves, head of the Manhattan Project, that the Soviets were using their scientists to ferret out information on U.S. atomic research.

American scientists visiting Moscow, Groves reported, had told the Manhattan Engineer District (MED) intelligence team that their Russian counterparts were "unduly curious in their questioning . . . concerning our work on uranium fission."[22] Wallace would, in voluntary testimony before the House Un-American Activities Committee on January 26, 1950, deny receiving this report, although Groves, in separate testimony, would confirm having personally delivered it to Wallace.[23] In any case, Stalin would, as his top secret bomb program shifted from research to actual design in early 1946, seek to isolate his scientists by banning their contacts with foreigners.[24]

Wallace, Gromov continued, was interested in the Soviet reaction to American discussions on safeguarding atom bomb secrets. "Keeping the technical [bomb] information in the USA leads, in Wallace's opinion, not only to a worsening of already highly strained Soviet-American relations, but gives the rest of the world the impression that the USA is the most potentially aggressive state on earth." The commerce secretary, Gromov went on, has been trying to get control of atomic energy for military use "handed over to the UN Security Council." His efforts had been unsuccessful. Wallace described Democratic senator Edward C. Johnson's atomic control bill as "a reactionary effort by the War Department" and "representatives of major industrial capital: DuPont, General Electric, Union Carbide, and Carbon Corporation."[25]

Gromov then asked how the president's statements on atomic questions, which at times seemed at cross-purposes, could be explained. Wallace hesitated, before opining that "Truman was a minor politico who had risen to his current post by chance." He frequently had "'good' intentions, but yields too easily to the influence of those around him." There were, Wallace went on, "two groups currently fighting for Truman's soul." The "more powerful and influential one," led by Byrnes, Hannegan, Clark, and Anderson, was "very anti-Soviet." They wished to build a "dominant Anglo-Saxon bloc which is decidedly hostile to the Slavic world." He, Wallace, was part of the opposing "smaller group," which "believes that there are only two great powers in the world, the USSR and the USA," and that "the well-being and fate of all mankind is dependent on good relations between them."

Such views, assuming the commerce secretary did indeed express them, were, at the least, highly indiscreet. Yet Wallace then, according to Gromov, went much further, calling on Moscow to aid his side of the internal debate. "You (that is, the USSR) could help this smaller group significantly," he told Gromov. "And we have no doubt of your desire to move in this direction."

Naturally curious, Gromov asked him to elaborate. But "Wallace declined, . . . and I felt it would be awkward to press him." Still, Wallace warned Gromov that congressmen returning from Russia and Western Europe were "spreading a lot of anti-Soviet tales."

Gromov cabled his account of the meeting to Moscow through the official NKID (foreign ministry) channel. From there, Molotov forwarded it to NKGB head Vsevolod Merkulov with the notation that it "should be sent to Comrade Stalin without fail."[26] Not long after, on December 7, Gromov, after learning of Bentley's defection to the FBI, would flee Washington for Moscow.[27]

As was his wont, Wallace addressed atomic matters in black-and-white. Absent U.N. control of atomic weapons, he warned a crowd of twenty thousand at Madison Square Garden on December 4, 1945 the bomb, uncontrolled, would become "the greatest evil which ever plagued man." Yet *with* U.N.

control, in stark contrast, atomic energy afforded the world "the unique opportunity to build one, single, human community on the highest spiritual
level, accompanied by unlimited material facilities."[28]

Forrestal, no less an internationalist than Wallace, would attack this position as unforgivably naïve. "Until the structure in which the United Nations
is to dwell is far more solidly established," he would say in a speech several
months later, the United States "must retain adequate military strength"—a
critical component of which was its atomic weapons. Good intentions were
not enough. "So long as power is necessary to obtain peace, it must reside
with those whose history shows that they have not abused power"—that is,
with the United States.[29]

For Wallace, two competing congressional bills offered right and wrong,
good and evil, approaches to managing atomic energy. The McMahon bill,
which prioritized civilian over military control, heralded "a new and un-
dreamed-of mastery of the secrets of the universe in the interest of a better
life for all."[30] The May-Johnson bill, in contrast, which provided for greater
military control, would enable the Army and the industrialists to establish
a "Fascist dictatorship in this country."[31]

Giving Senate testimony on October 11, 1945, Wallace called for "renunciation of the use and development of the atomic bomb." Still, he struggled
to explain just what "renunciation" meant.

"Do you think [the bomb] can just be outlawed?" asked fellow Democrat
William Fulbright of Arkansas, incredulous.

Of course it was not simple, Wallace clarified. "It would have to be backed
up by some adequate action of a very comprehensive sort."

But that was "nonsense," Fulbright put back. Wallace was falling victim
to the old utopian dream of renouncing war, as America had done with the
Kellogg-Briand Pact in 1928. And "look where we ended up," he chided the
witness—in another world war.

Wallace conceded that "politicians can't handle [atomic regulation] unless they have the most complete scientific knowledge."[32] The path to peace,
as he had long believed, lay not in spiritual faith alone, but in its marriage
to technocracy.

On January 31, 1946, he testified again—this time against the stifling restrictions surrounding the Manhattan Project. American military secrecy,
he said, was hampering creation of an international inspections regime for

atomic energy development. He called, therefore, for an early transfer of atomic authority to civilian control. He also argued that his department should acquire authority over patents derived from all government-financed research in nuclear physics—patents it could then use to disseminate knowledge to American business, making it more innovative.[33]

At a press conference on January 31, the president himself endorsed civilian atomic control through the McMahon bill.[34] This stance aligned him with Wallace, but only briefly. On March 12, the Senate Atomic Energy Committee, backed by Stimson's successor as secretary of war, Robert Patterson, voted 6–1 to approve "the Vandenberg amendment," establishing a Military Liaison Committee, appointed by the president, to comment on proposals going before the new U.S. Atomic Energy Control Commission. Before an audience of two hundred at an atomic energy development exhibit, Wallace, "his voice rising angrily," condemned the amendment, exhorting "the American people [to] rise up in their wrath." Though the committee was to be purely advisory, he insisted it would thrust the nation into "military fascism."[35]

Wallace's declarations on atomic matters were becoming increasingly emotional and intemperate. He invoked the word "fascism" with growing frequency, deriding the concerns of those calling for military input, even of a purely advisory nature. The New York Times attacked the "absurdity of Mr. Wallace's outburst" against the Vandenberg amendment, suggesting it was motivated by "love for Russia." However unfair the charge may have been, it is not surprising that the New Times, a Soviet magazine, cited his comments favorably, condemning U.S. military control of atomic energy as "fraught with grave consequences for the development of science."[36]

Truman would ultimately sign the amended McMahon Act into law on August 1, 1946. Despite Wallace's warnings against it, however, the country avoided, by most reasonable metrics, succumbing to "military fascism."

Back in March, another atomic policy clash was unfolding. Truman tapped the seventy-five-year-old financier, philanthropist, and veteran presidential counselor Bernard Baruch to serve as U.S. member of the new U.N. Atomic Energy Commission. Baruch had no expertise on atomic matters, but Truman, as always, had his eye on the Senate, where Byrnes' fellow South Carolinian was well regarded by many who opposed the McMahon Act, and who viewed a U.N. role with skepticism or alarm.[37] Though the self-regarding Baruch would ultimately champion proposals already formulated in a report by Dean Acheson and TVA chairman David Lilienthal, the "Baruch Plan" would part ways with it in trying to limit Moscow's ability, through use of its Security Council veto, to escape sanction for atomic violations. Baruch's nomination met scorn from prominent scientists fearing, rightly, that he would ignore them and, wrongly, that he would follow Wall Street and advisers beholden to the military. They urged, without success, that Wallace be appointed in his stead.[38] Still, the commerce secretary would, from the sidelines, make Baruch's job more difficult than would anyone else in America—save Andrey Gromyko.

On March 19, 1946, the American Society for Russian Relief put on a thousand-guest dinner in New York to honor Ambassador Averell Harriman, just returned from his posting in Moscow. Wallace, together with the ambassador, was asked to speak on U.S.-Russia relations.

Harriman spoke first. "I cannot stand before you," he told the Russo-friendly diners, "and minimize the differences that have arisen between our two governments since the end of the war." Moscow, he said, had repeatedly failed to carry out its agreements. He now shared the great "disappointment" of the American people "over the direction that some Soviet Government policies appear to be taking."

Wallace followed with a starkly different take. Russia, fearing "capitalist encirclement," he explained, now sought to make its "every boundary secure." That it did so by trying to take territory from others, such as Iran and Turkey, he did not mention. Instead, he attributed Soviet acquisitiveness, such as it was, to historic mistreatment by the West.

"The Soviet Union knows what the leading capitalist nations . . . tried to do to it from 1919 to 1921." And "they know what certain of the military . . . are thinking and saying today." These men, namely in the United States, want atom bombs, overseas airbases, "and huge appropriations for armaments and Arctic expeditions." The Russians may therefore feel that they can only find "peace and security" by giving "capitalist nations tit for every tat."

Stalin and the Soviet people, he assured the guests, want peace "above everything else." As in the United States, policy in the Soviet Union was directed at "the achievement of economic and social justice." Yet even if the

Soviet government were "wrong on every count," he explained, the United States still had "everything to lose by beating the tom-toms against Russia." War between the two nations was a "monstrous and preposterous" idea.[39]

Wallace laid the blame for growing U.S.-Soviet tensions squarely on Washington. In its hostility to the very birth of the Soviet Union, it had engendered the young multicultural nation's enduring mistrust. It therefore bore the onus of repairing relations by proving its peaceful intentions. Yet by arming for conflict instead, it was forcing Russia to push back. And since conflict with her was unwinnable, it had to be avoided at all costs.

The split in the Democratic Party between those supporting Harriman's views and those supporting Wallace's was now widening. On May 17, Senator Fulbright highlighted the growing rift at an arts awards event in New York. Stalin, he said, had adopted a policy of noncooperation with the West, for which he blamed the "weakness and vacillation" of the Truman administration. With Wallace in mind, he warned against suggesting that "our policy is peace at any price." The world must know that whereas "we do not seek war[,] we are willing and able to fight."[40]

But Senator Pepper condemned such belligerent talk. Acknowledging that Truman's odds of securing the Democratic nomination in 1948 were "overwhelming," he told *The New York Times* that he might not be able to back him, absent changes in foreign policy. As matters stood, he preferred Wallace.[41]

Russia bound Wallace and Pepper together, and in ways neither imagined. As with Wallace, Pepper's most trusted adviser and staff writer was, unbeknownst to him, an enthusiastic Communist and veteran NKGB agent.

The tall, slender, red-haired Charles Kramer—code name "Lot" (plumb) and "Krot" (mole)—joined the CPUSA in 1933 and, soon after, became an informant for Soviet military intelligence by way of the Hungarian-born Communist Josef Peters. Around 1939, he joined a party "informational" clique which evolved into the Perlo espionage group. Through Perlo's apparatus, Kramer interacted regularly with the man who would, from March 1946, become Wallace's lead counselor: Harry Magdoff.[42]

In May 1945, the month before becoming Pepper's chief of staff, Kramer became a direct Soviet intelligence source. In addition to writing Pepper's speeches and public statements, Kramer now provided intel on the senator direct to Washington NKGB station chief Anatoly Gromov—with whom Wallace would discuss atomic policy in October.[43]

In mid-1946, Kramer, serving as an agent of influence, began ghost-writing a book for Pepper championing a new Soviet-friendly U.S. foreign policy. By mid-1947, however, the ambitious Pepper would be angling to become the 1948 Democratic presidential candidate (or Eisenhower's running mate), and feared "sounding so at odds" with the public mood. Kramer assured Soviet diplomat Mikhail Vavilov, a Ministry of State Security (MGB) co-optee (code name "Oleg"), that he was "trying to convince P[epper] that this book needs to be published before the 1948 election." It was to no avail. The book was never published.

In August 1948, after Bentley's allegations against Kramer became public, Pepper would defend his adviser's "able and faithful service."[44] Wallace, more anxious than ever to burnish his image as the anti-Truman, would take on the Soviet agent as a researcher and speechwriter.[45]

On June 14, 1946, Baruch presented the U.S. atomic regulation plan to the new United Nations Atomic Energy Commission (UNAEC). Gromyko, now ambassador to the U.N., countered with the Soviet plan five days later.

The two plans were fundamentally different. The United States wanted internationalization of atomic energy control, but insisted on effective machinery for inspection and enforcement before giving up its bombs or the industrial technique to make them. The Soviets held that international inspection would constitute intolerable interference into national sovereignty. They wanted immediate American disarmament, and violations of any future treaty subject to remedy only by approval of the Security Council—and even then, only in cases involving "aggression."[46] This framework appeared to give Moscow carte blanche to develop and deploy atomic bombs while America disarmed. Even if the Soviets were to use such bombs for "aggression," they could veto any punishment.

Though the two sides were headed for stalemate, Baruch was unperturbed. "America can get what she wants if she insists on it," he said. "After all, we've got [the bomb] and they haven't, and won't for a long time to come."[47] His confidence, so widely shared within the embryonic U.S. intelligence community, would be misplaced.

On June 25, Felix Belair of *The New York Times* asked Wallace for his thoughts on the Soviet position. Their hard line, Wallace responded, showed that the Russians "had some very real and probably well-founded reasons for not trusting us." Belair tried to draw out those reasons, but Wallace, concerned that the *Times* was too close to Baruch, "refused to specify."[48]

Others in the government much closer to atomic matters than Wallace, notably the stern, brilliant Lieutenant General Leslie Groves, overlord of the mammoth Manhattan Project, also opposed Baruch's plan, but for the opposite reason. Groves was sure the Soviets were hell-bent on a bomb, and would accept international control only as a ruse to undermine a new key pillar of American self-defense. Yet even Groves underestimated how fast a Soviet bomb would be built.

At a cabinet meeting on July 19, the president asked everyone to send him their views on proposed instructions to the secretary of state. Jimmy Byrnes was set to return to Paris shortly, where he would continue haggling with Molotov over terms of peace treaties with Italy, Romania, Hungary, Bulgaria, and Finland. The entire cabinet approved the instructions, save Wallace—who, on July 23, handed a stunned Truman twelve pages laying out his deep concerns over foreign policy.

The two men now reenacted their established kabuki routine, with Wallace stressing the importance of good relations with Moscow and Truman agreeing for the sake of comity. But when Truman read the letter days later, he noted that its contents, covering "everything from Genesis to Revelation" were so out of step with approved policy that it could not have been intended to aid his decision-making. It was, instead, "a political document" for Wallace's own use.[49] As Wallace had, by one account, already decided to resign after the November midterm elections, intending to take his "fight for peace" out to the country, this judgment was almost surely correct.[50] In any case, Truman chose to file the letter and forget it. Or at least he hoped to forget it.

After thirteen years in Washington, the blue-eyed, thick-haired Wallace was grayer, thinner, more lined, yet still youthful and energetic in appearance. He was certainly more at ease back as a cabinet secretary than he had

been as vice president, a job whose schmoozing and ceremonial duties held
no interest for him. In interviews, his glance, writer and journalist Mildred
Adams noted, could still be oddly quizzical, as if he weren't quite sure why
he was being questioned. He often took refuge "behind a veil of abstraction." Sometimes, though, a new idea could suddenly animate him, taking
him off in a different, more interesting direction. Yet even then, he had a
habit of "letting a sentence trail away," obliging journalists to "supply new
bait" and refocus him.[51] He frequently espoused what appeared to be contradictory purposes—lifting industrial production and paring farm output,
cutting industrial prices and raising farm prices, boosting wages and ending unemployment, expanding trade and shrinking big business—yet did so
with such earnestness that it often seemed callous to challenge him.

In the nascent cold war between Wallace and the president over Russia
policy, August was deceptively quiet. Wallace spent the early part of the
month with his family at Farvue Farm in New York, testing radioactive soil
and tending chickens. On the 29th he left for Mexico, having been invited
by President Ávila Camacho to mark his political retirement. The official
functions bored him, but he found time to tour farms, as well as a Rockefeller Foundation–funded experimental corn-growing station. The latter
proved to be the highlight of his trip.[52]

During the month, his letter to the president was making its way through
the bureaucracy. Perhaps unwisely, Truman had sent a copy to the State Department, whose staff can only have been appalled by it.[53] Meanwhile, Commerce Department assistant solicitor Joel Fisher (at whose wedding Wallace
was best man) reported favorably on it to the Kremlin's friend at Treasury,
Harry Dexter White. "Very, very impressive," was Fisher's verdict, according to the FBI transcript of White's call to him on August 30. "Harry," he
added, "wait until you see the [secretary's] September 12 speech."[54]

Upon returning to Washington on September 10, Wallace requested
and received a fifteen-minute appointment with the president. After using
most of it up on Mexican politics, Wallace took from his pocket the speech
Fisher mentioned—the speech he planned to deliver at a rally for U.S.-Soviet
friendship at Madison Square Garden on the 12th.

Wallace reviewed it with the president "page by page," according to his
diary, with the latter repeatedly saying "that's right" and "yes, that is what I
believe."[55] Truman, in contrast, would record that he did no more than skim

it and endorse the part that "caught my eye"—a line saying that U.S. policy should be neither pro-British nor anti-Russian.

"There were one or two things in the paper which I thought were a little wild," Truman conceded, no doubt referring to Russia, "but I didn't interpret them as contrary to the general policy." So after forty-five minutes, Truman—now a half-hour behind schedule, with "important people" to see—sent Wallace on his way. "I don't think he would want to put anything over on me," Truman assured himself. Wallace, however, seemed to know that he had, later telling colleagues, smiling impishly, that whereas the president had approved the speech, "I don't think he understood it."

Strapped for time and anxious to avoid debate, Truman had once more yessed Wallace to speed his departure, heedless of the consequences. Still, he bemoaned Henry's "habit of attending to every member's business but his own."[56]

On September 12, reporters at the president's 4 p.m. press conference came armed with preview copies of Wallace's speech, "The Way to Peace." One pointed to Wallace's claim that he was "neither anti-Russian nor pro-Russian." It was followed by the statement that "when President Truman read these words, he said that they represented the policy of this administration."

Did that sentence, the reporter asked, refer just to the paragraph or to the whole speech?

"I approved the whole speech," Truman replied. There was no hesitation.

Another asked if the president regarded "Wallace's speech as a departure from Byrnes' policy . . ."

"I do not."

". . . toward Russia?"

"They are exactly in line."[57]

Reporters looked at each other, stunned. Six days earlier, Byrnes had given a speech in Stuttgart scolding the Soviets for breaching the Potsdam accords by obstructing German economic unification and transition to self-government. He had further condemned them for trying to reset Poland's border with Russia unilaterally.[58] Wallace's speech, in contrast, said that the United States had no business "in the political affairs of Eastern Europe," implying that it was a Russian sphere of interest, and condemned any sort of "Get tough with Russia" policy.[59]

When Clayton, in charge at State with Byrnes abroad, saw Wallace's text at 6 p.m., an hour before the speech was to be delivered, he was livid. "This will cut the ground right out from under Jimmy at Paris," he told a hurried staff meeting. The group agreed that he should urge White House press secretary Charlie Ross to intercede. Ross, however, insisted that the president had approved the speech. And he should not, in any case, be disturbed on his poker night.[60]

Truman would later admit to Ross that he had not read the whole speech, relying instead on Wallace's assurance that nothing was out of line. Yet since Wallace had crossed the line before, Truman should have expected consequences.

"Did I catch hell," Truman would lament of his failure.[61]

As it happened, Wallace, too, would catch hell. The rally, organized by the left-wing National Citizens Political Action Committee (NC-PAC) and the Independent Citizens Committee of the Arts, Sciences and Professions (ICCASP), filled the Garden with twenty thousand passionate pro-Russia activists. For them, Wallace had prepared plenty of red meat. But he was also looking to build a bridge between the activists and the party mainstream. And in so doing, he risked drowning in the currents between them.

Despite bowing to demands from the brusque, ever well-coiffed ICCASP leader Hannah Dorner, an FBI-tagged "concealed Communist" (a CPUSA member kept off the rolls), Wallace neglected to dilute his Kremlin rebukes sufficiently to keep the crowd onside.

The speech began smoothly enough. His assaults on "British balance-of-power manipulations" and "imperialistic policy" hit the mark, as did those aimed at "reactionaries" wanting to confront Russia. "The tougher we get, the tougher the Russians will get," Wallace warned, to the crowd's spirited approval. Yet as he groped toward evenhandedness, they turned on him.

Wallace pronounced himself "neither anti-Russian nor pro-Russian," calling forth hisses and hoots. Though he then insisted that Washington keep out of politics in Eastern Europe, he did so with the warning that Russia had "no business . . . in the political affairs of Latin America [and] western Europe." This suggestion—that America had a sphere of influence from which Communism was barred—provoked more angry cries.

Wallace was stunned. "Get the whole sentence!" he shouted back.[62]

Wallace had long championed Roosevelt's One World vision, yet his words now seemed at odds with it. Though Roosevelt had called for the

United States, the U.K., the Soviet Union, and China—the "four policemen" of the postwar era—each to keep the peace in their respective regions, he had never suggested parsing the globe into U.S. and Soviet spheres—as Wallace just had.

Wallace's notion that Moscow should be free to determine what sovereignty meant in Central and Eastern Europe also contradicted the Atlantic Charter. Roosevelt's brainchild, the charter asserted "the right of all peoples to choose the form of government under which they will live" and "to oppose territorial changes that do not accord with [their] freely expressed wishes." Wallace further appeared to be leaving the Near East and Mediterranean to Russian predations on the grounds that American interests there coincided with "British imperialism." Wallace's foreign policy vision was, the *Times* would conclude, one that would appeal to isolationists, pacifists, and "those who believe Russia is always right," but one which made a mockery of "the wartime pledges of the Great Powers."[63]

In Wallace's mind, he was merely recognizing a natural reality, and not renouncing One World principles. Had not Jesus, after all, he might well have reasoned, told his followers to render unto Caesar what is Caesar's? And was not Stalin a Caesar, and had not the world been so arranged by divine providence that the Soviet borderlands were his natural protectorate? And as for Jesus, was he not nonetheless still, in fact, a great advocate of One World, and in fact the greatest that had ever lived? Yet to Wallace's listeners, there was no reconciling his words with Roosevelt's. And in an interview years later, he would acknowledge, regretfully, that he had perhaps given "too much the impression that I stood for a world divided into segments."[64] He would pay a price for it.

Wallace's speech then shifted from warning Russia to censuring it, which further stoked the crowd's anger.

"We may not like what Russia does in eastern Europe," he said. "Her type of land reform, industrial expropriation, and suppression of basic liberties offends the great majority of the people of the United States. . . ."

"BOO, BOO! . . ."

Wallace looked up from his text. "Yes, I'm talking about people *outside of New York City*," he put back plaintively. "And I think I know about people outside of New York City."

"BOO, BOO! . . ."

But "any Gallup poll will reveal it!" he remonstrated. "We might as well face the facts."

"BOOOOO! . . ."

Desperate to appease them, he began rewriting his text on the fly.

"I realize that the danger of war is much less from communism than it is from imperialism," he ad-libbed, "whether it be of the United States or England." Yet war could still be avoided, he assured them, "if we can overcome the imperialistic urge in the Western world."[65]

It was, however, too late for redemption. Senator Pepper, before him, had roused the hall with a full-throated damnation of Truman foreign policy, and it was in no mood now for a speech full of "buts" and backtracks.

Hal Simon, trade union director of the Communist Party in New York State, would later describe to local members what happened. One of those members was a paid FBI informant, whose summary of Simon's observations would land on Hoover's desk:

> When [Wallace's] first unfavorable remarks toward Russia drew hisses, [he] apparently became unnerved; it is my impression that he then departed from his prepared text to avoid drawing any further unfavorable audience reaction. The remainder of his speech was characterized by extreme pussyfooting, which left the audience hazy as to what he actually meant. Many of the comrades were so confused by his remarks that they did not know whether to applaud or hiss.[66]

When Wallace tried returning to his text, it was to warn Russia not to meddle in Asia.

Though China "holds the longest frontier in the world with Russia," he said, "the interests of world peace demand that China remain free from any sphere of influence. . . ."

"BOOOOO! . . ."

"Mr. Truman read that particular sentence, and he approved of it. . . ."

"BOOOOO! . . ."

Floundering in his most important speech as a cabinet secretary, Wallace now began chopping his text.

After saying "we must have the basis of real peace with Russia—a peace that cannot be broken by extremist propagandists," he had *intended* to add that "we do not want our course determined for us by master minds operating out of London, Moscow, or Nanking." But he excised the line.

He further deleted "the Russians should stop conniving against us in certain areas of the world"; and then, too, that "the Russians should stop teaching that their form of communism must, by force if necessary, ultimately triumph over democratic capitalism."[67] He would later tell reporters he shortened the speech because of TV time constraints, but would privately admit this was untrue.[68]

Wallace did, however, dare to opine that "The Russians will be forced to grant more and more of the personal freedoms"—which set off a renewed chorus of boos.

"You don't like the word 'forced'?" he put back, shocked. "I say that in the process of time they will find it profitable enough and opportune to grant more and more of the personal freedoms," he explained. "Put it any way you want. That's the course of history just the same."[69]

"BOOOOO! . . ."

Wallace limped to the end without further incident, but the damage was done. Outside the hall, the reaction was swift and fierce.

Among the U.S. delegation accompanying Byrnes in Paris, the speech stirred bipartisan outrage. Texas Democrat Tom Connally, chairman of the Senate Foreign Relations Committee, insisted there was "no place in our international relations either for partisan politics or for intraparty division or personal ambitions." For the United States "to speak with a persuasive and influential voice in the peace conference, there must be no divisions behind the lines." Michigan Republican Arthur Vandenberg warned that Republicans could "only cooperate with one Secretary of State at a time."[70]

The British delegation, according to *The New York Times* reporter covering the Paris conference, Harold Callender, played to character, keeping calm. They expected Byrnes to win out, and Wallace to leave the cabinet, and could see no benefit in lashing out.[71] The British press, however, from right to left, condemned Wallace's attack on their country's "imperialist policy," stressing the government's consistent efforts to cooperate with the United States in Iran, Palestine, and around the globe.[72]

"The effect [of the speech] upon the small and friendly nations," Callender observed, was "particularly disastrous," leaving them fearful of the emboldening impact on Soviet policy.[73] South African prime minister Jan

Christiaan Smuts was livid over Wallace's distortions. British "militarism," he said, had "died with the Boer War." Britain had raised its colonies to independent, sovereign states, and was now doing so in India, Egypt, and elsewhere. No longer was there "any trace of British imperialism." In contrast, referring to Russia, he saw "a poison" spreading into "the heart of Europe."[74]

All in all, Callender concluded, "Wallace's speech was a setback" for U.S. influence "because it reinforced [concerns that] the President and his cabinet were split regarding foreign affairs."[75]

Only the Soviets were thrilled. In Paris, Molotov lunched with Jan Masaryk, the Czech foreign minister, the day following Wallace's speech. "Well, you see what has happened," Molotov told him. "The American people are revolting against their reactionary foreign policy."[76]

Back in Washington, Republicans condemned the speech while basking in the electoral lift it had given them. "If Mr. Truman permits Mr. Wallace to remain in the cabinet," said Ohio representative Clarence Brown, "it will be conclusive proof that the Democratic Administration values its alliance with the Left Wing element, as symbolized by Mr. Wallace, more than it does orderly government."[77] But Truman, of course, was damned if he did and damned if he didn't, looking either negligent or weak. Reaction from Democratic candidates campaigning in the November elections was also critical, with many feeling the speech, and the tempest that followed, had hurt the party's chances. "The people think it's a screwy mess," lamented New Jersey House aspirant John Zimmerman, "and so do I."[78]

What Wallace had surely not anticipated was the angry reaction that came from the non-Communist left. Even the Liberal Party, theretofore among Wallace's staunchest supporters, assailed the speech. "The Liberal Party profoundly disagreed," chairman John Child said, "with the dominant theme of Mr. Wallace's proposal"—namely to reconcile U.S. and Soviet geostrategic interests through "spheres of influence."[79] Veteran Socialist Party activist and journalist Algernon Lee said that Wallace's call for America to be neutral between Britain and Russia was tantamount to equating democracy with Communism. "Wallace properly condemns the lynching of four Negroes in Georgia, but does not mention the mass murder of political opponents in the Soviet sphere," Lee said. "He says the U.S.A. has no business intervening in Eastern Europe. This is urging the abandonment of the Atlantic Charter and our responsibilities to 12,000,000 who look to us as their only hope of liberation from Soviet domination." Shockingly, Lee observed, Wallace had declared Britain the main threat to peace, even though the Soviet Union had annexed 274,000 square miles of territory since the war while Britain had taken nothing. "Wallace embarrassed Truman, Byrnes and the State Department by his naïve and irresponsible statement. It is time that Truman should ask for his resignation if we are to follow a firm, clear-cut progressive foreign policy and not appeasement."[80]

In Moscow, at both the Foreign Ministry and the foreign policy department of the party Central Committee, Wallace's speech was followed by an explosion of interest in him. He became a prime subject in Soviet reporting on U.S. affairs. Anti-Truman rhetoric hardened. There also set in, however, a certain ambivalence over how to present the figure of Wallace to the masses in Soviet-dominated territories. Was he a friend of Russia? Or merely a rival of Truman?

Based on a leaked advance text of Wallace's speech, source unknown, TASS produced a private eight-page analysis for the Soviet top brass on September 11, highlighting not just his coming denunciations of U.S. policy but his criticisms of Moscow. "Unlike Wallace's previous [politically] correct statements," the report warned, "this speech includes a number of anti-Soviet invectives." Molotov took an intense interest in this and subsequent analyses, marking them up in red pencil and ordering retranslation of the speech by his personal translator.[81] Not until September 15 did *Pravda* make its first brief public mention of it. The U.S. chargé in Moscow, Elbridge Durbrow, cabled home his surprise over the contrast between Soviet media's extensive and effusive reporting on Pepper's speech and its cursory coverage of Wallace's.[82]

Subsequent Soviet commentary on Wallace was curiously diverse, given the normally suffocating central direction from the Kremlin. The Moscow-controlled Berlin paper *Nacht-Express* praised Wallace, its front page blaring: "Opposition Against Byrnes Grows, World Press Supports Wallace."[83] *Pravda* and Moscow Radio, in contrast, reserved their praise for the pro-Soviet New York crowd. Both reported, accurately, that "the audience loudly applauded Wallace's condemnation of imperialism, but punctuated his remarks against the U.S.S.R. with cries of disapproval."[84]

CPUSA commentary was similarly diffuse. At a sixteen-thousand-strong twenty-seventh-anniversary rally at Madison Square Garden a week after the speech, its chairman, William Z. Foster, said that the commerce secretary had been right to expose the dangers of U.S. policy. The administration, he said, was on a "drunken spree of Soviet-baiting" in pursuit of an "ill-fated project of establishing capitalist domination over the war-wracked world."[85] (A few left-wing, non-Communist papers sympathetic to Moscow, like *PM* in New York, also praised Wallace without reservation.)[86] The CPUSA's *Daily Worker* paper, however, denounced Wallace, saying that he had failed to demonstrate "any understanding of the role of American imperialism as the advance squadron of the international reaction."[87] Though Wallace had intended the speech to show he could unite the left under a progressive banner, it foreshadowed the immense difficulties he would face as a presidential candidate two years later.

The New York Times' Arthur Krock offered an incisive analysis of the crisis into which Wallace, in attacking his government's policy, and Truman, in allowing it, had thrust the administration. Unless Wallace retreated or Truman fired him, Krock surmised, "the Russians will construe this to mean that the country . . . is deeply divided on our foreign policy and will press harder for the obvious advantages that must accrue."[88]

At 2 p.m. on September 14, Truman tried to end the crisis by assuring reporters in his office that there had been "no change in the [nation's] established foreign policy." His comments before Mr. Wallace's speech had, he explained, produced "a natural misunderstanding." He had meant only to convey that Mr. Wallace had the right to "deliver" the speech, and not that he had approved of it.[89] Incredulous reporters tried to press him on his implausible clarification, but he took no questions.

Wallace phoned the president on the morning of September 16, hoping to put an impossibly positive possible spin on the hullabaloo he had created.

"This thing," he enthused, will "create an immense amount of interest" in our policies and "help get out the vote." Thanks to his speech, he explained, the Republicans could no longer "accuse the Democrats of warmongering."

The party, however, he insisted, had to go further. "If we are going to get the liberal elements, we will have to . . ."

But Truman stopped him.

"Let's you and I have a session on this," he offered, and "see what we can do without cutting the ground from under Byrnes."

Wallace assured the president that weakening Byrnes was not his "object."[90] On this basis, Truman was willing, for the time being, to suspend disbelief.

Just hours after the call, Wallace struck again, this time issuing a defiant public statement. "I stand upon my New York speech," he announced. He would address foreign policy further in "the near future."[91]

Truman, who had assumed Wallace would hold his tongue at least until they spoke again, was gobsmacked.[92] If Wallace's statement hadn't "cut the ground from under Byrnes," however, what transpired next would collapse it.

To cap off an eventful day, Charlie Ross called Wallace to say that journalist Drew Pearson had somehow gotten hold of his July 23 letter to the president. He planned to publish it imminently.

That letter, four thousand words in length, had been far more critical of U.S. policy than the speech. The discrepancy owed to the fact that whereas Wallace had written the speech, Magdoff, a committed Communist and longtime Soviet agent, had written the letter with his "gang."

FBI phone taps reveal that Magdoff and Alfred Van Tassel, assistant to Senator James Murray (D-MO) and, according to Perlo, a Soviet intelligence source, were disdainful of the speech. It had, they believed, shown the secretary to be unreliable and in need of firmer guidance. Wallace, Magdoff offered, "is a peculiar guy because he shifts around." Van Tassel agreed, noting that "the letter was far superior."

The speech, Magdoff explained, had been Wallace's "attempt to muddy the waters." He wanted to "be identified as 'middle of the road.'" The speech was, he said, "closer to the facts" than the letter. Yet it was also "closer to . . . Wall Street," and therefore damaging to the cause.[93]

But who had given Pearson the letter? It does not appear to have been Magdoff, but someone on the "right." Wallace's political adviser, the stout, affable, cigar-chomping Texan Harold Young, told him that Pearson had been overheard saying that the leaker was at State.[94] *PM* publisher Ralph Ingersoll, who phoned Wallace on September 17 to plead for a copy, also claimed to know that the leak came from State.[95]

Wallace told Ingersoll, without explanation, that he was unable to give him the letter. Later that day, however, Ross, hoping to deny Pearson his scoop, phoned Wallace again and told him to make the letter public.[96]

When informed after the fact, Truman was peeved. On principle, he opposed publication of a confidential letter, and, more pragmatically, he thought Pearson's poor record for journalistic probity would sow useful doubt over the letter's authenticity. He told Ross to stop distribution.

But it was too late. Joel Fisher, as the FBI learned from a tapped call to Harry Dexter White, had just given it "to all the news agencies."[97] When Ross called Wallace to halt the release, according to Truman's account, Wallace explained that *PM* already had a copy, and that at least one other had "gotten away."[98]

Together with the press release, Wallace had appended a claim that the letter, in the possession of a journalist, had been "filched from the files"—a claim Wallace knew to be false. With little concern for security, he had himself long ago distributed copies to six advisers. Pearson, who had planned to publish the letter the following day, threatened to sue for libel if Wallace did not retract his filching charge—which he did.[99]

Though the letter had been private, its mass publication on September 18 added pressure on Truman to silence Wallace.

In that letter, Wallace had placed the blame for the collapse in U.S.-Soviet relations squarely on Washington, and in particular on its exclusive possession of the atom bomb, its enormous military budget, and its menacing overseas airbases. Nowhere did he fault Russia's annexation of hundreds of thousands of square miles of territory; its occupation of Germany, which contradicted its pledges at Yalta and Potsdam to cooperate in its economic unification; its efforts to dominate the Balkans; its threats to Iran and Turkey; or its looting of Manchuria and coercive efforts to control its industry—which Wallace's own clandestine efforts in Chungking had helped set in motion.[100]

Wallace had admonished Truman to allay Russia's legitimate grounds "for fear, suspicion, or distrust" and to provide security "guarantees"—even if that meant "risking epithets of appeasement" from the right. He had called on the president to make deeper military cuts, to send high-level economic missions to Moscow, to break with Britain on matters where it was hurting U.S.-Soviet relations, and to make concessions to conclude an atomic control treaty under U.N. jurisdiction. Simply telling the Russians to be "good boys" before America turned over atomic secrets, Wallace argued, was counterproductive. It served only to compel Russia to boost its leverage by building its own bomb.[101]

This stance infuriated Forrestal. Following the letter's release the evening prior, he delivered a blistering extemporaneous speech before 1,200 industrialists and high-ranking naval officials praising Byrnes and, without naming him, disparaging Wallace. Handing power over atomic energy to the U.N. without "practicable and enforceable" controls, he said, would be dangerous and irresponsible.[102]

With the ongoing drama dominating the headlines, Truman was morose. "I'm still having Henry Wallace trouble," he lamented to his mother on September 18, "and it grows worse as we go along." The end, however, was in sight—or so he believed. "I think he'll quit today."[103]

Yet just as Wallace had refused to leave the vice presidential race in 1944, he had no intention of leaving the cabinet now. When he arrived in Truman's office at 3:30 p.m. that day he was in a buoyant mood.

"You are looking at the whole situation in too much of a negative light," Wallace scolded the president. The "emotional interest" would "help get out the vote" for Democrats.

Truman was now near his wit's end. "I'm not so sure he's as fundamentally sound intellectually as I had thought," he wrote of Wallace after the meeting. "Henry is a pacifist 100%. He wants us to disband our armed forces, give Russia our atomic secrets and trust a bunch of adventurers in the Kremlin Politburo who have no morals, personal or public. I don't understand a 'dreamer' like that." But Truman objected to more than just the man's "fuzzy" thinking. Wallace was, he suspected, being duplicitous. "I'm not so sure that Henry didn't purposely put it over on me with his Madison Square Garden speech," Truman continued. He had "absorbed some of the 'Commy'–'Jesuit' theory that the end justifies the means."[104]

Still, so fearful was Truman of losing the support of labor and the liberals that he could not bring himself to fire Wallace. Since the departure of Morgenthau and Ickes, Wallace had been guarding the government's left flank on his own. How much damage could he now do by bolting from the party—possibly fronting a progressive insurgency? Enemies put it at a million votes, friends at three million. Splitting the difference, two million, could have put Dewey in the White House in '44. Wallace knew this—and let it be known that he knew it.

In an interview with Mildred Adams earlier that month, Wallace had argued that the United States had "always been a progressive country underneath." Progressives were simply too "independent" to "stand up under regular party drudgery."

No one, of course, fit this description more clearly than he.

But what exactly, Adams asked, was a "progressive"?

"One who puts human rights over property rights," Wallace answered, with no hesitation. Yet he had used that same phrase before to define a "liberal," and even a "Democrat."

"Like Humpty Dumpty," Adams observed, Wallace "sometimes talks as though he believed that 'when I use a word it means just what I choose it to mean, neither more nor less.' This creates a trap for the researcher trying to trace a coherent and logical pattern of thought." Yet what Wallace wanted, it seemed, was not to define "progressive" so much as to make it his new brand.

And who were the progressives? Adams pressed on.

Well, they were everywhere, Wallace explained. Organized labor—though more CIO than AFL. Young people: two thirds of those under thirty-five. Their numbers were growing everywhere, even in the deep South.

Adams looked disbelieving, but Wallace doubled down. The South, he said, "showed signs of becoming one of the most progressive sections in the country." All that held them back was false consciousness: they needed "a better chance at education."

Progressives, he went on, now held the balance of power in America. Yet what they frequently faced was "little more than a choice between two evils": a Republican or a reactionary Democrat. Progressives will not, he clarified, vote Republican, but neither will they vote for Democrats who act like one. "The progressive who really wants to get something done," Wallace concluded, "had only two courses. Either he must work for a place within the [Democratic] party councils, or he must form his own party and work there."[105] There could be little doubt that the progressive of whom he spoke was Wallace himself.

Truman was acutely aware of the political risks of forcing Wallace out.

Yet he was also resolved to force Wallace back into his lane—at least until Byrnes returned home.

Jimmy is "giving me hell," Truman told Wallace on September 18. He was threatening to leave Paris. "I must ask you not to make any more speeches touching on foreign policy. We must present a united front abroad."

Wallace protested. In six days' time he was scheduled to speak in Providence, Rhode Island, where he intended to say that he "oppose[d] our present bipartisan, Republican-dominated foreign policy." He urged the president to break from it as well, insisting it would help him electorally. Truman needed only to bear in mind the "extraordinary demonstration" against his name when he spoke it at Madison Square Garden. Of course, there were "probably a number of commies present," but liberals were angry as well. Wallace offered, in any case, to make the disclaimer that his speech did not represent the president or administration policy.

Truman was stunned. Since the Madison Square Garden speech, he had endured "more sleepless nights than at any time since the Chicago convention." Yet Wallace now wanted his blessing to continue attacking the core of his foreign policy. "Henry is the most peculiar fellow I ever came in contact with," he would tell his mother after the meeting, using more civil language than he might have with someone else.

Truman vetoed the Providence speech, insisting that Wallace make no further public comments on foreign policy until the conclusion of the Paris conference—expected in mid-October. Chagrined, Wallace agreed, subject to the condition—which Truman accepted—that he be allowed to state that the decision to go silent was his.

Before departing, he told Truman a story that his economist Lewis Lorwin had learned in Moscow. Mikoyan, Wallace's Soviet counterpart, had been the only one of "19" (actually twenty-six) Baku rebels to survive execution by the "British" (actually Russian socialist and Menshevik revolutionaries) in 1918. His mangled story was meant to help Truman understand why Mikoyan supposedly harbored a distrust of the West (even if it had inspired Stalin's distrust of *Mikoyan*). Of Truman's reaction, Wallace recorded only "I don't think he was particularly interested." After a tense and difficult two hours and twenty minutes, the meeting ended.[106]

⁂

Forcing a grin from ear to ear, Wallace strode from the meeting into a throng of nearly one hundred reporters and flashing cameras. He opened a prepared text and read.

"The Secretary," he said, referring to himself, had, following a "friendly discussion" with the president, "reached the conclusion he would make no public statements or speeches until the Foreign Ministers' conference in Paris is concluded." Asked by a reporter why he had "decided to keep quiet," he responded only "Because I am an honest man."

He had *not*, however, "decided to keep quiet"—the president had decided for him. And with regard to his explanation, he would years later observe that the way in which the phrase "an honest man" was used in Washington always amused him. "It's a propaganda device, that's all."

He also told the reporters, truthfully, that he had not discussed resigning with the president. Back in March, however, he *had* called for the resignation of any Democrat who refused to conform to party policy on "fundamental" issues. And if foreign and atomic policy were not "fundamental," it was hard to imagine what was.

As the *Times*' Arthur Krock noted, Wallace's failure to resign suggested a "major inconsistency" in his position—though perhaps "not an unusual [one] in Mr. Wallace's career." Even back in March, when he called for rebels to resign, he was endorsing a radical candidate (and secret NKGB source), Johannes Steel (often spelled "Steele"), running for Congress in New York against the official Democratic one. Though this stance constituted a fundamental break with his party, he never entertained the thought of resigning. Wallace was, Krock observed, "very severe toward inconsistencies in others when they threaten any of the numerous causes he expounds," yet he gave himself carte blanche to support whomever or whatever he chose.[107]

The White House released its own official statement after the meeting— a joint declaration from the War and Navy secretaries repudiating a central contention of Wallace's New York speech: that "a school of military thinking" was "advocat[ing] a 'preventative war'" against Russia. No Army or Navy officer with whom the secretaries were familiar, their rebuttal said, "had ever advocated or even suggested" a policy or plan of attacking Russia.[108]

The *Times* blasted Truman's truce with Wallace, concluding that it would only weaken American influence and bargaining power. The Soviets knew that Wallace would resume his attacks on Byrnes' positions in a matter of weeks. "The issue is not free speech for Mr. Wallace," the editorial board said. He "can take his case to the country without being a member of the Cabinet. The issue is whether American foreign policy can stand the strain and endure the confusion of two officials of the same Cabinet advocating contradictory foreign policies simultaneously."[109]

The following day, September 19, Byrnes, in a teletype, urged Truman to issue a declaration stating that the secretary of state's policy in Paris was *his* policy; or, if he could not, to recall the U.S. delegation immediately. Though he did not mention Wallace by name, he said that the group's bargaining position and moral prestige had been undermined by the uncertainty about the president's views. He, Byrnes, could no longer function effectively without full public clarity.[110] Baruch was equally livid. Wallace's wild and inaccurate claims about U.S. atomic policy were undermining his efforts to secure credible international control through the U.N.

Sometime in the early morning hours of Friday, September 20, Truman decided he had heard enough. Yes, Wallace had a passionate following on the left that it was best not to alienate, particularly in the run-up to midterm elections, but the issues at stake were too important. He had been wrong to think he could maintain control of foreign policy while Wallace attacked it.

Truman, according to his own recollection,[111] phoned Wallace shortly after 10 a.m. With few preliminaries or acrimony, he asked for the secretary's resignation. Wallace was, according to aides, "astonished" but "unruffled." He had, with midterms just six weeks away, thought himself too important to the party for the president to cut loose. Still, he said he would comply with the president's request.[112]

Years later, however, Wallace would challenge this account. Truman had not called him, but had fired him in a *letter* "of a low level."[113] On the basis of multiple interviews, journalist Cabell Phillips concurred in Wallace's telling, describing Truman's unpreserved letter as "intemperate and bitter."[114]

Wallace says he then phoned *Truman* and advised him to take the letter back. "You don't want this thing out," he supposedly told the president. Truman, who allegedly acknowledged that he had been "hot-headed," thanked him and said he would "send a man over to pick it up."[115]

Phillips, however, rejects this part of Wallace's account, saying that the commerce secretary had instead phoned White House Press Secretary *Charlie Ross* and turned the letter over to him for disposal. The president later phoned Wallace to consummate his dismissal, but in more civil terms.[116]

However the firing occurred, Truman arrived twenty minutes late for his regular press conference—at 10:50 a.m. Packed into the room, 197 reporters scribbled as he read, calmly and confidently. "I have today asked Mr. Wallace to resign from the Cabinet":

> It had become clear that between his views on foreign policy and those of the Administration—the latter being shared, I am confident, by the great body of our citizens—there was a fundamental conflict.
>
> We could not permit this conflict to jeopardize our position in relation to other countries.
>
> I deeply regret the breaking of a long and pleasant official association, but I am sure that Mr. Wallace will be happier in the exercise of his right to present his views as a private citizen. . . .
>
> Our foreign policy as established by the Congress, the President, and the Secretary of State remains in full force and without change. . . .
>
> No member of the Executive branch of the government will make any public statements as to foreign policy which is in conflict with our established foreign policy.
>
> As I have frequently said, I have complete confidence in Mr. Byrnes and his delegation now representing this country at the Paris Peace Conference.
>
> Mr. Byrnes consults with me often, and the policies which guide him and his delegation have my full endorsement.

"That was it," he added. "Thank you, gentlemen."[117]

At 8 p.m., Wallace commented on his dismissal in a brief radio address, laying out his personal priorities and vision. "Winning the peace is more important than high public office," he said. "It is more important than any consideration of party politics":

The success or failure of our foreign policy will mean the differ-ence between life and death for our children and our grandchil-dren. It will mean the difference between the life or death of our civilization. . . . [W]e should every one of us regard it as a holy duty to join the fight for winning the peace. . . .

The action taken by the President this morning relieves me of my obligation of last Wednesday. I feel that our present foreign policy does not recognize the basic realities which led to two World Wars and which now threatens another war—this time an atomic war. However, I do not wish to abuse the freedom granted me by the President this morning by saying anything tonight which might interfere with the success of the Paris conference. . . .

I don't have to tell anyone who has followed my views on inter-national affairs that I began talking about "one world" more than fifteen years ago. I do not believe in two worlds. I have continu-ously and wholeheartedly advocated the principles of living in one world. We cannot have peace except in "one world."

I wish to make clear again that I am against all types of im-perialism and aggression, whether they are of Russian, British, or American origin. Also I wish to emphasize that the one world concept must be held steadfastly; and that any regionalism nec-essary to give practical form to world economic and political re-alities must take into account the rights of small nations, just as the nations of the Western Hemisphere have done under Franklin Roosevelt's "good neighbor" policy.

The success of any policy rests ultimately upon the confidence and the will of the people. There can be no basis for such success unless the people know and understand the issues—unless they are given all the facts—and unless they seize the opportunity to take part in the framing of foreign policy through full and open debate.

In this debate, we must respect the rights and interests of other peoples, just as we expect them to respect ours. How we resolve this debate, as I said in my New York speech, will determine not whether we live in "one world" or "two worlds"—but whether we live at all.

I intend to carry on the fight for peace.[118]

Henry A. Wallace resigning as secretary of commerce at the request of President Harry S. Truman. With him are his wife, Ilo (left), and their daughter, Jean, September 20, 1946.

Reaction to the firing was, predictably, radically split. Leading conservative DNC officials pledged to blackball Wallace during the election campaign. Republicans were pleased to see the president flounder, yet sorry to see the source of his troubles removed. Privately, Truman must have agreed with Senator Taft that trying to "keep Wallace [quiet] for thirty days and then let[ting] him oppose the President's foreign policy was stupid."

Labor and the left denounced the firing. The Brotherhood of Railroad Trainmen assailed Truman for "abett[ing] the forces of reaction" and invited Wallace to address their upcoming convention. Baldwin, now chairman of the National Citizens Political Action Committee, a left-wing arm of the CIO, called Wallace's firing "a blow to the progressive forces of the country and to the cause of peace." Communist Party national chairman William Foster condemned it as "a surrender to imperialist-minded big business, to the military brass hats and the Republican leaders who are now writing American foreign policy." Leo Krzycki, president of the left-leaning American Slav Congress, called for Wallace to be "nominated for president right now!"[119]

Top Left: Henry A. Wallace's grandparents, Henry "Uncle Henry" Wallace and Nancy Cantwell Wallace, sitting outside the family home at 756 16th Street, Des Moines, Iowa, c. 1905.

Top Right: Henry A. Wallace with his sister Annabelle, c. 1893.

Below Left: Henry A. Wallace (left) with his father Henry C. Wallace (center) and grandfather Henry "Uncle Henry" Wallace, c. 1908.

Above: Henry A. Wallace examining ears of corn at Clyde Herring's garage, Des Moines, Iowa, 1920s.

Left: Reception given by New York City mayor James Walker at City Hall in honor of Nicholas Roerich. From left to right, first row, starting with the second person: Louis Horch, James Walker, Nicholas Roerich, and Charles Crane. In the second row: Sina Lichtmann, Maurice Lichtmann, and George Roerich. In the third row, starting immediately behind George: Sofie Shafran and Nettie Horch, June 20, 1929.

Above: President Franklin D. Roosevelt and his cabinet. Seated, from left to right: Secretary of War George H. Dern, Secretary of State Cordell Hull, President Roosevelt, Secretary of the Treasury William Hartman Woodin, and Attorney General Homer S. Cummings. Standing, from left to right: Secretary of Agriculture Henry A. Wallace, Secretary of the Interior Harold Ickes, Secretary of the Navy Claude A. Swanson, Postmaster General James Farley, Secretary of Commerce Daniel C. Roper, and Secretary of Labor Frances Perkins, 1933.

Below Left: Secretary of Agriculture Henry A. Wallace reflects upon his late father's official portrait as secretary of agriculture, 1933.

Below Right: Nicholas Roerich, Naggar, India, 1932 or 1933.

Left: President Franklin D. Roosevelt (left) with Secretary of the Interior Harold L. Ickes (center) and Secretary of Agriculture Henry A. Wallace, August 1933.

Right: Secretary of State Cordell Hull (left) and Secretary of Agriculture Henry A. Wallace arriving in Washington, D.C.'s Union Station to greet President Roosevelt upon his return from a two-week vacation, May 14, 1937.

Left: Secretary of Agriculture Henry A. Wallace speaks over the *National Farm and Home Hour* broadcast, June 27, 1938.

Right: Secretary of Agriculture Henry A. Wallace and Senate Agriculture Committee chairman Ellison D. "Cotton Ed" Smith discuss the farm bill to be introduced during the new session of Congress, January 5, 1939.

Above: Vice presidential candidate Henry A. Wallace with his arm around President Franklin D. Roosevelt at Val-Kill Cottage in Hyde Park, New York, during the election campaign, August 8, 1940.

14

Right: Henry A. Wallace takes the oath of office as vice president from his predecessor, John Nance Garner, at the U.S. Capitol, January 20, 1941.

15

Left: Vice President Henry A. Wallace (center) talks with Chinese ambassador Wei Tao-ming (right) and Soviet ambassador Andrey A. Gromyko at a garden party in Washington, D.C., May 1, 1944.

Above: Vice President Henry A. Wallace with Colonel Ilya P. Mazuruk, Siberia, May 1944.

Right: Vice President Henry A. Wallace with Ivan Nikishov at Magadan, Siberia, May 1944.

Left: Vice President Henry A. Wallace with General Ilya S. Semenov, Siberia, May 1944.

19

Above: Vice President Henry A. Wallace with a group of men, Siberia, May 1944.

Below: Vice President Henry A. Wallace with Soviet government officials, Siberia, May 1944.

Above: Members of the Wallace mission to Russia pose with Soviet escorts at a party office. Vice President Henry A. Wallace is in the front row, third from left. In Seimchan, northeast Siberia, May 1944.

Below: Vice President Henry A. Wallace hoeing with a farmer, China, June 22, 1944.

Above: Vice President Henry A. Wallace pointing at the beaches of Normandy on a map, Siberia, June 1944.

Right: Vice President Henry A. Wallace (left) gestures in animated conversation with Chinese president Chiang Kai-shek (right) and Madame Chiang before an official banquet in Wallace's honor in Chungking, China, on June 30, 1944.

Above Left: Vice President Henry A. Wallace plays volleyball on the GI team against the officers' team in Chungking, China, July 1944.

Above Right: Vice President Henry A. Wallace at the 1944 Democratic National Convention in Chicago, July 20, 1944.

27

Above: Delegates show support for the renomination of Henry A. Wallace as vice president at the 1944 Democratic National Convention in Chicago. Soon after, Harry S. Truman is nominated in his stead, July 21, 1944.

Left: Vice President Henry A. Wallace sits alone at the 1944 Democratic Convention in Chicago. Around him are delegates chanting "We want Wallace!," July 21, 1944.

The New York Times reported that State Department officials were "outwardly" nonchalant but "elated" over the dismissal. Commerce officials, in contrast, were said to be "shocked."[120] The FBI, which continued to monitor Magdoff, knew this to be accurate.

In a long letter to Truman confidant George Allen, then director of the Reconstruction Finance Corporation, J. Edgar Hoover reported that Magdoff, who claimed to have written Wallace's July 23 letter with "his gang," was working with colleague and fellow "Soviet espionage agent" Edward Fitzgerald to "gear [up] public support" for Wallace.

For all Wallace's "screwiness" and "weaknesses," Hoover quoted Magdoff saying, the secretary was "just really a great man in every way." He offered this example: when a colleague suggested that staff line up and shake the secretary's hand as he departed, Wallace warned that those in line had "better watch out for the FBI." Magdoff was stunned, and deeply impressed. "That guy is no dope," he observed; "that was quite a remark."

Hoover no doubt agreed. He closed his letter by suggesting that the bureau's intel on Wallace's men would, in light of its ongoing investigation of Soviet espionage, "be of interest to the President."[121]

It may seem remarkable that Magdoff and other Soviet assets around Wallace were never prosecuted, but the evidence, however compelling it often appeared, was problematic. The phone tap records were inadmissible in court. The claims made by Elizabeth Bentley and Whittaker Chambers in 1948 amounted to hearsay. And the "Venona" decrypts of intercepted Soviet intelligence cables were top secret. But Hoover was far more interested in Wallace, and bureau surveillance of him would only intensify in the coming two years.[122]

Wallace's firing did not end the controversy over his letter. Byrnes had reached the end of his tether, having endured humiliation after humiliation in trying to conduct foreign policy with only tepid presidential support. He would ask to resign in December and, receiving no resistance from Truman, would depart in January—receiving *Time* "Man of the Year" honors as a farewell token.[123] As for Wallace's critique of U.S. atomic policy, it was sufficiently damaging to the administration's U.N. initiative that Baruch felt compelled to confront it publicly.

On September 19, 1946, the day between the letter's publication and Wallace's firing, Baruch called Wallace, at Truman's direction, to arrange a meeting to discuss atomic matters. "Friendly" though "upset," according to Wallace's phone log, Baruch offered to show him documents that might help him "come to a different conclusion" about U.S. policy. Wallace offered to send a telegram proposing a time.[124]

Despite his dismissal on September 20, Wallace agreed to meet with Baruch in New York the following Monday, the 23rd, and then again on Friday, the 27th. According to a later account of the second meeting by Gordon Arneson, a staff member of the U.S. delegation to the U.N. Atomic Energy Commission, Wallace conceded that he "had not had all the facts" on U.S. policy when he wrote to Truman, but still wanted Baruch to offer some "concession of Soviet mistrust."[125] Wallace told Baruch that the man who had drafted his letter to Truman was "abroad on an UNRRA mission," but offered to leave Phil Hauser behind to draft a statement correcting the misapprehensions in it.[126]

The only American writer who was abroad with UNRRA at the time was Wallace's collaborator on his Siberian memoir, *Soviet Asia Mission*. Andrew Steiger, an NKGB journalist source (code name "Fakir" and "Arnold"), had, in fact, written to Wallace from Minsk in June,[127] although there is no documentary evidence that he had been involved in the drafting of the July letter to Truman. FBI evidence points instead to the lead role of Magdoff.[128]

When, after three hours of talks, Wallace left Baruch's office, Hauser, over the next several hours, drew up the correction statement with Baruch's staff. He then tried in vain to reach Wallace Friday evening, and again over the weekend—or so he told Baruch.

But Hauser was lying. FBI taps of Magdoff's phone reveal that Hauser had called him on Saturday, September 28, the day after the meeting, explaining that Baruch's delegation had "turned [up] the heat . . . to persuade WALLACE to admit that he was mistaken in his letter of July 23." Magdoff, however, according to the FBI log, "strongly objected to the statement which HAUSER had drawn up with the members of the Commission." He insisted there was "no reason whatsoever for WALLACE to make an admission [of error] to the public"; it would only lead people to say he had made other mistakes. According to one FBI cable, Magdoff wanted Wallace to oppose the Baruch group, which meant "supporting [the] Russian view" that the United States should "destroy all [its] bombs" prior to an international agreement.

Magdoff insisted Hauser "should not involve himself in a controversy between BARUCH and WALLACE, and should tell BARUCH'S group that he is merely a go-between." Hauser promised to "delay any answer to BERNARD BARUCH until Monday, when he could see HENRY WALLACE." The men then agreed to meet in Magdoff's office the following day.

On Sunday, September 29, Magdoff met with Hauser and four other Commerce officials. At least two of them, like Magdoff, had also moonlighted for Soviet intelligence. Ed Fitzgerald, NKGB code name "Ted," was a leading figure in the Perlo espionage group, while Irving Kaplan, NKGB code name "Tino," was a member of the Silvermaster group[129] (though deactivated by Moscow after Bentley's defection in November 1945).

Magdoff argued that Wallace should make no statement unless Baruch attacked his stand, in which case Wallace "should retaliate with a strong press release." But the others insisted they needed an immediate alternative to Hauser's statement, given that Baruch was bound to make the latter public. Magdoff relented.[130]

On Monday, September 30, Wallace called Baruch and read him the new statement prepared by Magdoff's group on Sunday. Baruch, thinking he had resolved the matter with Hauser on Friday, was incensed. "Well, Henry," he said, "this is the parting of the ways. We are [now] going to get you any way we can."[131]

On Wednesday, October 2, Baruch held a press conference at which he released four documents: his letter to the president of September 24, correcting assertions in Wallace's letter of July 23; the statement agreed between Hauser and Baruch on September 27, but repudiated by Wallace on September 30; the statement issued by Wallace on September 30 in its stead; and a telegram from Baruch to Wallace, sent on October 2, recounting events and deploring the latter's actions and statements since September 30. All four documents appeared in *The New York Times* on October 3.[132] What emerges from them, concluded the *Times'* Arthur Krock, not unreasonably, is an unflattering portrait of a man "who constantly asserts his own high-mindedness," but who, "in his zeal for causes and for programs he does not fully comprehend," allows himself to be "swayed by bad advisers."[133] Krock was unaware that such advisers had also been Soviet agents.

Wallace had, in his July 23 letter to the president, attacked the U.S. atomic plan for its "fatal defect . . . of requiring other nations to enter into binding commitments not to conduct research into the military uses of atomic energy and to disclose their uranium and thorium resources while the United States retains the right to withhold its technical knowledge of atomic energy until the international control and inspection system is working to our satisfaction."

"Is it any wonder," Wallace asked rhetorically, "that the Russians did not show any great enthusiasm for our plan?" He predicted that the Russians would now "redouble their efforts to manufacture bombs," and "may also decide to expand their 'security zone' in a serious way." Such aggressive efforts would then be the fault of the United States.

Wallace had grossly mischaracterized the U.S. plan. Rather than the various stages of disarmament and information-sharing being set according to U.S. whim and diktat, as Wallace had charged, Baruch's plan called for staged action according to "pre-arranged schedules." This structure was precisely what Wallace was urging.

Wallace's (and Magdoff's) mischaracterizations were clearly taken from an article in the June 24 issue of *Pravda*, in which the Soviet journalist Boris Izakov charged, with no basis, that "the U.S. government [was] likely counting on determining *on its own discretion* the terms within which it will permit the international agency—'in successive stages'—to take a peek at [its atomic] secrets." It was, Izakov wrote, expecting "all other nations [to] show blind trust in [its] intentions."[134] Wallace had, in fact, discussed the *Pravda* "atomic blast" with the *Times*' Felix Belair back on June 25, and referred to it in his July 23 letter to Truman.

The resemblance between the *Pravda* and Wallace critiques of Baruch is uncanny. Wallace had simply accepted a Soviet caricature of U.S. policy as accurate, and had not even bothered to speak with his own country's U.N. delegation before sending his letter to the president.[135] Having been confronted with clear evidence from Baruch that his claims were *in*accurate, however, not to mention damaging to the credibility of U.S. negotiators, he might have been expected to concede his mistakes. Instead, he chose, after conferring again with Hauser, to retract his correction statement and reiterate his original position—that is, *Pravda*'s position.

In Hauser's September 27 statement draft, based on Wallace's belated acknowledgment of his mischaracterizations, Wallace would have admitted not having been "fully posted" on the U.S. position when he sent his objections to the president. But Magdoff and his "gang," as Magdoff called them, convinced Wallace not to sign the statement. Instead, they got him to sign a text lamenting "the absence . . . of mutual trust" between the United States and Russia, and appearing to lay blame, once again, on his own government. "We cannot hope to achieve success in our atomic energy association with Russia," Wallace's statement read, "until a plan is devised which will assure her, by deed as well as by words, of our sincere desire to pay due regard to Russia."

Wallace's July 23 letter had also offered a muddled defense of Gromyko's counterproposal. The Soviets wanted the United States to destroy all stocks of atomic weapons, finished or unfinished, within three months of an agreement's signing. In this respect, at least, according to Wallace, Moscow's plan "goes even further than our[s]" toward international control of atomic energy.

But this assertion was nonsensical, since Moscow's plan contained no provision for international inspection and no mechanism for punishing violations. What Wallace had not understood was that completing a Soviet bomb had, since Potsdam, become Stalin's overriding national objective. "International" control—which Stalin understood to be synonymous with American control—could not have been of less interest to him.

At Potsdam, on July 24, 1945, Truman, after receiving word of the successful test of the plutonium bomb in the New Mexico desert, revealed to Stalin only that his country had come to possess "a new weapon of unusual destructive force." Stalin, according to the independent accounts of Truman, Byrnes, and Bohlen, showed no surprise, or even curiosity, leading each of them to conclude that he had not registered the significance of the revelation. Years later, however, after reading Marshal Georgy Zhukov's account of the episode, Bohlen remarked that he "should have known better than to underrate the dictator."[136]

Stalin, in fact, had first been briefed on the U.S. atomic program three years before Truman—in a meeting with Beria in the spring of 1942.[137] In September of 1943, the GRU and NKGB informed him of the secret Anglo-

American agreement at Quebec not to reveal the program's existence to Moscow.[138] After Truman told Stalin of the "new weapon" in July 1945, the dictator—who had trusted neither his intelligence sources nor his scientists—silently resolved to catch up.

Returning to his quarters, Stalin recounted Truman's words to Molotov, who took them as a warning to Moscow not to step out of line. "They're puffing themselves up," he observed.

Stalin laughed. "Let them," he said. "We'll have to have a talk with [physicist Igor] Kurchatov today about speeding things up."[139]

Still, no one in the Soviet hierarchy had yet grasped the full magnitude of Truman's revelation. This would not come until two weeks later, with the shocking devastation of Hiroshima.

In its immediate aftermath, Alexander Werth, the London *Sunday Times* Moscow correspondent, found the Russian capital in a state of near-depression. "It was clearly realized," he wrote, "that this was a New Fact in the world's power politics, that the bomb constituted a threat to Russia." The country's "desperately hard victory over Germany was now," in the eyes of many, "'as good as wasted.'"[140] The Americans would use the bomb monopoly to dictate the postwar settlement.

A renewed sense of urgency gripped the government, from Stalin down. On August 20, Beria was appointed chair of a new special committee to direct "all work on the utilization of the intra-atomic energy of uranium." Two days later, the Soviet military attaché in Ottawa, and head of a GRU spy ring, Colonel Nikolai Zabotin, was given orders to accelerate the "acquisition"— that is, theft—of "technical process[es], drawings, and calculations" related to the atom bomb. Commands went out to boost uranium mining in Central Asia.[141] In Russia itself, vast industrial resources and pools of prison labor were harnessed to the mission of building the bomb faster. "Ask for whatever you like," Stalin told Kurchatov. "You won't be refused."[142]

With the aid of its spy network in Britain, Canada, and that embedded within the Manhattan Project, the Soviet bomb program had been moving forward far faster than the largely blind embryonic American intelligence apparatus had understood. Purloined British documentation on uranium processing alone, which Kurchatov first studied in late autumn 1942, had allowed the Soviet Union "to bypass many very labor-intensive phases."[143] The later efforts of Klaus Fuchs—the brilliant German-Jewish émigré physicist who worked at the Los Alamos atomic laboratory for two years, from August 1944—were particularly consequential. Operating first as a GRU source (code name "Otto"), and from 1944 as an NKGB source (code names "Rest" and "Charles"), Fuchs, who had been an active Communist in Germany, provided his American courier, Harry Gold, with detailed information and sketches on the U.S. implosion bomb in June and September 1945. These helped the Soviets to complete and successfully test their own weapon up to two years earlier than would otherwise have been possible—in August 1949.

The purpose of the Gromyko plan, unveiled in June 1946, was, the State Department's George Kennan argued, to exploit "the merciless spotlight of free information" in America to compel U.S. disarmament while the Soviets "proceed[ed] undisturbed with the development of atomic weapons in secrecy."[144] For Washington, therefore, any credible international plan to eliminate the weapons had to manage the processes of disarmament, inspection, and control simultaneously.

Underscoring the seriousness with which the Baruch plan took the integrity of such efforts, it required the permanent members of the U.N. Security Council to renounce their vetoes with respect to any agreement. This provision was meant to ensure that no U.N. member could stymie the legitimate sanctions authority of the new atomic control agency. But the Soviets refused to accept any weakening of veto rights. To do so, Izakov wrote in *Pravda*, would mean "renouncing their sovereignty . . . in favor of the USA." Wallace, notably, defended the Soviets by arguing that the veto was "completely irrelevant," since the treaty signatories could simply declare war on a violator. Yet this point underscored that no action *short of war*—war unsanctioned by any international authority—would be available to the signatories if a Security Council veto could block enforcement or punishment action.

The New York Times concluded, charitably, that the "vagueness" of Wallace's attack on U.S. policy reflected a failure to "fortify his idealism with the necessary facts." Moreover, in being "unpardonably careless with the deadly fireworks of atomic policy," he had undermined prospects for success in critical and delicate negotiations.[145] What even Baruch had not understood at the time, though, was that these negotiations never stood any practical chance of success.

On June 21, 1946,[146] two days after Baruch presented his plan to the UNAEC, Beria submitted to Stalin for approval a draft decree of the Council of Ministers of the USSR to begin actual production of atom bombs—the first one to be ready for testing by January 1, 1948 (too optimistic by twenty months).[147] All technical hurdles had been surmounted. Stalin was now sure he had his bomb in sight, and so his diplomacy aimed at pressuring the United States to disarm while spinning out U.N. negotiations until it could be completed.

The appointment of the relentless Gromyko as Soviet representative to the UNAEC was central to carrying out the strategy of badger and delay. "[T]he American project [remains] unacceptable in substance," according to instructions he received from the Soviet Foreign Ministry on December 27, 1946.[148] "For tactical reasons," however, "we believe that it is necessary not to decline discussion, but to suggest its discussion point by point, simultaneously insisting on introducing amendments. Such tactics are more flexible and may give better results." By rejecting Soviet counterproposals, the Americans would "bring odium on themselves for the break up."[149]

That, however, would not happen. On December 30, Baruch, with Truman's backing, demanded that the UNAEC vote. It went 10–0 in favor of the United States, with abstentions by the Soviet Union and Poland. The Soviet proposals of 1947, following a joint statement by Canada, China, France, and the U.K. condemning them, would be officially rejected on April 5, 1948 by a vote of 9–2.[150] The Soviets got their stalemate, but failed to achieve any propaganda victory.

It may be argued that since nothing like the Baruch plan could ever have secured Soviet support, given Stalin's determination to build the bomb, Wallace's attack on it did little damage.[151] The plan, however, represented a sincere and serious approach to marrying disarmament with a robust inspection regime, one widely supported by top peace-loving, internationalist-minded American scientists, as well as prominent liberal political figures such as Eleanor Roosevelt. As such, it deserved better than the glib treatment to which Wallace had subjected it.[152] At the very least, Wallace, by parroting *Pravda* and discrediting Baruch's efforts among many progressives, only helped the Soviets escape their share of responsibility for the horrific atomic arms race that followed.

Wallace's behavior naturally raised questions about what his real objectives were. Was it "peace"? Or was it aiding the Soviets?

Years later, in December 1949, the right-wing radio commentator Fulton Lewis Jr. would accuse Wallace of having abused his powers as a member of the War Production Board and chairman of the Board of Economic Warfare to send atomic secrets and uranium to Russia back in 1943 and early 1944. Lewis had supposedly learned these facts from former Air Force Major George Racey Jordan, who had already, shockingly, implicated Harry Hopkins before the HUAC. Jordan's stories, involving claimed discoveries of suitcases full of bomb-related materials bound for Russia, were widely deemed "inherently incredible," and were only made more so with Lewis' apparent embellishments. Wallace defended himself at length before HUAC on January 26, 1950, five months after the first successful Soviet atomic test, arguing credibly that he had had neither the power nor the knowledge to do what Lewis had charged.[153] No evidence has ever emerged of Wallace's role in the alleged improprieties, yet he would remain under a cloud of suspicion owing to the closeness of his positions on atomic matters to those proclaimed by the Soviet government. That closeness had owed much to his blind reliance, as commerce secretary, on handpicked advisers such as Harry Magdoff—a man who had betrayed his government, and Wallace personally, by passing his private cabinet papers to the NKGB.

Fourteen

THE NEW REPUBLIC

A week after Henry Wallace was fired, a dapper but nervous young man approached the door of the Wallace family apartment at the Wardman Park Hotel. Thirty-year old Michael Straight rang the bell, rehearsing his plea in his head.

As the door opened, a shaggy gray poodle shuffled by Mrs. Wallace, sniffing at the visitor's trousers with docile disinterest. Yet if dogs could smell secrets, Brutus would have smelled a trove. Straight had moved in an extraordinary circle, though it would be some years yet before the world would know it as such. As a student at Cambridge University in the mid-1930s, he had been welcomed into the secret society known as the Cambridge Apostles and, covertly, the British Communist Party.[1] At the urging of soon-to-be Cambridge Five double agents Guy Burgess and Anthony Blunt, he also agreed to spy on his native country.

Straight was less a political Communist than a romantic one. Still, after gaining an unpaid job at the State Department in 1938, through family ties to Roosevelt, he began meeting with a handler whom he knew as "Michael Green"—in fact, Soviet covert intelligence operative Iskhak Akhmerov. Straight would, four decades later, in 1983, publish a memoir in which he would confess to having transmitted to Moscow only his own unimportant reports. His Soviet intelligence files, however, would show that he, as agent "Nigel," had also provided departmental position papers, as well as some secret diplomatic communications and analyses.

After an uneventful stint on the home front with the Army Air Corps from 1942 to 1945, Straight took over the family business, becoming publisher of the influential, but unprofitable, left-leaning weekly political magazine *The New Republic* (*TNR*). By that time, he had begun a rightward march toward mainstream politics, coming to disdain the Communist parties of Britain and the U.S.—both of which he now saw as mindless tools of the Kremlin. Akhmerov lamented to Moscow that he had "turned into a bourgeois apologist."[2]

Straight had his differences with Wallace, namely on foreign policy. He had backed the Baruch atomic control plan, while Wallace had condemned it. Still, he saw the former vice president as Roosevelt's rightful liberal heir, and had admired his bravery in denouncing the poll tax at the '44 convention. That Communists had shouted down Wallace's Madison Square Garden speech was, in Straight's eyes, also a badge of honor.

Straight had now come hoping to hire Wallace. His magazine could not survive indefinitely on twenty thousand readers; with a liberal star like Wallace as editor, he reasoned, he could boost circulation fivefold.

Ilo Wallace led Straight out to the back terrace, where he saw, sitting in the soft-hued early-autumn sunlight, "the familiar unkempt figure."

Personal accounts of interactions with Wallace at the time suggest a man in transition—although toward what is unclear. Nearly fifty-eight, his hair is variously described as "light brown[,] just turning silver,"[3] "fast graying,"[4] and "very gray."[5] Weighing 190 pounds, his physique is described as "muscled,"[6] "robust,"[7] and "potbell[ied]."[8] To one observer, he had an "air of hearty friendliness"[9]; to another he was "self-intoxicated"[10]; to a third, "inarticulate and uncommunicative."[11] Wallace appeared to be a man headed for either soaring fame or plummeting fortune, and his own disposition toward his prospects, at any given point in time, seemed to affect what others saw.

Out on the terrace, the now former commerce secretary was sorting through letters and telegrams with Harold Young, the political adviser who had departed with him. For the diffident Wallace, the task must have brought great satisfaction, involving as it did the steady flow of fulsome praise without the need to reciprocate in small talk.

Straight spoke hurriedly, unfamiliar as he was with the Iowan's unnerving habit of studying his footwear as he listened. Young, a normally genial Texan, did his conspicuous best to ignore the youthful visitor, whose proposition held no interest for him. Straight watched anxiously as Young thumbed through the communications, among which, he could see, were proposals from agents and other prospective paymasters.

To Straight's surprise and delight, Wallace, at the end of the pitch, looked up from his shoes and recalled how his father and grandfather had, at difficult times in their lives, both turned to publishing. The prospect of preaching from *TNR*'s pulpit intrigued him. Its New York City offices were just fifty miles southwest of Wallace's new 118-acre farm, Farvue, in South Salem, near the Connecticut border. Being little concerned with money at this point, having earned $150,000 in dividends from Pioneer Hi-Bred that year alone, he asked for a modest salary of $15,000—equal to what he had earned at Commerce.

A week later, the deal was done. Straight scribbled out their understanding "on a grubby piece of paper,"[12] to which the new editor would be as allegiant as he'd been to Truman's foreign policy.

Beginning in December, Wallace spent three or four days a week in New York City, sleeping at a townhouse owned by Straight and walking the forty blocks each morning to the *TNR* offices at 40 East 49th Street. When not traveling, he would spend the rest of the week at Farvue, where he enjoyed alarming guests by telling them that the tomatoes they were eating were from radioactive soil.

Wallace, Straight would later write, "lived in his own world. He rarely read through the magazine, took little interest in the editors, [and] frequently forgot their names." The actual editor's work at the magazine continued to be handled by Wallace's predecessor, Bruce Bliven, who was retitled "editorial director." Bliven, Straight, and Wallace would typically discuss content matters over lunch, usually at some bistro chosen by the editor for the workout involved in jogging there. If Wallace took the check, one or the other fellow diner would, "surreptitiously," top up his 5 percent tip. Bliven loathed these midday "ordeals," as he called them.[13]

Straight saw soon enough that Wallace had no intention of separating his editorial responsibilities from his political ambitions—and that he saw the former as, in fact, inseparable from, and indeed subservient to, the latter. Soon after accepting his appointment, Wallace opened a second, private political office at 2500 Q Street, NW in Washington. That office, staffed by paid and volunteer aides under the direction of Harold Young, managed his speaking engagements and political correspondence. Seed funding for its activities arrived in the form of a $10,000 check from the industrial heiress Anita McCormick Blaine ($143,000 in today's money), accompanied by a note pledging allegiance to its astonished recipient. "You will lead us," she wrote worshipfully.[14]

Wallace took it to heart. "My job as editor of *The New Republic*," he would write, unabashedly, in his December 16, 1946 inaugural column, "is to help organize a progressive America." He addressed this movement as "we"—as in "we" who "are the captives of no party," and "we" who would, if the Democratic Party failed to become "militantly progressive . . . strike out along other lines."[15] The political message was clear: either Wallace would wrest the Democratic Party from Truman, or he would wrest the liberals from the party.

TNR staff, not to mention its owner, came to see their roles as pawns on the editor's political chessboard. As suggested in a March 1948 *Harper's* profile—written by William Harlan Hale, a former Wallace colleague who resigned in December 1947 to protest his dual role as candidate and columnist—Wallace "convert[ed] what had been a journal of opinion into [his] personal organ."[16] He skipped meetings. He failed to recognize colleagues in the hallways. His interest in them, they observed, lay only in ensuring that they hewed to his policy views—a curious stance from a man freshly fired for publicly opposing the president's policies. Colleagues frequented his office less and less often, replaced by visiting activists and sycophants agitating for his return to politics.[17]

One veteran *TNR* writer—the former *Time* foreign correspondent, and Kuomintang political adviser, Teddy White—observed that *TNR* under Wallace became as sympathetic to Stalin's interests as *Time* had been to those of Chiang Kai-shek. Immediately following Wallace's appointment, "The Editors," collectively, called for a "A New Deal with Russia," which amounted to little more than an apologia for the Soviet plunder of Central and Eastern Europe. Russia's getting "'tough' on the people of the areas they occupy," "The Editors" argued, was justified by "the losses suffered in the war," and by Washington's failure to offer reconstruction aid and trade credits. Such assistance would not only have softened Soviet behavior, "they" argued, but would have provided a huge boost to American jobs. Quoting Wallace's former Russia hand, Ernest Ropes, "they" insisted that there was "almost no limit to what the Russians would purchase in the United States" with a mere $1 billion trade credit. This assertion was testimony either to the terrible cost of the present conflict between Washington and Moscow or to the judgment of the Soviet consulate official who had labeled Ropes "politically naïve."[18] By late spring, Wallace was rejecting all editorial drafts critical of Soviet policies, insisting that he could only hope to affect policies in Washington.[19]

Beyond policy, White noted, "Wallace's bitterness at Harry Truman was unappeasable." His "hatred of Truman," Straight added, "was a virus that raged within his frame." By early 1947, White was "numb with shock" from the collapse in "intellectual tolerance" at the magazine, as well as with Wallace's incapacity for basic human warmth. The "self-intoxicated" editor enjoyed discussing only two things, neither of which could sustain White's interest: "plant genetics and himself." When White told Wallace he was to marry a young woman working for *Life*, a Henry Luce publication, Wallace responded with grim succinctness: "ah, conjugal infiltration." White, fed up, would resign that summer.[20]

Wallace's real job at *TNR* was to pen a weekly column, though his travels and speaking engagements sometimes left him insufficient time even for that. Straight brought in an "urbane intellectual," Jim Newman, to prepare first drafts of the pieces after the three men had talked through the editor's latest thoughts. Bliven often pitched in as well. Typically, one or the other would read these drafts aloud while Wallace, seated between the men on the couch, jingled keys in his pocket, his eyelids shutting, his chin slouching into his chest. The jingling would subside, die away, and finally stop. Minutes later, it would resume, the head would jerk up, and the editor would pronounce his verdict: typically, "that's fine." As Bliven noted, he would "rarely alter a word."

Newman's urbane influence notwithstanding, Straight thought some of Wallace's columns not merely "outspoken" but "insensitive," impugning the integrity of those rejecting his stern judgments. They could also be maddeningly "evasive," leaning on awkward phrasing to mask gaps in logic or evidence.[21] They made assertions that were, at once, sweeping and wonky, noble and trite, authentic and muddled. At their best, they shone a serviceable light on policies that were, at least in the area of foreign affairs, clearly shifting in far-reaching ways. But at their worst, they simply piled up lofty-sounding but dubious assertions.

Wallace's first column was a case in point, arguing that Russia, which considered its system "a higher form of democracy," would not "move toward greater political freedom" until we in America had rooted out "the weaknesses in *our* democracy." And it would never agree to "be part of One World in which there is not economic and social security." The welfare of the Common Man was, to Wallace's mind, central to Stalin's world vision.[22]

Wallace did, however, also have some concrete views on current events. Among the most impassioned of his commentary was that concerning Soviet arms control and atomic energy policy. It was also among his most ill-informed and misleading.

In his column of December 23, 1946, Wallace heaped praise on Soviet diplomacy for its role in the adoption by the U.N. General Assembly, nine days earlier, of a resolution entitled "Principles governing the general regulation and reduction of Armaments"—which he misrepresented as "the United Nations resolution for *disarmament*." Its adoption was, in Wallace's estimation, not only "the greatest accomplishment in the history of the UN to date," but possibly "one of the most important acts in all history."

"Russia really wants peace," Wallace declared. It had "met us halfway" in agreeing to an effective international inspection system for weapons of mass destruction. It was now time for the United States to reciprocate by putting all its atom bombs "in escrow," and then destroying them once disarmament had begun.

Back in June 1946, Wallace wrote, after Molotov had presented his disarmament proposal (the "Gromyko plan"), it had become "fashionable in Anglo-American circles to question his good faith." But it was now clear that Russia was "more interested in the barring of methods of mass destruction than either England or the United States."[23]

Even without the benefit of hindsight, Wallace's hyperbole was breathtaking. The U.N. General Assembly resolution was merely hortatory; it did not compel any government to do anything. Security Council action was necessary to effect an atomic inspection regime, and the Soviets had not changed their position—that the United States should destroy its atom bombs before such a regime could be discussed. Furthermore, the Soviets had, that June, just following presentation of the Gromyko plan to the

UNAEC, secretly initiated the production stage of their atomic weapons program.[24] They were determined to continue that program unimpeded.

"In contrast to the American plan," wrote Soviet nuclear physicist Dmitry Skobeltsyn in a memo dated October 12, 1946, "we will not be providing for the extension of [atomic] control to research activity, so as to facilitate our reaching the level America has already reached."[25] Molotov, on November 7, after reading the memo, cabled Stalin urging that the new Soviet U.N. proposal back a call for "special inspection bodies" in order to blunt U.S. criticisms that their earlier proposals had "said nothing about international control."[26] The two men understood that those bodies would never actually be created, given that the Soviets had veto power on the Security Council. Stalin approved the recommendation.[27] Finally, on December 27, just two weeks after adoption of the U.N. resolution hailed by Wallace, the Soviet foreign ministry instructed Gromyko to drag out UNAEC discussions indefinitely "for tactical reasons"—that is, to prevent impediment to the Soviet bomb project.[28]

In short, there was never an epiphanous moment in which Molotov "came out for peace," as Wallace had claimed. Molotov was, and always had been, fully committed to his country's atom bomb program. Rather, the Soviets would use the U.N. resolution for propaganda purposes, brandishing it to highlight the alleged "sabotage" of arms reduction by "the Western powers."[29]

Farming also featured in Wallace's commentary, and was tied to Russia policy in unusual ways. In an August 25, 1947 column, Wallace heaped praise on his rural Farvue neighbor, a Mr. Walter Bishop, for his insights on Russia. A stolid Republican chicken breeder, Mr. Bishop had been "convinced by personal contact that the Russians are like anyone else and . . . just as anxious for peace." That conclusion he had formed on the basis of selling them twenty thousand hatching eggs, after which he received an invitation to travel to Russia and "go over their poultry work." A busy man, he never went, but the experience prodded him to write "a plan for world security." That plan, which sounded remarkably like one from Henry Wallace, involved building a "world-armament force," distributed globally around "15 air bases," each to be run by a citizen of a different nation on a one-year term. "Mr. Bishop's plan," Wallace concluded, "might even solve the security problem if both the United States and Russia would agree to it."[30]

On economic policy, Wallace's columns broadly comprised attacks on "Wall Street" and hortations to bring forth "abundance." To the latter end, he called for greater state control of production and prices, guided by the visible hand of science. To increase world productivity, he explained, we needed "international planning through scientific technicians."[31] He praised Russia for pursuing a "program of planned abundance."[32] Stalin, he acknowledged, had "sacrificed many human rights [to] modernize Russian agriculture and industrialize." But his "success" had, in the end, "probably saved the lives of millions of American young men" in World War II.[33]

Wallace, in spite of the Kremlin's belief that he was a naïve Keynesian, showed little patience with Keynesian tinkering. He was much more of an avid planner. When prices rose too much, as he so judged, he expected government simply to cut and cap them. His critique of Italy's economy illustrated his blind spot on monetary policy. "Price controls and rationing are largely meaningless" in that country, he lamented; "no wonder Italy suffers so terribly from inflation."[34] But as any competent economist of the left or the right could have told him, this appraisal had matters backward. Black markets, such as Italy's, thrive where governments impose controls in lieu of tighter money. Wallace's diagnosis was therefore like blaming the patient's demise on his doctor's failure to leech.

As for his own country, Wallace preached unrelenting doom—at least for as long as it continued to be run by a reactionary Democrat or a Republican. "I stand by the prediction made in *Sixty Million Jobs*," he wrote in July 1947, "that we shall have a major depression in the early 1950's unless we act to avert it."[35] Though Washington would ignore his planning remedies, he was, thankfully, mistaken. From 1950 to 1953, a period during which the country would be run by a reactionary Democrat and a Republican, annual GDP growth would range from a robust 4.1 percent to a booming 8.7 percent.[36]

Wallace's analyses were also at times contradictory. His March 10, 1947 column asserted that Soviet leaders "have a vested interest in . . . continued American prosperity," and therefore "fear depression in the US."[37] Yet his July 28 column assured readers that the *opposite* was true—that "Russia and the Marxists await our economic crash," convinced "that the US will be easier and safer to deal with when 10 million men are out of work."[38] Contradictions were not of great concern to Wallace. Arguments were, to his way of thinking, merely the clothes the righteous man wears. He might change them daily, and did not thereby become less righteous. In any case, readers typically esteemed Wallace's devotion to liberalism more than they did his capacity for constancy. If he did not always reason clearly, he *felt* clearly. "Wallace's strength," wrote *New York Post* columnist Samuel Grafton, "is that he is *emotionally* right."[39]

Wallace could "write articles which [were] masterpieces of confusion, equivocation, and contradiction," observed the less sympathetic anti-Stalin socialist writer Dwight Macdonald, "but so long as he remains a symbol of hope and of dissidence, so long will he retain a mass following."[40] And so logical lapses in his columns were, from a business perspective, inconsequential. Even as Straight fretted over his editor's growing flirtation with a third-party presidential run, which he expected to rupture the liberal movement and damage his magazine, subscriptions would grow by a hearty fifty thousand.

On the foreign policy front, 1947 was momentous. It marked the launch of two historic American initiatives that would shape the Cold War and beyond: the Truman Doctrine and the Marshall Plan.

What came to be known as the Truman Doctrine comprised elements of a presidential address before a joint session of Congress on March 12, and was motivated by Britain's shock decision, just weeks earlier, to cease military and financial aid to Greece. Its forty thousand troops, defending the Greek government against Communist rebels, were set to leave the country by late March. Desperately short of dollars and gold, Britain had initiated the withdrawal as part of a global retrenchment which, the State Department feared, would tempt Soviet expansion into the Mediterranean and Middle East. Truman successfully alarmed Congress, which acceded to his request for $400 million in aid ($5.4 billion in today's money) to both Greece and Turkey—the latter of which a recent target of Soviet coercion. But Truman went much further, at least rhetorically. He called on the United States to protect, into the indefinite future, the "national integrity" of other nations "against aggressive movements that seek to impose upon them totalitarian regimes." This seemingly open-ended call for American readiness to intervene on behalf of "free peoples" worldwide received the lion's share of the media attention, both positive and negative. Less noticed, but still important, was the president's clarification that American "help should be primarily through *economic and financial aid*," which he deemed "essential to economic stability and orderly political processes." American aid, then, was not to be, in the main, military.

While Truman was delivering his speech, his new secretary of state, former Army Chief of Staff General George C. Marshall, was off in Moscow conducting difficult negotiations with Molotov, and later Stalin, over the future of Germany. After six weeks of lavish Russian hospitality and mulish diplomacy, Marshall left the country convinced that Stalin sought only chaos and disorder in the western zones of that country—those under American, British, and French occupation. Not only would turmoil in Germany aid a Communist takeover of the country, he reasoned, but it would undermine recovery and political stability in the wider Western Europe—the part of the continent not under Soviet domination.

He returned home in late April determined to commit as much economic aid as necessary to revive Western Europe, including western Germany, so as to allow it to defend itself against Soviet and domestic Communist subversion. The broad principles under which such a multiyear plan would be constructed and administered he laid out in a short address at Harvard on June 5. The Marshall Plan, as it came to be known, with Truman's full blessing, was to be open to *all* European nations willing to cooperate in a program that would integrate their economies, such that each would rely upon the openness of the others. Marshall, however, was under no illusion that the Soviet Union would join such a program except to wreck it. In July the British and French foreign ministries, under State Department prodding, undertook to lure Molotov to Paris for talks on Soviet participation, with the aim of revealing the Kremlin's purposes. It worked. Molotov stormed out, casting the Soviets as enemies of recovery. But it also hardened East-West divisions by spurring Stalin to impose greater domination over Czechoslovakia, Poland, and other "satellite" nations anxious for American aid.

For Henry Wallace, the Truman Doctrine constituted the clearest possible evidence that the president had allied himself with "fascists" and "reactionaries" in Congress, the military, and the State Department. Their actions, he asserted, would inevitably "bankrupt us morally and financially."[41]

Wallace scolded the "bipartisan bloc" who believed that we could only have "world welfare" after security is established. The experience of the late 1940s would, however, suggest the critical importance of security to recovery. Credible American defense guarantees, in the form of the April 1949 North Atlantic Treaty Organization (NATO) alliance commitments, would prove central to the integration and revival of Western Europe.[42]

Wallace claimed, further, that the United States was "destroying UNRRA," the United Nations Relief and Rehabilitation Administration, "and refusing to send food and supplies" abroad for fear that "relieving famine and misery" would boost the ability of prospective enemies to wage war. Yet it was Wallace, and not Truman, who opposed reconstruction in the cause of preventing rearmament. Wallace would remain a steadfast supporter of the Morgenthau Plan for German deindustrialization long after the U.S. military had reversed it, despite its contributing to famine and social breakdown in the country.

As for UNRAA, 73 percent of whose funding came from the United States, Truman only ceased backing it after four years of costly, disappointing, and often painful experience. By early 1947, contrary to Wallace's claim that UNRAA "had Europe on the road to recovery," Europe's nascent recovery had gone into reverse. Some governments, moreover, had ceased to cooperate with it. On August 9 and 19, 1946, for example, Yugoslavia shot down U.S. C-47 UNRRA relief transport planes inadvertently passing over its territory en route from Vienna to Udine. The attacks led Byrnes to insist that future relief aid should be provided directly by the United States.[43]

With regard to the Truman Doctrine, Wallace insisted that there would be "no more tragic victims of our insane policy than the Greek people."[44] U.S. Aid to the Greek government, he argued, amounted to unprovoked aggression against the populace. In evidence, he would point out that no foreign Communist forces—"no Yugoslavs, Bulgarians, Albanians or Russians"—would ever be "captured in the Greek fighting."[45] Yet no *Americans* would be captured there either. Those aiding each side were doing so with money and matériel, and not soldiers. The interventions by foreign Communist governments, moreover, had begun over a year before the American one.

U.S. aid to Greece, Wallace insisted, was not just immoral; it was counterproductive. "Who among us," he asked rhetorically in March 1947, "is ready to predict that . . . American dollars will outlast the grievances that lead to communism? I predict that Truman's policy will spread communism in Europe."[46] In January 1948, he would declare himself right. "[T]he guerrillas are stronger than ever," he wrote. Each death "by American bullets" had only brought forth ten more.[47] Yet such claims amounted to extreme artistic license. By October 1949, the Communist guerrillas would be defeated. And in February 1952, Greece would become a member of the new U.S.-led NATO alliance.

As for Greece's neighbor, which would also join the alliance at that time, Wallace observed that "there is no Communist problem in Turkey."[48] This statement was both true and beside the point. The Greek and Turkish problems were different, as Truman had made clear. In Greece, the challenge was local Communist guerrillas backed by foreign Communist governments; in Turkey, it was a direct Soviet military threat.

Stalin had kept out of the Greek conflict, staying allegiant to his secret October 1944 "percentages agreement" with Churchill—a deal whereby Britain would have "90 percent influence" in Greece, and the USSR 90 percent in Romania and Bulgaria.[49] But no such agreement existed with regard to Turkey, where Stalin had, just half a year earlier, demanded territorial concessions at gunpoint. Wallace insisted that "the Soviet Union [had] made no warlike moves,"[50] yet it had massed 300,000 troops on Turkey's borders.[51] Stalin only withdrew them when Truman sent a show of naval force to the region. "It was a good thing we retreated in time," Molotov would recall years later. "Otherwise it would have led to a joint [Anglo-American] aggression against us."[52] He was, unlike Wallace, insouciant in the face of Truman's new "doctrine," considering it little more than an obnoxious restatement of U.S. policy in the region.

Only outside the pages of *TNR* did Wallace acknowledge Turkey's strategic importance and vulnerability to Soviet predations. In spite of his writing that the country had no need of aid, and that Stalin had no designs on it, he would, at a news conference on June 16, 1947, stun his audience by stating that "a line should be drawn on Russian expansion"—a line running through "central Turkey," which was a critical gateway to "Saudi Arabian oil." The United States, he said, "should fight" if Russia overstepped that boundary—before reversing himself and saying it "*would* fight." He thereby downgraded an endorsement to a prediction.[53] In April, similarly, he had called for a large loan to Russia with no "political strings" attached, before saying it should "probably" be conditional on resolving German matters "and perhaps other points."[54] These were yet further instances in which Wallace would struggle to define U.S. interests and explain how he would defend them.

Much of that struggle could be explained by the fact that he did not take the details of foreign policy seriously, considering it the job of advisers to fill those in as necessary to support his convictions. Asked in January 1947 for his views on Byrnes' famous Stuttgart speech of September 1946, shortly before he, Wallace, was fired, a speech in which Byrnes had scolded the Soviets for breaking their commitments at Potsdam, Wallace responded, incredibly: "Byrnes at Stuttgart? I don't recall any such speech." Asked for his opinion on the Potsdam agreement itself—whether it was "too severe, not severe enough, or about right"—Wallace responded, more incredibly: "I guess I have no opinion for publication on that."[55] When asked in June how he explained the brutal "Russian tactics in Korea, Manchuria, the Balkans, Hungary, Austria, and Germany," he pled ignorance. "I have little first hand knowledge of these tactics," he said, but "I believe [they] are directed to providing the security she needs to rebuild." In any case, he added, "we can do a great deal to end any abuses on her part . . . through economic assistance and sincere pledges of friendship with the Russian people."[56]

"Politics stops at the water's edge," pronounced Arthur Vandenberg, the GOP's champion of bipartisan foreign policy, in 1947. It would fast become a mantra for those believing that Americans ought to present a united front to other countries.

As word spread in the State Department that Wallace planned to attack U.S. policy in England, Acheson raised concerns in cabinet on April 4. Truman, however, insisted it was best to "wait and see" what he actually did.[57] On April 10, two days after Wallace arrived in London, the president assured the press that, whatever differences there might be on policy, he fully expected the former commerce secretary to back the Democratic ticket in 1948.[58]

Claude Pepper shared Wallace's objections to the Truman Doctrine, yet seconded the president's faith in party loyalty. "We Democrats differ with each other sometimes during the primaries," the senator said, "but we don't leave the ancestral home." Wallace, however, would make no commitments to the party. "I will be campaigning for the ideals of the free world and the men who best express these ideas," he responded from London on April 11, "but I cannot guarantee that they will be on the Democratic ticket."

In venue after venue around England, Wallace blasted U.S. policy and touted his own. "The world is crying out, not for American guns and tanks to spread more hunger," he said in London, by way of reference to Greek and Turkish aid, "but for American plows and machines to fulfil the promise of peace." It was "futile," he added, to spend $400 million to "buy off" Communism. He accused his government of "ruthless imperialism."

Michael Straight was despondent. Though he had drafted Wallace's March 18 broadcast denouncing the Truman Doctrine, Straight had also warned him not to criticize Truman or his policies on foreign soil. What support Wallace was attracting, furthermore, was of the wrong kind. Among the unwanted visitors to his suite at the Savoy were Soviet spy Guy Burgess and (separately) the NKGB/MGB London station chief, Konstantin Kukin,[59] operating under the cover of embassy counselor. Straight, who would have recognized Kukin as the operative who tried to reengage him in Washington seven years earlier, whisked both of them down the elevator before they could be spotted near his editor.[60]

Back in Washington, the outcry over Wallace's words was swift and angry. "No American citizen," thundered Mississippi Democrat James Eastland on the Senate floor, "has the right to conspire with foreign peoples in order to . . . weaken the hand of the country." But Wallace responded with more defiance. "If it is a crime to work for peace in Britain," he said at Stoke-on-Trent the following day, then "I stand convicted."

Wallace now took up a favorite theme—how the United States and Britain were destroying cooperation with Russia. The League of Nations, he said, had failed because countries had used it "to gang up on Russia." Were we now to do the same, he asked, "in the United Nations?"[61] Both houses of Congress erupted, with member after member, Republican and Democrat, condemning Wallace. Vandenberg accused him of "treasonable utterances." It was, said The New York Times, "probably the most vehement congressional reaction in years to the pronouncements of a public figure."[62]

The transatlantic volley of attack and condemnation continued unabated. In Liverpool on April 13, Wallace dismissed Vandenberg and others as "hysterical," before going back on the offensive. Over BBC radio, he warned that if we embarked on an "American century of power politics rather than [one] of the Common Man," the result would be nations turning "to the Soviet Union as their only ally." Representatives J. Parnell Thomas (R-NJ) and John Rankin (D-MI) threatened to prosecute him under the Logan Act of 1799, which made it a criminal offense for private citizens to carry on "intercourse with any foreign government" with the intent to "defeat the measures of the United States."[63] In Walter Lippmann's view, Wallace, in going abroad to urge noncooperation with the United States, was at least guilty of interfering in European affairs in "a grossly embarrassing way."[64]

In London, Churchill dismissed Wallace's claims that war was inevitable under present policies, but insisted it would be "if Britain and the United States were to follow the policy of appeasement and one-sided disarmament which brought about the last war." Wallace's ideas, the former war leader said, appealed only to a "small minority of [British] crypto-Communists." Shortly after Wallace's departure for Scandinavia, the largest Labour Party convention in thirty years endorsed the Truman Doctrine and repudiated the views of its American visitor, whom Vandenberg now dismissed as an "itinerant saboteur."[65] The man whose policies Wallace was excoriating, however, kept his silence. Truman said he had no desire to call more attention to "Henry's wild statements."[66]

In Stockholm, Oslo, Copenhagen, and Paris, Wallace's speeches were much the same, with a few additions that kept him in the headlines back home. In Oslo he said "it would be unfortunate for world peace" if anything were, at that time, to "upset [Russia's] system of government."[67] In each of the capitals, U.S. officials avoided public contact with him—highly unusual treatment for a former vice president and cabinet official. In Paris, he was a virtual political leper. His visit had, unbeknownst to Straight, been arranged by the American journalist, novelist, and secret OGPU-NKGB agent Martha Dodd Stern (code name "Liza"), a friend of the Wallaces. Stern had written to the French radical socialist, and longtime Soviet asset, Pierre Cot asking him to invite Wallace, and to Wallace urging him to accept.[68] On the back of Cot's assurance that he would be received by "preeminent liberal people," Wallace cabled his acceptance.[69] Yet on arrival at the airport, a panicked Straight "looked in vain for Maurice Schumann, Jean Monnet, and other moderates who, we had been told, were sponsors of his visit." He recognized only the two Communist leaders: "the aged Marcel Cachin and the squat and ugly Jacques Duclos."[70] Of the four parties which had purportedly pledged to send representatives to Wallace's speech at the College of Sorbonne, only the Communists did so.[71]

The trip was, in the end, an unmitigated personal disaster. Wallace, Walter Lippmann wrote, had shown himself to be "a man trying earnestly to deal with a world which is too much for him," and who was now "cracking under the strain." In fleeing from "equal debate" and "tedious persuasion" to take refuge behind sanctimonious monologues, in "retreating to the comforting applause of coteries," in peddling "half-truths, myths, panaceas, nostrums, and quackery," in manufacturing constant "hubbub" and "provok[ing his own] persecution," in luxuriating in "martyr[dom]" and the "inner certitude that he is right," Wallace had shown himself "unfitted for prime responsibility in time of crisis." The self-inflicted damage to his reputation and political fortunes was "tragic" and perhaps "irreparable."[72] But from the time he was expelled from the protective cocoon Roosevelt had spun for him as vice president, it also seemed inevitable.

At the time Wallace penned his first column for *TNR* back in December 1946, Gallup had him trailing Truman 48 percent to 24 percent as the preferred Democratic presidential nominee. On arriving back on American soil at the end of April, Truman was trouncing him 79 percent to 9 percent.[73]

The trip did, however, help in uniting a Congress that had, prior to his departure, been far more divided on the question of aid to Greece and Turkey. On April 22, just a few hours after Wallace's speech at the College of Sorbonne, in which he called for a large U.S. loan to Russia through the U.N., the Senate approved Truman's aid package request by a majority of 67–23. On May 9, it would pass in the House 287–108.

In contrast to his harsh take on the Truman Doctrine, Wallace's initial response to the Marshall Plan was supportive. It "was a great advance over the Truman Doctrine," he enthused shortly after the Harvard speech. Unlike Truman, Wallace claimed, Marshall had "recognized that the fundamental problem [in Europe] is economic."[74] This contrast was, however, a false one.

Truman had, in fact, stressed that U.S. "help should be primarily . . . *economic and financial*." There was, as regards the primacy of economic over military assistance, no daylight between Truman and Marshall. Truman's sterner tone in March owed to the immediate need of securing Republican votes—votes from those more ready to confront Communists than to make gifts to capitalists. Come the fall, when Marshall would need to sell his plan to a GOP Congress, his tone would mirror Truman's.

Wallace also praised Marshall for seeing "that Europe must be aided *as a whole* and not country by country." European nations, he said, "must cooperate in efforts for recovery."[75] Marshall's call for Europe to produce an integrated recovery plan, which the United States would then fund, was indeed an innovation. Truman, however, had been dealing with a narrower and more immediate problem: defending Greece and Turkey. The difference between the two men's speeches, then, owed to the audience and timing rather than to principle.

Wallace supported the Marshall Plan, finally, because it "left the door open for Russia to join."[76] Indeed, Marshall *had* left that door open, but did so expecting Stalin to slam it. Marshall, unlike Wallace, had been under no illusion that Stalin would "cooperate in efforts for [European] recovery." To the contrary, he knew Stalin would sabotage them to undermine U.S. influence. Documentation on the internal Soviet debates, and its external communications, show Marshall to have been correct.[77] After digesting the American initiative, the Soviets, to Wallace's initial surprise and disquiet, condemned it and forbade its eager satellites from participating. Though they had pledged to defend Soviet interests, Stalin would not risk their succumbing, like the French and the British, to dollar vassalage.

Pravda attacked the Marshall Plan as a new element in Washington's "campaign against the forces of world democracy and progress." Its aim, *Pravda* said, was the "quick formation of a notorious western bloc under the unconditional and absolute leadership of American imperialism."[78] It was a "plan for political pressures with dollars and a program of interference in the internal affairs of other states."[79] At the United Nations, on September 18, Soviet assistant people's commissar of foreign affairs Andrey Vyshinsky rounded on the plan for a full ninety-two minutes.[80]

Wallace, now faced with the unresolvable dilemma of how to back Marshall without opposing Stalin, did a startling about-face. "[O]ur unilateral help to Europe intervenes in the internal politics of nearly every Western European nation," he now wrote, angrily. "[T]he ordinary European worker looks on it as naked imperialism—or even worse." He called for placing the Ruhr Valley under international control so that its output might aid European reconstruction and so that Germany would never again menace its neighbors.[81]

No longer, it seemed, was an American aid program desirable. It now constituted dictatorial unilateralism. No longer, it seemed, was it right to say that Europeans "must cooperate in efforts for recovery." This was now interference in their internal politics—even "naked imperialism." Neither should Germany be rehabilitated, but milked dry. Asked during House testimony how his new stance differed from that of Moscow, he demurred. "I'm not familiar with the Communist approach," he explained. He would later add that he did not "follow the Communist literature."[82] To many, it seemed strange that a former vice president should agitate so publicly and heatedly for peace with a regime about whose doctrines he pled ignorance.[83]

How was such a radical change in Wallace's perspective on the Marshall Plan to be explained? His own explanations echoed Keynes' observation that a sensible man changed his views with the facts. And since the Marshall Plan had changed in the months following Marshall's speech, so had Wallace's views on it.

Yet the facts of the plan had not altered when Wallace began attacking it. Marshall had avoided attaching conditions to it, beyond insisting that European nations make their aid request in concert, based on a cooperative blueprint—a blueprint sixteen of them concluded in Paris in September 1947. What *did* change over the summer, however, was Stalin's *reaction* to the plan, once he recognized that Marshall was in earnest about European integration. Stalin, in contrast to Marshall, wished to see Europe weak, divided, and dependent on Soviet goodwill.

Wallace's initial enthusiasm for the Marshall Plan must be understood in a domestic political context. Going back to January 1947, when Marshall became secretary of state, Wallace saw him as a useful political foil to Truman—one who could help him brand the president as an unprincipled warmonger.

"The *New Republic* may perhaps from time to time take issue with you on matters of foreign policy," Wallace warned gently in an "Open Letter to George Marshall" that month. Yet he, Wallace, would hold him always in "the highest personal esteem."[84] That reverential tone continued into the spring. "On behalf of America," Wallace wrote in March, just before the secretary left for Moscow, "George Marshall can be that man" who builds cooperation with Russia. "[W]e may hope that Stalin will establish the same fine personal relationship with Marshall that he had with Roosevelt."[85]

Yet once Stalin began denouncing the Marshall Plan in ever more strident tones, it became clear that no such relationship was in the offing. Wallace knew that he could not continue to support the plan while blaming Truman for the Cold War. He knew, further, that such support would kill any chance he had of getting an audience with Stalin in Moscow. And so he needed a compelling pretext to change course, a basis on which he could argue that a good Marshall Plan had been perverted by a bad president. He therefore concocted one.

"I was for the *spirit* of the *original* Marshall proposal, administered through the United Nations with no political strings attached," he explained to his patroness, Anita McCormick Blaine.[86] But since that proposal had been abandoned, his support naturally had to be withdrawn.

This claim, however, was nonsense. Neither the "spirit" nor the content of Marshall's proposal ever envisioned U.N. administration. To the contrary, a major impetus behind the Marshall Plan had been the perceived failure of UNRRA administration. The Marshall Plan, Clayton wrote in May 1947, was not to be "another UNRRA." The United States "must run this show."[87] In *TNR*, furthermore, Wallace questioned "the *motivation* of our so-called Marshall Plan," and not the evolution of it. As for political strings, Wallace had publicly backed Marshall's main requirement: that, in Wallace's own words, Europe must "be aided *as a whole* and not country by country." It had to be a unified program for an integrated European economy, and not what the State Department would call "sixteen shopping lists."[88] And so it was clear that it was not the Marshall Plan that had changed, but rather Wallace's political calculus. To win Stalin's trust, it was not enough to oppose Truman. He had to oppose anything which constrained Moscow's "sovereignty."

With that change in calculus, he embraced a very different program—

one that reflected Stalin's demands. "We propose a plan that will effectuate the fine words spoken by Secretary Marshall at Harvard," Wallace wrote in January 1948, referring to himself in the plural, and "not a plan whose deeds contradict those words." Marshall's plan, tragically, he now insisted, *did* contradict them, since it retained "the Truman Doctrine as its core."

Instead of the four years and $13.2 billion of Marshall grants Congress would approve ($165 billion in today's money), the United States should, Wallace said, finance a five-year, $50 billion "UN Reconstruction Fund" ($625 billion in today's money). That fund, over which the United States would have no control, would provide loans and grants "to those nations which suffered most severely from Axis aggression." By far the largest of these nations was, of course, the Soviet Union. "The UN agency," furthermore, Wallace added, "must not make aid conditional upon conformity by any nation with an over-all economic plan, but must leave each nation free fully to develop its own national economic plan."[89]

Wallace was now in wholesale contradiction with his earlier self. But, as recompense, he was getting the attention in Moscow he so craved. Molotov was being kept apprised of his attacks on the Plan through reports from the embassy in Washington, the Central Committee's foreign department, TASS, *Pravda*, and *Izvestia*.[90]

"In the long run," Wallace went on to warn, the foreign policy of the "bipartisan bloc" in Congress and the White House, of which the Marshall Plan was now the centerpiece, will, unless altered radically, "make us the most hated nation in the world."[91] Governments receiving Marshall Plan funds will "have no gratitude to the US," he asserted, because they will resent being used "as part of the program to fight Russia."[92] European "workers will hate us because they think we are trying to maintain or install reactionary governments and influence the economic system of Western Europe to the benefit of Wall Street." Yet not only would that program be rejected by the Common Man abroad, but by his brother at home in the United States. "Only a one-world policy of investment in peace," he wrote, referring to his own plan, "can win continued support from the American people."[93]

An election-time poll in November 1948, eight months after passage of the aid legislation, would show this claim to be mistaken. Gallup would find 62 percent of Americans satisfied with the Marshall Plan's performance, as against only 14 percent dissatisfied—an overwhelming positive margin for an aid project.[94] Liberals were especially supportive. In his efforts thus to show himself to the American public, and not just to the Kremlin, as a sound-thinking man of peace, Wallace had set himself against what would become the most popular and successful diplomatic initiative in American history—one that would result in abiding appreciation from succeeding generations in Western Europe. And, in the process, he would damage his standing among the liberals he so desperately wished to shepherd away from Truman.

Fifteen

GIDEON'S RED ARMY

Following the Tehran Allied war leaders conference in late 1943, the CPUSA was at a crossroads. Its general secretary, Earl Browder, a longtime enthusiast for U.S.-Soviet cooperation, believed that the joint declarations heralded a postwar world in which capitalism and socialism could coexist, and even work together in the cause of peace. In January 1944, he proposed to the party's National Committee that it be reconstituted as a less confrontational "political association," which would work alongside "a broad progressive and democratic movement." It was unanimously endorsed.

Browder's chief opponent, the doctrinaire Communist William Z. Foster, fought back in a letter to the committee rejecting his "Tehran Thesis." The war's end would, Foster insisted, sharpen class divisions and impel an imperialist drive in Washington that would make cooperation with Moscow impossible.[1]

The CPUSA's Politburo rejected Foster's hard line. But they would not have the last word. Over a year later, in April 1945, the French Communist leader, Jacques Duclos, published an article in his party's journal excoriating Browder for dissolving the CPUSA as a political party, and for his "erroneous conclusions" regarding the prospects for "peaceful coexistence and collaboration." The Tehran thesis, he wrote, represented a "notorious revision of Marxism," and had to be rejected. Duclos backed Foster, quoting his words favorably.[2]

Duclos' quoting of Foster was significant. Other than a handful of top CPUSA officers, the only people privy to Foster's letter were in the Kremlin. And since its argument contradicted the French Communist Party's own much more moderate line on cross-party cooperation, it was apparent that the article had not been written by Duclos. Unbeknownst to anyone but the seventy members of the Soviet Communist Party Central Committee and a few top Soviet officials, the article had first appeared in a January 1945 issue of a restricted-distribution Central Committee foreign-policy bulletin. Duclos had been sent a French translation and ordered to publish it in his name.

Not knowing the details of the article's origins, the State Department still recognized its provenance and diplomatic significance. The "Duclos letter," as it came to be known, indicated that Moscow intended to pursue its interests vigorously after the war, and was preparing for the likelihood of confrontation with Washington. Browder himself would later term it "the first public declaration of the Cold War."[3]

Given this context, Wallace's steadfast insistence that Stalin wanted only "peace," and that his aggressive behavior in Eastern Europe, Iran, Turkey, and Manchuria constituted *defensive* reactions to U.S. threats, rang hollow. "Peaceful coexistence" might, in Stalin's mind still be possible, but only to the extent that Washington and London accommodated his "desiderata." He was determined to lever ideological struggle as a means of weakening their ability to act cohesively and decisively against him.

The American Communists, interpreting the Duclos letter as an order from Moscow to "turn left," replaced Browder with a combination of Foster (as chairman of the National Committee) and Eugene Dennis (as general secretary) and, in 1946, expelled Browder from the party. Foster reversed Browder's reforms and reconstituted the CPUSA as a militant Stalinist party, committed to defeating "imperialism" and "monopoly capital." Whereas party publications had in April 1945 praised the new president, Harry Truman, as "a tireless worker for progress," he was by September being condemned as a "militant imperialist."

Under Foster's leadership, pragmatic cooperation with progressive groups remained an option, but only where such groups took no public issue with Soviet policy. So-called concealed Communists were embedded in other "Popular Front" leftist and labor groups to enforce discipline. Those liberals who called them out were denounced as "red baiters"; those Communists who counseled moderation were condemned for "Browderism."

Within both the CPSU[4] and the CPUSA, a clash of principle and pragmatism hampered adoption of a coherent postwar policy. It was impossible to achieve ideological purity while cooperating with others for political gain; one or the other had to take precedence. Where to draw the line was a constant source of division. Within the CPUSA, Foster put a premium on purity; Dennis put it on political success. Though they generally kept their disagreements quiet, these would surface in what was soon to be the most consequential question the party would face: whether and how to cooperate with Popular Front liberals to contest elections.[5]

The first test case came in February 1946, with a special congressional election in New York City. The Communists successfully pressed the American Labor Party (ALP) to back a pro-Communist journalist and radio commentator, Johannes Steel, over Democratic former congressman Arthur G. Klein. Klein, a well-regarded New Deal liberal, would normally have received the ALP's endorsement as a matter of course, but Communist influence within its ranks this time proved decisive.

Wallace, then commerce secretary, backed Steel over Klein—this in spite of Wallace's public insistence that Democrats breaking rank on major issues should resign. In his efforts to unite and mobilize the left, Wallace was also absorbing the Communists' vocabulary, hurling the terms "fascist," "reactionary," "imperialist," and "warmonger" at opponents with ever greater scope and frequency.

Years later, decoded Soviet intelligence cables, as well as records of conversations with Soviet diplomatic and VOKS cultural officials from 1944 to 1947, would show Steel to have been a valued confidential contact (under NKGB code name "Dicky") and mouthpiece for Moscow.[6] Though Klein ultimately won the election, it was unexpectedly close: 49.5 percent to 38.2 percent. (Republican William Shea garnered 12.3 percent.) CPUSA officials were elated by Steel's strong showing, convinced it was a harbinger of "a radical upsurge" among the American populace generally.[7]

The second test case came that spring, when CPUSA members and concealed Communists, working under orders from California party veteran Nemmy Sparks, bludgeoned liberal political and labor organizations into backing the candidacy of a longtime Communist ally, Congressman Ellis Patterson, in the state's Democratic primary for senator. The goal of their well-financed campaign was nothing less than to use his victory as a vehicle to take over the party of Roosevelt nationwide. "When we get through," crowed Los Angeles CIO-PAC officer Philip Connelly, a concealed Communist, "there won't *be* any Democratic Party."

In the end, Patterson, who campaigned on ideology rather than practical local concerns, lost every county in the state to his moderate opponent, Will Rogers Jr. (the entertainer's son). Republicans, however, successfully tarred *both* Democrats as "Communist sympathizers," paving the path to an easy general election victory for their candidate, William Knowland.

The disaster of Patterson's candidacy convinced Democrats of the need to keep the pro-Soviet left at bay. Prominent liberals, such as FDR son James Roosevelt and Hollywood director Philip Dunne, refused to have further dealings with organizations having Communist links. They "were not accepting leadership," Dunne would later write, "from any organization outside of the country." Many Communists, meanwhile, such as those editing the *Daily People's World*, concluded that the Democratic Party had become beholden to "Big Business" and "reactionaries," and that a new, militantly progressive third party would therefore be necessary to achieve electoral success.[8] Even for the ideological purists, this path now seemed inescapable, given that they expected their party soon to be outlawed.[9]

Wallace kicked off an undeclared presidential campaign in New York on December 29, 1946, featuring as the keynote speaker at a convention to merge two prominent but financially strapped Popular Front organizations: the ICCASP and the NC-PAC. ICCASP, founded in 1945 by Jo Davidson, sculptor of Wallace's vice presidential bust (titled *The Seer*), had aimed at promoting New Deal policies at home and peace policies abroad. NC-PAC, a CIO-linked lobbying group for nonunion professionals, backed by Wallace patron Anita McCormick Blaine, had originated in a committee to promote Roosevelt's reelection in 1944. The new merged organization, to be chaired by Davidson and NC-PAC chairman Frank Kingdon, would be named the Progressive Citizens of America (PCA).

Sidney Hillman, the NC-PAC founder who had died in July 1946, had opposed the merger on the grounds that the Communists, who were active in both organizations, would have outsize influence over the combined entity. NC-PAC's Beanie Baldwin and ICCASP's Hannah Dorner, who would become the PCA's workhorse executive vice presidents, were both friendly to the Communists, though claims that they were *of* them have never been documented.

Baldwin, a strong-jawed, intense but soft-spoken, Southern-drawling Virginian, with long ties to Wallace and the cause of small farmers and unions, had big plans for the PCA. Far from content to see it as a mere forum to promote progressive policies, he envisioned it as the embryo of a new party of the left. Based on his personal associations and his stalwart defense of Soviet espionage agent Gregory Silvermaster, some historians would later call Baldwin "a secret Communist"[10]—a term not as concrete as "concealed Communist" (which was an actual party member). Soviet Central Party Committee U.S. section head[11] Boris Vronsky, who traveled in the United States under the cover of an *Izvestia* correspondent, reported to Moscow that Baldwin was "close to the Communist party."[12] In any case, Baldwin had no qualms about enlisting Communist support for the PCA, for the party he hoped to create, and for the man he hoped to head it.

Wallace's speech to the convention, which he wrote himself,[13] offered clues as to his own thinking. Progressives, he said, preferred "a genuine two-party country," but would not tolerate "a fake one-party system under the guise of a bi-partisan bloc." This framing left the door open for him to run as leader of a refounded Democratic Party, if it would have him as such, or, if not, as leader of a pathbreaking new party.

Whereas both Wallace and the PCA proclaimed progressive values, they also made clear that they welcomed active Communist participation. The PCA's by-laws specified that it sought "to unite all progressive men and women in our nation, *regardless of . . . political affiliation*." "[T]he plutocrats and monopolists will try to brand us as Reds," Wallace warned in his speech. Yet this would not cow them. "If it is traitorous to believe in peace— we are traitors," he said defiantly. "If it is communistic to believe in prosperity for all—we are Communists. . . . On with the fight!"[14]

Foster, meanwhile, was determined to take utmost advantage of the PCA's openness to Communists. "The organization of [the PCA] is of major importance," he wrote in February 1947. "The experience is laying the foundation for the organization of a third party," and "Communists should constitute an active, recognized sector of the movement."[15] As Hale observed in his *Harper's* profile of Wallace, "Communists streamed into PCA as if by order," attracted by the prospect of political power unachievable through the CPUSA.[16] In Moscow, meanwhile, a Russian translation of Foster's words circulated within the party's Central Committee.[17]

Kingdon and other non-Communist PCA founders would soon enough be enmeshed in a bitter internal struggle.[18] Liberal luminaries, many of whom had respected Wallace, or in the past even been allied with him, were appalled by what was happening to the new organization. Ickes, who had resigned as ICCASP executive chairman the month prior, wrote that the PCA's "cornerstone . . . should have been a stern injunction that no Communist or sympathizer with Communism would be admitted for membership." It was inconsistent with progressive values. And just days after the PCA was launched, liberal activists led by Eleanor Roosevelt, economist John Kenneth Galbraith, labor leader Walter Reuther, historian Arthur Schlesinger, and theologian Reinhold Niebuhr launched a rival liberal association: Americans for Democratic Action (ADA). ADA shared much with PCA when it came to civil rights and economic policy. Yet in contrast, it rejected "any association with Communism," just as its predecessor Union for Democratic Action—which had two years earlier hailed Wallace's "simple courage" and "leadership"—had "rejected any association with fascists."[19] This rupture in the liberal camp, over Russia and Communism, would become a defining feature of home front Cold War politics.

For the CPUSA leadership, the first task in setting the United States on the path to Marxism-Leninism was to identify a cooperative political figure who could unite the left. Duclos' letter—that is, the Kremlin's letter—had praised a single American politician, suggesting that he, and possibly only he, would have Soviet support. That man, a man committed to fighting "fascism" and "tyranny" at home and abroad, was Henry Wallace.[20]

To Dennis and his comrades, Wallace met all the requirements. They needed "a coalition candidate," Dennis explained to a party plenum in August 1947. He should be "backed by the independent and third-party forces," though he should preferably run as a Democrat.[21] Given Wallace's history and status in the party, he was uniquely capable of leading an insurgency within it. Yet, if that failed, he could also lead an attack from without.

Wallace had always disclaimed any Communist connections or affections, which was essential to his ability to attract progressives and traditional

labor unionists. Yet he also routinely backed even the most controversial Soviet positions, denounced "red baiters," and attacked the evils of "monopoly
capitalism." He even openly welcomed Communist support.

To be sure, as CPUSA official George Charney later noted, Wallace had
shown some "lamentable lapses"—such as when he told the Madison Square
Garden crowd in September 1946 that Russia had "no business . . . in the
political affairs of Latin America [and] Western Europe." Still, he had directed the sharp "edge of his criticism" at U.S. foreign policy. It was therefore natural that Communists "came to embrace Wallace as the leader of a
new people's movement."[22]

The challenge was to shepherd Wallace onto their path. Fortunately,
Wallace showed a readiness to follow the lead of persons who flattered him;
who offered access to large, cheering crowds; and who would handle the
grubby registering, booking, marketing, fundraising, gladhanding, and
compromising required to advance his political ambitions. On all these
counts, the Communists were happy to oblige.

Working through concealed Communists within friendly liberal and
labor organizations such as ICCASP, NC-PAC, the National Council of
American-Soviet Friendship, the UAW, and the Amalgamated Clothing
Workers, they did "a superb 'snow job'" on Wallace, in Bliven's words. They
"convinc[ed] him that they were just a bunch of good liberals who liked and
admired him, and wanted to see more of him." Bliven guessed they had also
infiltrated *TNR*. During Wallace's tenure, he noted, "several [joined] the
editorial staff who in retrospect give evidence of having been planted by the
party," though he never had proof. Only one ever admitted to being a Communist, just before resigning. She was Wallace's private secretary.[23]

Following the creation of the PCA, the Soviets took great interest in the
organization—and Wallace's role in it. On March 21, 1947, Soviet embassy
official Anatoly Yermolaev and New York consulate official Pavel Fedosi-
mov met with Jo Davidson in New York to learn more about its composition
and aims. Davidson highlighted the "large group of Communists" among
its members. Asked what role Henry Wallace played in the organization,
Davidson explained that he was "not part of the leadership," although it
worked "under his close supervision and oversight."[24]

Over in Moscow, Kremlin officials plied American visitors on Wallace and the nascent third-party initiative. On March 18, VOKS deputy board chairman Alexander Karaganov, together with MGB foreign intelligence officer Sergei Kondrashov, interviewed Johannes Steel, who flew over and boarded at VOKS expense. Steel, the longtime NKGB source whom Wallace had supported for Congress in 1946, in preference to the official Democratic candidate, warned that "organization of the third party" would not necessarily "mean its immediate victory. But, at any rate," he assured Karaganov, "it will be helpful in making an impact on American policy."

Steel lavished praise on Wallace's latest speech condemning Truman's foreign policy, the text of which had just been published in a full-page ad taken out by the PCA in *The New York Times*.[25] That same day, back in Washington, Wallace's former Commerce colleague Ed Fitzgerald (NKGB code name "Ted") phoned the wife of fellow former colleague Harry Magdoff (code name "Tan") to discuss the ad and to arrange a meeting with Harry for the following day. With the FBI listening in, Fitzgerald enthused that "the thing"—that is, Wallace's third-party campaign—was "beginning to gather momentum."[26] Magdoff would soon be reunited with Wallace as a campaign adviser on economics and foreign policy.[27]

Before taking his leave of Karaganov on April 7, Steel asked for "bills" from his Intourist hotel—"in case of complications and attacks against him in connection with his trip to Moscow." His host agreed.[28] He was then granted audiences with Molotov and Vyshinsky. Steel told the latter that Wallace would be "considerably encouraged" if the Soviet chargé d'affaires in London might "pay a courtesy visit" during his stay the following month. (Michael Straight, we recall, would react in horror when NKGB/MGB London station chief Konstantin Kukin showed up at Wallace's hotel a few weeks later.) Vyshinsky summarized the meeting with Steel for Stalin, Molotov, Mikoyan, CPSU Central Committee Secretary Andrey Zhdanov, and other top officials, and instructed his staff to begin filing copies of all Wallace's statements.[29]

Morris Childs—a CPUSA National Committee member, editor of the *Daily Worker*, and future FBI informant[30]—met with Boris Vronsky five times between March 21 and April 26. On instructions from the CPUSA, Childs asked Vronsky for the Central Committee's view on the creation of a third party.[31] "In the field of international relations," he assured Vronsky, "the CPUSA [was] automatically following the policy of foreign Communist parties"—by which he meant, of course, the policy of the Kremlin.[32]

Realizing that the matter of a new "anti-imperialist" party in the United States was of great importance, Vronsky forwarded the question to Alexander Panyushkin, deputy director of the Foreign Policy Department. Panyushkin, in turn, submitted a summary of the interview to eight Politburo members, Stalin included, appending his department's view that "the USA [currently] lacked the prerequisites for the organization of a third, independent progressive party" owing to "the absence of unity in the labor movement."[33] The Politburo, seemingly, agreed. Solomon Lozovsky, a Central Committee member, subsequently warned Childs that the "radical political leaders" in the United States needed to win the support of the labor bosses. They could not simply hope for the bosses to rally to them.[34] In this regard, the Soviet Communists showed better practical judgment than their American comrades, who would instead try, and fail miserably, to *undermine* the pro-Truman union bosses among the rank and file.

Panyushkin, also a high-ranking foreign intelligence officer, would prove the most sober and objective among Soviet officials opining on third-party prospects. Appointed ambassador to the United States in October 1947, he would warn Vyshinsky, in an embassy political report, that "the backbone of Wallace's movement [was] not the working class, but a liberal-bourgeois intelligentsia." And this class, he added, had "always demonstrated hesitations and instability in periods of reaction."[35] Shorn of its obligatory ideological flourishes, this judgment, too, would be vindicated. Wallace's natural appeal was to pacifist intellectuals, and not to laborers.

Around the same time as the meetings of Steel and Childs in Moscow, Wallace called on Soviet U.N. ambassador Andrey Gromyko in New York, saying he wished to discuss "only one thing."

"What do you think," Wallace asked him eagerly, "of my chances in the 1948 presidential election?" Gromyko was uncertain how to respond. "I was frankly perplexed by the question," he later recalled, "for it showed that he did not have a very accurate knowledge of the mood of the electorate"— which was souring on his "peace" theme. "I had the impression not only that Wallace had lost contact with the pulse of [American] political life, but that he also lacked experienced advisers." Both impressions were true enough, though possibly enhanced by post-election hindsight. In any case,

Gromyko, knowing that Wallace could, win or lose, do much good in attacking U.S. policy as a candidate, "gave him an encouraging response."[36]

The Kremlin's concern over collapsing progressive influence within the Democratic Party had been mounting since Roosevelt's death. Its near-total absence, now, was fueling the emergence of a bipartisan U.S. foreign policy aimed at containing the expansion of Soviet territory and influence.

In April 1947, following Truman's "Doctrine" speech to Congress, the foreign department of the Central Committee of the Communist Party (CC VCP (b)) produced a report on "The Progressive Movement in the USA," blaming its disintegration and disorganization for the Republican capture of Congress the November prior. Progressive leaders such as Claude Pepper, the report lamented, could not let go of their "barren dream of making an 'impact' on the Democratic Party." It contrasted Pepper with Henry Wallace, whom it praised. His inaugural column as editor of *The New Republic* had argued that the American people would reject "a Democratic Party that is not militantly progressive." Should the party prove "incapable of change," therefore, he held, progressives would need to "strike out along other lines."[37] A further report from the Foreign Policy Department, produced that same month, observed that any third party "organized without the participation of Wallace and his followers will hardly receive popular support."[38]

The Bolsheviks had long been intrigued by the idea of steering U.S. foreign policy through covert support for a "third party." They had first begun taking the prospect seriously in 1924, when Robert "Fighting Bob" La Follette ran for president on a Progressive Party platform calling for nationalization of key industries and ending American "imperialism" in Latin America. Thereafter, the Kremlin, which supported the CPUSA with annual concealed financial allowances, distributed through intelligence operatives, urged it to infiltrate new leftist movements and co-opt their leadership and agendas.

Following Marshall's Harvard speech in June 1947, the Soviets came to see Truman as beyond redemption. Between an imperialist Democrat and a Republican, there was no meaningful difference. It was Tweedledum and Tweedledee—just as Wallace had been arguing.

The Kremlin therefore approved of the current interest among the American Communists in aiding the "consolidation of all progressive anti-monopolist forces and organizations into a unified progressive coalition." That coalition, the Central Committee report noted, might take the form of "a new, third, political party, which could oppose both the Republican and Democratic parties."[39] The CPUSA, which was "now in the period of its recovery," had "built the groundwork for projecting its influence on the development of the progressive movement."[40] Yet it had to be more proactive and creative. It needed to "demonstrate more flexibility in expanding the front of the progressive movement and in strengthening [its own] leading role in this struggle."[41]

"A characteristic feature of the struggle," said Panyushkin's embassy report to Vyshinsky, "was the formation of two warring political camps: the reactionary camp (the Republican and Democratic parties) and the progressive-democratic camp (Henry Wallace's movement)." The Republican and Democratic parties "represent[ed] a joint party of the super-giant monopoly capital of the USA."[42] A coalition between the CPUSA and the Wallace progressives was, therefore, according to "journalist" Boris Vronsky, citing favorably the Marxist historian and CPUSA official James Allen in New York, "the only possible road of resistance to reaction and fascism."[43]

In reality, the emerging unity among Republicans and Democrats reflected a growing consensus among the American public, not to mention diplomatic and military elites, that a "containment" policy—as elaborated by George Kennan, and as embodied by the Marshall Plan—held out the best prospect for halting Soviet expansion without a resort to war. In any case, Moscow's only hope for friendlier policies in Washington now seemed to lay in the creation of a new party.

Its presidential candidate, the Kremlin understood, faced tremendous hurdles in 1948. Yet the party could still accomplish much. It could show the world that America was at war with itself over foreign policy. It could undermine public support for the Marshall Plan, in the United States and abroad. It could, in the words of Eugene Dennis at Madison Square Garden on September 18, 1947, create "new opportunities ... for the election of a progressive, anti-war and anti-monopoly Congress in 1948."[44] It could prod the Democrats, if they lost the White House, to embrace a socialist "peace candidate" in 1952. And it could field such a candidate if the Democrats did not. Given that the United States, now in the final phase of capitalist collapse, was bound to be in another Great Depression by then, victory seemed assured.

⁂

Throughout the spring and summer of 1947, a battle raged within both the progressive movement and the CPUSA over whether to challenge Truman within the Democratic Party or from a distance, through a third party. Prominent California liberal Robert Kenny, a former state attorney general and failed gubernatorial candidate, led the drive for Wallace to challenge Truman in the Democratic primaries. Even if Wallace lost, he reasoned, Truman might be so weakened that he would give way to a candidate of the left. Speaking before a conference in Fresno on July 19, many of whose three hundred delegates were concealed Communists, Kenny argued against a third party. If the Democrats nominated Truman, he warned, there would be a Republican president. But "with Wallace," he said, "we can win everything!"

Kenny was misreading the electoral landscape. Yes, Wallace was bringing out large, enthusiastic crowds. But the Communists had packed the rallies and ordered their surrogates to shout scripted cheers. Polls showed that Wallace faced enormous odds. A June 1947 Gallup poll, when Wallace was at the height of his popularity that year, had him trailing Truman 71 percent to 12 percent. Given a menu of nine Democratic contenders, respondents gave Truman the highest "favorable" rating and Wallace the highest "unfavorable." As one party veteran put it, "they don't like this Bolshevik stuff. They like the way Truman has told Stalin to go jump in the Pacific Ocean."

A week after the Fresno conference, a special meeting of the state Democratic Central Committee endorsed the Truman Doctrine and the Marshall Plan, while equating Communism with fascism. The vote was 170–19.[45] Democrats were coming together around Truman and his foreign policy, even as Wallace was claiming that two thirds of Americans opposed the Truman Doctrine. Asked by a surprised journalist where he had gotten his figure, Wallace replied: "I got it from a newspaper man." Forcing a laugh, he then added, "I must not betray the source."[46] The *Newark Star-Ledger* was not amused. With "the two great parties . . . united on foreign policy," they wrote, Wallace was seeking to unite "the Communists, the fellow-travelers, the isolationists, the extreme pacifists, the confused, the despairing, the broken-hearted, the hysterical and the skeptical."[47]

✳

Two developments, one at home and one abroad, ultimately conspired to push the CPUSA into backing a Wallace third-party run.

At home, Truman and the labor movement reconciled after the president's veto of the union-curbing Taft-Hartley Act on June 20, 1947. Though Congress overrode the veto, with considerable Democratic support, union leaders now began seeing Truman's election as their best hope for repealing the act. The president's action had, in the words of A. F. Whitney, the long-time president of the Brotherhood of Railroad Trainmen, "vindicated him in the eyes of labor." Challenging him through a third party was now "out of the question." CIO president Philip Murray, too, welcomed Truman's action, and concluded that a third-party challenge could only lead to the election of an antiunion Republican. This meant that Communist-inspired anti-Truman influence within the CIO had to be excised. "If Communism is an issue in any of your unions," he told his executive board in July, "throw it to hell out."[48]

Abroad, developments out of Moscow strengthened the hand of those in the CPUSA wanting a clean break with mainstream American institutions. Having concluded that any further cooperation between the European Communist parties and their non-Communist counterparts would only aid implementation of the Marshall Plan, Stalin determined to end it. In Central and Eastern Europe, he therefore set out to impose full Communist Party control, while in France and Italy he demanded that the Communists abandon electoral politics and work to seize power by extralegal means.

Central to Stalin's new offensive strategy was the creation of a new institution—the Communist Information Bureau, or "Cominform"—to coordinate action among Europe's Communist parties and to reinforce Soviet control. To bring the Cominform to life, the Kremlin convened a six-day conference of nine such parties, beginning on September 22, in the scenic Polish mountain village of Szklarska Poręba—home of the first winter games of the International Workers Olympiad two decades prior.[49] Only the Soviet delegation to the conference, chaired by Andrey Zhdanov, was told in advance about the new organization, or that the gathering's main objective was to mobilize "the struggle against attempts by American imperialism to enslave economically the countries of Europe"—otherwise known as the Marshall Plan.[50]

The world, Zhdanov told the gathered, had become divided into two hostile and irreconcilable camps—the "democratic" camp led by the Soviet Union, and the "imperialist" camp led by the United States. For the former, the "motives of aggression and exploitation are utterly alien." For the latter, in contrast, aggression and exploitation were essential to forestall the crisis of monopoly capitalism.

The Marshall Plan, he explained, was a necessary reaction to "the unfavorable reception with which the Truman doctrine was met" owing to its "imperialistic character." But it was merely "a more carefully veiled attempt to carry through the same expansionist policy." Its aim was to "create a bloc of states bound . . . to the United States," bribing them to renounce their independence. The Americans would give aid "not to the impoverished victor countries, America's allies in the fight against Germany, but to the German capitalists."

Of course, the Soviet Union had been invited to discuss the Marshall initiative in Paris. But the purpose was merely "to mask the hostile nature of the proposals," as it was "well known beforehand that the USSR would refuse [Marshall's] terms." If the Soviet Union had consented to participate, it would have been "easier to lure the countries of East and South-East Europe into the trap." But the USSR would see to it that the plan is "doomed to failure."[51]

Prior to Zhdanov's performance in Poland, Foster had been supportive of the third-party initiative but hesitant to move forward. "The present situation," he had written back in February, requires workers "to break definitely with the capitalist-controlled Republican and Democratic parties and go about setting up an independent anti-fascist, anti-monopoly party of their own."[52] Yet in September, with Democrats still showing no signs of splintering, he was unsure that a third party was the better option for a Wallace challenge. A third party, he said, according to an FBI recording of him in a hotel room, could only succeed with support from the CIO—and that support now looked unlikely. "The Communist Party must not make the mistake it made twenty years ago," he said, referring to its backing of La Follette in 1924, "or history will repeat itself and [we] will be no further ahead twenty years from now."[53] It was a prescient observation, and one that he himself might have been wise to heed.

Though Stalin had not intended the Polish conference to send any political message to the American Communists, Foster understood otherwise. The new Cominform policy, he believed, now required the CPUSA to pursue power from outside the Democratic Party and to cease cooperation with the reactionary CIO leadership.

On December 15, according to Transport Workers Union president "Red Mike" Quill, Dennis informed allied labor figures that the CPUSA had "decided to form a Third Party led by Henry Wallace." The Central Committee expected them to "line up endorsements" for Wallace as soon as he declared. Quill was livid, insisting it would sunder the CIO into rival factions. "To hell with you and your central committee!" he shouted. For the Communists, however, there was no turning back. "Get busy and support it!" came the response.

The Communists had never considered Wallace entirely reliable, but were convinced they could keep him on message to the extent that their agents enveloped him with support and blandishments. They accepted that he might break with them at some point, but considered that a risk worth bearing—provided that he continued to promote the aims of Soviet foreign policy. Besides, with the loss of the CIO as a base from which to attack the Marshall Plan, there was simply no better option.

When Quill raised his objections with Gerhart Eisler, the German émigré Communist and ex-Comintern agent, the latter assured him it was "in the best interests of the Soviet bloc." That, he said, was "the only reason." But Quill was a union man to his core, and didn't give a damn about the Soviet bloc. He broke with the party soon after.

For the Communists, there was still the matter of getting Wallace to commit to leading a new party, now that it was decided he must. "[N]o other candidate," recalled Johnny Gates,[54] editor of the *Daily Worker*, "could have made a third party even appear viable." And so the Communists worked on Wallace through concealed members installed in Popular Front organizations, as well as within his inner circle of advisers. Indeed, such agents had been prepping Wallace for two years.[55]

In Washington, there was growing concern with Wallace's suspected Soviet ties. The State Department asked the FBI to open an envelope addressed to him and to photocopy its contents. Hoover kept the president apprised of his activities.[56]

※

For Henry Wallace, the path to the White House lay in convincing the American people that he was Roosevelt's rightful heir, and that Truman was, in contrast, a usurper leading them toward World War III. It was far from clear that Roosevelt, however, had he lived, would have been any less of a Cold Warrior than Truman. He had made concessions in the cause of wartime cooperation with Stalin, though these were largely concessions to the realities of geography. Truman, further, had consummated all of them, from Poland to Manchuria, and in drawing the line at Turkey, Iran, and Germany can hardly be said to have pursued his country's interests more pugnaciously than had his predecessor. As UAW president Walter Reuther put it, "the very people in the CIO convention who were calling Roosevelt a war monger" in 1940 were the ones "now calling Truman a warmonger" in 1947.[57] In any case, Wallace would, by the end of that year, have to judge whether the usurper could be so weakened politically that he, Wallace, could take the Democratic nomination, or whether he would need a new base from which to launch a challenge.

Wallace began his campaigning in earnest in May 1947, on his return from Europe. At this point, *The New Republic* and the PCA, in spite of Michael Straight's apprehensions as to where the awkward association would lead, were bound to each other. Straight reasoned that the PCA could bring out the crowds, which would boost his weekly's circulation and shrink its deficits. And though the PCA, under Baldwin's leadership, had shrunk its own inherited deficit, it needed the help of Wallace's employer to organize a major speaking tour. And so, while the candidate-editor was still in Europe, Baldwin and *TNR* Washington editor Helen Fuller mapped out a plan to sell him to the nation.[58]

The rallies moved from city to city, east to west, across the country. The better ones were impeccably choreographed. Starting in the early evening, local notables would work up the crowd, denouncing Truman and the militarists. Then, the lights would extinguish, the crowd would hush, and a single ray of light would descend upon a door by the stage. From there would emerge the striking figure of the tall, broad African-American singer Paul Robeson. A courageous and committed civil rights advocate, a self-proclaimed "violent anti-fascist," a staunch apologist for Soviet policy and future winner of the "International Stalin Prize" (1952), Robeson would spend much of the coming decade defending unpopular views in Washington, refusing to affirm or deny being a Communist. At Wallace rallies, his job was to warm up the faithful with his powerful, mellifluous baritone voice—always beginning with his famed rendition of "Ol' Man River." Once having completed his repertoire, he would wait, smiling, for the programmed chants to rise—"WAL-LACE FOR PRES-I-DENT! WAL-LACE FOR PRES-I-DENT!"—cup his hand theatrically behind his right ear, and yell out: "YES! The people want Wallace for president! And if they can't have him as a Democrat, they'll know where to go!"[59] Cheers would erupt. Beanie Baldwin loved this part.

Rare for political events, admission was charged, ranging from 60 cents to $3.60 ($49 in today's money). Collection baskets snaked through the crowd, often doubling the take. Still, the star speaker would not appear until after a final appeal from Clark Foreman, a fiery Georgia native who would soon become the new party's treasurer. Only then, perhaps a half-hour before midnight, would the hall darken once more, beckoning the amassed to cheer anew, summoning forth the floodlights one final time, and impelling Henry Wallace to amble into the illuminated center of the stage, his unruly gray forelock searching for his left temple, waving and grinning ear to ear.

"WAL-LACE IN '48!" came the chant from the crowd.

Wallace's speeches had two main elements. The first was to denounce anti-Communism, at home and abroad. At home, "99 percent of those being called Communists actually were not that," he assured a gathering in Minneapolis on May 12. But those who were "should be treated as human beings." Abroad, America had to abandon the "doctrine of unlimited aid to anti-Soviet governments," he told a Chicago crowd of 22,000 on May 14, and "use American money through the United Nations for plows and tractors, rather than for guns and fighter planes." The second element of his speeches was to ready the public for the emergence of a new party. "[I]f the Democratic Party succumbs to Wall Street domination," he said in Washington, America had to have "a new party to let the . . . world know [it] has not gone completely imperialistic and psychopathic."[60]

As much as Baldwin loved these lines, they made Michael Straight wince. The hatred between the PCA and ADA, Straight was sure, was just a warm-up for what was to come if the PCA formed a political party—staffed, funded, and steered by the Communists.

"Do you know what you're doing?" he asked Baldwin.

Baldwin nodded. Yes, indeed. The Wallace tour had raked in $300,000 ($4 million in today's money). "Without the threat of a third party, we haven't a chance," he explained. It is "the only way we can make the Democratic bosses listen." And he still thought they might listen, believing he already had 110 votes lined up for Wallace at the 1948 Democratic convention.

"[And] if it doesn't work?" Then what?

Baldwin just smiled.[61]

Straight understood; if Truman should prove a lock for the nomination, Beanie would have his new party—Beanie and the CPUSA, that was. And in so doing, they would lead *TNR*'s editor, and perhaps the magazine itself, into oblivion. His only chance to stop it was therefore by appealing to the editor himself.

Wallace arrived back at his office in mid-June, his tour having both exhilarated and exasperated him. There were the huge, cheering crowds, but also the sharp, stinging snubs and scathing editorials. At the University of Texas, he had been greeted with hammer-and-sickle flags and trucks blaring strains of "The Internationale." In California, he had, incredibly, been barred from speaking at UC Berkeley and the Hollywood Bowl. In Chicago, the press had excoriated him and his supporters. The *Chicago Daily News* accused him of "reckless demagogy." A *Herald-American* headline mocked the sycophantic "Claque" at the city's stadium that "'Nominate[d]' Wallace President." The "carefully planned" demonstration, the paper said, had been "dominated by Left Wing elements."[62] Straight knew this take to be fair. And he was determined to open Wallace's eyes.

He went through each city on the tour.

"What did you think of Cleveland?"

"It was fair," Wallace said.

"That was a broadly sponsored meeting," Straight explained. Many liberal groups, even the ADA, had backed it. But no Communists.

"What about Chicago?" he then asked.

"Much better," Wallace said.

That one "was organized by a number of Communist-led unions," Straight explained.

Silence.

And "Los Angeles?" Straight asked.

"A great rally," Wallace responded. Twenty-eight thousand had come out, film stars included. Even Katharine Hepburn had turned up to rail against HUAC.[63]

"Once again," Straight said, "Communist-led."

"Can you prove that?"

"No," Straight admitted. He knew only which meetings had Communist sponsorship. But he recognized their tactics, which he had learned in Cambridge and Washington. Of this education, he would say nothing to anyone—at least not until 1963 when, wishing to return to government, he faced a background check.

Wallace, in any case, was unmoved by Straight's claims. If you can't prove it, he told the young publisher, "then you shouldn't say it."

But Straight went on. How about Seattle and San Francisco?

"Fair," said Wallace.

No Communists. And Portland?

"Very good."

Communists.

Wallace shrugged. "They get out the crowds."

Not just that, Straight knew. They tell them what to yell and when to yell it. But, as Dwight Macdonald observed, Wallace had by that time come to see himself as "a Messiah" for whom all "who are with him are good" and "all against him are bad."[64] It was, to Wallace, inconceivable that those who cheered him were moved by anything more, or less, than a sincere desire for world peace and honest leadership.

Or as FDR Brain Truster Rex Tugwell had put it years earlier, Wallace had developed the "habit of rationalizing, as direct messages from God, the dirty deals and compromises" that drive politics. This habit explained why he did not want to know—or at least not yet—whether the men promoting him were Communists. For if he did know, his rationalizations might be that much harder to sustain.

At that moment, the publisher was torn. Should he give Wallace an ultimatum? Beanie or *The New Republic*?

Straight knew what Hale would later explain in *Harper's*: that "the invisible audience of a magazine meant less and less to Wallace" as he experienced more and more the thrill of a "visible audience to cheer him on."

Wallace had hardly been to the office for months. But Straight could not—at least not yet—afford to lose his celebrity editor. And, so, fearing Wallace's answer, Straight held his tongue.[65]

The summer was a quiet one for Wallace, spent mostly relaxing at Farvue and driving through New England. He wrote columns about farming—about "crossing and inbreeding chickens" and "experimenting with strawberries."[66] It seemed that even when his message was political, he couldn't help talking about farming—matters like the "great new progressive movement" taking shape in rural North Dakota.[67]

In June, following his national tour, support for Wallace heading a new party had reached a new high: 13 percent. But it started falling steadily from there.[68] The press, which had been hostile during Wallace's European tour, became indifferent after his American one. "For many months," Macdonald observed, "Wallace has had no front-page headlines and very few inside-page stories."

And the main reason was clear. "On both the domestic and the foreign-policy front, the Truman Administration [had] stolen his thunder."[69] With Truman's veto of Taft-Hartley, he was reconciling with labor. With the Marshall Plan, he was reconciling with liberals. Truman's vulnerability now, such as it was, seemed to lay on the *right*—with the Southern Democrats who voted to override his veto—rather than with the left. In the spring, Wallace had capitalized on a sense that Democrats were losing touch with FDR's base. But now, it was hardly enough for him to say he had fought for workers *before* Truman had, or that he had been for helping Europe *before* Marshall. Now, it seemed, he would have to contrive new battles, to make himself more radical, just to be heard.

As the summer came to a close, he was still undecided about a third-party run. He told associates he wanted to feel sure of winning at least three million votes before committing.[70] His Labor Day editorial in *The New Republic* showed that his hope still lay in defeating Truman on his own party turf. Progressives, he wrote, should be focused on "winning control of the Democratic convention." Yet he showed no willingness to compromise, or even to be civil, to make himself the party's choice. Instead, he blasted "the self-styled liberals" in his party who were "kowtowing to reaction."[71]

Whereas he affirmed that he "intended to stay in the Democratic Party and attempt to reform it,"[72] it was clear that he would not fight to lead it—he would expect the party to earn his candidacy.

By now, Hale observed, Wallace "had surrounded himself with . . . advisers . . . bent on getting him to break out of the Democratic party and wreak vengeance on it." They "knew his susceptibility as a discarded heir [to Roosevelt] who would like to see Harry Truman's house brought down."[73] And so, when it was announced that Wallace would begin speaking at PCA rallies once again, Straight despaired. "The progressive movement is disintegrating," he wrote to his mother on September 20.[74]

Anxious to lure Wallace off the PCA circuit, Straight soon found the perfect bait. On September 3, a special U.N. commission had recommended a plan to partition Palestine into two states, one Jewish and one Arab. On October 11, the Truman administration accepted partition in principle. Wallace strongly supported the creation of a Jewish state, and was fascinated by the agricultural challenges of the area. Straight reckoned, correctly, that Wallace would leap at the opportunity to travel there. PCA leaders initially resisted, but ultimately reasoned that the trip would boost Jewish donations.

On October 14, three days before his trip, Wallace, accompanied by Johannes Steel, visited the Soviet consulate in New York to meet with Vyshinsky and Deputy Minister of Foreign Affairs Valerian Zorin—both in town for the U.N. General Assembly meetings. Vyshinsky's account of the hour-long discussion, distributed to Stalin and the Kremlin elite, shows Wallace determined both to showcase his goodwill and to extract evidence of Stalin's.

"Wallace," reported Vyshinsky, "fully agreed" that the fault over the state of U.S.-Soviet relations lay with "the new course of Truman-Marshall." He wanted "assurance," however, "that Moscow did not give instructions to Communist parties in other nations." Wallace "knew such allegations were groundless," but was anxious for confirmation.

Vyshinsky, of course, was only too happy to comply. He did so notwithstanding the fact that Moscow had ordered Communist parties abroad to condemn the Marshall Plan, and would, in February 1948, order the CPUSA to "direct its entire activity toward reaching [the] goal [of] securing the election of progressive figures as president[,] vice-president[,] senators and members of the House of Representatives."

Cautiously, his report concluded that Wallace had made "a reasonably good impression." He had shown himself "an unpretentious and thoughtful man with a good understanding of politics." He was, also, and not incidentally, "sympathetic to us" and "somewhat naïve."[75]

Straight, anxiously preparing for the journey to the Holy Land, knew nothing of this meeting. He planned to use the flight over, on October 17, to convince Wallace that others were using him for ignoble ends, and that the result would be the demise of liberal solidarity and his own political fortunes. He needed to quash the new-party talk. Once on the plane, however, Wallace sat with his speechwriter, Lew Frank. Straight lost his chance.[76]

Or this, at least, is Straight's story. Given that he lived two weeks among Wallace's tiny entourage in Palestine, it is implausible that he could not find an opportunity to raise his concerns. More likely, the candidate-in-waiting was uninterested in them.

As for Palestine, Wallace billed the trip as an effort "to see whether in any way my knowledge of agriculture and industry would tend to facilitate the cause of peace in the Near East."[77] It did not, but neither did he set off diplomatic storms—as he had in Europe. He kept to a harmless agenda, visiting kibbutzim, tilling fields with Jewish farmers, and folk-dancing in battered tennis shoes. Though he met with a few labor leaders and politicians, he confined his public observations to what were, in the American political context of the time, banalities. He "saw evidence," he said, "that the Jew and the Arab get along very well, provided hatred and discord are not incited from the outside." He urged both peoples to "abide faithfully by the ultimate decisions of the United Nations." His one policy statement was a call for the creation of a Jordan Valley economic and environmental authority modeled on the TVA.

On his way home, Wallace stopped in Rome for a visit with Pope Pius XII. He learned nothing as to what His Holiness planned to "do for Palestine," but did return to New York on November 4 with two custom-blessed papal rosaries.[78] He penned a December column inspired by his trip, warning that governments following "the doctrine of Machiavelli instead of the doctrines of Christ" would mean "the perpetuation of . . . dictatorship and falsehood [and] war."[79] Wallace may have doubted Truman's commitment to Christ's doctrines, though he continued to show faith in Stalin's.

As for Stalin, his intelligence apparatus had been tailing Wallace in Rome. "Agent sources" reported "a confidential conversation" in which Wallace expressed confidence that, "in the case of his election as president, . . . relations between the USSR and the USA [could] be brought into normality within five years."[80] With each passing month, it seemed, the Kremlin was finding the prospect of a Wallace presidential run more and more intriguing.

On October 24, Straight was reading a translation of Zhdanov's speech introducing the manifesto of the new nine-nation Cominform. When he got to the part warning of the "danger to the international working class" in "underestimat[ing] its own power," it struck him. The American Communists, who invariably heard dog whistles in such talk, would take it as an order to abandon efforts at converting the reactionary union bosses.

Straight called Harold Young in Washington, telling him "there's going to be a third party." Young thought Straight "crazy," or at least he hoped he was. He had always found third-party talk useful as a club to wield against the Democrats, who might still be persuaded to dump Truman. But it was, to him, still no more than a toy club.

Baldwin, however, agreed with Straight. "You won't get the liberals," Straight warned him. "Don't count on *The New Republic*." Disappointed as he was, Baldwin was hardly shocked. He asked Straight to speak to John Abt. Abt, the sharp-witted general counsel for the Amalgamated Clothing Workers union, had been tasked by Baldwin with exploring how to get Wallace's name on state ballots. If Abt could not persuade Straight to back Wallace, Baldwin reasoned, he would at least get some insight into the media challenges the third party would face.

Straight found the lawyer quiet and respectful, but determined. "We'll go through with our plan," Abt told him, with or without *TNR* backing. "The world must be told that not all Americans have given up hope for peace."[81] He was convinced he could get Wallace on at least forty state ballots.

Abt would go on to become the new party's general counsel, after first warning Wallace of what he would inevitably find out—that his wife, Jessica Smith, was editor of *Soviet Russia Today*, and that his sister was the CPUSA's public relations director. Wallace could not have cared less. He was, in Abt's words, "no more alarmed than he would have been had I informed him of my admittance to the Illinois bar." Wallace would later explain that Abt, in spite of these associations, had assured him that he, Abt, was no Communist. And that assurance was more than sufficient.[82]

But Abt, an accomplished liar, was lying. He was a longtime concealed party member, having in the 1930s been an active Ware group adherent. He would go on to become the CPUSA's chief counsel in 1950, and only admit his earlier associations in a memoir published forty-six years later.

In his efforts to shepherd Wallace into the new party, Abt was ably aided by Lee Pressman. So wedded was the relentless CIO general counsel to Wallace's candidacy that he was prepared to sever his links with the powerful labor body. The CIO, which had backed Wallace for vice president against Truman in '44, but opposed him now, would fire Pressman in February 1948. Two years later, Pressman would—under pressure from the FBI, and anxious to avoid espionage charges—confess to Congress his CPUSA and Ware group memberships in the 1930s, as well as his covert CPUSA allyship in the late '40s. Yet agent "Vig," as he was soon to be known in Moscow, would successfully conceal his far more consequential history, over two decades, as part of the KGB's support network for its American spies. Although Wallace would claim to have seen no "evidence" of Pressman's Communist affiliation, his diary suggested otherwise. An October 1942 entry tagged Pressman as part of the CIO's "communist group."[83]

Others friendly to the Communists—Hannah Dorner, Jo Davidson, and Lew Frank—were, by late 1947, also important in persuading Wallace to break with the Democrats. The soft-spoken but persistent Frank, in his dual role with the magazine and the PCA, was particularly effective in "quashing editorial projects which might not serve [Wallace] politically," and in "isolating him from other influences"—including Straight himself. Whereas in early 1947 Wallace was willing to write about American suspicions of Soviet intentions (without validating them), by the late spring, with the PCA sentinels having closed in around him, he now considered such commentary unproductive. When his editors presented him with a draft piece highlighting areas where the Soviets might allay U.S. suspicions, he quashed it, saying he could not hope to influence matters in Moscow. He would stick to criticizing policy at home.[84]

Over in Moscow, on November 9, the newly named Soviet ambassador to Washington, Panyushkin, paid a protocol visit to his U.S. opposite number: Ambassador Walter Bedell Smith. Panyushkin sounded Smith out on the U.S. presidential election, asking for his take on Wallace.

Smith frowned. For Wallace, he said, "all was lost."

Panyushkin looked surprised. Surely, he said, Wallace's calls "for co-operation between our two nations should be positively received by broad circles within the American public?"

No, Smith insisted. As a cabinet member, Wallace had made an "irreme-diable political mistake"—attacking his government's foreign policy. Since that time, "Americans consider Wallace to be disloyal to the nation."[85]

Many, of course, considered Wallace an enlightened patriot for the forth-right way in which he had pursued the cause of peace. But many more had objected to the public manner in which he had fought his cause from within.

On November 21, 1947, Beanie Baldwin informed PCA state directors that efforts to secure a sizable bloc of delegates at the Democratic national con-vention were not bearing fruit. They, in turn, informed him that further delay in launching a third party would hurt morale among its backers and reduce the number of states in which Wallace could get on the ballot. Bald-win particularly feared losing a ballot spot in California.[86] On December 2, with pressure now rising on Wallace, much of it coming from Baldwin sur-rogates, he informed Baldwin that he would accept a third-party nomina-tion.

Wallace may have concluded that his three-million vote target was now achievable, yet he also knew he would need 20 million more to become presi-dent. So why did he actually decide to take on Truman from the outside? Wallace's later answers were curious, in that he claimed not to recall his own state of mind at the time. "There must have been something that caused me to think in December that the Democratic Party would not become a genuine peace party," he said in 1951. "I don't remember what it was, but there must have been something."[87] In Hale's view, Wallace's real reason was twofold.

The first was "vengeance," a view for which there is evidence.[88] When pressed privately by a businessman with a delegation of Massachusetts no-tables to explain why he wanted to run, Wallace did not fall back on wonk-ery or platitudes. "Harry Truman," he responded, "is a son-of-a-bitch."[89]

The second reason was more substantial, but not unrelated to the first.

Wallace was, Hale wrote, "willing to enter upon an adventure calculated simply to destroy his rival in the White House and to increase domestic tensions in preparation for another election in 1952."[90] A Republican president would, according to Wallace's neo-Marxian view, usher in a new depression that would demand a second, more robust, New Deal.[91] For this claim, too, there is much support in Wallace's own words. A year earlier, at the PCA inaugural convention, he had stated bluntly that "we, as progressives, would prefer the election of an out-and-out reactionary like Taft in 1948 to a luke-warm liberal."[92] Wallace's candidacy certainly appeared to increase the likelihood that Taft, or a fellow Republican "reactionary," would win the election. Wallace thought he could beat that reactionary in '52. This conclusion is borne out in Soviet intelligence from a French NKGB source (code name "Cyrano"). "Wallace thinks a Republican will be elected," read that report, based on an April 1947 conversation in Paris between Wallace and radical socialist Pierre Cot. "According to W[allace], a third party has no chance of succeeding in 1948." But the party "will exert influence on the Democrats and prepare for the 1952 election."[93]

The PCA was far from united on the third-party venture, however—or even on Wallace's candidacy. Kingdon, who had at Madison Square Garden on April 1 been cheered on as he urged Wallace to lead a "people's party," was by the fall opposed. Having concluded that public support for the venture was shallow and ebbing, he wrote a column in the *New York Post* on December 4 calling on Truman and Wallace to "sit down together" and "talk over 1948." At Jo Davidson's apartment the following day, Baldwin remonstrated Kingdon over the piece.

Many charged that the PCA co-chair had personal or financial reasons for changing his mind and opposing Wallace. Regardless, Baldwin had, in any case, infuriated many PCA notables by bypassing the organization's National Board and presenting the third party as a fait accompli.

At the heart of the battle within the PCA is the extent to which the organization and its candidate-in-waiting had become captives of outside forces—namely, the CPUSA. "Who asked Henry Wallace to run?" Kingdon demanded in the *Post* on December 31. The answer, he wrote, was clear: "The Communist Party, through William Z. Foster and Eugene Dennis, were the first."[94] CPUSA official Johnny Gates, who had in June been among those in the leadership calling for "the movement to build a third party [to] be accelerated," would years later claim that Baldwin had been one of them. "BB was a Communist," Gates would say. He was "the chief agent of Dennis . . . in influencing Wallace." Gates' wife would, after his death, swear that his statement had been "absolutely true."[95] Yet whether Baldwin was or was not himself a Communist, there is no doubt that he had worked closely with them in the effort.

Whereas Wallace never failed to point out his religious disagreements with Communists, he praised them for the passion of their wrong beliefs. "I admire their utter devotion to a cause they think is just," he said in December 1947.[96] They "are the closest things to the early Christian martyrs we have today."[97] This tendency of Wallace's, to elevate feeling over truth, intention over accomplishment, vision over reality, authenticity over objectivity, had long been hallmarks of his persona.

As to having Communists working for his campaign, "anyone who will work for peace is okay with me," he said.[98] The CPUSA, after all, had over sixty thousand acknowledged members[99]—highly motivated men and women who would organize events, ring doorbells, stuff envelopes, solicit money, and collect the hundreds of thousands of signatures required to get him onto state ballots. But Wallace was never clear as to what he meant by "work for peace." He had, after all, supported all-out *war* with Imperial Japan—and not peace; all-out *war* with Nazi Germany—and not peace. Did "peace" therefore simply mean "peace with the Soviet Union"? And was there no point at which the obligation to "work for peace" might collide with the imperative to avoid appeasement? And if such a collision were indeed possible, and perhaps even likely, were not there then grounds for rejecting the support of Communists—most of whom followed the Kremlin unfailingly? Wallace would never answer these questions.

Part of the problem with Wallace was psychological. He had great difficulty in recognizing duplicity. He had not recognized it in his Soviet handlers in Siberia. He had not recognized it in Roosevelt—at least not until the facts had rendered it unmistakable, by which time it was too late. And he did not recognize it in his supporters now, believing that their commitment to him evinced their honest devotion to the supreme moral goal of "peace." When delegations from local unions would show up at Wallace's office to tell him that the "rank and file" supported him, no matter what Phil Murray and the CIO said; when religious and ethnic group emissaries appeared to tell him the people were with him; when speechwriters arrived to volunteer their services—it would not occur to Wallace that they were other than the purest exemplars of Christian goodwill.

As for Wallace's belief that he spoke for "the people," even Marxist publications were disdainfully amused. "Populism, indeed!" exclaimed the Trotskyist *New International*, mocking Wallace's pretense to having imbibed this tradition. "Would William Jennings Bryan—who . . . could attract whole counties to his flaming speeches—have been taken in by delegations from . . . the New York District Council of the CIO Electrical Workers, the Slovenian section of the Passaic IWO, and the Freiheit Mandolin Society?" The PCA, unlike Bryan and the nineteenth-century populists, was almost entirely an upper-middle-class urban Protestant and Jewish intellectual phenomenon, with no rural or working-class roots. It further bore more connection with "Stalin than with Bryan," in that its emergence and transformation into a political movement was largely in obeisance to the dictator's growing animosity toward Truman.[100]

Warnings from old friends in Commerce, such as Phil Hauser, of the dangers inherent in the third party made no impact on Wallace. Pleas from liberal venerables, such as Eleanor Roosevelt and Claude Pepper, made no impact. Lectures from Straight and Bliven made no impact. If the eager new friends urging him on were Communists, Wallace explained to them, well, "nobody else comes forward to arrange meetings for me."[101] When combined with a flawed sense of self-interest—the sense that there was more to gain in embracing Communist support than in repudiating it—Wallace's inability to see how others might use him for purposes other than his own appeared, to many, to be setting him up for a career-ending failure.

Up to the last minute, Wallace kept everyone guessing. On December 13, he said publicly that he might, after all, support the "entire Democratic ticket in 1948." But Baldwin shut him up and pressed on. Fearing that the window of opportunity was closing rapidly, he refused demands from Helen Fuller and others that the PCA delay a decision on the third party until the scheduled National Board meeting in mid-January. Abt, ever the able lawyer, invoked an obscure bylaw to rule a motion to delay out of order. On December 15, Baldwin convened a PCA executive committee meeting to approve a statement urging Wallace to run. The debate was stormy, but the resolution passed with only Kingdon, among the members present, voting against. That same day, the CPUSA leadership directed its adherents in the labor movement to line up rank-and-file support for Wallace.

Kingdon and other PCA officials resigned in protest. Some of the dissidents objected to Wallace. Others supported Wallace, and might have backed him as a Democrat in '48 or '52, but believed that the third party would flop and destroy the PCA. Still others, such as New York State PCA chairman Raymond Walsh, worried that the party would become "a stalking horse for the Communists."[102]

But Baldwin cared little what the naysayers thought. He was ebullient. The "New Party," as it was to be provisionally known, was born, and Henry Agard Wallace was to be its leader.

Wallace officially announced his candidacy in a twenty-minute radio broadcast on December 29, 1947, the one-year anniversary of the PCA. Forgotten, it seems, was his stern warning, seventeen months prior, that a third-party contender would "guarantee a reactionary victory by dividing the votes of progressives."[103]

Truman offered no public comment, though he understood privately that having a "Dixiecrat" fighting him from the right (South Carolina Segregationist Governor Strom Thurmond) and a "Progressive" from the left made beating a Taft or a Dewey that much harder. Wallace, the president would write in his memoirs, "was not an opponent to be discounted." Though he had "transformed [himself] into a mystic with a zeal that verged on fanaticism," and had no chance of winning any states, he would "cost me votes."[104] Many of those would be in battleground states, and might therefore be decisive if, as expected, the race was hard-fought and close. Democrats, broadly, also feared the New Party's threat to oppose all of their candidates backing the Marshall Plan, which, if carried out, might hand winnable congressional seats to the GOP.

Republicans were, in consequence, giddy at Wallace's entry into the race. "Yes, Republicans, there is a Santa Claus," wrote one *Chicago Sun* wit. "His name is Henry Wallace."[105] The CPUSA, too, naturally, hailed Wallace's "momentous decision." The *Daily Worker* greeted his candidacy as "historic." Wallace was, in the words of Irwin Ross, a chronicler of the '48 campaign, "an enormous prize for the Communists." He was "a figure of international stature, a former Vice-President of the United States, and a man for whom the mantle of F.D.R. could be insistently claimed." Who better as a figurehead behind which to march into power, thereafter to remake the country's economic system and reorient its entire foreign-policy apparatus?

This logic prompted one mainstream reporter to ask Wallace if such backers might be agents of Moscow. Although Wallace had, a few months prior, claimed to have met only a single declared Communist in his life (a *Daily Worker* reporter), he responded now by saying that he had asked "every Communist" he met whether they were agents of Moscow. To his surprise, he explained, they all told him that "Moscow doesn't seem to want anything to do with them."[106] And given the Kremlin's desire to see Wallace portrayed in America as the embodiment of a grassroots rejection of the Marshall Plan, this statement rang true. When asked whether he repudiated Communist support, Wallace said he did not and would not. He would "do exactly as Roosevelt would have done." And for good measure, he added that they "could look up the record on that"—which they did. Roosevelt had declared, in October 1944, that he did "not welcome the support of any person or group committed to Communism."[107]

The rancorous split in the progressive field that Straight had so feared became a reality. Eleanor Roosevelt, who had been so pained by her husband's ditching of Wallace in '44, now took him to task in print. As her country's first representative on the U.N. Commission on Human Rights, she, unlike Wallace, had dealt with the Soviets firsthand. "[T]hey say many things they know are not true because they think they can make others believe they are true," she wrote. "They understand strength, not weakness." Wallace, unfortunately, was "doing more wishful thinking than realistic facing of facts." He had "never . . . been a good politician," had "never . . . been able to gauge public opinion," and had never "picked his advisers wisely." If he does not rethink his venture, she wrote, he would "merely destroy the very things he wishes to achieve."[108]

As for Straight, he would now have to reckon not only with the crushing of his hopes for a revived, unified progressive movement, but with the knotty consequences for his magazine. He could not allow candidate Wallace to continue on as "editor." He would, however, allow Wallace to continue writing weekly columns as a "contributing editor." This arrangement, which would survive until August 1948, would be awkward, as Straight intended for *TNR* to endorse Truman. Just how awkward would be made clear in Wallace's final column as editor, on January 5, in which he characterized the choice between Truman and a Republican as one "between two degrees of evil." As for those who now suggested that he and the third-party founders were "Russian tools" (among whom was Straight), they were, he wrote, "using the weapons of Adolf Hitler."[109]

For his part, Baldwin was determined to market Wallace as the true champion of the Common Man. "If you underestimate the rank-and-file feeling among American workers for Henry Wallace," he warned in a letter to *PM*, "you are making a cardinal political error. . . . By asserting ourselves *now* we can give organized, powerful, effective expression to the yearning for peace, jobs, and freedom among our people."

Public opinion was not bearing him out. Wallace's support had fallen through the autumn. On foreign policy, one October 1947 poll found that a mere 6 percent of Americans thought Truman "too tough" on the Soviets, while 62 percent thought him "*too soft.*" In one Washington-State special congressional election in June 1947, the PCA brought Wallace in to speak on behalf of Democrat Charles Savage—who proceeded to lose in spite of a two-to-one poll lead three weeks prior. In another race, in Pennsylvania, Wallace-camp activists infiltrating the campaign of Democrat Philip Storch so alienated voters that, in spite of the angry candidate buying ad space pledging support for the Marshall Plan, he went on to defeat in a landslide that defied even the most optimistic Republican predictions. By late December, Wallace was polling behind Taft, sponsor of the Taft-Hartley Act so loathed by labor, more than two to one *among union members.*[110] Whether the issue was "peace" or jobs, the Common Man seemed to have all but abandoned him.

Wallace would later claim that he "wasn't aware in those days of all the internal divisions in labor" or "how significant they were as political forces."[111] As remarkable as that seems, given the salience of such divisions in 1947 press accounts, it partly reflects the fact that his advisers only granted audiences to labor figures urging him to run. From all Wallace saw and heard, face-to-face, which was all that mattered to him, he was indeed the Common Man's candidate. And to the extent that polls suggested otherwise, it did not dishearten him. To the contrary, it fueled his sense of being on a selfless, righteous mission.

"We have assembled a Gideon's Army," Wallace said in his December 29 radio address, an army "small in number, powerful in conviction, ready for action."[112] That term, "Gideon's Army," referred to the tiny band of three hundred Israelites which, according to the Old Testament Book of Judges, defeated a vastly larger Midianite force in c. 1200 BC. But it was a somewhat awkward analogy. Gideon, on God's orders, had winnowed his force of ten thousand to a fanatically impassioned one of three hundred. But Wallace was no Gideon. Wallace, for want of men of faith, was scrounging for Communists.

Sixteen

COLLUSION

Though it had a mutual assistance treaty with the USSR, Czechoslovakia, which bordered both western Germany and Ukraine, was a weak link in Stalin's defensive perimeter. Its Communists trumpeted pursuit of the country's "own path" to socialism, which explained why they enjoyed greater popular support there than elsewhere in the East. But the United States and Britain had, according to a European Department official of the Soviet Foreign Ministry, worryingly "established their own centers of influence" in the country. "Reactionary forces" had become "more active in the struggle against progressive forces in the country"—that is, the Communists.[1] Given that Czechoslovakia was now one of the main sources of uranium for Moscow's atomic weapons program,[2] Stalin was on alert for signs of trouble.

These signs had been building since the previous summer. On the eve of the Cominform gathering in September 1947, Molotov had complained to Zhdanov about the unreliability of the Czechoslovak armed forces, and instructed him to raise the matter in Szklarska Poręba. Jan Masaryk, the non-Communist Czech foreign minister, meanwhile, continued to lament Stalin prohibiting Czech participation in the Marshall Plan. "We know that the United States will not consider us its favorite sons after the rejection of the Marshall Plan," he told the Czech paper *Svobodné Slovo* in October, "but we hope they will not completely forsake us."[3] In December, the Soviet embassy in Prague cabled Moscow about troubling political developments: "Reactionary elements within the country, actively supported by representatives of the West, [believe] that the parties of the right will receive a majority at the forthcoming [May 1948] elections and that the Communists will be thrown out of the government." Early in the new year, the National Socialists, the second largest party behind the Communists, expressed public regret about not having joined in the Marshall Plan.[4] Elements in the Communist Party now began agitating for Moscow to intervene. Stalin, who had been careful not to hand the West propaganda opportunities or to provoke anti-Communist underground forces in the East, decided it was now time to make clear to which bloc the country belonged.

George Kennan had warned this would happen back in November. "As long as communist political power was advancing in Europe, it was advantageous to the Russians to allow to the Czechs the outer appearances of freedom." It would permit the Czechs "to serve as bait for the nations further west." But once the "danger of the political movement proceeding in the other direction" became apparent in Moscow, the Russians would no longer be able to "afford this luxury." Czechoslovakia could stir liberal democratic forces elsewhere in the East. At that point, the Russians will "clamp down completely on Czechoslovakia," even though they "will try to keep their hand well concealed and leave us no grounds for formal protest."[5]

On February 18, 1948, the four National Socialist Party ministers—party chairman Peter Zenkl, Foreign Trade Minister Hubert Ripka, Justice Minister Prokop Drtina, and Education Minister Jaroslav Stránský—went to see the non-Communist president, Edvard Beneš, to express their alarm over the Communist purging of the Interior Ministry. Hard-line minister Václav Nosek was systematically replacing police commissioners with party loyalists, ignoring protests that his actions were illegal.[6] Above all else, Zenkl explained, it was "absolutely necessary to stop the communization of the police" and the distribution of their arms and ammunition. The National Socialists, Populists, and Slovak Democrats would therefore resign their twelve ministerial posts, amounting to half the cabinet, in advance of the Communist union congress on the 22nd. The mass resignation would prevent the Communists from shifting the spotlight from security to nationalization of industry, an issue on which they would gain support from the left-wing Social Democrats. The ministers wanted Beneš to demand the resignation of the remaining cabinet members from Communist prime minister Klement Gottwald, paving the way for either a new government that would reverse the security measures or new elections.

Beneš, who had previously said that he "would not stand for non-Communist parties being eaten up one by one as had occurred in other eastern European countries,"[7] buoyed them by agreeing to back new elections. The Communists, he said, would never give way, as they could not win elections without controlling the police. As for the Russians orchestrating the crisis, the brutal way they had blocked Marshall aid for the country still angered him. The Bolsheviks "shriek against Western imperialism to distract attention from their own aggressive expansionism," Beneš said. "They are provoking the whole world" with their behavior.[8]

The Soviet deputy foreign minister arrived in Prague unannounced the following day, February 19. Officially, Valerian Zorin was on a mission to inspect Russian grain supplies. Masaryk and Ripka were incredulous. They understood that Zorin's presence was meant to demonstrate Moscow's support for the new Communist security measures.

Zorin, according to U.S. ambassador Laurence Steinhardt, was "not a forceful, door-slamming type" like Vyshinsky. But he delivered his boss' messages clearly enough. Meeting with Gottwald, the Russian told him the time had come to "be firmer" and to stop making "concessions to those on the right." The premier had "to be ready for decisive action and for the possibility of breaching the formal stipulations of the constitution and the laws as they stand."

Gottwald, Zorin reported back to Molotov, did not want to move against the president, who had wide popular support. The premier still clung, Zorin lamented, to "the idea of a normal, parliamentary path . . . without any collisions." Yet he was ready to act more forcefully with Moscow's support. Gottwald wanted Soviet troop maneuvers on the country's borders to pressure Beneš. Stalin, however, still acting in accordance with Kennan's script, refused to provide such overt cover. As Washington had neither the will nor the means to resist, there was no need to put on a show of menace: he would rely on the Secret Police he had sent into Prague a few days earlier. Communist information minister Václav Kopecký, however, declared that the Red Army was massed on the frontiers, ready to intervene against the "reaction." The Soviet embassy remained silent.

On February 20, with no sign that the Communists would abandon their takeover of the police, the twelve non-Communist ministers submitted their resignations. Gottwald rejoiced at the naïveté of their tactic. "I could not believe it would be so easy. . . . I prayed that this stupidity over the resignations would go on." He denounced them as "lackeys of domestic and foreign reaction, traitors to the nation" who could never be part of a new government.

They want to make the country "a paradise for all the spies and saboteurs sent among us from abroad against our Republic and . . . the Soviet Union."

Beneš tried to reassure the democrats. "Naturally, I shall not accept your resignation[s]," he told the anxious ministers. "The Communists must give in," he insisted. "I will not compromise." But the president had also been speaking to Gottwald, and his public comments were less clear-cut. He told the press he would accept neither "a Cabinet of technicians"—which Gottwald falsely claimed his opponents wanted to impose—nor one without Communists. There was no defense of the democrats, nor any demand that the *entire* cabinet resign.

Meanwhile, the Communists were organizing Bolshevik-style "Committees of Action" around the country and ordering police officials to pledge their "loyal[ty] to the Government of Klement Gottwald" and to "obey all the orders of the Minister of the Interior." Workers were instructed to attend Communist rallies around the country. Those who refused were locked out or beaten. Ripka found the rhythmic ovations at the events terrifyingly similar to those delivered at demonstrations staged by the Nazi occupiers just a few years earlier.

On February 21, Gottwald told Beneš that if he refused to accept the resignations and allow the formation of a Communist government there would be a general strike and workers' militias in the streets. "Then there is also the Soviet Union!" he added pointedly.[9] The next day, Zorin and the entire Soviet embassy staff attended a Communist-organized congress of the Union of Soviet-Czechoslovak Friendship, timed to commemorate the thirtieth anniversary of the Red Army. Gottwald used the occasion to blast "the Western imperialists" who were "trying to revive capitalism" and fuel German "irredentism." It was, he said, necessary to stand with the country's Soviet ally. "The law," he closed, "should strike all those who undermine the basis of our foreign policy." *Pravda* and Radio Moscow backed the Czech Communists unreservedly, which was duly reported in the Czech Communist press. Still, Beneš insisted to the National Socialist ministers that he would not give way to a "*coup d'état*" or "second Munich."

But Beneš was ill and infirm, and the pressure around him was growing by the hour. On February 23, Minister of Defense General Ludvík Svoboda declared that the army "stands today, and will stand tomorrow, beside the U.S.S.R. and its other allies, to guarantee the security of our dear Czechoslovak Republic." The Communist-controlled Interior Ministry occupied the offices of the non-Communist press, instituting measures to prevent them "from disturbing public opinion by lies and provocations." By the 25th, they were taking the same editorial line as Moscow and the Communists.

Gottwald secured the cooperation of rebel members of the non-Communist parties, effectively making them part of his own party, and submitted a new cabinet list to the president. A communiqué declared the commitment of the new "Renovated National Front" to "the purging of the political parties, whose responsible leaders have abandoned the principles of the National Front," and to "tighten[ing] the alliance with the Soviet Union and the other Slav States." Steinhardt cabled Washington, comparing Gottwald's political tactics to those of Hitler.[10] Bohlen had years earlier opined that "a non-Communist Premier with Communist ministers would be like a woman trying to stay half-pregnant,"[11] but Gottwald's action suggested that a Communist premier with non-Communist ministers was also implausible.

At noon on February 25, to the shock of the now former National Socialist ministers, the country learned from the radio that Beneš had accepted their resignations. Telephoning his office, Ripka would be told only that the president had approved Gottwald's cabinet list. Swearing in the new ministers on the 27th, Beneš would explain that he was trying to prevent the crisis escalating. "[T]he people were so divided that everything might end in confusion." The chief of his Chancellery, Jaromír Smutný, later told foreign journalists that the president had "wanted to avoid the danger of a civil war."[12] Beneš would resign a few months later, on June 7. Gottwald would be elected president the following week.

"Ten years ago Czechoslovakia fell under the sword of the hereditary enemy who had threatened her throughout the centuries," Ripka wrote. "In 1948 she was subjected by Soviet Russia, her ally, from whom she had expected aid and protection against the German danger."[13] The Czech democrats had made a grievous miscalculation—both that a postwar Germany would threaten her security and that the Soviet Union would guarantee it.

In the weeks following the coup, there would be mass purges and arrests. These were followed by a rewriting of the constitution and rigged parliamentary elections. Masaryk accepted reappointment as foreign minister, explaining to Steinhardt tearfully that he wanted "to soften the impact of Communist ruthlessness . . . and perhaps aid others in leaving the country."[14] But his tenure was brief. In the early morning of March 10, his body was found on the ground below his third-story office in the Foreign Ministry. Steinhardt and Ripka thought it was suicide. Drtina had tried to kill himself in a similar fashion only two weeks prior.[15] A forensic investigation by the Prague police over half a century later, however, concluded what many had believed at the time, that Masaryk had been pushed.[16] An earlier journalist's investigation also concluded that the Soviets and the Czech Communists knew that Masaryk had been planning to flee the country, which threatened to turn him into an embarrassing cause célèbre. They therefore took preventive action.

Kennan would later write that Masaryk's death "dramatized, as few other things could have, the significance of what had just occurred" in Prague.[17] The Communist Vladimír Clementis took over as foreign minister. Washington's carefully assembled intelligence network in the country was dismantled, its leaders executed.[18] It also became clear that unless the United States took some decisive action, Stalin would repeat his Czech tactics to undermine democracies further west. The coup thus served as a stimulus for Congress to pass the Marshall aid legislation on April 2, 1948 and for twelve Western nations to launch its security counterpart, the North Atlantic Treaty Organization (NATO), a year later.[19]

Wallace's reaction to events in Czechoslovakia, which was to blame the Truman administration, constitutes among the least creditable episodes of his presidential campaign. A week after the resignations crisis in February, Wallace told the press that "the unfortunate Czechoslovak situation probably wouldn't have happened" had he, Henry Wallace, been president. "The Czech crisis," he explained, "is evidence that a 'get tough' [American] policy only provokes a 'get tougher' [Soviet] policy." "The men in Moscow, from their point of view," he clarified, "would be utter morons if they failed to respond [to American policy] with acts of pro-Russian consolidation."[20] The clear implication was that the Soviets, in orchestrating the Communist takeover, had acted in self-defense.

On March 7, 1948, Ambassador Panyushkin, writing in his capacity as chief *rezident* "Vladimir," reported to Moscow that agent "Krot" (Charles Kramer) was now working for Wallace, writing his speeches and statements. Of particular importance, Panyushkin noted, "Krot" had prepared

Wallace's Senate testimony of February 27, in which he condemned the Marshall Plan and proposed a counterplan under U.N. auspices—as the Soviets had been demanding.[21]

Also that month, Panyushkin reported to Moscow that Wallace friend and longtime Soviet source Martha Dodd Stern ("Liza") had told embassy second secretary Valentin Sorokin ("Snegirev") of her efforts to shape Wallace's statements on Czechoslovakia. Concerned over the "bad slant" Wallace had recently received on February's Communist takeover, she assigned a friend to prepare a corrective memo for him. Specifically, she told the friend to "give Wallace evidence that the coup . . . was aimed towards instilling democracy in Czechoslovakia."[22] Though Moscow considered Stern too talkative for agent work, she continued to report to Sorokin on goings-on within the campaign and pressing for a larger role in steering Wallace. In August, she would report that Wallace had offered her the chance to write his speeches, and she pleaded with Sorokin to supply her with drafts, or at least talking points. Moscow, continuing to see Stern as impetuous and undisciplined, rebuffed her.[23]

At a press conference on March 15, five days after Masaryk's death, reporters again grilled Wallace about the Czech crisis. This time, he was more specific. His earlier statements, he said, had been made before he "knew what [Ambassador] Steinhardt had been up to, before the rightists"—that is, the non-Communists—"staged their coup."

Reporters were incredulous. What, one asked, was this "rightist coup" to which he referred? Wallace assured him that his paper's foreign desk knew all about it. Steinhardt, he explained, had issued a statement intended to aid the "rightist cause [just] a day or two before the rightists resigned from the government, thereby precipitating a crisis."

Steinhardt's alleged interference on behalf of "the rightists" had been his saying, in an interview on February 20, that he hoped the Czech government "might still join" the Marshall Plan. As an angry Steinhardt would explain two days later, in response to Wallace, he had been out of the country for nearly three months before he had made his statement, and had made it two days *after*, and not before, the non-Communist ministers had told Beneš of their decision to resign. Wallace's charge that he had somehow precipitated the crisis was, therefore, farcical.

At this point in Wallace's press conference, his speechwriter Lew Frank slipped him a note. What it said is unknown, but Wallace announced that he had to "catch a train." As he began walking toward the door, a reporter yelled out "What about Masaryk's suicide?" Wallace now stopped, paused, and began speaking again. He ought to have just kept walking.

"I live in the house that [former U.S. ambassador to the U.K.] John G. Winant lived in," Wallace reflected, "and heard rumors why he committed suicide." Winant had shot himself a year prior. "One can never tell [why]," Wallace continued. "Maybe Winant had cancer, maybe he was unhappy about the fate of the world. Who knows?" With the eyes of stunned reporters upon him, Wallace walked out.[24]

Wallace's election-year columns, as a *TNR* contributing editor, continued to be, quite naturally, unrelentingly damning toward Truman's foreign policy, as well as toward those who backed and enabled it. America, he wrote in January, had succumbed to the historical tendency of victor nations to "take over the outstanding vices" of the vanquished—in this case, Nazi Germany. The United States, he wrote, was rapidly heading "in the direction of centralized Prussian bureaucracy and militarism."[25] It had adopted a "foreign policy based on hatred and fear," shaped by "men who opposed resistance to fascism."[26] Beholden to "big brass" (the military) and "big gold" (Wall Street), they were "imperialist, labor-hating, militaristic and reactionary" zealots, he explained in March, just prior to passage of the Marshall aid legislation. They were "out to set up [an American] police state" and gain "control of the entire world."[27]

Wallace often adorned his judgments in biblical prose. "As I watch this terrible drift toward war," he also wrote in March, "I am reminded of the proclamation of Isaiah as he saw the land of Judah trusting in force: 'Woe to those who trust in chariots, Because they are many, And in horsemen, because they are mighty; But they look not to the Holy One of Israel, Nor seek the Lord!'"[28] In more banal prose, but equally fuzzy logic, Wallace explained that "you get peace by preparing for peace rather than for war."[29] He thus denied any legitimate role for military readiness or deterrence, thereby contravening a basic tenet of thinking in international relations. As observed by the scholar Hans Morgenthau, "the political aim of military preparations is . . . to make the actual application of military force unnecessary by inducing the prospective enemy to desist from [its] use."[30] Wallace also contradicted his own past statements. In 1940, he had, under the banner of "total preparation," defended the buildup of American naval and air force bases in the Western Hemisphere. "If we are properly prepared, we shall not have war on this hemisphere."[31] And in June 1947, he had asserted that "a line should be drawn on Russian expansion."[32] Thus was his new political thinking becoming increasingly detached not just from conventional thinking but from his own repeated expressions of it.

In February 1948, Wallace's as yet unnamed New Party celebrated a vicarious victory of sorts. The socialist American Labor Party, founded in 1936, typically endorsed Democratic candidates but on occasion fielded its own. Now, in a Bronx special congressional election, it backed an energetic, handsome thirty-seven-year-old Zionist labor advocate, Leo Isacson, against a loyal, uninspiring "Flynn-machine" Democrat, Karl Propper. Smelling blood, New Party strategists embraced Isacson's campaign as its own, declaring the local skirmish to be a national referendum on Truman's program of "depression and war."

Communist-controlled unions put staff on paid leave to assist in electioneering. The *Daily Worker* admonished readers to volunteer. Funds flowed in, well in excess of those at Propper's disposal. To crown the effort, Wallace endorsed Isacson and stumped for him, plowing for Jewish votes by accusing Truman, and by association Propper, of "conspiring" with "feudal [Arab] lords" to deny the Jews a homeland. The New Party blasted the administration's arms embargo on the region, which threatened to undermine the Zionist effort to resist Arab attacks, evading press demands to explain why Wallace had supported it. Even the traditionally anti-Zionist CPUSA now embraced the cause in order to undermine the Truman candidate, whom the Isacson canvassers hammered with wild charges concocted to undermine Jewish and Black support.

On election day, February 17, Isacson beat his Democratic and Republican adversaries in a rout. Though he had won overwhelmingly on local issues—housing, jobs, and the cost of living—Isacson made sure to repay his New Party and Communist backers. "The people," he said on election night, "have gone to the polls to say 'No' to the Truman Doctrine [and 'No'] to the Marshall Plan, which plays politics with hunger!" That was said "for the record," one ALP official later explained. But, in truth, "half the voters [had] never heard of the Marshall Plan."

No matter; the Wallace forces were jubilant, having energized their base and filled them with hope. Over in Moscow, too, there was a sense that Isacson's victory was a watershed event. Sitting in his Kremlin office the day after the election, Molotov carefully reviewed a secret TASS report on its significance. The victorious American Labor Party, it said, was "one of the strongest supporters of . . . the presidential nomination of Henry Wallace." Its triumph was therefore "a demonstration of strength" for his movement. Reading the next paragraph, Molotov took up his red pencil and highlighted in the margins the report's observation that the ALP had campaigned in "resolute opposition to the U.S. imperialist adventures overseas and the Marshall Plan." Molotov's selections were published in *Pravda* the following day, February 19, to be followed by further pieces heralding "the immense significance of the third party's creation." Molotov's secretariat would thereafter collect, translate, and file copies of all Wallace's campaign speeches and addresses.[33] Meanwhile, Andrew Steiger, Wallace's collaborator on *Soviet Asia Mission*, began sending Wallace copies of the enthusiastic coverage from Moscow. "A rumor is circulating" in the Russian capital, Steiger told him, that "the latest public opinion polls in the U.S. are not being published since they show too favorable a trend for the third party."[34]

More clear-eyed observers, those outside Moscow and New York, preyed gleefully on what they saw as the naïveté of the pro-Wallace forces. "The 'century of the common man' is close at hand," Willard Townsend of the *Chicago Defender* enthused wryly. "The Bronx has capitulated, Harlem is tottering. Brooklyn is rushing to the barricades; and the only thing that is left is Greenwich Village and the rest of America."[35]

For years, Wallace had pined for an audience with Stalin. He had in March 1944, as vice president, asked Roosevelt to send him to Moscow, but the closest he was permitted to venture was Siberia. In June 1946, as commerce secretary, he had, with Truman's blessing, sent a trade mission to Moscow, hoping to come later that year as head of a U.S. conference delegation. But that mission was a failure. In Moscow in November, two months after Wallace's firing, Associated Press journalist Eddy Gilmore, who would shortly win a Pulitzer for his interview with Stalin, told Sergei Kondrashov, a young MGB foreign intelligence officer masking as a VOKS information officer, "strictly off the record" that Wallace now wished to visit Russia as a private citizen. Gilmore urged the VOKS to organize the trip,[36] but the Foreign Ministry saw no benefit in soliciting Wallace. And Wallace, for his part, saw no benefit in going as a tourist, having to beg for photo ops. Yet even as Soviet interest in Wallace rose with the prospect of his running for president, neither side would make a move. Until 1948.

Though the publicly released Soviet records are incomplete, we now know enough to tell a fairly complete story of what transpired in the spring of 1948, secretly, between Wallace and the Soviets. In mid-March of that year, Wallace approached the newly appointed Czech U.N. ambassador, Vladimír Houdek, asking for his mediation in making contact with his Soviet counterpart, Andrey Gromyko. How Wallace communicated with Houdek is not known, yet logs from FBI surveillance (prompted by Elizabeth Bentley's revelations) show that Houdek had contacts with Americans involved in left-wing politics and Soviet espionage—contacts who may also have interacted with Wallace.[37] In any case, Wallace seeking Houdek's intercession with Gromyko was, on the surface, strange and unnecessary. He had met Gromyko several times over the years, publicly and privately, and would have had no difficulty getting an appointment through official Soviet channels. This time, however, Wallace wished to keep the contact hidden.

On or around March 22, a day on which we know the two diplomats spoke, Houdek told Gromyko of Wallace's request. Some days later, Wallace and Gromyko met. Though there is no publicly accessible contemporaneous account of this particular encounter, it is referred to in a cipher cable which Gromyko sent to Moscow on April 2—a cable designated "Strictly Secret," a level beyond "Top Secret." It recounts details of a one-on-one dinner talk between Gromyko and Wallace at the ambassador's residence that very evening. In spite of Gromyko's memoirs noting meetings he had had with Wallace in 1945, 1946, and 1947, it fails to mention this or any other encounter he had with Wallace in 1948.

At Gromyko's previous meeting with Wallace in March, according to the cable, Wallace had told him he wished to go to Moscow, leaving open the questions of timing and itinerary. Molotov sent Gromyko instructions for a follow-up meeting, apparently directing him to be receptive but noncommittal. According to the ambassador, Wallace "expressed his satisfaction" with Moscow's response.

Gromyko asked Wallace when he wished to travel. As was standard for a Soviet diplomat, his mission was to get his subject to talk and to give nothing away himself. Wallace, however, was anxious to learn what the Kremlin was thinking. Did Stalin *really* want him to come? The *pas de deux* was much like that which Wallace had initiated with Roosevelt in June 1944, just before the Democratic convention. And so he now pressed Gromyko to reveal Moscow's thinking on the "appropriate time."

"It would be better for you to decide," Gromyko insisted. It was right out of the Kremlin playbook: Molotov had used the same strategy with Harriman, trying to get him to reveal the U.S. agenda in advance of Yalta.[38]

Beaten, Wallace offered that his trip ought to be before the Democratic and Republican conventions in mid-June.

Check. Gromyko now had his first intelligence nugget. Wallace wanted to upstage the conventions, and would doubtless pay a premium in policy concessions for an advance blessing from Stalin.

What then, Gromyko asked, was to be the purpose of this trip?

Wallace took pains, at first, to explain what the purpose was *not*. It was *not* to be "of a journalistic type," he insisted. Neither was it to be like that which Harold Stassen, the perennial Republican presidential aspirant, had taken the year prior. Nothing of political substance had been agreed there.

No, Wallace's trip was to be a historic mission. He, Wallace, "wanted to come to a definite agreement with . . . Generalissimo Stalin on *all major problems of Soviet-American relations*," with the aim of "maintaining international peace." It was to be a trip undertaken by a man "who had nominated himself as a U.S. presidential candidate." That is, he was to be treated as a president in waiting.

To Gromyko, such conceit must have seemed breathtaking. He had some time ago concluded that Wallace was, politically, no match for his own ambitions.[39] But he was still valuable as a stooge, and might, if used wisely, wreak havoc with American foreign policy—and even help replace the Democratic Party with a pro-Soviet one.

Wallace's aim, according to Gromyko's account for Moscow, was to use his "conversation with comrade Stalin . . . to make a definitive statement to the American people." He would show "that in the case of his election," there would be "an agreement with the USSR on such and such important issues." And the "more definitive such a statement would be in substance," Wallace explained, "the greater its effect will be on the American people."

Wallace stressed "that his Moscow trip would strengthen his position as a presidential candidate," but "only if he actually reached an agreement [with Stalin] on important issues." If "he failed" to do so, however, "his trip would mean more harm for him." He therefore wanted "to have a preliminary agreement on certain issues prior to his trip."

Wallace, Gromyko understood, wanted Stalin to help his campaign by reaching a private accord with him before his trip, and then making a joint statement at the trip's conclusion. The candidate, he emphasized for Moscow, "did not conceal that he considered such preliminary agreement as the guarantee of the successful outcome of his trip."[40]

If so, Wallace was skating at the borders of U.S. law. Although no one has ever been convicted under the Logan Act of 1799, Wallace was testing its prohibition against American citizens engaging in unauthorized negotiations with foreign governments. Lew Frank would warn him that *any* correspondence with Gromyko might be enough to land him in legal trouble.[41]

Gromyko pressed Wallace to explain his vision for the content of this prior agreement. Wallace, however, insisted "that he did not have in mind any particular issues." Instead, Gromyko wrote to Moscow, clearly surprised, Wallace wanted "us to list such issues."

Molotov's office at the People's Commissariat of Foreign Affairs consisted of three rooms. There was a conference room, dominated by a long table flanked by neat rows of chairs. There was a "rest" room with a couch, for napping, a small bathroom, and a small round table. The table always held a vase with fresh flowers and fresh fruit, delivered daily by special planes from the Caucuses and Central Asia, and a plate of unshelled walnuts. Then there was his work room, dominated by a tidy, orderly mahogany desk and small table off to the sides for more intimate discussions.[42]

Chairman of the Council of People's Commissars Vyacheslav Molotov at his desk, 1936.

Reading Gromyko's cable in his office the following day, Molotov would underline these words in red pencil: "<u>us to list such issues</u>." Like Gromyko, he was struck by Wallace's nonchalance on matters of policy substance.

Molotov read on. Wallace, the cable clarified, added only that he wanted the issues divided into two categories: those on which agreement "would be of significance before the presidential elections," and those on which final agreement could be expected "in case of his election."

This early part of the two men's secret dinner talk is of great importance in understanding Wallace's vision for "peace" with Russia. He had made clear to Gromyko that he sought *no actual concessions* from Stalin. Under a Wallace presidency, there was to be no Cold War irrespective of whether Stalin stopped his seizure of eastern German industry; no Cold War irrespective of whether he allowed free elections in Berlin; no Cold War irrespective of whether he stopped debasing the German currency. There was to be no Cold War irrespective of whether he ceased imposing Communist governments abroad; irrespective of whether he cooperated in reunifying Korea; irrespective of whether he, indeed, did *anything* that a responsible American government had cause to expect from a partner in peace. No. There was to be no Cold War simply because Henry Wallace needed American voters to believe it had been created by Harry Truman and his fascist accomplices, and that its termination required only Wallace's election. As for Stalin, all *he* had to do to bring it about was to write his own sequel to Yalta. It was, for the Generalissimo, a good deal.

The American mainstream press and foreign-policy establishment had for years disparaged Wallace's impassioned but woolly proclamations on "peace." What the Gromyko cable suggests is that they had been woolly by design. They were meant to encourage the belief that the United States could protect its economic and security interests without undertaking the hard business of diplomacy—the business of setting priorities and red lines, of cultivating allies, of deterring adversaries, and of backing these efforts with financial and military resources.

In the estimation of veteran journalist Vincent Sheean, a man of solid Rooseveltian-liberal convictions, Wallace had, particularly since Truman fired him in September 1946, come to see "peace" not as a reward for securing vital interests through strength and careful compromise, but as something synonymous with himself.[43] Those who supported Wallace supported "peace." That Stalin might see "peace" as no more than a means of extending his power and influence, and not as a worthy end in itself, never figured into Wallace's thinking. This fact constituted "the main reason why I will not vote for Mr. Wallace," Sheean wrote. "I consider his candidacy dangerous to the peace of the world." Even if Wallace loses, "a large popular vote" for him would make the Russians "harder to deal with than ever before. They would increase their demands, exaggerate their militancy, multiply insults and examples of belligerent intention, and thus, in all probability—taking advantage of some local dispute in Germany or Korea—force us into a war which it is my conviction nobody in this country wants."[44]

Gromyko remained cautious, even suspicious of Wallace. Why was Wallace not raising any issues of his own? Was he fishing for intelligence? Even after having "borrowed" and copied Wallace's private diary in Siberia, back in 1944, and finding nothing remotely suspicious, the Soviets could never quite believe that he did not, like all imperialists, have a hidden imperialist agenda. And so Gromyko pressed Wallace. "How," the ambassador asked him, was Moscow "to understand his statement that at present he did not mean to name *any* particular issues to be negotiated?" Did that mean "that in the future he *would* be able to name such issues?"

Wallace continued to insist that Moscow could name the issues. But he offered, by way of concession, that "disarmament" might be "one of such issues"—even if he "mentioned [it] only as an example." It was, Wallace pointed out, "necessary to build trust between the great powers." Disarmament went together with trust.

Whether Gromyko genuinely found these statements objectionable or whether he felt the need to demonstrate hypervigilance to Molotov, his cable warned that Wallace's views on trust and disarmament were "much like the official position of the Americans and the British, who consider trust a prerequisite for disarmament."

"I elucidated our position on this issue" for Wallace, his cable continued. That position was to demand *immediate* American nuclear disarmament while rejecting any international inspection regime—a regime which allegedly violated Soviet "national sovereignty."

The Soviets had been proposing "disarmament plans" since 1927, always against the backdrop of a relentless domestic arms buildup. And since mid-1945, it had been Stalin's top priority to reach atomic parity with the United States—even if it meant starving his people to achieve it. Consequently, his dual strategy was to build bombs as fast as possible while his diplomats lectured on the urgent need for America to destroy all of hers.

Gromyko now delivered such a lecture to Wallace, who acknowledged, in response, that the Soviet "position seemed to be as well reasonable." Given Wallace's seeming insouciance, Gromyko got the "impression that he was [simply] not adequately familiar with the issue." Wallace may, he warned Molotov, therefore still be "in the thrall of the U.S. and British official policy."

Kennan had remarked two years prior that even if the United States were to disarm entirely, deliver its "air and naval forces to Russia," and resign "powers of government to American Communists," the Soviets would "smell a trap."[45] Gromyko now bore him out, displaying remarkable wariness toward his country's most prominent American friend—one who actually *believed* in the vital necessity of unilateral American acts of goodwill.

No doubt feeling under pressure from Molotov's instructions, Gromyko continued to press Wallace to state the issues he wanted to discuss, to which

Wallace responded with three: "internationalization [of] the Dardanelles, Suez, and Panama channels"; "renunciation of supplying arms to other nations," particularly China; and defining the geographic "borders of Soviet political influence." The last of these, he suggested, might "result in a deal on the withdrawal of American forces" from Greece and other European countries. He stressed yet again "in every possible way the importance for him of reaching a preliminary agreement on major issues," whatever those issues were. He acknowledged that doing so would require "trust in him on the part of the Soviet Government and Generalissimo Stalin."

On this matter of trust, Wallace added, sheepishly, that the Communist takeover in Czechoslovakia had "somewhat undermined his position," but that he had tried to salvage it "by pointing to Ambassador Steinhardt's interference into the [country's] domestic affairs." By now knowing the exculpatory facts, however, he added that "his reference to Steinhardt [had been] a mistake." But he declined to specify why.

Wallace concluded by touting the success of his electoral campaign, which was "getting stronger." Seventy-five percent of Protestant clergymen now supported his nomination, he said, as did "rank-and-file [union] members"—in spite of their leaders' opposition.[46] Gromyko seemed little interested in such selective spotlighting, and ended the evening by securing his guest's promise to "send a list" of issues for future U.S.-Soviet negotiations.

"I will report to you immediately," he closed his cable to Molotov, "on the receipt of said list from Wallace."

Gromyko's two meetings with Wallace helped convince the Kremlin that his candidacy, while perhaps not putting him in the White House, would still be useful in undermining Truman—who was not yet even assured the Democratic nomination. On April 11, the *Red Star* (*Krasnaya Zvezda*), an official daily of the Soviet Ministry of Defense, made clear its support for Wallace in a piece titled "The Third Party in the USA." "[T]he electoral struggle for the election of Wallace as president," wrote "journalist" Boris Vronsky, is "the beginning of the consolidation of progressive forces in the USA. That burgeoning new movement, Vronsky assured readers, was "extraordinary in its sweep and depth."[47] The piece was intended to show Soviet readers that the American public, seeing the example of the "new democracies" of the Soviet Union and Eastern Europe, was turning away from capitalism and imperialism.

Wallace met Gromyko for a third time on April 20 (or possibly 21).[48] Though it had been nearly three weeks since their previous meeting, Wallace came poorly prepared. Used to having underlings prep him, he had, in this case, opted to keep knowledge of his outreach closely held. He confessed to Gromyko "that he had not yet had the time to prepare the final list of questions he wished to discuss [in] Moscow." Rummaging through his pockets, he pulled out wads of unorganized notes, "apologizing that he had [yet] to make sense of it all himself."

Having unexpectedly received from Moscow a list of questions Stalin was willing to discuss with candidate Wallace and, later, President Wallace, Gromyko was, in any case, now anxious to speak first.

"In accordance with your desire that we should as well name the questions for discussions," he told Wallace, "I am ready to name such questions" myself.

These had been prepared by Molotov, with Stalin penciling in subject headings, crossing out one item, and designating six others as appropriate for discussion prior to the U.S. elections.

The first of these was the "question of peaceful policy," which included "the banning of atomic weapons and the introduction of international control over atomic energy." This was code for saying that the United States should destroy its nuclear weapons before the USSR agreed to any inspection regime. Second was "the question of non-interference into the domestic affairs of other nations," which included the "preclusion of military bases in the territory of [other U.N. nations]" and "the use of . . . methods of economic pressure for political ends." This was code for saying that the United States should withdraw its forces from Europe and terminate the Marshall Plan. Third was "the question of European recovery," which included "restor[ing] UNRRA" to its predominant role. This was code for saying that the United States should revert to funding foreign relief and recovery assistance through the U.N. Fourth was "the question of Germany," which included "strict compliance with the decisions of the Crimean and Potsdam Conferences" and "institution of a united peace-loving German democratic government." This was code for saying that the United States should deliver expeditiously $10 billion in reparations from western Germany and accept the creation of a Soviet-friendly unified German government. Fifth was "the question of the Far East," including "withdrawal of armed forces" from China and Korea. This was code for saying that the United States should remove its troops from Asia. Sixth, and finally, was "the question of Japan," which included "the creation of a demilitarized, democratic and peace-loving" country. This was code for saying that Japan must not be made into a U.S. military ally.

Stalin indicated that "the question of the internationalization of the Dardanelles, the Suez, and the Panama channels" could be discussed *after* the elections, "as well as that of strategic air bases in Greenland, Iceland, Okinawa, etc." This was code for saying that the USSR should share power over key global water channels, and that the United States should abandon its foreign military airbases. Such matters Stalin may have thought too realpolitik for open discussion during the campaign.

Stalin had also considered Molotov's suggestion to allow dialogue over "the question of the borders of the political influence of the USSR," as Wallace had earlier proposed. Molotov had wanted to condemn the question by arguing that thinking along the lines of "spheres of political influence" was a legacy of the "fascist nations," and had no relevance to Soviet thinking or behavior. Stalin, however, decided to strike the paragraph entirely before authorizing the document's transmission to Gromyko.

Wallace listened approvingly as Gromyko read the list. When Gromyko finished, Wallace assured him that he himself "had planned [to raise] almost all those issues." Of these, he added, he felt disarmament the most important.

The ambassador, however, noted for Moscow that Wallace seemed "unclear about the substance of differences [between the two nations] at the UN Commission on Atomic Energy"—much as he had been in his bitter public dispute with Baruch back in September 1946. Wallace was "in particular [unclear] regarding [the issue of] inspection," which the Soviets had no intention of permitting. So "I gave [him] an appropriate explanation," Gromyko assured Molotov.

Gromyko also pressed Wallace to explain what he had meant when asking, at their last meeting, to discuss "the boundaries of political influence of the USSR." Gromyko stressed that it was "the U.S. ruling circles [who] were making the USSR responsible for [the] failures of their own policy in one or another country." It was not the USSR imposing its will abroad. Wallace assured him that "he did not believe what is said and written about the USSR" in the United States, but that "it might be worth saying something" about it.

Referring to his notes, Wallace stressed "the need for making a statement to the effect that the termination of the 'Cold War' . . . would not mean sacrificing by the United States any American principles or public interests."[49] The idea for such a statement had come from Lew Frank, one of several Soviet-friendly confidants to whom Wallace had written for advice after his last meeting with Gromyko.[50] This statement, Wallace suggested, could be "made either by comrade Stalin or by him, Wallace, with Stalin's approval."

Reading Gromyko's account of the meeting in his Kremlin office, sitting at a modest wooden desk topped by a green cloth, a brass lamp, three phones, and a glass bowl for his pipe ash, flanked by dark oak-paneled walls with insets of Karelian birch, Stalin underlined the words "by him, Wallace." He then scribbled in the margins, *"Better by Wallace"*—meaning that Wallace should make the statement on his own. Annoyed by the implication that the USSR bore any fault for worsening relations, Stalin also added: *"We are not waging any cold war. It is the USA that is waging it."*

Most of Wallace's proposals for the "agreement" with Stalin were innocuous, reflecting the Russophile outlook of those whose suggestions he had solicited. Stalin glossed over them. In a few cases, however, such as that above, he recorded his displeasure on Gromyko's cable. Beside Wallace's suggestion that it might be "worth discussing the issue of the [U.N. Security Council] 'veto,'" a veto the Soviets considered sacrosanct, Stalin wrote *"We are against."* Beside his suggestion that the Soviets say something "to convince U.S. public opinion that the information on the developments in Czechoslovakia disseminated [in the USA] was far from reality," Stalin wrote *"Rubbish."* Most important, however, was Stalin's response to Wallace's latest hint that he wanted an invite to fly to Moscow. *"The trip may do harm,"* Stalin wrote in a final, definitive veto. He was, it seemed, concerned that the optics of Wallace obeying a summons to the Kremlin might redound to Truman's

Soviet leader Joseph Stalin at his desk, 1936.

political benefit. "*A statement,*" however, he added, "*is useful.*" It is "*better [that it] be done by Wallace,*" he clarified, "*with Stalin stating his sympathy.*"[51] And so a statement it would be.

On or around April 26, Gromyko received an envelope from Ambassador Houdek, who had himself received it from two "minor Wallace aides" in the lobby of a New York hotel.[52] Inside were two similar documents, and Gromyko struggled to make sense of them. Wallace, wishing to leave no paper trail proving he had given the documents to the Soviets, enclosed no explanatory letter.

It seemed, Gromyko explained to Molotov in a cipher cable, that "the first document is a plan of the second document, which is entitled 'Open Letter to Premier Stalin.'" But what *was* an "Open Letter"? It must be something meant for public release, Gromyko reasoned. But the timing, too, was unclear. Did Wallace still wish to go to Moscow? Would this "letter" be made public before such a trip? After it? In lieu of it? Gromyko had no idea. "I will have to ask Wallace to specify," he told Molotov. "I will meet him [again] on May 8."

Over in Moscow, Molotov ordered copies of Wallace's documents distributed to Stalin and the Politburo. Stalin went through each one carefully, scribbling "*yes*" beside 90 percent of Wallace's statements. Covering disarmament, arms exports, international trade, the U.N., UNRRA aid, Germany, China, Korea, Japan, noninterference, and ideological rivalry, Wallace's statements were, for Stalin, mostly unobjectionable. Some Wallace had taken from Stalin's own earlier list—such as the call for the speedy creation of a united "peace-loving German government" dedicated to the fulfillment of Yalta and Potsdam obligations (which for Stalin included reparations). Some were to Stalin's advantage—such as Wallace's assertion that Russia could not "be held responsible for the excesses of local Communists." And others were sufficiently banal that Stalin could interpret them to his advantage. Still, Stalin wrote some testy notes in the margins.

"*We are not waging cold war*," Stalin wrote, yet again, in response to Wallace's call to end it. As for his call for "freedom of movement for citizens, students and journalists," Stalin deemed it "*not appropriate*." With regard to "freedom of speech and political democracy," Stalin saw these matters as "*the business of each particular nation*." And as for a bilateral "trade agreement [to] secure a healthy market for American goods [and] to facilitate the recovery and further industrialization of the USSR," this Stalin branded, simply, "*wrong*." Trade, he insisted, must be purely on a "*mutually beneficial basis*,"[53] and Wallace's formulation failed to conform to his Bolshevik conception of such.

The Wallace campaign was, for Stalin, only one gift the Americans had handed him to undermine their foreign policy. Another was a diplomatic blunder by the State Department.[54]

In a Policy Planning Staff paper written during the February Czech coup, Kennan had suggested that the success of the Marshall Plan might help bring the Soviets to the table for substantial discussions over policy differences. Shortly after, he gave an off-the-record press briefing in which he opined, with uncharacteristic optimism, that a "spectacular retreat of Soviet and Communist influence in Europe may be expected" within six months.[55]

Determined to help it along, he advised a quiet démarche to Moscow in March. Truman approved it late the following month, and Marshall instructed Ambassador Smith in Moscow to approach Molotov with a carefully drafted oral statement. After warning Molotov at length that Moscow would be making "a tragic error" in assuming Washington would not defend its interests, Smith was to tell him that "the door" was nonetheless "always wide open for full discussion and the composing of our differences."[56]

Molotov readily agreed to receive the "old spy,"[57] as he called the general. Armed with intercepts of French cables from Berlin to Paris, he was aware of Franco-American tensions over the pace of western German unification, which Paris still opposed, and suspension of reparations to Moscow.[58] The meeting was thus a golden opportunity to rupture Allied solidarity. Molotov greeted Smith on May 4, in a manner the latter described as "grave, attentive and courteous."

Chief of staff to Eisenhower during the war, Smith was able, orderly, candid, straight-talking, "all business." He had a harsh, powerful voice, intimidated subordinates, and made little effort to personate a diplomat. Upon learning that Smith would be sent to Moscow in the spring of 1946, Eisenhower remarked that it would "serve those bastards right."[59]

Script in hand, Smith assured Molotov that America's "entire history was [a] refutation of any suspicion of a policy which involved aggressive war." But he stressed his country's concern over Soviet behavior in Czechoslovakia. The United States, he said, "did not oppose Communism because of its Marxian ideology, but purely and simply because we had seen repeated instances," as in Prague, "of Communist minorities coming into power by illegal means and against the will of the majority." It remained convinced that such "minority coup[s] d'etat" could never have occurred "without the moral and physical support of the USSR."

"No one," Molotov responded in a May 9 follow-on meeting, had "been able to find any facts to prove these false allegations. Nor can anyone state with authority that the Communists have used illegal means." The fault lay instead, he said, with "rightist circles . . . that wish to induce changes by violence." As for the United States, "it was well-known that the western European and American press were saying openly" that the military alliance and bases it was establishing "were directed against the USSR." And "events in Greece are not the only example of [its] interference in the internal affairs of other states."[60]

The two agreed on nothing, though Smith fulfilled his mission by transmitting the open-door message. Molotov ran the text up to Stalin, who read that part with delight—scribbling *Ha-ha!* in the margins.[61] Here, he saw, was a chance to undermine Truman with American allies and voters. By publishing this off-the-record text, he could make it seem as if the repentant Americans had come to him pleading for peace talks. He, Stalin, could then appear magnanimous by accepting the "invitation," thereby forcing Truman to come to the table with concessions in order to avoid the public impression of diplomatic failure. If Truman disowned the "invitation," however, he would look to the world like a skulking bluffer, making conciliatory proposals behind the backs of America's allies and then disclaiming them once their conniving had been revealed. Kennan, in short, had been wrong. "Spectacular retreat" was not on Stalin's agenda.

TASS published the highly selective Soviet version of the confidential talks, and Moscow Radio publicized it, on May 11,[62] catching the Truman administration unprepared.[63] "The Russians," Truman fumed to his diary, had acted without "ethics or moral considerations."[64] Stalin, the State Department understood, was trying "to create the impression . . . that the US had been forced to appeal to the USSR for a settlement." This impression, Stalin hoped, would "undercut US leadership . . . by sowing distrust among our friends who were not consulted in advance."[65] Indeed, two days later Ernest Bevin was, thanks to the TASS release, subjected to angry questioning in Parliament over what he had known and when he had known it.[66]

Stalin had been well aware that May 11 was also the day Wallace was to read and distribute his Open Letter at a nineteen-thousand-strong campaign rally at Madison Square Garden. It was the perfect opportunity to undermine U.S. policy by showing the world the contrast between an outwardly belligerent but cowardly Harry Truman and a bold, peace-loving Henry Wallace.

Molotov presumably informed Gromyko of Moscow's reaction to Wallace's proposed Open Letter texts, but no cipher cable has been found to document this. We further have no record from Gromyko of a May 8 meeting with Wallace. Whether that is because it did not occur, or because the ambassador's account has gone astray, or because it has been withheld from public view, we cannot say. What we do have, however, is Mikoyan's marked-up copy of a draft letter from Stalin to Wallace, which had been sent to Politburo members for review on May 10—the day before the TASS release on the Smith-Molotov talks and the publication of Wallace's Open

Letter. This letter shows that communication efforts between Moscow and Wallace continued right up until the day that Wallace's letter was made public.

The core of the draft, translated from the Russian, reads as follows:

> The statement outlined in your letter is very important and has a serious impact both for the international relations and the relations between the Soviet Union and the USA.
>
> Even before the receipt of your letter, the Soviet Government had received through the U.S. Ambassador Mr. Smith a statement of the U.S. Government, in which the U.S. government expressed its desire to improve the Soviet-American relations and for this purpose to get down to the discussion and resolution of the controversies existing between the USSR and the USA.
>
> This is all good. But to translate these wishes into reality it is necessary to find a way forward, to map an agreement. Your letter is timely. In this respect, it is making a step forward, creating a foundation for improvement of our relations. This is a serious difference between your move and the move of the U.S. Government. If the content of your letter is taken as a foundation for the agreement between the USSR and the USA, then settling our differences will be possible. We approve such a road to settlement.
>
> In your letter, you touch upon a number of important issues which may be discussed between us and resolved in the spirit of mutual sympathy, in the interest of both of our nations and universal peace.
>
> I would think it necessary to make one addition to your proposals, namely to supplement a point on resuming unlimited commerce between our two nations with the words "excluding any discrimination."[67]
>
> I. STALIN

Though we do not know if or when[68] this, or a similar, message was communicated to Wallace, we do know that an important element of it *was* communicated. Wallace included Stalin's final phrase "excluding any discrimination" in the published version of his Open Letter to Stalin. Stalin's draft message, therefore, constitutes documentary evidence of his personal involvement in the writing of Wallace's Open Letter.

Stalin's draft message also shows that he wished Wallace to know of the confidential Smith-Molotov exchange, as well as how he, Stalin, saw Wallace's Open Letter as "a step forward" from that exchange. How and when Wallace received such a message is, again, unknown, but he understood the linkage as being important enough that he added a new last-minute introduction to what he called "the most significant [speech] I have ever given."[69]

"Although the notes of Ambassador Bedell Smith and Foreign Minister Molotov are both characterized by the same self-righteousness which has led to the international crisis," he would tell his massed supporters in New York on May 11,

they represent great hope to those of us who have consistently maintained that peace is possible and they represent a severe blow to the propagandists on both sides who have insisted that the two nations cannot live at peace in the same world. The two letters assume what we have long contended—that the wartime cooperation between the two great powers can be rebuilt and strengthened in time of peace. The exchange of notes, opening the door to negotiations, must be followed by a meeting—an open, fully reported meeting of representatives of both the United States and the Soviet Union. With the prospect of such a meeting, I present my thoughts on the steps necessary to achieve the Century of Peace.[70]

That meeting, Wallace still hoped, would take place between himself and Generalissimo Stalin.

Down in Washington, administration officials saw that the timing of Stalin's radio bombshell was meant to "strengthen the public influence and following of Henry A. Wallace."[71] Suspecting collusion between Wallace and the Soviets, the State Department subjected his Open Letter (see Appendix 1) to intense study. "Although almost all of Wallace's proposals had been promoted by Moscow at one time or another," the Department's textual assessment would conclude, "we should not assume with any degree of certainty that the letter was directly inspired by Moscow. It's more probable that Wallace's proposals were prepared by his advisers and experts on the

USSR on the basis of [their] analysis of Soviet foreign policy."[72] This conclusion was correct in that Wallace's inspiration was largely his own, and in that he deferred to his advisers in the drafting. But it was incorrect insofar as it failed to detect Moscow's hand in that drafting.

Subsequent investigation with the assistance of the FBI, however, *did* turn up evidence pointing at collusion between the Wallace campaign and the Soviet Union. The first public airing of the Smith-Molotov exchange had been over Moscow Radio early on the morning of May 11 (Moscow time). FBI agents planted in the New York print shop after the Madison Square Garden event, however, documented that the text of the Open Letter had arrived an hour and a half *before* the broadcast.[73] Assuming this discovery was accurate, the Wallace campaign had to have been given details of the exchange before Moscow broke it to the world. On this basis, a State Department security investigator would, on June 7, report to Kennan that "we have very convincing evidence that Wallace has a direct communication line with Moscow"[74]—which, through Gromyko, we now know he did. Attorney General Tom Clark ordered a secret investigation of Wallace's ties to the Soviet Union.[75]

Curtis MacDougall, a 1948 Illinois Progressive Party senatorial candidate, observed of Wallace that whereas he "would have little or nothing to do with organizational details," he was, when it came to major political initiatives, never the mere "dupe" of advisers his critics made him out to be. He pursued such initiatives of his own convictions, and brought in advisers only to furnish facts to justify them or policies to support them. And so it was with the Open Letter.

Particularly given the secrecy required to engage Stalin without tipping off U.S. authorities, Wallace kept most of his campaign team in the dark throughout the process. When a week or so before the event he revealed to Baldwin his plans to release such a letter, Baldwin urged him to make certain Stalin would actually respond. Otherwise, he, Wallace, would be left to dangle in harsh political winds. Wallace, according to Baldwin, assured him that all was in hand.

When MacDougall would, years later, write to Wallace asking whether "[you had] contact[ed] anyone in the Soviet Embassy . . . to make sure your open letter to Stalin would get a reply," Wallace denied it. "I had no assurances from anyone," Wallace wrote back, "and made no effort to get assurances that Stalin would reply to my open letter which was released in May of 1948 but which was never sent to Stalin."[76] This statement, we now know from Soviet records, was materially false. Stalin had studied and edited the letter in advance. Presumably, Gromyko had also provided Wallace with the assurances he had repeatedly sought regarding Stalin's "preliminary agreement" on the issues detailed in the letter.

When Stalin's response to the Open Letter finally came over Moscow Radio on May 18, it was everything Wallace had hoped for. The Soviet leader was at last acknowledging him before the world as a statesman with whom he could do business.

"[T]he open letter of Mr. Wallace, Presidential candidate of the United States third party," Stalin said, "is the most important document" among those aimed at the "consolidation of peace [and] the setting up of international cooperation." Stalin contrasted the promise of Wallace's "concrete program for peaceful settlement of the differences between the U.S.S.R. and the United States" with "the inadequacy of the statement" of the U.S. government. He highlighted over a dozen of Wallace's proposals (the ones requiring only U.S. concessions), concluding that they represented "a good and fruitful basis" for an agreement between the two countries.

When asked by reporters for his reaction to Stalin's statement, Wallace, campaigning in California, did his best to put on an air of humility and surprise. "If I have done anything that moves the world further toward peace," he told them, "I feel that my campaign will have been a success."

"The significance of Premier Stalin's reply," Wallace added before an Oakland Auditorium Arena crowd that evening, "lies in the fact that the Russian government is truly prepared to discuss issues on their merit and is genuinely interested in finding a way for the two great powers to live at peace."[77] He did not mention that the issues Stalin had singled out were largely those which Stalin himself had offered for inclusion in the letter. Two days later, in San Diego, Wallace would tell the press he was willing to fly to Moscow and meet with Stalin if it would "advance the cause of peace."[78] But Stalin was still set against such a meeting.

The administration's public response to Stalin's duplicity, which was to deny that Smith had put forth a change in U.S. foreign policy, was poorly received by much of the U.S. and international press. Truman and Marshall appeared both clumsy in their conduct of diplomacy and mulish in their refusal to pursue a diplomatic opening which they themselves had initiated. The State Department conceded that Stalin had "scored a temporary propaganda victory."[79] Yet Marshall's assertion that "the overwhelming majority" of Americans still supported their position[80] was correct.

"No one could expect Mr. Marshall to accept the Wallace formula, which was in fact heavily weighted in favor of Moscow," opined Freda Kirchwey of *The Nation*—a journal solidly of the left.[81] In fact, a poll taken two weeks before the Stalin-Wallace spectacle of May 11 showed that only 10 percent of Americans believed the United States should be "more willing to compromise" with the Soviet Union, whereas 61 percent thought it "should be *even firmer*."[82] The Madison Square Garden rally may have energized the candidate's supporters, yet the image of Wallace welcoming, if not collaborating in, Stalin's election meddling hardly helped him with the vast remainder of the electorate. "The whole business," Vincent Sheean wrote in *The Saturday Evening Post*, "was simply a mechanism for giving Stalin's approval to an American presidential candidate."[83]

The Kremlin, however, was too caught up in celebrating its propaganda coup to think rationally about the electoral dynamics. At the Central Committee's Foreign Policy Department, a new profile of Candidate Wallace was quickly assembled, this one celebrating evidence of his fitness to serve Soviet interests. "After his visit to the USSR in 1944," it noted, "Wallace made friendly public statements about the Soviet Union." His "diary, which was obtained through agent sources, contains notes on his meetings with Soviet people and his visits to collective farms and industrial enterprises. The nature of these notes testifies to the objectivity and friendly attitude of the author to the Soviet Union in that period. . . . 'We should learn a lot from the Russians.'" Wallace wrote in the purloined diary, "'Their viewpoint is broader and in some respects more scientific than ours.'"[84]

Molotov seemed smitten by the notion that Wallace could now, with the Kremlin's help, actually be elected. Between May 12 and 18, he built up a file of personally annotated memos and reports on the Open Letter and drafts of Stalin's response to it. *Pravda* and *Izvestia* began publishing near-daily TASS reports on the Wallace campaign—reports that Molotov, and in some cases Stalin, would necessarily have edited.[85] On May 17, Andrew Steiger wrote to Wallace from Moscow telling him of the "instantaneous and warm welcome" his Open Letter had received in the Russian press.[86] "So volu-

minous has been the press reaction," he followed up on June 4, "that I am
sending you the latest batch of clippings immediately in the hope that you
will find them of interest and value."[87]

Back in May 1947, the populist muckraking journalist Westbrook Pegler
published the first of what would be, by July 1948, three dozen columns excoriating Wallace over his relationship with Nicholas Roerich, his deception
of the American taxpayer in sending the "Russian god-man" to Asia, and
his refusal to acknowledge authorship of the "Guru letters." In March 1948,
Pegler published photos of the letters themselves. On July 23, at a press conference on the opening day of the New Party convention in Philadelphia,
with over four hundred in attendance, a journalist asked Wallace to answer
Pegler's question—did he or did he not write the letters?

Wallace had dodged the matter for eight years, but the media's klieg light
now shone upon him. "I never comment on Westbrook Pegler," he replied.
To gasps of surprise, Pegler himself then rose and repeated the question.
"I will never engage in any discussion whatsoever with Westbrook Pegler,"
Wallace put back. Two more newsmen tried, prompting him to call them
"stooges of Westbrook Pegler." Finally, the legendary cultural critic H. L.
Mencken stood, asking if Wallace thought him a "Pegler stooge" as well.
Wallace laughed. No, he did not; Mencken was nobody's stooge. "Well,
then," Mencken said, "it's a simple question."

"Why don't you answer?" yelled out Doris Fleeson, Washington correspondent for the *Daily Boston Globe*. "I'll answer in my own time," Wallace
put back, defiant to the end.

Wallace's "tumultuous" conference was recounted in a front-page piece
the next day in *The New York Times*. Mencken called Wallace an "imbe-
cile" for his handling of the letters controversy. Around the country, the
commentariat condemned Wallace's lack of candor—not just about past ties
to mystics, but present ties to Communists. Wallace acknowledged having
"a lot" of Communist support for his candidacy, but refused to take questions about it. He welcomed votes, he said, from anyone with an "interest in
peace."[88] Yet he was losing such votes at an alarming pace.

On June 26, 1948, Hilde Spiel, a Vienna-born novelist and journalist who had settled in London before the war, talked her way onto an American military aircraft from Frankfurt to Berlin. Warned of the risk of hostile Soviet air maneuvers, she was ordered to don a parachute. The plane shook violently as it entered the narrow, turbulent corridor permitted by the Soviets.

Disembarking unsteadily after vomiting, she found a city in a state of high tension. Berliners out scavenging for food returned to crumbling homes with no electricity, the main source having been cut off in the East. The drone of Allied supply planes overhead was relentless. The roars frightened Spiel, reminding her of the Blitz. But, strangely, the enemy was still invisible. She didn't know what to make of it.[89]

A currency war had just broken out, but the effects had yet to sink in. A week earlier, on June 18, the American military governor General Lucius Clay, together with the British and French military governors, had given their Soviet counterpart, General Vasily Sokolovsky, a mere few hours' notice before publicly declaring a currency changeover in the west of the country (though not yet in Berlin), which would take place on Sunday the 20th. The unilateral western reform was necessitated by Soviet indifference to soaring German inflation, which had led to a carton of cigarettes selling for the equivalent of $2,300[90] ($28,000 in today's money). The angry Russian general called the move "illegal" and promised "actions to protect the economy of the Soviet zone."[91] But Truman and Marshall were, by this point, prepared to split Germany in two if that is what it took to revive and secure the western half.

On June 19, the Soviets announced that "banknotes issued in the Western occupation zones will not be allowed to circulate in the Soviet zone or in 'Greater Berlin,' which is situated in the Soviet zone and is economically a part thereof." Fearing disorder in the Eastern zone, which would be flooded with old reichsmarks declared worthless in the West, Moscow also blocked all interzonal passenger traffic and incoming road traffic, while instituting an inspection regime for inbound trains. Use of the deutschmark in the East was banned.

Refusing to acknowledge the legitimacy of the transport restrictions, Clay, after warning Soviet officials, sent in a train to challenge them. Following a thirty-six-hour standoff, its crew was overpowered and a Soviet locomotive hauled it back to Helmstedt, on the western frontier.

Unable to provision his garrison by ground, Clay began ferrying in supplies by air.[92] As tensions climbed, currency experts from each side argued over solutions for Berlin. On June 22, the Americans offered a proposal for a new Berlin currency, under four-power administration. The Soviets rejected it. The British offered a compromise, with the Allies accepting the Soviet mark but placing it under four-power control. Western access rights would be restored. The Soviets, however, spurned all notions of combined control or guaranteed access rights. "We give notice to you and to the German population of Berlin," they told the Allies, "that we shall apply . . . sanctions that will ensure that only one currency will circulate in Berlin" as of June 26, "the currency of the Soviet zone."[93] This, Clay concluded, would have placed Berlin under effective Soviet control.[94] The Allied governors declared the Soviet decree invalid in the west of the city, and threatened to introduce the deutschmark in their sectors if the Soviets went ahead.

The local Berlin city government, the Magistrat, which functioned with limited authority allowed it by the Allied Control Council, now found itself in an impossible political situation. Whose orders would it obey? After emotional debate, it ruled that the Soviet order did not apply outside the Soviet sector. But the elected City Council had the final word. On June 23, the Soviets shuttled in hundreds of SED (Communist) demonstrators in army trucks hours in advance of its 4 p.m. meeting. With raucous commotion in the hall delaying the start for several hours, the members voted to back the Magistrat. As legislators exited the building into the throngs of protesters, Soviet-sector police helped them identify those who had voted with the West. Many were severely beaten.

That same day, the Soviets announced the introduction of their own East mark into Berlin and eastern Germany, effective June 24. Gummed stamps were attached to old reichsmark bills until new bills were ready. On the 24th, Allied officers declared the Soviet initiative null and void in West Berlin and introduced the deutschmark into the city. To keep room for compromise, though, the bills were stamped with a "B" to distinguish them from non-Berlin deutschmarks. This marking would facilitate withdrawal at a later date.

Sokolovsky announced that the Allied military government had ceased to exist, and began isolating the three Western sectors with a full-scale blockade. He suspended all road, rail, and barge traffic to and from the sectors owing to unspecified "technical difficulties." He cut off electricity and food supplies from the East because of "coal shortages" and the need to prevent Western currency from circulating illegally. He moved eight Soviet combat divisions into assembly points near the interzonal border. Reports emerged of Russian barrage balloons being placed near Tempelhof airfield in the American sector to disrupt landings.

French Berlin commandant General Jean Ganeval warned Clay of "incalculable consequences which will undoubtedly not be confined to Berlin." French foreign minister Georges Bidault thought "the Western powers [would] find it very difficult to stay there for more than a few weeks unless there [were] a radical change in relations with the Soviet authorities." Those authorities were in turn receiving reports from their "leading comrades in [eastern] Germany," indicating that "the Western powers would [soon] be forced to . . . surrender their positions in Berlin to the Soviet Union."

But Clay remained defiant. By the end of June, 480 relief flights were landing each day, one plane every three minutes. "I may be the craziest man in the world," he told Berlin's Social Democratic Party leader Ernst Reuter, "but I'm going to try the experiment of feeding this city by air."[95] It was the beginning of one of the most remarkable Western logistical and diplomatic feats of the Cold War: the Berlin Airlift.[96]

Accepting the nomination as the presidential candidate of his newly christened Progressive Party on July 24, 1948, Henry Wallace addressed the Berlin crisis. That crisis "need not have happened," he told the 32,000-strong crowd in Philadelphia's Shibe Park. In fact, "Berlin did not *happen*. Berlin was *caused*," he corrected. It was caused by Truman's "get tough" policy.

"I assure you," he went on, "that if *I* were president, there would be no crisis in Berlin." The Russians would have no cause for a blockade. They had, after all, shown great "eagerness" in accepting Ambassador Smith's "invitation to talk over the problems," conveyed over Moscow Radio on May 11. Yet President Truman, inexplicably, then "slammed the door." He, Wallace, tried to salvage peace when he "addressed an open letter to Stalin" later that same day. Stalin responded positively, once more, but Truman simply "slammed the door *again*."

What, then, of Germany's future? Of Europe's future? The "so-called 'just peace'" America had established through its occupation "is not just" at all, Wallace insisted. "It is a peace that," in the service of "Wall Street," merely "rebuilds the war-making potential of German industry in the western zone." America now had no moral standing in Europe. "Our prestige in Germany went sinking when we divided Germany and established the western sector as an American and British Puerto Rico"—that is, as "a colony."[97] Not incidentally, much of the party convention was, to the dismay of the young British journalist Alistair Cooke, "dedicated to liberating Puerto Rico."[98]

Wallace's words played well in the Kremlin; less well in the park. Despite a raucous welcome, Wallace proceeded to suck the spirit out of the gathering. The speech was ill-focused and too long, and the candidate seemed unable to muster enough conviction to sustain even a loyal crowd. His call for withdrawal from Berlin, to which he added a pause to accommodate applause, was met with embarrassing silence. By the time he had moved on from Berlin to random recollections of the words and deeds of Jefferson, Lincoln, and the Roosevelts, the crowd had begun heading for the doors. And by the time he had finished, a third of them had disappeared.[99]

One reason for Wallace's dead delivery may have been that the speech had been thrust upon him. He never quite embraced it as his own. Ilo, his wife, routinely blamed campaign writers for his poor perorations, claiming that they put unnatural words in his mouth. She was not always aware that his most inflammatory slogans, those she hated the most (such as "merchants of death"), were of his own inspiration.[100]

According to later testimony from the media scriptwriter, and erstwhile Communist, Allan Sloane, he and fellow Communist writer Millard Lampell had rewritten Wallace's "terrible" acceptance speech text at the behest of Hannah Dorner.[101] Wallace appeared to be growing inured to his own by-now-ritual denunciations of "big brass" and "the banking house boys," and they came out—well, scripted. As Max Hall of the Associated Press put it, "the blow-torch phrases . . . seem much more inflaming on paper than they do when Wallace reads them. . . . [D]roningly, he plows on through the denunciations" until, eventually, he just stops, "grins, nods, and waves."[102]

Typically, if the Communist contingent were large enough, a little droning did not dampen the crowd's spirited cheers. At Shibe Park, however, the denunciations actually plowed on from July 24 into July 25. It was not until 12:09 a.m. that Wallace arrived at his closing call to arms.

Right: President Franklin D. Roosevelt speaks into radio microphones from his open car in the rain. Vice President–elect Harry S. Truman sits between Roosevelt and outgoing Vice President Henry A. Wallace, November 10, 1944.

Left: President Harry S. Truman listens to a speech by Secretary of Commerce Henry A. Wallace at the Jefferson-Jackson Day Dinner, March 27, 1946.

Left: Singer and actor Paul Robeson (left), Senator Claude Pepper (D-FL) (center), and Secretary of Commerce Henry A. Wallace at Madison Square Garden, New York, September 12, 1946.

Right: Henry A. Wallace resigns as secretary of commerce, with his wife Ilo (left) and daughter Jean by his side, on September 20, 1946.

Left: Cartoonist Clifford Berryman depicts Henry A. Wallace pleading for $17 billion in aid to the Soviet Union as Senator Arthur Vandenberg (R-MI) delivers $400 million to President Truman for Greece and Turkey, April 24, 1947.

Right: Henry A. Wallace (right) shakes hands with Senator Claude Pepper (D-FL) while waving to the 12,000 people who heard his address at the Watergate Amphitheater in Washington, D.C., June 16, 1947.

Above: Henry A. Wallace (left) leans on his pitchfork as he works with Michael Straight (center), publisher of *The New Republic*, in the fields of the Afikim settlement in Lower Galilee during his Palestine trip, November 3, 1947.

Right: "New Party" (soon to be Progressive Party) presidential candidate Henry A. Wallace (left) puts his arm around the shoulder of Senator Glen H. Taylor (D-ID), soon to be his running mate, in a Washington, D.C. hotel, February 23, 1948.

Left: Progressive Party presidential candidate Henry A. Wallace (in front of tree) visits William Penn College president Cecil Hinshaw (far left) and students on the campus grounds in Oskaloosa, Iowa, 1948.

Right: A political cartoon by Clifford Berryman shows Progressive Party presidential candidate Henry A. Wallace "flip-flopping" on defense policy from his time as vice president to his presidential run, April 1, 1948.

Left: Soviet leader Joseph Stalin's copy, with notations, of the seventh page of Permanent Representative to the United Nations and Deputy Foreign Minister Andrey Gromyko's cipher cable to Foreign Minister Vyacheslav Molotov, dated April 21, 1948, reporting on Gromyko's secret April 20 meeting with Progressive Party presidential candidate Henry A. Wallace. See Appendix 2 for translation.

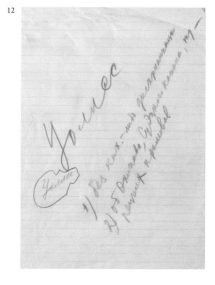

Right: Soviet leader Joseph Stalin's undated notes, likely scribbled on the night of May 9, 1948, while reading the Foreign Ministry's early draft of his answer to Progressive Party presidential candidate Henry A. Wallace's draft "Open Letter."

Translation:
Wallace
1) Excluding any discrimination
2) on Okinawa, the Suez Channel, Turkish Straits

13

Left: Progressive Party presidential candidate Henry A. Wallace is serenaded by Manuel Olvera (left), who, between songs, calls Wallace "the friend of the poor man," and Arnold Gonzalez at La Bonita restaurant in Denver, Colorado, May 13, 1948.

14

Right: Progressive Party presidential candidate Henry A. Wallace addressing a gathering of followers at a picnic at Asbury Park, New Jersey, July 18, 1948.

Below: Progressive Party leaders at the Philadelphia convention. Seated left to right: Chairman Rexford Tugwell, vice presidential candidate and senator Glen H. Taylor (D-ID), presidential candidate Henry A. Wallace, and singer and actor Paul Robeson, July 1948.

15

Above: Presidential candidate Henry A. Wallace (holding hat) and running mate Glen H. Taylor walk the streets of Philadelphia as the nominees of the Progressive Party for the 1948 election, July 1948.

Below: Delegates wait to hear from Henry A. Wallace and his running mate, Senator Glen H. Taylor (D-ID), during the Progressive Party National Convention at the Philadelphia Convention Hall, July 23, 1948.

Above: Progressive Party presidential candidate Henry A. Wallace delivers a vigorous speech in front of the courthouse during a campaign stop in Charlotte, North Carolina, August 31, 1948.

Right: Progressive Party presidential candidate Henry A. Wallace and his wife Ilo cast ballots in White Plains, New York, November 2, 1948.

Left: Henry A. Wallace working in his garden.

Below: Henry A. Wallace at his Farvue Farm in South Salem, New York, 1962.

"All you who are within the sound of my voice tonight," he finally intoned, as the numbers within that sound continued to dwindle, "have been called to serve, and to serve mightily, in fulfilling the dreams of the Prophets and the founders of the American system."[103] Scattered claps pierced the drowsy night.

Polls following the convention showed Wallace isolating himself on Berlin—isolating himself from all, that is, but the Communists, who would endorse him at their own convention in early August. A striking 90 percent of the American public backed Truman's resolve to remain in Berlin. Eighty percent said the president should hold firm *even if it meant war with Russia.* Seventy-six percent wanted U.S. military strength *increased.* Ominously, nearly half of *Wallace supporters* opposed their candidate's calls for withdrawal from Berlin, and half supported the Marshall Plan.

Wallace had been steadily losing the support of his early and most ardent booster groups since he had declared the previous December. Among the young and the blue-collar, his poll numbers had halved. Despite the CIO having led the drive to make him FDR's running mate in 1944, a mere 10 percent of its members, and 7 percent of union members overall, now backed him for president. And notwithstanding his awkward efforts to deny Communist influence over his party, while at the same time embracing Communist support, half the public thought his new party "communist controlled."

"Mr. Wallace," Eleanor Roosevelt wrote in her daily column, "should really take a good look at those who controlled his convention."[104] Such warnings, charges, and insinuations frustrated Wallace. "The Progressive Party is *not* controlled by Communists," he insisted, "nor was its convention or program dictated by them."[105] He was willing to disown the support of any who owed their "allegiance to some foreign capital," but denied that most Communists did so. There was, he contended, "as much variation in the beliefs of Communists as in the beliefs of Democrats and Republicans," yet he continued to decry Democrats and Republicans for pursuing identical reactionary policies. As for the atrocities being committed abroad in the name of Communism, he "doubt[ed] if any Marxists today [were] as violent as Lincoln and Jefferson were in their day." This latter comment provoked considerable anger and dismay on the left. "How," Socialist Party veteran and columnist Norman Thomas asked the distraught Rex Tugwell, chairman of the Progressive Party's platform committee, "can you trust a man . . . guilty of comparing . . . Jefferson and Lincoln with a dictator [Stalin] who, on coming to power, liquidated all his original associates?"

As for the American Communist leaders themselves, many, fearing that their own party would soon be banned, were more interested in winning control of the new party than in winning votes for Wallace.[106] Little more could explain the remarkable similarity between the platforms of the Progressive and Communist parties, both of whom backed Wallace.[107] Liberals such as Tugwell were, in the end, simply steamrolled by Lee Pressman, the secret-Communist secretary of the platform committee; ALP congressman Vito Marcantonio, the Communist-backed chairman of the rules committee; and John Abt, the secret-Communist roving stage manager. The unified Communist contingent even succeeded in crushing a meek proposal from the Vermont delegation not "to give blanket endorsement to the foreign policy of any nation," insisting that it constituted a shocking and unwarranted criticism of the Soviet Union.[108] These men were not out to convince liberal voters, but to act as parasites, taking over the body of a host left-liberal party—just as their Communist brethren had done in Germany.[109]

In any case, the policy territory onto which the new party could expand was shrinking to electoral insignificance. Truman had pacified labor. He had convinced news readers and listeners of his soundness on foreign affairs. In the words of Progressive campaign chronicler Curtis MacDougall, "Gideon's Army" had, by the time of the convention, been "reduced to those who sympathized with all or most of Wallace's criticisms of the Truman foreign and domestic policies"—a small number indeed.

These true believers, however were out in force among the convention's 3,200 delegates and alternates. "If the people's movement continues to spread," enthused one disciple from North Carolina, "Wallace will carry at least forty states."[110] The candidate, for his part, also remained upbeat. He took little interest in the Communist-instigated platform brawls over matters such as Puerto Rican and Macedonian independence (the latter of which was never resolved, owing to Communist confusion as to whether it served Stalin or Yugoslavia Premier Josip Tito). For Wallace, "*le parti, c'est moi.*" He *was* the party. It could not bind him. As for the poor polling, it constituted merely proof of his army's uncontaminated Christian virtue. "We have said with Gideon," he proclaimed, "'Let those who are fearful and trembling depart.' . . . A just cause is worth a hundred armies."[111]

"In his inexplicable way," observed journalist James Wechsler, "Wallace gloried in the fact" of his declining popularity. He might not win, this time out, but, "dispossessed of the faint-hearted, he and the others could go on to build the third party for the future."[112]

Wallace's Olympian detachment distressed his most able and devoted backers. The candidate took no interest in campaign tactics or logistics, and even refused to discuss them. "He places his cause on such a high plane," observed Bob Kenny, one of his most important boosters in California, "that we . . . cannot 'sully' it by discussing the crass issues of political strategy with him. When we [try], he falls asleep."[113]

Seventeen

THE PEOPLE SPEAK

Henry Wallace, now approaching age sixty, remained a fine specimen of health and vigor. Entering the seventh decade of life, he might still have reflected that his choice of running mate would be a matter of concern to the prudent voter. To Wallace's own mind, after all, he himself should *already have been president*. That is, he *would have been president*, had the sixty-two-year-old Franklin Roosevelt chosen a running mate more responsibly.

Yet Wallace hardly thought of his own running mate as a president in waiting. Instead, he seemed to think of him more as comic relief. The flamboyant, voluble Glen Taylor, known to the media as "the singing cowboy," was a self-educated, showboating, banjo-strumming, horse-trekking, hairpiece-sporting forty-four-year-old first-term Democratic senator from Idaho. Wallace's temperamental opposite, Taylor still shared with the Iowan a penchant for hurling invectives at bankers and generals, as well as a higher regard for ideological purity than for pedantic accuracy. Colleagues and relations had warned Taylor that leaving his party to run with Wallace would mean political suicide, but a Quixotic streak, and a love of the spotlight, trumped any fear of losing his cherished Senate seat (which he would indeed lose in 1950).

Taylor could, at times, veer inexplicably into the ludicrous, as when he chose to don lipstick for some presumed camera effect at the Philadelphia convention. The humor engendered thereby prompted second-order jokes about "red smears" and the like.

Still, Taylor brought a certain kinetic energy to the campaign which the chicken-rearing, God-fearing Wallace could not. In his defense of the Soviet Union, Taylor could be even more doctrinaire than Wallace, and even more vitriolic toward American policies which offended it. The Cold War,

Senator Glen H. Taylor (D-ID), Henry A. Wallace's running mate in 1948, sings his own version of "Home on the Range" with his family on the Capitol steps, January 1945.

Taylor argued, was entirely America's fault. Communists were, after all, unlike capitalists, peace-loving people, since "they don't need markets." In the Soviet Union, unlike in the United States, he explained, "nobody gets rich from wars." Stock prices, in truth, typically fainted at the sight of military conflict, yet this line nonetheless remained a staple of his speeches. On the Marshall Plan, Taylor was similarly more immoderate than Wallace, calling it "the greatest fraud, the greatest steal ever perpetrated in all history." It was, he said, "a futile effort to bribe whole nations into becoming our mercenaries in a senseless struggle for world domination." And though his positions on foreign policy differed little from Wallace's, Taylor appealed to Progressives of the liberal-isolationist variety in a way in which the more evangelically internationalist Wallace could not.[1]

As for Wallace, his grasp of Soviet doctrine seemed to fall further and further behind his ever-strengthening convictions. At his July 23 press conference, he contended that Yugoslavia's expulsion from the Cominform was owed to its attachment to a "medieval" feudal land ownership system—an attachment which, he alleged, offended the Soviets. He seemed to see Stalin as a sort of Slavic Robin Hood, one who had expected Tito to take land from the large estates and give it to the peasants. Stalin, however, had in fact wanted the opposite—for Tito to force the peasants, 90 percent of whom had owned small farms before the war, onto collectives.[2]

Wallace conceded that the Soviets had not lived up to their Yalta commitments to allow free elections in the liberated countries, but suggested that the problem was mainly one of language. "Important words like 'free,'" he offered, "should be carefully defined before another conference is held." If he were president, he explained, there would be no such problem. "I'd sit down with the Russians, and ask them what they *mean* by free elections. They would find out what *we* mean. . . . And then we'd simply write down our agreement."[3]

The press was incredulous. "It was somewhat painful and embarrassing," observed columnist Joseph Alsop, who had first witnessed Wallace's ingenuousness in China, "to see the press conference of a former Vice President [turned] into something [like] the baiting of a village idiot."[4] Ickes, though far more sympathetic to Wallace, also lost patience with the candidate's inability to "explain definitely what his blueprint for world peace [actually] *is*." Peace required hard, concrete compromises. Without addressing this reality, his foreign policy amounted to little more than "the frenzied shouting of a political dervish." The cost to his campaign of shunning honest facts and reasoned prescriptions, Ickes believed, would become all the more obvious "as election time draws near."[5]

Just days after Wallace's nomination, that campaign was hit by a blow from Washington. In the midst of the growing controversy over Communist control of his party and his policies, newspaper headlines blared stunning new allegations of widespread Soviet infiltration of the U.S. government. Beginning on July 31, and extending into late August, Elizabeth Bentley made five appearances, and Whittaker Chambers six, before the House Un-American Activities Committee. The two confessed former Soviet spies named names—many names—including a number close to Wallace and integral to his campaign. Lee Pressman, John Abt, and Charles

Kramer were all subpoenaed, and all invoked their Fifth Amendment right against self-incrimination.

On August 13, the most prominent among the FBI suspects—Wallace's old friend and confidant from Treasury, Harry Dexter White—voluntarily defended himself before the committee. Three days later, he was dead of a heart attack.[6] Also accused was former State Department Latin America specialist Laurence Duggan, another longtime friend of Wallace's who accompanied him on his Latin American tour in 1943. Duggan would be interviewed by the FBI on December 11. Nine days later, he would plunge to his death from his office window. Police would never determine whether he had fallen or jumped.

Thanks to later U.S. military decrypts of Soviet intelligence cables, as well as revelations from former Soviet intelligence agents, we now know that White (NKGB code names "Richard" and "Lawyer") gave the Soviets secret information, advocated for their desired U.S. policies, and promoted their agents within the U.S. government.[7] These activities he carried on over the better part of eleven years, from 1935 to 1946. White denied all the allegations, and surely lied in saying that he did not "recollect" having ever met Whittaker Chambers—his Communist underground contact (and Soviet military intelligence agent) from 1935 to 1938. We likewise know that Duggan (NKGB code names "19th," "Frank," "Sherwood," and "Prince")—from 1936 to 1939, and 1942 to 1944—also gave the Soviets secret information.[8] He acknowledged to the FBI having twice been recruited by Soviet intelligence (unsuccessfully, he said), though he also acknowledged never reporting this fact to the State Department.

According to press reports and other accounts of his various statements, Henry Wallace, had he become president, would have made White his treasury secretary and Duggan his secretary of state.[9]

Wallace opponents made good use of the hearings, highlighting the roles in his campaign played by Pressman, Abt, and economist Victor Perlo (NKGB code name "Raid").[10] They also called attention to Wallace's statements regarding White as a future treasury secretary. Mississippi Dixiecrat John Rankin wanted Wallace to be subpoenaed so that he could "tell us why . . . Communists who were plotting the overthrow of the government were placed in key positions in his [Commerce] Department at a time when our young men were fighting and dying on every battle front in the world for the protection of this country."[11]

Years later, Wallace would tell Glen Taylor that "no fair minded person [could] laugh off the testimony of Bentley."[12] At the time, however, Wallace was less than fair-minded. He insisted that White had been "killed by [HUAC]," killed by the "poisonous slander, [the] venomous rumors, [and] the vicious gossip of self-confessed spies." No doubt White's health had been strained by the hearings, yet he had been ailing for some time. Following a severe heart attack a year prior, he had been bedridden for three months. As for the veracity of the espionage allegations against him, documentary evidence would emerge after his death.

Following the hearings, John Abt reluctantly offered to resign as party general counsel, but Wallace "would hear nothing of it." Abt was naturally relieved. He reflected decades later, after acknowledging having been a Communist Party member continually since 1934, that it "seem[ed] one further illustration of Wallace's impracticality as a politician."[13] The problem was not merely one of "impracticality," though, but an unwillingness, at least prior to 1949, to entertain facts at odds with his faith that Communists were serving his interests—rather than the reverse.

Progressive playwright and donor Lillian Hellman, a Westchester neighbor of Wallace's, recalled lunching with the candidate late in the campaign, following which he asked her to walk with him. After topping up his miserly tip, she caught up with him.

Was it true, he asked, "what they're saying"—that "many . . . in the [party] were Communists?"

Hellman laughed. Of course, she said. Who did he think did all "the hard, dirty work in the office"? It was, she added pointedly, the same bunch who gave him "a good deal of [his] bad advice."

"I see," Wallace said. He asked no more.

Years later, after Wallace had "turned bitter" toward the party, proclaiming that he had known nothing of Communists invading it, Hellman recalled her final encounter with this man who so baffled her—a man who applied "odd pieces of knowledge" to great practical effect, as well as to cultivating a "wacky" mysticism. Having learned that she was in need of cash and obliged to sell her farm, following her refusal to testify as a "friendly" witness before the HUAC, Wallace invited her to dinner at his house. He served her a single egg over shredded wheat, and himself a double portion. Hellman lost her appetite, wanting only a stiff drink. None was forthcoming. On her departure, Wallace loaded a farewell gift on top of her car. Unwrapping it the next day, she found fifty pounds of manure.[14]

No part of Wallace's campaign presented such a stark contrast between courage and nobility of purpose, on the one hand, and stubborn denial of unpalatable truth, on the other, as the candidate's brutal weeklong slog through the South, beginning on August 29, 1948.

The tone was set from the start, in Virginia, with the campaign denouncing and rejecting audience segregation laws and canceling a hotel refusing to serve its Black staff. To be sure, practical and strategic considerations were not entirely absent. The Wallace team did not openly flout segregation laws, but instead skirted them by issuing "invitations." This contrivance transformed illegal rallies into legal "private gatherings." As for hotels, it did not escape notice that the candidate had never challenged segregation policies in the *North*. Even sympathetic locals accused the ardent New York "volunteers," many of whom were concealed Communists or sympathizers, of behaving as "carpetbaggers" or "occupying troops."[15] Nonetheless, Wallace's vocal support of racial equality in the land of Jim Crow was, in the political environment of the time and the place, courageous and creditable.

At the various rally stops, the white population received him with reactions ranging from apathy to anger. Still, the first evening appearance, at North Carolina's Durham Armory, began amiably enough. Guitarist Pete Seeger led a smartly dressed, well-mannered crowd of 1,500—Black and white alike—in the singing of campaign-themed folk songs. The atmosphere changed, however, just before Wallace's arrival. Dixiecrat extremists began storming the hall, assaulting Progressives with fists, banners, chairs, and knives. As the police struggled to regain control, Wallace mounted the stage, a gun-ready National Guardsman and four plainclothesmen at his side. Under a hail of raucous cheers and heckles, he approached the microphone.

"Well," the candidate yelled to the crowd, grinning absurdly, as if exiting a wild amusement ride, "this is the most unique introduction I have ever experienced!"

Shouting erupted anew. Eggs flew in through an entryway.

Feigning unconcern, Wallace took up his speech as if he had been in

Portland, or Chicago, or any number of places where the crowds had been drafted and scripted by friendly local Communists. In one breath, he denounced segregation; in the next, he called for the South to receive $4 billion in federal development aid. Yet few heard a word he said.

Certain he could still win over the noisy throng, Wallace looked up from his text and yelled: "WHAT DO WE WANT FOR THE SOUTH?"

The cry duly came back: "WE WANT THURMOND!"

Wallace left the hall, after first leading a short prayer—also drowned out. But the violence soon spilled onto the streets, this time wrought with clubs and stones.[16]

The next day, Wallace laid blame on corporate interests. The Durham fiasco, he explained to the press, had been "a planned attack" in "reprisal for [my] long and bitter fight against tobacco trusts." By no means, therefore, had he "lost faith in the essential liberalism of the South."[17]

That liberalism was hardly manifest in the receptions he received in North Carolina's tobacco and textile country. In Burlington, Greensboro, High Point, Charlotte, and Hickory the crowds pelted him with eggs and tomatoes, shouting "nigger lover!," "Communist!," and "kill Wallace!" Though clearly shaken at times—his hair caked in egg yolk and sweat, his automobile rocked and pounded—he persevered. "[I have] a pretty good idea," he would say of the experience, "of what it must have felt like to be an early Christian martyr." Still, he never blamed "the great, glorious and God-loving people of the South."[18] They, too, were victims, he explained—victims of "Wall Street" and "outside corporations." Even his physical attackers were blameless. Though by all appearance ruddy and robust, "most of them," Wallace said, had "not had enough to eat." This observation evoked howls of laughter from the purportedly underfed.[19]

Along the tour, Wallace professed a unique brand of quasi-Marxist economic determinism, one in which there ran "a long chain that links unknown hoodlums in a North Carolina or Alabama mill town with men in . . . finely tailored business suits—men who are in the great financial centers of New York and Boston—men who make a . . . profit by setting race against race in the faraway South." The "deliberate falsehoods and lies" they spread "had inflamed the passions" of a "proud and courageous people," impelling them "to act against their deepest Christian principles."[20] As for the racism which had long plagued the South, it would, he insisted, vanish once Northern predations ceased, aid flowed in, and good jobs became plentiful.

To tour the South in 1948 was in reality to travel through a world in which the term "white supremacy" was still invoked with pride. To many white Southerners along Wallace's route, the candidate's sympathy came across as ignorant, patronizing, and even threatening to their way of life. Wallace's policy fixes—in particular, imposing levies on Northern firms operating in the South, and distributing the take to local ones—seemed equally off the mark. Southern firms were hardly renowned for progressive labor or race policies, and so it was far from apparent why subsidizing them, at the expense of Northern investors, should have improved wages or race relations.

As with Stalin's Russia, Wallace was navigating the Jim Crow South with a mental map that bore little relation to reality. It was yet another instance of The World That Wasn't. The Common Man of his imagination needed only leaders devoted to peace and planning in order to thrive beside his neighbor, a neighbor whom he, the noble commoner, mistakenly considered the alien "other"—thanks only to the evil of corporate-induced false consciousness. Racism, like anti-Communism, was, for Wallace, a political disease, yet one reliably cured through the patient provision of jobs and Christian goodwill.

In any case, white Southerners, following the North Carolina debacles, largely lost interest in Wallace. His appearances in Louisiana, Arkansas, and Tennessee were sparsely attended and—beyond the ritual deprecations and occasional flying egg—mostly peaceful. As for Black Southerners, who were broadly appreciative of his forthright stance for civil rights, they proved a greater disappointment to Wallace than the whites who egged him. They were, and would remain, strongly supportive of Truman.[21]

For all the president's ingrained biases and, at times, distinctly un-progressive habits of speech, he had, back in February, put forth the most far-reaching civil rights program of any president in the nation's history. His message to Congress was forthright. "The Federal Government," he said, had "a clear duty to see that the Constitutional guarantees of individual liberties and of equal protection under the laws are not denied or abridged anywhere in the Union." He demanded a federal antilynching law. He demanded statutory protections for the right to vote, including the abolition of poll taxes. He proposed a new Fair Employment Practices Committee to stop bias at work. He insisted that interstate rail, bus, and plane travel be free of racial inequities. And he called on the secretary of defense to put a definitive end to discrimination in the military.

When Southern Democrats pressed him to scale back his ambitions, he refused. Though his own forebears had been Confederates, he reminded them, "my stomach turned over when I learned that Negro soldiers, just back from overseas, were being dumped out of army trucks in Mississippi and beaten. . . . I shall fight to end evils like this." Even to wary friends back home, he was frank and unapologetic. "[T]he South," he wrote to one, was "eighty years behind the times and the sooner they come out of it the better it will be for the country and themselves." He could not, he insisted, turn his eyes from the violence and injustices perpetrated on Black citizens. "I am going to try to remedy it," he concluded, "and if that ends up in my failure to be reelected, that failure will be in a good cause."[22]

The civil rights record of Truman's Republican adversary, New York governor Thomas Dewey, had been strong. Yet Dewey chose, thinking the election all but won, to appease the Taft wing of his party through virtual silence on the subject. This choice would prove a momentous miscalculation. Taft, in arguing, uncontested by Dewey, that Republicans were "far more in accord with the views of the [white] South than the policies of the Truman administration," convinced Blacks that the party opposed their interests.[23]

As for Wallace, Black leaders, such as the NAACP's William Hastie, governor of the U.S. Virgin Islands, warned that support for his candidacy could only mean the election of a "reactionary Republican Administration." Notwithstanding Wallace's brave pronouncements, Hastie dismissed him for having been "notoriously disinterested in civil rights and the needs of the Negro when he was vice president and in the Cabinet." Wallace had, in fact, declined NAACP speaking invitations for years, displaying little interest in its concerns before 1944.[24] Civil rights activist Walter White condemned his "refusal to do anything about segregation and discrimination in the Departments of Commerce and Agriculture," in contrast to Ickes at Interior and Morgenthau at Treasury. Wallace himself would later acknowledge that it was not until 1944 that he began to take a strong interest in race matters.[25] In any case, Hastie was right that domestic affairs were, at best, a secondary concern for Wallace. And when Hastie condemned the Progressive Party as "a political puppet securely tied to the Communist party line," he was reflecting the strong anti-Communism prevalent among African Americans at the time.[26]

All in all, it was a rough summer for Wallace, capped off by the brutal Dixie tour. And so he was relieved to return to New York after Labor Day. For nearly two years now, he had been sculpting his political persona in the city. It had become his sanctuary. Home to concentrations of social activists and liberal intellectuals—not to mention, of course, Communists—New York enveloped Wallace with men and women among whom his convictions and policies found resonance.

Wallace was particularly thrilled to return to the Bronx. The borough had been the source of his campaign's earliest triumph back in February— or, to be accurate, *Leo Isacson's* triumph, which Wallace adopted as his own. Isacson, now the American Labor Party representative for the 24th Congressional District (The Bronx), and Vito Marcantonio, its Communist-backed representative for the 18th (Harlem), were the sole third-party members of Congress. They offered both hope and support for Wallace and his own new party.

At Yankee Stadium, 11:30 on the night of September 10, 48,000 Wallace supporters, two thirds of whom in their early twenties or younger, cheered as their candidate emerged from the home dugout. Waving and grinning, he made his way through the handmade confetti wafting down from the upper levels, amidst a growing chant of "WE WANT WALLACE! WE WANT WALLACE!" This, the most lucrative of his rallies, would add a remarkable $100,000 ($1.2 million in today's money) to the party coffers.[27]

Wallace's speech that night was of his own hand. It was also the most caustic and polemical of his campaign. Wallace repeated the charges he had made down South that its "proud and courageous" people were victims of the Northern "owners of the mines and mills, the great plantations, and [the] newspapers which incite violence." Whereas these enterprises did not "*personally* engage in lynching either free speech or human beings," he qualified, they "inflame[d] the passions of others."

He blasted the "corrupt and dangerous" men—the Democrats, Republicans, and "self-styled Liberals"—who "have joined hands in their bipartisan wrath against" Leo Isacson and Vito Marcantonio, "real servants of the people." Those gathered, he said, were proud to make enemies of men "who support fascists in Greece and China," men "who hated Franklin Roosevelt and the New Deal." These were men abetted by "cheap political tricksters," men "who all their lives have practiced black reaction."[28]

For those planning to vote for either main party on November 2, Wallace's speech would have sounded self-righteous and repellent. Yet for those cheering Wallace in the stands that night, it was simply and upliftingly righteous. As they made for the exits, they broke into spirited song. To the tune of the "Battle Hymn of the Republic," they sang:

From the village, from the city, all the nation's voices roared.
Down the rivers, 'cross the prairies, like a torrent it has poured.
We will march like Gideon's Army.
We will fight with Gideon's Sword,
For the people's march is on!
Glory, Glory Hallelujah,
Glory, Glory Hallelujah,
Glory, Glory Hallelujah,
The people's march is on![29]

Unfortunately for Wallace, the people's march ended at the borders of New York City. His national poll numbers continued to fall: from 7 percent in January, to 6 percent in June, to 5 percent in August, to 3.5 percent in October. On Truman's signature issues, particularly foreign policy, Wallace was losing the country. Support for the Marshall Plan was high and growing, particularly among those most familiar with it.

In the South, Wallace was anathema. In the vast middle of the country, he was an object of apathy. At his party's state convention in Nebraska, on the same night as the Yankee Stadium rally, barely a third of the 750 souls required to qualify the party for the ballot turned out. In California, prominent liberal Democrats, such as Helen Gahagan Douglas and Chet Holifield, refused to allow their names to be cross-listed on the Progressive line. "I did not seek the endorsement of the third party and do not desire it," declared Douglas—who had, in 1944, strongly supported Wallace for vice president. "My differences with the third party are well known. I strongly support the

Marshall Plan and believe the present Russian attitude is a threat to world peace."

Such repudiations put the party in an awful bind, as it had either to run its own candidates against them, making the election of Republicans more likely, or to abandon its line on the ballot and face charges of aiding "reactionaries"—that is, those who backed Truman's foreign policy. Baldwin tried to quell the growing crisis on a case-by-case basis, but ultimately began conceding ballot lines around the country, even when the local Democrat renounced his party's endorsement, to staunch rising anger over Progressives boosting Republican fortunes. This climbdown led to conflict with the more purist Wallace, who insisted he could never ally with Democrats who "opposed peace."

The liberal press, too, had turned against Wallace. *The Nation, PM,* and even *The New Republic,* so recently his own personal bullhorn, opposed his candidacy. Among dailies, he was backed by only the Communist *Daily Worker* and *People's World* of San Francisco, as well as the tiny *Gazette and Daily* of York, Pennsylvania.[30]

The clearer it became that his campaign was collapsing, the more Wallace fell back on his Bronx rhetoric. Those who "hate" him, his "enemies," wished to turn the nation over "to slavery or to war." The "bipartisan reactionaries" in Washington were fashioning a "phony war scare" in Berlin to erect a "smoke screen" for the monopolists and moneymen, a smoke screen behind which they hoped to "create a new Nazi state in the heart of Europe." Having earlier scolded Truman for abandoning the U.N. as a means of resolving disagreements, he now—in a head-snapping twist—scolded the president for taking the Berlin crisis to the new body, "where it cannot be solved." Only direct bilateral talks with Moscow, he now insisted, could end it. Remarkably, he even celebrated the news that Mukden had fallen to Mao and his Communists: "Chiang Kai-shek is on his way out!"

When chastised by the press for unsubstantiated charges and inconsistencies, the candidate contested their quotes or condemned their bad faith. Wallace, chided the *Los Angeles Times,* had "been chased out on a limb by facts" and "does not know how to get back, except by denying that the facts exist." He would years later blame ghostwriters, who routinely assisted in providing the Kremlin's version of facts. Wallace approved their work, of course, but, in his defense, he was at times asleep while hearing it. In any case, the overwrought denunciations were his own peculiar specialty, and he required no outside assistance in their conjuring.[31]

On October 26, a week before election day, with the polls looking bleak, Wallace returned to his old safe space, Madison Square Garden, for one last rally of the faithful. Marcantonio was to have introduced him, but instead sent a telegram, which Wallace read to the crowd, explaining the need to man his own electoral battlelines in the 18th District. Skeptics may have speculated that the congressman was loath to nail his mast to a sunken ship. Wallace, however, wore a bold—one might even say brazen—air. Before a crowd of nineteen thousand, he declared victory; victory not for himself, but for his vision.

"Because of the Progressive Party," he said, Americans, Black and white, stood "on the threshold of a new and richer freedom." Because of the Progressive Party, the "fighters for freedom" in Greece and in China (that is, the Communists and their allies) knew that the American people supported their struggle. And because of the Progressive Party, "there shall," above all, "*be no war.*" The crowd cheered.

Most, while no doubt heartened by the news that they had stopped a war, must still have been surprised by it. But Wallace doubled down. The Progressive Party, he declared, had "stopped the cold war in its tracks."[32]

These stunning statements were likely motivated by the recent revelations that Truman had considered—though, owing to objections from Marshall, also quickly rejected—sending Supreme Court Justice Fred Vinson to Moscow as a personal envoy.[33] Wallace was sure that Truman's latest effort to renew a dialogue with Stalin, however halfhearted and half-baked, owed to his, Wallace's, shaming of the president as a warmonger.

Of course, Wallace knew, bad men might yet make the world go bad. Yet whatever might happen in Berlin, whatever might happen in Greece, whatever might happen in China, whatever might happen in Korea, he had, at least for a brief time, thanks to the power of his ideas, the power of his words, and the power of his Army of Gideon, brought peace. He had changed the world. As he walked off, smiling, waving, down from his favorite pulpit for the final time, this was the truth he wished the world to know.

On the night of Monday, November 1, 1948, the eve of the election, Wallace addressed street rallies in Harlem and the Bronx. People all over the globe, he told them, "were rebelling against the Truman Doctrine and the Marshall Plan." America had become "a symbol of oppression" in Greece and China. Votes for Vito Marcantonio, Leo Isacson, and Henry Wallace were, therefore, votes against "the war and anti-labor policies of Wall Street." Virtually conceding the election to Dewey, however, he implored them, in any case, not to "waste" their ballots on Truman. "Truman is going to lose."[34]

Pravda agreed. Its final elections article was devoted almost entirely to the Progressive Party, which had already "gained a significant victory" by getting Wallace on forty-five state ballots. Dewey and the Republicans were mentioned only in passing; Truman and the Democrats not at all.[35]

At eight the following morning, November 2, Henry and Ilo Wallace arrived at the polling place for their local constituency—a 148-year-old white colonial structure that was the South Salem Public Library. After casting their votes, they returned to Farvue for breakfast, following which the candidate passed some hours reading telegrams, talking with neighbors, and tending to experimental chickens. In the late afternoon, the couple headed to Manhattan by car. Driving through Brooklyn, "at least half a million people greeted Wallace," according to a report exclusive to *Trud*, the Soviet trade union newspaper. The candidate's vehicle was, the report continued, "accompanied by 50 machines decorated with banners and posters appealing for support of the Progressive Party." Eager locals "rushed up to Wallace in order to shake his hand."[36]

At 6 p.m., the Wallaces ate dinner at the Hotel Russell and watched the early election returns. At one point, the columnist Drew Pearson came on air and predicted that Henry Wallace would, within six months, disown the Communists and ditch the Progressive Party, which was headed for total defeat. Annoyed, Wallace turned to his wife, saying plaintively, "I couldn't do it if I wanted to." Ilo, who loathed Communists, and preferred experimental chickens to experimental parties, smiled uneasily.[37] As for Pearson's prognostications, only his timing would be slightly off.

At 8:30 p.m., the Wallaces arrived at Progressive Party headquarters at Park Avenue and 36th Street. Among the crowd, many Soviet assets who had aided the campaign and shaped its policy positions, such as Alfred and Martha Stern, were on hand to welcome them.[38] Paul Robeson sang. The mood was buoyant. The returns were dismal, yet the final result, whichever way it went, could still be spun to happy effect. If Dewey won, it would show the price to be paid for abandoning liberalism. If Truman won, it would show that Democrats could be shamed back to liberalism. For the Progressive optimist, any outcome signaled success.

Such a fortuitous state of affairs did not, however, commend itself to Mrs. Wallace. As she watched the returns, she sobbed openly. "I told him so all the time!" she cried, speaking of how she had begged her husband not to engage with the new party. "He should never have done it!"[39]

At 10:45 p.m., an unrepentant Mr. Wallace gave a radio address, calling forth the wrath of the righteous and pledging their ultimate victory. "Today I say that the cup of iniquity of both the old parties will overflow," he intoned. "Unless this bipartisan foreign policy of high prices and war is promptly reversed," he warned, "I predict that the Progressive party will rapidly grow into the dominant party." They would therefore continue the "fight to save the nation and the world."[40]

By the early hours of November 3, it was looking as if a monumental upset might be in the offing—just not the one Gideon's Army had envisioned. On the back of a spirited campaign, topped off by a relentless six-week whistle-stop tour, Harry Truman, the accidental president, was defying the polls and Wallace's prophecy. His lead in the popular vote was solid, though the electoral math would remain murky until well after sunrise.

From Harlem, happier tidings were flowing in. Six-term representative Vito Marcantonio was headed for reelection, narrowly, on the American Labor Party line. Technically, there was no Progressive Party in New York, and Wallace had piggybacked on the ALP ballot. He thus embraced their victory as his own, much as he had done with Isacson's in February, and decided to head north and join their celebration at 2 a.m.

As for Isacson, he was, after just nine months in the House, headed for a thrashing by his Democratic rival, lawyer Isidore Dollinger. "[V]irtually the only difference on issues" between the men, noted *The New York Times*, was that Isacson opposed the Truman Doctrine and the Marshall Plan.[41] Wallace would observe his loss with a demure silence.[42]

Shortly before Wallace left his supporters, John Abt handed him the draft of a telegram he might send to Truman, should the president emerge victorious. Wallace passed it to Clark Foreman, the party's national treasurer, who thought it ungracious. It was in fact, as concession letters go, obnoxious.

It read:

> The people of America and particularly the farmers, workers and Negro people look to you and to the new Democratic Congress to implement [your] declarations by enacting the necessary legislation.
>
> These goals cannot be realized and the bankruptcy of the American economy avoided so long as the policy of the Cold War is continued and we spend increasing billions of American dollars to support reactionary regimes abroad, arm Western Europe, and militarize America.
>
> A comprehensive program of assistance to farmers, rollback of consumer prices, public housing, social security, conservation, irrigation, and public power development is possible only under a foreign policy of one world at peace, not two hostile worlds arming for war.
>
> Therefore the Progressive party calls upon you, as you enter upon your first elected term, to repudiate the bipartisan foreign policy, to remove the military from the civilian branch of government, and the bankers from the State Department, and to return to the Roosevelt policy of friendship and collaboration among nations through the United Nations for the establishment of one world at peace. Only in this way can the mandate which you have received from the American people be fulfilled.

Beyond the problem of tone, Foreman explained, the message lacked the basic word "congratulations"—which was de rigueur in such things.

Wallace, however, was in no mood to be civil. "Under no circumstances," he said, "will I congratulate that son of a bitch."[43] And with that, he departed the building. A few hours later, the telegram followed.

At 8:30 A.M., the media called Ohio for Truman, sealing his victory. In the end, he would capture 303 electoral votes to Dewey's 189 and Thurmond's 39 (from Alabama, Louisiana, Mississippi, and South Carolina). Wallace failed to win a single electoral vote.

Overall, Truman received 24,179,347 popular votes (49.5 percent) to Dewey's 21,991,292 (45.1 percent), Thurmond's 1,175,930 (2.4 percent), and Wallace's 1,157,328 (2.4 percent). Wallace had, in the end, become the "fourth party" candidate. Progressive cognoscenti had, at polling time, been anticipating 5 to 10 million Wallace votes, or four to nine times more than he got.[44]

Between Truman and Dewey, it had been a close contest. A shift in votes to Dewey of a mere 7,000 in Ohio, 17,000 in California, and 33,000 in Illinois would have given him the election. Had two of those three states gone to Dewey, the election would have been thrown to the House of Representatives.[45]

As for Wallace, he polled poorly even in comparison with the century's two earlier independent progressive presidential candidates. In 1912, Teddy Roosevelt garnered 88 electoral votes, and 27 percent of the popular vote, finishing second to Woodrow Wilson. In 1924, "Fighting Bob" La Follette, with solid union backing, took the 13 electoral votes of his home state, Wisconsin, and 16.6 percent of the total popular vote. Wallace's best performance by far was in his adopted state of New York, where he took 8.1 percent of the vote—amounting to half of his national total.

Almost the entirety of Wallace's support was urban. A remarkable 37 percent of his nationwide vote came from New York City *alone*. No major farm organization backed him, and his rural support was trifling. In his home state of Iowa, he took a mere 1.17 percent of the vote. Farm policy had, in fact, played a negligible role in his campaign, and to the extent that it did he was not helped by his own words. After suggesting, off the cuff, that the federal government buy up submarginal agricultural land, he added that to the extent that "people insist on living on such land . . . the government should not let them have children." These people, he emphasized, sounding more fascist than liberal, had "no right to have children."[46]

Wallace was bitter over his lack of union support. The only unions that backed him would later be expelled from the CIO for being Communist-dominated.[47] And though Wallace had been commerce secretary for nearly a year and a half, no prominent industrial interests rallied to him. In short, farmers, workers, and business opposed his candidacy—a trifecta of failure.

Wallace was also resentful over his pitiful tally of Black votes. About 77 percent went to Truman and 21 percent to Dewey, leaving Wallace with the remaining 2 percent or so.[48] Blacks, Wallace would later say, had "had their chance" and "let me down." Truman, in fact, polled about 10 points better than had FDR in 1944. Given the slim majorities by which Truman won Ohio, California, and Illinois, that strong Black support, at a time in which Democrats could hardly take it for granted, was critical to the election outcome.[49]

Wallace's strongest support came from Jewish voters—roughly 18 percent of whom backed him (versus 60 percent for Truman). Jews, disproportionately progressive, appreciated Wallace's ardent New Dealism, as well as his forthright backing for the creation and defense of the new state of Israel. Precise figures are impossible to come by, but it would appear that Jews may have accounted for more than a third of Wallace's total votes.

In stark contrast to those numbers, not even one percent of Wallace's Protestant coreligionists backed him (Thurmond took 3 percent, Truman and Dewey 48 percent each). Though Wallace had been vocally critical of the Vatican's anti-Sovietism, his Catholic support, at 2.3 percent, roughly matched his overall support. It is possible, however, that Truman's overwhelming Catholic support (70 percent, versus 27 percent for Dewey) was helped by Wallace's bolstering of Truman's anti-Communist credentials.[50]

In terms of gender, Wallace's support was split almost perfectly (51 percent male). Truman's and Dewey's support leaned slightly more male (52.8 percent and 53.4 percent, respectively). Thurmond's support was overwhelmingly male (66.1 percent). In terms of age, Wallace voters were considerably younger: 35 years old on average, compared with 42 for Truman voters, 45 for Thurmond voters, and 46 for Dewey voters. In terms of economic class, Truman's support came most heavily from the poor: 62.3 percent. 52.9 percent of Wallace voters were classified as poor, as compared to 46.4 percent of Thurmond voters and 38.1 percent of Dewey voters. 3.5 percent of Dewey voters were classified as wealthy, as compared to 3.6 percent of Thurmond voters, 2 percent of Wallace voters, and a mere 0.7 percent of Truman voters. In terms of education, Wallace and Dewey voters were almost equally likely to have college degrees (20 percent and 21.6 percent, respectively). (If college students are included in those numbers, Wallace probably tops Dewey.) 17.9 percent of Thurmond voters had college degrees, and only 9.6 percent of Truman voters.[51] Overall, Truman clearly had a better claim to being the candidate of the Common Man than did Wallace, his self-declared champion.

There is a certain irony in the fact that the Dewey camp credited Truman's victory to corn and Russia—these being the two great objects that bookended Wallace's career. "The farm vote switched in the last ten days," Dewey would write to Henry Luce. "You can analyze figures from now to kingdom come and all they will show is that we lost the farm vote." Indeed, corn prices had fallen in the four-month run-up to the poll, and farmers saw Truman and the Democrats as more likely to safeguard their incomes than Dewey and the Republicans. Truman won six of the eight largest corn-producing states.[52]

Then there was the crisis in Europe. Although Wallace had scorned the Marshall Plan and the Berlin Airlift, the public saw them both, by election time, as noble and effective responses to Soviet aggression. In the end, "the bear got us," concluded Dewey adviser Elliott Bell.[53] Wallace had built his campaign on the contention that Truman was a dangerous, incompetent, and irrational anti-Communist warmonger. Yet the president had succeeded, in spite of the diplomatic hiccups with Ambassador Smith and Justice Vinson, in establishing himself as a sound-minded steward of the nation's foreign affairs.

As for the Progressive Party broadly, all of their 114 House and nine Senate candidates went down to defeat. None even polled sufficient votes to affect the outcome of their races. After two years in the minority, the Democrats once again dominated both houses of Congress: 54–42 in the Senate, and 263–171 in the House.

Part of the problem for the Progressives in 1948 was that "protest parties . . . have never done well in periods of prosperity"[54] and that, in spite of Wallace's repeated prophesies of imminent economic doom, the United States was in the midst of just such a period. But the Progressive wipeout also owed much to the fact that the party had been created largely to support the ambitions of one man—a man who cared little about domestic policy. Without the name of Henry Wallace, and his Soviet-friendly agenda, the CPUSA would never have worked to build, to staff, and to finance that party. Their work, however, as important as it was in getting the party off the ground and onto the ballots, helped shape the fatal public perception that its candidates were not merely sympathetic to Moscow but controlled by it. The Communists had set themselves to dominating the new party, hoping to use it to bring down Truman, the Marshall Plan, and the CIO leadership. Now, with the election over, they found themselves grasping an empty husk.

Many Progressives would naturally claim that their party's great success had been tugging Truman to the left, particularly on economic issues. The Progressives were, in Wallace's words, "the chief moving force in causing the American people to reverse their fatally reactionary 1946 trend. They voted for the Democratic candidate for President only after we had forced him to compete with us on the same program."[55]

Wallace had, however, campaigned to the bitter end for controversial policies, such as extensive price controls, that Truman refused to back. There is, further, scant evidence that Truman had taken the electoral threat from Wallace seriously enough to bend his policies against it.[56] On domestic policy, his leftward shift, which was apparent by 1947, is easily explained by the change in economic and political circumstances. As the strike wave of 1945–46 fell away, it freed him to indulge his pro-labor instincts and to stand against the excesses of Taft-Hartley. In the realm of foreign affairs, Wallace was, for Truman, political manna from heaven. Whereas Wallace's votes in New York, Michigan, and Maryland—all close contests—were sufficient to hand 74 electoral votes to Dewey, it is more difficult to quantify those votes Truman may have *gained* by Wallace robbing Dewey of the argument that the president was a weak and dangerous leftist.

"In so far as [Wallace successfully] identified liberal opinion with Communist opinion," wrote Margaret Marshall in *The Nation*, he "made it tragically easy for [Truman] to ignore it and even to condemn it."[57]

Eighteen

BELIEF BETRAYED

On a Sunday morning in 1953, Michael Straight met with the sixty-four-year-old Henry Wallace, for the first time in four years, at the home of the Swiss minister married to Wallace's sister. Wallace had wanted to see documents Straight had found undermining charges by Fulton Lewis Jr., the anti-Communist shock jock, that Wallace had aided Communists in the Roosevelt administration.

But Wallace also had some questions to ask—painful questions—about the '48 election.

"Was John Abt a Communist?"

Straight nodded. "I think so."

"And Paul Robeson?"

"I'm afraid so."

"What about Lew Frank?"

Straight frowned. "I've asked myself that many times. I just don't know."

"And Beanie Baldwin?"

"Beanie wasn't a Communist—in my opinion. He thought he could use them."

Wallace nodded. "I blame Beanie for a lot."

Heads bowed, the two walked together to the dining room, joining Wallace's wife, his brother-in-law, his daughter, and daughter-in-law.

It was a somber, joyless dinner.

"Wallace sat in silence in the candlelight," Straight recorded. "The gloom that exuded from him spread like a black cloth, smothering all conversation."[1]

Nothing, it seems, so sears the soul like belief betrayed.

❧

Five years earlier, in December 1948, the month following his electoral gutting, Henry Wallace was still in a fighting mood. He was determined to rebrand himself yet again, this time as a mediator. News reports said he hoped the president would send him "on a peace mission to Moscow."[2] Through personal agents, such as patron Anita McCormick Blaine, who wrote multiple letters to Truman's appointments secretary, he set out to market his services.

"The President," the White House told Blaine, "was delighted" to hear from her. No mention was made of Henry Wallace.[3]

The aspiring peacemaker was, however, also feverishly working the other side. On November 7, a week after the election, Wallace was the star guest at a caviar-and-sturgeon reception at the Soviet embassy, commemorating the Bolshevik Revolution.[4] On December 7, the day following the White House brush-off, Wallace invited the Soviet ambassador, Alexander Panyushkin, to lunch at his Farvue Farm the following Sunday. The ambassador, a veteran intelligence officer, accepted gratefully.[5]

On December 13, the day following the lunch, Wallace denounced American "imperialists and militarists" at a twenty-thousand-strong National Council of American-Soviet Friendship rally at Madison Square Garden, and urged the president to abandon his Cold War.[6] At Yale Law School, he called on Truman to ignore "militarists" at the National Security Council and to send a civil representative to Moscow for talks with Stalin. This call was duly publicized in *Pravda*.[7]

On or around Christmas, Panyushkin had Wallace to dinner at the Soviet embassy, where the Iowan offered to mediate secretly between the Kremlin and the White House. According to the ambassador's cable reporting the encounter to Moscow, Wallace claimed there was a "new situation" in the White House, now that Marshall had left the State Department. Truman would, Wallace said, hereafter be more "independent and resourceful in foreign policy." This was a remarkable claim for a man who had always held that Truman, and not Marshall, was the reactionary force preventing peace.

Panyushkin, however, "did not exclude" the possibility that Wallace was acting "on behalf of more constructive-thinking members of the administration." He therefore advised Moscow "to treat Wallace's statements with attention."[8]

Shortly after New Year's 1949, Molotov cabled back instructions to accept Wallace's offer of "non-official mediation." No doubt anticipating Stalin's skepticism, however, he added that Panyushkin should proceed "only if Wallace himself believes in this business."

But Wallace did not believe in it; he knew the White House would not even speak to him. He was trying, instead, to get Stalin to believe in it.

Meeting with the ambassador a few days later, he urged the Kremlin to reach out and "capture Truman's imagination." Stalin, he suggested, might offer "guarantees as to the limits of Soviet expansion." Wallace pledged his assistance in "correcting" any proposals the Kremlin might make in advance of their submission to the White House.

As Stalin had edited an "open letter" from Wallace to him, Wallace was now offering to edit a private letter from Stalin to Truman. Still, Wallace put his odds of success at only "one in four."

Reading Panyushkin's new cable, Molotov was incredulous. In his draft orders for Stalin's approval, he insisted that the ambassador not let Wallace "get away with general phrases." What "we are interested in obtaining, with Wallace's cooperation, in an unofficial way," Molotov explained, is "more convincing information on Truman's current position, and whether there is a trend [in thinking] towards any improvement of relations [with us], since we are not in possession of any such information."

It was testimony to the complete collapse of the Soviet spy network in Washington since late 1945, following the defection of Elizabeth Bentley, that the Kremlin could even imagine that Henry Wallace might be a credible informant, let alone mediator. Yet in spite of that hope, Stalin's innate paranoia ruled the day. "Wallace thinks of using his mediation only for [the benefit of] his own party," the *vozhd* scribbled contemptuously on Molotov's draft, "without much thought to the outcome of this mediation for the USSR."

Wallace, however, was not thinking of his party—a party which had let him down, just as the Democrats and Republicans had done before it. Wallace was thinking of himself, and his next shot at the White House in 1952. The party was merely one possible vehicle, and certainly no end in itself.

In any case, Stalin had little use for Wallace at this point. With all his friendly talk, the peace-man had never delivered. "We should not open all our cards to Wallace," Stalin concluded. "Let Wallace screw around as he pleases."9

And so on January 14, 1949, Stalin, together with the six other Politburo members handling major foreign policy decisions, voted to cease contacts with Wallace. Dealings with "leaders of an opposition party in the USA," they reasoned, would only "provide a pretext for U.S. reactionary circles" to threaten the USSR.[10]

Unaware of Stalin's disdain, Wallace wrote to his former Russian teacher, Arthur Saul, that same day. "[F]or the first time in five years I strongly feel the urge to study Russian again," the letter said. "The need for promoting understanding between the US and the USSR has never seemed to me to be as great as right now."[11] Four days later, Wallace wrote an open letter to Truman and the Congress calling on them to "reject the proposal for a North Atlantic military alliance" (NATO), and for the U.S. and USSR to sign a "peace treaty." Declaring peace, for Wallace, was a wholly viable alternative to resolving differences. The Soviet embassy, also seemingly unaware of Stalin's edict, forwarded his peace petition to Moscow.[12] It sent no response.

Over the subsequent months, Wallace continued to reach out to Panyushkin on minor matters. On March 14, he wrote to him asking for an English copy of a Russian book entitled *The Truth About American Diplomats*. Published in Moscow the previous month, the book was a hyperbolic anti-American screed revealing alleged anti-Soviet intrigues at the State Department. Its putative author, a former junior U.S. embassy official in Moscow named Annabelle Bucar, had been recruited by the MGB (counterintelligence) Second Directorate using a male "honey trap" to secure her defection. The MGB report on Bucar makes clear that she had no useful writing talents, and could not have authored a tabloid op-ed, let alone a political tell-all.[13] The book was a transparent Soviet counterintelligence product, copies of which had been sent to the embassy in Washington for distribution to those whom Lenin might have called "useful idiots." Panyushkin sent a copy to Wallace, promising to send an English version as soon as one became available.[14]

Throughout the spring, Wallace campaigned vigorously, on radio and at live nationwide "Peace Tour" rallies, against NATO, the Marshall Plan, and even the Berlin Airlift—the high cost of which he blamed on the American "policy of containment." That policy, he said, was bound to "end in absolute failure."[15] There were, he thundered at a rally in Cleveland, "more warmongers concentrated in the USA than in any other nation of the world."[16]

Before the Senate Foreign Relations Committee on May 5, he blamed "the Catholic church," "British imperial interests," and "American big business interests" for "consciously and carefully" conducting an anti-Communist "propaganda campaign." He denounced NATO as "a military alliance designed for aggression."

A stunned Connecticut Democrat Brien McMahon observed that Wallace seemed to be accusing the State Department of "treasonable conduct."

Wallace agreed; he was indeed. "I will be glad to give you documentation along that line," he offered.

Arkansas Democrat William Fulbright asked if Russia's own actions in the Balkans might have inspired anti-Communism in the United States. Wallace responded by reversing chicken and egg: The problem, he said, went back to 1919, when "various nations were trying to choke the Bolsheviks."

Texas Democrat Committee chairman Tom Connally pressed Wallace on how his program of resolving conflicts through the United Nations would work. "Did Russia consult us," he asked, "before she incorporated [Czechoslovakia,] Hungary, and Bulgaria into her system, and made them a complete tool of Russia?"

"These were local communists that did the work," Wallace objected. "It was not done by Russia as Russia."

Connally was incredulous. Russia "is the greatest land force in the world, is it not?"

"I think undoubtedly," Wallace answered.

"Is it just for protection, for defense?"

"I think so."

And on it went in such vein, for four hours.[17]

By the early fall of 1949, however, there was a curious shift—subtle but noticeable—in Wallace's rhetoric. Speaking at a Progressive Party dinner in his honor in September 1949, Wallace was, *The New York Times* noted, "more critical [of] Russia's policies than in any speech he [had] made since 1946." Condemning power politics in international aid and menacing displays of military strength, he said repeatedly that "this goes for Russia" as much as it did the United States.[18] And at an American Labor Party rally the following month, he "denounce[d] both the United States and Russia for needless acts of provocation."[19] Shock and anger toward Wallace spread through the Progressive camp.

Wallace himself later acknowledged a shift in his thinking around that time. "Beginning in late 1949," he would write in September 1950 correspondence, "I began to think that Russia wanted the cold war and perhaps even the hot war eventually."

But what could have caused such a shift? "This was partly based on information coming to me from Czechoslovakia," Wallace explained. "The brutal elimination of all except the Moscow-trained in positions of power in a country with democratic traditions convinced me that Russia would stop at nothing."[20] Writing in *New Leader* magazine around that same time, he clarified the source of his epiphany: the accounts of "Progressive party people of Czech origin" regarding the travails of their relatives after the Communist takeover.[21]

This statement was a seeming confession that he had been grievously wrong when, following the February 1948 Communist coup in Prague, he had publicly blamed the U.S. ambassador and "rightist" forces within the Czech government. "The Czech crisis is clearly another fruit," he had concluded in April of that year, "of the utterly stupid and possibly suicidal Truman Doctrine."[22] That Wallace should have done an about-face eighteen months later, and blamed the Soviets, only after hearing anecdotes from Progressives "of Czech descent," constitutes, too, an indictment of his standards of political evidence—surprisingly low standards for a man who had built his reputation as an agro-scientist based on the gathering and study of empirical data.

Speaking on the CBS television program *Face the Nation* years later, in October 1955, Wallace would go further in detailing his turn against Moscow, explaining that he had only become aware of the "character" of the regime in 1949—after learning that it had engineered the Prague coup. "That was more than I could stand," Wallace said.[23] From that time on, he began blaming Moscow for the Cold War generally.

Wallace never acknowledged that he was wrong, however, in his relentless condemnation of Truman's foreign policy. He would insist that he had been right to press for "a peace treaty with Russia when she was weak," just after the war, "before she had an atom bomb. We could have arrived at an agreement then, which would have been to the interest of all members of the United Nations."[24] This statement seems to acknowledge that American strength was *conducive* to peace at the time—and not a barrier to it. Yet for three years, from 1946 to 1948, he had opposed American military preparedness and atomic diplomacy efforts on the grounds that they were aggressive, and *antithetical* to peace.

Wallace's correspondence in late 1949 makes clear that it was not just bitterness toward Moscow's Communists that had begun weighing on him, but bitterness toward its American brethren, who had led him into the political wilderness. "[T]o the extent that the communists took me over," according to media and public impression, he wrote to Lew Frank on October 15, "to that extent I lost influence." He was particularly critical of Beanie Baldwin, who had "not seen with sufficient clarity what identification with Communism in the public mind would do to us." The effect of this rising bitterness was not merely to turn him against Communists, but to begin turning him against politics broadly, and back toward his roots in farming. "The more I see of humanity both east and west right now," he closed, "the better I am impressed with gladioli, strawberries and chickens."[25]

Following Wallace's adoption of a new, more critical tone on Soviet culpability, in the fall of 1949, the Kremlin began to register concern. Would Moscow lose its sway over the Progressive Party? A Committee of Information (KI) report to Stalin, Molotov, Beria, and others dated October 23, for example, notes disturbing disclosures from Communists within the Progressive camp.

"[T]he prominent lawyer John Abt and his wife, Jessica Smith, the editor of the magazine *Soviet Russia Today*," the report said, revealed "that Wallace has been displaying a desire more and more clearly of late to drop out from active politics." He had "adamantly refused" multiple appeals from Abt to lobby the Senate against military aid to Greece and Turkey. Likewise, Abt's "proposal for a trip to the USSR and the people's democracies was categorically rejected." And "despite the fact that [Wallace's] finances have improved a great deal, he is not giving the [Progressive] party monetary assistance." His "farming associates," who were presumably anti-Communist, were "exerting heavy influence on him."[26] In November, a Soviet embassy official noted that Wallace had "refused" a request from the National Council of American-Soviet Friendship to speak at a Madison Square Garden rally[27]—the first time he had ever declined such a request.

On February 24, 1950, Wallace gave a long radio address, covered critically in Moscow by a top secret TASS report, in which he tried to distance himself and his party from the Soviet Union and Communism. "The Progressive Party," Wallace said, "believes . . . that American foreign policy should be based on friendship and mutual understanding." That "position," he said, had been "used by enemies, working inside the Progressive Party, to charge that the [party] is a simple proponent of Russia and communism." This charge was false. The "party's outlook," Wallace insisted, "is neither Marxism, nor Leninism, nor socialism, but a progressive capitalism." The TASS report noted with particular concern that Wallace claimed there were "no democratic freedoms in the people's democracy."[28]

To be sure, Wallace continued to criticize the United States. "Both nations," he said during a radio address on April 9, "are meddling into the affairs of other nations."[29] And the price, he lamented, would be borne by "the common man," who "has not gained from the building of the A-bomb or the [Communist] victory in China."[30] Proliferation of atomic know-how was inevitable, and threatened humanity globally. Within the United States, he condemned both business *and* labor leaders for recklessly seeking prosperity through cold war. He lodged his faith increasingly in religious leaders and intellectuals.

Still, there was no mistaking the fact that Wallace's disapproval and disparagement were more and more frequently and pointedly directed at Moscow and the Communist movements it supported.

On June 1, Jessica Smith reported to a Soviet embassy official on tensions within the CPUSA over how to manage the Progressive Party, now that Wallace had "moved considerably in the right-wing direction and [was] trying to purge Communists." Her husband, John Abt, was likely to leave the party. Some within the CPUSA leadership, she reported, now wanted to "liquidate" the Progressive Party entirely. Nineteen fifty being an election year, however, "it was decided to preserve [it] and target its activities exclusively on domestic policy."[31] It was best for the Communists, they believed, to bide their time and wait for new world developments that would, once again, make the Progressives useful in the cause of undermining U.S. foreign policy. Such developments were, in fact, poised just on the horizon.

※

"Now that China was finishing its liberation," Kim Il-sung told Soviet officials in Pyongyang in January 1950, "it is the turn of the liberation of the Korean people in the South."[32] Installed as North Korean leader by the Soviets in 1945, Kim was sure his time had come. He accelerated the buildup of his army and made secret trips to Moscow to press Stalin for permission to invade the South.

The Soviet leader was chary, unwilling to risk military confrontation with the United States. In a diplomatic blunder of great consequence, however, Secretary of State Dean Acheson made a speech on January 12, 1950, in which he left Korea out of the American "defensive perimeter" in Asia.[33] The omission emboldened both Stalin and Mao, the latter of whom shared Kim's view that the Americans would not intervene in a Northern invasion of the South.

Stalin authorized clandestine shipments of heavy weapons to Pyongyang, and assigned Russian generals to advise Kim, but made clear that the Soviets would not join the fighting. "If you should get kicked in the teeth I shall not lift a finger," he warned Kim. "You have to ask Mao for all the help." Stalin's main aim was not to unify Korea under Kim, but rather to draw the United States into protracted deadly conflict with China. Doing so would, he believed, give the Soviet Union a freer hand in Europe, and elsewhere in Asia.

On May 13, Kim held a secret meeting with Mao in Beijing, following which Mao offered to put Chinese troops on the Korean border to deter—and if necessary confront—the Americans. Kim—"arrogantly," according to Mao—dismissed the offer. He was sure he could liberate the South on his own, within three weeks.

Stalin gave Kim permission to launch his invasion, likely directing him to do so in late June. On the morning of the 25th, the North Korean leader ordered a massive artillery barrage, following which more than 100,000 elite troops crossed the 38th parallel. Two more days passed before he informed the Chinese ambassador of the invasion, claiming—contrary to the ambassador's knowledge—that the South had attacked his forces first.[34] On July 5, Stalin cabled Mao urging him "to immediately concentrate nine Chinese divisions on the Korean border for volunteer actions in case the adversary crosses the 38th parallel." Stalin said he would try "to provide air cover for [Chinese] forces."[35]

Back on January 13, 1950, the day following Acheson's fateful speech, Stalin, too, made what seemed a historic diplomatic error. Against the advice of Andrey Gromyko (now First Deputy Minister of Foreign Affairs), he ordered the USSR to boycott the U.N. Security Council on the grounds that the United States and its allies refused to admit the representative of the new People's Republic of China to the body.[36] When, two days after the North Korean invasion, on June 27, the U.N. Security Council considered a U.S.-initiated resolution calling on member states to provide South Korea with military assistance, no Soviet representative was present to veto it. The resolution therefore passed, and the multination United Nations Command, under General MacArthur, would begin slowing the Northern advance in August—before reversing it in September.

Three weeks after the Northern invasion, on July 15, Henry Wallace made the most dramatic policy pivot of his career. Insisting that the Soviets could "undoubtedly" have prevented the invasion, and could "stop the attack any time they wish," he offered wholehearted support for military efforts to defeat it.[37] Three weeks later, *The New York Times*, with both shock and hearty approval, quoted his call for the United States to "continue [the] fight against North Korean troops in South Korea until such time as Russia is willing to use her influence to stop the fighting."[38]

In a dramatic departure from myriad earlier statements on conflict between Washington and Moscow, Wallace offered no hint that he considered Truman at fault. He declared an unambiguous allegiance to his government's foreign policy, recognizing full well what it meant for him: the end of his reign as America's apostle of peace, its Cassandra of Cold War. If the Progressive Party would not back him, he explained, he was prepared to leave it.[39]

The Washington Post, no fan of Wallace, praised his stand. "It could not have been easy for him to relinquish [the] glory" of being "a great popular leader marching at the head of Gideon's army," the paper said. But that army was being "commanded, in fact, by the propagandists who created it."[40] Wallace had merely been their tool. As for the rank and file, they had taken him at his word that Harry Truman was the great enemy of peace, and that he, Henry Wallace, was its guarantor. Peace needed only a peace*maker*. Yet the Wallace they beheld was now, apparently, no less willing to fight Communists than he had been to fight fascists.

It did not help Wallace that his statement of reasoning angered the party masses even more than did the stance itself. "I want to make it clear," he said, "that when Russia, the United States and the United Nations appeal to force, I am on the side of the United States and the United Nations."[41] Supporters, or rather former supporters, understood him to be saying "my country, right or wrong." Not surprisingly, his mailbox quickly filled with angry letters demanding to know how he could make such jingoistic proclamations.[42]

There was also seeming disingenuity in his reference to "the United Nations." The Security Council, after all, had only been empowered to back the South thanks to the Soviet boycott. And Wallace had never considered the Council credible without Soviet participation. All in all, then, his statement lent the impression that war in Korea was, for him, simply a convenient pretext for shedding a political millstone—that of friendship with an awkwardly aggressive Soviet regime.

On August 6, the Progressive Party's two-day annual convention, attended by one hundred delegates, condemned Wallace for his support of the U.S. and U.N. military action.[43] Two days later, with the party's Communist-dominated national committee also firmly against him, Wallace resigned his membership.[44] As for his longtime aide Beanie Baldwin, whatever the true nature of his ties with the Communists, it speaks volumes of his ideological priorities that he chose to back the committee's continued stance against America's "bi-partisan cold-war foreign policy." He expressed only "deep regret" at Wallace's resignation.[45]

The *Post* yet again praised Wallace, backhandedly, for breaking "with the comrades." In so doing, the paper said, he had "managed to salvage something of his reputation for genuine, if muddle-headed, idealism." Still, in having now, over the course of his career, renounced the Republicans, the Democrats, and the Progressives, Wallace had likely "ceased forever to be an important factor in American political life."[46] There was simply nowhere left for him to go.

At the time, no one understood what drove Wallace to his latest resignation better than fellow Progressive, and later chronicler of his presidential campaign, Curtis MacDougall. "My feeling," MacDougall wrote to him on August 11, "is that your action has been caused both by the understandable disappointment and discouragement following the 1948 results and because of growing disgust with Communists within the Progressive party."[47] Indeed, he might have gone further, and suggested that Wallace's turn against the Soviets was driven by these same factors.

Wallace continued to obliterate Progressive Party taboos. On August 10, 1950, he said that "Russian aggression" had caused him to reverse his opposition to the atom bomb. Korea, he explained, "justified" holding on to it. Now, he hoped merely that "we never have to drop it again."[48] In a further turn toward realism some months later, he would add, seemingly wistfully, that the Japanese Empire had served as "a real threat" to Soviet domination of Asia.[49]

On September 30, Wallace wrote an open letter to Mao, "as one farmer to another," urging his Communist Party to halt what seemed, to many in the United States, the imposition of "complete obedience to the Soviet Union" on the Chinese people. "I can understand how Russia, under her present leadership, might want to get China into a war with the U.S.," he wrote. "But I am sure that no responsible leader in China wants to see anything of that sort happen."[50]

On November 12, he called on the United States to boost its armed strength "as fast as possible." It was yet another radical turn for a man who had, just a few years prior, insisted that "you get peace by preparing for peace rather than for war."[51] Had the Truman administration taken that advice, it would have been in even worse position to do what Wallace was demanding now: that is, to beat back a Chinese- and Soviet-backed invasion of South Korea.

Wallace acknowledged changing his mind about the need both to meet Russia "halfway" in the cause of peace and to back U.N. admission for Communist China. Peace, he now said, could never be achieved through appeasement. Russia had to be assured "of our united determination to take effective action to nip future Koreas in the bud." Only through firmness would "peace be brought nearer."[52]

"When Russia permitted the North Koreans to attack and when Chinese troops entered North Korea [on October 19], it became clear to me that Russia is eager to use other people to heat up the cold war." And when it "incites China to bloody conflict with the United States [it] is committing a criminal act."[53] On December 3, he added that he was now "convinced that Russia is out to dominate the world."[54]

Wallace would also show foresight on the future path of Sino-Soviet relations. "Mao Tse-tung may be utterly loyal to Moscow," he said in a speech on January 2, 1951, "but sooner or later the Chinese people themselves will get rid of their Russian masters."[55] Indeed, relations between the two great Communist powers would steadily deteriorate after Stalin's death in 1953.

The Soviet publication *New Times* accused Wallace of "committing rank treason and embracing the cause of the warmongers." Wallace, the magazine said, "knows perfectly well that Washington launched unprovoked aggression against Korea."[56] The Communist Sunday paper *The Worker* assailed him for "support[ing] the war now being waged against the Korean people."[57] *Literaturnaya Gazeta* (Literary Gazette), a Soviet propaganda weekly, listed Wallace among its "Enemies of Mankind."[58]

Henry Wallace clearly suffered from the realization that he had been used and manipulated by Communists, foreign and domestic. Yet once he had come to terms with this fact, and had abandoned his Jamesian belief in the mystical capacity of the will to peace, he became notably clear-sighted about Stalin's aims.

Though Wallace had no access to secret Soviet communications now available to scholars, he correctly reasoned that Stalin was using North Korea to manipulate China into war with the United States. These aims were, in fact, evident in this secret telegram which Stalin sent to his ambassador in Czechoslovakia, for transmission to the Communist Czech president Klement Gottwald, on August 27, 1950:

> Following our withdrawal from the Security Council, America became entangled in a military intervention in Korea and is now squandering its military prestige and moral authority. . . . [I]t is clear that the United States of America is presently distracted from Europe to the Far East. Does it not give us an advantage in the global balance of world forces? It undoubtedly does.

Let us suppose that [the] American government continues to be tied down in the Far East and also pulls China into the struggle for the freedom of Korea and its own independence. What might come of this?

First, America, just like any other country, cannot cope with China, a country with such large armed forces at the ready. It follows that America would overextend itself in this struggle. Second, having overextended itself in this matter, America would be incapable of [launching] a third world war in the near future. Therefore, a third world war would be postponed for an indeterminate period, which would provide the time necessary to strengthen socialism in Europe, not to mention that the struggle between America and China would revolutionize the entire Far East.[59]

What the telegram shows is that Stalin's apparent hesitations and blunders over Korea, such as boycotting the Security Council, were actually part of a grand strategy for doing just as Henry Wallace had reasoned—drawing China and America into war with each other. In this aim, Stalin was successful. On November 25, Mao, having been assured that Stalin "stands by his ally,"[60] ordered a massive Chinese counterattack against MacArthur's advancing forces in North Korea. By the time the fighting would end in stalemate two and a half years later, over 2.5 million Koreans, Chinese, Americans, and American-allied troops would lose their lives through it.

In setting aside Jamesian belief for evidential belief, Wallace had shown himself capable of political judgment commensurate with his considerable intelligence. Still, he did not abandon his faith in semi-utopian peace plans.

On January 21, 1951, he called for "a really big P.W.A. (Public Works Administration) project for the whole world," to be funded by the United States through the United Nations, at a cost of $10 billion a year ($117 billion today). It would, he estimated, be three to four times cheaper than war preparations—an estimate which assumed that a World PWA obviated the possibility of war. "It is cheaper to win the hearts of men," he said, "than to kill them."

The subsequent history of the Marshall Plan would suggest that security, in the form of NATO, was critical to its success—that security was a prerequisite for economic flourishing.[61] Wallace would not have disagreed with this premise, but believed that peace needed instead to be kept by "a United Nations police force stronger than the armed might of any individual nation." Needless to say, such an entity found little support in Washington, and less in Moscow.

In any case, there was an element of Soviet-skeptical realism underlying Wallace's call for a World PWA that was distinctly new. As a condition for participation, "the Iron Curtain countries" would, he said, have to "join all the United Nations agencies, agree to a program of disarmament, park the atom bombs, discontinue fifth column activities and agree to [the proposed] United Nations police force."[62] He had not previously set conditions on Soviet access to his peace bounty, and the mere fact of their inclusion showed a material change in his thinking.

Notwithstanding Wallace's tentative embrace of mainstream Washington views of Russia, his relations with the political establishment remained rocky. In January 1950, he defended himself before Congress against charges, never proven, that he had aided the shipment of uranium to the Soviet Union in 1943.[63] He also denied learning from General Groves, during a period when he was pushing for more exchanges between Soviet and American scientists, that Soviet scientists were probing for information on U.S. uranium fission work.[64] In October 1951, he went before Congress once again, this time to defend himself against more absurd charges: that he had, in recommending the replacement of General Stilwell with the anti-Communist Wedemeyer in China in 1944, intended to boost the Communists.[65] In March of 1952, he reacted angrily to publication of a book containing direct and indirect references to him—to his alleged pacifism and friendliness to Moscow—from the president's diary.[66] In each of these instances, and many less important ones, Wallace parried his critics with vigor.

Yet he also showed a willingness to acknowledge some significant errors of past judgment, and to account for them. In September 1952, he even wrote an article entitled "Where I Was Wrong." The piece was notable for a man who had so recently run for president on the grounds that the incumbent was grievously and dangerously wrong.

Wallace began by acknowledging that "many people" did not understand how he reconciled his "stand before Korea" with his "uncompromising anti-

Communist attitude" since then. "The answer was simple," he said. He had, "before 1949," believed that "Russia really wanted and needed peace." After 1949, however, he "became convinced that the Politburo wanted the Cold War continued indefinitely, even at the peril of accidentally provoking a hot war." This epiphany was occasioned by "the shocking revelations of the activities of Russia's atomic spies" and, then, "reports of friends" regarding the actions of the "Moscow-trained Communists" in Czechoslovakia. "I now feel," he wrote, "that my greatest mistake was in not denouncing the Communist take-over [of the country] in 1948."

"Time," he said, had also given him "new understanding of the Korean question." "[K]nowing more about Russia's methods" in 1952, he was "sure it was a serious mistake when we withdrew our troops" in 1949.

Writing of his four-week tour of Soviet Asia in 1944, Wallace confessed to having "had not the slightest idea" that Magadan was "the center" of a vast "slave labor" complex. The subsequent writings of prisoners such as Elinor Lipper, however, convinced him that the Kremlin had built "a Potemkin village for [his] inspection." He had, he said, been "altogether too much impressed by the show put on by high Russian officials." "What I did not see," he added, "was the Soviet determination to enslave the common man morally, mentally, and physically for its own imperial purposes."

Wallace had come a long way since the days when he lauded the Soviet commitment to "economic democracy." "More and more," Wallace now wrote, "I am convinced that Russian Communism in its total disregard of truth, in its fanaticism, its intolerance and its resolute denial of God and religion is something utterly evil."

Still, he concluded, inexplicably given such sentiments, that "the whole course of history" would have been different had Roosevelt "remained alive and in good health." The United States would not, he said, "be spending $60 billion a year on arms"—as it was under Truman.[67] Such spending would, presumably, be unnecessary thanks to peace between the United States and Russia.

That Wallace's faith in Roosevelt's peacemaking powers—and his own, for that matter—could co-reside with belief in an "utterly evil" Soviet ideology shows clearly that he never wholly abandoned his mystical mindset. He could simply not accept that the choice between Roosevelt's "One World" and Truman's "Two Worlds" was *not* a choice between an attainable good and an avoidable evil, but a choice between a *preferred world order* and the *best order attainable*, given incompatible American and Russian interests.

Politically homeless, Henry Wallace publicly endorsed no one in the 1952 presidential race. In a letter to Democratic candidate Adlai Stevenson, for whom a biographer-duo claims Wallace voted,[68] Wallace called it "the dirtiest campaign in history."[69] Less than two weeks later, however, he sent a glowing telegram of congratulations to Stevenson's victorious Republican rival.[70] "The nation is fortunate," Wallace wrote to Dwight D. Eisenhower, "that a man of peace has been elected president." In correspondence with a friend, he hailed "the majesty of the Eisenhower victory."[71]

Wallace flirted with both candidates again in 1956, but this time saw fit to endorse Eisenhower. "It is my belief that Eisenhower commands more prestige for peace in Europe, both East and West," he wrote to Glen Taylor by way of explanation, "than any other man who could possibly be elected."[72] Over the coming three years, he would write the president at least six letters. These offered an admixture of paean and advice. He praised Eisenhower's "profound faith in God," comparing him to George Washington,[73] and opined that he would "lead the whole world into a New Era of Freedom and Prosperity."[74] He urged the president to improve relations with Indian Prime Minister Jawaharlal Nehru and India,[75] and expressed pessimism over Russia's prospects vis-à-vis China—the latter of which he saw, much earlier than most, as a rising great power.[76] In 1958, a few months shy of his seventieth birthday, he said publicly that the next century might well be "the Chinese century." He made outstandingly accurate predictions on China's population growth, and hailed "their very great abilities."[77] He was less prescient when he predicted, in 1961, however, that the United States and Russia would, within his lifetime, enter into alliance "against the Chinese horde."[78]

After the 1956 election, Wallace also developed a surprisingly warm and respectful relationship with the arch-anti-Communist Richard Nixon. At a dinner honoring the vice president in December of that year, the two had a congenial discussion on Near East and Middle East policy, including the role of foreign aid.[79] In March 1960, as Nixon prepared for his presidential run, he invited Wallace for a secret talk in Washington, which lasted forty minutes, covering foreign policy, disarmament, farm programs—and the political opponent Nixon expected to face that fall: Jack Kennedy. Wallace seemed to know little of the Massachusetts senator, reminiscing instead about dealings with his father.[80] Though Wallace refused to make an endorsement that year,[81] he leveled some sharp public criticism at Kennedy's farm program—opining that it might "require stricter controls than they have in most Communist countries,"[82] and would still push up food prices 25 percent.[83] Whom Wallace actually voted for is uncertain. A *New York Times* piece said it was Kennedy;[84] a later one said Nixon.[85]

In any case, Kennedy bore no grudge over the swipe at his farm policy, inviting Wallace and his wife to the inauguration ceremony and luncheon— the first Wallace had attended in sixteen years. Wallace subsequently became a penpal of the new secretary of agriculture, Orville Freeman, and his fears over the direction of farm policy died away.[86] In Freeman's effort to couple production control with price supports, he was, Wallace concluded, "on the right track."

In the 1964 race, Wallace decried Republican candidate Barry Goldwater's reliance on "demagogic appeal," and backed Lyndon Johnson.[87] He subsequently exchanged friendly correspondence with the president on farm policy, but privately criticized his ever-deepening military intervention in Vietnam.

One suspects that Wallace would, had he lived longer, have spoken out publicly against the war. He hated the way it was dividing the country and would surely never have accepted domino logic.[88] By the early 1960s, however, in the last years of his life, his focus was overwhelmingly on improving features of plants and animals. At his sprawling 118-acre hilltop Farvue Farm, he conducted careful hybridization experiments to create tastier strawberries; heartier, cold-resistant gladioli; and more efficient chickens. The chicken breeding was particularly successful, resulting in strains which eat less food and lay more eggs. Not surprisingly, they today dominate the U.S. market.[89] Wallace also lectured widely on agricultural innovation— even traveling to Cuba, Honduras, Guatemala, and El Salvador to speak at farms and schools.[90] By 1962, he was at work on a book (never completed) examining the history of the strawberry.[91] Having set aside his political passions, he was visibly more at ease with himself, and the world, than he had been since his days, four decades earlier, at *Wallaces' Farmer*.

≈✤↶

On October 6, 1963, one day shy of Wallace's seventy-fifth birthday, *The New York Times* ran a feature piece on him. Veteran Washington correspondent Cabell Phillips described his subject's rise to power, from "the New Dealingest of New Dealers" in the 1930s to political celebrity at "the peak of his radicalism" in 1948. But "when his light went out," the author observed, "it went out for good." In the wake of his electoral thumping, Henry Wallace quickly became "the most forgotten of forgotten men."

Perhaps Phillips underestimated his subject's potential, for future generations of idealistic undergraduates, as martyr to peace. But there can be no doubt that the Henry Wallace whom he encountered at the "unpretentious" tree-shaded, white-sided, green-shuttered nineteenth-century South Salem farmhouse sought no veneration, nor even attention. He rather implored Phillips not to reveal his local post office, for fear it might attract too much mail—mail that would take up "time which I would rather spend with my agricultural projects."

Truly, Wallace wanted nothing more than to return to his one lifelong love: solitary scientific farming. It was a love that had rewarded him with both inner peace and the satisfaction of knowing he had measurably improved the lives of millions.

Serenaded by the screeching of a thousand experimental pullets and roosters, Phillips approached the house by way of rows of carefully labeled seedbeds, colorful glistening gladioli, and seven-foot corn stalks, redolent of the owner's native Iowa. Greeted by Wallace at the front door, Phillips was struck by how little he had changed in the dozen years since they had last met. The full head of thick hair was white now, but the sturdy frame, ruddy complexion, determined gait, careless dress, and shy, awkward speech were just as Phillips had remembered.

Wallace's Pioneer Hi-Bred Corn Company, which had branched out into all manner of genetically groomed plants and poultry, was flourishing. Politics, Phillips sensed, had become for him a sort of embarrassing accident he had stumbled into long ago—one which he had little urge to recall. He looked "back upon the whole episode regretfully, as a virtuous husband might upon an extramarital fling with the office widow." The analogy applied particularly well to his impassioned politics of peace.

"I was mistaken," Wallace confessed, readily but wearily, "in my esti-mate of the Russians' intentions. I believed then that Stalin was prepared to be the kind of partner in peace that he had been in war. I believed that, if we could overcome the Russians' centuries-old distrust of Western imperial-ism and their later fear of Western capitalism, they would collaborate in the rebuilding of a truly democratic world."

These beliefs changed in 1949, Wallace explained in his by-now tidy, well-practiced account, when he learned the truth behind the Czech coup. "I lost faith in [Russia's] intentions" after that, he explained. "They smashed a truly democratic regime there and installed a totalitarian government of their own."

But hadn't his misestimation of Russia, Phillips pressed, amounted to a fundamental failing, one which undermined the very notion that a "third-party movement" had been "wise or useful"? The question pained Wallace. He went silent. His eyes, which seemed to radiate a "perpetual sadness," set themselves "for a long moment" on "the distant blue hills." Then he spoke again. "I was out to dramatize the necessity of peace," he explained, and the importance of "avoid[ing] atomic war."[92] Or as Cold Warrior Dean Ache-son would put it, though in making very different political arguments, one sometimes had to be "clearer than truth."[93]

Wallace, Phillips could see, wanted to speak no more of the Progressives. But he did want Phillips to understand that he had been right to seek peace with Stalin—at least until the Soviet leader had shown himself committed to confrontation.

For Truman and Marshall, that moment had come in April 1947—with Marshall's failed mission to Moscow. For Wallace, the moment had not come until February 1948—with the Czech coup. And even then, by his own admission, it still took a further year and a half to experience epiphany.

"Maybe I was ahead of my time," Wallace finally lobbied in self-defense, after considerable thought.[94] Maybe, he seemed to say, it was not that he had seen the truth too late, but that he had seen the opportunity for peace *too early*, before the establishment was capable of grasping it.

Phillips, ever the skeptical, courtly Southerner,[95] was not quite buying it. But neither did he see the need to press further. Clearly, peace and politics were, for Wallace, qualitatively different subjects. He could never renounce the striving for the one, even as the other failed to deliver it.

★

While climbing a pyramid in Guatemala in the spring of 1964, Henry Wallace experienced a strange sensation. His left foot dragged; it was unresponsive. It did not improve. Typical for Wallace, though, he remained active, even playing his trademark vigorous tennis—the version he had gleaned from a Spalding rulebook six decades earlier—at least until July, when he could no longer manage it. In August, he finally submitted to testing at a hospital in Danbury, Connecticut. The attending physician diagnosed the problem correctly, but decided against revealing it to him at that time.

Wallace cut back his athletic activities, but continued with speaking engagements into the fall. By then, his voice was raspy, and his movements strained. In November, he visited the Mayo Clinic for more tests, after which he finally learned the source of his ailments.[96]

Wallace was suffering from amyotrophic lateral sclerosis (ALS), otherwise known as Lou Gehrig's disease—a rare nervous system disorder causing progressive loss of muscle control. At the time, patients with the fatal disease typically survived only about two years. The diagnosis was a grave shock to a man who had, until the previous spring, been supremely healthy and active—having told a student audience in 1960 that he planned "to go right on living until I'm 100."

"Every year I know I have to be around next year to see what's going to happen in my garden," he said, "to see what will come up, with the sort of interest with which we can hope God looks down on us."[97]

Wholly in character, Wallace sought out treatments from the orthodox to the radical, the speculative to the mystical, across the United States and in Switzerland. He exercised when and where he could, climbing steps and doing push-ups, keeping careful notes on his declining performance. The pain he could endure, one of his doctors recorded, was extraordinary.

By the spring of 1965, he could barely move on his own, except, gingerly, with a foot brace and walker. In August he wrote to President Johnson, warning that the growing urban-rural wage gap was threatening to worsen the problem of slums and, under doctor's orders, regretfully declining an invitation to the White House.[98] By the autumn, his body was failing him completely, making it impossible for him even to eat or drink except through an opening cut into his esophagus from his neck. But he continued correspondence, typing slowly with his still functional right hand. His Swedish great-nephew, economist Per Magnus Wijkman, visited him at Bethesda National Hospital, just outside Washington, in October. Though bedridden, largely paralyzed, and unable to speak, Wallace gave him a book entitled *The City Man's Guide to the Farm Problem* and a notepad on which he had written "Good book!" Per Magnus was stunned and moved. "Scientific curiosity and personal courage," he recorded, "drove him to the end."[99]

On October 28, Wallace was transferred by ambulance from Bethesda back to his home in Farvue. On the morning of November 18, with his breathing now labored, he was rushed back to Danbury Hospital. At 11:15 a.m., with his wife and sister at his bedside, Henry Wallace died. He was seventy-seven.

The funeral service two days later, at St. Stephen's Episcopal Church in Ridgefield, Connecticut, was simple and brief—as he had wished.[100]

At the time of his death, Henry Wallace was still a controversial figure. Obituaries highlighted his earlier clashes over foreign policy with major elements of the liberal coalition, such as labor and the intellectuals.[101] Over time, however, particularly following the disastrously divisive war in Vietnam, which undermined the idea of a benign "American Century," it was perhaps natural that the image of Wallace as foresighted champion of peace would come to dominate. The chaotic 1944 Democratic convention provided the perfect backdrop for the tragic narrative of The World That Wasn't—the narrative that the Cold War had been brought on by a corrupt coterie of party oligarchs who bribed delegates with sinecures and ambassadorships. It is a narrative contradicted by the evidence, as we have seen, but one which has endured thanks to its usefulness in delegitimizing the presidency of Harry Truman.

Politically, Henry Wallace deserves to be remembered as a distinctly American progressive idealist who staked his career on a categorical error of judgment. Wallace misunderstood "peace" as a policy choice—a policy choice which Harry Truman, under malign conservative influence, allegedly rejected in favor of an unnecessary and devastating Cold War with Russia. Peace between conflicting sovereign nations is *not* a policy choice, however, but a state of affairs which obtains when each sublimates the will to act for the purpose of avoiding war. When sublimation is unilateral, it is not peace, but appeasement. And given Stalin's designs on Turkey, Iran, Greece, Germany, Manchuria, and Korea, the only alternatives to Cold War were hot war and appeasement.

In the 1950s, Henry Wallace came to acknowledge his earlier misapprehensions regarding Soviet expansionism, while still maintaining that peace had been possible, at least until 1948, on the basis of superior American power. The flaw in such reasoning is now apparent, given what we also know of Stalin's resolve to close the power gap—particularly through the rapid building of atom bombs.

If the colorful career of Henry Agard Wallace shows anything clearly, it is this: that, as the ancient Stoic philosophers recognized, success in life requires conforming desires to realities. One can neither will corn to higher yields, nor will a dictator to compromise. Wallace accepted the former, and labored within the timeless laws of genetics;[102] he denied the latter, and labored beyond the timeless principles of statesmanship. The results were predictable: success as agriculturist, failure as statesman.

We have reaped the blessings of his successes. May we learn from his failures.

ACKNOWLEDGMENTS

When some eight years ago John Lewis Gaddis first suggested that I write a political biography of Henry Wallace, I was flattered but dismissive. Surely, I thought, this was not an undertaking for someone doctorized in financial economics. Yet he persisted, and by 2018 I was all in. Completing this book has, since then, been the most challenging, and commensurately rewarding, project of my career, and I am existentially grateful to John for his confidence, prodding, and guidance.

Enormous thanks go also to Russian historian Svetlana Chervonnaya, who scoured government and private archives in Moscow, not to mention her library of a mind, and assembled thousands of pages of documents, notes, translations, and detailed commentary. She then critiqued every chapter of this book. I could never have seriously undertaken, let alone completed, this work without her.

But many other people also availed me of their talents and energies along the way. My brilliant research associates at the Council on Foreign Relations, Lila Rosenzweig and her two immediate predecessors, Benjamin Beames and Scott Remer, contributed enormously by tracking down and organizing research material from Iowa City to Hyde Park. They also ably supervised my fabulous semester interns: Lily Zhang (Spring 2023), Emily Kohn (Fall 2022), Christopher Shim (Summer 2022), Alexandre Edde (Spring 2022), Kuangye Wang (Fall 2021), Tathagat Bhatia (Fall 2020), Kashif Azam (Spring 2020), Alexis Tsapralis (Fall 2019), Coleman Sherry (Summer 2019), Hiba Ismail (Spring 2019), Jacqueline Samuel (Fall 2018), Katie Gillis (Spring 2018), and Anamaria Lopez (Fall 2017). They aided with everything from identifying source materials to preparing summaries, and in some cases even translating articles and diary entries.

Thanks, too, go to Fred Qin, who translated Chinese-language archival material, and to my CFR colleague Zongyuan Zoe Liu, who gave me valuable feedback on the China historical material.

I further had the sage guidance of a CFR study group of policy experts and scholars under the chairmanship of former World Bank president Robert Zoellick: Gary Bass, Charles Boustany, John Gaddis, Jeffrey Garten, Thomas Graham, Martin Indyk, Anne Kornhauser, Massimo Pigliucci, Alex Raskolnikov, Scott Shapiro, and Arne Westad. Their comments and critiques were invaluable in refining the research project and polishing the final text. Two keen-eyed anonymous reviewers commissioned by CFR also provided insightful feedback on the manuscript. At the end, CFR president Richard Haass, director of studies James Lindsay, and deputy director of studies Shannon O'Neil made sure I cut no corners on clarity and context. My thanks to all of them. I am also grateful for the financial support provided for my research, over the period 2018 to 2020, from CFR's Historian-in-Residence Fellowship. The fellowship is made possible through generous funding from David Rubenstein.

Finally, my warmest thanks to my agent, Andrew Wylie, who encouraged me to follow my instincts and passions, and my brilliant editor, Ben Loehnen, who proved me wrong each time I thought I couldn't be more concise.

Errors and other failings in this, the final product, are, of course, mine and mine alone.

CAST OF CHARACTERS

Abt, John Jacob (1904–1991). American lawyer. Concealed Communist from 1934. General counsel for the Amalgamated Clothing Workers Union, 1938–1948; general counsel for Wallace's Progressive Party, 1948. Became CPUSA chief counsel in 1950.

Acheson, Dean Gooderham (1893–1971). American statesman. Undersecretary of state, 1945–1947; secretary of state, 1949–1953. A principal architect of the Truman Doctrine and the Marshall Plan. Opposed Wallace's vice presidential nomination in 1944.

Allen, George Edward (1896–1973). American lawyer, businessman, and Democratic political figure. Commissioner of the District of Columbia, 1933–1939; Democratic National Committee treasurer, 1940–1945, and secretary, 1943. A director of the Reconstruction Finance Corporation, 1946–1947. Opposed Wallace's vice presidential nomination in 1944.

Alsop, Joseph Wright V (1910–1989). Journalist and military aide to General Chennault in China in 1944. Met with Wallace on his China trip, successfully urging him to recommend General Stilwell's dismissal. Later an influential political columnist.

Anderson, Clinton Presba (1895–1975). American politician. Congressman (D-NM), 1941–1945; secretary of agriculture, 1945–1948; senator, 1949–1973. Clashed with Wallace over Soviet policy in the Truman administration.

Appleby, Paul Henson (1891–1963). Wallace's executive assistant, and de facto political adviser, in the Department of Agriculture, 1933–1940; undersecretary of agriculture, 1940–1944.

Baldwin, Calvin Benham "Beanie" (1902–1975). Left-wing government, labor, and political official. Administrator of the Farm Security Administration, 1940–1943. Manager of Wallace's Progressive Party presidential campaign in 1948. Widely accused of being a Communist, although no hard evidence has ever surfaced.

Bankhead, John Hollis, II (1872–1946). American politician. Senator (D-AL), 1931–1946. Conservative Southern Democrat who opposed Wallace during the latter's time as secretary of agriculture. Vice presidential aspirant in 1944.

Barkley, Alben William (1877–1956). American politician. Congressman (D-KY), 1913–1927; senator, 1927–1949, 1955–1956; Senate majority leader, 1937–1947. Vice presidential aspirant in 1944, and vice president under Truman, 1949–1953.

Baruch, Bernard Mannes (1870–1965). American financier, philanthropist, and foreign policy adviser to Presidents Wilson, Roosevelt, and Truman. American member of the U.N. Atomic Energy Commission in 1946. Clashed with Wallace over atomic and Soviet policy.

Beneš, Edvard (1884–1948). Czechoslovak politician and statesman. President, 1935–1938 and 1945–1948. Reestablished the independent state of Czechoslovakia after World War II and led the country until shortly after the February 1948 Communist coup.

Bentley, Elizabeth Terrill (1908–1963). CPUSA member and Soviet spy from the late 1930s to 1945. Fell out with her Soviet handlers and became a U.S. government informant.

Beria, Lavrenty Pavlovich (1899–1953). Soviet government official. Head of the NKVD, 1938–1945; deputy prime minister of the USSR, 1941–1953; member of the Politburo, 1946–1953; marshal of the USSR, 1945–1953. Supervised the Soviet atomic bomb project. Directed Ivan Nikishov to oversee Wallace's 1944 visit to Siberia.

Boettiger, John Clarence (1900–1950). FDR's son-in-law and veteran Chicago newspaper reporter. Military officer during World War II.

Bogomolov, Dmitry Vasilievich (1890–1938). Soviet career diplomat, 1920–1937. Ambassador to China, 1933–1937.

Borodin, Dmitry Nikolaevich (1887–1957). Russian entomologist and U.S.-based agronomist and plant physiologist. Head of the Russian Agricultural Bureau in New York, 1920–1926. Urged Wallace to visit New York's Roerich Museum in 1927, which marked the beginning of Wallace's fateful relationship with Nicholas Roerich.

Bressman, Earl Norman (1894–1985). Wallace's coauthor on *Corn and Corn-Growing* (1923). Scientific adviser and special assistant to Wallace in the Department of Agriculture, 1933–1940. Handled administration of Nicholas Roerich's expedition to Asia in 1934–1935.

Browder, Earl Russell (1891–1973). CPUSA general secretary, 1930–1944. During World War II, came to believe in a postwar cooperation between the Soviet Union and the United States.

Brown, Walter Jay (1903–1995). Assistant to the director of the Office of War Mobilization and Reconversion, 1943–1945; special assistant to the secretary of state, 1945.

Bruenn, Howard G. (1905–1995). Naval cardiologist. Attended to FDR in the year before his death.

Bruggmann, Carl "Charles" (1889–1967). Swiss minister to the United States, 1939–1954. Wallace's brother-in-law.

Bush, Vannevar (1890–1974). American engineer, inventor, and science administrator. President of the National Defense Research Committee, 1940–1941; behind the early push for a full-scale atomic program.

Byrd, Harry Flood (1887–1966). Governor of Virginia, 1926–1930; senator (D-VA), 1933–1965.

Byrnes, James (Jimmy) Francis (1882–1972). American politician, jurist, and statesman. Congressman (D-SC), 1911–1925; senator, 1931–1941; Supreme Court justice, 1941–1942; director of the Office of Economic Stabilization, 1942–1943; director of the Office of War Mobilization, 1943–1945; secretary of state, 1945–1947; considered by FDR for the Democratic vice presidential ticket in 1944. Clashed with Wallace over Soviet policy in the Truman administration.

Carver, George Washington (c. 1864–1943). Born into slavery, he became an eminent agricultural chemist, botanist, and expert in plant modification and soil conservation. Director of the Department of Agriculture at the Tuskegee Normal and Industrial Institute, 1896–1943. A friend and mentor to Wallace from the latter's childhood.

Casey, Eugene (Gene) (1904–1986). Multimillionaire D.C.-area builder and investor. Director of the Farm Credit Administration, 1940–1941. White House agricultural adviser.

Chang, Kia-ngau (1888–1979). Chinese government official. Minister of railways, 1935; minister of communications, 1935–1943; minister of transportation, 1935–1943; chairman of the Manchuria Economic Counsel, 1945–1946; governor of the Bank of China, 1947–1948. Met with Wallace in Washington in September 1945.

Chase, Stuart (1888–1985). Engineer, economist, and member of FDR's "Brain Trust." Published *The Tragedy of Waste* in 1925, about the appeal of instituting Soviet economic planning in America. In 1927, he traveled to the Soviet Union and coauthored a book praising Soviet experiments in agricultural and social management (*Soviet Russia in the Second Decade*).

Chennault, Claire Lee (1890–1958). World War II leader of the famed Flying Tigers in China. Chiang Kai-shek's chief aviation adviser.

Chiang Kai-shek (1887–1975). Chinese and Taiwanese military leader and statesman. President of China, 1928–1949; president of Taiwan, 1950–1975. Met with Wallace on the latter's 1944 trip to China.

Chicherin, Georgy Vasilyevich (1872–1936). Russian revolutionary, statesman, and diplomat. The second Soviet people's commissar of foreign affairs, 1918–1930. Nicholas Roerich met with him in Moscow in 1926.

Churchill, Winston Leonard Spencer (1874–1965). British statesman and prime minister, 1940–1945 and 1951–1955. Led the United Kingdom during World War II. Deeply concerned by Wallace's views on the British Empire and the Soviet Union.

Chuvakhin, Dmitry Stepanovich (1903–1997). Soviet diplomat. First secretary of the Soviet embassy in the U.S., 1938–1942; assistant head of the USA department, NKID, 1942–1945. Later served as ambassador in Canada and Israel. Accompanied Wallace during his 1944 trip to Siberia.

Clayton, William Lockhart (1880–1966). American diplomat and assistant secretary of state for economic affairs, 1944–1946; undersecretary of state, 1946–1947. A principal architect of the Marshall Plan.

Collins, Perry McDonough (1813–1900). Entrepreneur and American commercial agent to the Amur River, 1856–1857. Launched the failed project to create the Russian-American telegraph, 1865–1867.

Connally, Thomas (Tom) Terry (1877–1963). American politician. Senator (D-TX), 1929–1953. He and Wallace had major disagreements on policy toward the Soviet Union.

Coolidge, Calvin (1872–1933). President, 1923–1929. Promoted a laissez-faire orientation in government policy. His first secretary of agriculture was Henry A. Wallace's father, Henry C. Wallace.

Crowley, Leo Thomas (1889–1972). American businessman and government official. Chairman of the Federal Deposit Insurance Corporation, 1934–1945. Member of FDR's expanded wartime cabinet.

Currie, Lauchlin Bernard (1902–1993). Economist. FDR's special adviser on economic affairs, 1939–1945. Sent on special missions to China in 1941 and 1942. In early 1944, was involved in the organization of Wallace's China trip.

Dahl, Roald (1916–1990). Famed author of children's books. Assistant air attaché for the British embassy in Washington and spy for British Security Coordination (BSC), 1942–1943. Reported on Wallace to the BSC and attempted to influence American policy through him.

Daniels, Jonathan Worth (1902–1981). American writer and editor. Served as one of FDR's administrative assistants.

Davies, John Paton, Jr. (1908–1999). Foreign Service officer, State Department, 1931–1954. Political aide to General Stilwell in China. Influential "China Hand," critical of Chiang Kai-shek and wary of Soviet ambitions in Asia.

Davies, Joseph Edward (1876–1958). American lawyer and diplomat. Soviet-friendly ambassador to the Soviet Union, 1936–1938.

Dewey, Thomas Edmund (1902–1971). American lawyer and politician. Governor of New York, 1943–1945. Republican candidate for president in 1948, defeated by Truman.

Dies, Martin Jr. (1901–1972). American politician. Congressman (D-TX), 1931–1945 and 1953–1959; founder and chairman of the House Committee to Investigate Un-American Activities (later renamed House Un-American Activities Committee), 1938–1944. Accused Wallace of employing Communist affiliates in the Board of Economic Warfare (BEW).

Douglas, William (1898–1980). Supreme Court justice, 1939–1975. Considered by FDR for the Democratic vice presidential nomination in 1944.

Duclos, Jacques (1896–1975). French Communist politician. Communist Party member from 1920, member of its Central Committee from 1926; deputy of the French National Assembly, 1926–1969. A staunch Stalinist, he was involved in the Comintern and Cominform.

Duggan, Laurence Hayden (1905–1948). American diplomat and Latin America specialist. Chief of the Division of American Republics Affairs, State Department, 1935–1944. In late 1936, was recruited by Soviet foreign intelligence and provided information until December 1939. A longtime friend of Wallace, he accompanied him on his Latin American tour in 1943. Widely believed to have been Wallace's choice for secretary of state, had Wallace become president.

Eisenhower, Dwight David (1890–1969). President, 1953–1961. Considered a national hero for his role as commanding general of the victorious forces in Europe during World War II.

Eisenhower, Milton Stover (1899–1985). Brother of Dwight Eisenhower. American civil servant and academic administrator. Director of information at the Department of Agriculture, 1928–1941. For three months in 1942, he was the first director of War Relocation Authority; then served at the Office of War Information until he left government service in 1943.

Ezekiel, Mordecai Joseph Brill (1899–1974). American agricultural economist. Architect of the Agricultural Adjustment Administration. Economic adviser to the secretary of agriculture, 1933–1944. Wallace's primary economic adviser, 1933–1940.

Farley, James Aloysius (1888–1976). American politician. Chairman of the Democratic National Committee, 1933–1940; postmaster general, 1933–1940. Tried to dissuade FDR from selecting Wallace as his running mate in 1940.

Faymonville, Philip Ries (1888–1962). Soviet-friendly American military and diplomatic official. First U.S. military attaché to the Soviet Union, 1934–1939. Unknowingly provided Soviet disinformation about the Roerich family and expedition to the U.S. government.

Ferris, Benjamin Greeley (1892–1982). U.S. brigadier general. Deputy chief of staff to General Stilwell in China, Burma, and India.

Flynn, Edward Joseph (1891–1953). American politician. Democratic Party chairman in the Bronx, 1922–1953; New York secretary of state, 1929–1939. A close associate of FDR; accompanied him to the Yalta Conference.

Forrestal, James Vincent (1892–1949). American financier and government official. Secretary of the Navy, 1944–1947; secretary of defense, 1947–1949. Opponent of Wallace's Soviet-friendly policy views in the Truman cabinet.

Foster, William Zebulon (1881–1961). Militant American labor organizer and CPUSA official.

Frank, Lewis Crown (1916–1970). Staff writer for *The New Republic* when Wallace became its editor in late 1946. Went on to become a speechwriter for Wallace during the latter's 1948 presidential bid.

Gardner, Oliver Max (1882–1947). American politician. Delegate at the 1944 Democratic convention; governor of North Carolina, 1929–1933; undersecretary of the treasury, 1946. Named ambassador to the U.K. in 1946, but died before taking up his post.

Garner, John Nance (1868–1967). Conservative Texas Democrat. Speaker of the House, 1931–1933. FDR's first vice president, 1933–1941.

Garrels, Arthur (1873–1943). American diplomat. U.S. consul general in Tokyo, 1930–1938. Reported unfavorably to Secretary of State Hull on the activities of Nicholas Roerich.

Gauss, Clarence Edward (1886–1960). American diplomat. Ambassador to China, 1941–1944. Met with Wallace in Chungking in June 1944.

Goebbels, Joseph (1897–1945). Minister of public enlightenment and propaganda for the Third Reich of Germany, 1933–1945.

Goglidze, Sergei Arsenievich (1901–1953). Soviet state security official from 1921. Head of the NKVD in Georgia, 1934–1938; head of the NKVD Leningrad Directorate, 1938–1941; chief of the NKGB-MGB security apparatus in the Far East, 1941–1951. Member of Beria's inner circle. Accompanied Wallace during his 1944 trip to Siberia.

Gottwald, Klement (1896–1953). Czechoslovak Communist politician. Deputy prime minister, 1945–1946; prime minister, 1946–1948; president, 1948–1953. Helped orchestrate the February 1948 Communist coup.

Grant, Frances Ruth (1896–1993). American journalist and follower of Nicholas and Helena Roerich. Vice president and trustee of the Roerich Museum, 1922–1935. Close friend of Wallace and liaison between him and the Roerichs until their falling-out in 1935.

Gridasova, Alexandra Romanovna (1915–1982). Chief of the Magadan camp branch (Maglag) of the North-eastern Camp (SVITL) of Dal'stroi, 1943–1948. Managed Magadan theater using prisoner musicians, singers, and actors. Civil wife of Ivan Nikishov, chief of Dal'stroi.

Gromyko, Andrey Andreyevich (1909–1989). Soviet diplomat and statesman. Ambassador to the United States, 1943–1946; Soviet U.N. Security Council representative, 1946–1948, deputy foreign minister, 1946–1949, first deputy foreign minister, 1949–1952 and 1953–1957; Soviet ambassador to London, 1952–1953; foreign minister, 1957–1985. Member of the Central Committee CPSU, 1956–1959; member of the Politburo CC CPSU, 1973–1988. Corresponded and met with Wallace in 1943–1946; secretly met with Wallace during the latter's 1948 presidential campaign.

Guffey, Joseph Finch (1870–1959). Senator (D-PA), 1935–1947. Backed Wallace for the vice presidential nomination at the 1944 Democratic convention.

Hale, William Harlan (1910–1974). American writer, journalist, and editor. Colleague of Wallace at *The New Republic*, turning against him in protest over his dual role as journalist and presidential candidate.

Roosevelt, Anna Eleanor (1906–1975). Writer and newspaper editor, daughter of FDR.

Hannegan, Robert (Bob) Emmet (1903–1949). American politician. Helped Truman get elected to the U.S. Senate in 1934. Commissioner of Internal Revenue, 1943–1945; postmaster general, 1945–1947; chairman of the Democratic National Committee, 1944–1947. Worked to keep Wallace off the Democratic ticket in 1944.

Harding, Warren Gamaliel (1865–1923). President, 1921–1923. Henry C. Wallace, father of Henry A. Wallace, served as his first secretary of agriculture. Harding died in office.

Harriman, Averell William (1891–1986). American businessman, politician, and diplomat. Served as FDR's special envoy to Britain and the Soviet Union on coordination of the Lend-Lease program, 1941–1942. U.S. ambassador to the Soviet Union, 1943–1946; ambassador to Great Britain, 1946; secretary of commerce, 1946–1948.

Hauser, Philip Morris (1909–1994). American sociologist and government official. Deputy director of the U.S. Census Bureau, 1946–1947; acting director, 1949–1950. Worked concurrently as assistant to Wallace during his time as secretary of commerce, 1945–1947.

Hazard, John Newbold (1909–1995). Soviet-law scholar, Russian-language interpreter, and adviser to the State Department. Chief liaison officer of the Foreign Economic Administration's Division for Soviet Supply, 1941–1945. Wallace's Russian translator and adviser on his 1944 trip to Siberia and China.

Hillman, Sidney (1887–1946). American labor leader. Founder of the Congress of Industrial Organizations (CIO). Initially backed Wallace during the 1944 Democratic convention, but switched to Truman after concluding that Wallace had lost too much party support.

Hitler, Adolf (1889–1945). Leader of the German Nazi Party, 1921–1945; chancellor and führer of Germany, 1933–1945.

Hoover, Herbert Clark (1874–1964). American statesman. Secretary of commerce under Presidents Harding and Coolidge, 1921–1929; president, 1929–1933. Rival of Henry C. Wallace, Henry A. Wallace's father, opposing his fight for "farm relief" in the 1920s.

Hoover, J. Edgar (1895–1972). Director of the Federal Bureau of Investigation, 1924–1972. Distrusted Wallace, secretly investigating him from at least 1943.

Hopkins, Harry Lloyd (1890–1946). American statesman. Secretary of commerce, 1938–1940. One of FDR's closest aides and confidants. FDR's personal manager at the 1940 Democratic National Convention. Though apprehensive about Wallace, he helped organize the latter's 1940 vice presidential nomination.

Horch, Louis L. (c. 1888–1979). Currency trader. Spiritual follower and financial sponsor of Nicholas Roerich. One of the founders and the primary financier of the Roerich Museum in New York. In July 1935, closed down the museum and its affiliated institutions, eventually taking possession of the building and its art collections.

Horch, Nettie S. (c. 1896–1991). Wife of Louis Horch. Former classmate of Frances Grant, spiritual follower and patron of Nicholas Roerich. Trustee and shareholder in the Roerich Museum and its affiliated institutions.

Hornbeck, Stanley Kuhl (1883–1966). American diplomat and scholar. Chief of the Division of Far Eastern Affairs, State Department, 1928–1937. Opposed the Roerichs' participation in the Wallace-sponsored agricultural expedition to Manchuria in 1934. Served as one of the four special advisers on political questions to Secretary of State Cordell Hull, 1937–1944.

Houdek, Vladimir (1912–2006). Czechoslovak diplomat. Counselor at the Czechoslovak embassy in Washington, 1946–1947; permanent Czechoslovak representative to the United Nations, 1948–1950, when he asked for and was granted political asylum in the United States. Served as a secret liaison between Gromyko and Wallace during the latter's 1948 presidential campaign.

Hull, Cordell (1871–1955). American statesman. Congressman (D-TN), 1907–1930; senator, 1931–1933; secretary of state, 1933–1944. Reputedly favored for the Democratic vice presidential nomination by FDR in 1940 but refused it. Won the Nobel Peace Prize in 1945.

Hurley, Patrick Jay (1883–1963). American lawyer, military officer, and military diplomat. Secretary of war, 1929–1933. Served as FDR's personal representative to Europe, the Middle East, and Asia, including to China in 1943. U.S. ambassador to China, 1944–1945.

Ickes, Harold LeClair (1874–1952). American lawyer and government official. One of FDR's closest advisers and confidants. Ardent New Dealer. Secretary of the interior, 1933–1946. Clashed often with Wallace.

Jackson, Samuel Dillon (1895–1951). American lawyer and politician. Senator (D-IN), 1944; chairman of the Democratic National Convention, 1944.

James, William (1842–1910). American philosopher and psychologist. Argued for the possibility of rational belief without evidence. Was a significant intellectual influence on Wallace.

Jones, Jesse Holman (1874–1956). American businessman and government official. Director of the Reconstruction Finance Corporation, 1933–1939; administrator of the Federal Loan Agency, 1939–1944; secretary of commerce, 1940–1945. Clashed vehemently and publicly with Wallace when the latter was vice president.

Kelly, Edward Joseph (1876–1950). American politician. Mayor of Chicago, 1933–1947. Close confidant of FDR.

Kennan, George Frost (1904–2005). One of the most influential American diplomats of the twentieth century. Chargé d'affaires in Moscow, 1944–1946; director of policy planning at the Department of State, 1947–1949; ambassador to the Soviet Union, 1952–1953. Architect of Truman's containment policy and a staunch critic of Wallace's views on the Soviet Union.

Kenny, Robert (Bob) Walker (1901–1976). Prominent California lawyer, judge, and politician. Attorney general of California, 1943–1947. Chairman of the California delegation during the 1944 Democratic convention.

Kight, Richard Thomas (1913–2001). U.S. Air Force brigadier general. Wallace's pilot on his 1944 Siberia travels.

Kramer, Charles (1906–1992). American left-wing economist. Worked for government agencies and congressional committees during the New Deal and World War II, taking an active part in the labor and Communist movements of the period. A CPUSA member from 1933, he was part of the "Ware group" of Communist operatives and, in 1944–1945, served as an NKGB foreign intelligence source (agent "Lot," later "Krot"). Worked on Wallace's 1948 presidential election campaign.

Krestinsky, Nikolai Nikolayevich (1883–1938). Russian lawyer, Bolshevik revolutionary, and statesman. People's commissar of finance, 1918–1922; ambassador in Germany, 1922–1930; deputy and first deputy people's commissar of foreign affairs, 1930–1937. Met with Nicholas Roerich in Berlin on Christmas Eve 1924. Arrested in 1937 on falsified charges and executed in 1938.

Krock, Arthur Bernard (1886–1974). Influential *New York Times* political columnist.

Kung, H.H. (1880–1967). Prominent Chinese banker and statesman, husband to Soong Ai-ling. Head of Sun Yat-sen's central bank and minister in Kuomintang party governments. President of the Nationalist government, 1938–1939.

La Follette, Robert Marion "Fighting Bob," Sr. (1855–1925). American lawyer and politician. Progressive Party presidential candidate in 1924; senator from Wisconsin, 1906–1925.

Landon, Alfred (Alf) Mossman (1887–1987). American oilman and politician. Republican governor of Kansas, 1933–1937; Republican nominee for president, 1936.

Lattimore, Owen (1900–1989). Central Asia scholar, fluent in Chinese, Mongolian, and Russian. Political adviser to Chiang Kai-shek, 1941–1942; director of Pacific Operations at the U.S. Office of War Information, 1942–1944. Diplomatic adviser to Wallace on his 1944 trip to Siberia and China.

Leahy, William Daniel (1875–1959). American fleet admiral, diplomat, and presidential aide. Chief of Naval Operations, 1937–1939; governor of Puerto Rico, 1939–1940; ambassador to Vichy France, 1940–1942; chief of staff to FDR, 1942–1945; chief of staff to Truman, 1945–1949.

Lenin, Vladimir Ilyich (1870–1924). Russian Bolshevik revolutionary and Soviet leader. Led Bolshevik forces to victory in the coup of October 1917 and became the first Soviet head of state.

Lewis, John Llewellyn (1880–1969). American labor leader. President of the United Mine Workers of America (UMWA), 1920–1960. Founding president of the Congress of Industrial Organizations (CIO).

Lichtmann, Esther (1892–1990). Sister of Maurice Lichtmann. Patron and spiritual follower of Nicholas and Helena Roerich, board member of and shareholder in New York's Roerich Museum.

Lichtmann, Maurice (1887–1948). Brother of Esther Lichtmann and the first husband of Sina Lichtmann. Patron and spiritual follower of Nicholas and Helena Roerich, board member of and shareholder in New York's Roerich Museum.

Lichtmann, Sina (c. 1887–1983). Russian-born musician, concert pianist, and music teacher. Her first marriage was to Maurice Lichtmann; became Sina Fosdick after her second. Spiritual follower of Nicholas and Helena Roerich, director of the Master Institute of United Arts, and board member of and shareholder in New York's Roerich Museum.

Lipper, Elinor (1912–2008). Dutch-born socialist who served eleven years in the Magadan labor camp on falsified charge of "counterrevolution." Author of *Eleven Years in Soviet Prison Camps* (1951). Fierce critic of Wallace's account of his 1944 Siberian travels.

Lippmann, Walter (1889–1974). American writer and columnist. A founding editor of *The New Republic*. Two-time Pulitzer Prize winner noted for his analysis of U.S. foreign policy.

Littell, Norman Mather (1899–1994). FDR's assistant attorney general, 1939–1944. Wallace ally.

Lorwin, Lewis L. (1883–1970). Left-wing economist and labor historian. Adviser to the Office of International Trade of the Department of Commerce, 1945–1952. Accompanied Ernest Ropes on a trade mission to Moscow organized by Wallace in 1946.

Lozovsky, Solomon Abramovich (1878–1952). Bolshevik revolutionary and Soviet statesman. General secretary of the Red International Labor Union (Profintern), 1921–1937; deputy people's commissar of foreign affairs handling the Far East, 1939–1946; head of the Sovinformburo, 1945–1948; member of the Central Party Committee, 1939–1949.

Lucas, Scott Wike (1892–1968). American attorney and politician. Senator (D-IL), 1939–1950; Senate majority leader, 1948–1950.

Luce, Henry Robinson (1898–1967). American publishing magnate. Cofounder of *Time* magazine and founder of *Fortune* and *Life* magazines. Coined the phrase "the American Century."

MacArthur, Douglas (1880–1964). U.S. Army general who commanded the Pacific theater during World War II.

MacDougall, Curtis Daniel (1903–1985). Nineteen forty-eight Illinois Progressive Party senatorial candidate, journalist, and author. Chronicled Wallace's 1948 presidential campaign.

MacMillan, Howard Gove (1890–1985). Botanist at the U.S. Department of Agriculture, 1915–1934. Accompanied Nicholas Roerich's expedition to Manchuria and Mongolia as the principal agriculture explorer in the Division of Plant Exploration and Introduction, but split from Roerich's party several months into it.

Magdoff, Harry Samuel (1913–2006). Influential American Marxist economist and CPUSA member. NKGB agent ("Tan" and "Kant"), 1944–1945. Trusted adviser to Henry Wallace, 1945–1946. Betrayed Wallace by passing his cabinet papers to the NKGB.

Mao Tse-tung (1893–1976). Chinese Communist revolutionary and founder of the People's Republic of China.

Marcantonio, Vito Anthony (1902–1954). American lawyer and politician. CPUSA-backed American Labor Party congressman from New York, 1947–1949.

Marsh, Charles Edward (1887–1964). Texas publishing magnate, well connected in the Democratic Party. Patron of Wallace. Mentor to Roald Dahl, the British embassy official who spied in Washington during World War II.

Marshall, George Catlett, Jr. (1880–1959). American military leader and statesman. Army chief of staff, 1939–1945; secretary of state, 1947–1949; secretary of defense, 1950–1951. Received the Nobel Peace Prize in 1953 for his efforts in creating the European Recovery Program, aka the Marshall Plan.

Masaryk, Jan Garrigue (1886–1948). Czechoslovak diplomat and politician. Foreign minister of Czechoslovakia, 1945–1948. Son of the country's post–World War I founder, he sought to preserve his country's independence from the Soviet Union.

McCarthy, Joseph Raymond (1908–1957). American politician. Senator (R-WI), 1947–1957. Known for the "Red Scare" movement that alleged massive infiltration of the U.S. government by Communists and Soviet spies.

McCullough, David Gaub (1933–2022). American popular historian and Truman biographer.

McIntire, Ross T. (1889–1959). Vice admiral of the U.S. Navy. Surgeon general of the Navy, 1938–1946; personal physician to FDR, 1932–1945.

McNutt, Paul Vories (1891–1955). American diplomat, politician, and conservative Democrat. Indiana governor, 1932–1937; administrator of the Federal Security Commission, 1939–1945; chairman of the War Manpower Commission, 1942–1945; ambassador to the Philippine Republic, 1946–1947. Opposed Wallace's vice presidential nomination in 1944.

Merkulov, Vsevolod Nikolayevich (1895–1953). Soviet state security official. Head of the People's Commissariat of State Security (NKGB), 1941 and 1943–1946. Dismissed by Stalin in 1947 and executed in 1953 along with Lavrenty Beria. In 1944, he was in charge of security for Wallace's Siberia trip.

Mikoyan, Anastas Ivanovich (1895–1978). Bolshevik revolutionary, Communist Party leader, and Soviet statesman. Member of the Politburo, 1926–1966; people's commissar of trade and foreign trade, 1926–1930; of procurement, 1930–1934; of food processing industry, 1934–1938; of foreign trade, 1938–1946; minister of foreign trade, 1946–1949; deputy chairman of the Soviet government, 1937–1953. Met with Wallace's trade mission officials in Moscow in 1946.

Molotov, Vyacheslav Mikhailovich (1890–1986). Bolshevik revolutionary, Soviet government and Communist Party leader. Chairman of the Soviet Government (Council of People's Commissars), 1930–1941; first chairman of the Council of People's Commissars, 1941–1946; Council of Ministers, 1946–1957; people's commissar of foreign affairs, 1939–1946; minister of foreign affairs, 1946–1949, 1953–1956. A doctrinaire Marxist and loyal to Stalin, he was renowned among contemporary statesmen for his stubborn but effective anti-Western diplomacy.

Morgenthau, Henry, Jr. (1891–1967). Secretary of the treasury, 1934–1945. One of FDR's closest confidants; introduced him to Wallace in 1933. Was instrumental in financing World War II, served as chairman of the Bretton Woods Conference in 1944, and lent his name to the plan that sought to de-industrialize postwar Germany.

Murphy, Charles Francis (1858–1924). New York politician and Tammany Hall "chief," 1903–1924.

Murray, Philip (1936–1952). American labor leader. President of the Congress of Industrial Organizations (CIO), 1940–1952; vice president of the United Mine Workers of America (UMWA), 1920–1942; president of the United Steel Workers of America (USWA), 1942–1952. In 1948, Murray endorsed Truman for president and expelled left-leaning unions that supported the Wallace campaign.

Mussolini, Benito (1883–1945). Prime minister of Italy, 1922–1943. Dictator and leader of the Italian Fascist Party.

Nelson, Donald Marr (1888–1959). American business executive and public servant. Director of the Supply Priorities and Allocation Board, 1941–1942; chairman of the War Production Board, 1942–1944.

Nikishov, Ivan Feodorovich (1894–1958). Cadre OGPU-NKVD officer, 1924–1948. From 1939 through 1948, he served as director of Dal'stroi, a state trust for road and industrial construction of the Kolyma region, including gold exploration and mining, which relied on prisoner labor in its vast North-Eastern Camp (*Sevvostlag*). Wallace's host in Magadan.

Panyushkin, Alexander Semenovich (1905–1974). Soviet foreign intelligence officer, diplomat, and Communist Party official. Soviet ambassador and NKVD chief *rezident* in China, 1939–1944; deputy head of the Department of International Information (later Foreign Policy Department) of the Central Committee of VCP (b), 1944–1947; ambassador to the U.S. and chief Committee of Information (KI) *rezident* ("Vladimir"), 1947–1952. Ambassador in China, 1952–1953. Returned to the CPSU Central Committee's apparatus in 1955 until his retirement in 1962. Wallace was meeting with Panyushkin in late 1948 and maintained occasional correspondence with him for three more years.

Pauley, Edwin Wendell (1903–1981). American oil magnate, Democratic politician, and presidential adviser. Treasurer of the Democratic National Committee, 1942–1948, and a friend and confidant of Senator Truman. Opponent of Wallace's nomination for vice president in 1944.

Pendergast, Thomas (Tom) Joseph (1873–1945). Powerful Missouri political boss, 1925–1939. Supported Truman's early political career.

Pepper, Claude Denson (1900–1989). American lawyer and left-wing politician. Senator (D-FL), 1936–1951; Congressman (D-FL), 1963–1989. Prominent supporter of Wallace for the 1944 vice presidential nomination.

Perkins, Frances (1882–1965). American workers' rights advocate and government official. Secretary of labor, 1933–1945, prominent New Dealer, and the first woman to serve as a cabinet secretary.

Perkins, Milo Randolph (1900–1972). American economist. Wallace aide at the

Department of Agriculture, 1935–1940; executive director of the Board of Economic Warfare (BEW), 1942–1944.

Perlo, Victor (1912–1999). American Marxist economist and civil servant. Member of the CPUSA from 1932. Consultant to the Agricultural Adjustment Administration (AAA), 1934–1935. Member of the "Ware group" of Communist operatives. Alternate member of the Committee for Reciprocity Information, Monetary Research division of the Treasury Department, 1945–1947. Worked for NKGB operatives as agent "Raid" from 1944 to 1945. In 1948, became an economist for Wallace's Progressive Party, drafting its economic platform.

Powell, John B. (1886–1947). Shanghai correspondent for the *Chicago Tribune*, 1918–1938. Published a damning article about Nicholas Roerich's mission to Manchuria and Mongolia in 1935.

Pressman, Lee (1906–1969). Labor lawyer. General counsel of the Agricultural Adjustment Administration (AAA), 1933–1935; general counsel of the Congress of Industrial Organizations (CIO), 1936–1948. Member of the Communist-led "Ware group" at the Department of Agriculture, member of CPUSA from 1935, and confidential contact of Soviet intelligence ("Vig"). Resigned from the CIO to become the secretary of Wallace's 1948 campaign platform committee.

Rayburn, Samuel Taliaferro (1882–1961). American politician. Congressman (D-TX), 1912–1961; speaker of the House, 1940–1947, 1949–1953, and 1955–1961. Vice presidential aspirant in 1944.

Reinsch, Leonard James (1908–1991). Radio adviser to the White House, 1945–1952; executive director of the Democratic National Convention, 1960 and 1964.

Rerikh, Boris Konstantinovich (1885–1945). Youngest brother of Nicholas Roerich, he worked as an artist, architect, and then movie art director in Russia. In 1926, he took part in Nicholas' Central Asian expedition, representing the latter's interests with Soviet institutions. Arrested by OGPU in 1927 and 1931 on charges of association with foreign organizations.

Rerikh, Vladimir Konstantinovich (1882–1951). Younger brother of Nicholas Roerich. Worked as a manager of agricultural estates while in Russia. A monarchist, he followed White forces to Siberia and eventually to Harbin, China. From Harbin, in 1930, he began collaborating with Nicholas in the development of a Manchurian agricultural co-op. In 1934, briefly took part in the Manchurian leg of Nicholas' expedition.

Roach, Neale (1913–1979). Manager of the Democratic National Conventions, 1948, 1952, and 1956.

Roerich, George (1902–1960). Russian name: Yury Konstantinovich Rerikh. Russian-born, European- and U.S.-educated son of Nicholas and Helena Roerich. Fluent in dozens of European and Asian languages and dialects, he was expert in Asian culture, religion, and philosophy. Assisted his father on the Wallace-sponsored Central Asian expedition of 1934–1935.

Roerich, Helena (1879–1955). Russian name: Elena Ivanovna Rerikh. Russian theosophist and Asian explorer, best known for her Agni Yoga ("Live Ethic") teaching. Wife of Nicholas Roerich. From 1933 to 1935, corresponded with Wallace, trying to influence him both spiritually and politically.

Roerich, Nicholas (1874–1947). Russian name: Nikolai Konstantinovich Rerikh. Russian artist, archaeologist, explorer, writer, and public figure. Founded the Master Institute of United Arts and the Roerich Museum in New York in the early 1920s. In the early 1930s, he was a great influence on Wallace as his spiritual guide ("Guru") and confidant. In 1934, Wallace appointed him to lead a Central Asian seed-gathering expedition that acted as a cover for his ambition to re-create the legendary earthly paradise of Shambhala.

Roerich, Svetoslav (1904–1993). Russian name: Svyatoslav Nikolaevich Rerikh. Russian-born younger son of Nicholas and Helena Roerich. Artist and architect who in the 1920s took an active part in the work of the New York Roerich Museum and cultural institutions. In 1931, he moved to India, which became his second motherland.

Roosevelt, Eleanor Anna (1884–1962). American diplomat and humanitarian activist. Wife of FDR and first lady, 1933–1945; delegate to the United Nations General Assembly, 1945–1953.

Roosevelt, Franklin Delano (1882–1945). President, 1933–1945. Led the United States through the Great Depression and World War II. Appointed Wallace secretary of agriculture in 1933. Went against his advisers and insisted upon Wallace as his running mate in 1940, but failed to do so in 1944. Appointed Wallace as commerce secretary in 1945.

Ropes, Ernest C. (1877–1949). Expert at the Russian Division of the Bureau of Foreign and Domestic Commerce, Commerce Department, 1923–1947, becoming chief in 1946. Accompanied economist Lewis Lorwin on a trade mission to Moscow organized by Wallace in 1946.

Rosenman, Samuel Irving (1896–1973). American lawyer, judge, and Democratic politician. Member of the New York State Assembly, 1922–1926; FDR speechwriter from 1928; New York State Supreme Court justice, 1936–1943; special counsel to FDR, 1943–1945, and to President Truman, 1945–1946. Featured in legal and political issues related to Nicholas Roerich and Wallace's controversial relations with him.

Ryerson, Knowles A. (1893–1990). Chief of the USDA's Bureau of Plant Industry under Wallace, 1933–1934; chief of the Office of Tropical and Subtropical Horticulture, Department of Agriculture, 1934–1937; professor and director of the

Davis campus of the University of California, 1937–1942. Wallace fell out with him over Roerich's leadership of the Central Asian expedition of 1934–1935, to which Ryerson strongly objected.

Semenov, Ilya Sergeyevich (1904–1971). High-ranking official of Soviet Civil Aviation, head of the Krasnoyarsk–Uelkal Airway, 1943–1944. Greeted Wallace during his 1944 trip to Siberia.

Service, John Stewart (1909–1999). Foreign Service officer, 1935–1951 and 1957–1962. One of the State Department's influential "China Hands." Born and raised in China by missionary parents.

Sgovio, Thomas (1916–1997). American Communist and artist who served sixteen years in Siberia's Kolyma labor camp. Wrote about the Soviet deception of Wallace during the latter's Siberian tour of 1944.

Sheng, Shicai (1895–1970). Left-wing Chinese warlord and military governor of Sinkiang, 1933–1944, under whom the Soviets enjoyed a trade monopoly and exploited natural resources. In 1942, he eradicated Communist influence in his government and pledged allegiance to the National Government. When the Soviets invaded Sinkiang in 1944, the Chinese government removed him from his post and named him minister of agriculture and forestry.

Sherwood, Robert Emmet (1896–1955). American playwright and screenwriter. FDR speechwriter.

Silvermaster, Nathan Gregory (1989–1964). Leader of a CPUSA informational group while working as an economist in the U.S. government. From 1944, he was directly under the control of NKGB operatives as an agent-group leader. Silvermaster and his networks were betrayed by Elizabeth Bentley in November 1945.

Skvortsov, Tikhon Fedorovich (1900–1972). Soviet career diplomat, 1935–1956. Chargé d'affaires of the Soviet embassy in China, 1942–1945. Reported to Moscow on Wallace's China trip, including intelligence on Wallace's diplomatic efforts with Chiang Kai-shek.

Smith, Alfred (Al) Emanuel (1873–1944). American politician. Democratic governor of New York, 1919–1921 and 1923–1929. Failed 1928 presidential candidate.

Smith, Harold Dewey (1898–1947). American public administrator. Director of the Federal Bureau of the Budget, 1939–1946. Brokered agreements that gave Wallace more power within the Board of Economic Warfare (BEW).

Soong, Ai-ling (1890–1973). Eldest daughter of Charlie Soong. Personal assistant to Sun Yat-sen, 1911–1914, wife of H.H. Kung. Matriarch of the Soong business empire after Charlie Soong's death.

Soong, Charlie (1863–1918). Wealthy Chinese entrepreneur and businessmen educated in the United States. Methodist patriarch of a powerful family in

China. Financier of Sun Yat-sen's revolution to create the National Republic of China.

Soong, Ching-ling (1893–1981). U.S.-educated middle daughter of Charlie Soong. Third wife of Sun Yat-sen. After her husband's death, she became an influential political leader in China, supporting the left wing of the Nationalist Party.

Soong, Mei-ling (1897–2003). First lady of the Republic of China, 1927–1949. U.S.-educated youngest daughter of Charlie Soong. Second wife of Chiang Kai-shek and major Chinese political figure, influential in the United States. Together with Chiang Kai-shek, she launched the New Life Movement to counter Communism in 1934. Met with Wallace on his 1944 trip to China, interpreting for her husband.

Soong, T.V. (1894–1971). Son of Charlie Soong. Prominent Chinese businessman and politician. Took over financing of China's Nationalist Party alongside Ai-ling after Charlie Soong's death in 1918. Finance minister of the Nationalist government, 1925–1931; foreign minister, 1942–1945.

Spilvanek, Ivan Ivanovich (1883–?). Soviet diplomat. Acted as the Soviet consul general in Peking and simultaneously Tianjin, 1926–1929; official at the Soviet embassy in China, Nanking, 1933; consul general in Shanghai, 1933–1937; consul general in Peking, 1937–1939.

Stalin, Iosif (Joseph) Vissarionovich (1879–1953). Bolshevik revolutionary, Communist Party leader, and Soviet statesman who built a murderous and repressive totalitarian regime. Secretary general of the Soviet Communist Party, 1922–1953; chairman of the Council of People's Commissars/Council of Ministers, 1941–1953; supreme commander in chief of the Armed Forces, 1941–1945; chairman of the State Committee of Defense (GKO), 1941–1945; people's commissar of defense, 1941–1946, minister of the Armed Forces of the USSR, 1946–1947; Generalissimo, 1945.

Steel, Johannes (1908–1988). Left-wing American journalist and writer. An occasional confidential contact of Soviet diplomats and intelligence operatives. Wallace backed his unsuccessful run for a New York congressional seat in 1946 as the American Labor Party candidate.

Steiger, Andrew Jacob (1900–1970). Longtime Moscow-based journalist. Louis Budenz testified that he had been a secret Communist in the 1930s. Recruited by Soviet intelligence in 1940. Venona decrypts suggest that he passed foreign-policy-related information to the NKGB in 1943–1944. In 1945–1946, collaborated with Wallace in writing *Soviet Asia Mission*.

Stephens, James L. (1902–1982). Botanist at the Department of Agriculture. Assistant to Howard MacMillan. Accompanied MacMillan on Nicholas Roerich's mission to Manchuria and Mongolia in 1934, but the Americans split from Roerich's party several months into the expedition.

Stettinius, Edward Reilly (1900–1949). American businessman and diplomat. CEO of General Motors and U.S. Steel Corporation, 1934–1940; chairman of the War Resources Board, 1939; chairman of the Priorities Board and director of Priorities Division, Office of Production Management, 1941; director of Lend-Lease Administration and special assistant to the president, 1941–1943; under-secretary of state, 1943–1944. Though Wallace wanted to succeed Cordell Hull as secretary of state in 1944, FDR chose Stettinius, who served from 1944 to 1945.

Stilwell, Joseph Warren "Vinegar Joe" (1883–1946). American general who served in China and Burma during World War II. Trained the Chinese Nationalist army. Owing to strategic and temperamental differences, Chiang Kai-shek pushed FDR for his removal.

Stimson, Henry Lewis (1867–1950). American statesman, lawyer, and politician. Secretary of state, 1929–1933; secretary of war, 1940–1945; chairman of the Stimson Committee for the Marshall Plan to Aid European Recovery, 1947–1948. Instrumental in the decision to drop the atomic bomb on Japan.

Straight, Michael Whitney (1916–2004). Publisher of *The New Republic*, 1941–1956. Hired Wallace to be the magazine's editor in late 1946. U.K.-educated, Straight became a Communist in the 1930s and, from 1937 to 1939, a recruit of Soviet foreign intelligence ("Nigel"). Moved toward mainstream politics in the 1940s, and worked assiduously to persuade Wallace not to run as the presidential candidate of the Communist-infiltrated Progressive Party in 1948.

Sun Yat-sen (1866–1925). Chinese revolutionary, instrumental in overthrowing the Qing dynasty in 1911. First provisional president of the Republic of China, 1911–1912. Founded the Nationalist Party (Kuomintang/KMT) in 1912 and became its first leader. In his final years he reorganized the KMT and arranged an alliance with the Communist Party to fight for reunification of China.

Taft, Robert Alphonso (1889–1953). American politician. Senator (R-OH), 1939–1953. Staunch conservative.

Taylor, Glen Hearst (1904–1984). American politician and entertainer. Senator (D-ID), 1945–1951. Wallace's vice presidential running mate in 1948.

Thurmond, James Strom (1902–2003). American politician. Governor of South Carolina, 1947–1951; senator (D-SC), 1954–1964; senator (R-SC), 1964–2002. Ran as the States' Rights Democratic ("Dixiecrat") candidate for president in 1948 on a segregationist platform, garnering more votes than Wallace.

Trotsky, Lev Davidovich (1879–1940). Russian revolutionary and Soviet statesman. Leader in the October 1917 Bolshevik coup. Soviet commissar of foreign affairs, 1917–1918; of war and navy, 1918–1925; member of the Politburo, 1919–1926, and one of the organizers of the Comintern. Stalin's opponent from 1923, banished from Moscow in January 1928 and from the USSR in 1929. Murdered on Stalin's order in 1940.

Truman, Harry S. (1884–1972). American politician and statesman. Senator (D-MO), 1935–1945; vice president, 1945; president, 1945–1953. Led the United States through the end of World War II and the beginning of the Cold War. Won out over Wallace to become the Democratic vice presidential candidate during the tumultuous Democratic convention of 1944. Retaining Wallace as commerce secretary in 1945, Truman clashed with him repeatedly on policy toward the Soviets. Fired Wallace in September 1946.

Tugwell, Rexford Guy (1891–1979). American economist, part of FDR's "Brain Trust." Assistant secretary of agriculture under Wallace, 1933–1934; undersecretary of agriculture, 1934–1935; director of the Resettlement Administration, 1935–1936; chairman, New York Planning Commission, 1938; governor of Puerto Rico, 1942–1946; chairman of the platform committee of the Progressive Party, 1948.

Tully, Grace G. (1900–1984). Personal secretary to FDR from 1928. Principal personal secretary, 1941–1945.

Vandenberg, Arthur Hendrick (1884–1951). American politician. Senator (R-MI), 1928–1951; chairman of the Senate Foreign Relations Committee, 1947–1949. An isolationist turned internationalist and a hawk on Soviet policy. Accused Wallace in 1947 of "treasonable utterances" for his support of the Soviet Union.

Vincent, John Carter (1900–1972). Career foreign service officer. Head of the Division of China Affairs, State Department, 1945–1947. Wallace's adviser on Chinese affairs during the latter's 1944 trip to China. One of the famous "China Hands" attacked by Senator McCarthy for defeatism over Chiang's regime and alleged Communist leanings.

Vinson, Frederick (Fred) Moore (1890–1953). American lawyer, Democratic politician, and jurist. Treasury secretary, 1945–1946; chief justice of the Supreme Court, 1946–1953. Close friend of Truman.

Vyshinsky, Andrey Januarievich (1883–1954). Soviet lawyer, diplomat, and statesman. Prosecutor of the USSR, 1935–1939; assistant chairman of the Council of People's Commissars, 1939–1944; assistant people's commissar of foreign affairs/assistant foreign minister, 1940–1949; foreign minister, 1949–1953; deputy foreign minister, 1953–1954; Soviet permanent representative at the United Nations, 1949–1954. Prosecuting attorney in the notorious Moscow show trials of 1934–1938 and Stalin's "Great Purge." Oversaw Wallace's 1944 Siberian trip as the first assistant people's commissar of foreign affairs.

Walker, Frank Comerford (1886–1959). American lawyer and politician. Adviser to FDR. Postmaster general, 1940–1945; chair of the Democratic National Committee, 1943–1944. Opposed Wallace's vice presidential nomination in 1944.

Wallace, Henry (Harry) Cantwell (1866–1924). American journalist, farmer, and father of Henry A. Wallace. Editor of the influential *Wallaces' Farmer* agricultural journal, 1916–1921. Republican secretary of agriculture under Warren G. Harding and Calvin Coolidge, 1921–1924. Backed efforts to increase agricultural prices and played an important part in framing agricultural legislation.

Wallace, Henry "Uncle Henry" (1836–1916). Grandfather of Henry A. Wallace. Farmer and Presbyterian minister. Founded the influential *Wallaces' Farmer* agricultural journal. Republican activist, reportedly considered twice for the new office of secretary of agriculture.

Wallace, Ilo Browne (1888–1981). Wife of Henry A. Wallace and mother of his three children.

Watson, Edwin Martin "Pa" (1883–1945). U.S. Army major general. FDR's senior military aide from 1933, and from 1938 simultaneously his appointments secretary. Opposed Wallace's renomination as vice president in 1944. Died on the way back from the Yalta Conference.

Wedemeyer, Albert Coady (1897–1989). U.S. Army general and military leader. Principal author of the 1941 Victory Program, a war plan for U.S. entry into World War II. Chief of staff to General Chiang Kai-shek and commander of U.S. forces in China, 1944–1946.

White, Harry Dexter (1892–1948). Soviet-friendly American Keynesian economist and U.S. Treasury Department official, 1934–1946. Chief architect of the 1944 Bretton Woods international monetary conference. U.S. executive director at the newly established International Monetary Fund, 1946–1947. Considered a valuable agent of influence by Soviet intelligence. A friend of Wallace from 1940, White was widely believed to be his choice as treasury secretary in a Wallace administration.

White, Theodore (Teddy) Harold (1915–1986). American political journalist and historian best known for his *Making of the President* series. Kuomintang political adviser. Foreign correspondent for *Time* magazine in East Asia, 1939–1945. Worked under Wallace at *The New Republic*.

Willkie, Wendell Lewis (1892–1944). American lawyer and politician. Republican presidential candidate, 1940. Represented the liberal, internationalist wing of the Republican Party. Willkie preceded Wallace in 1942 in touring the Soviet Union and China as FDR's personal representative.

Winant, John Gilbert (1889–1947). American politician and diplomat. Republican governor of New Hampshire, 1925–1927 and 1931–1935; first chairman of the Social Security Board, 1935–1937; assistant director, International Labor Organization, Geneva, 1936–1939, and third director, 1939–1941; ambassador to the U.K., 1941–1946.

Zhdanov, Andrey Alexandrovich (1896–1948). Soviet Communist Party leader and statesman. First secretary of the Leningrad regional and city committees of VCP (b), 1934–1945; member of the Politburo, 1939–1948; chief of the office of propaganda and agitation of VCP (b) Central Committee, 1939–1940; secretary of the Central Committee responsible for ideology, 1944–1948. From 1946, on Stalin's orders, he launched ideological campaigns against Soviet writers, musicians, and artists.

Zhou Enlai (1898–1976). Leading member of the Chinese Communist Party. First premier of the People's Republic of China, 1949–1976, and simultaneously its foreign minister, 1949–1958. Close associate of Mao Tse-tung.

Zorin, Valerian Alexandrovich (1902–1986). Soviet diplomat and statesman. Ambassador to Czechoslovakia, 1945–1947; assistant foreign minister, 1947–1955, 1956–1960, and 1963–1965; head of the Committee of Information under the Ministry of Foreign Affairs, 1949–1952; Soviet permanent representative at the United Nations, 1952–1953 and 1960–1963; ambassador to the Federal Republic of Germany, 1955–1956; France, 1965–1971; ambassador-at-large, 1971–1986. Infamous for his October 25, 1962 U.N. dialogue with Adlai Stevenson.

APPENDIX 1

HENRY A. WALLACE'S
"OPEN LETTER" TO JOSEPH STALIN
May 11, 1948

The following is the text of Henry A. Wallace's "open letter to Premier Stalin," as distributed on May 11, 1948 at the Wallace rally at Madison Square Garden:
The New York Times, May 12, 1948

A CENTURY OF PEACE

Although the notes of Ambassador Bedell Smith and Foreign Minister Molotov are both characterized by the same self-righteousness which has lead to the international crisis, they represent great hope to those of us who have consistently maintained that peace is possible, and they represent a severe blow to the propagandists on both sides who have insisted that the two nations cannot live at peace in the same world. The two letters assume what we have long contended—that the wartime cooperation between the two great powers can be rebuilt and strengthened in time of peace. The exchange of notes, opening the door to negotiations, must be followed by a meeting—an open, fully reported meeting of representatives of both the United States and the Soviet Union. With the prospect of such a meeting, I present my thoughts on the steps necessary to achieve the Century of Peace.

THE COLD WAR MUST STOP

The United States of America and the Union of Soviet Socialist Republics must take immediate action to end the cold war. This involves taking definite, decisive steps looking toward the following objectives:

- General reduction of armaments—outlawing all methods of mass destruction.

- Stopping the export of weapons by any nation to any other nation.

- The resumption of unrestricted trade (except for goods related to war) between the two countries.

- The free movement of citizens, students and newspaper men between and within the two countries.

- The resumption of free exchange of scientific information and scientific material between the two nations.

- The re-establishment of a reinvigorated United Nations Relief and Rehabilitation Administration or the constitution of some other United Nations agency for the distribution of international relief.

Neither the United States of America nor the Union of Soviet Socialist Republics should interfere in the internal affairs of other nations. Neither the United States of America nor the Union of Soviet Socialist Republics should maintain military bases in other United Nations countries. Neither the United States of America nor the Union of Soviet Socialist Republics should terrorize the citizens of member states of the United Nations by massing land forces, establishing air bases, or making naval demonstrations. Neither the United States of America not the Union of Soviet Socialist Republics should use financial pressure, economic pressure or the pressure of secret agents to obtain political results in other countries. Both the United States of America and the Union of Soviet Socialist Republics, in the spirit of the United Nations Charter, should collaborate to the limit in furthering the political, economic and cultural health of the world. To that end the United States of America and the Union of Soviet Social Republics should join the various subsidiary agencies of the United Nations, such as the World Health Organization, the Food and Agricultural Organization, and The United Nations Educational, Scientific and Cultural Organization.

REHABILITATION OF EUROPE

It is to the advantage of both the United States of America and the Union of Soviet Socialist Republics to give maximum economic help to Europe as promptly as possible within the framework of the United Nations, proportioned to the devastation and economic need. As soon as possible the European Cooperation Administration and the United Nations and the Economic Commission for Europe should be converted into a reinvigorated and expanded United Nations Relief and Rehabilitation Administration for the purpose of building a highly productive, economically unified Europe in which there would be no barriers of trade, communication or culture between Eastern Europe and Western Europe.

SPEEDY PEACE WITH GERMANY

The Union of Soviet Socialist Republics, the United States of America, Great Britain and France should conclude a peace treaty with Germany at the earliest possible moment. The objective is the prompt re-establishment of a peace-loving German government in charge of a united Germany which is obligated to the strict fulfillment of the Yalta and Potsdam agreements. Russian, French, British and American troops should be withdrawn from Germany within one year after the signing of the German peace treaty.

PEACE IN THE FAR EAST

Neither the United States of America nor the Union of Soviet Socialist Republics should send arms into China. Both the United States of America and the Union of Soviet Socialist Republics should withdraw troops from both China and Korea. There should be set up as soon as possible a government for all of Korea. Both the United States of America and the Union of Soviet Socialist Republics should adhere to the principle of equal rights for all nations in China, with respect for the sovereignty of China, and refrain from interference in the internal affairs of China. Both the United States of America and the Union of Soviet Socialist Republics can benefit from a

China which is strong and unified on the basis of economic and political democracy.

JAPAN

A peace treaty with Japan based on agreements heretofore arrived at should be made at the earliest possible moment. Both the United States of America and the United Soviet Socialist Republics have a vital interest in a democratic and peace-loving Japan. All nations having occupation troops in Japan should withdraw them within a year after the signing of the peace treaty with Japan.

VETO AND ATOMIC ENERGY CONTROL

The excessive use of the veto and the impasse with regard to certain phases of atomic energy control are the expression of the lack of confidence between the two nations. They are symptoms, not causes. Both can be handled constructively once confidence is established in the major issues. The door should be promptly opened to the extraordinary benefits which atomic energy can bring to mankind at peace. Atomic energy for war is a crime and a curse. Atomic energy for peace can be science's greatest blessing.

ACCESS TO RAW MATERIALS

The Atlantic Charter has provision for freedom of access to raw materials by the nations of the world. This is very important for the smaller nations and both the United States of America and the Union of Soviet Socialist Republics should carry out the spirit of Article 4 of the Atlantic Charter.

There are possibilities of increasing interchange of goods between the United States of America and the Union of Soviet Socialist Republics to a volume many times the pre-war figure. Such an increase in trade excluding any discrimination will promote friendly relations between the two countries and thereby strengthen the cause of world peace.

ASSURANCE WITH REGARD TO RUSSIAN AND AMERICAN INTENTIONS

Millions of citizens in the United States of America believe it is the settled purpose of Soviet leaders to conquer the world. Millions of citizens in the United Soviet Socialist Republics believe it is the settled purpose of the United States of America to invade the Union of Soviet Socialist Republics. Both point to specific instances to make their point. Each nation should state definitively and categorically that it has no design on the territorial integrity of any other nation.

COMMUNISM AND CAPITALISM

The ideological competition between communism and capitalism is a different matter from the misunderstanding between the Union of Soviet Socialist Republics and the United States of America. The latter can be solved in a way that will preserve peace. But the competition between the capitalist and Communist systems is never ending. It is the concern of both nations to see that this competition remains constructive and that it never degenerates into the status of such a religious war as the Thirty Years War which so devastated Europe at the beginning of the seventeenth century.

Russia cannot be held responsible for the excesses of local Communists any more than the United States of America can be held responsible for the reprehensible exploitation of backward peoples by many capitalists who are not citizens or only nominally citizens of the United States of America.

Undoubtedly many Communists and capitalists have expressed the belief that their particular system will inevitably dominate the world. But that does not mean that the Union of Soviet Socialist Republics and the United States of America must engage in perpetual conflict. The two countries can agree to a modus vivendi while the slow process of time determines the strong and weak points of the two economic systems and the free peoples of the world today make day by day the small choices which eventually will evolve, on the basis of empiricism, systems which will be best adapted for the various individual countries.

THE CENTURY OF PEACE MUST COME

There is no misunderstanding or difficulty between the United States of America and the Union of Soviet Socialist Republics which can be settled by force or fear and there is no difference which cannot be settled by peaceful, hopeful negotiation. There is no American principle or public interest, and there is no Russian principle or public interest which would have to be sacrificed to end the cold war and open up the Century of Peace which the Century of the Common Man demands.

APPENDIX 2

TRANSLATION OF SOVIET CYPHER CABLE

[STALIN'S NOTATIONS:]

1) *A trip may do harm*
2) *A statement is useful*

[GROMYKO'S WORDS:]

In conclusion, Wallace said that he had not definitively decided if he should go to Moscow. An address with a statement, he said, on the major issues of Soviet-American relations might definitely help him. Such statement, he said, could be made either by Generalissimo Stalin or by him, Wallace, with the approval of I.V. Stalin. He still tends to think that the effect would be greater if such statement would result from his trip to Moscow.

He said that he would be leaving New York for long periods of time to speak at all kinds of meetings and rallies, but he would be in New York in early May and in early June. He promised to get in touch with us afterward.

That was the end of the conversation.

21.IV.48. G R O M Y K O

REFERENCE: No. 519/ref. number No. 7345/ from 14.04.48: com. Molotov provided ["SPRAVKA"] instructions for conversation with Wallace.

No. 513/ ref. number No. 7279/ from 13.04.48: com. Molotov transmitted a list of issues to be discussed with Wallace before and after the US elections.

17 copies typed Apr. 21, 21:20 [9:20 p.m.] issued [by] Penkin

[Stalin drew a line from "or by him, Wallace," at the top of the page, to the bottom of the page, where he wrote:]

It is better [that it] be done by Wallace, with Stalin stating his sympathy.

REFERENCES

Archival Material

The American Presidency Project, University of California Santa Barbara, Santa Barbara, California.

Amherst Center for Russian Culture [ACRC], Amherst, Massachusetts.
    Roerich Collection

The Archive of the Nicholas Roerich Museum (NRM), New York.
    Roerich Collection

Archives Nationales, Paris, France.
    Private Archives of M. Georges Bidault

Arkhiv museiia Rerikha, filial Rossiiskogo gosudarstvennogo museia Vostoka (The Archive of the Roerich Museum, an Affiliate of the Russian State Museum of the Orient), Moscow, Russia.

Arkhiv Prezidenta Rossiiskoi Federatsii (The Archive of the President of the Russian Federation) [AP RF], Moscow, Russia.

Arkhiv vneshnei politiki Rossiiskoi Federatsii (The Archive of the Foreign Policy of the Russian Federation) [AVP RF], Moscow, Russia.

Columbia Center for Oral History [CCOH], Columbia University, New York, New York.
    Reminiscences of Henry Agard Wallace, 1951–1953
    Reminiscences of Paul H. Appleby

FBI Records: The Vault [FBI FOIA], Federal Bureau of Investigations, Winchester, Virginia.
    Henry A. Wallace
    Rosenberg File

Franklin D. Roosevelt Presidential Library and Museum [FDRL], Hyde Park, New York.
    Diaries of Henry Morgenthau Jr.
    Map Room Papers
    Henry A. Wallace Papers
    John Toland Papers
    President's Secretary's Files
    Samuel I. Rosenman Papers

George Washington University, Washington, DC.
    Eleanor Roosevelt Papers

Gosudarstvennyi arkhiv Khabarovskogo kraiia (The State Archive of the Khabarovsk Region) [GAHK], Khabarovsk, Russia.

Gosudarstvennyi arkhiv Rossiiskoi Federatsii (The State Archive of the Russian Federation) [GARF], Moscow, Russia.

Harry S. Truman Library and Museum, Independence, Missouri.
    Clark M. Clifford Papers
    George M. Elsey Papers
    Harry S. Truman Papers
    Oral History Interviews

White House Central Files: Official File [WHCF: OF]
White House Central Files: Confidential File
Hoover Institute Library and Archives, Stanford University, Stanford, California.
Allen Weinstein Papers
Diaries of General Joseph W. Stilwell, 1900–1946
Houghton Library, Harvard University, Cambridge, Massachusetts.
Robert E. Sherwood Papers
Library of Congress, Washington, DC.
Alexander Vassiliev Papers
Miller Center, University of Virginia, Charlottesville, Virginia.
National Archives and Records Administration [NARA], College Park, Maryland.
Record Group 46
Record Group 56
Record Group 59
Record Group 77
Record Group 226
Record Group 260
National Museum of History, Taipei, Taiwan.
National Security Administration [NSA], Fort Meade, Maryland
Declassified Documents
Penn State University Libraries, Philadelphia, Pennsylvania
Health and Retirement Funds Record, 1940–1993.
Rossiiskii gosudarstvennyi arkhiv economiki (The Russian State Archive of the Economy)
[RGAE], Moscow, Russia.
Rossiiskii gosudarstvennyi arkhiv sotsialno-politicheskoi istorii (The Russian State
Archive of Social and Political History) [RGASPI], Moscow, Russia.
Rossiiskii gosudarstvennyi musei Vostoka (The Russian State Museum of Orient) Moscow,
Russia.
Memorial'nyi kabinet N.K. Rerikha (Roerich Memorial Room)
Rutgers University Special Collections [RUSC], New Brunswick, New Jersey.
Frances R. Grant Papers [FGP]
Smithsonian Libraries and Archives, New York, New York.
Tsentralnyi arkhiv Sluzhby vneshnei razvedki RF (The Central Archive of the Foreign
Intelligence Service of RF) [SVR RF], Moscow, Russia.
University of California, Davis Library, Davis, California
Knowles A. Ryerson Papers
University of Iowa, Iowa City, Iowa.
Henry A. Wallace Collection
Henry A. Wallace Papers
Wilson Center Digital Archive, Washington, DC.

Published Primary Sources and Databases

Atomnyi proekt SSSR: dokumenty i materialy: [v 3 t.] / Pod obshch. red. Ryabev, L.D.—
1998–2009. T. 1. 1938–1945: v 2 ch. Chast' 1. Moskva: Nauka, Fizmatlit, 1998; Chast' 2.
Moskva: Izdatel'stvo MFTI, 2002; T.II. Atomnaia bomba. 1945–1954. Kniga 1. Sarov:
RFYaTs-VNIIEF, 1999. (*The Atomic Project of the USSR, Documents and Materials*, 3
volumes. Under the general editorship of L.D. Ryabev. Vol. 1. 1938–1945, in 2 parts:

Part 1, Moscow: Nauka, Fizmatlit, 1998; Part 2, Moscow: MFTI Publishers, 2002; Vol. 2, The Atomic Bomb, 1945–1954, Book 1, Sarov: RFYaTs-VNIIEF, 1999.

Blum, John Morton. *From the Morgenthau Diaries: Years of War, 1941–1945*. Boston: Houghton Mifflin, 1967.

———(ed.). *The Price of Vision: The Diary of Henry A. Wallace*. Boston: Houghton Mifflin, 1973.

Bureau of Agricultural Economics. "The Wheat Situation." United States Department of Agriculture. Washington, DC: November 1941. https://downloads.usda.library.cornell .edu/usda-esmis/files/cz30ps64c/1z40kw273/ bc386m938/WHS-11-14-1941.pdf.

Downey, Fredrick J. (ed.). *Selected Papers of Will Clayton*. Baltimore: Johns Hopkins University Press, 1971.

Department of State Bulletin, 1939–1989. Washington, DC: U.S. Government Printing Office.

Drury, Allen. *A Senate Journal, 1943–1945*. New York: McGraw-Hill, 1963.

Federal Bureau of Investigation. "Philip Faymonville." http://www.personal.psu.edu /dmc166/Philip%20Faymonville.pdf.

Forrestal, James, with Walter Millis (ed.). *The Forrestal Diaries*. New York: Viking, 1951.

Fosdick, Z.G. *Moi uchitelya. Vstrechi s Rerikhami. Po stranitsam dnevnika 1922–1934*. Moskva: Sfera, 2002. (Fosdick, Sina. *My Teachers. The Meetings with the Roerichs. Diary Leaves, 1922–1934*. Moscow: Sphere, 2002.)

Gallup, George H. (ed.). *The Gallup Poll: Public Opinion, 1935–1971, Vol. I: 1935–1948*. New York: Random House, 1972.

Geselbracht, Raymond H. (ed.). *The Memoirs of Harry S. Truman: A Reader's Edition*. Columbia, Missouri: University of Missouri Press, 2019.

Gillin, Donald G., and Ramon H. Myers (eds.). *Last Chance in Manchuria: The Diary of Chang Kia-ngau*. Stanford, CA: Hoover Institution Press, 1989.

GULAG (Glavnoe upravlenie lagerei). 1918–1960. Dokyumenty / Sost. Kokurin, A.I., Petrov, N.V. Moskva: MFD, 2000. (*GULAG [The Main Directorate of the Camps], 1918–1960*. Documents / Compiled by A.I. Kokurin and N.V. Petrov. Moscow: MFD, 2000.)

House Committee on Appropriations. *Department of Commerce Appropriation Bill for 1947: Hearings Before the Subcommittee of the Committee on Appropriations*. 79th Congress, 2nd Session. Washington, DC: U.S. Government Printing Office, 1946.

House Committee on Foreign Affairs. *The Strategy and Tactics of World Communism: Report [of] Subcommittee No. 5, National and International Movements*. Washington, DC: U.S. Government Printing Office, 1948.

House Committee on Un-American Activities. *Hearings Regarding Communist Espionage in the United States Government*. 80th Congress, 2nd Session. Washington, DC: U.S. Government Printing Office, 1948.

House Committee on Un-American Activities. *Hearings Regarding Shipment of Atomic Material to the Soviet Union During World War II*. 81st Congress, 1st and 2nd Sessions. Washington, DC: U.S. Government Printing Office, 1950.

House Committee on Un-American Activities. *Hearings Regarding Communist Methods of Infiltration (Entertainment—Part 1)*. 83rd Congress, 2nd Session. Washington, DC: U.S. Government Printing Office, 1954.

House Committee on Un-American Activities. *Proceedings Against Mrs. Louise Berman— Report No. 2906*. 81st Congress, 2nd Session. Washington, DC: U.S. Government Printing Office, 1950.

House Committee on Ways and Means. *1945 Extension of Reciprocal Trade Agreements*

Act, Hearings Before the Committee on Ways and Means. 79th Congress, 1st Session. Washington, DC: U.S. Government Printing Office, 1945.

Huston, John W. *American Airpower Comes of Age: General Henry H. "Hap" Arnold's World War II Diaries, Vol. I.* Honolulu: University Press of the Pacific, 1998 [2004].

The Iowa Board of Immigration. "Iowa: The Home for Immigrants, Being a Treatise on the Resources of Iowa and Giving Useful Information with Regard to the State, for the Benefit of Immigrants and Others." Des Moines, IA: Mills & Company, 1870. In *Iowa: The Definitive Collection*, edited by Zachary Michael Jack. North Liberty, IA: Ice Cube Press, 2009.

"Istoriia Karlaga v arkhivnyh dokumentah." 29 oktiabria 2013. Ofis General'nogo prokurora Respubliki Kazakhstan. ("The History of Karlag in archival documents." October 29, 2013. Prosecutor General's Office of the Republic of Kazakhstan.) https://web.archive.org/web/20190816030956/http://pravstat.prokuror.gov.kz/rus/sub/news/istoriya-karlaga-v-arhivnyh-dokumentah.

Joint Committee on Atomic Energy. *Soviet Atomic Espionage.* 82nd Congress, 1st Session. Washington, DC: U.S. Government Printing Office, April 1951.

Qin, Xiaoyi (ed.) *The First Edition of Important Historical Materials of the Republics of China: The Period of the Anti-Japanese War, Part Three, Wartime Diplomacy, Vol. I.* Taipei: Kuomintang Committee on Party History, 1980.

Rerikh, E.I. *Pis'ma. Tom I (1919–1933).* Moskva: Mezhdunarodnyi Tsentr Rerikhov, 2011 (Roerich, Helena. *Letters, Vol. I [1919–1933].* Moscow: The International Centre of the Roerichs (IRC), 2011.)

———. *Dnevniki Ye.I. Rerikh.* Zhivaya Etika v Mire. (*Diaries of Helena Roerich.* Living Ethics in the World. (website). https://lebendige-ethik.net/index. php/ biblioteka/ dnevniki-e-i-rerikh.

Rerikh, N.K. *Urusvati.* Moskva: Mezhdunarodnyi Tsentr Rerikhov, 1993. (Roerich, Nicholas. *Urusvati.* Moscow: The International Centre of the Roerichs [IRC], 1993.)

———. *Listy dnevnika, Tom II (1936–1941).* Moskva: Mezhdunarodnyi Tsentr Rerikhov, 2002. (Roerich, Nicholas. *Diary Leaves, Vol. II (1936–1941).* Moscow: The International Centre of the Roerichs (IRC), 2002.)

———. *Dnevnik Manchzhurskoi ekspeditsii (1934–1935).* Moskva: Mezhdunarodnyi Tsentr Rerikhov, 2015. (Roerich, Nicholas. *The Diary of the Manchurian Expedition (1934–1935).* Moscow: The International Centre of the Roerichs [IRC], 2015.)

Rerikh, Yurii Nikolajevich. *Pis'ma. Tom I (1919–1935).* Moskva: Mezhdunarodnyi Tsentr Rerikhov, 2002. (Roerich, Yury Nikolayevich. *Letters. Vol. I (1919–1935).* Moscow: The International Centre of the Roerichs [IRC], 2002.)

Roerich v. Helvering, 115 F.2d 39 (D.C. Court of Appeals, 1940).

Roerich v. Horch, 279 N.Y. 668 (New York Court of Appeals, 1938).

Roosevelt, Eleanor. "Plain Talk About Wallace." *Courage in a Dangerous World: The Political Writing of Eleanor Roosevelt.* Edited by Allida M. Black. New York: Columbia University Press, 1999.

Senate Committee on Commerce. *Administration of Certain Lending Agencies of the Federal Government: Hearings Before the Committee on Commerce.* 79th Congress, 1st Session. Washington, DC: U.S. Government Printing Office, 1945.

Senate Committee on Finance. *1945 Extension of Reciprocal Trade Agreements Act: Hearings Before the Committee on Finance.* 79th Congress, 1st Session. Washington, DC: U.S. Government Printing Office, 1945.

Senate Committee on Foreign Relations. *North Atlantic Treaty: Hearings Before the Committee on Foreign Relations.* 81st Congress, 1st Session. Washington, DC: U.S. Government Printing Office, 1949.

Senate Committee on Interior and Insular Affairs. *Accessibility of Strategic and Critical Materials to the United States in Time of War and Our Expanding Economy.* 83rd Congress, 2nd Session, No. 1627. Washington, DC: U.S. Government Printing Office, 1955.

Senate Committee on Labor and Public Welfare. *Hearings, Reports and Prints of the Senate Committee on Labor and Public Welfare, Vols. 4–6.* Washington, DC: U.S. Government Printing Office, 1964.

Senate Special Committee on Atomic Energy. *Atomic Energy Act: Hearings Before the Special Committee on Atomic Energy.* 79th Congress, 2nd Session. Washington, DC: U.S. Government Printing Office, 1946.

Senate Subcommittee of the Committee on Military Affairs. *Hearings on Science Legislation.* 79th Congress, 1st Session. Washington, DC: U.S. Government Printing Office, 1945.

Senate Subcommittee to Investigate the Administration of the Internal Security Act and Other Internal Security Laws of the Committee on the Judiciary. *Institute of Pacific Relations: Hearings Before the Subcommittee to Investigate the Administration of the Internal Security Act and Other Internal Security Laws of the Committee on the Judiciary.* 82nd Congress, 1st Session. Washington, DC: U.S. Government Printing Office, 1951.

Senate Subcommittee to Investigate the Administration of the Internal Security Act and Other Internal Security Laws of the Committee on the Judiciary. *Institute of Pacific Relations: Hearings Before the Subcommittee to Investigate the Administration of the Internal Security Act and Other Internal Security Laws of the Committee on the Judiciary.* 83rd Congress, 1st Session. Washington, DC: U.S. Government Printing Office, 1953.

Sistema ispravitel'no-trudovyh lagerei v SSSR, 1923–1960: spravochnik. Obshchestvo "Memorial" - Gosudarstvennyi arkhiv Rossiiskoi Federatsii./ Sostavitel' Smirnov, M.B. Moskva: Zveniia, 1998. (*The System of Labor Camps in the USSR, 1923–1960: A Data Book.* "Memorial" Society - The State Archive of the Russian Federation. / Compiled by M.B. Smirnov. Moscow: Zvenya, 1998.)

Smith, Jean Edward (ed.). *The Papers of General Lucius D. Clay: Germany 1945–1949, Vol. 2.* Bloomington: Indiana University Press, 1974.

Sovetskii faktor v Vostochnoi Evrope 1944–1953. Tom 1 1944–1948: Dokumenty / Otv. red. Volokitina, T.V. Moskva: ROSSPEN, 1999. (*The Soviet Factor in Eastern Europe, 1944–1953,* 2 volumes. Vol. I, 1944–1948. Editor in chief, Volokitina, T.V. Moscow: ROSSPEN, 1999.)

Sovetsko-amerikanskie otnosheniia. Gody nepriznanija 1918–1926: Dokumenty / Pod red. Sevostianova G.N. i Hezlema, Dzh. Mezhdunarodnyi fond "Demokratiia" [MFD], Guverovskii in-t voiny, revolutsii i mira, Stenfordskii un-t. Moskva: MFD, 2002 (*Soviet-American Relations: Years of Non-Recognition 1918–1926: Documents* / Ed. by Sevostyanov, G.N. and Jonathan Haslam. International Foundation "Democracy," Hoover Institution of War, Revolution and Peace, Stanford University. Moscow: MFD, 2002.)

Sovetsko-amerikanskie otnosheniia 1939–1945: Dokumenty / Pod obshchei redaktsijei Yakovleva A.N. Mezhdunarodnyi fond "Demokratiia," Moskva. Moskva: "Materik," 2004. (*Soviet-American Relations 1939–1945: Documents* / Under the general editorship of Yakovlev, A.N. International Foundation "Democracy." Moscow: "Materik," 2004.)

Sovetsko-amerikanskie otnosheniia 1945–1948: Dokumenty / Pod obshchei redaktsijei Yakovleva A.N. Mezhdunarodnyi fond "Demokratiia." Moskva: "Materik," 2004. (*Soviet-American Relations 1945–1948: Documents* / Academic editor Sevostianov, G.N. International Foundation "Democracy." Moscow: "Materik," 2004.)

Sovetsko-izrail'skie otnosheniia: Sbornik dokumentov. Tom I: 1941–1953, Kniga 1: 1941–mai 1949 / Ministerstvo inostrannykh del Rossiiskoi Federatsii; Ministerstvo inostrannykh del Gosudarstva Israil'. Moskva: Mezhdunarodnye otnosheniia, 2000. (*Documents on Israeli-Soviet Relations 1941–1953 [DISR], Part I: 1941–May 1949.* Edited by the Russian Academy of Sciences; The Cummings Center for Russian Studies; The Foreign Ministry of the Russian Federation; The Israel Foreign Ministry; The Oriental Institute, The Russian Federation; and the University of Tel Aviv, Israel. London: Frank Cass, 2000.)

Stalin, Joseph. *Stalin's Correspondence with Roosevelt and Truman: 1941–1945.* New York: Capricorn, 1965.

Stilwell, Joseph W. *The Stilwell Papers.* Edited by Theodore H. White. New York: Sloane Associates, 1948.

Truman, Harry S. *Public Papers of the Presidents of the United States: Harry S. Truman.* Vols. 1, 2, and 4. Washington, DC: U.S. Government Printing Office, 1961–1964.

United States Department of Agriculture, Agriculture Marketing Service. "Farm Population: Annual Estimates by States, Major Geographic Divisions, and Regions, 1910–50." Washington, DC, 1953.

United States Department of Commerce, Bureau of the Census. "Unemployed Persons, by Duration of Unemployment: 1946–1954." *Statistical Abstract of the United States.* Washington, DC, 1955.

United States Department of State. *The China White Paper.* Washington, DC: U.S. Government Printing Office, 1949.

United States v. Butler. 297 U.S. 1 (1936).

USA FACTS. *Federal Farm Subsidies: What the Data Says.* Published on June 4, 2019 [republished September 29, 2020].

U.S. Department of State Archive. *The Tehran Conference, 1943.* Last updated January 20, 2009.

The World Almanac and Book of Facts for 1935. New York: New York World Telegram, 1934.

Ye, Huifen (ed.). *Diaries of President Chiang Kai-Shek: Book 57.* Taipei: Academia Historica, 2011.

Books, Selections in Books, and Theses

Abt, John J., with Michael Myerson. *Advocate and Activist.* Urbana: University of Illinois Press, 1993.

Acheson, Dean. *Present at the Creation: My Years in the State Department.* New York: W. W. Norton, 1969.

Allen, George E. *Presidents Who Have Known Me.* New York: Simon & Schuster, 1960.

Andrew, Christopher, and Vasily Mitrokhin. *The Sword and the Shield: The Mitrokhin Archive and the Secret History of the KGB.* New York: Basic Books, 1999.

Andreyev, Alexander. *The Myth of the Great Master Revived: The Occult Lives of Nikolai and Elena Roerich.* Eurasia Studies Library, Vol. 4. Leiden and Boston: Brill, 2014.

Arnold, Thurman W. *The Folklore of Capitalism.* New Haven: Yale University Press, 1937.

Bailey, Stephen Kemp. *Congress Makes a Law: The Story Behind the Employment Act of 1946.* New York: Columbia University Press, 1950.

Baime, A.J. *The Accidental President: Harry S. Truman and the Four Months That Changed the World.* Boston: Houghton Mifflin Harcourt, 2017.

———. *Dewey Defeats Truman: The 1948 Election and the Battle for America's Soul.* Boston: Houghton Mifflin Harcourt, 2020.

Barkley, Alben W. *That Reminds Me.* Garden City, NY: Doubleday, 1954.

Barnet, Richard. *The Alliance: America-Europe-Japan, Makers of the Postwar World.* New York: Simon & Schuster, 1983.

Batiuk, V.I. "Plan Barukha i SSSR"—*Kholodnaia Voina. Novye podkhody. Novye dokumenty.* Moskva: Institut Vseobshchei istorii RAN, 1995. (Batiuk, V.I. "The Baruch Plan and the USSR," in *The Cold War. New Approaches. New Documents.* Moscow: The Institute of General History, Russian Academy of Sciences, 1995.)

Behrman, Greg. *The Most Noble Adventure.* New York: Free Press, 2007.

Beisner, Robert L. *Dean Acheson: A Life in Cold War.* New York: Oxford University Press, 2006.

Bentley, Elizabeth. *Out of Bondage: The Story of Elizabeth Bentley.* New York: Devin-Adair, 1951.

Berezhkov, V. M. *Kak ya stal perevodchikom Stalina.* Moskva: DEM, 1993. (Berezhkov, Valentin. *How I Became Stalin's Translator.* Moscow: DEM, 1993.)

Beschloss, Michael R. *The Conquerors: Roosevelt, Truman and the Destruction of Hitler's Germany.* New York: Simon & Schuster, 2002.

Bien, George Z. *Lost Years: A Hungarian Student's Ten Years in the Siberian Gulag in Kolyma, Eastern Siberia, 1945–1955.* Self-published, 2003.

Biles, Roger. "Edward J. Kelly: New Deal Machine Builder." In *The Mayors: The Chicago Political Tradition,* edited by Paul M. Green and Melvin G. Holli. Carbondale: Southern Illinois University Press, 1987.

Bliven, Bruce. *Five Million Words Later: An Autobiography.* New York: John Day, 1970.

Bohlen, Charles E. *Witness to History, 1929–1969.* New York: W. W. Norton, 1973.

Boia, Lucian. *Romania: Borderland of Europe.* Translated by James Christian Brown. London: Reaktion Books, 2001.

Bradley, James. *The China Mirage: The Hidden History of American Disaster in Asia.* New York: Little, Brown, 2015.

Brinley, John Ervin. "Government and Labor: The Coal Industry, 1946–1947." Master's thesis, University of Utah, August 1967.

Brinton, Christian. *The Nicholas Roerich Exhibition, With Introduction and Catalogue of the Paintings.* New York: Redfield-Kendrick-Odell Company, 1920.

Brown, Walter J. *James F. Byrnes of South Carolina: A Remembrance.* Macon, GA: Mercer University Press, 1992.

Buchheim, Christoph. "The Establishment of the Bank Deutscher Länder and the West German Currency Reform." In *Fifty Years of the Deutsche Mark,* edited by Deutsche Bundesbank. Oxford: Oxford University Press, 1999.

Buck, Pearl S. *China as I See It.* New York: John Day, 1970.

Buxton, D.F. *The Challenge of Bolshevism: A New Social Ideal.* London and New York: George Allen & Unwin, 1928.

Byrnes, James F. *All in One Lifetime.* New York: Harper & Brothers, 1958.

———. *Speaking Frankly.* New York: Harper & Brothers, 1947.

Chase, Stuart. *A New Deal.* New York: Macmillan, 1932.

Chen, Chieh-ju, with Lloyd E. Eastman (ed.). *Chiang Kai-shek's Secret Past: The Memoir of His Second Wife.* Boulder: Westview Press, 1993.

Chuev, F. *Sto sorok besed s Molotovym: Iz dnevnika F. Chujeva.* Moskva: Terra, 1991 (Chuev, Felix. *One Hundred Forty Conversations with Molotov: From the Diary of F. Chuev.* Moscow: Terra, 1991.)

Clay, Lucius D. *Decision in Germany.* Garden City, NY: Doubleday, 1950.

Collins, Perry M. *A Voyage Down the Amoor.* New York: D. Appleton & Co., 1860.

Conant, Jennet. *The Irregulars: Roald Dahl and the British Spy Ring in Wartime Washington.* New York: Simon & Schuster, 2008.

Cooke, Alistair. *Six Men*. New York: Alfred A. Knopf, 1977.

Crowder, Richard. *Aftermath: The Makers of the Postwar World*. London: I. B. Tauris, 2015.

Culver, John C., and John Hyde. *American Dreamer: The Life and Times of Henry A. Wallace*. New York: W. W. Norton, 2000.

Dallek, Robert. *Franklin D. Roosevelt: A Political Life*. New York: Viking, 2017.

Daniels, Jonathan. *White House Witness, 1942–1945*. Garden City, NY: Doubleday, 1975.

Davies, John Paton, Jr. *China Hand, An Autobiography*. Philadelphia: University of Pennsylvania Press, 2012.

———. *Dragon by the Tail: American, British, Japanese, and Russian Encounters with China and One Another*. New York: W. W. Norton, 1972.

Davis, Joseph S. *Wheat and the AAA*. Washington, DC: The Brookings Institution, 1935.

Davis, Kenneth S. *FDR: Into the Storm, 1937–1940*. New York: Random House, 1993.

Degtyarev, Klim, and Kolpakidi, Alexandr. *Vneshniaia razvedka SSSR. INO-PGU-SVR*. Moskva: Yauza, Eksmo, 2009. (Degtyarev, Klim, and Alexander Kolpakidi. *The Foreign Intelligence of the USSR. INO-PGU-SVR*. Moscow: Yauza, Eksmo, 2009.)

Devine, Thomas W. *Henry Wallace's 1948 Presidential Campaign and the Future of Postwar Liberalism*. Chapel Hill: University of North Carolina Press, 2013.

Donovan, Robert J. *Conflict and Crisis: The Presidency of Harry S. Truman, 1945–1948*. New York: W. W. Norton, 1977.

Dorn, Frank. *Walkout with Stilwell in Burma*. New York: Thomas Y. Crowell, 1971.

Drayer, Ruth A. *Nicholas & Helena Roerich: The Spiritual Journey of Two Great Artists and Peacemakers*. Wheaton, IL: Quest Books, 2005.

Duranty, Walter. *USSR: The Story of Soviet Russia*. London: Hamish Hamilton, 1944.

Elleman, Bruce A. "Soviet Sea Denial and the KMT-CCP Civil War in Manchuria, 1945–1949." In *Naval Coalition Warfare: From the Napoleonic War to Operation Iraqi Freedom*, edited by Bruce A. Elleman and S.C.M. Paine. London: Routledge, 2008.

Engerman, David C. *Modernization from the Other Shore: American Intellectuals and the Romance of Russian Development*. Cambridge: Harvard University Press, 2003.

Farley, Jim. *Jim Farley's Story: The Roosevelt Years*. New York: Whittlesey, 1948.

Feierabend, Ladislav Karel. *Politické Vzpomínky III. (Political Memories III.)* Brno, Czech Republic: Atlantis, 1996.

Feigel, Lara. *The Bitter Taste of Victory: Life, Love, and Art in the Ruins of the Reich*. New York: Bloomsbury, 2016.

Feis, Herbert. *The China Tangle*. Princeton: Princeton University Press, 1953.

Fenberg, Steven. *Unprecedented Power: Jesse Jones, Capitalism, and the Common Good*. College Station: Texas A&M University Press, 2011.

Fenby, Jonathan. *Chiang Kai Shek: China's Generalissimo and the Nation He Lost*. New York: Carroll & Graf, 2004.

Ferrell, Robert H. *Choosing Truman: The Democratic Convention of 1944*. Columbia: University of Missouri Press, 1994.

———. *Ill Advised: Presidential Trust and Public Trust*. Columbia: University of Missouri Press, 1992.

Fielding, Raymond. *The March of Time, 1935–1951*. New York: Oxford University Press, 1978.

Flynn, Edward J. *You're the Boss*. New York: Viking, 1947.

Foo, Yee-Wah. *Chiang Kaishek's Last Ambassador to Moscow: The Wartime Diaries of Fu Bingchang*. New York: Palgrave Macmillan, 2010.

Fossedal, Gregory A. *Our Finest Hour: Will Clayton, the Marshall Plan, and the Triumph of Democracy*. Stanford, CA: Hoover Press, 1993.

Foster, John Bellamy. "Harry Magdoff." In *A Biographical Dictionary of Dissenting Economists*, edited by Philip Aretis and Malcolm C. Sawyer. Cheltenham, UK: Edward Elgar, 2000.

Fox, John Francis, Jr. "'In Passion and in Hope:' The Pilgrimage of an American Radical, Martha Dodd Stern and Family, 1933–1990." PhD thesis, Durham: University of New Hampshire, 2001.

Frank, Waldo. *Dawn in Russia: The Record of a Journey*. New York: Charles Scribner's Sons, 1932.

Fraser, Steven. *Labor Will Rule: Sidney Hillman and the Rise of American Labor*. New York: Free Press, 1991.

Fraser, T.G. "Roosevelt and the Making of America's East Asian Policy, 1941–45." In *Conflict and Amity in East Asia: Essays in Honour of Ian Nish*, edited by T.G. Fraser and P. Lowe. London: Palgrave Macmillan, 1992.

Freeman, Joshua B. *Working-Class New York: Life and Labor Since World War II*. New York: New Press, 2000.

Friedman, Milton, and Anna J. Schwartz. *A Monetary History of the United States, 1867–1960*. Princeton: Princeton University Press, 1963.

Gaddis, John Lewis. *The United States and the Origins of the Cold War, 1941–1947*. New York: Columbia University Press, 1972.

Garthoff, Raymond L. "The Soviet Intervention in Manchuria, 1945–46." In *Sino-Soviet Military Relations*, edited by Raymond L. Garthoff. New York: Praeger, 1966.

Garver, John. *Chinese Soviet Relations*. Oxford: Oxford University Press, 1988.

Gilbert, Jess. *Planning Democracy: Agrarian Intellectuals and the Intended New Deal*. New Haven: Yale University Press, 2015.

Goodwin, Doris Kearns. *No Ordinary Time, Franklin & Eleanor Roosevelt: The Home Front in World War II*. New York: Simon & Schuster, 1994.

Gormly, James L. *From Potsdam to the Cold War: Big Three Diplomacy, 1945–1947*. Wilmington: SR Books, 1990.

Grammatchikov, N.V. *Derzhava Rerikha*. Chicago: Rassvet, 1935 [1994]. (Grammatchikov, N.V. *The State of Roerich*. Chicago: Rassvet [Dawn], 1935 [1994].)

Green, Michael. *By More Than Providence: Grand Strategy and American Power in the Asia Pacific Since 1783*. New York: Columbia University Press, 2017.

Gromyko, A.A. *Pamyatnoe*. Kniga 1. Moskva: Politizdat, 1988. (Gromyko, Andrey Andreevich. *Memorable*. Book 1. Moscow: Politizdat, 1988.)

———. *Memoirs*. Foreword by Henry Kissinger. New York: Doubleday, 1989.

Guffey, Joseph F. *Seventy-five Years on the Red-Fire Wagon from Tilden to Truman Through New Freedom and the New Deal*. Privately published, 1952.

Halle, Louis J. *The Cold War as History*. New York: Harper & Row, 1967.

Halpern, Martin. *UAW Politics in the Cold War*. Albany: State University of New York Press, 1988.

Hamby, Alonzo. *Man of the People: A Life of Harry S. Truman*. New York: Oxford University Press, 1995.

Harmsen, Peter. *Shanghai 1937: Stalingrad on the Yangtze*. Havertown, PA: Casemate, 2013.

Harriman, W. Averell, and Elie Abel. *Special Envoy to Churchill and Stalin, 1941–1946*. New York: Random House: 1975.

Haslam, Jonathan. *Russia's Cold War: From the October Revolution to the Fall of the Wall*. New Haven: Yale University Press, 2011.

Hastings, Max. *Retribution: The Battle for Japan, 1944–45*. New York: Alfred A. Knopf, 2007.

Haynes, John Earl, and Harvey Klehr. *Venona: Decoding Soviet Espionage in America*. New Haven: Yale University Press, 1999.

Haynes, John Earl, Harvey Klehr, and Alexander Vassiliev. *Spies: The Rise and Fall of the KGB in America*. New Haven: Yale University Press, 2009.

Hazard, John N. *Recollections of a Pioneering Sovietologist*. New York: Oceana Publications, 1984.

Heimann, Mary. *Czechoslovakia: The State That Failed*. New Haven: Yale University Press, 2009.

Heinemann-Grueder, A. "Sovetskii atomnyi proekt i nehvatka urana. Dobycha urana v Vostochnoi Germanii i v Chekhoslovakii posle 1945 g." – Mezhdunarodnyi symposium: *Nauka i obshchestvo: istoriia sovetskogo atomnogo proekta (40-e – 50-e gody)*, Trudy. Tom 2. Moskva: IZDAT, 1999. (Heinemann-Grueder, A. "The Soviet Atomic Project and the Shortage of Uranium: Uranium Mining in the GDR and Czechoslovakia After 1945." In *Science and Society: History of the Soviet Atomic Project [40's–50's]*: Proceedings of the International Symposium. Vol. 2. Moscow: IZDAT, 1999.)

Heins, Marjorie. *Priests of Our Democracy: The Supreme Court, Academic Freedom and the Anti-Communist Purge*. New York: New York University Press, 2013.

Hewlett, Richard G., and Oscar E. Anderson. *The New World, 1939–1946: A History of the United States Atomic Energy Commission*. University Park: Pennsylvania State University Press, 1962.

Higgs, Robert. *Depression, War, and Cold War*. Oakland: The Independent Institute, 2006.

Hollander, Paul. *Political Pilgrims: Western Intellectuals in Search of the Good Society*. New Brunswick: Transaction Publishers, 1997.

Holloway, David. *Stalin and the Bomb*. New Haven: Yale University Press, 1994.

Houghton, Vince. *The Nuclear Spies: America's Atomic Intelligence Operation Against Hitler and Stalin*. Ithaca, NY: Cornell University Press, 2019.

Hsü, Immanuel C.Y. *The Rise of Modern China*. New York: Oxford University Press, 1970.

Hurt, R. Douglas. *Problems of Plenty: The American Farmer in the Twentieth Century*. Chicago: Ivan R. Dee, 2002.

Irwin, Douglas A., "From Smoot-Hawley to Reciprocal Trade Agreements: Changing the Course of U.S. Trade Policy in the 1930s." In *The Defining Moment: The Great Depression and the American Economy in the Twentieth Century*, edited by Michael D. Bordo, Claudia Goldin, and Eugene N. White. Chicago: University of Chicago Press, 1998.

———. *Clashing over Commerce: A History of U.S. Trade Policy*. Chicago: University of Chicago Press, 2017.

Irwin, Douglas A, Petros C. Mavroidis, and Alan O. Sykes. *The Genesis of the GATT*. Cambridge: Cambridge University Press, 2008.

Isaacson, Walter, and Evan Thomas. *The Wise Men: Six Friends and the World They Make*. New York: Simon & Schuster, 1986 [2012].

Isaev, V.I. *Kommuna ili kommunalka? Izmenenie byta rabochikh Sibiri v gody industrializatsii*. Novosibirsk: Nauka, 1996. (Isaev, V.I. *Commune or a Shared Apartment? The Changes of Everyday Life of Siberian Workers in the Years of Industrialization*. Novosibirsk: Nauka, 1996.)

Istoricheskaia hronika Magadanskoi oblasti: sobytiia i fakty: 1917–1972. Sostavitel' Bogdanov, A.D. Magadan: Magadanskoye knizhnoye izd-vo, 1975. (*Historical Chronicle of the Magadan Region: Events and Facts, 1917–1972*. Compiled by A.D. Bogdanov. Magadan: Magadan Book Publishing House, 1975.)

Jaffe, Philp J. *The Rise and Fall of American Communism*. New York: Horizon Press, 1975.

James, Harold. *Europe Reborn: A History, 1914–2000*. New York: Routledge, 2003 [2014].

James, William. *The Varieties of Religious Experience: A Study in Human Nature*. New York, London, and Bombay: Longmans, Green, 1902.

———. *The Will to Believe*. New York, London, and Bombay: Longmans, Green, 1896 [1912].

Jones, Jesse. *Fifty Billion Dollars: My Thirteen Years with the RFC*. New York: Macmillan, 1951.

Josephson, Matthew. *Sidney Hill: Statesman of American Labor*. Garden City, NY: Doubleday, 1952.

Kaplan, Karel. *The Short March: The Communist Takeover in Czechoslovakia, 1945–1948*. London: C. Hurst, 1987.

Kennan, George F. *Memoirs, Vol. I: 1925–1950*. Boston: Little, Brown, 1967.

Kotkin, Stephen. *Stalin: Paradoxes of Power, 1878–1928*. New York: Penguin, 2014.

Kotljarchuk, Andrej, and Olle Sundström (eds.). *Ethnic and Religious Minorities in Stalin's Soviet Union: New Dimensions of Research*. Huddinge, Sweden: Södertörn University, 2017. http://umu.diva-portal.org/smash/get/diva2:1166475/FULLTEXT02.pdf.

Kravchenko, Victor. *I Chose Freedom*. Garden City, NY: Garden City Publishing Company, 1946.

Krock, Arthur. *Memoirs: Sixty Years on the Firing Line*. New York: Funk & Wagnalls, 1968.

Kunetka, James. *The General and Genius*. Washington, DC: Regnery History, 2015.

Laufer, Jochen P. "From Dismantling to Currency Reform: External Origins of the Dictatorship, 1944–1948." In *Dictatorship as Experience: Towards a Socio-Cultural History of the GDR*, edited by Konrad H. Jarausch. Translated by Eve Duffy. New York: Berghahn, 1999.

Lazell, Frederick John. "Some Autumn Days in Iowa." Cedar Rapids, IA: The Torch Press, 1906. In *Iowa: The Definitive Collection*, edited by Zachary Michael Jack. North Liberty, IA: Ice Cube Press, 2009.

Lea, Albert M. "Notes on the Wisconsin Territory Particularly with Reference to the Iowa District of Black Hawk Purchase." Philadelphia: H.S. Tanner, 1836. In *Iowa: The Definitive Collection*, edited by Zachary Michael Jack. North Liberty, IA: Ice Cube Press, 2009.

Leahy, William D. *I Was There: The Personal Story of the Chief of Staff to Presidents Roosevelt and Truman Based on His Notes and Diaries Made at the Time*. New York: Whittlesey House, 1950.

Lelyveld, Joseph. *His Final Battle: The Last Months of Franklin Roosevelt*. New York: Vintage, 2016.

Leuchtenberg, William. *Franklin D. Roosevelt and the New Deal: 1932–1940*. New York: Harper & Row, 1963.

Levine, Steven I. *Anvil of Victory: The Communist Revolution in Manchuria*. New York: Columbia University Press, 1987.

Liang, Chin-tung. *General Stilwell in China, 1942–1944: The Full Story*. New York: St. John's University Press, 1972.

Lilienthal, David Eli. *The Journal of David Eli Lilienthal: The Atomic Energy Years, 1945–1950*. New York: Harper & Row, 1964.

Lipper, Elinor. *Eleven Years in Soviet Prison Camps*. Chicago: Regnery, 1951.

Littell, Norman M. *My Roosevelt Years*. Seattle: University of Washington Press, 1987.

Lord, Russell. *The Wallaces of Iowa*. Boston: Houghton Mifflin, 1947.

Lukes, Igor. *On the Edge of the Cold War: American Diplomats and Spies in Postwar Prague*. New York: Oxford University Press, 2012.

Lyon, Leverett S., Paul T. Homan, Lewis L. Lorwin, George Tebororgh, Charles L. Dearing, and Leon C. Marshall. *The National Recovery Administration: An Analysis and Appraisal*. Washington, DC: The Brookings Institution, 1935.

Macdonald, Dwight. *Henry Wallace: The Man and the Myth*. New York: Vanguard Press, 1947.

MacDougall, Curtis D. *Gideon's Army*. Three Volumes. New York: Marzani & Munsell, 1965.

Mal'kov, V.L. "Igra bez myacha: sotsial'no-politicheskii kontekst sovetskoi 'atomnoi diplomatii' (1945–1949)." *Holodnaia voina 1945–1963. Istoricheskaia retrospektiva: Sbornik statei* pod red. Jegorova, N.I., Chibarian, A.O. Moskva: OLMA-Press, 2003. (Malkov, V.L. "Off the Ball Game: Social-Psychological Context of the Soviet 'Atomic Diplomacy' (1945–1949)." In *The Cold War 1945–1963. Historic Retrospective*, edited by N.I. Jegorova and A.O. Chubaryan. Moscow: OLMA-Press, 2003.)

Markowitz, Norman D. *The Rise and Fall of the People's Century: Henry A. Wallace and American Liberalism, 1941–1948*. New York: Free Press, 1973.

Martin, George Whitney. *Madam Secretary: Frances Perkins*. Boston: Houghton Mifflin Harcourt, 1976.

Martin, Joe. *My First Fifty Years in Politics*. New York: McGraw-Hill, 1960.

Masters, Charles J. *Governor Henry Horner, Chicago Politics, and the Great Depression*. Carbondale: Southern Illinois University Press, 2007.

May, Gary. *China Scapegoat: The Diplomatic Ordeal of John Carter Vincent*. Washington, DC: New Republic Books, 1979.

———. "The China Service of John Carter Vincent, 1924–1953." PhD thesis, University of California, Los Angeles, 1974.

McCannon, John. *Nicholas Roerich: The Artist Who Would Be King*. Pittsburgh: University of Pittsburgh Press, 2022.

McCullough, David. *Truman*. New York: Simon & Schuster, 1992.

McLynn, Frank. *The Burma Campaign: Disaster into Triumph, 1942–45*. New Haven: Yale University Press, 2011.

Medvedev, Roi. *Blizhnii krug Stalina: soratniki vozhdia*. Moskva: EKSMO, 2005. (Medvedev, Roy. *Stalin's Close Circle: The Chief's Close Associates*. Moscow: EKSMO, 2005.)

Michael, Franz H., and George E. Taylor. *The Far East in the Modern World*. New York: Holt, Rinehart & Winston, 1956.

Minahan, James. *Encyclopedia of the Stateless Nations: Ethnic and National Groups Around the World*. Westport, CT: Greenwood Press, 2002.

Moley, Raymond. *After Seven Years*. New York and London: Harper & Brothers, 1939.

———. *27 Masters of Politics*. New York: Funk & Wagnalls, 1949.

Morgan, Ted. *FDR: A Biography*. New York: Simon & Schuster, 1985.

Morgenthau, Hans J. *Politics Among Nations: The Struggle for Power and Peace, Brief Edition*. Revised by Kenneth W. Thompson. New York: McGraw-Hill, 1948 [1993].

Narinsky, Mikhail M. "The Soviet Union and the Berlin Crisis, 1948–9." In *The Soviet Union and Europe in the Cold War, 1943–53*, edited by Francesca Gori and Silvio Pons. London: Palgrave Macmillan, 1996.

Neiberg, Michael. *Potsdam: The End of World War II and the Remaking of Europe*. New York: Basic Books, 2015.

Nicholas Roerich Museum (New York, N.Y.). *Proceedings at the Laying of the Cornerstone of the Roerich Museum, New York, March 24, 1929*. New York: Roerich Museum Press, 1929.

Ocherki istorii rossiiskoi vneshnei razvedki. V 6 t. T. 5. 1945-1965. Glavnyiv redaktor Lebedev, S.N. Moskva: Mezhdunarodnye otnosheniia, 2003. (*The Essays on the History of Russian Foreign Intelligence*, in 6 volumes. Vol. 5, 1945–1965. Lead editor S.N. Lebedev. Moscow: International Relations, 2003.)

Paarlberg, Donald. "Tarnished Gold: Fifty Years of New Deal Farm Programs." In *The New Deal and Its Legacy: Critique and Reappraisal*, edited by Robert Eden. Westport, CT: Greenwood Press, 1989.

Pakula, Hannah. *The Last Empress: Madame Chiang Kai-shek and the Birth of Modern China*. New York: Simon & Schuster, 2009.

Parker, Nathan Howe. "Iowa as It Is in 1855." Chicago: Keen and Lee, 1855. In *Iowa: The Definitive Collection*, edited by Zachary Michael Jack. North Liberty, IA: Ice Cube Press, 2009.

Pcchatnov, Vladimir O. "The Soviet Union and the World, 1944–1953." In *The Cambridge History of the Cold War, Vol. I: Origins*, edited by Melvyn P. Leffler and Odd Arne Westad. Cambridge: Cambridge University Press, 2010.

———. *Stalin, Ruzvel't, Trumen: SSSR i SShA v 1940-h gg.: dokumental'nye ocherki*. Moskva: TERRA-Knizhnyi Klub, 2006. (*Stalin, Roosevelt, Truman: The USSR and the USA in the 1940s: Documentary Essays*. Moscow: TERRA-Book Club, 2006.)

Pechatnov, Vladimir O., and C. Earl Edmondson. "The Russian Perspective." In *Debating the Origins of the Cold War: American and Russian Perspectives*, by Ralph B. Levering, Vladimir O. Pechatnov, Verena Botzenhart-Viehe, and C. Earl Edmondson. Lanham, MD: Rowman & Littlefield, 2001.

Pepper, Claude Denson, and Hays Gorey. *Pepper: Eyewitness to a Century*. San Diego: Harcourt Brace Jovanovich, 1987.

Perkins, Frances. *The Roosevelt I Knew*. New York: Viking, 1946.

Petrov, N.V., Skorkin, K.V. *Kto rukovodil NKVD 1934–1941*. Spravochnik. Moskva: Zvenia, 1999. (Petrov, N.V., and K.V. Skorkin. *Who Were the Leaders of the NKVD, 1934–1941: Reference Book*. Moskva: Zvenia, 1999.)

———. *Istoriia imperii "GULAG."* (*The History of the GULAG Empire*). Pseudology, accessed on April 28, 2023: https://www.pseudology.org/GULAG/.

Phillips, Cabell. *The Truman Presidency: The History of a Triumphant Succession*. New York: Macmillan, 1966.

Pogue, Forrest C. *George C. Marshall, Vol. IV: Statesman, 1945–1959*. New York: Viking, 1987.

Powell, John B. *My 25 Years in China*. New York: Macmillan, 1945.

Reinsch, J. Leonard. *Getting Elected: From Radio and Roosevelt to Television and Reagan*. New York: Hippocrene, 1988.

Repetto, Thomas A. *Shadows Over the White House: The Mafia and the Presidents*. New York: Enigma Books, 2015.

Rerikhi. Mify i fakty. Sbornik statei. Red. Andreyev, Alexandr, Savelli, Dany. Sankt-Peterburg: Nestor-Istorija, 2011. (*The Roerichs: The Myths and the Facts*. Edited by Alexander Andreyev and Dany Savelli. St. Petersburg: Nestor-History, 2011.)

Richards, Henry I. *Cotton Under the Agricultural Adjustment Act; Developments Up to 1934*. Washington, DC: The Brookings Institution, 1934.

Ripka, Hubert. *Czechoslovakia Enslaved. The Story of the Communist Coup d'état*. London: Victor Gollancz, 1950.

Robbins, Louise. *The Librarian Spies: Philip and Mary Jane Keeney and Cold War Espionage.* Westport, CT: Praeger Security International, 2009.

Roberts, Geoffrey. *Stalin's Wars: From World War to Cold War, 1939–1953.* New Haven: Yale University Press, 2006.

Robertson, David. *Sly and Able: A Political Biography of James F. Byrnes.* New York: W. W. Norton, 1994.

Roerich, George N. *Trails to Inmost Asia: Five Years of Exploration with the Roerich Central Asian Expedition.* New Haven: Yale University Press, 1931.

Romanus, Charles F., and Riley Sunderland. *Stilwell's Command Problems.* U.S. Government Printing Office, 1956.

Roosevelt, Eleanor. *This I Remember.* New York: Harper, 1949.

Roosevelt, Elliott, with a foreword by Eleanor Roosevelt. *As He Saw It.* New York: Duell, Sloan & Pearce, 1946.

Rose, Lisle A. *After Yalta: America and the Origin of the Cold War.* New York: Charles Scribner, 1973.

Rosenman, Samuel. *Working with Roosevelt.* New York: Harper & Brothers, 1952.

Rosov, V.A. *Nikolai Rerikh: Vestnik Zvenigoroda.* 2 toma. Moskva: Ariavarta-Press, 2002–2004. (Rosov, V.A. *Nicholas Roerich: the Herald of Zvenigorod.* 2 vols. Moscow: Ariavarta-Press, 2002–2004.)

Ross, Irwin. *The Loneliest Campaign: The Truman Victory of 1948.* New York: New American Library, 1968.

Schaller, Michael. "FDR and the 'China Question.'" In *FDR's World: War, Peace, and Legacies,* edited by David B. Woolner, Warren F. Kimball, and David Reynolds. New York: Palgrave Macmillan, 2008.

———. *The U.S. Crusade in China, 1938–1945.* New York: Columbia University Press, 1979.

Schapsmeier, Edward L., and Frederick H. Schapsmeier. *Henry A. Wallace of Iowa: The Agrarian Years, 1910–1940.* Ames: Iowa State University Press, 1968.

———. *Prophet in Politics: Henry A. Wallace and the War Years, 1940–1965.* Ames: Iowa State University Press, 1970.

Schlesinger, Arthur M. *The Coming of the New Deal.* Boston: Houghton Mifflin, 1958.

Schlesinger, Arthur M., Jr. *A Life in the 20th Century: Innocent Beginnings, 1917–1950.* Boston: Houghton Mifflin, 2000.

Schmidt, Karl M. *Henry A. Wallace: Quixotic Crusade 1948.* Syracuse: Syracuse University Press, 1960.

Scott, James C. *Seeing Like a State: How Certain Schemes to Improve the Human Condition Have Failed.* New Haven: Yale University Press, 1998.

Seagrave, Sterling. *The Soong Dynasty.* New York: Harper & Row, 1985.

Service, John S. *Lost Chance in China: The World War II Despatches of John S. Service.* New York: Random House, 1974.

Sevareid, Eric. *Not So Wild a Dream.* New York: Alfred A. Knopf, 1946 [1969].

Sgovio, Thomas. *Dear America! Why I Turned Against Communism.* Kenmore, New York: Partners Press, 1979.

Shannon, David A. *The Decline of American Communism.* New York: Harcourt, Brace, 1959.

Sherwood, Robert E. *Roosevelt and Hopkins: An Intimate History.* New York: Enigma Books, 1948 [2008].

Simonov, Konstantin. *Through The Eyes of a Man of My Generation.* Moscow: Kniga, 1989.

Sirevag, Torbjorn. *The Eclipse of the New Deal and the Fall of Vice-President Wallace, 1944.* New York: Garland, 1985.

Smith, Jean Edward. *Lucius D. Clay: An American Life*. New York: Henry Holt, 1990.

Spalding, Elizabeth. *The First Cold Warrior: Harry Truman, Containment, and the Remaking of Liberal Internationalism*. Lexington: University Press of Kentucky, 2006.

Steil, Benn. *The Battle of Bretton Woods: John Maynard Keynes, Harry Dexter White, and the Making of a New World Order*. Princeton: Princeton University Press, 2013.

———. *The Marshall Plan: Dawn of the Cold War*. New York: Simon & Schuster, 2018.

Stimson, Henry L., and McGeorge Bundy. *On Active Service in Peace and War*. New York: Harper, 1948.

Stone, I.F. *A Non-Conformist History of Our Times: The War Years, 1939–1945*. Boston: Little, Brown, 1988.

Stone, Oliver, and Peter Kuznick. *The Untold History of the United States*. New York: Gallery Books, 2012.

Straight, Michael. *After Long Silence*. New York: W. W. Norton, 1983.

Sutherland, Jonathan, and Diane Canwell. *The Berlin Airlift: The Salvation of a City*. Barnsley, South Yorkshire, UK: Pen & Sword Aviation, 2007.

Taylor, Jay. *The Generalissimo: Chiang Kai-Shek and the Struggle for Modern China*. Cambridge, MA: The Belknap Press, 2009.

Thomas, S. Bernard. *Season of High Adventure: Edgar Snow in China*. Berkeley: University of California Press, 1996.

Tihvinskii, S.L. *Put' Kitaiia k ob'edineniiu i nezavisimosti, 1898–1949: Po materialam biografii Chzhou En'laiia*. Moskva: Vostochnaia literature, RAN, 1996. (Tikhvinsky, S.L. *The Road of China Towards Unification and Independence, 1898–1949. A Case Study of the Biographical Materials of Zhou Enlai*. Moscow: Oriental Literature, RAN, 1996.)

Timmons, Bascom N. *Jesse Jones: The Man and the Statesman*. New York: Henry Holt, 1956.

Toll, Ian W. *Twilight of the Gods: War in the Western Pacific, 1944–1945*. New York: W. W. Norton, 2020.

Trine, Ralph Waldo. *In Tune with the Infinite*. Indianapolis: Bobbs-Merrill, 1897 [1908].

Truman, Harry S. *Memoirs by Harry S. Truman*. Two Volumes. New York: Doubleday, 1955–56.

———, with Robert H. Ferrell (ed.). *Off the Record: The Private Papers of Harry S. Truman*. Columbia: University of Missouri Press, 1980 [1997].

Tuchman, Barbara W. *Stilwell and the American Experience in China, 1911–45*. New York: Macmillan, 1970.

Tugwell, Rexford. *The Industrial Discipline and the Government Arts*. New York: Columbia University Press, 1933.

———. *Roosevelt's Revolution: The First Year, a Personal Perspective*. New York: Macmillan, 1977.

Tully, Grace. *F.D.R. My Boss*. New York: Charles Scribner's Sons, 1949.

Vaksberg, Arkadi. *Stalin's Prosecutor: The Life of Andrei Vyshinsky*. Translated by Jan Butler, foreword by Robert Conquest. New York: Grove Press, 1991.

van de Ven, Hans. *China at War: Triumph and Tragedy in the Emergence of the New China*. Cambridge: Harvard University Press, 2018.

van Minnen, Corenlis A., and John F. Sears (ed.). *FDR and His Contemporaries: The World of the Roosevelts*. London: Palgrave Macmillan, 1992.

Van Vechten, Carl. "In the Garret." New York: Alfred A. Knopf, 1920. In *Iowa: The Definitive Collection*, edited by Zachary Michael Jack. North Liberty, IA: Ice Cube Press, 2009.

Veblen, Thorstein. *The Engineers and the Price System*. New York: B. W. Huebsch, 1921 [2001].

Walker, Frank C., with Robert H. Ferrell (ed.). *FDR's Quiet Confidant: The Autobiography of Frank C. Walker.* Niwat: University Press of Colorado, 1997.

Walker, J. Samuel. *Henry A. Wallace and American Foreign Policy.* Westport, CT: Greenwood Press, 1976.

Wallace, Henry A. *Agricultural Prices.* Des Moines: Wallace Publishing Company, 1920.

———. *America Must Choose; The Advantages and Disadvantages of Nationalism, of World Trade, and of a Planned Middle Course.* New York: Foreign Policy Association, 1934.

———. *New Frontiers.* New York: Reynal & Hitchcock, 1934.

———. *Statesmanship and Religion.* New York: Round Table Press, 1934.

———. *Whose Constitution: An Inquiry into the General Welfare.* New York: Reynal & Hitchcock, 1936.

———. *The Price of Freedom.* Chevy Chase, MD: National Home Library Foundation, 1940.

———. "Practical Religion in the World of Tomorrow." In *Christian Bases of World Order: The Merrick Lectures.* New York: Abingdon-Cokesbury Press, 1943.

———, with Russel Lord (ed.). *Democracy Reborn.* New York: Reynal & Hitchcock, 1944.

———. *Our Job in the Pacific.* New York: American Council Institute of Pacific Relations, June 1944.

———. *Sixty Million Jobs.* New York: Simon & Schuster, 1945.

———, with Andrew Steiger. *Soviet Asia Mission.* New York: Reynal & Hitchcock, 1946.

———. *Toward World Peace.* New York: Reynal & Hitchcock, 1948.

Wallace, Henry ("Uncle Henry"). *Uncle Henry's Own Story of His Life: Personal Reminiscences, Volumes 1–3.* Des Moines: The Wallace Publishing Company, 1917.

Walton, Richard J. *Henry Wallace, Harry Truman, and the Cold War.* New York: Viking, 1976.

Waterhouse, Amanda Carroll. *Food & Prosperity: Balancing Technology and Community in Agriculture.* New York: The Rockefeller Foundation, 2013.

Weinstein, Allen, and Alexander Vassiliev. *The Haunted Wood: Soviet Espionage in America—The Stalin Era.* New York: Modern Library, 2000.

Werth, Alexander. *Russia at War, 1941–1945.* London: Pan, 1964.

Westad, Odd A. *Cold War and Revolution: Soviet-American Rivalry and the Origins of the Chinese Civil War, 1944–1946.* New York: Columbia University Press, 1993.

White, Ann Folino. *Plowed Under: Food Policy Protests and Performance in New Deal America.* Bloomington: University of Indiana Press, 2014.

White, Graham, and John Maze. *Henry A. Wallace: His Search for a New World Order.* Chapel Hill: University of North Carolina Press, 1995.

White, Theodore H. *In Search of History: A Personal Adventure.* New York: Warner Books, 1978.

Wicksteed, Alexander. *Life Under the Soviets.* London: J. Lane, 1928.

Zhukov, Georgii Konstantinovich. *The Memoirs of Marshal Zhukov.* New York: Delacorte, 1971.

Znamenski, A. *Red Shambhala: Magic, Prophecy, and Geopolitics in the Heart of Asia.* Wheaton, IL: Quest Books, 2011.

Articles

Adams, Frank S. "Wallace, Truman Cheered by 20,000 at Liberal Rally: They Enter Garden Arm in Arm but Vice President Fails to Return Nominee Praise." *New York Times.* November 1, 1944.

——. "Forrestal Voices Praise of Byrnes; 'Annoyed' by Wallace Incident." *New York Times*. September 18, 1946.

Adams, Mildred. "Wallace: Liberal or Star-Gazer." *New York Times*. September 15, 1946.

Alsop, Joseph. "Budenz and Morris." *Washington Post*. September 14, 1951.

——. "The Strange Case of Louis Budenz." *The Atlantic*. April 1952.

——, and Stewart Alsop. "The Meaning of Wallace." *Washington Post*. July 26, 1948.

American Farm Bureau Federation. "Official News Letter." March 21, 1933.

Appleby, Paul H. "Roosevelt's Third-Term Decision." *The American Political Science Review*. Vol. 46, No. 3 (September 1952). https://www.jstor.org/stable/1952282.

Army and Navy Journal. "Patents for Military Inventions." November 3, 1888.

Arnesen, Eric. "The Traditions of African American Anti-Communism." *Twentieth Century Communism*. Vol. 2014, No. 6 (January 2014).

Atomic Heritage Foundation. "Bombings of Hiroshima and Nagasaki—1945." June 5, 2014. https://ahf.nuclearmuseum.org/ahf/history/bombings-hiroshima-and-nagasaki-1945/.

Baldwin, Hanson W. "Feud on Atom Control Centers on Authority." *New York Times*. March 17, 1946.

——. "Atomic Energy Control: The Points in Dispute." *New York Times*. October 6, 1946.

Ballis, William B. "The Pattern of Sino-Soviet Treaties, 1945–1950." *The Annals of the American Academy of Political and Social Science*, Vol. 277 (September 1951): 167–76. http://www.jstor.org/stable/1030262.

Barnes, Bart. "Claude Pepper, Crusader for Elderly, Dies." *Washington Post*. May 31, 1989.

Bazelon, David T. "The Faith of Henry Wallace: The Populist Tradition in the Atomic Age." *Commentary*. April 1947.

Bean, L.H. "Post-War Interrelations Between Agriculture and Business," *Proceedings, International Conference of Agricultural Economists*. Vol. 2 (1930): 178–97.

Beevor, Antony. "Eisenhower's Pit Bull." *Wall Street Journal*. October 23, 2010.

Belair, Felix, Jr. "Plea to Give Soviets Atom Secrets Stirs Debate in Cabinet." *New York Times*. September 22, 1945.

——. "Truman Predicts Wallace Aid in '48." *New York Times*. April 11, 1947.

Bell, Jack. "Truman Seen as FDR's Running Mate." *Star*. April 12, 1944.

Benson, Robert L. "The Venona Story." Center for Cryptologic History, National Security Agency. 2001. https://www.nsa.gov/portals/75/documents/about/cryptologic-heritage/historical-figures-publications/publications/coldwar/venona_story.pdf.

Berg, Manfred. "Black Civil Rights and Liberal Anticommunism: The NAACP in the Early Cold War." *The Journal of American History*. Vol. 94, No. 1 (June 2007).

Bernstein, Richard. "Assassinating Chiang Kai-shek." *Foreign Policy*. September 3, 2015.

Birstein, Vadim J. "Three Days in 'Auschwitz Without Gas Chambers': Henry A. Wallace's Visit to Magadan in 1944." Wilson Center, January 2012. https://www.wilsoncenter.org/publication/three-days-auschwitz-without-gas-chambers-henry-wallaces-visit-to-magadan-1944.

Boston Globe. "Wallace Sees China Pushing Russia Out." March 28, 1960.

Boyd, James. "In Search of Shambhala? Nicholas Roerich's 1934–5 Inner Mongolian Expedition." *Inner Asia*. Vol. 14, No. 2 (2012): 267–68. https://www.jstor.org/stable/24572064.

Boyle, James E. "The AAA: An Epitaph." *The Atlantic*. Vol. 157, No. 2 (February 1936). https://www.theatlantic.com/culture/archive/2021/01/poem-epitaph-tyrant-sort-of/617713/.

Bridgeport Post. "Russia Starting to Fear China, Says Henry Wallace." November 26, 1962.

Brodkin, M.S. "Iz istorii snavzheniia Dal'stroiia NKVD SSSR v 1941–1945 godah" / Vestnik Novosibirskogo gosudarstvennogo universiteta. Seriia: Istoriia, filologiia, 2008. T.7, vyp. 1: Istoriia, s. 180–184. (Broadkin, M.S. "From the History of Supplying Dalstroy to the USSR in 1941–1945." *Vestnik NGU [The NGU Bulletin], History, Philology Series*. Vol. 7, No. 1 [2008: 180–184].)

Browder, Earl. "How Stalin Ruined the American Communist Party." *Harper's Magazine*. March 1960.

Buhle, Paul. "Harry Magdoff." *The Guardian*. February 20, 2006.

Callender, Harold. "Reds in China Seen in an Uneasy Truce." *New York Times*. February 18, 1943.

———. "Byrnes Deeply Disturbed by Wallace's Policy Talk; Truman Under Fire for It." *New York Times*. September 14, 1946.

———. "Byrnes Expected to Restate Policy in Paris Promptly." *New York Times*. September 16, 1946.

———. "Paris Expects Truman to Support Byrnes and Ask Wallace to Resign." *New York Times*. September 17, 1946.

———. "Wallace Silence Held Inadequate." *New York Times*. September 19, 1946.

———. "Truman Reassures Byrnes That Policy Stands Unchanged." *New York Times*. September 20, 1946.

Cameron, Rob. "Police Close Case on 1948 Death of Jan Masaryk—Murder, Not Suicide." *Radio Prague*. January 6, 2004.

Carpenter, Frederic I. "William James and Emerson." *American Literature*. Vol. 11, No. 1 (March 1939): 39–57. https://www.jstor.org/stable/2920693.

Catholic Advance. "Robert E. Hannegan Dies; Was Postmaster General." October 14, 1949.

Catledge, Turner. "President's Word on Wallace Choice Not Believed Order." *New York Times*. July 17, 1944.

———. "Democrats Press 'War Chief' Issue: Second Place Open." *New York Times*. July 20, 1944.

———. "Vote is 1,086 to 90." *New York Times*. July 21, 1944.

———. "2D Ballot Decides." *New York Times*. July 22, 1944.

Chang, Jui-Te. "Nationalist Army Officers During the Sino-Japanese War, 1937–1945." *Modern Asian Studies*. Vol. 30, No. 4 (1996): 1033–56. https://www.jstor.org/stable/312958.

Chervonnaya, Svetlana. "Alexander Vassiliev's Notes, Venona and Laurence Duggan." *Documentstalk.com*. 2008. http://www.deadlypass.com/wp/alexander-vassilievs-notes-venona-and-laurence-duggan/.

———. "Duggan, Laurence Hayden (1905–1948)." *Documentstalk.com*. 2008. http://www.deadlypass.com/wp/duggan-laurence-hayden/.

———. "Gorsky, Anatoly Veniaminovich (1907–1980)." *Documentstalk.com*. 2008. http://www.deadlypass.com/wp/gorsky-anatoly-veniaminovich-1907-1980/.

Chicago Daily Tribune. "Democrats Name Truman." July 22, 1944.

Chossudovsky, E.M. "Lenin and Chicherin: The Beginnings of Soviet Foreign Policy and Diplomacy." *Millennium: Journal of International Studies*. Vol. 3, No. 1 (1974): 1–16. https://journals.sagepub.com/doi/pdf/10.1177/03058298740030010101.

Cincinnati Enquirer. "Newspapers Attack Wallace Appointment as Jolt to Nation." January 23, 1945.

Clapper, Raymond. "Depth Noted in Wallace Speech." *Buffalo Evening News*. May 15, 1942.

Conklin, William R. "Russia's Policies Praised at Rally." *New York Times*. December 14, 1948.

Cook, Joan. "John J. Abt, Lawyer, Dies at 87; Communist Party Counsel in U.S." *New York Times.* August 13, 1991.

Cooke, Alistair. "The Disciples of Mr. Wallace." *Manchester Guardian.* July 24, 1948.

Davis, Joseph S. "AAA as a Force in Recovery." *Journal of Farm Economics.* Vol. 17, No. 1 (February 1935): 1–14. https://www.jstor.org/stable/1231028.

Deane, Michael J. "The Soviet Project of 'Correlation of Forces.'" Strategic Research Institute, Stanford Strategic Studies Center, Stanford University. May 1976. https://apps.dtic.mil/dtic/tr/fulltext/u2/a027223.pdf.

Dennis, Eugene. "Concluding Remarks on the Plenum Discussion." *Political Affairs.* Vol. 26, No. 8 (August 1947).

Des Moines Register. "Mystic Cult Letters of Early New Deal Era Harass Wallace." April 4, 1948.

Des Moines Register. "Wallace Sees a Chinese Era." June 11, 1958.

D'Mello, Bernard. "Tribute Harry Magdoff (1913–2016)." *EPW Commentary.* January 24, 2006. http://users.wfu.edu/cottrell/ope/archive/0601/0127.html.

Duclos, Jacques. "On the Dissolution of the Communist Party of the United States." *Cahiers du Communisme.* April 1945. Reprinted in *Marxism-Leninism vs. Revisionism,* by William Z. Foster et al. New York: New Century Publishers (February 1946). https://www.marxists.org/history/usa/parties/cpusa/1945/04/0400-duclos-ondissolution.pdf.

Duranty, Walter. "Stalin's War Sec in Long-Range Aim." *New York Times.* February 7, 1943.

Eagleton, Thomas F., and Diane L. Duffin. "Bob Hannegan and Harry Truman's Vice-Presidential Nomination." *Missouri Historical Review.* Vol. 90, No. 3 (April 1996).

Edwards, Sebastian. "Academics as Economic Advisers: Gold, the 'Brains Trust,' and FDR." *NBER Working Paper,* No. 21380 (July 2015). https://www.nber.org/papers/w21380.

Egan, Charles E. "Wallace Disowns Third Party Aim; Vandenberg Prods Truman on Him." *New York Times.* April 13, 1947.

Ek, Carl. "Speech." *Herald-News.* May 21, 1942.

Era. "Wallace Trip Sets Off New Speculation." April 13, 1944.

Ezekiel, Mordecai. "The Agricultural Problem." *New York Herald Tribune.* May 11, 1933.

Faber, Harold. "Papers of Flynn Go to Hyde Park." *New York Times.* May 20, 1984.

Fahan, R. "What Makes Henry Run? Wallace's Social and Political Role." *New International.* Vol. 14, No. 123 (February 1948).

Feinberg, Alexander. "Contrasting Views on Russian Moves." *New York Times.* March 20, 1946.

Fleeson, Doris. "Wallace Lectures Press, Mum on Own Affairs." *Boston Daily Globe.* July 24, 1948.

Flint, Peter B. "Glen H. Taylor of Idaho Dies; Wallace Running Mate in '48." *New York Times.* May 5, 1984.

Folsom, Merrill. "Wallace Is Silent on Voting Choice." *New York Times.* October 20, 1960.

———. "Henry Wallace Assays Candidates' Farm Plans." *New York Times.* October 27, 1960.

———. "Library Is Begun in Westchester." *New York Times.* September 5, 1962.

Foo, Yee-Wah. "Fu Bingchang, Chiang Kai-shek and Yalta," *Cold War History.* Vol. 9, No. 3 (August 2009): 389–409.

Fortune. "U.S. Opinion on Russia." Vol. 32 (September 1945).

Fossedal, Gregory A., and Bill S. Mikhail. "Marshall Plan Commemorative Section: A Modest Magician: Will Clayton and the Rebuilding of Europe." *Foreign Affairs.* May/June, 1997.

Foster, John Bellamy. "The Optimism of the Heart: Harry Magdoff (1913–2006)." *Monthly Review.* January 2, 2006. https://mronline.org/2006/01/02/the-optimism-of-the-heart-harry-magdoff-1913-2006/.

Foster, William. "On Building a People's Party." *Political Affairs.* February 1947.

Frank, Richard B. "Ending the Pacific War: Harry Truman and the Decision to Drop the Bomb." *Foreign Policy Research Institute.* April 28, 2009.

Garver, F.B., and Harry Trelogan. "The Agricultural Adjustment Act and The Reports of the Brookings Institution." *The Quarterly Journal of Economics.* Vol. 50, No. 4 (August 1936): 594–621. https://www.jstor.org/stable/1891095.

Gazette. "Wallace Trip Raises Political Conjectures." April 13, 1944.

Gerber, Larry G. "The Baruch Plan and the Origins of the Cold War." *Diplomatic History.* Vol. 6, No. 1 (Winter 1982): 69–95. http://www.jstor.org/stable/24911302.

Glushchenko, Alexandr. "'Lapsha' dlya vitse-prezidenta. O vizite vitse-presidenta SShA Genri A. Uollesa na Kolymu v 1944 godu." (Glushchenko, Alexander, "Pulling Wool Over the Ears of the Vice-President. On the Visit of the U.S. Vice President Henry A. Wallace to Kolyma in 1944.") *Samizdat* (blog). Originally published April 14, 2013, updated October 16, 2017. http://samlib.ru/g/glushenko_a_g/lapsha_dlja_vice-prezidenta.shtml.

Goldschmidt, Bertrand. "A Forerunner of the NPT? The Soviet Proposals of 1947." *International Atomic Energy Agency Bulletin,* Vol. 28, No. 1 (March 1986).

Golodnikova, I. Yu. "The Final Version of Roerich Expedition Map in Central Asia." International Cartographic Association.

Gruson, Sydney. "'Humane' Treatment for Germany Urged by Smuts to Win Her Aid." *New York Times.* September 17, 1946.

Grutzner, Charles. "Wallace Asserts He Ended Cold War." *New York Times.* October 27, 1948.

Hachey, Thomas E. "American Profiles on Capitol Hill: A Confidential Study for the British Foreign Office in 1943." *The Wisconsin Magazine of History.* Vol. 57, No. 2 (Winter 1973–1974): 141–53. http://www.jstor.org/stable/4634869.

Hagerty, James. "Sharp Race Looms for Second Place." *New York Times.* July 20, 1944.

———. "President Favors Truman, Douglas." *New York Times.* July 21, 1944.

———. "Big City Bosses Won over Hillman." *New York Times.* July 22, 1944.

———. "Wallace Warns on 'Tough' Policy Toward Russia." *New York Times.* September 13, 1946.

———. "Wallace Renews His Red Vote Stand." *New York Times.* July 24, 1948.

———. "48,000 Hear Wallace Assert Prejudice Will Fail in South." *New York Times.* September 11, 1948.

———. "Wallace Supports Our Fight in Korea." *New York Times.* July 16, 1950.

Hale, William Harlan. "What Makes Wallace Run?" *Harper's Magazine.* March 1948.

Hamilton, Thomas J. "Baruch Counters Wallace, Says Atomic Policy Stands." *New York Times.* September 20, 1946.

Harkness, Richard, and Daz Harkness. "Where Are Those Rampaging New Dealers?" *New York Times.* May 22, 1960.

Hartford Courant. "Soviet Press Takes Note of Election." November 3, 1948.

Harvard Crimson. "F.B.I. Agent Says Student's Spouse Preached Revolt." April 13, 1949.

Hasegawa, Tsuyoshi. "Soviet Policy Toward Japan During World War II," *Cahiers du Monde Russe.* Vol. 53, No. 2/3 (2011): 245–71. http://www.jstor.org/stable/41708322.

Hauser, Ernest O. "China's Soong: Chiang's Mysterious Brother-in-Law Finds Funds to Keep China Fighting." *Life.* March 24, 1941.

Hausman, Joshua K., Paul W. Rhode, and Johannes F. Wieland. "Recovery from the Great Depression: The Farm Channel in Spring 1933." *American Economic Review.* Vol. 109, No. 2 (2019): 427–72. https://pubs.aeaweb.org/doi/pdfplus/10.1257/aer.20170237.

Hazlitt, Henry. "A Vain Search for a Wage Price Formula." *New York Times.* October 22, 1945.

Heaster, Brenda L. "Who's on Second: The 1944 Democratic Vice-Presidential Nomination." *Missouri Historical Review.* Vol. 80, No. 2 (January 1986). https://digital.shsmo.org/digital/collection/mhr/id/42287.

Hellman, Lillian. "On Henry Wallace." *New York Times.* April 11, 1976.

Herrington, Boze. "The Seven Signs That You Are in a Cult." *The Atlantic.* June 18, 2014.

Hetzel, Robert L. "German Monetary History in the First Half of the Twentieth Century." *Federal Reserve Bank of Richmond Economic Quarterly.* Vol. 88, No. 1 (Winter 2002): 1–35.

Hoffman, Michael G. "Europe Will Feel Loss." *New York Times.* October 15, 1947.

Holley, Joe. "Gulag Survivor George Z. Bien Dies at 76." *Washington Post.* June 20, 2005.

Huang, Ray. "Chiang Kai-shek and His Diary as a Historical Source, Part II." *Chinese Studies in History.* Vol. 30, Nos. 1–2 (Fall–Winter 1996–1997).

Hulen, Bertram D. "Truman Supports Byrnes, Says Policy Is Unchanged; Explains Stand on Wallace." *New York Times.* September 15, 1946.

———. "Wallace Stands on Policy Speech, Plans a New Talk." *New York Times.* September 17, 1946.

———. "President Exhorts Party Candidates." *New York Times.* September 18, 1946.

Hurd, Charles. "Wallace Talks with President: Insists That China Was Sole Topic." *New York Times.* July 11, 1944.

Irish Echo. "Ed Flynn, the Bronx Boss at FDR's Side." March 12, 2012.

Irwin, Don. " 'Progressive' Name Taken by Wallace Party." *New York Herald Tribune.* July 24, 1948.

"Istoriia teatra," Magadanskii gosudarstvennyi musykal'nyi i dramaticheskii teatr. ("Theater History." Magadan State Musical and Drama Theater.) Accessed April 28, 2023. https://mmdt.ru/o-teatre/istoriya-teatra.

Izakov, Boris. "Mezhdunarodnoe obozrenie." "Pravda," 24 ijunia 1946. (Izakov, Boris. "International Review." *Pravda.* June 24, 1946.)

Jackson, Brooks. "Blacks and the Democratic Party." *Factcheck.org.* April 18, 2018. https://www.factcheck.org/2008/04/blacks-and-the-democratic-party/.

Jalil, Andrew, and Gisela Rua. "Inflation Expectations and Recovery from the Depression in 1933: Evidence from the Narrative Record." *Finance and Economics Discussion Series 2015-029.* Washington, DC: Board of Governors of the Federal Reserve System, 2015. https://www.federalreserve.gov/econresdata/feds/2015/files/2015029pap.pdf.

Kaplan, Morris. "A.L.P. Rally Hears Attack on Dulles." *New York Times.* October 25, 1949.

Kirchwey, Freda. "Moves Toward Peace." *The Nation.* May 29, 1948.

Klehr, Harvey, and John Earl Haynes. "Two Gentlemen of Venona." *Washington Examiner.* May 13, 1996.

Krebs, Albin. "Rexford Tugwell, Roosevelt Aide, Dies." *New York Times.* July 24, 1979.

Krock, Arthur. "What the BEW Order Did to the State Department." *New York Times.* April 28, 1942.

———. "Truman Cabinet Reflects a National Cleavage." *New York Times.* September 25, 1945.

———. "Forrestal Considered for a Political Role." *New York Times.* October 28, 1945.

———. "Broken Alignments on the Atomic Issue." *New York Times*. March 15, 1946.

———. "Wallace; His Speech Poses Test of His Relations with President." *New York Times*. September 15, 1946.

———. "A Cabinet Divided Against Itself and Its Chief." *New York Times*. September 17, 1946.

———. "A Formula That Is Not Self-Operating." *New York Times*. September 19, 1946.

———. "Mr. Wallace Contributes to a Growing Impression." *New York Times*. October 4, 1946.

———. "Kremlin's Release of Note Held Breach of Diplomacy." *New York Times*. May 12, 1948.

———. "The Ever More Mysterious East." *New York Times*. October 11, 1951.

Kuhn, Ferdinand, Jr. "American Officials Embarrassed by Moscow Broadcast of 'Acceptance.'" *Washington Post*. May 12, 1948.

Larson, Edward J., and Larry Witham. "Leading Scientists Still Reject God." *Nature*. Vol. 394, No. 313 (July 23, 1998). https://www.nature.com/articles/28478.

Lattimore, Owen. "New Road to Asia." *National Geographic Magazine*. December 1944.

Lawrence, W.H. "Wallace Accepts, Calling on Allies to Give Up Berlin." *New York Times*. July 25, 1948.

———. "Similarities Noted in Left Platforms." *New York Times*. July 28, 1948.

Lehmann-Haupt, Christopher. "Michael Straight, Who Wrote of Connection to Spy Ring, Is Dead at 87." *New York Times*. January 5, 2004.

Leviero, Anthony. "Voice for Military on Atom Approved." *New York Times*. March 13, 1946.

Lippmann, Walter. "Henry Wallace." *New York Herald Tribune*. July 11, 1944.

———. "Wallace in a China Shop." *Washington Post*. April 15, 1947.

Lissner, Will. "Wallace Vote Is Far Short of His Party's Expectations." *New York Times*. November 3, 1948

Los Angeles Times. "Wallace Again Shows His Pro-Russian Bias." September 29, 1948.

Los Angeles Times. "Madame Chiang Kai-shek of Taiwan Dies at 105." October 24, 2003.

Lowitt, Richard. "Henry A. Wallace and the 1935 Purge in the Department of Agriculture." *Agricultural History*. Vol. 53, No. 2 (July 1979): 607–21. https://www.jstor.org/stable/3742758.

Lukes, Igor. "The 1948 Coup d'Etat in Prague Through the Eyes of the American Embassy." *Diplomacy & Statecraft*. Vol. 22, No. 3 (September 2011): 431–49.

Macdonald, Dwight. "Henry Wallace." *Politics*. March–April 1947.

Mallon, Winifred. "Wallace Backs Science Program." *New York Times*. October 12, 1945.

Marshall, Margaret. "Notes by the Way." *The Nation*. June 26, 1948.

Marshfield News-Herald. "U.S., Russian Alliance Seen." March 29, 1961.

Martin, Douglas. "Harry Magdoff, Economist, Dies at 92." *New York Times*. January 9, 2006.

McCormick, Anne O'Hare. "Old Circus Goes on, but War Has Floor." *New York Times*. June 27, 1944.

McCullough, John M. "New Progressive Party Must Conquer Internal Pressure if It Is to Survive." *Philadelphia Inquirer*. July 27, 1948.

McNair, Marie. "Henry Wallace Attends Soviet Embassy Party." *Washington Post*. November 8, 1948.

Meerovich, M.G. "Kontseptsiia sotsialisticheskogo rasseleniia." —*Arkhitekton: izvestiia vizov*, 2008, No. 3. (Meerovich, Mark. "The Concept of Socialist Settlement." *Architecton: Newsletter of the Institutes of Higher Learning*, No. 3 [September 2008].)

Middleton, Drew. "U.S. Study Finds Soviet Needs Help." *New York Times*. July 31, 1946.

———. "Smith Asks the Russians About It." *New York Times*. March 16, 1947.

———. "Soviet Proclaims New Berlin Money." *New York Times*. June 23, 1948.

Miller, John R. "The Chiang-Stilwell Conflict, 1942–1944." *Military Affairs*. Vol. 43, No. 2 (April 1979): 59–62. https://www.jstor.org/stable/i308054.

Misselwitz, Henry F. "Shanghai Mob Raids Soviet Consulate to Avenge Czarists." *New York Times*. November 8, 1927.

Monnay, Tatyana. "A Program That Pays Farmers Not to Farm Isn't Saving the Planet." *Politico*. August 29, 2021. https://www.politico.com/news/2021/08/29/usda-farmers-conservation-program-507028.

Morain, Tom. "Connection Between Norman Borlaug and George Washington Carver." *AgBioWorld*. 2011. http://www.agbioworld.org/biotech-info/topics/borlaug/connection.html.

Morrow, Edward A. "Communists Halt Berlin Assembly." *New York Times*. June 24, 1948.

Moscow, Warren. "Wallace Through, Opponents Assert." *New York Times*. July 18, 1944.

———. "Wallace Accuses U.S. in Czech Coup." *New York Times*. March 16, 1948.

———. "Wallace Deserts Progressive Party in Split on Korea." *New York Times*. August 9, 1950.

Newman, Robert P. "Clandestine Chinese Nationalist Efforts to Punish Their American Detractors." *Diplomatic History*. Vol. 7, No. 3 (July 1983): 205–22.

News and Observer. "How They Voted." July 22, 1944.

New York Herald Tribune. "The Amazing Farm Bill." March 18, 1933.

New York Herald Tribune. "Roerich Cleared of Politics Charge on Oriental Quest." February 5, 1936.

New York Sun. "U.S. Discharges Artist in Asia: Mysterious Spy Charge Was Lodged Against Nicholas Roerich in Manchukuo." January 30, 1936.

New York Sun. "Action Threatened Against Agriculture Department." January 31, 1936.

New York Sun. "Capital Denies Roerich Report." January 31, 1936.

New York Sun. "20 seed packages Cost U.S. $35,000." February 1, 1936.

New York Times. "Chiang Weds Mme. Sun Yat-sen's Sister; 3,000 See Rites for Wellesley Girl Bride." December 2, 1927.

New York Times. "India Said to Regard Roerich as Pro-Soviet; Artist's Aide Here Amazed at Refusal of Visa." July 18, 1930.

New York Times. "Roerich Activities 'Embarrass' the U.S." June 24, 1935.

New York Times. "Injunction Denied to Roerich Group." February 12, 1936.

New York Times. "Text of Wallace Speech Accepting Nomination for the Vice Presidency." August 30, 1940.

New York Times. "Roosevelt Urges Speed in BEW Drive." April 24, 1942.

New York Times. "Costa Ricans Mass to Cheer Wallace." March 19, 1943.

New York Times. "Delegates Awaken at Night Session." July 20, 1944.

New York Times. "Wallace Is in Fight to Finish, Directing Convention Contest." July 20, 1944.

New York Times. "Wrong Place for Mr. Wallace." January 23, 1945.

New York Times. "Truman to Settle Atom Bomb Policy." September 24, 1945.

New York Times. "Lewis and Murray Clash over Wages at Labor Meeting." November 9, 1945.

New York Times. "Wallace Renews Auto Wage Debate." November 10, 1945.

New York Times. "Collective Bargaining." November 11, 1945.

New York Times. "Wallace Stresses Trade War Perils." November 13, 1945.

New York Times. "Fatherland Front Victor in Bulgaria." November 20, 1945.

New York Times. "Texts of the UAW and Romney Statements on Auto Union Demands." November 20, 1945.

New York Times. "Truman Points Way to High Production." December 1, 1945.

New York Times. "Congress Bill Sets Swiss Watch Limit." January 19, 1946.

New York Times. "Byrnes Aids China." March 6, 1946.

New York Times. "Mr. Wallace's 'Fascists.'" March 14, 1946.

New York Times. "Baruch Selection Scored." March 21, 1946.

New York Times. "Soviet Organ Sees 'Atomic Dictatorship' Aim." March 21, 1946.

New York Times. "Wallace Says U.S. Force Should Quit Iceland Base." March 22, 1946.

New York Times. "Forrestal Pleads for Strong Nation." March 24, 1946.

New York Times. "Fulbright Warns of Soviet Attitude." May 18, 1946.

New York Times. "Wallace Opposes Third Party in U.S." May 25, 1946.

New York Times. "Two Americans Leave Today for Moscow Trade Talks." June 20, 1946.

New York Times. "'Boom and Bust' On, Wallace Warns." August 4, 1946.

New York Times. "Pepper Favors Wallace." August 14, 1946.

New York Times. "Algernon Lee Calls for Wallace Ouster." September 15, 1946.

New York Times. "British Press Irate at 'Imperialist' Barb." September 15, 1946.

New York Times. "Connally, Vandenberg Urge Bipartisan Foreign Policy." September 15, 1946.

New York Times. "Soviet Brief on Wallace: Moscow Radio Says Audience Disliked Anti-Russian Words." September 15, 1946.

New York Times. "Liberals Assail Wallace." September 18, 1946.

New York Times. "Text of Secretary Wallace's Letter to President Truman on U.S. Foreign Policy." September 18, 1946.

New York Times. "Dr. Wang Asserts 'Open Door' Policy." September 19, 1946.

New York Times. "Mr. Truman and Mr. Wallace." September 19, 1946.

New York Times. "Communists Assail Truman at Rally." September 20, 1946.

New York Times. "Anti–New Dealers Acclaim Dismissal." September 21, 1946.

New York Times. "Russians in Berlin Upbraid Churchill." September 21, 1946.

New York Times. "Text of Truman Statement." September 21, 1946.

New York Times. "Statement by Baruch on Controversy with Wallace and Texts of Exchanges Between Them." October 3, 1946.

New York Times. "Some Facts for Mr. Wallace." October 4, 1946.

New York Times. "Baruch vs. Wallace." October 6, 1946.

New York Times. "Assembly in Sofia Has Red Majority." October 29, 1946.

New York Times. "Henry Wallace Answers President Truman." March 18, 1947.

New York Times. "Wallace Implies Arms Lead to War." April 21, 1947.

New York Times. "Text of Wallace's Letter to Stalin Calling for Peace Program." May 12, 1948.

New York Times. "Text of Wallace's Acceptance Speech in Which He Charged American People Are Being Betrayed." July 25, 1948.

New York Times. "Pepper Lauds Kramer's Work." August 13, 1948.

New York Times. "Text of Wallace's Speech at Yankee Stadium." September 11, 1948.

New York Times. "Hastie Sees Negroes Voting for Truman." October 14, 1948.

New York Times. "Dollinger Served 12 Years in Albany." November 3, 1948.

New York Times. "Wallace Votes, then Tends Farm." November 3, 1948.

New York Times. "Panyushkin, 'Red Dean,' Wallace to Talk at Rally." November 18, 1948.

New York Times. "'Budding Fascism' Seen by Wallace." September 13, 1949.

New York Times. "Robert Hannegan Dies in Home at 46." October 7, 1949.

New York Times. "Wallace Willing to Quit." July 17, 1950.

New York Times. "Robeson's Wife Hits U.S., U.N., on Korea." August 7, 1950.

New York Times. "The Return of Henry Wallace." August 10, 1950.

New York Times. "Russia Says Korea Justifies Atom Bomb." August 11, 1950.

New York Times. "Worker Assails Wallace." August 13, 1950.

New York Times. "Wallace Urges Red China to Shun a 'Slavish Obedience' to Moscow." September 30, 1950.

New York Times. "Soviet Calls Wallace Disloyal." November 24, 1950.

New York Times. "Wallace Says Russia Seeks to Rule World." December 4, 1950.

New York Times. "Wallace Sees China Dropping Soviet Link." January 3, 1951.

New York Times. "Wallace Asks for Peace Through 'World P.W.A.'" January 22, 1951.

New York Times. "Texts of Documents Outlining Wallace's Position on China Policy." September 24, 1951.

New York Times. "Wallace Disowns 'Soft' China Policy." September 24, 1951.

New York Times. "Wallace Asserts He Backed Chiang." October 10, 1951.

New York Times. "Wallace Defends His China Mission." October 18, 1951.

New York Times. "Wallace Declares 'Mr. X' Story False." March 18, 1952.

New York Times. "Wallace First 'Saw' Soviet Aims in '49." October 31, 1955.

New York Times. "The Activities for the Week." January 15, 1956.

New York Times. "Cubans Hear Wallace." June 9, 1957.

New York Times. "Kennedy Farm Plan Worries Wallace." October 6, 1960.

New York Times. "Gen. Bedell Smith Is Dead in Capital." August 10, 1961.

New York Times. "Henry A. Wallace Is Dead at 77." November 19, 1965.

New York Times. "Fulton Lewis Jr. Is Dead at 63." August 22, 1966.

New York Times. "Gerhart Eisler, Top Communist Who Fled U.S. Persecution, Dies." March 22, 1968.

New York Times. "Dr. Lewis L. Lorwin, Economist and Labor Historian, 86, Dies." June 7, 1970.

New York Times. "George Allen, Presidents' Crony, Dies." April 24, 1973.

New York Times. "Samuel I. Rosenman, 77, Dies." June 25, 1973.

New York Times. "Louis L. Horch, 90, Founder of Museum." April 16, 1979.

New York Times. "F.B.I. Kept Watch on Henry Wallace." September 6, 1983.

New York Times. "Trenchcoats, Then and Now." June 24, 1990.

"Novoe vremia," "O dezertirstve Genri Uollesa." 23 noiabria, 1950. (*New Times.* "On the Desertion of Henry Wallace." November 23, 1950.)

Parke, Richard H. "Wallace Demands U.S. Rearm Quickly." *New York Times.* November 13, 1950.

Paterson, Thomas G. "The Abortive American Loan to Russia and the Origins of the Cold War, 1943–1946." *The Journal of American History.* Vol. 56, No. 1 (June 1969): 70–92. https://www.jstor.org/stable/1902064.

Pearson, Drew. "Rep. Thomas Reminded of Trial Rights." *Washington Post.* November 11, 1948.

Pearson, Richard. "Political Journalist Theodore H. White Dies at 71." *Washington Post.* May 17, 1986.

Pegler, Westbrook. "Rosette Is Hung on Bubblehead Wallace." *Knoxville Journal.* June 2, 1948.

Pepper, Claude, and Robert A. Taft. "'Sixty Million Jobs': Pro and Con." *New York Times.* September 9, 1945.

Peterson, Osler L. "Henry Wallace: A Divided Mind." *The Atlantic.* August 1948.

Petrov, Nikita. "Piry rabovladel'tsev na nevol'nichikh rudnikah." "Novaiia gazeta," No. 133, 28 noiabria 2011. (Petrov, Nikita. "Slaveholders' Feasts at Slave Labor Mines." *New Gazette*, No. 133 [November 28, 2011].) https://www.novayagazeta.ru/articles/2011/11/28/47010-piry-rabovladeltsev-na-nevolnichih-rudnikah.

Phelps, Christopher, and Harry Magdoff. "An Interview with Harry Magdoff." *Monthly Review*. May 1, 1999. https://monthlyreview.org/1999/05/01/an-interview-with-harry-magdoff/.

Phillips, Cabell. "At 75, Henry Wallace Cultivates His Garden." *New York Times*. October 6, 1963.

Pigliucci, Massimo. "The Ethics (or Lack Thereof) of Belief." *Philosophy as a Way of Life* (blog), August 31, 2022. https://philosophyasawayoflife.medium.com/the-ethics-of-belief-f1d459c572e3.

Pittsburgh Post-Gazette. "Truman Wins Vice Presidential Nomination on Second Ballot." July 22, 1944.

PM. "Wallace Calls for an American Policy." September 13, 1946.

PM. "Wallace Is Heckled Often." September 13, 1946.

Pollin, Robert. "Remembering Harry Magdoff." *Counterpunch*. January 6, 2006. https://www.counterpunch.org/2006/01/06/remembering-harry-magdoff/.

Popham, John N. "Tennesseans Give Wallace Cheers." *New York Times*. September 5, 1948.

Porter, Russell. "Physical Progress More Rapid than Expected but Some Industrial Problems Remain." *New York Times*. November 4, 1945.

———. "We Have the 'Can Do' We Need the 'Will Do.'" *New York Times*. December 2, 1945.

———. "Wallace's Employment Goal Is Reached Four Years Early." *New York Times*. July 7, 1946.

Powell, John. "Japanese Expel Explorers Sent by Sec. Wallace." *Chicago Tribune*. June 24, 1935.

"Pravda," "Massovyi miting v Medison skver garden." 15 sentiabria, 1946. (*Pravda*. "The Mass Rally at Madison Square Garden." September 15, 1946.)

"Pravda," "Na podstupah k vyboram v SShA". "Pravda", 1 noiabria 1948. (*Pravda*. "In the Run-up to the Elections in the USA." November 1, 1948.)

"Pravda," "Izbiratel'naiia kampaniia Progressivnoi partii." 2 noiabria, 1948. (*Pravda*. "The Election Campaign of the Progressive Party." November 2, 1948.)

Pulliam, Walter. "Wallace Wants to Halt Soviet Expansion at Central Turkey." *Washington Post*. June 16, 1947.

Radosh, Ronald. "A Story Told Before." *The Weekly Standard*. November 12, 2012.

Raine, Fernande Scheid. "Stalin and the Creation of the Azerbaijan Democratic Party in Iran, 1945." *Cold War History*. Vol. 2, No. 1 (October 2001).

Raskin, A.H. "200,000 Quit in 16 States." *New York Times*. January 16, 1946.

Rasmussen, Wayne D. "The New Deal Farm Programs: What They Were and Why They Survived." *American Journal of Agricultural Economics*. Vol. 65, No. 5 (December 1983). https://www.jstor.org/stable/1240440.

"Razoruzhenie." *Bolshaya Sovetskaia Encyclopedia*, tretie izdanie. Tom 21, chast' 30. ("Disarmament." *Big Soviet Encyclopedia*, 3rd edition, Vol. 21, part 3.)

Reston, James. "Wallace May Win Part of Jones' Job." *New York Times*. January 19, 1945.

———. "Senators Start Fight on Wallace to Succeed Jobs." *New York Times*. January 23, 1945.

———. "Wallace Speech Is Seen Embarrassing to Byrnes." *New York Times*. September 13, 1946.

——— . "Prior Objection by Clayton to Wallace Talk Disclosed." *New York Times.* September 14, 1946.

———. "Wallace Airs Issues in Our Soviet Policy." *New York Times.* September 15, 1946.

———. "Capital Faces Hang-over on Wallace-Truman Issue." *New York Times.* September 16, 1946.

———. "U.S., Britain Said to Use Balance-of-Power System." *New York Times.* September 19, 1946.

———. "Position Clarified: President Acts to Avoid Misconceptions, Denies Hostility to Soviet." *New York Times.* May 12, 1948.

Evening Review. "Wallace's China Trip Hints at His Removal by Democratic Party." April 12, 1944.

Rosenman, Sam. "Franklin Roosevelt: One Year After." *New York Times.* April 7, 1946.

Rosenof, Theodore. "The Economic Ideas of Henry A. Wallace, 1933–1948." *Agricultural History.* Vol. 41, No. 2 (April 1967): 143–54. http://www.jstor.org/stable/3739869.

Rosov, V.A. Amerikanskoe obshchestvo "Belukha" i proekt N.K. Rerikha "Jedinaiia Aziia."—*Vestnik Sankt-Peterburgskogo Universiteta, Seriia 2, vypusk 2* (2005). ("American 'Belucha' Association and the 'United Asia' Project of N.K. Roerich." *The Newsletter of the St.-Petersburg University,* Series 2, Issue 2 [2005]).

———. Arhitektor B.K. Rerikh. Rassekrechennoe arhivnoe delo # 2538.—*Vestnik Araivarty,* No. 10 (2008). ("Architect B.K. Rerikh. Declassified archival case file No. 2538." *Bulletin of Ariavarta,* No. 10 [2008].) http://www.aryavest.com/partlink/156.pdf.

Ruleva, I.V., A.A. Abaimova. "Ideinye predposylki kontseptsii sotsgoroda."—*Sovremennye problemy nauki i obrazovania,* No. 6 (30 Dekabrya 2012). (Ruleva, I.V., and A.A. Abaimova. "Ideological Prerequisites of the Concept of Sotsgorod." *The Modern Problems of Science and Education,* No. 6 [December 30, 2012].)

Ryan, Thomas G. "Farm Prices and the Farm Vote in 1948." *Agricultural History.* Vol. 54, No. 3 (July 1980): 387–401. http://www.jstor.org/stable/3742831.

Salisbury, Harrison E. "Soviet Fills Press with Peace Theme." *New York Times.* October 4, 1950.

Saraswati, Purohit. "A Review: Asperger Syndrome." *Biomedical Journal of Scientific & Technical Research.* January 3, 2018.

"Savoyeva Nina Vladimirovna (1916–2003)." Sakharovskii Tsentr. Vospominaniia o GULAGe. ("Savoyeva Nina Vladimirovna," Sakharov Center. Memories of GULAG.) https://www.sakharov-center.ru/asfcd/auth/?t=author&i=279.

Saxon, Wolfgang. "Cabell Phillips, Newsman, Dead." *New York Times.* November 15, 1975.

———. "Edwin Wendell Pauley Sr., 78." *New York Times.* July 29, 1981.

Schonberger, Howard. "T.A. Bison and the Limits of Reform in Occupied Japan." *Bulletin of Concerned Asian Scholars.* Vol. 12 (1980).

Schwarz, Benjamin. "Clearer than the Truth." *The Atlantic.* April 2004. https://www.theatlantic.com/magazine/archive/2004/04/clearer-than-the-truth/302928/.

Selgin, George. "The New Deal and Recovery, Part 9: The AAA." *Alt-M: Ideas for an Alternative Monetary Future* (blog). January 11, 2021. https://www.alt-m.org/2021/01/11/the-new-deal-and-recovery-part-9-the-aaa/#_ftn2.

Sfeckas, Stanley. "Roerich's Theosophy." Paper Prepared for the 7th Annual English Conference "Nicholas Roerich—Messenger of Beauty and Peace." University of Indianapolis, Athens Campus. April 9, 2011. https://www.researchgate.net/publication/286417736_ROERICH'S_THEOSOPHY.

Shalett, Sidney. "Patterson Backs Civil Atom Board." *New York Times.* March 16, 1946.

Sheean, Vincent. "Why I Will Not Vote for Wallace." *Saturday Evening Post*. September 18, 1948.

Shephard, John E., Jr. "Warriors and Politics: The Bitter Lessons of Stilwell in China." *Defense Technical Information Center*. March 1989.

Shuit, Douglas. "Edwin Pauley, 78, Calif. Oilman Who Advised Presidents." *Washington Post*. July 30, 1981.

Sitkoff, Harvard. "Harry Truman and the Election of 1948: The Coming of Age of Civil Rights in American Politics." *The Journal of Southern History*. Vol. 37, No. 4 (November 1971). https://www.jstor.org/stable/2206548.

Stalin, I.V. "God velikogo pereloma: K XII godovshchine Oktiabria" (1929). Soch., Tom 12, ss. 118–35. Moskva: Gospolitizdat, 1949. (Stalin, Joseph. "The Year of the Great Breakthrough" (1929), in *Works*, Vol. 12, pp. 118–35. Moscow: Gospolitizdat, 1949.)

Stark, Louis. "Basic Talks Begin." *New York Times*. November 6, 1945.

The State. "Henry Wallace Sees Rise of Red China." May 13, 1960.

Steil, Benn. "Why the Marshall Plan Worked—and Why It Won't in Today's Warzones." *Defense One*. April 2, 2018. https://www.defenseone.com/ideas/2018/04/why-marshall -plan-worked-and-why-it-wont-todays-warzones/147127/.

Stevens, Donald G. "Organizing for Economic Defense: Henry Wallace and the Board of Economic Warfare's Foreign Policy Initiatives, 1942." *Presidential Studies Quarterly*. Vol. 26, No. 4 (Fall 1996): 1126–29. https://www.jstor.org/stable/27551675.

St. Louis Star Times. "Partial Text of Wallace's Attack on Jesse Jones." June 29, 1943.

Stout, David. "John Hazard, 86, Law Professor and a Top Sovietology Scholar." *New York Times*. April 11, 1995.

Sulzberger, C.L. "All-out War Set." *New York Times*. December 2, 1943.

———. "Paris Sees Byrnes' Policy Reinvigorated by Truman." *New York Times*. September 21, 1946.

Tamer, Hasper. "Why Do Taxpayers Subsidize Rich Farmers?" *Washington Post*. March 15, 2018. https://www.washingtonpost.com/lifestyle/food/why-do-taxpayers-subsidize -rich-farmers/2018/03/15/50e89906-27b6-11e8-b79d-f3d931db7f68_story.html.

TASS. "K sovetsko-amerikanskin otnosheniiam,"—"Krasnaiia Zvezda," 11 maiia, 1948. (TASS. "On Soviet-American Relations." *Red Star*, May 11, 1948.)

The Telegraph. "Michael Straight." January 17, 2004.

Thomas, Reginald. "Claude Pepper, Fiery Fighter for Elderly Rights, Dies at 88." *New York Times*. May 31, 1989.

Time. "U.S. at War: Globaloney." February 22, 1943.

Time. "High Wind in Tihwa." July 3, 1944.

Time. "James F. Byrnes, Man of the Year." January 6, 1947.

The New Republic. "A New Deal with Russia: I." December 16, 1946.

Topping, Simon. "'Never Argue with the Gallup Poll': Thomas Dewey, Civil Rights and the Election of 1948." *Journal of American Studies*. Vol. 38 (August 2004): 179–98. https://www.cambridge.org/core/services/aop-cambridge-core/content/view/ S0021875804008400.

Tower, Samuel A. "Truman for Civil Control of Atomic Energy in U.S." *New York Times*. February 1, 1946.

Trohan, Walter. "Truman Bested Stalin to Establish U.S. as Boss of Pacific." *Times Herald*. August 18, 1945.

Trussell, C.P. "Ex-Major Says Hopkins Sped Uranium to Soviet in 1943; Wallace Named; Denies Role." *New York Times*. December 6, 1949.

Tsou, Tang. "The Quemoy Imbroglio: Chiang Kai-Shek and the United States." *The Western Political Quarterly*. Vol. 12, No. 4 (December 1959): 1075–91. https://www.jstor.org/stable/443798.

Tuttle, Frederic, "Wallace Refuses to Disavow Reds' Support of His Political Party." *Fort Worth Star-Telegram*. July 24, 1948.

United Press International. "Lovett and Wallace Join Soviet Anniversary Party." *New York Times*. November 8, 1948.

———. "Edwin Pauley, a Millionaire Oilman Who Put Together . . ." July 28, 1981. http://www.upi.com/Archives/1981/07/28/Edwin-Pauley-a-millionaire-oilman-who-put-together-the/6580365140800/.

U.S. Department of Energy. "The Atomic Bombing of Hiroshima." Accessed April 30, 2023. https://www.osti.gov/opennet/manhattan-project-history/Events/1945/hiroshima.htm.

U.S. News & World Report. "Was A-Bomb on Japan a Mistake?" August 15, 1960: 62–76.

Vronskii, Boris. "Tretiia partiia v Soedinennykh Shtatah."—"Krasnaiia Zvezda," 11 aprelia, 1948. (Vronsky, Boris. "The Third Party in the United States." *Red Star*, April 11, 1948.)

Waggoner, Walter H. "Wallace Creates Foreign Trade Job." *New York Times*. December 2, 1945.

Waldron, Arthur. "How China Was 'Lost.'" *The Weekly Standard*. January 28, 2013.

Walker, J. Samuel. "'No More Cold War': American Foreign Policy and the 1948 Soviet Peace Offensive." *Diplomatic History*. Vol. 5, No. 1 (Winter 1981).

———. "The New Deal and the Guru." *American Heritage*. Vol. 40, No. 2 (March 1989).

Walker, T.J. "The Untold Story of Key New Dealer, Frank Walker." Accessed April 29, 2023. https://livingnewdeal.org/stories/untold-story-key-new-dealer-frank-walker/.

Wallace, Henry A. "Wallace Warns Against a 'New Isolationism.'" *New York Times*. July 12, 1942.

———. "Trade-Pact Law Renewal Vital to World Progress." *Foreign Commerce Weekly*. May 5, 1945.

———. "The Way to Peace: Division of World Between Russia and United States." *Vital Speeches of the Day*. Vol. 12, No. 24 (October 1, 1946).

———. "Jobs Peace Freedom." *The New Republic*. December 16, 1946.

———. "The UN and Disarmament." *The New Republic*. December 23, 1946.

———. "Henry Wallace's Forum." *The New Republic*. December 30, 1946.

———. "An Open Letter to Secretary Marshall." *The New Republic*. January 20, 1947.

———. "The Moscow Conference Can Succeed." *The New Republic*. March 10, 1947.

———. "The Fight for Peace Begins." *The New Republic*. March 24, 1947.

———. "Bevin Muddies the Waters." *The New Republic*. June 30, 1947.

———. "Keeping 60 Million Jobs." *The New Republic*. July 28, 1947.

———. "Summer Vacation at Farvue." *The New Republic*. August 25, 1947.

———. "Come Out Fighting!" *The New Republic*. September 1, 1947.

———. "Trust Busters and Planners." *The New Republic*. September 8, 1947.

———. "Too Little, Too Late." *The New Republic*. October 6, 1947.

———. "Radioactivity and Plant Growth." *The New Republic*. October 13, 1947.

———. "Thoughts at Christmas." *The New Republic*. December 22, 1947.

———. "I Shall Run in 1948." *Vital Speeches of the Day*. Vol. 14, No. 6 (January 1, 1948).

———. "Stand Up and Be Counted." *The New Republic*. January 5, 1948.

———. "My Alternative to the Marshall Plan." *The New Republic*. January 12, 1948.

——. "Militarization in the United States." *The New Republic*. January 26, 1948.

——. "Whipped-up Hysteria." *The New Republic*. March 29, 1948.

——. "Buying Foreign Elections." *The New Republic*. April 5, 1948.

——. "Count the Cost!" *The New Republic*. April 12, 1948.

——. "Henry Wallace's Column." *The New Republic*. April 19, 1948.

——. "On Testifying in Washington." *The New Republic*. April 26, 1948.

——. "American Fiasco in China." *The New Republic*. July 5, 1948.

——. "Farewell and Hail." *The New Republic*. July 19, 1948.

——. "Why a Third Party in 1948?" *Annals of the American Academy of Political and Social Science*. Vol. 259 (September 1948): 10–16.

——. "Where I Stand." *The New Leader*. August 26, 1950.

——. "Where I Was Wrong." *The Week Magazine*. September 7, 1952.

Wallaces' Farmer and Iowa Homestead. April 19, 1930.

Wallaces' Farmer and Iowa Homestead. October 11, 1930.

Wallaces' Farmer and Iowa Homestead. "Odds and Ends." October 29, 1932.

Wallaces' Farmer and Iowa Homestead. "Odds and Ends." November 26, 1932.

Wallaces' Farmer and Iowa Homestead. "Odds and Ends." December 3, 1933.

Washington Post. "New Deal Symbol." January 25, 1944.

Washington Post. "Pay-Off." January 23, 1945.

Washington Post. "Wallace's Reconversion." July 20, 1950.

Washington Post. "The Turning Worm." August 10, 1950.

Washington Post. "Wallace on China." November 16, 1950.

Washington Post. "Stifling Wallace." October 11, 1951.

Washington Post. "Facts vs. Fiction." October 20, 1951.

Washington Post. "Gen. Walter Bedell Smith." August 11, 1961.

Washington Post. "Ex–Vice President Henry Wallace Dies at 77 After Long Illness." November 19, 1965.

Washington Star. "Commerce Officials Reach Soviet with Wallace Trade Plans." July 7, 1946.

Wechsler, James A. "The Philadelphia Payoff." *The Progressive*. September 1948.

Wellerstein, Alex. "FDR and the Bomb." *Restricted Data: The Nuclear Secrecy Blog*. September 30, 2016. https://blog.nuclearsecrecy.com/2016/09/30/fdr-and-the-bomb/#identifier_6_6424.

White, Donald W. "The 'American Century' in World History." *Journal of World History*. Vol. 3, No. 1 (Spring 1992).

White, J. Patrick. "New Light on Yalta." *Far Eastern Survey*. Vol. 19, No. 11 (May 31, 1950): 105–12.

White, William S. "Senators and Wallace Clash on His Atlantic Pact Stand." *New York Times*. May 6, 1949.

Whitney, Robert F. "Wallace Explains." *New York Times*. September 21, 1946.

Wijkman, Per Magnus. "Henry A. Wallace as Vice President: The Last New Dealer." *The American Economist*. Vol. 65, No. 1 (February 22, 2019).

Wilentz, Sean. "Cherry-Picking Our History: Oliver Stone and Peter Kuznick's 'The Untold History of the United States.'" *New York Review of Books*. February 21, 2013.

Williams, Oliver P. "The Commodity Credit Corporation and the 1948 Presidential Election." *Midwest Journal of Political Science*. Vol. 1, No. 2 (August 1957): 111–24.

Wilson, Theodore A. "Parsifal in Politics: Henry Agard Wallace, Mysticism and the New Deal." *Irish Journal of American Studies*. Vol. 5 (1996): 1–31.

Wood, Lewis. "Wallace Reveals He Bade President Treat with Soviets." *New York Times*. September 18, 1946.

———. "Truman Silences Wallace Until After Paris Parley." *New York Times*. September 19, 1946.

———. "Agreement Is Reported." *New York Times*. September 20, 1946.

———. "The President Acts." *New York Times*. September 21, 1946.

Wool, Harold, and Calman Winegarden. "Recent Unemployment Trends: Historical Changes, Sources of Unemployment in 1946–48, Characteristics of the Unemployed, and Geographic Differentials." *Monthly Labor Review*. Vol. 70, No. 5 (1950): 485–96. http://www.jstor.org/stable/41832033.

Young, Kenneth Ray. "The Stilwell Controversy: A Bibliographical Review." *Military Affairs*. Vol. 39, No. 2 (April 1975): 66–68. https://www.jstor.org/stable/i308038.

Yukiko, Kitamura. "The Survey of the Japanese Publications About N.K. Rerikh," in *Rerikhi: Mify I fakty*. Red. Andreyev, Alexandr, Savelli, Dany. Nestor-Istorija, 2011. (*The Roerichs: The Myths and the Facts*, edited by Alexander Andreyev and Dany Savelli, Nestor-History, 2011), pp. 196–210.

"Za pobedu," "Slavnyi put' nashego zemliaka." 14 marta, 2009. (*For Victory*. "The Honorable Life Story of Our Fellow Countryman." March 14, 2009.) http·//www.gazeta-ibresi .cap.ru/Publication.aspx?id=119201.

Zemskov, V.N. "GULAG (Istoriko-sotsiologicheskii aspect),"—"Sotsiologicheskie issledovaniia," Nos. 6–7 (iun'–iul' 1991). (Zemskov, V.N. "GULAG [The Historical-Sociological Aspect]." *Soviet Union Sociological Studies*. Nos. 6–7 [June–July 1991].)

———. "Zakliuchennye, spetsposelentsy, ssyl'no poselentsy, ssyl'nye i vyslannye (Statistiko-geografícheskii aspect)."—"Istoriia SSSR," 1991, No. 5, ss. 151–65. ("Prisoners, Special Settlers, Exiled Settlers and Exiled [Statistical and Geographic Aspect]." *The History of the USSR*, No. 5 [1991: 151–165].)

Znamenski, Andrey. "The Sacred Union of the East: Great Depression, New Deal, and Roerich-Wallace Spiritual Utopia." Paper prepared for the "Arts and Letters Conference" at the University of North Georgia. March 2, 2014.

Speeches and Statements

Acheson, Dean. "Excerpts from Acheson's Speech to the National Press Club." January 12, 1950. https://web.viu.ca/davies/H102/Acheson.speech1950.htm.

Byrnes, James M. "Stuttgart Speech (Speech of Hope)." Stuttgart, Germany. September 6, 1946. https://ghdi.ghi-dc.org/sub_document.cfm?document_id=2300.

Churchill, Winston. "Sinews of Peace." Fulton, Missouri. March 5, 1946. https://www .nationalchurchillmuseum.org/sinews-of-peace-iron-curtain-speech.html.

Hepburn, Katharine. "Katharine Hepburn Progressive Party Speech 1947." May 19, 1947. YouTube. Posted December 9, 2015. https://www.youtube.com /watch?v=KN5q0Am_-e8.

Roosevelt, Franklin D. "Address at University of Virginia." June 10, 1940. https://www .presidency.ucsb.edu/documents/address-university-virginia.

———. "Annual Message to Congress (Four Freedoms)." January 6, 1941. https://69494391 .weebly.com/dr-win-the-war.html.

Wallace, Henry A. "The Century of the Common Man." New York City. May 8, 1942. https://www.americanrhetoric.com/speeches/henrywallacefreeworldassoc .htm#:~:text=Some%20have%20spoken%20of%20the,the%20common%20man%20 must%20live.

———. "Address Before Congress of American Soviet Friendship." New York City. November 8, 1942. http://www.ibiblio.org/pha/policy/1942/421108f.html.

———. "What We Fight for: Each Age Demands a New Freedom." Chicago, Illinois. September 11, 1943. http://www.ibiblio.org/pha/policy/1943/1943-09-11a.html.

———. "The Era of the Pacific." *Report on Trip to Serbia and China.* Broadcast over NBC. Seattle, Washington. July 9, 1944. http://www.ibiblio.org/pha/policy/1944/1944-07-09a.html.

———. "The Liberal Platform: Democratic Party Cannot Be Conservative." Delivered at the Democratic National Convention. Chicago, Illinois. July 20, 1944. Delivered at the Democratic State Platform Convention. Des Moines, Iowa. July 29, 1944. http://www.ibiblio.org/pha/policy/1944/1944-07-20d.html.

———. "Unity for Progress." University of Iowa, Iowa City, Iowa. December 29, 1946.

Vyshinsky, Andrey. "Vyshinsky at UN (1947)." September 1947. YouTube. Posted April 13, 2014. https://www.youtube.com/watch?v=6f7qIPODFfg.

Plays

Rocco, Danny. *Convention.* Directed by Shannon Fillon. New York: Irondale Center. June 7, 2019.

NOTES

1. Why Wallace?

1. The Brooklyn play *Convention* (Rocco [2019]), according to its creators, tells the "true-and-overlooked" story of Wallace's defeat in 1944: https://playbill.com/article/an-excl usive-look-at-convention-at-brooklyns-irondale-center.
2. Stone and Kuznick collaborated on a book and a film of the same name, *The Untold History of the United States* (Stone and Kuznick [2012]).
3. See, for example, Wilentz (February 21, 2013).
4. Reminiscences of Henry Agard Wallace, CCOH, pp. 4567–70.
5. Churchill, speech, "Sinews of Peace," March 5, 1946: https://www.nationalchurchillmu seum.org/sinews-of-peace-iron-curtain-speech.html.
6. See, in particular, Culver and Hyde (2000); White and Maze (1995); Walker (1976); Walton (1976); Schmidt (1960); Lord (1947); Schapsmeier and Schapsmeier (1968); Schapsmeier and Schapsmeier (1970); Markowitz (1973); and MacDougall (1965). Bliven (1970: 268–69). Ross (1968: 145).
7. "People with this condition may be socially awkward and have an all-absorbing interest in specific topics." Saraswati (January 3, 2018).
8. Adams (September 15, 1946).

2. Of Maize, Math, and Mysticism

1. Lord (1947: 107).
2. *Army and Navy Journal* (November 3, 1888).
3. The Iowa Board of Immigration (1870).
4. Lea (1836). Parker (1855). Lazell (1906). Van Vechten (1920).
5. Henry Wallace ("Uncle Henry") (1917: 82).
6. The McNary-Haugen Farm Relief Act, S. 4808, 70th Congress (1927) and S. 3555, 70th Congress (1928). Macdonald (March–April 1947). Bazelon (April 1947).
7. Lord (1947: 170).
8. Reminiscences of Henry Agard Wallace, CCOH, pp. 2–3, 27–29.
9. Reminiscences of Henry Agard Wallace, CCOH, p. 4.
10. Lord (1947: 143–50).
11. Reminiscences of Henry Agard Wallace, CCOH, p. 17.
12. Culver and Hyde (2000: 33).
13. Reminiscences of Henry Agard Wallace, CCOH, pp. 41–42. Culver and Hyde (2000: 30–35). Lord (1947: 158, 183).
14. Trine (1897 [1908]: 25).
15. Reminiscences of Henry Agard Wallace, CCOH, p. 42.
16. Larson and Witham (July 23, 1998).
17. Wallace, lecture at the Pacific School of Religion, Berkeley, California, "Church and School in Democratic Capitalism," February 23, 1938, in Box: Series 10, Box 35, Henry A. Wallace Papers, University of Iowa.

18. Walker (1976: 51).
19. Carpenter (March 1939).
20. See, for example, Reminiscences of Henry Agard Wallace, CCOH, pp. 47–49.
21. See, in particular, James (1902).
22. James (1896 [1912]): https://www.gutenberg.org/files/26659/26659-h/26659-h.htm. For an excellent critique of James' "ethics of belief," see Pigliucci (August 31, 2022): https://philosophyasawayoflife.medium.com/the-ethics-of-belief-f1d459c572e3.
23. James (1896 [1912]).
24. Correspondence from Henry Wallace (grandfather) to Henry A. Wallace dated October 7, 1909, Henry A. Wallace correspondence [reel 1], 1888–April 1929—Ia01-0005, Henry A. Wallace Collection, University of Iowa.
25. Culver and Hyde (2000: 36).
26. Wallace (1944: 97).
27. Culver and Hyde (2000: 37–40).
28. Hellman (April 11, 1976).
29. Culver and Hyde (2000: 41–42).
30. Culver and Hyde (2000: 49).
31. Culver and Hyde (2000: 50–53).
32. Russell Lord, introduction to Henry A. Wallace, *Democracy Reborn* (1944: 8).
33. Wallace (1920: 108–10).
34. Lord (1947: 234). Culver and Hyde (2000: 56–57).
35. Correspondence from Henry A. Wallace to L. Edward Johndro dated October 24, 1931, Henry A. Wallace correspondence [reel 10], October 6, 1931–Nov. 25, 1931—Ia10-0238, Henry A. Wallace Collection, University of Iowa. Culver and Hyde (2000: 82–83, 90).
36. Wallace (1934 [*Statesmanship and Religion*]: 47).
37. Culver and Hyde (2000: 78–81).
38. Reminiscences of Henry Agard Wallace, CCOH, p. 117.
39. Walker (1976: 19).
40. Correspondence from Henry A. Wallace to L. Edward Johndro dated February 24, 1932, Henry A. Wallace correspondence [reel 13], February 23, 1932–April 13, 1932—Ia13-0029, Henry A. Wallace Collection, University of Iowa.
41. Reminiscences of Henry Agard Wallace, CCOH, p. 4.
42. Reminiscences of Henry Agard Wallace, CCOH, p. 117.
43. Walker (1976: 11, 15).
44. Walker (1976: 13, 17).
45. Correspondence from Henry A. Wallace to Charles Brand dated July 7, 1930, Henry A. Wallace correspondence [reel 3], July 1930–October 1930—Ia3-0028, Henry A. Wallace Collection, University of Iowa. Walker (1976: 20–21).
46. Walker (1976: 13, 16).
47. Walker (1976: 13, 25–26).
48. *Wallaces' Farmer and Iowa Homestead* (October 11), 1930 (italics added).
49. Walker (1976: 27, 28, 30).
50. *Wallaces' Farmer and Iowa Homestead* (April 19, 1930). Walker (1976: 28).
51. Scott (1998: 202–3).

3. The Farmer's New Deal

1. Dallek (2017: 113–15, 121).
2. The rival paper, *Iowa Homestead*, had been owned by Dante M. Pierce (Schapsmeier and Schapsmeier [1968: 121–22]).
3. Correspondence from Henry A. Wallace to Henry Jr. Morgenthau dated July 28, 1932, Henry A. Wallace correspondence [reel 15], June 14, 1932–August 1932—Ia15-0374, Henry A. Wallace Collection, University of Iowa. Schapsmeier and Schapsmeier (1968: 152).
4. Schapsmeier and Schapsmeier (1968: 153–55). Gilbert (2015: 32).
5. *Wallaces' Farmer and Iowa Homestead* (October 29, 1932: 565).
6. Schapsmeier and Schapsmeier (1968: 158, 161). *Wallaces' Farmer and Iowa Homestead* (November 26, 1932: 517).
7. See, for example, Reminiscences of Henry Agard Wallace, CCOH, p. 191.
8. Schapsmeier and Schapsmeier (1968: 160). Gilbert (2015: 5, 46).
9. Correspondence from Raymond Moley to Henry A. Wallace dated November 29, 1932, Henry A. Wallace correspondence [reel 17], October 19, 1932–December 9, 1932—Ia17-0818, Henry A. Wallace Collection, University of Iowa.
10. Decades later, Wallace remained convinced that Morgenthau opposed his nomination as agriculture secretary (Reminiscences of Henry Agard Wallace, CCOH, p. 169, 182.) Culver and Hyde (2000: 105–6).
11. See, for example, Reminiscences of Henry Agard Wallace, CCOH, p. 184.
12. Correspondence from Franklin D. Roosevelt to Henry A. Wallace dated February 3, 1933, Henry A. Wallace correspondence [reel 59], December 1931–1964—Ia59-0600, Henry A. Wallace Collection, University of Iowa.
13. Wilson (1996: 11). Henry A. Wallace to Daniel Wallace, April 6, 1920, Box 1, Henry A. Wallace Papers, Henry A. Wallace Collection, University of Iowa.
14. Moley credits Wallace's procrastination over accepting the appointment to standard "etiquette to be observed on the receipt of an offer of high office." But Wallace was hardly one to stand on "etiquette." (Moley [1939: 123–24]).
15. Correspondence from Henry A. Wallace to Franklin D. Roosevelt [document undated], 1933, Henry A. Wallace correspondence [reel 59], December 1931–1964—Ia59-0601, Henry A. Wallace Collection, University of Iowa. Moley (1949: 80). Reminiscences of Henry Agard Wallace, CCOH, p. 190. Culver and Hyde (2000: 107–8). Schapsmeier and Schapsmeier (1968: 161–62).
16. United States Department of Agriculture, Agricultural Marketing Service (November 1953: 2).
17. Walker (1976: 37).
18. Hurt (2002: 44–51, 63, 66).
19. Schlesinger (1958: 42–44).
20. Walker (1976: 35).
21. Reminiscences of Henry Agard Wallace, CCOH, p. 86.
22. Culver and Hyde (2000: 76).
23. Reminiscences of Henry Agard Wallace, CCOH, p. 281.
24. Culver and Hyde (2000: 112–13, 120, 187–89).
25. Reminiscences of Henry Agard Wallace, CCOH, p. 512.
26. Hurt (2002: 67–68).
27. Moley (1939: 84).

28. Tugwell (1977: 53, 68).
29. American Farm Bureau Federation (March 21, 1933).
30. *New York Herald Tribune* (March 18, 1933).
31. Ezekiel (May 11, 1933).
32. Schlesinger (1958: 40, 46).
33. Leuchtenberg (1963: 73).
34. Wallace, (1934 [*New Frontiers*]: 174–75).
35. See, for example, Tamer (March 15, 2018); and Monnay (August 29, 2021).
36. White (2014: 9).
37. Leuchtenberg (1963: 73).
38. Dallek (2017: 145).
39. Reminiscences of Henry Agard Wallace, CCOH, p. 263.
40. Tugwell (1933: 228). Krebs (July 24, 1979).
41. Paarlberg (1989).
42. Dallek (2017: 146).
43. Hurt (2002: 73–74).
44. Reminiscences of Henry Agard Wallace, CCOH, p. 282.
45. The first lady's letters were dated June 7 and June 15, 1939. White (2014: 12–13).
46. Reminiscences of Henry Agard Wallace, CCOH, p. 438.
47. Wallace, diary entry, February 2, 1935, reprinted in Lowitt (July 1979: 613).
48. Wallace, diary entry, February 1, 1935, reprinted in Lowitt (July 1979: 611).
49. Wallace, diary entry, February 2, 1935, reprinted in Lowitt (July 1979: 612–13).
50. McDonald (1947: 42).
51. Gilbert (2015: 85). Hurt (2002: 4).
52. Reminiscences of Henry Agard Wallace, CCOH, p. 457.
53. See, for example, Scott (1998: 200, 267).
54. Schapsmeier and Schapsmeier (1968: 199–200).
55. Boyle (February 1936).
56. Schapsmeier and Schapsmeier (1968: 202).
57. Schlesinger (1958: 80) (italics added).
58. Schlesinger (1958: 79).
59. Wallace diary entry, February 2, 1935, reprinted in Lowitt (July 1979: 614).
60. Wallace diary entry, February 11, 1935, reprinted in Lowitt (July 1979: 619).
61. Schlesinger (1958: 80).
62. Wallace diary entry, February 7, 1935, reprinted in Lowitt (July 1979: 617).
63. Wallace diary entry, February 5, 1935, reprinted in Lowitt (July 1979: 616).
64. Correspondence from Henry A. Wallace to Franklin D. Roosevelt dated September 29, 1933, Henry A. Wallace correspondence [reel 18], December 10, 1932–September 1933—Ia18-0995, Henry A. Wallace Collection, University of Iowa; enclosed, Correspondence from Henry A. Wallace to Cordell Hull dated September 29, 1933, Henry A. Wallace correspondence [reel 18], December 10, 1932–September 1933—Ia18-0996–Ia18-0997, Henry A. Wallace Collection, University of Iowa.
65. Walker (1976: 36).
66. Walker (1976: 38–39).
67. Bureau of Agricultural Economics (November 1941: 1). Hurt (2002: 76).
68. Garver and Trelogan (August 1936).
69. Hurt (2002: 76).
70. Hausman, Rhode, and Wieland (2019).

71. Davis (1935: 366–68). Garver and Trelogan (August 1936: 602). Hausman, Rhode, and Wieland (2019).
72. Garver and Trelogan (August 1936: 614–15).
73. Wallace (1934 [*New Frontiers*]: 174) (italics added).
74. Davis (February 1935: 7–8).
75. Lyon et al. (1935). Selgin (January 11, 2021).
76. Boyle (February 1936).
77. White (2014: 10).
78. White (2014: 11).
79. Wallace (1934 [*New Frontiers*]: 177–78).
80. Bean (1930). Davis (February 1935: 1–14).
81. Hausman, Rhode, and Wieland (2019).
82. Friedman and Schwartz (1963).
83. Edwards (July 2015: 29).
84. Leuchtenberg (1963: 38).
85. Jalil and Rua (2015: 80–82).
86. "The act invades the reserved rights of the states. It is a statutory plan to regulate and control agricultural production, a matter beyond the powers delegated to the federal government. The tax, the appropriation of the funds raised, and the direction for their disbursement, are but parts of the plan. They are but means to an unconstitutional end." *United States v. Butler*, 297 U.S. 1 (1936).
87. Wallace, radio address, "The New Farm Legislation," March 3, 1936, in Box: Series 10, Box 29, Henry A. Wallace Papers, University of Iowa (italics added).
88. Culver and Hyde (2000: 162).
89. Wallace (1936: 87, 92–93, 187–27, 272–325).
90. Schapsmeier and Schapsmeier (1968: 221).
91. Wallace (1934 [*New Frontiers*]: 263) (italics added).
92. Wallace (1934 [*America Must Choose*]: 12–13) (italics added).
93. Wallace (1934 [*Statesmanship and Religion*]: 93–94, 96–97, 100–101, 104) (italics added).
94. Wallace (1934 [*New Frontiers*]: 274).
95. Reminiscences of Henry Agard Wallace, CCOH, p. 249.
96. Wallace (1934 [*New Frontiers*]: 263).
97. Gilbert (2015: 1).
98. Gilbert (2015: 6).
99. Gilbert (2015: 18).
100. Gilbert (2015: 48).
101. Gilbert (2015: 155).
102. Gilbert (2015: 154).
103. See Richards (1934).
104. Schlesinger (1958: 72–73).
105. Irwin (1998).
106. Schapsmeier and Schapsmeier (1968: 238, 241–43).
107. Hurt (2002: 92).
108. Culver and Hyde (2000: 170).
109. Schapsmeier and Schapsmeier (1968: 204).
110. *USA FACTS* (June 4, 2019 [September 19, 2020]). (Graph—Government payments [excluding crop insurance payments] to farms): https://usafacts.org/articles/federal-farm-subsidies-what-data-says/.

111. Leuchtenburg (2009: 256).
112. Between 1930 and 1940, gross farm income rose from $11.2 billion to $11.3 billion, and net farm income rose from $4.2 billion to $4.4 billion. The parity price index fell from 83 to 81. Hurt (2002: 93).
113. Leuchtenburg (2009: 256).
114. Rasmussen (December 1983: 1161).
115. Dallek (2017: 146).
116. Hurt (2002: 93–96).

4. The Guru and the New Country

1. Frances Grant, letter to Henry A. Wallace, April 4, 1927, folder 31, Box 15, FGP, RUSC. Citation from Rosov II (2004: ch. 3, footnote 3). Frances Grant, "Henry Wallace's First Visit to the Roerich Museum," p. 9, folder 83, Box 14, FGP, RUSC. *Wallaces' Farmer and Iowa Homestead* (December 3, 1933). Frances R. Grant to Wallace, October 25 1929, Box 2, Henry A. Wallace Papers, University of Iowa. Wilson (1996: 9) dates Wallace's first visit to the museum as being in October 1929, and Walker (1989) dates it to 1928, but on the basis of Rosov and Grant these appear to be an error: it was April 1927.
2. It seems highly unlikely that the decidedly unromantic Wallace, in spite of the unusually personal nature of his letters to Frances Grant, and his many private meetings with her, carried on any romantic relationship with her. Wallace's letters to Helena Roerich, whom he never met, were similar in tone and substance.
3. Wilson (1996: 14).
4. The Archive of the Roerich Museum, Fond 01:2, file 144 and file 535; Fond 02-2, file 386 and file 386a; Fond 07, file 90 and file 133; Fond 08, file 128 [copies in folder "Guru Letters" (Henry A. Wallace), Container 9, Samuel I. Rosenman Papers, (FDRL)].
5. Reminiscences of Paul H. Appleby, CCOH, 1957, interview 1, side 2, January 12, 1952, pp. 35–37.
6. Culver and Hyde (2000: 96–98).
7. Brinton (1920).
8. Sfeckas (April 9, 2011).
9. Fosdick (2002: 316).
10. Andreyev (2014: 87–88), citing Roerich (2011: 53, 54, 55–56, 58).
11. Andreyev (2014: 93–94), citing Rosov I (2002: 45).
12. Nicholas, Helena, and Svyatoslav sailed from New York City on May 8, 1923. They stayed in Europe until November 17, when they sailed to India, arriving on December 2. Fosdick (2002: 195).
13. Fosdick (2002: 206).
14. Fosdick (2002: 208, 210).
15. Rosov I (2002) and Andreyev (2014: 198) write that Roerich offered "intelligence" on British activities, but that is unsubstantiated.
16. Memorandum [Reference] prepared by The Archive of the Foreign Policy of the USSR, The Archive of the Roerich Museum, Fond 08, file 55, pp. 1–2.
17. N.N. Krestinsky to G.V. Chicherin, Berlin, January 2, 1924, AVP RF, Fond 04, op. 13, P 87, file 50117, p. 13A. Rosov (2005).
18. See *Equitable Envoy* (February 1946) for one description of the expedition: https://roerichs museum.website.yandexcloud.net/DE/DE-042.pdf (in The Archive of the Roerich Museum, Fond 08, file 42). Roerich (1931).

19. Helena Roerich, diary entry, May 21, 1925, notebook 22, *Diaries of Helena Roerich*. It can be viewed here: http://lebendige-ethik.net/index.php/biblioteka/dnevniki-e-i-rerikh/192-tetrad-22-21-05-1925-12-08-1926.
20. Chossudovsky (1974).
21. Helena Roerich, diary entry, April 5, 1926, notebook 22, *Diaries of Helena Roerich*. It is possible, though we have no evidence, that the "Mahatmas' message" was transcribed by George Roerich, who could read and write in the Tibetan language. The Mahatmas' letter to G.V. Chicherin, 1925, AVP RF, Fond of the Department of the Far East, NKID, op. 1, P 4, file 25, p. 8; typed Russian translation copy at The Archive of the Roerich Museum, Fond 08, file 261; the text is identical with the writing as "given" to Helena Roerich, described in the entry for April 5, 1926. Memorandum prepared by The Archive of the Foreign Policy of the USSR, "On the meetings of N.K. Roerich with the Soviet diplomatic representatives in 1924–1927," The Archive of the Roerich Museum, Fond 08, file 55, p. 5.
22. That plan was transcribed by Helena, as (allegedly) dictated by Morya. Helena Roerich, diary entry, March 18, 1926, notebook 22, *Diaries of Helena Roerich*.
23. Memorandum [Reference] prepared by The Archive of the Foreign Policy of the USSR, "On the meetings of N.K. Roerich with the Soviet diplomatic representatives in 1924–1927," The Archive of the Roerich Museum, Fond 08, file 55, pp. 5–6; original AVP RF citation: G.V. Chicherin letter to V.M. Molotov, June 13, 1926, AVP RF, Fond of the Department of the Far East, NKID, op. 1, P 4, file 35, p. 6.
24. Rosov I (2002: ch. 4, endnotes 9, 10), citing L. Horch, M. Lichtmann, F. Grant, Letter to the Main Concession Committee, May 27, 1925, GA RF, Fond 8350, op. 1, file 730, pp. 3–13, typed, English; Memorandum of the Beluha Corporation, New York, the USA, regarding the concessions in South-Western Altai, May 1, 1925, GA RF, Fond 8350, op. 1, file 730, pp. 14–24. Fosdick (2002: 206, 208, 221, 224, 229, 231, 239, 240).
25. Rosov I (2002: ch. 3, endnotes 13, 14), citing Certificate of Incorporation of Beluha Corporation, November 11, 1924, NRM; Certificate of Increase of Capital Stock of Beluha Corporation, November 25, 19 1924, NRM.
26. Letter from the vice president of the Nicholas Roerich Museum in New York, Maurice Lichtmann, to the Main Concession Committee of the Council of People's Commissars of the USSR about the expedition to the Altai of the Museum staff, May 6, 1928, The Archive of the Roerich Museum, Fond 08, file 8. Rosov I (2002: ch. 3, endnote 2), citing Z.G. Fosdick (Lichtmann), Diary 1924–1925, p. 250, notebook 2, NRM.
27. A.E. Minkin, member of the GKK to NKID, Concession Commission of the Commissariat of Agriculture, June 15, 1925, AVP RF, Fond 04, op. 58, P 377, file 56190, p. 204 (original). Published in *Soviet-American Relations* II (2002).
28. Extract from protocol No. 29 of the meeting of the Smaller Main Concession Committee under the SMK, July 12, 1926, GA RF, Fond 8350, op. 1, file 729, p. 81.
29. Helena Roerich, diary entries, April 17 and April 25, 1927, notebook 24, *Diaries of Helena Roerich*. M.I. Skobelev, M.S. Yapolsky, et al., letter to M. Lichtmann, July 14, 1926, GA RF, Fond 8350, op. 1, file 729, p. 83.
30. Helena Roerich, diary entries, September 17, 18, 26, and 27, 1926, notebook 23, *Diaries of Helena Roerich*.
31. Helena Roerich, diary entries, October 19, 25, 26, 28, 30, and 31, 1926, notebook 23, *Diaries of Helena Roerich*.
32. Helena Roerich, diary entry, April 17, 1927, notebook 24, *Diaries of Helena Roerich*; Helena Roerich, diary entry, June 3, 1927, notebook 24, *Diaries of Helena Roerich*.
33. Golodnikova (2009: 9).

34. Rosov (2008: 41–42, 46). Extract from protocol No. 29 of the plenum of the Main Concession Committee from June 9, 1927, GA RF, Fond 8350, op. 3, file 246, p. 8.

35. Letter from the vice president of the Nicholas Roerich Museum in New York, Maurice Lichtmann, to the Main Concession Committee of the Council of People's Commissars of the USSR about the expedition to the Altai of the Museum staff, May 6, 1928, The Archive of the Roerich Museum, Fond 08, file 8, p. 5.; original at GA RF, Fond 8350, op. 1, file 729, p. 193.

36. L.L. Horch, Letter to the GKK, September 24, 1928, GA RF, Fond 8350, op. 1, file 729, .p. 202.

37. M.M. Lichtmann, Letter to the Main Concession Committee, July 8, 1929, GA RF, Fond 8350, op. 1, file 729, p. 212.

38. Fosdick (2002: 421–23).

39. Nicholas Roerich Museum (New York, N.Y.) (1929), sourced from the Smithsonian Libraries and Archives.

40. Henry A. Wallace to Frances Grant, April 15, 1929, folder 31, Box 15, FGP, RUSC.

41. Henry A. Wallace to Dr. Nicholas Roerich, November 28, 1931, The Archive of the Roerich Museum, Fond 01-2, file 535, p. 1.

42. Fosdick (2002: 515–16).

43. Lewis Horch to the Secretary of State, April 17, 1925, The Archive of the Roerich Museum, Fond 08, file 5, p. 1.

44. The first mortgage of $2 million was signed on May 31, 1928 to begin construction and the second of $500,000 on July 1, 1928. Financial statements of the Roerich Museum in New York, 1928–1934, The Archive of the Roerich Museum, Fond 07, file 64, pp. 12, 14–17.

45. For example, see L.L. Horch to N.K. Roerich, April 22, 1931, The Archive of the Moscow Roerich Museum, Fond 01-2, file 568, p. 53.

46. "Logvan," Sina recorded way back in 1924, referring to Horch by his occult name, "said in passing that he was asking N.K. [Nicholas] to give him a letter in which he thanked Logvan for 10-year delay with *repaying debt*! That is that N.K. owed him some sum! N.K. and myself sensed some hidden danger immediately." Fosdick (2002: 229, 231) (italics added).

47. Fosdick (2002: 530).

48. L.L. Horch's telegram to all members of the Bondholders' Committee, April 1, 1932, The Archive of the Roerich Museum, Fond 07, file 081, pp. 29–30.

49. L.L. Horch to the Holders of the Bonds, July 1, 1932, The Archive of the Roerich Museum, Fond 07, file 081, p. 33.

50. *New York Times* (July 18, 1930); Nicholas Roerich (2002). Andreyev and Savelli (2011: 121–36).

51. Andreyev (2014: 357).

52. The full name was Urusvati Himalayan Research Institute of the Roerich Museum.

53. Andreyev (2014: 359–62).

54. Roerich (1993: 77).

55. Helena Roerich, diary entry, May 24, 1933, notebook 37, *Diaries of Helena Roerich*.

56. Helena Roerich, diary entry, June 20, 1933, notebook 37, *Diaries of Helena Roerich*.

57. See, for example, Wallace (1944 [*Democracy Reborn*]: 228).

58. Helena Roerich, diary entry, August 18, 1933, notebook 37, *Diaries of Helena Roerich*.

59. Helena Roerich, diary entry, June 20, 1933, notebook 37, *Diaries of Helena Roerich*.

60. Helena Roerich, diary entry, December 22, 1933, notebook 38, *Diaries of Helena Roerich*.

61. See, for example, Herrington (June 18, 2014).

62. Helena Roerich, diary entry, November 11, 1933, notebook 38, *Diaries of Helena Roerich*.

63. Helena Roerich, diary entry, December 6, 1933, notebook 38, *Diaries of Helena Roerich*.

64. G. (Galahad/Henry A. Wallace) to M. (Modra/Frances Grant), January 8, 1934, The Archive of the Roerich Museum, Fond 07, file 48, p. 53.

65. Henry A. Wallace to Frances Grant, July 1, 1933, Samuel I. Rosenman Papers, FDRL.

66. Correspondence from Henry A. Wallace to Dal Lee dated February 6, 1951, Henry A. Wallace Correspondence [reel 48], February 1951–August 1952—Ia48-0017, Henry A. Wallace Collection, University of Iowa.

67. Znamenski (March 2, 2014: 15–16).

68. G. (Galahad/Henry A. Wallace) to M. (Modra/Frances Grant), undated, February (?) 1934, The Archive of the Moscow Roerich Museum, Fond 07, file 048.

69. Henry A. Wallace to Frances Grant, July 1, 1933, Samuel I. Rosenman Papers, FDR Library.

70. Cordell Hull to Henry A. Wallace, October 18, 1933, The Archive of the Roerich Museum, Fond 07, file 048, pp. 118–19.

71. Rosov II (2004: 88), citing Sina Lichtmann to Helena and Nicholas Roerich, December 13, 1933, The Archive of the Roerich Museum, Fond 01-2, file 548, p. 208.

72. Helena Roerich, diary entry, December 19, 1933, notebook 38, *Diaries of Helena Roerich*.

73. Knowles A. Ryerson Papers, University of California, Davis Library, p. 98.

74. Knowles A. Ryerson to Henry A. Wallace, October 14, 1934, The Archive of the Roerich Museum, Fond 07, file 70, p. 101.

75. G.[Galahad] to M.[Modra], March 1934, The Archive of the Roerich Museum, Fond 07, file 48, p. 8.

76. Henry Wallace to Nicholas Roerich, March 16, 1934, folder 32, Box 15, FGP, RUSC. Wilson (1996: 18). Henry A. Wallace to Frances Grant, undated, Box 13, Samuel I. Rosenman Papers, FDR Library.

77. G[alahad] to Dear Guru, March 12, 1933, The Archive of the Roerich Museum, Fond 07, file 48, p. 172.

78. See, for example, Henry A. Wallace to Frances Grant, undated, likely late May 1933, The Archive of the Roerich Museum, Fond 07, file 48, pp. 97, 98. See also Henry A. Wallace to Madam and Professor Roerich, July 2, 1933, The Archive of the Roerich Museum, Fond 07, file 90, p. 13; another copy in folder 34, Box 15, FGP, RUSC (italics added).

79. Modra [Frances Grant] to Nicholas Roerich, July 4, 1933, The Archive of the Roerich Museum, Fond 01-2, file 278, pp. 27–29.

80. Modra [Frances Grant] to N.K. Roerich, July 10, 1933, The Archive of the Roerich Museum, Fond 01-2, file 279, pp. 93–94.

81. Modra [Frances Grant] to N.K. Roerich, October 26, 1933, The Archive of the Roerich Museum, Fond 01-2, file 279, pp. 127–28.

82. Correspondence from Henry A. Wallace to Franklin D. Roosevelt dated September 29, 1933, Henry A. Wallace correspondence [reel 18], December 10, 1932–September 1933—Ia18-0993–Ia18-0995, Henry A. Wallace Collection, University of Iowa.

83. Modra [Frances Grant] to N.K. Roerich, December 28, 1933, The Archive of the Roerich Museum, Fond 01-2, file 279, p. 148.

84. G.[Galahad] to M.[Modra], undated (late 1933 or early 1934), The Archive of the Roerich Museum, Fond 08, file 48, p. 81.

85. Modra [Frances Grant] to N.K. Roerich, January 3, 1934, The Archive of the Roerich Museum, Fond 01-2, file 279, pp. 152–53 (italics added).

86. G.[Galahad] to M.[Modra], undated (February 1934), The Archive of the Roerich Museum, Fond 07, file 48, p. 131.

87. Rosov II (2004: ch. 4), citing N.K. Roerich, letter to V.K. Roerich, October 5, 1933, NRM; V.K. Roerich, Manchurian Agricultural Cooperative, folders 30–31, Box 14, FGP, RUSC. Fosdick (2002: 610).

88. Fosdik (2002: 608–9). Andreyev (2014: 372).

89. Helena Roerich, diary entry for September 22, 1932, notebook 35, *Diaries of Helena Roerich*.

90. Andreyev (2014: 373–74). Andreyev and Savelli (2011: 196).

91. Fosdick (2002: 619–20).

92. George Roerich's appointment approved on April 7, 1934, Ryerson Plant Industry to Dr. George Roerich, Washington, April 7, 1934, The Archive of the Roerich Museum, Fond 08, file 121.

93. Henry A. Wallace to George Roerich, undated (mid-April 1934), The Archive of the Roerich Museum, Fond 07, file 48, pp. 61–69. Walker (March 1989).

94. Knowles A. Ryerson to Henry A. Wallace, October 13, 1934, The Archive of the Roerich Museum, Fond 07, file 070, p. 98. Culver and Hyde (2000: 137–38). Walker (March 1989).

95. Henry Wallace to George Roerich, undated (c. April 18, 1934), The Archive of the Roerich Museum, Fond 08, file 121, p. 111.

96. G.[Galahad] to M.[Modra], undated, likely earlier than May 17, 1934, The Archive of the Roerich Museum, Fond 07, File 48, p. 82 (italics added).

97. Helena Roerich, diary entry, May 15, 1934, notebook 39, *Diaries of Helena Roerich* (italics added).

98. Fosdik (2002: 667). Andreyev (2014: 377).

99. Dispatch from the U.S. embassy in Peking to the U.S. Department of State regarding the activities of N.K. Roerich and other members of the expedition from April 28 to August 2, 1934, The Archive of the Roerich Museum, Fond 08, file 88, pp. 1–11.

100. Andreyev (2014: 377).

101. Telegram (No. 95) from Cordell Hull to the American Ambassador at Tokyo dated June 11, 1934, The Archive of the Roerich Museum, Fond 07, file 070, p. 15. McCannon (2022: 396). White and Maze (1995: 88). Walker (1989). Culver and Hyde (2000: 138).

102. McCannon (2022: 401).

103. Correspondence from H.G. MacMillan to Knowles A. Ryerson dated June 5, 1934, Henry A. Wallace correspondence [reel 19], October 1933–July 1935—Ia19-0263, Henry A. Wallace Collection, University of Iowa.

104. White and Maze (1995: 88). Andreyev (2014: 381–82).

105. Henry Wallace to Frances Grant, undated (June 1934), The Archive of the Roerich Museum, Fond 07, file 48, p. 122.

106. Nicholas Roerich, letter, July 8, 1934, The Archive of the Roerich Museum, Fond 07, file 50, p. 50/33.

107. Correspondence from Georges de Roerich to Knowles A. Ryerson dated June 5, 1934, Henry A. Wallace correspondence [reel 19], October 1933–July 1935—Ia19-0264, Henry A. Wallace Collection, University of Iowa.

108. Walker (1989). Culver and Hyde (2000: 139).

109. Nicholas Roerich to "My dear ones," June 23, 1934, The Archive of the Roerich Museum, Fond 07, file 50, p. 32 (italics added).

110. Correspondence from H.G. MacMillan to Arthur Garrels dated June 26, 1934, Henry A. Wallace correspondence [reel 19], October 1933–July 1935—Ia19-0326, Henry A. Wallace Collection, University of Iowa. Correspondence from H.G. MacMillan to Arthur Garrels

dated July 20, 1934, Henry A. Wallace correspondence [reel 19], October 1933–July 1935—Ia19-0362–Ia19-0365, Henry A. Wallace Collection, University of Iowa. Correspondence from H.G. MacMillan to Knowles A. Ryerson dated July 20, 1934, Henry A. Wallace correspondence [reel 19], October 1933–July 1935—Ia19-0358, Henry A. Wallace Collection, University of Iowa. Correspondence from H.G. MacMillan to Knowles A. Ryerson dated June 9, 1934, Henry A. Wallace correspondence [reel 19], October 1933–July 1935—Ia19-0273–Ia19-0282, Henry A. Wallace Collection, University of Iowa.

111. N.K. Roerich to the staff of the New York Museum, July 26, 1934, The Archive of the Roerich Museum, Fond 07, file 24, p. 7.

112. Helena Roerich, diary entry, July 1, 1934, notebook 39, *Diaries of Helena Roerich*.

113. Henry A. Wallace to Helena Roerich, received on August 7, 1934, The Archive of the Roerich Museum, Fond 02-2, file 386, p. 1 (italics added).

114. *Harbinskoe Vremya* (Harbin Times), June 6, 1934 [issue #147], The Archive of the Roerich Museum, Fond 08, file 181b.

115. The expedition gear was bought, almost certainly secondhand, at a cheap Harbin store owned by a Mr. M.A. Shitukhin: http://myharbin.name/magaziny/252-spisok-torgovykh-predpriyatij, The Archive of the Roerich Museum, Fond 08, file 64 and file 65.

116. Nicholas Roerich, letter to America, August 19, 1934, The Russian State Museum of Orient, Roerich Memorial Room, Box "The letters of N.K. and Yu.K. Rerikhs to America," file 36, p. 2/reverse. Nicholas Roerich to the staff of the New York Museum, August 19, 1934, The Archive of the Roerich Museum, Fond 07, file 36, pp. 1–4.

117. Correspondence from Nicholas Roerich to Henry A. Wallace dated October 1, 1934, Henry A. Wallace correspondence [reel 19], October 1933–July 1935—Ia19-0518–Ia19-0524, Henry A. Wallace Collection, University of Iowa.

118. Correspondence from Henry A. Wallace to Nicholas Roerich dated August 6, 1934, Henry A. Wallace correspondence [reel 19], October 1933–July 1935—Ia19-0414, Henry A. Wallace Collection, University of Iowa.

119. Ryerson to MacMillan, August 11, 1934, The Archive of the Roerich Museum, Fond 08, file 121, p. 36. White and Maze (1995: 91).

120. Nicholas Roerich, letter, August 27, 1934, The Archive of the Roerich Museum, Fond 07, file 50, p. 50/40. Nicholas Roerich to the staff of the New York Museum, August 19, 1934, The Archive of the Roerich Museum, Fond 07, file 036, pp. 3–4.

121. Nicholas Roerich, letter to America, August 19, 1934, The Russian State Museum of Orient, Roerich Memorial Room, Box "The letters of N.K. and Yu.K. Rerikhs to America," file 36, p. 2/reverse; handwritten. Nicholas Roerich to the staff of the New York Museum, August 19, 1934, The Archive of the Roerich Museum, Fond 07, file 036, p. 4.

122. Helena Roerich to Henry A. Wallace, September 3, 1934, The Archive of the Roerich Museum, Fond 02-2, file 132, pp. 2–3.

123. M. Modra/Frances Grant to Mother [Helena Roerich], October 5, 1934, The Archive of the Roerich Museum, Fond 02-2, file 208, p. 143.

124. "Report to Trustees: Washington Trip," September 18, 1934, The Archive of the Roerich Museum, Fond 08, file 131. M.[Modra/Frances Grant] to Mother [Helena Roerich], September 8, 20, 27, 28, and October 5, 1934, The Archive of the Roerich Museum, Fond 02-2, file 208, pp. 131, 135–38, 141–43. Sina Fosdick, Report to the New York Roerich Museum Board on the outcome of the negotiations of Frances Grant with Henry Wallace on the recall of the American Botanists from the Manchurian expedition of Nicholas Roerich, The Archive of the Roerich Museum, Fond 08, file 131, pp. 1–2.

125. Correspondence from Knowles A. Ryerson to H.G. MacMillan dated September 18,

1934, Henry A. Wallace correspondence [reel 19], October 1933–July 1935—Ia19-0484, Henry A. Wallace Collection, University of Iowa.

126. Correspondence from Henry A. Wallace to H.G. MacMillan dated September 20, 1934, Henry A. Wallace correspondence [reel 19], October 1933–July 1935—Ia19-0488, Henry A. Wallace Collection, University of Iowa. Correspondence from Henry A. Wallace to Nicholas Roerich dated September 20, 1934, Henry A. Wallace correspondence [reel 19], October 1933–July 1935—Ia19-0490, Henry A. Wallace Collection, University of Iowa.

127. Correspondence from Henry A. Wallace to Nicholas Roerich dated September 27, 1934, Henry A. Wallace correspondence [reel 19], October 1933–July 1935—Ia19-0510, Henry A. Wallace Collection, University of Iowa.

128. M.[Modra/Frances Grant] to M. [Mother/Helena Roerich], The Archive of the Roerich Museum, Fond 02-2, file 208, p. 138.

129. M.[Modra/Frances Grant] to M. [Mother/Helena Roerich], The Archive of the Roerich Museum, Fond 02-2, file 208, pp. 141–43.

130. Henry A. Wallace to Helena Roerich, September 30, 1934, The Archive of the Roerich Museum, Fond 02-2, file 386, pp. 2, 5–6.

131. Helena Roerich to Francis Grant, October 3, 1934, The Archive of the Roerich Museum, Fond 02-2, file 386, pp. 2, 5.

132. M.[Modra/Frances Grant] to M. [Mother/Helena Roerich], October 5, 1934, The Archive of the Roerich Museum, Fond 02-2, file 208, p. 142/reverse.

133. Sina Lichtmann's Report to Trustees, September 18, 1934, The Archive of the Roerich Museum, Fond 02-2, file 131, pp. 2. Henry A. Wallace to Col. Saito, September 27, 1934, The Archive of the Roerich Museum, Fond 08, file 132, p. 1.

134. Henry A. Wallace to Helena Roerich, October 10, 1934, The Archive of the Roerich Museum, Fond 02-2, file 386, pp. 3–4.

135. Helena Roerich to Franklin D. Roosevelt, October 10, 1934, The Archive of the Roerich Museum, Fond 02-2, file 114, pp. 1–3; English translation in folder "Roerich Peace Pact," Official File 723, FDRL.

136. Louis Horch, "Visit on November 7th 1934 to the Mother and the Meeting with her Son," The Archive of the Roerich Museum, fond 02-2, file 411, pp. 177–86.

137. McCannon (2022: 409–10).

138. Por. Porooma/Nettie Horch], October 18, 1934, The Archive of the Roerich Museum, Fond 02-2, file 412, p. 198 (italics added).

139. Helena Roerich to Henry A. Wallace, December 27, 1934, The Archive of the Roerich Museum, Fond 02-2, file 132, p. 8.

140. Letter from Knowles Ryerson to Henry A. Wallace, October 13, 1934, The Archive of the Roerich Museum, Fond 07, file 70, pp. 98–101.

141. Correspondence from Henry A. Wallace to Knowles A. Ryerson dated October 20, 1934, Henry A. Wallace correspondence [reel 19], October 1933–July 1935—Ia19-0551, Henry A. Wallace Collection, University of Iowa.

142. Correspondence from Henry A. Wallace to Earl N. Bressman dated October 22, 1934, Henry A. Wallace correspondence [reel 19], October 1933–July 1935—Ia19-0552, Henry A. Wallace Collection, University of Iowa.

143. Correspondence from Nicholas Roerich to Henry A. Wallace dated October 1, 1934, Henry A. Wallace correspondence [reel 19], October 1933–July 1935—Ia19-0518–Ia19-0524, Henry A. Wallace Collection, University of Iowa.

144. Introduction by O.A. Lavreneva in Roerich (2015: 19).

145. A draft of a memo on Nicholas Roerich's lecture at the Russian Club of Harbin on November 7, 1934, "Irreconcilability Day," GAHK, Fond R-830, op. 3, file 40194, pp. 1–2.

146. Nicholas Roerich, diary entry, October 30, 1934, The Archive of the Roerich Museum, Fond 07, file 50, pp. 50/54, 50/55.

147. Boyd (2012: 267–68).

148. Nicholas Roerich, diary entries for November 14, 18, 19, 26, The Archive of the Roerich Museum, Fond 08, file 50, pp. 58–61. The latter was written "from the steamer on the way to Taku-tsinging," describing a week-long "unheard-of persecution on the side of the Japanese papers . . . and the Fascist *Nash Put*. . . : According to these newspapers it follows that I am a sort of a head of a masonic kingdom in Siberia, that I am the representative of the universal Jewish committee, that I am a powerful American agent, a mason, a Rosicrucian, at the head of America and USSR, I am destroying Nippon and some such unheard of absurdities."

149. Znamenski (2011).

150. Helena Roerich, Writings of conversations with the Teacher [series "Teaching"], notebook 27, 1934–1935, The Archive of the Roerich Museum, Fond 02-1, file 27, pp. 50/reverse, 51.

151. George Roerich to Frances Grant, March 19, 1936, The Archive of the Roerich Museum, Fond 08, file 087, pp. 8, 8/reverse.

152. Nicholas Roerich, diary entry, November 27, 1934, The Archive of the Roerich Museum, Fond 7, file 50, pp. 62–63.

153. Nicholas Roerich, diary entry, December 6, 1934, The Archive of the Roerich Museum, Fond 7, file 50, p. 9; original in folder 56, Box 15, FGP, RUSC.

154. Nicholas Roerich, diary entry, July 8, 1934, The Archive of the Roerich Museum, Fond 07, file 50, p. 50/53.

155. George Roerich to Sina Lichtmann, December 7, 1934, in Yury Roerich (2002) (italics added).

156. Nicholas Roerich, diary entry, December 8, 1934, in Roerich (2015).

157. File 82, Box 14, FGP, RUS.

158. The Archive of the Roerich Museum, Fond 07, file 39, pp. 3–4.

159. Nicholas Roerich, diary entry, c. December 29, 1934, The Archive of the Roerich Museum, Fond 07, file 50, p. 78.

160. Helena Roerich to Franklin D. Roosevelt, November 15, 1934, The Archive of the Roerich Museum, Fond 02-2, file 114, pp. 13–14.

161. Helena Roerich to Franklin D. Roosevelt, November 15, 1934, The Archive of the Roerich Museum Fond 02-2, file 114, pp. 4–5.

162. Louis Horch, "Report of the visit [FDR] on Dec. 19, 1934," prepared for Mme H. de Roerich at 11:00 a.m., The Archive of the Roerich Museum, Fond 02-2, file 411, pp. 195, 195/reverse, 177–79.

163. Helena Roerich to Sina Lichtmann, December 3, 1935, The Archive of the Roerich Museum, Fond 02-2, file 137, p. 9.

164. Rosov II (2004: ch. 5), citing Louis Horch "Visit on November 7th 1934 to the Mother (Sara Roosevelt) and the Meeting with her Son (F.D. Roosevelt)," Autograph, Gray Box, Roerich Collection, ACRC: 3-8.

165. *Star of the Hero* is the title of a famous Roerich painting. G.[Galahad] to M.[Modra], undated notes, early 1935, The Archive of the Roerich Museum, Fond 07, File 48, pp. 41, 43, 44, 46, 47.

166. Wallace to Frances Grant, received Feb. 15, 1935, The Archive of the Roerich Museum, Fond 07, File 48, p. 155.

167. George Roerich to Sina Lichtmann, January 19, 1935, in Yury Roerich (2002).

168. G.[Galahad] to M.[Modra], undated notes, early 1935, The Archive of the Roerich Museum, Fond 07, File 48, pp. 41, 155.

169. Henry Wallace to Frances Grant, received February 15, 1935), The Archive of the Roerich Museum, Fond 07, file 48, p. 155.

170. G.[Galahad] to M.[Modra], either January or February 1935, The Archive of the Roerich Museum, Fond 07, file 48, p. 71.

171. Henry A. Wallace to Helena Roerich, February 3, 1935, The Archive of the Roerich Museum, Fond 02-2, file 386, p. 7.

172. Louis Horch, Visit to Galad[Galahad], January 31, 1935, The Archive of the Roerich Museum, Fond 02-2, file 411, pp. 224–27, 228.

173. Nicholas Roerich to Henry A. Wallace, March 1, 1935, The Archive of the Roerich Museum, Fond 01-2, file 144, p. 7.

174. Visit to Mur.[Mrs. Murray/FDR], March 8, 1935, The Archive of the Roerich Museum, Fond 02-2, file 411, p. 203. Autograph, Gray Box, Roerich Collection, ACRC: 3–6.

175. Helena Roerich to Franklin D. Roosevelt, February 4, 1935, The Archive of the Roerich Museum, Fond 02-2, file 114, pp. 8–11.

176. Louis Horch, "A number of Meetings held with Gal.[Galahad]," The Archive of the Roerich Museum, Fond 02-2, file 411, pp. 209, 209/reverse.

177. Esther Lichtmann to Helena Roerich, March 9, 1935, The Archive of the Roerich Museum, Fond 02-2, file 279, pp. 60, 60/reverse.

178. "Visit to Mur.[Mrs. Murray/FDR] on March 14th 1935 with Oj[Ojana] and Logv.[Logvan]," The Archive of the Roerich Museum, Fond 02-2, file 411, pp. 209, 209/reverse (italics added). Esther Lichtmann to Helena Roerich, March 16, 1935, "Second visit," The Archive of the Roerich Museum, Fond 02-2, file 279, pp. 66, 66/reverse.

179. Nicholas Roerich, diary entries for March 28, 29, 30, and 31, 1935, The Archive of the Roerich Museum, Fond 07, file 50, p. 50/108. George Roerich, diary entries for March 28, 29, 30, and 31 in Roerich (2012: 166–67).

180. McCannon (2022: 420–21).

181. Frances Grant to Helena Roerich, May 29, 1935, The Archive of the Roerich Museum, Fond 02-2, file 209, pp. 92, 92/reverse, 93.

182. "[T]he New Co. [country] is the c. country] of F. [Fujama/Nicholas Roerich]," Helena Roerich to Nettie Horch, May 14, 1935, The Archive of the Roerich Museum, Fond 02-2, file 144: pp. 59, 59/reverse.

183. Frances Grant to Nicholas Roerich, April 5, 1935, The Archive of the Roerich Museum, Fond 07, file 50, pp. 50/111–50/112.

184. Esther Lichtmann to Helena Roerich, April 5, 1935, The Archive of the Roerich Museum, Fond 02-2, file 279, pp. 111–12.

185. Helena Roerich to Louis Horch, April 8, 1935, The Archive of the Roerich Museum, Fond 02-2, file 144, pp. 51–52.

186. Nicholas Roerich diary entry for April 14, 1935, The Archive of the Roerich Museum, Fond 07, file 50, p. 122.

187. Helena Roerich to Louis Horch, April 16 and 24, 1935, The Archive of the Roerich Museum, Fond 02-2, file 144, pp. 53, 55, 55/reverse.

188. Drayer (2005: 308).

189. Frances Grant to Helena Roerich, July 4, 1935, The Archive of the Roerich Museum, Fond 02-2, file 209, pp. 108–9.
190. Esther Lichtmann to Helena Roerich, April 30, 1935, The Archive of the Roerich Museum, Fond 02-2, file 279, p. 73/reverse.
191. Esther Lichtmann to Helena Roerich, April 18, 1935, The Archive of the Roerich Museum, Fond 02-2, file 279, pp. 70, 70/reverse.
192. Helena Roerich to "Fiery Warriors [Louis Horch and Esther Lichtmann]," April 24, 1935, The Archive of the Roerich Museum, Fond 02-2, file 144, p. 55.
193. Helena Roerich to Nettie Horch, May 14, 1935, The Archive of the Roerich Museum, Fond 02-2, file 144, p. 57.
194. Helena Roerich to Louis Horch, June 5, 1935, The Archive of the Roerich Museum, Fond 02-2, file 144, pp. 63, 63/reverse.
195. Esther Lichtmann to Helena Roerich, June 7, 1935, The Archive of the Roerich Museum, Fond 02-2, file 279, pp. 76–77. Steil (2013: 47–49).
196. Louis Horch to Helena Roerich, June 8, 1935, The Archive of the Roerich Museum, Fond 02-2, file 411, p. 136.
197. Helena Roerich to Louis Horch, June 24, 1935, The Archive of the Roerich Museum, Fond 02-2, file 144, pp. 67, 67/reverse, 68, 68/reverse; Helena Roerich to coworkers at the New York Museum, June 24, 1935, The Archive of the Roerich Museum, Fond 02-2, file 157, pp. 174, 174/reverse, 175, 175/reverse.
198. O.A. Lavreneva, introduction in Roerich (2015: 30). The Archive of the Roerich Museum, Fond 08, file 181c, pp. 81–83, 90.
199. Powell (June 24, 1935).
200. *New York Times* (June 24, 1935).
201. Nikolai Ivanovich Grammatchikov and Mikhail Nikolaevich Chuvstvin.
202. Victor Ivanovich Gribanovksy.
203. Alexander Moiseeff (Moiseev).
204. Details of the expedition staff in: The Archive of the Roerich Museum, Fond 08, file 065; Grammatchikov (1935 [1994]).
205. Nicholas Roerich to Henry A. Wallace, July 27, 1935, The Archive of the Roerich Museum, Fond 08, file 175, pp. 1–2.
206. Kotkin (2014: 404).
207. Nicholas Roerich to Henry A. Wallace, July 27, 1935, The Archive of the Roerich Museum, Fond 08, file 175, p. 2.
208. Powell (1945: 201–3).
209. Misselwitz (November 8, 1927).
210. Powell (1945: 202–3).
211. Thomas (1996: 54).
212. Powell (1945: 201–3, 222–23).
213. Radna (Sina Fosdick) to Helena Roerich, July 2, 1935, The Archive of the Roerich Museum, Fond 02-2, file 397, p. 191.
214. Frances Grant to Helena Roerich, June 28, 1935, The Archive of the Roerich Museum, Fond 02-2, file 209, pp. 105–6.
215. Henry A. Wallace to Frances Grant, July 2, 1935, The Archive of the Roerich Museum, Fond 07, file 90, p. 4.
216. Frances Grant to Helena Roerich, July 4, 1935, The Archive of the Roerich Museum, Fond 02-2, file 209, pp. 108–9, 109/reverse, 110.

217. Correspondence from Henry A. Wallace to Nicholas Roerich dated July 3, 1935 (cable), Henry A. Wallace correspondence [reel 19], October 1933–July 1935—Ia19-0947, Henry A. Wallace Collection, University of Iowa.

218. Correspondence from Earl N. Bressman to Frances R. Grant dated July 8, 1935, Henry A. Wallace correspondence [reel 19], October 1933–July 1935—Ia19-0950, Henry A. Wallace Collection, University of Iowa.

219. Correspondence from Henry A. Wallace to Louis L. Horch dated July 3, 1935, Henry A. Wallace correspondence [reel 19], October 1933–July 1935—Ia19-0946, Henry A. Wallace Collection, University of Iowa (italics added).

220. G.[Galahad] to Helena Roerich, July 4, 1935, The Archive of the Roerich Museum, Fond 2-02, file 386, p. 10.

221. The Archive of the Roerich Museum, Fond 07, file 61, p. 408. Nicholas Roerich to Louis Horch, cable from Peking, undated, after August 14, 1935, The Archive of the Roerich Museum, Fond 07, file 61, p. 422.

222. The Archive of the Roerich Museum, Fond 07, file 61, pp. 412, 414. Nicholas Roerich to Louis Horch, September 11, 1935, in response to Horch's from August 7, 1935, The Archive of the Roerich Museum, Fond 07, file 33.

223. Radna (Sina Lichtmann) to Helena Roerich, July 8, 1935, The Archive of the Roerich Museum, Fond 02-2, file 397, pp. 192–93.

224. Frances Grant to Helena Roerich, July 9, 1935 (Hotel Roosevelt, Washington, D.C.), The Archive of the Roerich Museum, Fond 02-2, file 209, pp. 117, 117/reverse. Frances Grant to Helena Roerich, July 10, 13, 1935 (Hotel Roosevelt, Washington, D.C.), The Archive of the Roerich Museum, Fond 02-2, file 209, pp. 122, 125.

225. Esther Lichtmann to Helena Roerich, July 10, 1935, The Archive of the Roerich Museum, Fond 02-2, file 279, p. 80.

226. Lewis Horch to Helena Roerich, July 30, 1935, The Archive of the Roerich Museum, Fond 02-2, file 411, p. 166.

227. Helena Roerich to Sina Lichtmann, December 3, 1935, The Archive of the Roerich Museum, Fond 02-2 file 137, pp. 9, 9/reverse, 10, 10/reverse.

228. Correspondence from R. Walton Moore to Henry A. Wallace dated August 24, 1935, Henry A. Wallace correspondence [reel 20], August 1935–January 1937—Ia20-001 7-Ia20-0019, Henry A. Wallace Collection, University of Iowa.

229. Federal Bureau of Investigation, "Philip Faymonville."

230. Correspondence from Henry A. Wallace to George Dern dated September 17, 1935, Henry A. Wallace correspondence [reel 20], August 1935–January 1937—Ia20-0050, Henry A. Wallace Collection, University of Iowa. Correspondence from Cordell Hull to Henry A. Wallace dated September 17, 1935, Henry A. Wallace correspondence [reel 20], August 1935–January 1937—Ia20-0051, Henry A. Wallace Collection, University of Iowa. Correspondence from Henry A. Wallace to Georges de Roerich dated September 18, 1935, Henry A. Wallace correspondence [reel 20], August 1935–January 1937—Ia20-0054, Henry A. Wallace Collection, University of Iowa. Correspondence from F.D. Richey to George Roerich dated September 19, 1935, Henry A. Wallace correspondence [reel 20], August 1935–January 1937—Ia20-0059, Henry A. Wallace Collection, University of Iowa.

231. Correspondence from Cordell Hull to Henry A. Wallace dated August 27, 1935, Henry A. Wallace correspondence [reel 20], August 1935–January 1937—Ia20-0022, Henry A. Wallace Collection, University of Iowa, transmitting telegram from Peiping [Peking] with the text of Yury Roerich cable from August 24—Correspondence from Nelson T.

Johnson to Cordell Hull dated August 27, 1935, Henry A. Wallace correspondence [reel 20], August 1935–January 1937—Ia20-0023, Henry A. Wallace Collection, University of Iowa. Correspondence from Henry A. Wallace to Georges de Roerich dated August 31, 1935, Henry A. Wallace correspondence [reel 20], August 1935–January 1937—Ia20-0027, Henry A. Wallace Collection, University of Iowa. Correspondence from Henry A. Wallace to Louis L. Horch dated September 18, 1935, Henry A. Wallace correspondence [reel 20], August 1935–January 1937—Ia20-0058, Henry A. Wallace Collection, University of Iowa.

232. Correspondence from G.F. Allen to Nicholas Roerich dated August 21, 1935, Henry A. Wallace correspondence [reel 20], August 1935–January 1937—Ia20-0018, Henry A. Wallace Collection, University of Iowa.

233. Correspondence from Earl N. Bressman to Nicholas Roerich dated September 17, 1935, Henry A. Wallace correspondence [reel 20], August 1935–January 1937—Ia20-0052, Henry A. Wallace Collection, University of Iowa. (The letter was addressed to Prof. N. Roerich, Naggar Kulu, Punjab, British India.)

234. Correspondence from Henry A. Wallace to Mrs. Nicholas Roerich dated September 24, 1935, Henry A. Wallace correspondence [reel 20], August 1935–January 1937—Ia20-0087, Henry A. Wallace Collection, University of Iowa.

235. Correspondence from Henry A. Wallace to Louis L. Horch dated September 18, 1935, Henry A. Wallace correspondence [reel 20], August 1935–January 1937—Ia20-0058, Henry A. Wallace Collection, University of Iowa.

236. Correspondence from Earl N. Bressman to C. Burnett dated September 25, 1935, Henry A. Wallace correspondence [reel 20], August 1935–January 1937—Ia20-0089, Henry A. Wallace Collection, University of Iowa (italics added).

237. "[A] new 24 story structure [was] erected, the lower three and one half stories of which were to be used for cultural and educational purposes..." (Roerich v. Horch, 279 NY 668 [New York Court of Appeals, 1938]: p. 1876).

238. Citation from the website of the former International Roerich Center, original in Russian; the letter does not appear in Sina Fosdick letters to N.K. Roerich in the Archive of the Roerich Museum, Fond 01-2, files 547–48.

239. L.L. Horch to Professor Nicholas and Mme. Helena Roerich, Naggar, Kulu, September 27, 1935, The Archive of the Roerich Museum, Fond 07, file 61, p. 416.

240. The Archive of the Roerich Museum, Fond 07, file 057, p. 6.

241. Fosdick (2002: 178).

242. Fosdick (2002: 178).

243. Rosov II (2004: ch. 6, endnote 22), citing Louis L. Horch, "Visit of E.J.L[ichtmann] and L.L.H[orch] to Hyde Park to see Pres. F.D.R[oosevelt] on September 9, 1935," Gray Box, Roerich Collection, ACRC: 4.

244. Nicholas Roerich to Franklin Roosevelt, c. January 3, 1936, The Archive of the Roerich Museum, Fond 01-2, file 125, pp. 2–4.

245. Helena Roerich to Franklin D. Roosevelt, December 12, 1935, The Archive of the Roerich Museum, Fond 02-2, file 114, pp. 29–30; Helena Roerich to Franklin D. Roosevelt, January 11, 1936, The Archive of the Roerich Museum, Fond 02-2, file 114, pp. 35, 37.

246. Correspondence from Henry A. Wallace to Guy T. Helvering dated October 1, 1935, Henry A. Wallace correspondence [reel 20], August 1935–January 1937—Ia20-0104–Ia20-0105, Henry A. Wallace Collection, University of Iowa.

247. Roerich v. Helvering, 115 F.2d 39 (D.C. Court of Appeals, 1940).

248. Correspondence from T.J. Coolidge to Henry A. Wallace dated January 17, 1936, Henry

A. Wallace correspondence [reel 20], August 1935–January 1937—Ia20-0392, Henry A. Wallace Collection, University of Iowa.

249. Correspondence from Henry A. Wallace to Henry Morgenthau Jr. dated January 23, 1936, Henry A. Wallace correspondence [reel 20], August 1935–January 1937—Ia20-0373, Henry A. Wallace Collection, University of Iowa.

250. Correspondence from Henry A. Wallace to Louis Horch dated January 23, 1936, Henry A. Wallace correspondence [reel 20], August 1935–January 1937—Ia20-0372, Henry A. Wallace Collection, University of Iowa.

251. Fosdick (2002: 179).

252. Correspondence from T.J. Coolidge to Henry A. Wallace dated February 7, 1936, Henry A. Wallace correspondence [reel 20], August 1935–January 1937—Ia20-0414–Ia20-0416, Henry A. Wallace Collection, University of Iowa.

253. Roerich v. Helvering, 115 F.2d 39 (D.C. Court of Appeals, 1940).

254. Rosov II (2004: ch. 6, endnote 24), citing Louis L. Horch, "Visit of E.J. Lichtmann and L.L. Horch to Steph. (F.D.R[oosevelt]) on January 15, 1936," Louis L. Horch, "Visit [to F.D.R[oosevelt] on January 28, 1936 [with] O[jana], G[alahad] and L[ogvan]," Gray Box, Roerich Collection, ACRC. Samuel I. Rosenman, interview by Jerry N. Hess, October 15, 1968, and April 23, 1969, Oral History Interviews, Truman Library; *New York Times* (June 25, 1973).

255. Rosov II (2004: ch. 6, endnote 24) citing Louis L. Horch, "Visit of E.J. Lichtmann and L.L. Horch to Steph. (F.D.R[oosevelt]) on January 15, 1936," Gray Box, Roerich Collection, ACRC.

256. *New York Sun* (January 30, 1936), in The Archive of the Roerich Museum, Fond 07, file 057, p. 7.

257. The Archive of the Roerich Museum, Fond 07, file 057, p. 8.

258. *New York Sun* (["Action Threatened Against Agriculture Department"] January 31, 1936), in The Archive of the Roerich Museum, Fond 07, file 057, p. 11.

259. Yury Roerich to Frances Grant, February 4, 1935, The Archive of the Roerich Museum, Fond 08, file 87, pp. 1–2.

260. The Archive of the Roerich Museum, Fond 07, file 057, p. 11.

261. *New York Sun* (["Capital Denies Roerich Report"] January 31, 1936). A more formal denial appears to have come from the Department of Agriculture on February 4: *New York Herald Tribune* (February 5, 1936).

262. *New York Times* (February 12, 1936).

263. Rosov II (2004: ch. 6, endnote 30), citing Louis L. Horch, "Visit to S[tephan] (F.D.R[oosevelt]) on March 5, 1936," Gray Box, Roerich Collection, ACRC.

264. Fosdick (2002: 179–80).

265. *New York Sun* (February 1, 1936).

266. Yury Roerich to Frances Grant, February 26, 1936, The Archive of the Roerich Museum, Fond 08, file 87, pp. 4, 4/reverse.

267. Correspondence from W.E. Whitehouse to Earl N. Bressman dated September 23, 1935, Henry A. Wallace correspondence [reel 20], August 1935–January 1937—Ia20-0063, Henry A. Wallace Collection, University of Iowa.

268. George Roerich to Dr. E.N. Bressman, September 20, 1935, The Archive of the Roerich Museum, Fond 08, file 150, p. 78.

269. Yury Roerich to Miss Grant, Naggar, February 26, 1936, The Archive of the Roerich Museum, Fond 08, file 87, pp. 4, 4/reverse. Roerich (2015:3). Reports on the outcomes of the expedition, Manchurian Expedition, The Archive of the Roerich Museum, Fond

08, files 135, 136, 137. List of Systematic herbarium gathered by the Roerich Expedition to North Manchuria, The Archive of the Roerich Museum, Fond 08, file 138A. List of the plants of the herbarium collected by I.V. Kozlov in the vicinity of Kalgan in 1934, March 27, 1935, The Archive of the Roerich Museum, Fond 08, file 141. List of seeds collected by the N.K. Roerich Expedition in Inner Mongolia from July 24 to October 4, 1935, The Archive of the Roerich Museum, Fond 08, file 143. List of seeds collected by the N.K. Roerich during Manchurian Expedition in the area of Spiti in the period from September 21 to October 8, 1935, The Archive of the Roerich Museum, Fond 08, file 144. List of boxes with Nos. of species collected by the expedition of N.K. Roerich, The Archive of the Roerich Museum, Fond 08, file 146.

270. *New York Times* (April 16, 1979).

271. Drayer (2005: 319–20).

272. Correspondence from Henry A. Wallace to Knowles A. Ryerson dated October 11, 1935, Henry A. Wallace correspondence [reel 20], August 1935–January 1937—Ia20-0108, Henry A. Wallace Collection, University of Iowa.

273. Correspondence from Henry A. Wallace to J.L. Stephens dated November 19, 1935, Henry A. Wallace correspondence [reel 20], August 1935–January 1937—Ia20-0296, Henry A. Wallace Collection, University of Iowa.

274. "Scientific Progress for 1934," in *World Almanac and Book of Facts for 1935* (1934: 185).

275. Correspondence from Earl N. Bressman to C. Burnett dated September 25, 1935, Henry A. Wallace correspondence [reel 20], August 1935–January 1937—Ia20-0089, Henry A. Wallace Collection, University of Iowa (italics added).

276. Correspondence from Henry A. Wallace to Prince Teh-Wang dated October 24, 1935, Henry A. Wallace correspondence [reel 20], August 1935–January 1937—Ia20-0155, Henry A. Wallace Collection, University of Iowa.

277. Correspondence from Henry A. Wallace to Alexander Troyanovsky dated October 24, 1935, Henry A. Wallace correspondence [reel 20], August 1935–January 1937—Ia20-0238, Henry A. Wallace Collection, University of Iowa.

278. A local Tarrytown newspaper, January 31, 1936, preserved in the Archive of the Roerich Museum, Fond 07, file 057, p. 6.

279. New York *Sun* (February 1, 1936).

280. Correspondence from Henry A. Wallace to Louis L. Horch dated September 18, 1935, Henry A. Wallace correspondence [reel 20], August 1935–January 1937—Ia20-0058, Henry A. Wallace Collection, University of Iowa.

281. Helena Roerich to Sina Lichtmann, December 3, 1935, The Archive of the Roerich Museum, Fond 02-2, file 137, pp. 9, 9/reverse, 10, 10/reverse.

5. Fighting Fascists, Planning Peace

1. Roosevelt, speech, June 10, 1940: https://www.presidency.ucsb.edu/documents/address-university-virginia. Roosevelt (1949: 212).

2. Sherwood (1948 [2008]: 137).

3. Morgan (1985: 529–30). Sherwood (1948 [2008]: 139). Reminiscences of Paul H, Appleby, CCOH, 1957, pp. 185–93.

4. See, for example, Rosenman (1952: 205).

5. Hull I (1948: 858–61).

6. See, for example, Harold Ickes, diary entry, July 16, 1944, Box 12, reel 6, Harold L. Ickes Papers, Library of Congress and Rosenman (1952: 205–6).

7.   Perkins (1946: 127).

8.   Rosenman (1952: 213). Farley (1948: 293–94).

9.   Fosdick (2002: 618, 634, 654).

10. Reminiscences of Paul H. Appleby, CCOH, 1957, p. 166.

11. Reminiscences of Paul H. Appleby, CCOH, 1957, p. 163.

12. Reminiscences of Paul H. Appleby, CCOH, 1957, p. 168.

13. Reminiscences of Paul H. Appleby, CCOH, 1957, pp. 166–82.

14. Culver and Hyde (2000: 197).

15. Farley (1948: 184). Culver and Hyde (2000: 200).

16. Louis H. Bean, interview by Jerry N. Hess, September 11, 1970, Oral History Interviews, Truman Library: 36–38.

17. The diary entry was December 11, 1939. Reminiscences of Henry Agard Wallace, CCOH, pp. 558, 609.

18. Reminiscences of Paul H. Appleby, CCOH, 1957, p. 174.

19. See, for example, Perkins (1946: 126–29); Reminiscences of Paul H. Appleby, CCOH, 1957, p. 211; Reminiscences of Henry Agard Wallace, CCOH, p. 609; and Appleby (September 1952: 759).

20. Appleby (September 1952: 759). Reminiscences of Paul H. Appleby, CCOH, 1957, p. 223.

21. Martin (1976: 434). Roosevelt (1949: 218). Appleby (September 1952: 760–61). Culver and Hyde (2000: 219–21).

22. Culver and Hyde (2000: 222–23).

23. See, for example, *Des Moines Register* (April 4, 1948).

24. The Archive of the Roerich Museum, Fond 01:2, file 144 and file 535; Fond 02-2, file 386 and file 386a; Fond 07, file 90 and file 133; Fond 08, file 128 [copies in folder "Guru Letters" (Henry A. Wallace), Container 9, Samuel I. Rosenman Papers, (FDRL)].

25. Morgan (1985: 531–33).

26. The Reminiscences of Paul H. Appleby, Oral History Office, Columbia University, 1957, pp. 35–37.

27. Morgan (1985: 533).

28. *Des Moines Register* (April 4, 1948). Martin (1960: 117).

29. White House—conversation in President's office with Lowell Mellett and others (poor) (30 minutes), 1940/08/23-27, Recorded Speeches and Utterances of Franklin D. Roosevelt, 1920–1945, Audio/Visual Collections, FDRL. Morgan (1985: 533–34).

30. Reminiscences of Henry Agard Wallace, CCOH, p. 5107.

31. Wallace (1943).

32. Davis (1993: 613).

33. *New York Times* (August 30, 1940).

34. Morgan (1985: 539).

35. White and Maze (1995: 140).

36. Election Year 1940 Statistics, The American Presidency Project.

37. Reminiscences of Henry Agard Wallace, CCOH, p. 1400.

38. Reminiscences of Henry Agard Wallace, CCOH, pp. 1300–1305.

39. Stevens (Fall 1996: 1127).

40. Table No. 186, "Paid Employees in the Executive Branch of the Federal Government, by Agency for June 1941 to 1944," untitled census.gov (https://www2.census.gov/prod2 /statcomp/documents/1944-04.pdf), p. 179; including 2,885 in Washington, D.C. Metropolitan Area.

41. Sirevag (1985: 120).

42. See, for example, Wallace's letter to Roosevelt, April 16, 1942, quoted in Sirevag (1985: 112).

43. Correspondence from Henry A. Wallace to Arthur Krock dated December 31, 1942, Henry A. Wallace correspondence [reel 24], November 1942–July 15, 1943—Ia24 -0221-Ia24-0222, Henry A. Wallace Collection, University of Iowa.

44. Blum (1973: 68–70). Krock (April 28, 1942). Krock (1968: 205–7). Stevens (Fall 1996: 1131–33).

45. *New York Times* (April 24, 1942).

46. Franklin D. Roosevelt, Press Conference #823, May 1, 1942, Series 1: Press Conference Transcripts, Press Conferences of President Franklin D. Roosevelt, 1933–1945, FDRL: 313–15.

47. Timmons (1956: 303).

48. Reminiscences of Henry Agard Wallace, CCOH, p. 1450.

49. See, for example, letter of Army representative Daniel F. Margolies to Harold W. Starr, October 14, 1943, quoted in Sirevag (1985: 119).

50. Wallace (July 12, 1942).

51. Jones (1951: 422–26). Timmons (1956: 324). Culver and Hyde (2000: 288–89). Sirevag (1985: 122–23).

52. Sirevag (1985: 120).

53. Culver and Hyde (2000: 295–96).

54. *St. Louis Star Times* (June 29, 1943).

55. Secretary of Commerce Washington, RFC-1847, Henry A. Wallace correspondence [reel 67], 1934–1965—Ia67-0067, Henry A. Wallace Collection, University of Iowa.

56. Sherwood (1948 [2008]: 578).

57. Reminiscences of Henry Agard Wallace, CCOH, pp. 2549–54. Byrnes (1958: 192–93). Sirevag (1985: 127–28). Culver and Hyde (2000: 304–7).

58. Correspondence from Henry A. Wallace to Franklin D. Roosevelt dated July 12, 1943, Henry A. Wallace correspondence [reel 24], November 1942–July 15, 1943—Ia24-0937, Henry A. Wallace Collection, University of Iowa.

59. Correspondence from Franklin D. Roosevelt to Jesse Jones dated July 15, 1943, Henry A. Wallace correspondence [reel 24], November 1942–July 15, 1943—Ia24-0992, Henry A. Wallace Collection, University of Iowa.

60. Correspondence from Franklin D. Roosevelt to Henry A. Wallace dated July 28, 1943, Henry A. Wallace correspondence [reel 59], December 1931–1964—Ia59-0685, Henry A. Wallace Collection, University of Iowa.

61. Byrnes (1958: 193–94). Sirevag (1985: 130–32). Jones (1951: 503–6).

62. Jones (1951: 503).

63. Wallace, speech, "The Century of the Common Man," May 8, 1942: https://www .americanrhetoric.com/speeches/henrywallacefreeworldassoc.htm#:~:text=Some%20 have%20spoken%20of%20the,the%20common%20man%20must%20live.

64. Blum (1973: 363).

65. Clapper (May 15, 1942). Ek (May 21, 1942).

66. Correspondence from Henry A. Wallace to Henry R. Luce dated May 16, 1942, Henry A. Wallace correspondence [reel 23], November 1941–October 1942—Ia23-0519, Henry A. Wallace Collection, University of Iowa.

67. White (Spring 1992: 125).

68. Wallace, speech, November 8, 1942 (italics added): http://www.ibiblio.org/pha/policy /1942/421108f.html.

69. Correspondence from Henry A. Wallace to Fred W. Henshaw dated May 7, 1943, Henry A. Wallace correspondence [reel 24], November 1942–July 15, 1943—Ia24-0656, Henry A. Wallace Collection, University of Iowa.

70. For example, in January 1944 he still referred to the TVA as "a model for decentralization, for true economic democracy." Correspondence from Henry A. Wallace to Bruce Bliven dated January 7, 1944, Henry A. Wallace correspondence [reel 25], July 16, 1943–February 1944—Ia25-0715, Henry A. Wallace Collection, University of Iowa.

71. Wallace, speech, "What We Fight For: Each Age Demands a New Freedom," September 11, 1943: http://www.ibiblio.org/pha/policy/1943/1943-09-11a.html.

72. Wallace, speech, November 8, 1942 (italics added): http://www.ibiblio.org/pha/policy/1942/421108f.html. Correspondence from Henry A. Wallace to Paul Novick dated November 1, 1943, Henry A. Wallace correspondence [reel 25], July 16, 1943–February 1944—Ia25-0384, Henry A. Wallace Collection, University of Iowa.

73. See, for example, Kotljarchuk and Sundström (2017).

74. Correspondence from William D. Hassett to Elmer Davis dated February 26, 1943, Henry A. Wallace correspondence [reel 24], November 1942–July 15, 1943—Ia24-0458, Henry A. Wallace Collection, University of Iowa.

75. Wallace (1943: 9–20). Wallace (1944: 214–19). Culver and Hyde (2000: 297).

76. A. Gromyko, "Record of conversation with Counsel (in the rank of Minister) of the Mexican government in Washington—Don Louis Quintanilla," September 30, 1942, AVP RF, Fond 0129, op. 26, P 143, file 2, p. 27.

77. A. Gromyko, Counsel, Soviet Embassy in the USA, to A.Ja. Vyshinsky, Assistant People's Commissar of Foreign Affairs, November 13, 1942, AVP RF, Fond 0129, op. 26, P 143, file 6, p. 28 (NKID US Department entry stamp—January 23, 1943).

78. Correspondence from Henry A. Wallace to Cordell Hull dated December 16, 1940, Henry A. Wallace correspondence [reel 22], July 1940–October 1941, 1943—Ia22-0268–Ia22-0270, Henry A. Wallace Collection, University of Iowa.

79. Correspondence from Henry A. Wallace to Cordell Hull dated December 16, 1940, Henry A. Wallace correspondence [reel 22], July 1940–October 1941, 1943—Ia22-0276–Ia22-0279, Henry A. Wallace Collection, University of Iowa.

80. Correspondence from Santiago Reachi to Henry A. Wallace dated December 7, 1940, Henry A. Wallace correspondence [reel 22], July 1940–October 1941, 1943—Ia22-0290–Ia22-0314, Henry A. Wallace Collection, University of Iowa. Correspondence from Franklin D. Roosevelt to Henry A. Wallace dated January 10, 1941, Henry A. Wallace correspondence [reel 22], July 1940–October 1941, 1943—Ia22-0408-Ia22-0411, Henry A. Wallace Collection, University of Iowa. Correspondence from Henry A. Wallace to Franklin D. Roosevelt dated December 29, 1940, Henry A. Wallace correspondence [reel 22], July 1940–October 1941, 1943—Ia22-0351–Ia22-0355, Henry A. Wallace Collection, University of Iowa.

81. Waterhouse (2013: 114).

82. Morain (2011).

83. The Acting Secretary of State to Certain Diplomatic Representatives in the American Republics, March 11, 1943, in FRUS, 1943, V: 59.

84. See, for example, Reminiscences of Henry Agard Wallace, CCOH, p. 417.

85. The Minister in Costa Rica (Scotten) to the Secretary of State, March 18, 1943, in FRUS, 1943, V: 61. New York Times (March 19, 1943).

86. The Minister in Costa Rica (Scotten) to the Secretary of State, March 20, 1943, in FRUS, 1943, V: 61.

87.   Wallace (1944: 227).

88.   Culver and Hyde (2000: 298).

89.   The Minister in Costa Rica (Scotten) to the Secretary of State, March 20, 1943, in *FRUS, 1943*, V: 61.

90.   The Ambassador in Panama (Wilson) to the Secretary of State, March 22, 1943, in *FRUS, 1943*, V: 62. The Ambassador in Panama (Wilson) to the Secretary of State, March 24, 1943, in *FRUS, 1943*, V: 62.

91.   The Ambassador in Chile (Bowers) to the Acting Secretary of State, April 3, 1943, in *FRUS, 1943*, V: 66.

92.   Subject: Henry Wallace, Part 01 of 02 and Part 04 of 05, FBI FOIA.

93.   Wallace (1944: 228).

94.   Subject: Henry Wallace, Part 04 of 05.

95.   Lord (1947: 502–3).

96.   Report from La Paz, Bolivia, April 16, 1943, Subject: Henry Wallace, Part 04 of 05, FBI FOIA: 75–80.

97.   John Edgar Hoover, Memorandum for the Attorney General, May 3, 1943, Subject: Henry Wallace, Part 04 of 05, FBI FOIA: 115–16. See also Subject: Henry Wallace, Part 04 of 05, FBI FOIA: 112.

98.   Report to John Edgar Hoover from San Jose, Costa Rica, April 5, 1943, Subject: Henry Wallace, Part 04 of 05, FBI FOIA: 57–62.

99.   27th July, 1943—31st July—3rd August, 1943, 1 Peruvian Reaction to Henry Wallace Visit, Subject: Henry Wallace, Part 04 of 05, FBI FOIA: 6–10.

100. "Political Matters in Ecuador," report from Quito, Ecuador, April 1, 1943, Subject: Henry Wallace, Part 01 of 02, FBI FOIA.

101. Subject: Henry Wallace, Part 04 of 05, FBI FOIA: 66–74.

102. Lord (1947: 504–5).

103. The Ambassador in Colombia (Lane) to the Secretary of State, Bogota, May 7, 1943, in *FRUS, 1943*, V: 73. See also, regarding Wallace's earlier brief stop in Colombia: The Ambassador in Colombia (Lane) to the Secretary of State, March 26, 1943, in *FRUS, 1943*, V: 63.

104. Correspondence from Charles E. Marsh to Henry A. Wallace dated February 11, 1943, Henry A. Wallace correspondence [reel 24], November 1942–July 15, 1943—Ia24-0383-Ia24-0387, Henry A. Wallace Collection, University of Iowa. Correspondence from Charles E. Marsh to Helen Rogers dated February 10, 1943, Henry A. Wallace correspondence [reel 24], November 1942–July 15, 1943—Ia24-0388, Henry A. Wallace Collection, University of Iowa.

105. Correspondence from Gabriel Pascal to Charles E. Marsh dated December 30, 1942, Henry A. Wallace correspondence [reel 24], November 1942–July 15, 1943—Ia24-0210, Henry A. Wallace Collection, University of Iowa. Correspondence from Gabriel Pascal to Henry A. Wallace dated June 8, 1943, Henry A. Wallace correspondence [reel 24], November 1942–July 15, 1943—Ia24-0812, Henry A. Wallace Collection, University of Iowa.

106. Correspondence from Charles E. Marsh to Gabriel Pascal dated January 3, 1943, Henry A. Wallace correspondence [reel 24], November 1942–July 15, 1943—Ia-0233, Henry A. Wallace Collection, University of Iowa. Correspondence from Gabriel Pascal to Henry A. Wallace dated June 8, 1943, Henry A. Wallace correspondence [reel 24], November 1942–July 15, 1943—Ia24-0812, Henry A. Wallace Collection, University of Iowa.

107. Conant (2008: 46–49).

108. *Time* (February 22, 1943).
109. Conant (2008: 146).
110. Conant (2008: 62).
111. Blum (1973: 201–2).
112. This material is quoted from the actual publication, which was not released until June 1944. It may or may not have been in the same exact form in the draft which Dahl read.
113. Conant (2008: 121–24, 145).
114. Conant (2008: 195, 214).
115. Conant (2008: 240).
116. Wallace's letter was written on March 29, 1942 in response to an earlier claim of Dies', in a letter to Wallace dated March 28, 1942, alleging to have identified "at least 35 high [BEW] officials [affiliated] with front organizations of the Communist Party." (Correspondence from Martin Dies to Henry A. Wallace dated March 28, 1942, Henry A. Wallace correspondence [reel 23], November 1941–October 1942—Ia23-0383-Ia23-0387, Henry A. Wallace Collection, University of Iowa). Dies raised the figure to 39 in his speech before the House of Representatives on February 1, 1943. Wallace's letter is here: Correspondence from Henry A. Wallace to Ben Hibbs dated March 28, 1942, Henry A. Wallace correspondence [reel 23], November 1941–October 1942—Ia23-0390-Ia23-0392, Henry A. Wallace Collection, University of Iowa.
117. Virginius Frank Coe, then executive secretary of the Joint War Production Committee of the United States and Canada and an assistant to the executive director of the Board of Economic Warfare (BEW), until he moved to the Treasury Department as its director of the Division of Monetary Research in 1944. He later became the first secretary of the International Monetary Fund. Code-named "Peak," he worked under the delusion that "he was working for the 'Helmsman'" (CPUSA secretary general Earl Browder). Vassili Zarubine to V.N. Merkulov, September [no day given] 1944, Alexander Vassiliev's White Notebook No. 1, p. 5, Alexander Vassiliev Papers, Library of Congress, referring to SVR RF No. 35112, Vol. 1, pp. 400–401. Vadim to the Moscow Center, October 1, 1945, Alexander Vassiliev's White Notebook No. 3, p. 82, Alexander Vassiliev Papers, Library of Congress.
118. Charles Flato had been an open Communist Party member, joining the party in May 1935 under the party name C.D. Manchester; later assigned to the Harvard unit of the CPUSA. Although spotted by NKGB "illegal" resident Itskhak Akhmerov, Moscow decided not to proceed with the recruitment. RGASPI, Fond 515, op. 1, file 4003, pp. 31–36.
119. Michael Greenberg joined the British Communist Party while a Trinity College student. He moved to the U.S. in 1939, and briefly worked as Lauchlin Currie's assistant at the White House. In 1942, he was employed by the Board of Economic Warfare as its China expert, and later by the Foreign Economic Administration (Administrative Division, Enemy Branch). Greenberg was a knowing and enthusiastic Soviet source. In Alexander Vassiliev's notes, his code name may have been "Yank." Vassiliev White Notebook No. 2, pp. 9, 33, Alexander Vassiliev Papers, Library of Congress; Vassiliev White Notebook No. 1, pp. 52–53, Alexander Vassiliev Papers, Library of Congress.
120. Thomas Arthur Bisson was a principal economic analyst at BEW, where he was engaged in a major study on the most effective strategy for blocking the flow of essential war supplies to Japan and disrupting the Japanese economy. His code name was "Arthur" [Artur]. Schonberger (1980).
121. David R. Wahl was a librarian by education and occupation. He was recruited by the GRU while at the Library of Congress, moving to the BEW in 1942 and likely report-

ing to the GRU until early 1945. Robbins (2009). Alexander Vassiliev Black Notebook, p. 74, referring to KGB file 43173, Vol. 2v, p. 202, Alexander Vassiliev Papers, Library of Congress.

122. SVR RF File 43173, Vol. 1, pp. 8, 8a, 9, 9a (Xerox copies from the typed original, taken in the early 1990s for subsequent release to Alexander Vassiliev; sketchy notes in Vassiliev's Black Notebook.) The left-hand bottom of p. 1 has a declassification date of June 1, 1994. Courtesy of the late Theodore Gladkov to Svetlana A. Chervonnaya.

123. Annotation for the materials of the U.S. Board of Economic Warfare for February 1943, c. July 9, 1943, AVP RF, Fond 06, op. 5, P 30, file 347, pp. 3–7.

124. Benson (2001).

125. Correspondence from Henry A. Wallace to Ben Hibbs dated March 28, 1942, Henry A. Wallace correspondence [reel 23], November 1941–October 1942—Ia23-0391-Ia23-0393, Henry A. Wallace Collection, University of Iowa.

6. Into Siberia

1.   Particularly, February 9, 1944. PRES-CHIANG. (#4473) American Observer Mission to China; February 22, 1944. PRES-CHIANG. (#4473) American Observer Mission to China; March 1, 1944. PRES-CHIANG. (#4646). American Observer Mission to China, FDR and Chiang Kai-Shek, 1944, Box 10, Map Room Papers, FDRL.

2.   Blum (1973: 308–9).

3.   Memorandum by the Chief of the Division of Eastern European Affairs (Bohlen) to the Secretary of State, April 20, 1944, in *FRUS, 1944*, VI: 222.

4.   AVP RF, Fond 0129, op. 28, P 158, file 32, p. 4.

5.   Memorandum by the Under Secretary of State (Stettinius) to the Secretary of State, March 8, 1944, in *FRUS, 1944*, VI: 216.

6.   Henry Morgenthau, diary entry, May 18, 1944, Book 733, Series 1: Morgenthau Diaries, Diaries of Henry Morgenthau, Jr., FDRL: 33–34 (italics added). May (1974: 292). Blum (1967: 120).

7.   May (1974: 292–93). Culver and Hyde (2000: 330–31).

8.   Bell (April 12, 1944: 8). See also *Evening Review* (April 12, 1944: 1, 6); *Era* (April 13, 1944); and *Gazette* (April 13, 1944).

9.   Allen (1960: 126).

10. Ferrell (1994: 6).

11. Blum (1967: 308–10).

12. Tuchman (1970: 574).

13. Blum (1967: 120).

14. Reminiscences of Henry Agard Wallace, CCOH, p. 3199.

15. Brown (1992: 184). Ferrell (1994: 18).

16. Memorandum by the Under Secretary of State (Stettinius) to the Director of the Office of Far Eastern Affairs (Grew), *FRUS, 1944,* VI: 230.

17. Feis (1953: 145).

18. "The Ministry of Foreign Affairs Counselor Liu Kai submitted a report from Washington to the Ministry of Foreign Affairs that the purpose of US Vice President Wallace's visit to China was to observe the agricultural conditions in China and inspect the US military in China," in Qin (1980: 859). "Ambassador to the United States, Wei Daoming, reports from Washington to Chairman Jiang that US Vice President Wallace appears to be interested in discussing Sino-Soviet relations and CCP issues in China," in Qin (1980: 861).

602   Notes to Pages 152–159

19. Memorandum for the Director, May 12, 1944, "Re: Vice President Henry Wallace's Trip to China and Russia, Information concerning," Subject: Henry Wallace, Part 04 of 05, FBI FOIA: 143–48.

20. Correspondence from Henry A. Wallace to Stephen Early dated May 19, 1944, Henry A. Wallace correspondence [reel 26], March 1944–July 1944—Ia26-0467, Henry A. Wallace Collection, University of Iowa. The statements of the president and vice president appear in *FRUS, 1944*, VI: 228–29 (The Secretary of State to the Ambassador in China [Gauss], Washington, May 23, 1944).

21. Wallace (1946: 20).

22. Wallace (1946: 21–23).

23. Wallace (1946: 96–97).

24. Wallace (1949: 77–78). Perry quote from Collins (1860: 52).

25. Wallace (1946: 21–23).

26. Secret Report by Captain Kennith Knowles, Observer and Military Secretary of the Wallace Mission, July 15, 1944, File 811.003/Wallace, Henry A./7-2944; Box 3498, Central Decimal File, 1940–1944, Record Group 250, NARA: 2.

27. Memorandum for the Director, "Re: Vice President Henry Wallace's Trip to China and Russia," Federal Bureau of Investigation, May 12, 1944, Subject: Henry Wallace, Part 04 of 05, FBI FOIA: 143–48.

28. Secret Report by Captain Kennith Knowles, Observer and Military Secretary of the Wallace Mission, July 15, 1944, File 811.003/Wallace, Henry A./7-2944; Box 3498, Central Decimal File, 1940–1944, Record Group 250, NARA: 9.

29. Wallace (1946: 31).

30. This was its original full name. From 1938 to 1945 it was "The Main Directorate on Construction in the Far North of the NKVD of the USSR."

31. Bogdanov (1975: 120).

32. Wallace wrongly identified Semenov, whom he called "Semeonov," as "commander of the vast Yakutsk military area." Wallace (1946: 31,118). Lipper (1951: 98). Secret Report by Captain Kennith Knowles, Observer and Military Secretary of the Wallace Mission, July 15, 1944, File 811.003/Wallace, Henry A./7-2944; Box 3498, Central Decimal File, 1940–1944, Record Group 250, NARA: 9.

33. The title "president" was not used in this era; Goglidze may actually have been introduced to Wallace as "chairman."

34. Wallace (1946: 31–33, 81–83). Secret Report by Captain Kennith Knowles, Observer and Military Secretary of the Wallace Mission, July 15, 1944, File 811.003/Wallace, Henry A./7-2944; Box 3498, Central Decimal File, 1940–1944, Record Group 250, NARA: 13).

35. Wallace (1946: 33).

36. Wallace (1946: 33–34).

37. Nikishov to People's Commissar of Internal Affairs Comrade Beria, June 3, 1944, cc to Stalin, Molotov, June 6, 1944, GA RF, Fond R-9401, op. 2, file 65, p. 193. Wallace (1946: 27–40, 127–28).

38. Wallace (1946: 34–36).

39. Wallace (1946: 36–37).

40. Wallace (1946: 41–44, 90).

41. Wallace (1946: 44–46, 242).

42. Wallace (1946: 50–51).

43. Wallace (1946: 21–23).

44. Wallace (1946: 84).

45. Wallace (1946: 84–85, 118–20). Birstein (2012: 16).
46. Wallace (1946: 112).
47. Wallace (1946: 132).
48. Wallace (1946: 57–60, 62, 64–66).
49. Wallace (1946: 121).
50. GA RF, Fond R6822, op. 1, files 81, 409, and 410.
51. Wallace (1946: 93, 118). Birstein (2012: 4).
52. Wallace (1946: 93–95). Engerman (2003: 154).
53. Wallace (1946: 87–89).
54. Wallace (1946: 239).
55. Wallace (1946: 68–69).
56. Wallace (1946: 110, 142).
57. Wallace (1946: 146–50).
58. Culver and Hyde (2000: 332).
59. Blum (1973: 347).
60. Hazard (1984: 65).
61. Sir Fitzroy Maclean, quoted in Vaksberg (1991: 115).
62. Wallace (1946: 31–33, 81–83). Birstein (2012: 5). Lipper (1951: 193). AVP RF, Fond 0129, op. 28, P 158, file 32, p. 79.
63. This rank is the rough equivalent of a U.S. army lieutenant general. Birstein (2012: 3–5). Wallace (1946: 33, 73, 89). Lipper (1951: 111–12).
64. Wallace (1946: 127–28).
65. Birstein (2012: 13). Lipper (1951: 113).
66. Russian landscape in embroidery, Magadan, Siberia, 1944, Box 3, Series 7, Henry A. Wallace Collection, University of Iowa.
67. Lipper (1951: 113).
68. Another example: "Former Dalstroi worker M. KRAINII. . . was fired because he lived with GRIDASOVA. She asked him to make her pregnant in order to bind NIKISHOV more tightly to her." The source is a December 1945 anonymous letter from someone at *Dal'stroi* to the chief of the Cadre Department of the Central Committee of VCP (b), with a copy to the People's Commissar of Internal Affairs L.P. Beria, I.F. Nikishov, and chief of the Office of the Magadan ITL [Correctional Labor Camp] A.R. Gridasova. Signed copy sent to Beria: GA RF, Fond R-9401, op. 1, file 4932, pp. 515–18. Original in VCP (b) Central Committee Cadre Department files: RGASPI, Fond 17, op. 127, file 1129, pp. 35–37/reverse. First published by Petrov (November 28, 2011).
69. Degtyarev and Kolpakidi (2009).
70. Wallace (1946: 108, 110, 147). Petrov and Skorkin (1999).
71. Wallace (1946: 84).
72. Wallace (1946: 87–89).
73. Smirnov (1998). Other sources give slightly different figures. Petrov writes that by the beginning of 1945, *Dal'stroi* camps had 91,215 prisoners. Kokurin and Petrov (2000); Petrov (The History of the GULAG Empire: ch. 11).
74. Zemskov (July 1991). Zemskov (1991). Lipper (1951: 146).
75. Sgovio (1979: 250).
76. Wallace (1946: 35). Lipper (1951: 110, 112).
77. Holley (June 20, 2005).
78. Bien (2003: vi).
79. Birstein (2012: 5).

80. Nikishov to Beria, Stalin, and Molotov, GA RF, Fond R-9401, op. 2, file 65, pp. 191–93.
81. Wallace (1946: 84–85, 118–19).
82. Sgovio (1979: 150).
83. Birstein (2012: 6). Khakimov surely exaggerated in writing "everybody. . . ate" imported food, but locally produced food was severely insufficient. An authoritative source is Brodkin (2008).
84. Lipper (1951: 268).
85. Secret Report by Captain Kennith Knowles, Observer and Military Secretary of the Wallace Mission, July 15, 1944, File 811.003/Wallace, Henry A./7-2944; Box 3498, Central Decimal File, 1940–1944, Record Group 250, NARA: 6.
86. Lipper (1951: 268).
87. Birstein (2012: 6).
88. Wallace (1946: 36). Sgovio (1979: 251).
89. Wallace (1946: 131).
90. Birstein (2012: 14).
91. Sgovio (1979: 251).
92. Wallace (1946: 36).
93. Magadan State Musical and Drama Theater, "Theater History."
94. Glushchenko (April 14, 2013, updated October 16, 2017).
95. Sakharov Center, "Savoyeva Nina Vladimirovna (1916–2003)."
96. Sgovio (1979: 251).
97. Nikishov to Beria, copy to Stalin and Molotov, GA RF, Fond R-9401, op. 2, file 65, pp. 191–93.
98. Wallace (1946: 92).
99. Wallace (1946: 34, 73, 222). Birstein (2012: 6, 7–9). Lipper (1951: 103, 111–12, 268).
100. Wallace (1946: 44).
101. Wallace (1946: 108, 117, 123, 140).
102. Engerman (2003: 99–101).
103. Lattimore (December 1944: 646). Prosecutor General's Office of the Republic of Kazakhstan (October 29, 2013). Wallace (1946: 87–89). Birstein (2012: 18).
104. Isaev (1996).
105. Ruleva and Abaimova (December 30, 2012).
106. Meerovich (September 2008).
107. Report on the activities of the American Society of Cultural Relations with the USSR for 1929, GA RF, Fond 5283, op. 3, p. 104/reverse.
108. Stalin (1949: 118–35).
109. Engerman (2003: 143).
110. Veblen (1921 [2001]: 86–104).
111. Chase (1932: 155–56).
112. Engerman (2003: 168, 179–81, 184, 188–89).
113. Engerman (2003: 241).
114. Engerman (2003: 214).
115. Engerman (2003: 234).
116. Duranty (1944: 161).
117. Engerman (2003: 200, 211–15).
118. *New York Times* (June 24, 1990).
119. Engerman (2003: 128–46, 151–54, 160–73, 179–81, 184, 188–89, 193). George F. Kennan, Memorandum for the Minister, in Robert Skinner to the Secretary of State, August 19,

1932, Decimal File 1932, 861.5017 Living Conditions/510, Record Group 59, NARA. Stalin (1949: 118–35).

120. George F. Kennan, Memorandum for the Minister, in Robert Skinner to the Secretary of State, August 19, 1932, Decimal File 1932, 861.5017 Living Conditions/510, Record Group 59, NARA.

121. See, for example, Hollander (1997).

122. Wallace (1946: 93–95). Engerman (2003: 194).

123. Engerman (2003: 216).

124. Wallace (1946: 137).

125. Wallace (1946: 136–39).

126. Top Secret reference, "Wallace, Henry Agard, 1948 Presidential candidate from third party," May 1948, Soviet Central Committee "Henry Wallace" file, held at the foreign policy department of the central committee of VCP (b), RGASPI, Fond 495, op. 261, file 60, part 1, p. 34.

127. Secret Report by Captain Kennith Knowles, Observer and Military Secretary of the Wallace Mission, July 15, 1944, File 811.003/Wallace, Henry A./7-2944; Box 3498, Central Decimal File, 1940–1944, Record Group 250, NARA: 75.

128. Hollander (1997: 107, 129).

129. Frank (1932: 135).

130. Buxton (1928: 71).

131. Wallace (1940: 17).

132. Kravchenko (1946: 469).

133. Wicksteed (1928: 189).

134. Wallace (1946: 110, 142).

135. Minahan (2002: 345).

7. China, Through a Glass Darkly

1. Roosevelt (1946: 143).

2. Tuchman (1970: 481).

3. Davies (1972: 322).

4. Bradley (2015: 85–92).

5. Pakula (2009: 64).

6. See Walker (1976: 17–18). Green (2017:140).

7. Chen (1993: 155).

8. On Mei-ling's rise and influence, see Pakula (2009).

9. Fenby (2004: 166).

10. Bradley (2015: 103–4). Chen (1993: 244–51).

11. Taylor (2009: 61).

12. Bradley (2015: 105).

13. Seagrave (1985: 284). *Los Angeles Times* (October 24, 2003).

14. White (1978).

15. *New York Times* (December 2, 1927).

16. Bradley (2015: 115–17, 148, 197). Fielding (1977: 134).

17. Stimson and Bundy (1948: 243).

18. Bradley (2015: 127).

19. Tikhvinsky (1996).

20. Buck (1970: 135).

21. Chang (1996: 1033–56). Harmsen (2013).
22. Taylor (2009: 169).
23. Bradley (2015: 139, 217).
24. Schaller (1979: 104–5).
25. Schaller (1979: 98). Hauser (March 24, 1941).
26. White (1978: 76).
27. Pearson (May 17, 1986).
28. Bradley (2015: 201).
29. Schaller (1979: 88).
30. Blum (1973: 119). Speech reprinted in Wallace (1944: 200).
31. Correspondence from Henry A. Wallace to Elmer Davis dated September 28, 1943, Henry A. Wallace correspondence [reel 25], July 16, 1943–February 1944—Ia25-282, Henry A. Wallace Collection, University of Iowa. *New York Times* (October 11, 1943).
32. Davies (1972: 223–24) (italics added). Useful pieces on the making of Roosevelt's China policy include "Ch'I, Hsi-sheng, Chiang Kai-shek and Franklin D. Roosevelt," in van Minnen and Sears (1992); Fraser (1992); Miller (April 1979: 59–62); Shephard (March 1989); Tsou (December 1959: 1075–91); Newman (July 1983: 205–22); Schaller (2008: 145–74); and Young (April 1975: 66–68).
33. Tuchman (1970: 293–95).
34. Stilwell (1948: 26).
35. Huston (1998 [2004]: 452).
36. Fenby (2004: 400).
37. McLynn (2011).
38. Blum (1973: 126).
39. Schaller (1979: 143, 159–60).
40. May (1974: 303–4).
41. *Time* (July 3, 1944: 20).
42. Summary Report of Vice President Wallace's Visit in China, July 10, 1944, Subject file "Henry A. Wallace" (1940–44), Box 190, President's Secretary's File, FDRL. Correspondence from Henry A. Wallace to Franklin D. Roosevelt dated July 10, 1944, Henry A. Wallace correspondence [reel 59], December 1931–1964—Ia59-0781, Henry A. Wallace Collection, University of Iowa. Liang (1972: 193).
43. Blum (1973: 348).
44. Sevareid (1946 [1969]: 310). Service (1974: 100). Taylor (2009: 216–17).
45. News clip video of Wallace's arrival and various events (including volleyball games) in Chungking can be seen here: https://www.youtube.com/watch?v=Uy0N0PtVqb0&feature=youtu.be and here: https://www.youtube.com/watch?v=QqF-ItEOQVA&feature=youtu.be.
46. *For Victory* (March 14, 2009).
47. Record of conversation of the Soviet Charge d'affaires in China T.F. SKVORTSOV with the American Ambassador in China Gauss and the head of the Chinese sector of the US State Department ["Ministry of Foreign Affairs"] Vincent, June 20, 1944, AVP RF, Fond 06, op. 6, P 39, file 498, p. 182.
48. T.F. Skvortsov, charge d'affairs of the USSR in China to People's Commissar of Foreign Affairs of the USSR, V.M. Molotov, July 5, 1944, AVP RF, Fond 0100, op. 32a, P 298, file 1, p. 242. *Time* (July 3, 1944: 20). May (1974: 307), based on an interview with Vincent, March 17, 1972.
49. John Davies to Harry Hopkins, "Chiang Kai Shek and China," December 31, 1943, Harry L. Hopkins, Memorandum for the President, February 7, 1944, Box 27, President's

Secretary's File, FDRL. "Report by Mr. Hall of the National City Bank on his observations in Chinese Communist controlled areas in the course of his journey from Peiping to Chungking," memorandum submitted by Embassy at Chungking, March 4, 1943, in Correspondence from John Carter Vincent to Lauchlin Currie dated January 28, 1944, Henry A. Wallace correspondence [reel 25], July 16, 1943–February 1944—Ia25-0874-Ia25-0879, Henry A. Wallace Collection, University of Iowa. John Davies, "The American Stakes in Chinese Unity: Proposals for Preliminary American Action," File #30127P, Henry A. Wallace Papers, University of Iowa: 3.

50. Memorandum by the Second Secretary of Embassy in China (Davies), "Observers' Mission to North China," January 15, 1944, in *FRUS, 1944*, VI: 307–8. May (1974: 298–99).

51. Bulletin #1634, June 21, 1944, The Chinese Information Committee, Fond 0100, Referentura on China, the 1st Far Eastern Department, NKID, AVP RF, Fond 0100, op. 35, P 237, file 12.

52. *Time* (July 3, 1944: 20). May (1974: 307), based on an interview with Vincent, March 17, 1972.

53. Correspondence from Henry A. Wallace to Franklin D. Roosevelt dated July 10, 1944, Henry A. Wallace correspondence [reel 59], December 1931–1964—Ia59-0781, Henry A. Wallace Collection, University of Iowa. Summary report of Vice President Wallace's Visit in China, July 10, 1944, Subject File "Henry A. Wallace" (1940–1944), Box 190, President's Secretary's File, FDRL: 3.

54. Dorn (1971: 77–79). Taylor (2009: 257). Schaller (1979: 130–31, 153). Bernstein (September 3, 2015).

55. Tuchman (1970: 384, 317). Taylor (2009: 2,10, 99).

56. May (1974: 312–13). Ye (2011: 303–4).

57. "Summary Notes of Conversation between Vice President Henry A. Wallace and President Chiang Kai-shek," by John Carter Vincent, in United States Department of State (1949: 550). Davies (1972: 306). May (1974: 314).

58. Record of conversation of the Soviet Charge d'affaires in China C.[Comrade] Skvortsov with Gauss [phonetic], Lattimore, Hazard, Kight, June 21, 1944, AVP RF, Fond 06, op. 6, P 39, file 498, pp. 183–84.

59. May (1974: 315), based on interviews with John Carter Vincent on July 1, 1971. Correspondence from Henry A. Wallace to Franklin D. Roosevelt dated July 10, 1944, Henry A. Wallace correspondence [reel 59], December 1931–1964—Ia59-0781, Henry A. Wallace Collection, University of Iowa. Summary report of Vice President Wallace's Visit in China, July 10, 1944, Subject File "Henry A. Wallace" (1940–1944), Box 190, President's Secretary's File, FDRL: 3.

60. Discussion with Pres. Chiang on June 22, Subject File "Henry A. Wallace," Box 190, President's Secretary Files, FDRL: 3–11. Harriman to FDR, June 11, 1944, Box 11, Map Room Papers, FDRL.

61. Hazard (1984: 74).

62. Stout (April 11, 1995). Hazard (1984).

63. Record of conversation of the Soviet Charge d'affaires in China T.F. Skvortsov with the head of the section on Lend-Lease supplies to the USSR . . . J. Hazard, June 23, 1944, AVP RF, Fond 06, op. 6, P 39, file 498, pp. 186, 188.

64. Hazard (1984: 74).

65. Record of conversation of the Soviet Charge d'affaires in China T.F. Skvortsov with the head of the section on Lend-Lease supplies to the USSR . . . J. Hazard, June 23, 1944, AVP RF, Fond 06, op. 6, P 39, file 498, p. 187; "In their progressive development," Wallace said on June 23, 1944, "the Chinese people will meet the hearty support of Americans." A

record of his statement was underlined in red pencil in an NKID report. AVP RF, Fond 0100, op. 35, P 237, file 12, p. 64.

66. Record of conversation of the Soviet Charge d'affaires in China T.F. Skvortsov with the head of the section on Lend-Lease supplies to the USSR . . . J. Hazard, June 23, 1944, AVP RF, Fond 06, op. 6, P 39, file 498, pp. 187–88.

67. Hazard (1984: 74).

68. Hazard (1984: 74).

69. "The Trip of Vice-President Wallace to China," informational memo, August 17, 1944, AVP RF, Fond 0100, opp. 35, P 237, file 12, pp. 31–39.

70. Record of conversation of the Soviet Charge d'affaires in China T.F. Skvortsov with the head of the section on Lend-Lease supplies to the USSR . . . J. Hazard, June 23, 1944, AVP RF, Fond 06, op. 6, P 39, file 498, p. 188.

71. May (1974: 321). Notes on the Vice President's Conversation with President Chiang, June 21 at President Chiang's Residence, Subject File "Henry A. Wallace," Box 190, President's Secretary's File, FDRL: 11–13.

72. Westad (1993: 71) documents the political strategy of Mao and the CCP in 1944–45, which prioritized moderation in policy ambition, cooperation with the United States, and coalition with the KMT.

73. Notes on the Vice President's Conversation with President Chiang, June 23, Subject File "Henry A. Wallace," Box 190, President's Secretary Files, FDRL: 16–17. Harriman to FDR, June 11, 1944, Box 11, Map Room Papers, FDRL. Davies (1972: 392). May (1974: 323–25). Diary entry, March 14, 1944, reprinted in Reminiscences of Henry Agard Wallace, CCOH, p. 3207. Reminiscences of Henry Agard Wallace, CCOH, pp. 4025–4036. Ballis (September 1951: 170).

74. Notes on the Vice President's Conversation with President Chiang, June 23, Subject File "Henry A. Wallace," Box 190, President's Secretary Files, FDRL: 17–18. Wallace, statement before the Senate Subcommittee to Investigate the Administration of the Internal Security Act and Other Internal Security Laws of the Committee on the Judiciary, October 17, 1951, in Senate Subcommittee to Investigate the Administration of the Internal Security Act and Other Internal Security Laws of the Committee on the Judiciary (1951: 1368–69). May (1974: 329–32).

75. Tuchman (1970: 557–58). Schaller (1979: 135).

76. Correspondence from Henry A. Wallace to Harry S. Truman dated September 19, 1951, Henry A. Wallace correspondence [reel 48], February 1951–August 1952—Ia48 -0387-Ia48-0390, Henry A. Wallace Collection, University of Iowa.

77. Mission of Vice President Wallace to China, June 1944; Conversations between Vice President Wallace and Generalissimo Chiang Kai-shek, in FRUS, 1944, VI: 216–46.

78. Alsop, statement before the Senate Subcommittee to Investigate the Administration of the Internal Security Act and Other Internal Security Laws of the Committee on the Judiciary, October 17, 1951, in Senate Subcommittee to Investigate the Administration of the Internal Security Act and Other Internal Security Laws of the Committee on the Judiciary (1951: 1444–48). Alsop (April 1952: 31). May (1974: 331–37). Stilwell, diary entry, May 19, 1943, Diaries of General Joseph W. Stilwell, 1900–46, Hoover Institution Library and Archives. Correspondence from Henry A. Wallace to Harry S. Truman dated September 19, 1951, Henry A. Wallace correspondence [reel 48], February 1951–August 1952—Ia48-0388-Ia48-0389, Henry A. Wallace Collection, University of Iowa.

79. Memorandum for the President for the U.S. Chiefs of Staff, July 4, 1944, folder 17, Box 87, Marshall Papers, George C. Marshall Foundation; Stimson, diary entry, August 2, 1944, Stimson, Henry L. Diary Excerpts, Box 124, John Toland Papers, FDRL.

80. Gillin and Myers (1989: 3–4).
81. Stilwell, diary entry, July 8, 1944, Diaries of General Joseph W. Stilwell, 1900–46, Hoover Institution Library and Archives. F.D.R. to Chiang Kai-Shek, cable, July 7, 1944, Box 10, Map Room Papers, FDRL. Generalissimo Chiang Kai-shek to President Roosevelt, Chungking, July 8, 1944, in *FRUS, 1944*, VI: 121–22.
82. Hurd (July 11, 1944). Huang (Fall–Winter 1996–97: 102).
83. Taylor (2009: 283, 292).
84. Liang (1972: 242–43).
85. Stilwell, diary entries, September 25 and 26, 1944, Diaries of General Joseph W. Stilwell, 1900–46, Hoover Institution Library and Archives. President Roosevelt to Generalissimo Chiang Kai-shek, October 5, 1944, in *FRUS, 1944*, VI: 165–66.
86. van de Ven (2018: 193).
87. Romanus and Sunderland (1956: 468, footnote 73). Liang (1972: 271–72).
88. Stilwell, diary entry, October 20, 1944, Diaries of General Joseph W. Stilwell, 1900–46, Hoover Institution Library and Archives.
89. Davies (2012: 45).
90. Davies (2012: 140).
91. Davies (2012: 139).
92. Davies (2012: 150).
93. Meeting of the Joint Chiefs of Staff, November 24, 1943, in *FRUS: The Conferences at Cairo and Tehran*: 32.
94. Roosevelt-Churchill-Stalin Luncheon Meeting, November 30, 1943, in *FRUS: The Conferences at Cairo and Tehran*: 565–68. The Tehran Conference, 1943, Milestones, *FRUS* U.S. Department of State Archive (January 20, 2009).
95. Tripartite Political Meeting, December 1, 1943, in *FRUS: The Conferences at Cairo and Tehran*: 600–60.
96. Davies (2012: 189, 212).
97. May (1974: 292–93).
98. Lozovsky was born "Solomon Dridzo," later assuming the pen name "A. Lozovsky" with "A" standing for "Alexei."
99. AVP RF, Fond 06, op. 7, P 7, file 82, pp. 6–18. Published in *Soviet-American Relations* V (2004a: 605–12).
100. Davies (2012: 253).
101. Davies (1972: 424).
102. See, for example, Ballis (September 1951: 170), and White (May 31, 1950: 106).
103. May (1974: 293, 329, 356) references his interviews with Vincent on July 1, 1971, and March 17, 1972.
104. "China Officially Announces the Key Points of Common Talks to the Press When US Vice President Wallace Left Chongqing," in Qin (1980: 869–71).
105. Chang diary entry in Gillin and Myers (1989: 63).
106. Wallace (June 1944).
107. AVP RF, Fond 06, op. 7, P 7, file 82, pp. 6–18. Published in *Soviet-American Relations* V (2004a: 605–12).
108. "On the other side of China lie Port Arthur, which Russia lost in her war with Japan in 1905, and Manchuria, long regarded as a sphere of rival Russian-Japanese influences. Some believe that when Japan is defeated, especially if this is achieved with Russian participation, Moscow will evince more than an academic interest in these regions on China's borders. Russia would then be the greatest Asiatic power." Callender (February

18, 1943). "Russia wants the Liaotang Peninsula, her lost fortress of Port Arthur and the great port of Dairen, which in Russian is known as Dalny, meaning 'far off.' That is what the Russians want, the control of the West Pacific; that is, of the China coast." Duranty (February 7, 1943).

109. Davies (2012: 260). Schaller (1979: 150).

110. AVP RF, Fond 06, op. 7, P 7, file 82, pp. 6–18. Published in *Soviet-American Relations* V (2004a: 605–12) (italics added). Sulzberger (December 2, 1943).

111. Blum (1973: 333).

112. Davies (2012: 248).

113. Blum (1973: 473).

114. Blum (1973: 473).

115. "Chiang Kai-Shek and Henry Wallace's Conversation in the Counselor's Office," June 16, 1944, Revolutionary Documents—American Diplomacy: Wallace's Visit to China, Chiang Kai-Shek Cultural Artifacts, National Museum of History, 002-020300-0038-007, translated by Fred Qin. In 1942, Currie had, according to one Chinese Nationalist account, told Chiang that "Washington" thought it might "not be a bad idea to make Manchuria a buffer state between Japan and Russia." Chiang reacted angrily (Liang [1972: 77–82]).

116. Department of State, memorandum of conversation, "Re: China," June 1945, Box 1928, Harry S. Truman Papers, WHCF: OF. Leahy (1950: 381). Baime (2017: 271–72).

8. History's Pivot

1. Blum (1973: 360).

2. Donovan (1977: xii).

3. Hachey (Winter 1973–1974: 141–53). Blum (1973: 363). Brown (1992: 188). Hamby (1995: 278–79). Guffey's autobiography enthuses at length about his warm friendship with Harry Truman. Referring to the 1944 Democratic convention, Guffey does not even mention Wallace. He says only that he did not openly back Truman after the latter entered the vice presidential race because he had already "committed" himself to a nameless someone else. Guffey (1952: 167).

4. Allen (1960: 129).

5. Henry Morgenthau, diary entry, July 6, 1944, Presidential Diary, Vol. 6, Morgenthau Presidential Diaries, Diaries of Henry Morgenthau, Jr., FDRL: 1382. Brown (1992: 190).

6. Goodwin (1994: 491).

7. Goodwin (1994: 493–97). Ferrell (1994: 3).

8. Lelyveld (2016: 23, 102–3).

9. Gromyko (1988: 120–24). Significant parts of the "Bungalow dinner" account were omitted in the English version of Gromyko's memoir: Gromyko (1989: 47).

10. Tully (1949: 275).

11. Ferrell (1994: 20).

12. Lippmann (July 11, 1944).

13. Lelyveld (2016: 13, 157, 358). [Interview with Robert E. Hannegan]. TS.; Washington, 25 May 1946, Box 40, Robert E. Sherwood Papers, Houghton Library.

14. MacDougall I (1965: 14).

15. Daniels (1975: 231).

16. Rosenman (1952: 439).

17. Reminiscences of Henry Agard Wallace, CCOH, pp. 3661, 3666.

18. Daniels (1975: 231).
19. Rosenman (1952: 441).
20. Blum (1973: 360–61). Rosenman (1952: 442).
21. Brown (1992: 190). Daniels (1975: 231). Wallace, speech, "The Era of the Pacific," July 9, 1944: http://www.ibiblio.org/pha/policy/1944/1944-07-09a.html.
22. Blum (1973: 361).
23. "Roosevelt—Politics," August 8, 1944, Reminiscences of Henry Agard Wallace, CCOH, p. 3444.
24. Blum (1973: 361). "Mark Etheridge," July 25, 1944, Reminiscences of Henry Agard Wallace, CCOH, p. 3401. Allen (1960: 129). Rosenman (1952: 442–43).
25. Blum (1973: 361–62).
26. Harold Ickes, diary entry, July 16, 1944, Box 12, reel 6, Harold L. Ickes Papers, Library of Congress.
27. Daniels (1975: 235).
28. Blum (1973: 362).
29. Blum (1973: 362–63).
30. *New York Times* (October 7, 1949).
31. Flynn (1947: 180). Faber (May 20, 1984). *Irish Echo* (March 12, 2012).
32. Allen (1960: 118, 136). *New York Times* (April 24, 1973). George E. Allen, interview by Jerry N. Hess, May 15, 1969, Oral History Interviews, Truman Library.
33. Edwin W. Pauley with Richard English, "Why Truman is President," 2-2A, undated, "The President," Box 30, White House Central Files: Confidential Files, Truman Library. Edwin W. Pauley, interview by J.R. Fuchs, March 3, 1971, Oral History Interviews, Truman Library: 1–3. Saxon (July 29, 1981). Allen (1960:122). Shuit (July 30, 1981). United Press International (July 28, 1981).
34. Biles (1987: 111–21). Masters (2007: 116).
35. Walker (1997: vii–ix, xiii–xix, 138–42). Walker, "The Untold Story of Key New Dealer, Frank Walker." "Frank C. Walker (1945)," Harry S. Truman—Administration, Miller Center, University of Virginia.
36. Lelyveld (2016: 165). Edwin W. Pauley, "Life and Times of EWP," pp. 42–43, folder 4, Box 88, Truman Library.
37. Lelyveld (2016: 165–66). Brown (1992: 185–87, 191–95, 198).
38. Edwin W. Pauley,, "Life and Times of EWP," pp. 44–45, folder 4, Box 88, Truman Library. Barkley (1954: 169–73).
39. Lelyveld (2016: 165–66). Edwin W. Pauley with Richard English, "Why Truman is President," pp. 13–14, undated, "The President," Box 30, White House Central Files: Confidential Files, Truman Library.
40. Brown (1992: 195). Edwin W. Pauley with Richard English, "Why Truman is President," 14, undated, "The President," Box 30, White House Central Files: Confidential Files, Truman Library. Edwin W. Pauley, "Life and Times of EWP," p. 43, folder 4, Box 88, Truman Library.
41. Edwin W. Pauley, "Life and Times of EWP," pp. 46–48, folder 4, Box 88, Truman Library.
42. Letter from Special Agent Rudolph H. Hartmann regarding his investigation into Tom Pendergast, Inmate #55295, June 6, 1939, Pendergast, Tom, 1870–1945, Notorious Offenders Files, 1919–1975, Records of the Bureau of Prisons, 1870–2009, NARA.
43. Eagleton and Duffin (April 1996: 269–74). Allen (1960: 128–29). Harold Ickes, diary entry, July 16, 1944, Box 12, reel 6, Harold L. Ickes Papers, Library of Congress. Walker (1997: 138–40). McCullough (1992: 221–22, 285–86, 288, 300–301, 323). Ferrell (1994: 7).

Lelyveld (2016: 165–67). Edwin W. Pauley with Richard English, "Why Truman is President," 14–15, undated, "The President," Box 30, White House Central Files: Confidential Files, Truman Library. Allen (1960: 126).

44.   Blum (1973: 364). "Mark Etheridge," July 25, 1944, Reminiscences of Henry Agard Wallace, CCOH, pp. 3401–3402. Byrnes (1958: 222). McCullough (1992: 302). Culver and Hyde (2000: 349).

45.   Blum (1973: 365–66). Barkley (1954: 188).

46.   Blum (1973: 366–67). Allen (1960: 130). Byrnes (1958: 222). "Gallup Poll," March 5, 1944, Reminiscences of Henry Agard Wallace, CCOH, p. 3147. "Gallup Poll," March 14, 1944, Reminiscences of Henry Agard Wallace, CCOH, p. 3208. Correspondence from Jake S. More to Henry A. Wallace dated July 18, 1944, Henry A. Wallace correspondence [reel 26], March 1944–July 1944—Ia26-0933, Henry A. Wallace Collection, University of Iowa. Culver and Hyde (2000: 350).

47.   Byrnes (1958: 223–25). Walker (1997: 140). Ferrell (1992: 33).

48.   My recounting of the train episode leaves out one matter of intense historical controversy. Grace Tully, FDR's private secretary, has claimed that the president's handwritten version of the letter had Douglas' name before Truman's (as on the July 11 "envelope" note), but that Hannegan told her the boss wanted them reversed when typed. Tully claims that Douglas would have become vice president, and thence president, save for the change. There are four major problems with her account, however. The first is why she did not challenge Hannegan or speak to the president, for whom she worked loyally, if she believed Hannegan was mischaracterizing his preferences. The second is that the Hannegan family has denied the story. The third is that both the final typewritten *and* a handwritten version have survived, each with Truman's name first—supporting the Hannegan family account. The fourth is that FDR signed both versions, indicating his approval of the text. McCullough, strangely, notes the existence of the handwritten letter, but defends Tully's account on the grounds that she "was not known for fabricating." He makes no effort to resolve the discrepancy between the two. See Eagleton and Duffin (April 1996: 274–80); McCullough (1992: 306–7); Hamby (1995: 280–81); and Heaster (January 1986: 168).

The discrepancies regarding the letter are only one example of the challenges facing a historian in writing a definitive account of all the major events leading to Wallace's departure from the vice presidency. George Allen put it best in his memoirs: "It is one of the episodes in American history that will baffle scholars of the future because no two accounts of it agree completely and some vary widely. I am not particularly worried about tomorrow's historians. It is not my ambition to make things easy for them. Let them work for their pay. Anyway, they'll pick the accounts that best suit their own preconceptions of what happened, as historians always have, and then defend their own pet versions in learned and heated tracts, thus holding their franchises as creative writers" (Allen 1950: 120–21). I have done my best not to be one of such historians, and to identify the accounts, in each case, that cohere most logically and factually. As always, readers will be the judge.

49.   Brown (1992: 206). Ferrell (1992: 38). Lelyveld (2016: 171).

50.   "Barkley," August 1, 1944, Reminiscences of Henry Agard Wallace, CCOH, pp. 3437–38.

51.   Byrnes (1958: 226).

52.   Eagleton and Duffin (1996: 276).

53.   See, for example, Ferrell (1994: 35–36).

54.   See, for example, McCullough (1992: 306–7). McCullough's account of the train story and its aftermath is perhaps the most confused and unconvincing part of his celebrated biography of Truman.

55. See, for example, Eagleton and Duffin (1996: 271) and this statement of Hannegan's daughter: https://www.pbs.org/video/american-experience-truman-and-unity-a-com promise-candidate/.

56. Walker (1997: 139). Byrnes (1958: 229).

57. Ferrell (1994: 39).

58. Robertson (1994: 357).

59. Brown (1992: 198).

60. Flynn (1947: 182).

61. Ferrell (1994: 3).

62. Byrnes (1958: 223–25).

63. Walker (1997: 142).

64. Byrnes (1958: 226–29). Flynn (1947: 182). Ferrell (1994: 44–48). Walker (1997: 146). Robertson (1994: 358).

65. McCullough (1992: 308–9).

66. Ferrell (1994: 52).

67. "Senator Truman," August 3, 1944, Reminiscences of Henry Agard Wallace, CCOH, p. 3443.

68. Letter on the Vice-Presidential Nomination, July 14, 1944, Franklin D. Roosevelt, The American Presidency Project.

69. McCullough (1992: 310). Culver and Hyde (2000: 351–52).

70. Drury (1963: 218).

71. Drury (1963: 218). Culver and Hyde (2000: 351).

72. Barkley (1954: 189).

73. Moscow (July 18, 1944).

74. McCullough (1992: 310).

75. Blum (1973: 374). *New York Times* (November 11, 1945).

76. Flynn (1947: 181). Ferrell (1994: 48–49).

77. "Mark Etheridge," July 25, 1944, Reminiscences of Henry Agard Wallace, CCOH, p. 3402. Ferrell (1994: 53–54).

78. Ferrell (1994: 55–56). Fraser (1991: 531). Josephson (1952: 619–22). "Mark Etheridge," July 25, 1944, Reminiscences of Henry Agard Wallace, CCOH, p. 3406.

79. *New York Times* (July 20, 1944), "Delegates Awaken at Night Session." "Time Magazine," July 31, 1944, Reminiscences of Henry Agard Wallace, CCOH, p. 3430. Blum (1973: 368). Jonathan Daniels, interview by J.R. Fuchs, October 4, 1963, Oral History Interviews, Truman Library: 93. McCullough (1992: 313).

80. In Truman's account, his first words were actually "Jesus Christ!" Truman I (1955: 193). McCullough (1992: 314). Ferrell (1992: 61–62).

81. Edwin W. Pauley with Richard English, "Why Truman is President," 26, undated, "The President," Box 30, White House Central Files: Confidential Files, Truman Library.

82. Brown (1992: 208). Ferrell (1994: 62).

83. Blum (1973: 368). Ferrell (1994: 64, 66, 69). Hagerty (July 21, 1944).

84. Edwin W. Pauley with Richard English, "Why Truman is President," 16, undated, "The President," Box 30, White House Central Files: Confidential Files, Truman Library.

85. Edwin W. Pauley with Richard English, "Why Truman is President," 19, undated, "The President," box 30, White House Central Files: Confidential Files, Truman Library. "C.B. Baldwin," August 11, 1944, Reminiscences of Henry Agard Wallace, CCOH, p. 3454.

86. Hagerty (July 21, 1944). Hagerty (July 20, 1944). Catledge (July 20, 1944). *New York Times* (July 20, 1944), "Delegates Awaken at Night Session." *New York Times* (July 20, 1944), "Wallace Is in Fight to Finish, Directing Convention Contest." Ferrell (1994: 82).

87. McCullough (1992: 313). McCormick (June 27, 1944).

88. Edwin W. Pauley with Richard English, "Why Truman is President," 20–21, undated, "The President," Box 30, White House Central Files: Confidential Files, Truman Library.

89. *Washington Post* (January 25, 1944).

90. Roosevelt, speech, "Annual Message to Congress (Four Freedoms)," January 6, 1941: https://69494391.weebly.com/dr-win-the-war.html.

91. Peterson (August 1948).

92. "Phillip Murray of the C.I.O.," August 8, 1944, Reminiscences of Henry Agard Wallace, CCOH, p. 3447.

93. Catledge (July 21, 1944). Reminiscences of Henry Agard Wallace, CCOH, "Time Magazine," July 31, 1944, p. 3430.

94. *Congressional Record,* 78th Congress, 2nd Session, XC, Part 11, 1944: A3490. Wallace, speech, "The Liberal Platform: Democratic Party Cannot Be Conservative," July 29, 1944: www.ibiblio.org/pha/policy/1944/1944-07-20d.html. Peterson (August 1948).

95. Ferrell (1994: 79–80). Neale Roach, interview by Jerry N. Hess, January 21, 1969, Oral History Interviews, Truman Library: 24–25. Edwin W. Pauley with Richard English, "Why Truman is President," 12, undated, "The President," Box 30, White House Central Files: Confidential Files, Truman Library. Edwin W. Pauley, interview by J.R. Fuchs, March 3, 1971, Oral History Interviews, Truman Library: 31–32. J. Leonard Reinsch, interview by J.R. Fuchs, March 14, 1967, Oral History Interviews, Truman Library: 128.

96. Blum (1973: 370). Baldwin says that "the occupants of the gallery," though having obtained their tickets from Kelly's office, "underst[ood] that the will of the rank and file was being thwarted by the political bosses" and "expressed their resentment" by "join[ing] the parade." "Report by C.B. Baldwin on Democratic National Convention, 1944," February 27, 1951, Reminiscences of Henry Agard Wallace, CCOH, p. 3413.

97. McCullough (1992: 315). Flynn (1947: 281) says that "Kelly really wanted Scott Lucas," but had "persuaded Allen to support Truman."

98. Edwin W. Pauley with Richard English, "Why Truman is President," 21, undated, "The President," Box 30, White House Central Files: Confidential Files, Truman Library. J. Leonard Reinsch, interview by J.R. Fuchs, March 13, 1967, Oral History Interviews, Truman Library: 29. Neale Roach, interview by Jerry N. Hess, January 21, 1969, Oral History Interviews, Truman Library: 24.

99. Ferrell (1994: 78).

100. Ferrell (1994: 118).

101. Repetto (2015: 105).

102. Edwin W. Pauley with Richard English, "Why Truman is President," 20–22, undated, "The President," Box 30, White House Central Files: Confidential Files, Truman Library. Edwin W. Pauley, interview by J.R. Fuchs, March 3, 1971, Oral History Interviews, Truman Library: 31. Neale Roach, interview by Jerry N. Hess, January 21, 1969, Oral History Interviews, Truman Library: 24.

103. Thomas (May 31, 1989). Barnes (May 31, 1989).

104. J. Leonard Reinsch, interview by J.R. Fuchs, March 13, 1967, Oral History Interviews, Truman Library: 28–29. Reinsch (1988: 5–7). Neale Roach, interview by Jerry N. Hess, January 21, 1969, Oral History Interviews, Truman Library: 24–26. Edwin W. Pauley with Richard English, "Why Truman is President," 22, undated, "The President," Box 30, White House Central Files: Confidential Files, Truman Library. McCullough (1992: 316–17). Ferrell (1994: 80). Pepper and Gorey (1987: 135). The dramatic audio can be heard here: https://www.youtube.com/watch?v=eKRdrQGGg9c&feature=youtu.be.

105. Drury (1963: 220).
106. "Time Magazine," July 31, 1944, Reminiscences of Henry Agard Wallace, CCOH, p. 3429. Edwin W. Pauley with Richard English, "Why Truman is President," 22–23, undated, "The President," Box 30, White House Central Files: Confidential Files, Truman Library.
107. The second ballot was a chaotic affair, with many delegation votes changing—some multiple times. Accounts of who-voted-which-way-when differ across sources. I have done my best to piece together an accurate picture across many of them. *News & Observer* (July 22, 1944). *Chicago Daily Tribune* (July 22, 1944). *Pittsburgh Post-Gazette* (July 22, 1944). Littell (1987: 281–82). Edwin W. Pauley with Richard English, "Why Truman is President," 24–26, undated, "The President," Box 30, White House Central Files: Confidential Files, Truman Library. McCullough (1992: 319–20). Culver and Hyde (2000: 365–66).
108. MacDougall I (1965: 21).
109. McCullough (1992: 318) provides no reference, but his words are almost identical to those of Culver and Hyde (2000: 364), who in turn cite "Report by C.B. Baldwin on Democratic National Convention, 1944," February 27, 1951, Reminiscences of Henry Agard Wallace, CCOH, pp. 3383–88. Culver and Hyde not only claim that ambassadorships and "postmaster positions" were "handed out," but that "cold cash changed hands." There is no basis whatsoever for the postmaster claims. The cash claims seem to be based on Baldwin's unsubstantiated statement that he "was satisfied that the votes of delegates were actually bought outright." McCullough evidently thought the cash part too much of a stretch, so left it out. The *New York Times*' James Hagerty, whom McCullough does quote, says only that "it took a good deal of talking and a good deal of pressure" to bring around the delegates. Hagerty (July 22, 1944).
110. Hagerty (July 22, 1944).
111. Tennessee recorded all its 26 votes for Cooper in both rounds.
112. In round 1, the New York delegation voted 69½ for Truman, 23 for Wallace, ½ for Barkley, and 3 "absent." In round 2, the vote was 74½ for Truman, 18 for Wallace, ½ for Barkley, and 3 "absent." It is unrecorded how the individual delegates voted.
113. In round 1, the Indiana delegation voted 21 for McNutt and 5 for Wallace. In round 2, it voted 19 for McNutt, 6 for Wallace, and 1 for Truman.
114. "Report by C.B. Baldwin on Democratic National Convention, 1944," February 27, 1951, Reminiscences of Henry Agard Wallace, CCOH, p. 3388.
115. "Report by C.B. Baldwin on Democratic National Convention, 1944," February 27, 1951, Reminiscences of Henry Agard Wallace, CCOH, pp. 3386–87.
116. MacDougall I (1965: 21).
117. Catledge (July 22, 1944).
118. "Report by C.B. Baldwin on Democratic National Convention, 1944," February 27, 1951, Reminiscences of Henry Agard Wallace, CCOH, pp. 3386–87.
119. Hagerty (July 21, 1944).
120. Catledge (July 17, 1944). Hagerty (July 20, 1944). Edwin W. Pauley, interview by J.R. Fuchs, March 3, 1971, Oral History Interviews, Truman Library: 14.
121. Correspondence from Henry A. Wallace to Harry S. Truman dated July 21, 1944, Henry A. Wallace correspondence [reel 26], March 1944–July 1944—Ia26-0947, Henry A. Wallace Collection, University of Iowa.
122. Littell (1987: 284–85).
123. Drury (1963: 220).
124. Correspondence from Eleanor Roosevelt to Henry A. Wallace dated July 22, 1944,

Henry A. Wallace correspondence [reel 59], December 1931–1964—Ia59-0707, Henry A. Wallace Collection, University of Iowa. McCullough (1992: 322).

125. *Catholic Advance* (October 14, 1949). Edwin W. Pauley, interview by J.R. Fuchs, March 3, 1971, Oral History Interviews, Truman Library: 17. Edwin W. Pauley with Richard English, "Why Truman is President," 27, undated, "The President," Box 30, White House Central Files: Confidential Files, Truman Library. Flynn (1947: 180).

126. Allen (1960: 118–19).

127. MacDougall I (1965: 15).

128. Rosenman (April 7, 1946).

129. Drury (1963: 220).

130. Reminiscences of Henry Agard Wallace, CCOH, p. 3473. Culver and Hyde (2000: 370).

131. Blum (1973: 371). Wallace Diaries, January 19, 1945, Series 6, Box 19, Henry A. Wallace Papers, University of Iowa. Culver and Hyde (2000: 378).

132. Allen (1960: 126, 130) (italics added). "Had [Roosevelt] chosen to oppose the advice of the party spokesmen," wrote Tully, "I am sure he could have kept Wallace on the ticket" (Tully 1949: 275). McCullough agrees: "Roosevelt would have had no trouble whatever getting [Wallace] nominated" (1992: 322).

133. "I remembered that in 1940, after Mr. Roosevelt had been nominated, he told me that he would decline to run if the convention refused to accept his recommendation of Wallace for Vice President. I knew how effective his threat had been" (Byrnes 1958: 223).

134. FDR's son Jimmy believed his father "really preferred Justice William O. Douglas," which is consistent with numerous firsthand accounts. "I think if Roosevelt could have had his own way and if he felt he could get the support of the convention, he would have selected Bill Douglas as vice president," wrote Walker. "He indicated that more than once" (1997: 138). Other than Truman, the only other one on the president's short list, at least until July 17, was Byrnes (McCullough 1992: 323).

135. On July 11, Gene Casey asked Roosevelt whether he really intended to let the convention decide the vice presidential nominee. "Yes," Roosevelt responded wryly, though "of course, there are some people I wouldn't run with." Tammany Hall boss Charlie Murphy had similarly told people, according to Roosevelt, that the convention would choose the New York lieutenant governor. "And he got away with it for years" (Daniels, 1975: 235). Pepper observed that whereas Roosevelt "might bow to the delegates by not taking a candidate who was objectionable to them, he would never take one whom he did not want" (Barkley 1954: 190).

136. To quote Walker again: "[T]o have it known, and without impugning anyone's good faith it would most certainly have been known, that Roosevelt did not want Byrnes or anyone else to run with him would have had violent political repercussions" (1997: 142).

9. Keeping Up with the Joneses

1. Correspondence from Henry A. Wallace to Grace Tully dated August 16, 1944, Henry A. Wallace correspondence [reel 27], August 1944–January 22, 1945—Ia27-0626, Henry A. Wallace Collection, University of Iowa. Reminiscences of Henry Agard Wallace, CCOH, p. 3390.

2. Blum (1973: 367).

3. Correspondence from Harry S. Truman to Henry A. Wallace dated July 25, 1944, Henry A. Wallace correspondence [reel 26], March 1944–July 1944—Ia26-0979, Henry A. Wallace Collection, University of Iowa. Correspondence from Harold L. Ickes

to Henry A. Wallace dated July 24, 1944, Henry A. Wallace correspondence [reel 26], March 1944–July 1944—Ia26-0978, Henry A. Wallace Collection, University of Iowa. Correspondence from Robert E. Hannegan to Henry A. Wallace dated August 8, 1944, Henry A. Wallace correspondence [reel 27], August 1944–January 22, 1945—Ia27-0068, Henry A. Wallace Collection, University of Iowa.

4. Correspondence from Henry A. Wallace to Curtis D. MacDougall dated December 11, 1952, Henry A. Wallace correspondence [reel 49], September 1953–May 1954—Ia49-0193, Henry A. Wallace Collection, University of Iowa.

5. Blum (1973: 375, 381–84). Jones (1951: 288–90). Culver and Hyde (2000: 373).

6. Blum (1973: 388–89).

7. Culver and Hyde (2000: 374), citing Campaign address at the Liberal Party Rally, New York City, October 31, Box 58, Series 10, Henry A. Wallace Papers, University of Iowa.

8. Allen (1960: 146–47).

9. Campaign address at the Liberal Party Rally, New York City, October 31, Box 58, Series 10, Henry A. Wallace Papers, University of Iowa (italics added). Culver and Hyde (2000: 374).

10. Adams (November 1, 1944).

11. Blum (1973: 390–91).

12. See, for example, Goodwin (1994: 575).

13. Blum (1973: 405–6).

14. Blum (1973: 401). Blum (1973: 419). Sirevag (1985: 164). Blum (1973: 426). Memorandum on reorganization of the Commerce Department, in Correspondence from Frank D. Richardson to Mildred M. Eaton dated November 29, 1944, Henry A. Wallace correspondence [reel 27], August 1944–January 22, 1945—Ia27-0533-Ia27-0537, Henry A. Wallace Collection, University of Iowa.

15. Blum (1973: 406–13). See, for example, Fossedal (1993: 63).

16. Reston (January 19, 1945).

17. Franklin Delano Roosevelt to Jesse Jones, January 20, 1945, folder "Commerce—Jones, Jesse," Box 54, Departmental Correspondence, President's Secretary's File, FDRL.

18. *Congressional Record*, 79th Congress, 1st Session, XCI, 1945: 365–66.

19. *Washington Post* (January 23, 1945). *Cincinnati Enquirer* (January 23, 1945), quoting *Cleveland News*. *New York Times* (January 23, 1945). Drury (1963: 345).

20. Drury (2963: 346).

21. Reston (January 23, 1945). Drury (1963: 346–47, 354). *Congressional Record*, 79th Congress, 1st Session, XCI, 1945: 370.

22. Reston (January 23, 1945).

23. Jones, statement before the Senate Committee on Commerce (1945: 56). Fenberg (2011: 514–17). Drury (1963: 347, 352).

24. Drury (1963: 349–50).

25. *Congressional Record*, 79th Congress, 1st Session, XCI, 1945: 1616. Drury (1963: 354–55, 373). Byrnes (1958: 255–56). Truman I (1955: 195). Sirevag (1985: 169–70). Culver and Hyde (2000: 383–84).

26. Reminiscences of Henry Agard Wallace, CCOH, p. 3643.

27. Goodwin (1994: 602–3).

28. McCullough (1992: 346–47).

29. Acheson (1969: 104).

30. Stone (1988: 274).

31. Reminiscences of Henry Agard Wallace, CCOH, p. 3692.

10. "60 Million Jobs," Four Million Strikers

1.   McCullough (1992: 260).
2.   McCullough (1992: 229, 420).
3.   MacDougall I (1965: 85–86). Straight (1983: 204–5).
4.   Beschloss (2002: 249).
5.   Blum (1973: 466). Steil (2018: 9, 90). McCullough (1992: 388, 404).
6.   Toll (2020: 642).
7.   Wallace, statement before the House Committee on Appropriations, January 25, 1946, in House Committee on Appropriations (1946: 3). Schapsmeier and Schapsmeier (1970: 134). Culver and Hyde (2000: 393–94).
8.   Bailey (1950: 42–43).
9.   Wallace (1945: 6–7, 9, 20, 45–46, 48, 77, 83, 92, 126, 145, 168–69, 203, 216).
10. Pepper and Taft (September 9, 1945). Correspondence from Claude Pepper to Henry A. Wallace dated August 4, 1945, Henry A. Wallace correspondence [reel 36], July 23, 1945–September 1945—Ia36-0240, Henry A. Wallace Collection, University of Iowa. Stalin conversation with Senator Pepper, September 14, 1945, RGASPI, Fond 558, op. 11, file 374, pp. 93–94. Telephone conversation, Senator Guffey to Henry A. Wallace, September 12, 1945, Henry A. Wallace correspondence [reel 65], March 22, 1945–December 29, 1945—Ia65-0442, Henry A. Wallace Collection, University of Iowa.
11. Cabinet Meeting Minutes, Friday, October 19, 1945, folder "October 19, 1945," Notes on Cabinet Meetings I, 1945–1946, Matthew J. Connelly Papers, Truman Library. Blum (1973: 495).
12. Biography of "Tan" and his wife (January 1945), Alexander Vassiliev Yellow Notebook No. 2 p. 67, referring to SRV, File 40623, Vol. 1 "Tan" ("Kant"), pp. 30–32, Alexander Vassiliev Papers, Library of Congress. Phelps and Magdoff (May 1, 1999).
13. Re: Harry Magdoff, Serials 465 to 466, Vol. 19, Subject "Silvermaster," Rosenberg Files, FBI FOIA: 83; hereinafter this collection is cited as "FBI Silvermaster File." Foster (January 26, 2006). Phelps and Magdoff (May 1, 1999). Foster (2000: 386).
14. Martin (January 9, 2006). Phelps and Magdoff (May 1, 1999).
15. "Harry Samuel Magdoff," Serials 1364, Vol. 60, File No. 65-56402, FBI Silvermaster File: 86, 87, 88.
16. "Edward Fitzgerald," Serials 1364, Vol. 60, FBI Silvermaster File: 5.
17. Memo on H.D. White, Serials 561 to 573, Vol. 23, FBI Silvermaster File: 29, 30. J.E. Hoover to Brigadier General Harry Hawkins Vaugan, Nov. 8, 1945, Serials 376 to 420, Vol. 16, FBI Silvermaster File: 98–100; "Underground Soviet Espionage organization (NKVD) in Agencies of the United States Government, February 21, 1946," sent to Brigadier General Harry Hawkins Vaughan, Military Aide to the President, February 25, 1946, to Attorney General and to Secretary Byrnes on February 25, 1946, Serials 561 to 573, File, Vol. 023, FBI Silvermaster File: 55–276.
18. Teletype New York to Washington HQ and Field, November 21, 1945, Serials 51 to 108, Vol. 2, FBI Silvermaster File: 8.
19. Note by "X" dated 11.01.45, Alexander Vassiliev Yellow Notebook No. 2, p. 66, Alexander Vassiliev Papers, Library of Congress, referring to SVR RF File 40623, Vol. 1, p. 22.
20. "List of materials," undated, Alexander Vassiliev Yellow Notebook No. 2, p. 66, Alexander Vassiliev Papers, Library of Congress, referring to SVR RF File 40623, Vol. 1, p. 44.
21. Serial EBF 621, Part 2, Vol. 25, FBI Silvermaster File: 188.

22. "Harry Samuel Magdoff," March 16–31, 1946, Serial 1009, Vol. 43, FBI Silvermaster File: 67; "Re Harry Magdoff," Serials 465 to 466, Vol. 19, FBI Silvermaster File: 83.

23. Correspondence from Henry A. Wallace to Harland H. Allen dated June 17, 1948, Henry A. Wallace correspondence [reel 45], June 1948–March 1949—Ia45-0095, Henry A. Wallace Collection, University of Iowa.

24. Testimony of Harry Magdoff, accompanied by Joseph Rotwein, before the Senate Subcommittee to Investigate the Administration of the Internal Security Act and Other Internal Security Laws of the Committee on the Judiciary, May 1, 1953, in Senate Subcommittee to Investigate the Administration of the Internal Security Act and Other Internal Security Laws of the Committee on the Judiciary (1953: 286–96). Martin (January 9, 2006).

25. Correspondence from Henry A. Wallace to Homer Ferguson dated May 5, 1953, Henry A. Wallace correspondence [reel 49], September 1953–May 1954–Ia49-0449-Ia49-0450, Henry A. Wallace Collection, University of Iowa.

26. Correspondence from Henry A. Wallace to Homer Ferguson dated May 5, 1953, Henry A. Wallace correspondence [reel 49], September 1953–May 1954—Ia49-0448-Ia49-0449, Henry A. Wallace Collection, University of Iowa. Buhle (February 20, 2006). Foster (2000: 386). D'Mello (January 14, 2006).

27. Harry S. Truman, Letter to the President, Society for the Advancement of Management, Concerning Full Employment, November 30, 1945, in Truman I (1961: 514). *New York Times* (December 1, 1945).

28. Wallace (1948). Wallace (September 1948). Wallace (December 30, 1946). Wallace (September 8, 1947). Wallace (April 19, 1948). Rosenof (April 1967). Arnold (1937).

29. Senator Ferguson, "Misleading Official Reports Affecting the Automobile Industry," in *Congressional Record*, 79th Congress, 2nd Session, XCII, Part 2, 1946: 2417–20.

30. McCullough (1992: 470). Freeman (2000).

31. Correspondence from Henry A. Wallace to Karl Haartz dated June 28, 1946, Henry A. Wallace correspondence [reel 41], June 1946–August 8, 1946—Ia41-0391-Ia41-0392, Henry A. Wallace Collection, University of Iowa.

32. Hazlitt (October 22, 1945). Blum (1973: 518). Porter (November 4, 1945). Stark (November 6, 1945). *New York Times* (November 10, 1945). *New York Times* (November 11, 1945). *New York Times* (November 9, 1945). Senator Ferguson, "Misleading Official Reports Affecting the Automobile Industry," in *Congressional Record*, 79th Congress, 2nd Session, XCII, Part 2, 1946: 2417–20.

33. Serials 465 to 466, Vol. 19, FBI Silvermaster File: 84–85.

34. Senator Ferguson, "Misleading Official Reports Affecting the Automobile Industry," in *Congressional Record*, 79th Congress, 2nd Session, XCII, Part 2, 1946: 2417–20. Correspondence from Henry A. Wallace to Karl Haartz dated June 28, 1946, Henry A. Wallace correspondence [reel 41], June 1946–August 8 1946—Ia41-0391-Ia41-0392, Henry A. Wallace Collection, University of Iowa. "Edward Fitzgerald," FBI Silvermaster File, Vol. 060, Serials 1364, p. 5.

35. *Congressional Record*, 79th Congress, 1st Session, XCI, 1945:12521–22. *New York Times* (November 20, 1945), "Texts of the UAW and Romney Statements on Auto Union Demand." Porter (December 2, 1945).

36. Telephone conversation between Henry A. Wallace and Phil Hauser dated December 26, 1945, Henry A. Wallace correspondence [reel 65], March 22, 1945–December 29, 1945—Ia65-0680, Henry A. Wallace Collection, University of Iowa.

37. Serial EBF 621, Part 2, Vol. 25, FBI Silvermaster File: 18.

38. ". . . On Dec 27, 1945 . . . MAGDOFF told CHARLES KRAMER of MAGDOFF's appointment on the Staff of the General Motors Fact Finding Committee . . . Mrs. Magdoff told [telephone surveillance] . . . that the subject's name apparently was suggested to WILLIAM LLOYD GARRISON, a member of the . . . Committee, by Secretary of Commerce Wallace. . . ," "Re: Harry Magdoff," Serials 465 to 466, Vol. 19, FBI Silvermaster File: 83–84.

39. Senator Ferguson, "Misleading Official Reports Affecting the Automobile Industry," in *Congressional Record*, 79th Congress, 2nd Session, XCII, Part 2, 1946: 2417–20. Hallpern (1988: 84).

40. McCullough (1992: 481).

41. Raskin (January 16, 1946).

42. Correspondence from Willard Monroe Kiplinger to Henry A. Wallace dated May 22, 1946, Henry A. Wallace correspondence [reel 40], April 4, 1946–May 1946—Ia40-0833-Ia40-0835, Henry A. Wallace Collection, University of Iowa.

43. "Re: Harry Dexter White," phone surveillance, January 2, 1946, Serials 465 to 466, Vol. 19, FBI Silvermaster File: 177–78.

44. The President's News Conference of January 24, 1946, in Truman II (1962: 92).

45. Blum (1973: 540, 541–42).

46. Blum (1973: 373).

47. Truman diary entry in Geselbracht (2019: 294).

48. Hallpern (1988: 84, 87, 88, 89, 93, 95).

49. McCullough (1992: 492).

50. Brinley (August 1967: 7–8).

51. In the case of the Soviet blockade of Berlin in 1948–49, Truman wisely persisted with the airlift, rather than shifting to more radical action, even though no one believed that the airlift constituted a "strategy" to end the crisis. The combination of a U.S. counterblockade and horrific public relations for Moscow, however, wore Stalin down, motivating him to lift the blockade in May 1949. See Steil (2018: chs. 11–12).

52. Executive Order No. 9727, Possession, Control, and Operation of Certain Railroads, Signed, May 17, 1946, Executive Orders Disposition Tables, Office of the Federal Register, NARA. McCullough (1992: 495).

53. Blum (1973: 571).

54. McCullough (1992: 501). Cabinet Meeting Minutes, May 24, 1946, Matthew J. Connelly Papers, Personal Papers, Truman Library.

55. "Radio Address to the American People on the Railroad Strike Emergency," May 24, 1946 (Broadcast from the White House at 10 p.m.), Public Papers, Truman Library; Special Message to the Congress Urging Legislation for Industrial Peace, May 25, 1946 [As delivered in person before a joint session], in Truman II (1962: 277–80).

56. Blum (1973: 575–76). McCullough (1992: 503–6). United Mine Workers of America, Health and Retirement Funds records, 1940–1993, Penn State University Libraries.

57. U.S. Department of Commerce, Bureau of the Census (1955: 189). Wool and Winegarden (May 1950: 488).

58. U.S. Department of Commerce, Bureau of the Census (1955: 189).

59. Wallace, speech before the Michigan Citizens' Committee in Detroit, May 7, 1946, reprinted in *Congressional Record*, 79th Congress 2nd Session, XCII, Part 11, 1946: A2773–A2774. Porter (July 7, 1946). Higgs (2006: 133, 151).

60. *New York Times* (August 4, 1946).

61. Adams (September 15, 1946).

62. Wallace (1945: 3–9, 12–13, 20, 33, 45–46, 48–49, 51, 73, 77–78, 81, 83, 87–89, 93, 99, 124–26, 130, 144–45, 152–53, 160–64, 168–69, 179, 195, 203–4, 207, 214, 216). Pepper and Taft (September 9, 1945).

11. Mission to Moscow

1. In early March 1945, U.S. Office of Strategic Services (OSS) agents in Switzerland notified Washington that German General Karl Wolff had arrived in Berne to discuss a possible surrender. U.S. officials then informed Moscow within two days (Gaddis 1972: 92).
2. Drury (1963: 313).
3. Under Soviet influence, Romania formed what appeared to be a "broad coalition government," which included members of the Liberal and National Peasant parties, on March 6, 1945. However, the important government posts were held by Communists. Communists and their allies claimed a big victory in the election of November 1946, which was marked by propaganda and intimidation of the opposition. King Michael attempted to block a total Communist takeover but was forced to abdicate on December 30, 1947. That day, the Romanian People's Republic was declared. Boia (2001: 11–115).
4. The four-party "Fatherland Front" coalition was installed in a bloodless coup on September 9, 1944. It included the Communist Bulgarian Workers' Party, the Agrarian Party, the Socialist Party, and the "People's Union *Zveno.*" ("Current Intelligence Study Number 28," June 29, 1945, Research and Analysis Branch 1930–1946, Office of Strategic Services, Record Group 226, NARA). The Communist Party came to dominate the coalition; it won an absolute majority of seats (277 of 465) in the elections of October 27, 1946. However, they continued to operate through the "Fatherland Front." (*New York Times* [November 20, 1945], "Fatherland Front Victor in Bulgaria"; *New York Times* [October 29, 1946]).
5. The United States Political Adviser for Germany (Murphy) to the Secretary of State, June 6, 1945, in *FRUS, 1945*, III: 331.
6. The Deputy Director of the Office of European Affairs (Hickerson) to the Secretary of State, January 8, 1945, in *FRUS: Conferences at Malta and Yalta, 1945*: 93–96.
7. Truman I (1955: 36–38).
8. Bohlen (1973: 223).
9. This is Truman's account (Truman I [1955: 79–82]). Bohlen's is milder, but it is indisputable from Molotov's own version that the president was undiplomatically harsh. Bohlen (1973: 213); AVP RF, Fond 05, op. 7, P 2, file 30, pp. 53–55.
10. Stalin to Truman, April 24, 1945, in Stalin (1965: 219–20).
11. Memorandum by the Acting Secretary of State and the Foreign Economic Administrator (Crowley) to President Truman, May 11, 1945, in *FRUS, 1945*, V: 999–1000.
12. Truman diary entry in Geselbracht (2019: 364–65). Rose (1973: 188–89). Blum (1973: 451). Gaddis (1972: 219).
13. Sherwood (1948 [2008]: 690–705. Rose (1973: 191–92).
14. Truman (1980 [1997]: 49).
15. Truman (1980 [1997]: 44). Neiberg (2015: 59, 103–4). Gaddis (1972: 239).
16. Truman I (1955: 402).
17. Rose (1973: 303). Toll (2020: 675).
18. Gaddis (1972: 214–15).
19. Truman diary entry in Geselbracht (2019: 191) (italics added).
20. Memorandum of Conversation, by the First Secretary of Embassy in the Soviet Union (Bohlen), November 5, 1943, in *FRUS, 1943*, III: 781–86.

21. Gaddis (1972: 86, 179–81). The Ambassador in the Soviet Union (Harriman) to Mr. Harry L. Hopkins, Special Assistant to President Roosevelt, September 10, 1944, in *FRUS, 1944*, IV: 989.

22. Memorandum for the President, "A $10 Billion Reconstruction credit for the U.S.S.R.," by H.D. White, January 5, 1944, folder "January–May 1944", Box 15, Staff Memoranda of H.D. White, January 1941–June 1946, Records of Assistant Secretary of the Treasury, Monetary and International Affairs, Record Group 56, NARA; Henry Morgenthau, diary entry, January 5, 1944, Book 691, Series 1: Morgenthau Diaries, Diaries of Henry Morgenthau, Jr., FDRL: 104–21. Gaddis (1972: 184–86).

23. V.G. Dekanozov to V.M. Molotov, December 29, 1945, AVP RF, Fond 06, op. 7, P 19, file 19, pp. 14–16. James (1996: 70).

24. See, for example, Deane (May 1976).

25. Chuev (1991). Raine (October 2001: 1).

26. From the diary of V.M. Molotov, reception of Turkish ambassador Selim Sarper, June 7, 1945, AVP RF, Fond 06, op. 7, P 2, file 31, pp. 2–6; Acheson (1969: 199–200).

27. Chuev (1991).

28. Gaddis (1972: 286–90, 315).

29. *Congressional Record*, 79th Congress, 2nd Session, XCII, 1946: 1692–95.

30. Byrnes' address at the Overseas Press Club of America, February 28, 1946, reprinted in *Congressional Record*, 79th Congress, 2nd Session, XCII, 1946: 1056–58. Gaddis (1972: 295, 305).

31. Truman II (1956: 93); Roberts (2006: 309); Halle (1967: 99–100). Ertegün died in 1944, not 1946—as claimed in the otherwise useful account of the Iran Crisis in Sebestyen (2014: 190–99). His body was not repatriated earlier because of the war.

32. Beisner (2006: 38–39).

33. *Fortune* (September 1945). Gaddis (1972: 321).

34. Beisner (2006: 39–43). Acheson, interview by Theodore A. Wilson and Richard D. Mckinzie, June 30, 1971, Oral History Interviews, Truman Library: 2–3; Isaacson and Thomas (1986 [2012]: 370–72); McCullough (1992: 369).

35. Wallace to Truman, March 14, 1946, in Truman diary entry in Geselbracht (2019: 295).

36. Downey (1971: 216).

37. Statement by Assistant Secretary Clayton made before the House Ways and Means Committee April 18, 1945, *The Department of State Bulletin* (April 22, 1945: 757).

38. Irwin (2017: 464–65, 467). Senate Committee on Finance (1945: 20).

39. Wallace (May 5, 1945).

40. *New York Times* (November 13, 1945).

41. Waggoner (December 2, 1945) (italics added). Paul indicated that the 1,500 staff from the FEA would be halved by the end of 1945.

42. House Committee on Ways and Means (1945: 180). *Congressional Record*, 79th Congress, 1st Session, XCI, 1945: 5259. *New York Times* (January 19, 1946).

43. Fossedal (1993: 197–98). "Veto of the Wool Act," June 26. 1947, Public Papers, Truman Library.

44. Telephone conversation between Henry A. Wallace and Joseph Davies dated June 12, 1946, Henry A. Wallace correspondence [reel 66], January 2, 1946–September 20, 1946—Ia66-0435, Henry A. Wallace Collection, University of Iowa.

45. *New York Times* (June 20, 1946).

46. The $500 million two-way trade projection was reported in *The Washington Star* on July 7, 1946, and noted in the *Congressional Record*: "Another Mission to Moscow," Ex-

tension of Remarks of Hon. Reid F. Murray of Wisconsin, in *Congressional Record*, 79th Congress, 2nd Session, XCII, Part 12, 1946: A4029.

47. Ladd to FBI Director, c. November 26, 1945, Serials 51-108x/6, Vol. 2, FBI Silvermaster File: 217.

48. Photocopy of Bentley's Nov. 8, 1945 statement is at: E.E. Conroy to Director, FBI, November 13, 1945, Serials 574 to 630, Vol. 24, FBI Silvermaster File: 14–44. Steil (2013: 294).

49. Re: Anatoli Borisovich Gromov, December 18, 1945, Serial EBF 621, Part I, Vol. 25, FBI Silvermaster File: 429.

50. Serial EBF 621, Part I, Vol. 25, FBI Silvermaster File: 429. S. Tsarapkin to Kemenov, August 28, 1945, GA RF, Fond 5283, op. 22a, file 46, p. 173. Alexander Vassiliev Black Notebook, p. 55, ref. to SVR RF File 43173 Vol. 1, pp. 155–60, Alexander Vassiliev Papers, Library of Congress.

51. Alexander Vassiliev, 1996 draft chapter, "Golos-Bentley-Browder," grace of Dr. Svetlana A. Chervonnaya (originally part of the "Jury Bundle" during Vassiliev's libel litigation in London in 2002–2003; from 2010, part of Alexander Vassiliev Papers at the Library of Congress). Vassiliev refers to SVR RF File 70545, pp. 57, 71, 162, 178–79, 397–401, 410–14; file 70994, pp. 327, 339, 360–71. Weinstein and Vassiliev (2000: 99–104). Haynes and Klehr (1999: 96–97, 122).

52. "Re—Confidential Informant Gregory [i.e., Elizabeth Bentley], from April 10 to May 4, 1946," Serial 1158, Vol. 49, FBI Silvermaster File: 67, 69. Bentley (1951: 307).

53. House Committee on Un-American Activities (1950), *Proceedings Against Mrs. Louise Berman—Report No. 2906*.

54. New York Consul General Yakov Lomakin to Solomon Lozovsky, Deputy Minister of Foreign Affairs, July 7, 1946, GA RF, Fond 5283, op. 22, file 14a, p. 172.

55. "Who Went on the Second 'Mission to Moscow'?" Extension of Remarks of Hon. Reid F. Murray, July 31, 1946, in *Congressional Record*, 79th Congress, 2nd Session, XCII, Part 12, 1946: A4678; *New York Times* (June 7, 1970).

56. Telephone conversation between Henry A. Wallace and Lewis L. Lorwin dated May 17, 1946, Henry A. Wallace correspondence [reel 66], January 2, 1946–September 20, 1946—Ia66-0383, Henry A. Wallace Collection, University of Iowa.

57. "Another Mission to Moscow," Extension of Remarks of Hon. Reid F. Murray in *Congressional Record*, 79th Congress, 2nd Session, XCII, Part 12, 1946: A4029. *Congressional Record*, 79th Congress, 2nd Session, XCII, Part 12, 1946: A4678. *Washington Star* (July 7, 1946).

58. Medvedev (2005: 36).

59. There was no official record of Stalin's speech at the 1952 plenum of the CPSU Central Committee: it is mostly known from the memoirs of Nikita Khrushchev and (more reliably) from writer Konstantin Simonov. According to the latter, Stalin's denouncement of Mikoyan, although shorter than that of Molotov, was "even more vicious and disgraceful." Simonov (1989).

60. RGASPI, Fond 84, op. 3, file 16, pp. 152, 155. "Record of the conversation of the Minister of Foreign Trade A.I. Mikoyan with officials of the US Ministry of Commerce E.C. Ropes and L.L. Lorwin," July 15, 1946, AVP RF, F. 06, op. 8, P 47, file 790, pp. 6–8.

61. "Record of the conversation of the Minister of Foreign Trade A.I. Mikoyan with officials of the US Ministry of Commerce E.C. Ropes and L.L. Lorwin," July 24, 1946, AVP RF, F. 06, op. 8, P. 47, file 790, pp. 10–16.

62. With credits, as opposed to loans, interest only begins accumulating at the time import orders are placed.

63. Mikoyan's dictations on misc subjects, incl. war-time Soviet-American negotiations. . . , [dictated] February 11, 1965–December 30, 1966, RGASPI, Fond 84, op. 3, file 116, p. 170.

64. Mikoyan's record of his conversation with Harriman on February 1, 1944, AVP RF, Fond 06, op. 6, P 17, file 175, pp. 1–6, 8–10; Mikoyan's dictations on misc. subjects. . . , RGASPI, Fond 84, op. 3, file 116; *FRUS, 1944*, IV: 1043, 1054–55. Paterson (June 1969: 73).

65. Henry Morgenthau, diary entry, January 5, 1944, Book 691, Series 1: Morgenthau Diaries, Diaries of Henry Morgenthau, Jr., FDRL: 104–21.

66. Memorandum, Harry Dexter White to Henry Morgenthau, March 7, 1944, Part II: 23, Harry D. White Papers, reprinted in Senate Committee on Interior and Insular Affairs (1955), *Accessibility of Strategic and Critical Materials to the United States in Time of War and Our Expanding Economy.*

67. New York to Moscow #590, April 29, 1944, Venona, Declassified Documents, NSA.

68. New York to Moscow, #1119–21, Venona, Declassified Documents, NSA. Folder "January–May 1944," Box 15, Harry Dexter White records, Record Group 56, NARA.

69. Henry Morgenthau, diary entry, January 5, 1944, Book 691, Series 1: Morgenthau Diaries, Diaries of Henry Morgenthau, Jr., FDRL: 104–21.

70. Folder "January–May 1944," Box 15, Staff Memoranda of H.D. White, January 1941–June 1946, Records of Assistant Secretary of the Treasury, Monetary and International Affairs, Record Group 56, NARA.

71. New York to Moscow #83, January 18, 1945, Venona, Declassified Documents, NSA.

72. The Assistant Secretary of State (Clayton) to the Secretary of State, January 20, 1945, in *FRUS, Conferences at Malta and Yalta, 1945*: 318–19.

73. *FRUS, 1945*, V: 996, 845.

74. Truman I (1955: 80).

75. Folder "Inter Treasury Memoranda (Secretary) Mr. Coe 1945," Box 17, Harry Dexter White records, Record Group 56, NARA.

76. From Vyshinsky's diary, "Reception of American Senator Pepper, September 21, 1945," AVP RF, Fond 0129, op. 29, P 166, file 4, pp. 53–55.

77. A.I. Mikoyan dictation on October 10, 1966, "Soviet-American war-time negotiations," RGASPI, Fond 84, op. 3, file 116, pp. 173–78; Paterson (June 1969: 84, 87–88).

78. Middleton (July 31, 1946) (italics added).

79. "Special Message to the Congress Requesting Extension of the Reciprocal Trade Act," March 1, 1948, in Truman IV (1964: 169); Irwin, Mavroidis, and Sykes (2008: 93). The GATT was intended as a stopgap until the Truman administration could get ratification of the International Trade Organization through Congress; the ITO, however, was never ratified owing to concerns over usurpation of U.S. sovereignty and congressional power. See, for example, Kaplan (1996: 52–53) and Gerber (2012: 46–47).

80. Hoffman (October 15, 1947); Fossedal and Mikhail (May–June 1997).

81. The $500 million two-way trade projection was reported in *The Washington Star* on July 7, 1946, and noted in the *Congressional Record*: "Another Mission to Moscow," Extension of Remarks of Hon. Reid F. Murray of Wisconsin, in *Congressional Record*, 79th Congress, 2nd Session, XCII, Part 12, 1946: A4029. According to Soviet data, two-way U.S.-Soviet trade in 1950 was 231.7 million rubles. At the exchange rate of 14 rubles to the dollar devised by Soviet economists, based on purchasing power parity, that was the equivalent of about $16 million. "Section on the USA in the Survey of commercial and political relations of the USSR with capitalist nations in 1950," prepared at the Ministry of Foreign Trade of the USSR, March 22, 1951, RGAE, Fond 413 sch [secret file keeping], op. 25, file 986, p. 89.

12. The Odd Tale of the Sino-Soviet Treaty

1. AVP RF, Fond 06, op. 7, P 7, file 82, pp. 6–18. Published in *Soviet-American Relations* V (2004a: 605–12) (italics added). Sulzberger (December 2, 1943).

2. The Commanding General, United States Military Mission in the Soviet Union (Deane), to the Joint Chiefs of Staff, Moscow, October 17, 1945, in *FRUS, Conferences at Malta and Yalta, 1945*: 371–73.

3. "Conversation: MILEPOST," December 14, 1944, Harriman Papers, Moscow Files, in *FRUS, Conferences at Malta and Yalta, 1945*: 378–79. Harriman and Abel (1975: 379–80).

4. See, for example, Foo (2009: 395).

5. Harriman and Abel (1975: 397–99).

6. Westad (1993: 32).

7. There is some controversy among scholars as to the means by which Chiang may have learned of the precise contents of the secret Yalta deal before June 1945. See, for example, Foo (2009: 395–403).

8. Record of conversation of I.V. Stalin with H. Hopkins, May 28, 1945, RGASPI, Fond 558, op. 11, file 374, pp. 33–45. Sherwood (1948 [2008]: 700). Garthoff (1966: 61).

9. Department of State, memorandum of conversation, re: China, June 1945, Box 1928, Harry S. Truman Papers, WHCF: OF, Truman Library; Leahy (1950: 381); Baime (2017: 271–72).

10. United States Department of State (1949: 115–18). Westad (1993: 35–36).

11. Westad (1993: 43).

12. See, for example, Byrnes (1947: 208).

13. Record of Soong conversation with Molotov (et al.), July 10, 1945, RGASPI, Fond 558, op. 11, file 322, p. 48.

14. Secretary of State to Ambassador Hurley for Chiang Kai-shek, July 23, 1945, Folder: "Volume X—The President's correspondence: With Chiang Kai-shek," Berlin Conference file, 1945, Harry S. Truman Papers, Staff Member and Office Files: Naval Aide to the President Files, Harry S. Truman Papers, Truman Library. Westad (1993: 45).

15. Foo (2010: 164). Foo (August 2009: 391, 397–98). Garver (1988: 210–12). Westad (1993: 46–48).

16. Kunetka (2015: 357–67). Hastings (2007: 477, 481). Atomic Heritage Foundation (June 5, 2014). U.S. Department of Energy, "The Atomic Bombing of Hiroshima."

17. Stalin's willingness to attack the Japanese in Manchuria without a Sino-Soviet treaty was a major change in his approach to Chungking. See, for example, Foo (2009: 394).

18. Westad (1993: 49, 77).

19. Toll (2020: 704).

20. Japanese deaths in the Soviet invasion of Manchuria would total 84,000 soldiers and up to 400,000 noncombatants (Frank [April 28, 2009]).

21. From the Diary of V.M. Molotov. Reception of the Japanese Ambassador Kaotake Sato at 17.00 [5 p.m.], August 8, 1945, AVP RF, Fond 06, op. 7, P 54, file 895, pp. 40–44. Toll (2020: 680–81, 705–6). Hastings (2007: 460, 466–67, 472, 480–81).

22. Hasegawa (2011). Hastings (2007: 504–6). Toll (2020: 680–81, 706, 720–25).

23. Blum (1973: 473–74, 477–78). Trohan (August 18, 1945). Toll (2020: 726–28).

24. Westad (1993: 52–53). Hastings (2007: 487, 507–8).

25. Hastings (2007: 523).

26. Gillin and Myers (1989: 101, 111–15, 153). United States Department of State (1949: 123).

27. Gillin and Myers (1989: 21).

28. Chang Kia-ngau's official title was chairman, Northeast (Manchuria) Economic Commission.

29. Gillin and Myers (1989: 63).

30. Gillin and Myers (1989: 1–2, 23, 63). Westad (1993: 86–87, 90). Blum (1973: 483–84).

31. "Report on Japanese Assets in Manchuria to the President of the United States, July, 1946," by Edwin W. Pauley, November 12, 1946; "Report on Japanese Assets in Soviet-Occupied Korea to the President of the United States, June, 1946," by Edwin W. Pauley, October 25, 1946, Box 19, Allied Commission on Reparations File, 1932–1971, Pauley, Edwin W. Papers, Truman Library. Raphael Green, interview by Neil M. Johnson, May 4, 1991, Oral History Interviews, Truman Library: 23.

32. Blum (1973: 520). Garthoff (1966: 74). Gillin and Myers (1989: 61).

33. Longhand Note of President Harry S. Truman, September 19, 1946, Folder: September 19, 1946, Harry S. Truman Papers: President's Secretary's Files, Harry S. Truman Papers, Truman Library.

34. See, for example, "Record of Conversation between Soviet Ambassador in China Apollon Petrov and Mao Zedong, Zhou Enlai, and Wang Roufel," September 6, 1945, Wilson Center Digital Archive. Perov notes that he "repeatedly stressed [to Mao] that the Soviet Union would like to see China politically united, that the talks [with the KMT] must continue, and an agreement between the parties must be reached through reciprocal concessions.

35. Gillin and Myers (1989: 75, 100, 105–6). Elleman (2008: 199).

36. Telegram from Molotov to Stalin (draft reply to Commander Malinovsky), October 30, 1945, Wilson Center Digital Archive. The actual cable was sent by Stalin on November 16, 1945.

37. Ballis (September 1951: 172).

38. Chang diary entries in Gillin and Myers (1989: 68, 95, 152–55).

39. The Secretary of State to the Embassy in China, February 9, 1946; The Secretary of State to the Chargé in the Soviet Union (Kennan), February 9, 1946; The Secretary of State to the Chargé in the Soviet Union (Kennan), March 5, March 7, 1946, in *FRUS, 1946*, X: 1104, 1104–5, 1112, 1113–14, 1115–16 (see "Manchurian War Booty"). *The New York Times* (March 6, 1946).

40. Chang diary entries in Gillin and Myers (1989: 66, 115, 222, 244).

41. Wallace (1946: 77–78). Perry quote from Collins (1860: 52).

42. Chang diary entries in Gillin and Myers (1989: 97, 238, 256–57).

43. Gillin and Myers (1989: 243–44, 272, 297).

44. *FRUS, 1946*, IX: 143, 427–28 [Levine (1987: 74–75)]. *New York Times* (September 19, 1946), "Dr. Wang Asserts Open Door Policy."

45. Gillin and Myers (1989: 243–44, 272, 297).

46. Gillin and Myers (1989: 310, 330).

47. Gillin and Myers (1989: 6–7, 13, 20, 37, 48–49, 61).

48. Levine (1987: 71, 79). Gillin and Myers (1989: 18). United States Department of State (1949: 125–26).

49. United States Department of State (1949: 122–23).

50. Levine (1987: 13). Michael and Taylor (1956: 440). Hsü (1970: 721).

51. See, for example, May (1979).

52. Davies (2012: 301). See also Waldron (January 28, 2013).

53. Westad (1993: 160–61).

54. Levine (1987: 242).

55. Stilwell died in 1946.

56. Wallace (July 5, 1948).
57. Pechatnov (2010: 108–9).

13. The Nuclear Option

1. Blum (1973: 152). Reminiscences of Henry Lewis Stimson, CCOH, p. 22. Hewlett and Anderson (1962: 45).
2. Wallace (July 19, 1948).
3. See, for example, Oliver Stone: http://www.peacecouple.com/2012/11/17/oliver-stone -discusses-pacifist-presidential-candidate-henry-wallace-on-dn/ and Oliver Stone, *The Untold History of the United States*, 12-chapter documentary series (2012) and companion book (Stone and Kuznick [2012]).
4. Reminiscences of Henry Agard Wallace, CCOH, pp. 3977–78. Culver and Hyde (2000: 396).
5. Blum (1973: 471).
6. Blum (1973: 475–76). Wallace, statement before a subcommittee of the Senate Committee on Banking and Currency, August 28, 1945, in Senate Committee on Labor and Public Welfare (1964: 2270–78).
7. Byrnes (1958: 373).
8. Blum (1973: 481–84) (italics added).
9. Belair (September 22, 1945).
10. "In August 1945, at a Cabinet meeting, Mr. Truman brought up the question of exploring the advisability of giving to Russia the secrets of the atom bomb." Crowley said after the meeting: "It was stated that it would take about $3.000.000.000 for Russia to build the bomb unless they were given economic aid. Acheson, who was sitting for Mr. Byrnes, said that he knew Mr. Byrnes would oppose the idea but that he (Acheson) thought it should be considered. Mr. Wallace made similar remarks.... Crowley said that the question was never brought up again and that neither Acheson nor Wallace had ever actually urged giving the atom bomb to Russia." Leo T. Crowley's speech in Milwaukee, October 15, 1951, in *Congressional Record*, 82nd Congress, 1st Session, XCVII, Part 15, 1951: A6540.
11. Forrestal (1951: 95). Blum (1973: 491). Gaddis (1972: 249) (italics added).
12. Blum (1973: 485–87).
13. Stimson and Bundy (1948: 642–46). Gaddis (1972: 248).
14. Truman diary entry in Geselbracht (2019: 330). Blum (1973: 496) (italics added).
15. Correspondence from Henry A. Wallace to Harry S. Truman dated September 24, 1945, Henry A. Wallace correspondence [reel 36], July 23, 1945–September 1945—Ia36-0892-Ia36-0893, Henry A. Wallace Collection, University of Iowa.
16. *New York Times* (September 24, 1945).
17. Krock (October 28, 1945).
18. Reminiscences of Henry Agard Wallace, CCOH, pp. 4108, 4174. Blum (1973: 485–87).
19. Krock (September 25, 1945). Gaddis (1972: 257).
20. Alexander Vassiliev, "Sources in Washington," pp. 122–23, referring to SVR RF "Tan" ("Kant") File No. 40623, Vol. 1, p. 44, "Summary Chapters," Alexander Vassiliev Papers, Library of Congress. "List of materials," Alexander Vassiliev, Yellow Notebook No. 2, p. 67, referring to SVR RF "Tan" ("Kant") File No. 40623, Vol. 1, p. 44, Alexander Vassiliev Papers, Library of Congress.
21. Blum (1973: 499–500).

22. Leslie Groves to Henry Wallace, Henry Stimson, and George Marshall, "Present Status and Future Program," August 23, 1943, roll 5, Correspondence ("Top Secret") of the Manhattan Engineer District, 1942–1946, National Archives microfilm publications, NARA. Houghton (2019: 106).

23. House Committee on Un-American Activities (1950: 1076), *Hearings Regarding Shipment of Atomic Material to the Soviet Union During World War II.* Joint Committee on Atomic Energy (April 1951: 954), *Soviet Atomic Espionage.*

24. Ryabev II (1999: 428), sourced from AP RF, Fond 93, file 99/46, p. 12; Malkov (2003: 311); RGASPI, Fond 17, op. 125, file 452, p. 5; AVP RF, Fond 06, op. 8, P 7, file 101, p. 66.

25. Alexander Vassiliev Black Notebook, p. 55, Alexander Vassiliev Papers, Library of Congress, referring to SVR RF File 43173, Vol. 1, pp. 155–60.

26. To Comrade Beria L.P. from Merkulov, undated, Alexander Vassiliev Black Notebook, p. 55, referring to SVR RF File 43173, Vol. 1, pp. 155–60, Alexander Vassiliev Papers, Library of Congress.

27. Chervonnaya (2008), Gorsky, Anatoly Veniaminovich (1907–1980). Serials 51-108x/b, Vol. 2, FBI Silvermaster File: 217. Serial EBF 621, Part 1, Vol. 25, Part 1, FBI Silvermaster File: 429. S. Tsarapkin to Kemenov, August 28, 1945, GA RF, Fond 5283, op. 22a, file 46, p. 173. Alexander Vassiliev Black Notebook, p. 55, Alexander Vassiliev Papers, Library of Congress, referring to SVR RF File 43173, Vol. 1, p. 155–60.

28. Wallace speech, "Peaceful Atomic Abundance," December 4, 1945, Series 10, Box 62, Henry A. Wallace Papers, University of Iowa.

29. *New York Times* (March 24, 1946).

30. Wallace speech, "Peaceful Atomic Abundance," December 4, 1945, Series 10, Box 62, Henry A. Wallace Papers, University of Iowa.

31. Telephone conversation between Henry A. Wallace and Harold Smith dated November 7, 1945, Henry A. Wallace correspondence [reel 65], March 22, 1945–December 29, 1945—Ia65-0573, Henry A. Wallace Collection, University of Iowa.

32. Henry Wallace, statement before the Senate Subcommittee of the Committee on Military Affairs (1945: 158–59). Mallon (October 12, 1945).

33. Wallace, statement before the Senate Special Committee on Atomic Energy, January 31, 1946, in Senate Special Committee on Atomic Energy (1946: 219–46).

34. Tower (February 1, 1946). MacDougall I (1965: 74).

35. Leviero (March 13, 1946). Shalett (March 16, 1946).

36. *New York Times* (March 14, 1946). Krock (March 15, 1946). Baldwin (March 17, 1946). *New York Times* (March 21, 1946), "Soviet Organ Sees 'Atomic Dictatorship' Aim."

37. See, for example, Truman diary entry in Geselbracht (2019: 340–43).

38. *New York Times* (March 21, 1946), "Baruch Selection Scored." Blum (1973: 438).

39. Feinberg (March 20, 1946). *New York Times* (March 22, 1946).

40. *New York Times* (May 18, 1946).

41. *New York Times* (August 14, 1946).

42. "Re: Harry Magdoff," Serials 465 to 466, Vol. 19, FBI Silvermaster File: 83; "Harry Samuel Magdoff" in "Underground Soviet Espionage Organization in Agencies of the United States Government," Serial 3620, Vol. 144, FBI Silvermaster File: 170. Teletype New York to Washington HQ and Field, November 21, 1945, Serials 51-108, Vol. 2, FBI Silvermaster File: 8. Haynes, Klehr, and Vassiliev (2009: 279–83).

43. Alexander Vassiliev's 1996 Russian manuscript, Istochniki v Vashingtone (*The Sources in Washington*), Allen Weinstein Papers, Hoover Institution Library and Archives: 112, referring to SVR RF "Krot" File 55302, Vol. 1, p. 68.

44. *New York Times* (August 13, 1948).

45. Cipher cable to Vadim dated November 23, 1945, Alexander Vassiliev White Notebook No. 3, p. 3, Alexander Vassiliev Papers, Library of Congress, referring to SVR RF File 70545 ("Mirna"/Elizabeth Bentley), p. 405. Haynes, Klehr, and Vassiliev (2009: 210, 279–83). *New York Times* (August 13, 1948).

46. Gerber (Winter 1982). Hamilton (September 20, 1946).

47. Lilienthal (1964: 123).

48. Blum (1973: 581–82).

49. Correspondence from Henry A. Wallace to Harry S. Truman dated July 23, 1946—Henry A. Wallace correspondence [reel 41], June 1946–August 8, 1946—Ia41-0761-Ia41-0772, Henry A. Wallace Collection, University of Iowa. Blum (1973: 588). Longhand Note of President Harry S. Truman, September 17, 1946, Harry S. Truman Papers: President's Secretary's Files, Harry S. Truman Papers, Truman Library.

50. Lord (1947: 561).

51. Adams (September 15, 1946).

52. Reminiscences of Henry Agard Wallace, CCOH, p. 4941. Culver and Hyde (2000: 418).

53. Truman wrote up at least three versions of the meeting, one six days after it, one seven days after it, and one years later—in his memoirs. They differ slightly in account and emphasis. Here, I am relying on the two more contemporaneous accounts: Longhand Notes of President Harry S. Truman, September 16 and 17, 1946, Box 274, Harry S. Truman Papers: President's Secretary's Files, Harry S. Truman Papers, Truman Library.

54. Harry Dexter White investigation report, transcript of H.D. White's telephone call to Joel Fisher, August 30, 1946, Serial 1673, Vol. 77, FBI Silvermaster File: 226.

55. Blum (1973: 612).

56. Longhand Note of President Harry S. Truman, September 16, 1946, Harry S. Truman Papers: President's Secretary's Files, Harry S. Truman Papers, Truman Library. MacDougall I (1965: 61).

57. The President's News Conference, September 12, 1946, Public Papers, Truman Library.

58. Byrnes, speech, "Stuttgart Speech (Speech of Hope)," September 6, 1946: http://ghdi.ghi-dc.org/sub_document.cfm?document_id=2300.

59. Wallace, speech, September 12, 1946, in *Vital Speeches of the Day* (October 1, 1946: 738–42). Reston (September 13, 1946). Hagerty (September 13, 1946). Reston (September 14, 1946). Callender (September 14, 1946). Hulen (September 15, 1946). Krock (September 15, 1946). Reston (September 15, 1946). Reston (September 16, 1946). Callender (September 17, 1946).

60. Phillips (1966: 151). Culver and Hyde (2000: 420).

61. Longhand Note of President Harry S. Truman, September 17, 1946, Box 274, Harry S. Truman Papers: President's Secretary's Files, Harry S. Truman Papers, Truman Library. McCullough (1992: 514).

62. Blum (1973: 660–69). *PM* (September 13, 1946), "Wallace Is Heckled Often."

63. *New York Times* (September 19, 1946), "Mr. Truman and Mr. Wallace."

64. Reminiscences of Henry Agard Wallace, CCOH, p. 3997.

65. Blum (1973: 660–69). *PM* (September 13, 1946), "Wallace Is Heckled Often."

66. D.M. Ladd, Memorandum for the Director, September 30, 1946, Subject: Henry Wallace, Part 04 of 05, FBI FOIA.

67. Blum (1973: 660–69). *PM* (September 13, 1946), "Wallace Is Heckled Often."

68. Culver and Hyde (2000: 420).

69. Blum (1973: 666–69).

70. *New York Times* (September 15, 1946), "Connally, Vandenberg Urge Bipartisan Foreign Policy."

71. Callender (September 19, 1946).

72. *New York Times* (September 15, 1946), "British Press Irate at 'Imperialist' Barb."

73. Callender (September 19, 1946).

74. Gruson (September 17, 1946).

75. Callender (September 16, 1946).

76. Sheean (September 18, 1948: 23).

77. Hulen (September 17, 1946).

78. Hulen (September 18, 1946).

79. *New York Times* (September 18, 1946), "Liberals Assail Wallace."

80. *New York Times* (September 15, 1946), "Algernon Lee Calls for Wallace Ouster."

81. On September 11, a new file was opened at Molotov's office at the Ministry of Foreign Affairs, entitled "Wallace's addresses, September 11–September 25, 1946," AVP RF, Fond 06, op. 8, P 48, file 804 (this file was released for the first time to the archive's reading room for this book).

82. *Pravda* (September 15, 1946: 4); The two semi-columns in the paper's fourth and last "international" page mostly cites from Pepper's speech, with the piece on Wallace's address so small that it prompted Durbrow to send a message to Washington: The Chargé in the Soviet Union (Durbrow) to the Secretary of State, September 16, 1946, in *FRUS, 1946*, VI: 782.

83. *New York Times* (September 21, 1946), "Russians in Berlin Upbraid Churchill."

84. *New York Times* (September 15, 1946), "Soviet Brief on Wallace: Moscow Radio Says Audience Disliked Anti-Russian Words."

85. *New York Times* (September 20, 1946).

86. *PM* (September 13, 1946), "Wallace Calls for an American Policy."

87. London radio report, September 14, 1946, in TASS #216, September 16, 1946, report, "Further comments on Wallace's speech," RGASPI, Fond 495, op. 261, file 60, part IV, p. 347.

88. Krock (September 17, 1946).

89. The President's News Conference, September 12, 1946, Public Papers, Truman Library. Hulen (September 15, 1946).

90. Blum (1973: 613–15).

91. Hulen (September 17, 1946). Blum (1973: 614).

92. Longhand Note of President Harry S. Truman, September 17, 1946, Box 274, Harry S. Truman Papers: President's Secretary's Files, Harry S. Truman Papers, Truman Library.

93. "Harry Samuel Magdoff," Serial 1638x, Vol. 73, FBI Silvermaster File: 99.

94. Blum (1973: 615).

95. Telephone conversation between Ralph Ingersoll to Henry A. Wallace dated September 17, 1946, Henry A. Wallace correspondence [reel 66], January 2, 1946–September 20, 1946—Ia66-0663-Ia66-0664, Henry A. Wallace Collection, University of Iowa.

96. Telephone conversation, Charles Ross of the White House to Henry A. Wallace dated September 17, 1946, Henry A. Wallace correspondence [reel 65], March 22, 1945 December 29, 1945—Ia65-0449, Henry A. Wallace Collection, University of Iowa. McCullough (1992: 515).

97. "Harry Dexter WHITE, Synopsis," entry for September 17, 1946, Serials 1908-1908x3, Vol. 84, FBI Silvermaster File: 153.

98. Longhand Note of President Harry S. Truman, September 17, 1946, Box 274, Harry S. Truman Papers: President's Secretary's Files, Harry S. Truman Papers, Truman Library.

99. Wood (September 19, 1946).

100. Reston (September 19, 1946).

101. *New York Times* (September 18, 1946), "Text of Secretary Wallace's Letter to President Truman on U.S. Foreign Policy." Wood (September 18, 1946).

102. Adams (September 18, 1946).

103. Harry Truman to Martha Ellen Truman, September 18, 1946, Correspondence from Harry S. Truman to Mary Jane Truman, 1945–1948, Papers of Harry S. Truman Pertaining to Family, Business, and Personal Affairs, Harry S. Truman Papers, Truman Library.

104. Longhand Note of President Harry S. Truman, September 19, 1946, Box 274, Harry S. Truman Papers: President's Secretary's Files, Harry S. Truman Papers, Truman Library.

105. Adams (September 15, 1946).

106. Blum (1973: 617–26). Longhand Note of President Harry S. Truman, September 19, 1946, Box 274, Harry S. Truman Papers: President's Secretary's Files, Harry S. Truman Papers, Truman Library. Wood (September 19, 1946).

107. Krock (September 19, 1946).

108. Wood (September 19, 1946). Callender (September 20, 1946). Wood (September 20, 1946). Culver and Hyde (2000: 411).

109. *New York Times* (September 19, 1946), "Mr. Truman and Mr. Wallace."

110. On September 20, Truman wrote to his wife that he "was in communication with Byrnes yesterday and assured him that the ground would not be cut from under him . . . ," Letter from Harry S. Truman to Bess W. Truman, September 20, 1946, Papers of Harry S. Truman Pertaining to Family, Business, and Personal Affairs, Harry S. Truman Papers, Truman Library. Sulzberger (September 21, 1946).

111. Truman (1980 [1997]: 96–97).

112. Wood (September 21, 1946).

113. Reminiscences of Henry Agard Wallace, CCOH, p. 5028.

114. Phillips (1966: 153–54).

115. Reminiscences of Henry Agard Wallace, CCOH, p. 5028.

116. Phillips (1966: 153–54).

117. Statement by the President on Foreign Policy, September 20, 1946, in Truman II (1962: 431).

118. Whitney (September 21, 1946).

119. *New York Times* (September 21, 1946), "Anti-New Dealers Acclaim Dismissal."

120. *New York Times* (September 21, 1946), "Text of Truman Statement."

121. "Clyde Tolson, Memorandum for the Director, September 25, 1946," Serial 1596, Vol. 72, FBI Silvermaster File: 55–61.

122. See, for example, *New York Times* (September 6, 1983).

123. *Time* (January 6, 1947). Brown (1992: 350–51).

124. Telephone conversation between Henry A. Wallace and Edward U. Condon dated September 19, 1946, Henry A. Wallace correspondence [reel 66], January 2, 1946–September 20, 1946—Ia66-0667–Ia66-0668, Henry A. Wallace Collection, University of Iowa.

125. R. Gordon Arneson, interview by Neil M. Johnson, June 21, 1989, Oral History Interviews, Truman Library: 50–51.

126. Krock (October 4, 1946).

127. Correspondence from Andrew J. Steiger to Henry A. Wallace dated June 15, 1946,

Henry A. Wallace correspondence [reel 41], June 1946–August 8, 1946—Ia41-0632. Henry A. Wallace Collection, University of Iowa.

128. For example, see "Re: Harry Samuel Magdoff," Serial 1638x, Vol. 73, FBI Silvermaster File: 99.

129. Haynes, Klehr, and Vassiliev (2009: 268).

130. "NY from Washington Field; teletype, October 2, 1946," Serials 1596–1638, Vol. 72, FBI Silvermaster File: 109–10. "RE: Harry Samuel Magdoff," Serial 1638x, Vol. 72, FBI Silvermaster File: 2, 104–7.

131. "Harry Samuel Magdoff," Serials 1596–1638, Vol. 72, FBI Silvermaster File: 105–10.

132. *New York Times* (October 3, 1946).

133. Krock (October 4, 1946).

134. Izakov (June 24, 1946) (italics added).

135. Krock (October 4, 1946). Blum (1973: 581–82).

136. Truman I (1955: 416). James Byrnes, interview in *U.S. News & World Report* (August 15, 1960: 67–68); version I in Byrnes (1947: 263). Zhukov (1971: 674–75). Bohlen (1973: 247–48).

137. V.M. Molotov to I.V. Stalin, September 27, 1942, Ryabev I (1998: 268–69); sourced from AP RF, Fond 22, op. 1, file 95, p. 103.

138. Wellerstein (September 30, 2016).

139. Zhukov (1971: 674–75).

140. Werth (1964: 925).

141. Decision of the GOKO [State Committee on Defense] No 9887/ss/op "On the Special Committee under GOKO," Moscow, Kremlin, August 20, 1945, Top Secret (Special File), RGASPI, Fond 644 (GOKO), op. 2, file 533, pp. 80–84. Holloway (1994: 115, 129–30).

142. Holloway (1994: 132).

143. I.V. Kurchatov's memorandum for V.M. Molotov with analysis of intelligence materials and proposals on organization of the works on building atomic weapons in the USSR, November 27, 1942, Ryabev I (1998: 276–80), referring to AP RF, Fond 3, op. 47, file 24, pp. 94–98. Holloway (1994: 91).

144. Memorandum for Under Secretary of State Dean Acheson, July 18, 1946, in *FRUS, 1946*, I: 861–62.

145. *New York Times* (October 3, 1946). *New York Times* (September 18, 1946), "Text of Secretary Wallace's Letter to President Truman on U.S. Foreign Policy." *New York Times* (October 4, 1946). *New York Times* (October 6, 1946). Krock (October 4, 1946). Baldwin (October 6, 1946). Izakov (June 24, 1946).

146. It may have been shortly before June 21, 1946, but no later than that date.

147. The letter of L.P. Beria to I.V. Stalin, submitting for [his] approval the draft of the Decision of SM [Council of Ministers] of the USSR, "On the plan for the development of works of CB [Construction Bureau]-11 under Laboratory No. 2 of the AN USSR Academy of Sciences of the USSR," no later than June 21, 1946. Strictly Secret (Special File), referring to Ryabev II (1999: 432–34); sourced from AP RF, Fond 93, file 99/46, p. 20.

148. Malkov (2003: 311).

149. *Soviet-American Relations* (2004b: 356–57).

150. Goldschmidt (March 1986: 62–63).

151. For a Russian (post-Soviet) statement of this position, see Batiuk (1995: 85–98).

152. Gerber (Winter 1982) argues, unconvincingly, that Baruch's position was so unyielding that it never represented a credible effort to reach agreement with the Soviets. But Baruch was always willing to negotiate within the confines of the U.N. General Assembly's

mandate to the UNAEC, to which the Soviet Union subscribed, which included setting up "effective safeguards" to prevent the misuse of atomic energy. The Soviets never made a counterproposal which encompassed such safeguards.

153. Joint Committee on Atomic Energy (April 1951), *Soviet Atomic Espionage*. Trussell (December 6, 1949). *New York Times* (August 22, 1966). Wallace, statement before the House Committee on Un-American Activities, January 26, 1950, in House Committee on Un-American Activities (1950: 1069–99).

14. The New Republic

1. At age nineteen, he was technically too young to be an official party member.
2. Haynes, Klehr, and Vassiliev (2009: 248–49, 251). Straight (1983: 134). Bernstein (January 6, 2004). *The Telegraph* (January 17, 2004). Lehman-Haupt (January 5, 2004).
3. White (1978: 257).
4. Hale (March 1948: 242).
5. Schlesinger, Jr. (2000: 414).
6. White (1978: 257).
7. Hale (March 1948: 242).
8. Schlesinger, Jr. (2000: 414).
9. Hale (March 1948: 242).
10. White (1978: 257).
11. Schlesinger, Jr. (2000: 414).
12. Straight (1983: 203–4). Culver and Hyde (2000: 431–32).
13. Bliven (1970: 268–69). Hellman (April 11, 1976). Ross (1968: 145). Culver and Hyde (2000: 448–49).
14. Correspondence from Anita M. Blaine to Henry A. Wallace dated September 22, 1946, Henry A. Wallace correspondence [reel 42], August 9, 1946–January 1947—Ia42-0595, Henry A. Wallace Collection, University of Iowa. Wallace (October 13, 1947). Culver and Hyde (2000: 429, 431–32).
15. Wallace (December 16, 1946).
16. Hale (March 1948: 243).
17. Hale (March 1948: 243).
18. New York Consul General Yakov Lomakin to Solomon Lozovsky, Deputy Minister of Foreign Affairs, July 7, 1946, GA RF, Fond 5283, op. 22, file 14a, p. 172.
19. Hale (March 1948: 247).
20. White (1978: 256–57). *TNR* (December 16, 1946). Straight (1983: 204–6).
21. Straight (1983: 204). Bliven (1970: 268).
22. Wallace (December 16, 1946) (italics added).
23. Wallace (December 23, 1946).
24. Ryabev II (1999: 432–34); sourced from AP RF, Fond 93, file 99/46, p. 20.
25. Batiuk (1995: 88), referring to "From com. Skobeltsyn, Oct. 12, 1946. On the issue of control over atomic energy," AVP RF, Fond 47, Referentura on the UNO, op. 1, P 12, file 210, pp. 31–33.
26. Molotov to Druzhkov (Stalin), November 7, 1946, RGASPI, Fond 558, op. 11, file 102, p. 37.
27. Druzhkov (Stalin) to Molotov, RGASPI, Fond 558, op. 11, d. 102, pp. 33–36/reverse.
28. *Soviet-American Relations* (2004b: 356–57).
29. *Big Soviet Encyclopedia*, "Disarmament."
30. "I am in favor of World Federation, with world law and a world police force stronger than

the military might of either the United States or Russia. I am for internationalization of . . . all strategic air bases" (Henry A. Wallace to Mrs. Anita McCormick Blaine dated April 2, 1948, Henry A. Wallace correspondence [reel 44], May 1947–May 1948—Ia44-0810, Henry A. Wallace Collection, University of Iowa). Wallace (August 25, 1947).

31. Wallace (January 5, 1948).
32. Wallace (December 23, 1946).
33. Wallace (April 26, 1948).
34. Wallace (April 5, 1948).
35. Wallace (July 28, 1947).
36. Amadeo (May 26, 2022).
37. Wallace (March 10, 1947).
38. Wallace (July 28, 1947).
39. Devine (2013: 66).
40. Macdonald (1947: 166).
41. Wallace (January 12, 1948).
42. Steil (2018: 369, 375). Steil (April 2, 2018). Wallace (December 16, 1946).
43. Wallace (December 16, 1946). Wallace (January 12, 1948) (italics added).
44. Wallace (January 12, 1948).
45. Wallace (April 12, 1948).
46. H.A. Wallace first made this statement on March 13, on NBC radio: "Radio address concerning President Truman's proposed loan of $400 million to Greece and Turkey," March 13, 1947, reprinted in the *Congressional Record*, 80th Congress, 1st Session, XCII, Part 10: A1329. Wallace (March 24, 1947).
47. Wallace (January 5, 1948).
48. Wallace (March 24, 1947).
49. Minutes of the conversation of Comrade I.V. Stalin with Churchill, October 9, 1944, at 10 p.m., AVP RF, Fond 06, op. 7a, P 58, file 15, pp. 2–10.
50. Wallace (March 24, 1947).
51. Gormly (1990: 182).
52. Pechatnov and Edmondson (2001: 119).
53. Pulliam (June 16, 1947).
54. MacDougall I (1965: 142).
55. Macdonald (1947: 149).
56. MacDougall I (1965: 170–71).
57. Cabinet Meeting Minutes, April 4, 1947, folder "April 1947," Notes on Cabinet Meetings II, 1946–1953, Matthew J. Connelly Papers, Personal Papers, Truman Library.
58. Belair (April 11, 1947).
59. "Red Professor" Kukin Konstantin Mikhailovich (1897–1979), Soviet party functionary, diplomat, intelligence officer, head of the London "legal" residency. "Cambridge 5" web project of the Russian Intelligence Service (SVR): https://cambridge5.ru/page8808630 .html.
60. Straight (1983: 207–9).
61. MacDougall I (1965: 134–36).
62. Egan (April 13, 1947).
63. MacDougall I (1965: 136).
64. Lippmann (April 15, 1947).
65. MacDougall I (1965: 136–39).
66. Culver and Hyde (2000: 441).

67. *New York Times* (April 21, 1947).
68. Straight (1983: 210).
69. Correspondence from Pierre Cot to Henry Wallace dated February 14, 1947, Henry A. Wallace correspondence [reel 43], February 1947–April 1947—Ia43-0054, Henry A. Wallace Collection, University of Iowa. Correspondence from Henry Wallace to Pierre Cot dated February 14, 1947, Henry A. Wallace correspondence [reel 43], February 1947–April 1947—Ia43-0072, Henry A. Wallace Collection, University of Iowa.
70. Straight (1983: 210).
71. MacDougall I (1965: 139–40).
72. Lippmann (April 15, 1947).
73. Culver and Hyde (2000: 443).
74. Wallace (June 30, 1947), "Bevin Muddies the Waters."
75. Wallace (June 30, 1947), "Bevin Muddies the Waters" (italics added).
76. Wallace (June 30, 1947), "Bevin Muddies the Waters."
77. Steil (2018: 117–21, 135).
78. *Pravda Ukraine*, June 11, 1947, quoted in Pogue (1987: 220).
79. *Pravda*, June 17, 1947, quoted in Behrman (2007: 80–81).
80. Vyshinsky, speech, September 1947 (in Russian): https://www.youtube.com/watch?v=6f7qIPODFfg; Partial text (in English): https://sites.temple.edu/immerman/vyshinsky-speech-to-u-n-general-assembly-2.
81. Wallace (January 12, 1948).
82. Belair (September 22, 1945).
83. Ross (1968: 155).
84. Wallace (January 20, 1947).
85. Wallace (March 10, 1947).
86. Correspondence from Henry A. Wallace to Mrs. Anita McCormick Blaine dated April 2, 1948, Henry A. Wallace correspondence [reel 44], May 1947–May 1948—Ia44-0710, Henry A. Wallace Collection, University of Iowa. (Italics added).
87. Clayton memorandum, "The European Crisis," May 27, 1947, in *FRUS, 1947*, III: 230–32 (italics in original). Steil (2018: 100).
88. Wallace (June 30, 1947), "Bevin Muddies the Waters" (italics added). Wallace (October 6, 1947) (italics added).
89. Wallace (January 12, 1948).
90. "Henry Wallace," RGASPI, Fond 495, op. 261, file 60, part IV, p. 197/reverse. RGASPI, 495-261-60, part V, pp. 265, 265/reverse. RGASPI, 495-261-60, part V, pp. 244, 244/reverse, 245. RGASPI, 495-261-60, part V, p. 243. RGASPI, 495-261-60, part V, pp. 241, 241/reverse, 242. RGASPI, 495-261-60, part V, pp. 199. RGASPI, 495-261-60, part V, p. 137. RGASPI, 495-261-60, part V, pp. 135–36. RGASPI, 495-261-60, part V, p. 133. "Political report of the Soviet Embassy in the USA for 1947," AVP RF, Fond 0129, op. 31a, P 241, file 1, pp. 70–71. AVP RF, Fond 07, op. 21d, P 53, file 20, p. 8. AVP RF, F. 06, op. 10, P 69, file 967, p. 7.
91. Wallace (January 5, 1948).
92. Wallace (January 26, 1948).
93. Wallace (October 6, 1947). Wallace (January 12, 1948).
94. Gallup I (1972: 770–71).

15. Gideon's Red Army

1. The letter can be seen here: https://www.marxists.org/archive/foster/1944/01/22.htm.
2. Duclos (April 1945).
3. Browder (March 1960: 45).
4. Known until 1952 as the VCP (b).
5. Duclos (April 1945). Devine (2013: 3–7).
6. See, for example, New York to Moscow, No. 734, May 21, 1944, Venona, Declassified Documents, NSA; New York to Moscow, No. 1039–41, July 24–25, 1944, Venona, Declassified Documents, NSA; New York to Moscow, No. 1393, October 3, 1944, Venona, Declassified Documents, NSA; and New York to Moscow, No. 1814, 1815, December 23, 1944, Venona, Declassified Documents, NSA.
7. Devine (2013: 13–14).
8. Devine (2013: 9–11).
9. Bliven (1970: 269).
10. Haynes and Klehr (1999: 132, 136). Haynes, Klehr, and Vassiliev (2009: 266).
11. A fuller title would be head of the USA section of the Foreign Policy Department of the Soviet Central Party Committee.
12. Boris Vronsky, Information Memorandum on his trip to the USA, December 18, 1947, RGASPI, Fond 17, op. 128, file 1128, p. 269.
13. MacDougall I (1965: 114).
14. Wallace, speech, "Unity for Progress," December 29, 1946.
15. Foster (February 1947: 114, 116).
16. Hale (March 1948).
17. Russian translation of Foster's article at the Soviet Central Committee's Foreign Policy Department, N. Pukhlov to G.M. Shucklin, May 17, 1947, RGASPI, Fond 17, op. 128, file 1128, pp. 74–294.
18. Hale (March 1948: 243).
19. Schlesinger, Jr. (2000: 412–13). MacDougall I (1965: 127).
20. Duclos (April 1945).
21. Dennis (August 1947). Devine (2013: 20).
22. Devine (2013: 17).
23. Bliven (1970: 230, 269) does not provide her name or resignation date.
24. GA RF, Fond 5283, op. 22a, file 25, pp. 136–39.
25. From the books [diary] of Alexander V. Karaganov, VOKS Deputy Board Chairman, "Record of conversation with Johannes Steele," March 18, 1947, GA RF, Fond 5283, op. 22a, file 25, pp. 100, 102. New York Times (March 18, 1947).
26. Serials 2310 to 2325, Vol. 110, FBI Silvermaster File: 32.
27. Foster (January 2, 2006). Pollin (January 6, 2006).
28. From the books [diary] of Karaganov, "Record of conversation with Steele," April 7, 1947, GA RF, Fond 5283, op. 22a, file 20, p. 102.
29. From the books [diary] of Vyshinsky, "Reception of American journalist Iohannes Steele," April 7, 1947, AVP RF, Fond 07, op. 12, P 2, file 24, pp. 10–11/reverse; AVP RF, Fond 07, op. 21d, P 53, file 20.
30. Childs was recruited by the FBI in 1952.
31. A. Panyushkin to A.A. Kuznetsov, April 10, 1947; cc to A.A. Zhdanov, RGASPI, Fond 17, op. 128, file 408, p. 8.
32. Boris Vronsky's memo, "Conversations with the member of the US Politburo Morris Childs on March 26 and April 1, 1947. . . ," RGASPI, Fond 17, op. 128 file 1128, pp. 62–68.

33.   A. Panyushkin to Secretaries of CC VCP (b) Zhdanov A.A., Kuznetsov A.A., April 10, 1947—RGASPI, Fond 17, op. 128, file 1128, pp. 60–61.

34.   Devine (2013: 18–19).

35.   Ambassador A. Panyushkin to Assistant Minister of Foreign Affairs A.Ja. Vyshinsky, submitting Political Report of the Soviet Embassy in the USA for 1947, AVP RF, Fond 0129, op. 31a, P 241, file 1, p. 72.

36.   Gromyko (1989: 48). Gromyko says the meeting was in "early 1946" (and the American translation just says "1946"), but this is clearly an error. Both Gromyko and Wallace were living in Washington at the time, and the PCA had not yet been created. Early 1947 is far more likely, specifically around March 18, the date the PCA took out a full-page ad in *The New York Times* containing a transcript of Wallace's recent radio address criticizing Truman's foreign policy.

37.   *Bulletin of the Information Bureau of the CC VCP (b), The Issues of Foreign Policy* (April 15, 1947), in RGASPI, Fond 17, op. 128, file 265. pp. 124/reverse, 127/reverse. Wallace (December 16, 1946).

38.   *Bulletin of the Information Bureau of the CC VCP (b), The Issues of Foreign Policy* (April 15, 1947), in RGASPI, Fond 17, op. 128, file 265. p. 124. Wallace (December 16, 1946).

39.   *Bulletin of the Bureau of Information of the CC VCP (b), The Issues of Foreign Policy* (January 15, 1947: 25), in RGASPI, Fond 17, op. 128, file 26.

40.   *Bulletin of the Bureau of Information of the CC VCP (b), The Issues of Foreign Policy* (April 15, 1947), in RGASPI, Fond 17, op. 128, file 265, p. 122/reverse.

41.   *Bulletin of the Bureau of Information of the CC VCP (b), The Issues of Foreign Policy* (January 15, 1947: 25), in RGASPI, Fond 17, op. 128, file 26.

42.   "Political report of the Soviet Embassy in the USA for 1947," AVP RF, Fond 0129, op 31a, P 241, file 1, p. 64.

43.   V. Moshetov to A.A. Zhdanov, submitting Boris Vronsky's memo on his trip to the USA as Izvestia correspondent at the session of the General Assembly, December 18, 1947, RGASPI, Fond 17, op. 128, file 1128, p. 272/10.

44.   "The Communists in 1948," from Vronsky's materials brought from the USA, January 26, 1948, RGASPI, Fond 17, op. 128, file 1128, pp. 276–83.

45.   Devine (2013: 21–23).

46.   MacDougall I (1965: 160).

47.   MacDougall I (1965: 166).

48.   Devine (2013: 28–30).

49.   The countries participating were Bulgaria, Czechoslovakia, France, Hungary, Italy, Poland, Romania, and the Soviet Union. "Memorandum by A.A. Zhdanov to I.V. Stalin on the anticipated program of the conference of nine Communist parties in Poland," RGASPI, Fond 77, op. 3, file 90, undated (not earlier than September 1947), pp. 1–5.

50.   L. Baranov to Zhdanov, untitled instructions for the delegates of VCP (b) at the conference of the Communist parties in Poland, August 15, 1947, RGASPI, Fond 575, op. 1, file 3, pp. 1–3.

51.   Zhdanov, "On the International Situation," reprinted in House Committee on Foreign Affairs (1948); Russian original of Zhdanov's report in RGASPI, Fond 575, op. 1, file 1, pp. 154–94.

52.   Foster (February 1947: 109).

53.   Devine (2013: 24).

54.   Gates was born Solomon Regenstreif.

55.   Devine (2013: 26–27, 31–33). *New York Times* (March 22, 1968).

56. *New York Times* (September 6, 1983).
57. Devine (2013: 30).
58. MacDougall I (1965: 147–48, 152–53).
59. Straight 1983: 213). Devine (2013: 69).
60. Culver and Hyde (2000: 447).
61. Straight (1983: 214). MacDougall I (1965: 162). Hale (March 1948: 244).
62. MacDougall I (1965: 156).
63. Hepburn, speech, May 19, 1947: https://www.youtube.com/watch?v=KN5q0Am_-e8. Straight (1983: 214–15).
64. MacDonald (1947: 161).
65. MacDonald (1947: 158–59, 161). Straight (1983: 214–15). MacDougall I (1965: 210). Hale (March 1948: 244).
66. Wallace (August 25, 1947).
67. Wallace (June 30, 1947), "Report on the Farmers."
68. Gallup I (1972: 663).
69. MacDonald (1947: 169).
70. MacDougall I (1965: 176).
71. Wallace (September 1, 1947).
72. MacDougall I (1965: 199).
73. Hale (March 1948: 244).
74. Culver and Hyde (2000: 453).
75. "Record of conversation of Assistant Foreign Minister A.J. Vyshinsky and V.A. Zorin with US politician H. Wallace on Soviet-American relations, New York, October 14, 1947, Top Secret," RGASPI, Fond 82, op. 2, file 1308, p. 68. L. Baranov to M. Suslov, February 27, 1948, RGASPI, Fond 17, op. 128, file 1138, p. 59.
76. Straight (1983: 217–18).
77. Macdonald (1947: 170).
78. MacDougall I (1965: 211–12).
79. Wallace (December 22, 1947).
80. RGASPI, Fond 495, op. 261, file 60, part 1, p. 37.
81. Straight (1983: 217). Devine (2013: 37). Haynes and Klehr (1999: 63–64).
82. Reminiscences of Henry Agard Wallace, CCOH pp. 5067–59. Abt (1993: 144). Devine (2013: 37).
83. Blum (1973: 115). Haynes, Klehr, and Vassiliev (2009: 426). Devine (2013: 133–34).
84. Hale (March 1948: 246–47).
85. "Record of conversation of the Soviet Ambassador in the USA A.S. Panyushkin with US Ambassador W.B. Smith on Soviet-American relations, November 21, 1947," AVP RF, Fond 06, op. 9, P 68, file 1048, pp. 52–54.
86. Devine (2013: 38–39).
87. Reminiscences of Henry Agard Wallace, CCOH, p. 5083.
88. Hale (March 1948: 248).
89. MacDougall I (1965: 82).
90. Hale (March 1948: 248).
91. Ross (1968: 149).
92. Wallace, speech, "Unity for Progress," December 29, 1946.
93. Alexander Vassiliev, Yellow Notebook #4, p. 120, Alexander Vassiliev Papers, Library of Congress, referring to SVR RF File 40961, Vol. 2, pp. 1–5.
94. Schmidt (1960: 271).

95. Devine (2013: 19, 40).
96. Shannon (1959: 144).
97. Devine (2013: 45).
98. Devine (2013: 46).
99. Shannon (1959: 97).
100. Fahan (February 1948).
101. Bliven (1970: 269). Devine (2013: 47).
102. Straight (1983: 219). Devine (2013: 50–52).
103. *New York Times* (May 25, 1946).
104. Truman diary entry in Geselbracht (2019: 518–19).
105. Devine (2013: 59).
106. Devine (2013: 45, 63).
107. Ross (1968: 143). MacDougall I (1965: 303–4). Devine (2013: 63).
108. January 2, 1948, "My Day" by Eleanor Roosevelt, Eleanor Roosevelt Papers, George Washington University. Roosevelt (1999: 245). Devine (2013: 68).
109. Wallace (January 5, 1948).
110. Devine (2013: 55–57).
111. Reminiscences of Henry Agard Wallace, CCOH, p. 5083.
112. Wallace (January 1, 1948: 172–74).

16. Collusion

1. "Proposal of the IV ED of the MID of the USSR regarding the major direction of the Czechoslovak policy following the February crisis, March 2, 1948," in Volokitina (1999: 553–55). Haslam (2011: 98–99).
2. Heinemann-Grueder (1999: 334, 336); Gottwald to Stalin, November 25, 1947, RGASPI, Fond 558, op. 11, file 393, p. 124; Stalin to Gottwald, November 29, 1947, RGASPI, Fond 558, op. 11, file 393, p. 126.
3. Feierabend (1996: 362).
4. Ross (January 18, 1948).
5. Policy Planning Staff, "Résume of World Situation," November 6, 1947, in *FRUS, 1947*, I: 771, 773.
6. Heimann (2009: 172); James (2003 [2014]: 283).
7. Charles Yost to Marshall, September 15, 1947, in *FRUS, 1947*, IV: 231.
8. Ripka (1950: 210–20).
9. Laurence Steinhardt to Marshall, April 30, 1948, in *FRUS, 1948*, IV: 750. Haslam (2011: 99–100). Ripka (1950: 222, 227, 231–36). Kaplan (1987: 179).
10. Crowder (2015: 215).
11. Isaacson and Thomas (1986 [2012]: 243). Bohlen (1973: 170).
12. Ripka (1950: 240–41, 250–51, 265, 267, 278–79, 281, 284–85, 293, 296, 307). Lukes (September 2011: 443). Spalding (2006: 100).
13. Ripka (1950: 7).
14. Laurence Steinhardt to Marshall, February 27, 1948, in *FRUS, 1948*, IV: 741–42.
15. Laurence Steinhardt to Marshall, March 10, 1948, in *FRUS, 1948*, IV: 743–44. Laurence Steinhardt to Marshall, April 30, 1948, in *FRUS, 1948*, IV: 751.
16. Cameron (January 6, 2004).
17. Kennan (1967: 422).
18. Lukes (2012: 15).

19. The Czech crisis and its role in the creation of the Marshall Plan and NATO are covered in detail in Steil (2018).

20. Devine (2013: 109).

21. Record of conversations between the 1st Secretary of the Soviet Embassy in Washington, M.S. Vavilov, and "Krot" ["Mole"] on July 1 and 5, 1947, Alexander Vassiliev, White Notebook No. 3, p. 103, Alexander Vassiliev Papers, Library of Congress, referring to SVR RF File 55302 ("Mole"), Vol. 1, pp. 103, 106.

22. Fox (2001: 269).

23. Alexander Vassiliev, White Notebook No. 2, p. 69, Alexander Vassiliev Papers, Library of Congress, referring to SVR RF File 14 449 ("Liza"), Vol. 2, pp. 64–72, 76–78.

24. Moscow (March 16, 1948).

25. Wallace (January 26, 1948).

26. Wallace (January 5, 1948).

27. Wallace (March 29, 1948).

28. Wallace (March 29, 1948).

29. Wallace (January 5, 1948).

30. Morgenthau (1948 [1993]: 34).

31. Schapsmeier and Schapsmeier (1968: 259).

32. Pulliam (June 16, 1947).

33. "Victory of the nominee of the American Workers Party in additional elections in NYC," TASS, February 18, 1948, p. 88-0, AVP RF, Fond 06, op. 10, P. 69, file 967, pp. 1–3.

34. Correspondence from Andrew Steiger to Henry A. Wallace dated March 28, 1948, Henry A. Wallace correspondence [Reel 44], May 1947–May 1948—Ia44-0675, Henry A. Wallace Collection, University of Iowa.

35. Devine (2013: 71–82).

36. From the diary of S. Kondrashov, "Record of conversation with Eddy Gilmore, the Associated Press correspondent," November 8, 1946, GA RF, Fond 5283 [VOKS], op. 22, file 17, pp. 195–96.

37. These include Wallace Connecticut campaign organizer and Yale Russian Studies professor John Marsalka and Zionist Soviet intelligence source David Wahl. See, for example, Serials 2126 to 2181, Vol. 96, FBI Silvermaster File: 120, 135; Serials 2183 to 2210, Vol. 98, FBI Silvermaster File: 3; "Re: John Paul Milan Marsalka," Serial 1638x, Vol. 73, FBI Silvermaster File; Heins (2013: 79); *The Harvard Crimson* (April 13, 1949); "FBI Washington Field to Director, June 2, 1947," Serials 2478 to 2529, Vol. 120, FBI Silvermaster File; Haynes, Klehr, and Vassiliev (2009: 208, 210); Robbins (2009); Russian Academy of Sciences et al. (2000); and Serial 2849, Vol. 129, FBI Silvermaster File: 170.

38. From the diary of V.M. Molotov: Reception of the US Ambassador Harriman, January 3, 1945, AVP RF, Fond 06, op. 7, P 2, file 29, pp. 45–46.

39. Gromyko (1989: 48).

40. Record of the conversation of A.A. Gromyko with Henry Wallace, April 2, 1948, Strictly secret, RGASPI, Fond 82, op. 2, file 1308, pp. 70–73.

41. Correspondence from Lewis C. Frank to Henry A. Wallace dated April 14, 1948, Henry A. Wallace correspondence [reel 44], May 1947–May 1948—Ia44-0749, Henry A. Wallace Collection, University of Iowa. MacDougall II (1965: 359).

42. Valentin (1993: 64). Berezhkov (1993: 171–250).

43. Sheean (September 18, 1948: 23).

44. Sheean (September 18, 1948: 154).

45. The Chargé in the Soviet Union (Kennan) to the Secretary of State, March 20, 1946, in *FRUS, 1946*, VI: 721–23.

46. "Record of the conversation of A.A. Gromyko with Henry Wallace, April 2, 1948, Strictly secret," RGASPI, Fond 82, op. 2, file 1308, pp. 70–73.

47. Vronsky (April 11, 1948).

48. A.A. Gromyko's informational memorandum ["Spravka"] on his conversation with Henry A. Wallace, April 21, 1948 (date of the memo; its first page is missing in the file, hence untitled and uncertain if the conversation took place on April 20 or 21), RGASPI, Fond 558, op. 11, file 387, pp. 5–10. Molotov to Gromyko, cipher cable No. 519/ref. number No. 7345, from April 14, 1948; this cable has not been released, citing a brief reference to it in Stalin files, RGASPI, Fond 558, op. 11, file 387, p. 10.

49. Information memorandum from A.A. Gromyko, April 21, 1948, sent to the Foreign Ministry (Molotov) in cipher cables #13755–13790, transmitted to Stalin after deciphering. (Citation from a copy in Stalin Papers, where its first page is missing; hence untitled), RGASPI, Fond 558, op. 11, file 387, pp. 5–10.

50. Correspondence from Lewis C. Frank to Henry A. Wallace dated April 14, 1948, Henry A. Wallace correspondence [reel 44], May 1947–May 1948—Ia44-0749-Ia44-0750, Henry A. Wallace Collection, University of Iowa. Another correspondent Wallace had turned to regarding matters to raise with Stalin was Harvard scientist Harlow Shapley, described in Soviet profiles as a "great friend of the Soviet Union." Correspondence from Harlow Shapley to Henry A. Wallace dated April 12, 1948, Henry A. Wallace correspondence [reel 44], May 1947–May 1948—Ia44-0736, Henry A. Wallace Collection, University of Iowa.

51. Information memorandum from A.A. Gromyko, April 21, 1948, "Henry Wallace's list of issues with Stalin's notations," RGASPI, Fond 558, op. 11, file 387, pp. 6–8, 10.

52. MacDougall II (1965: 360).

53. A.A. Gromyko to V.M. Molotov, Special cc [cipher cables] # 1254–1263, designated as "Accord precedence" ["Out of turn"—the highest degree of expediency], April 27, 1948, RGASPI, Fond 558, op. 11, file 387, pp. 11–21.

54. What follows is mostly taken from Steil (2018: 265–67).

55. Policy Planning Staff, report, "Review of Current Trends: U.S. Foreign Policy," February 24, 1948, in FRUS, 1948, I: 522–23.

56. Marshall (approved by Lovett) to Smith, urgent telegram, undated 1948, Folder: "Russia [7 of 8]," Box 15, Subject File, Clark M. Clifford Papers, Truman Library.

57. "Molotov's reception of Romanian Ambassador [Iorgu] Iordan, October 3, 1947, 3:00 PM," AVP RF, Fond 06, op. 9, P. 2, file 23, p. 14.

58. Lebedev (2003: 551–56).

59. Washington Post (August 11, 1961). New York Times (August 10, 1961). Middleton (March 16, 1947). Beevor (October 23, 2010).

60. Smith to Marshall, telegram, marked with a circled "3," May 10, 1948, Folder: "Russia [7 of 8]," Box 15, Subject File, Clark M. Clifford Papers, Truman Library. For the Soviet version of the conversations, see Record of conversation with the U.S. Ambassador W. B. Smith on the positions of the US Government on international problems and foreign policy of the USA, May 4, 1948, AVP RF, Fond 06, op. 10, P. 1, file 4, pp. 1–12; and Record of conversation with the U.S. Ambassador W. B. Smith on the state of Soviet-American relations, May 9, 1948, AVP RF, Fond 06, op. 10, P. 1, file 4, pp. 19–29. Kuhn (May 12, 1948).

61. From the Diary of V.M. Molotov, "Reception of US Ambassador Smith, May 4, 1948," RGASPI, Fond 558, op. 11, file 387, pp. 22–33, 26. Pechatnov and Edmondson (2001: 140).

62. TASS (May 11, 1948), in RGASPI, Fond 558, op. 11, file 387, pp. 44–45.

63. Reston (May 12, 1948).

64. Truman diary entry, May 11, 1948.

65. State Department Weekly Review, Europe and the British Commonwealth: Smith-Molotov Exchange, undated, Folder: "Foreign Relations—Russia (1948)," Box 64, Subject File, George M. Elsey Papers, Truman Library: 3.

66. Douglas to Marshall, transcript of U.K. House of Commons questioning on the Smith-Molotov meeting, May 14, 1948, Folder: "Telegrams: London [England]: Winant," Box 166, Foreign Affairs File, Subject File, President's Secretary's Files, Harry S. Truman Papers, Truman Library.

67. "The draft of Stalin's letter about Soviet-American relations" with A.I. Mikoyan's notations, RGASPI, Fond 84, op 1, file 142, p. 42. The document has a handwritten notation in the bottom by Mikoyan's assistant: "*10/V-48 for PB Notes by Com. Mikoyan*" "for PB"—suggesting the date of the discussion at Politburo. In the logs of Stalin's Kremlin office, on May 10, the eight Politburo members were present from 6 to 8:30 p.m. The list of visitors began with Molotov—an indication of the discussion of "the question of the Foreign Ministry." Besides the "Politburo eight," there was Vyshinsky—suggestive that he might be the writer of the draft. No formal record was kept, hence no record exists in the Politburo files. It was likely too sensitive even for its "Special File" (RGASPI, Fond 17, op. 166).

68. Based on undated handwritten notes of Stalin's referring to Wallace's meeting with Gromyko on April 20 (or 21), in which he scribbles "without any discrimination," we may speculate that Gromyko communicated this edit to Wallace at their scheduled May 8 meeting (RGASPI, Fond 558, op. 11, file 387, p. 4).

69. Correspondence from Henry A. Wallace to Anna T. Davis dated May 10, 1948, Henry A. Wallace correspondence [reel 44], May 1947–May 1948—Ia44-0874, Henry A. Wallace Collection, University of Iowa.

70. *New York Times* (May 12, 1948).

71. Krock (May 12, 1948).

72. Pechatnov (2006: 540, 729, footnote 45), citing J. Morrison to G. Kennan, May 19, 1948, Box 23, Country and Area Files (USSR 1946–1950), Records of Policy Planning Staff, 1947–1952, Record Group 59, NARA.

73. Pechatnov (2006: 540, 729, footnote 46), citing J. Morrison to G. Kennan, May 19, 1948, Box 23, Country and Area Files (USSR 1946–1950), Records of Policy Planning Staff, 1947–1952, Record Group 59, NARA.

74. Pechatnov (2006: 729, footnote 46), citing J. Morrison to G. Kennan, May 19, 1948, Box 23, Country and Area Files (USSR 1946–1950), Records of Policy Planning Staff, 1947–1952, Record Group 59, NARA.

75. *New York Times* (September 6, 1983).

76. MacDougall II (1965: 360–61).

77. MacDougall, II (1965: 354–56).

78. MacDougall, II (1965: 361).

79. *FRUS, 1948*, IV: 860–61.

80. George C. Marshall, "Memorandum for the President," May 11, 1948, Confidential File (State Department Correspondence, 1948–1949), Harry S. Truman Papers, Truman Library.

81. Kirchwey (May 29, 1948).

82. Walker (Winter 1981: 90) (italics added).

83. Sheean (September 18, 1948: 153).

84. RGASPI, Fond 495, op. 261, file 60, part 1, pp. 20–39.

85. AVP RF, Fond 06, op. 10, P 66, file 925, pp. 5–7. AVP RF, Fond 06, op. 10, P 66, file 930.

86. Correspondence from Andrew J. Steiger to Henry A. Wallace dated May 17, 1948, Henry A. Wallace correspondence [reel 44], May 1947–May 1948—Ia44-0910, Henry A. Wallace Collection, University of Iowa.

87. Correspondence from Andrew J. Steiger to Henry A. Wallace dated June 4, 1948, Henry A. Wallace correspondence [reel 45], June 1948–March 1949—Ia45-0022, with enclosures Ia45-0023–Ia45-0025, Henry A. Wallace Collection, University of Iowa.

88. Hagerty (July 24, 1948). Pegler (June 2, 1948). Tuttle (July 24, 1948). Cooke (July 24, 1948). Fleeson (July 24, 1948). McCannon (2022: 336–39).

89. Feigel (2016: 305–6, 319).

90. Barnet (1983: 40).

91. Editorial Note, "The Establishment of the Berlin Blockade," in *FRUS, 1948*, II: 909.

92. Murphy to Marshall, June 19, 1948, in *FRUS, 1948*, II: 910. Harrington (2012:71–72). Clay to Bradley, CC-4843, June 23, 1948, Folder: "AG 319.1 Transportation Situation Reports, Vol. II, 1948," Box 427, OMGUS AGO General Correspondence, Record Group 260, NARA. Murphy to Marshall, June 21, 1948, in *FRUS, 1948*, II: 911–12. Narinsky (1996: 66).

93. Narinsky (1996: 66). "The German question," AVP RF, Fond 048/3, op. 11zh, P 70, file 17, p. 454.

94. Smith (1990: 492). Clay to Royall, CC-4880, June 25, 1948, in Smith II (1974: 675–78).

95. Feigel (2016: 301, 312). Sutherland and Canwell (2007: 37). Narinsky (1996: 66–67). Jean Ganeval to Bidault, June 24, 1948, Fonds 457, Carton AP-18, Private Archives of M. Georges Bidault, Archives Nationales. Bidault to Henri Bonnet, June 27, 1948, Fonds 457, Carton AP-18, Private Archives of M. Georges Bidault, Archives Nationales. M. Senin, "Memorandum on the Berlin question, 1950," AVP RF, Fond 082, op. 37, P 216, file 112, p. 21. Caffery to Marshall, June 24, 1948, in *FRUS, 1948*, II: 916–17. Hetzel (Winter 2002: 27). Buchheim (1999: 94). Clay (1950: 364). Narinsky (1996: 61, 66). Laufer (1999: 80–84). Middleton (June 23, 1948). Morrow (June 24, 1948).

96. A detailed account of the Berlin Blockade and Airlift can be found in Steil (2018).

97. *New York Times* (July 25, 1948).

98. Cooke (1977: 104).

99. McCullough (July 27, 1948). Devine (2013: 170).

100. MacDougall II (1965: 430, 600).

101. House Committee on Un-American Activities (1954: 3869–70), *Hearings Regarding Communist Methods of Infiltration (Entertainment—Part 1)*.

102. Devine (2013: 281).

103. Lawrence (July 25, 1948). *New York Times* (July 25, 1948).

104. July 19, 1948, "My Day" by Eleanor Roosevelt, Eleanor Roosevelt Papers, George Washington University.

105. Schmidt (1960: 253).

106. Devine (2013: 124–25, 168–70, 197–98, 205, 212, 336).

107. Lawrence (July 28, 1948).

108. Wechsler (September 1948).

109. Steil (2018: 80).

110. MacDougall II (1965: 534). Devine (2013: 150, 180).

111. Ross (1968: 149).

112. Devine (2013: 278, endnote 22).

113. Walton (1976: 167). Devine (2013: 54).

17. The People Speak

1. Flint (May 5, 1984). Devine (2013: 84, 167).
2. Irwin (July 24, 1948).
3. Devine (2013: 131).
4. Alsop and Alsop (July 26, 1948: 9).
5. Devine (2013: 172).
6. See Steil (2013: 318–22).
7. See Steil (2018: 35–46, 53–59, 318–29).
8. Views differ as to how seriously to take Duggan's oral disclosures to the Soviets during the years 1942 to 1944. Haynes and Klehr (1999: 201–4) take a considerably harder line than Chervonnaya (2008), "Alexander Vassiliev's Notes, Venona and Laurence Duggan" and "Duggan, Laurence Hayden (1905–1948)."
9. Andrew and Mitrokhin (1999: 133). Radosh (November 12, 2012). Devine (2013: 228). Klehr and Haynes (May 13, 1996).
10. Victor Perlo in HUAC session: ". . . I am now a consulting economist in New York, employed for the current campaign by the Progressive Party." Ladd to Fletcher, August 9, 1948, "Subject: Whittaker Chambers," Vol. 139, FBI Silvermaster File: 81.
11. House Committee on Un-American Activities (1948: 623).
12. Correspondence from Henry A. Wallace to Glen H. Taylor dated April 18, 1956, Henry A. Wallace correspondence [reel 59], December 1931–1964—Ia59-0795, Henry A. Wallace Correspondence, University of Iowa.
13. Cook (August 13, 1991). Steil (2018: 318, 324–29). Abt (1993: 155). Devine (2013: 229).
14. Hellman (April 11, 1976).
15. Devine (2013: 235, 237, 240–41, endnotes 8, 21, 32).
16. MacDougall III (1965: 709). Devine (2013: 242–243, endnotes 38–41).
17. Devine (2013: 244). Schmidt (1960: 205–6).
18. Popham (September 5, 1948).
19. Devine (2013: 246).
20. Devine (2013: 253).
21. MacDougall III (1965: 653).
22. Sitkoff (November 1971).
23. Topping (August 2004: 192).
24. Judge William H. Hastie, interview by Jerry N. Hess, January 5, 1972, Oral History Interviews, Truman Library: 72–73. Topping (August 2004: 193).
25. MacDougall III (1965: 655–56, 667).
26. Arnesen (January 2014). *New York Times* (October 14, 1948). Berg (June 2007).
27. Hagerty (September 11, 1948).
28. *New York Times* (September 11, 1948).
29. Devine (2013: 271).
30. Ross (1968: 152, 156).
31. Reminiscences of Henry Agard Wallace, CCOH, pp. 5077–78. *Los Angeles Times* (September 29, 1948). MacDougall III (165: 752, 765, 837). Devine (2013: 271–74, 278–81, 284).
32. Grutzner (October 27, 1948).
33. Steil (2018: 293–95).
34. Grutzner (October 27, 1948). TASS (night time report), November 1, 1948, RGASPI, Fond 495, op. 261, file 60, part 7, p. 204. *Pravda* (November 2, 1948).

35. *Pravda* (November 1, 1948).
36. *Hartford Courant* (November 3, 1948). Baime (2020: 325).
37. *New York Times* (November 3, 1948), "Wallace Votes, then Tends Farm." MacDougall III (1965: 600, 602–3, 881).
38. Fox (2001: 267).
39. MacDougall III (1965: 603, 883). Lissner (November 3, 1948).
40. MacDougall III (1965: 881).
41. *New York Times* (November 3, 1948), "Dollinger Served 12 Years in Albany."
42. Marcantonio would, too, in 1950, lose his seat to a Democratic rival, James Donovan. The Communists would soon after withdraw their backing for the ALP, and the latter would disband in 1956.
43. MacDougall III (1965: 882–83). MacDougall ends his three-volume book with the text of another, longer, much more moderate letter, which he says Wallace wrote in pencil later that night on the back of a copy of the telegram. He doesn't say whether it was sent.
44. Jaffe (1975: 121).
45. McCullough (1992: 711).
46. Ross (1968: 156).
47. Ross (1968: 156).
48. Jackson (April 18, 2018). Topping (August 2004: 196).
49. Jackson (April 18, 2018). Some estimates were higher: Topping (August 2004: 196).
50. The figures used are from the post-election poll of the American Institute of Public Opinion (see below). Regarding the Jewish vote, Gallup and American National Election Studies showed that around 75% of sampled Jewish citizens voted. Given that 3.53 million American adults identified as Jewish in 1948, based on data from the Pew Research Center, roughly 2.6 million Jews voted in 1948. If 18 percent of those voted for Wallace, we get roughly 475,000 Jewish votes for Wallace—or 40 percent of his total: https://www.pewresearch.org/wp-content/uploads/sites/7/2013/10/jewish-american-full-report-for-web.pdf. This estimate is consistent with those from Samuel Lubell and Arthur Kahn, cited in MacDougall III (1965: 645, 858).

Religion (% within total)

		Catholic	Protestant	Jewish	Other
Candidate	Truman	363 69.5%	760 47.6%	74 60.2%	29 58.0%
	Dewey	140 26.8%	777 48.6%	25 20.3%	18 36.0%
	Wallace	12 2.3%	14 0.9%	22 17.9%	3 6.0%
	Thurmond	7 1.3%	47 2.9%	2 1.6%	0 0.0%
	Total	522 100.0%	1598 100.0%	123 100.0%	50 100.0%

American Institute of Public Opinion (November 3–8, 1948); N=2293

51. American Institute of Public Opinion, Survey #432.
52. Ryan (July 1980: 387–401). Williams (August 1957: 111–24). McCullough (1992: 712–13).
53. McCullough (1992: 713–14).
54. Professor Russell B. Nye, quoted in MacDougall III (1965: 878).
55. MacDougall III (1965: 859).
56. MacDougall III (1965: 769).
57. Marshall (June 26, 1948).

18. Belief Betrayed

1. Straight (1983: 222–23). On Baldwin, see also Reminiscences of Henry Agard Wallace, CCOH, pp. 219–20.
2. Pearson (November 11, 1948).
3. Correspondence from Henry A. Wallace to Anita M. Blaine dated November 29, 1948, Henry A. Wallace correspondence [reel 45], June 1948–March 1949—Ia45-0532, Henry A. Wallace Collection, University of Iowa. Correspondence from Anita M. Blaine to Matthew Connelly dated December 6, 1948, Henry A. Wallace correspondence [reel 45], June 1948–March 1949—Ia45-0533–Ia45-0534, Henry A. Wallace Collection, University of Iowa. Correspondence from Anita M. Blaine to Harry S. Truman dated December 6, 1948, Henry A. Wallace correspondence [reel 45], June 1948–March 1949—Ia45-0537–Ia45-0538, Henry A. Wallace Collection, University of Iowa. Correspondence from Matthew J. Connelly to Anita M. Blaine dated December 6, 1948, Henry A. Wallace correspondence [reel 45], June 1948–March 1949—Ia45-0539, Henry A. Wallace Collection, University of Iowa. Correspondence from Anita M. Blaine to Matthew J. Connelly dated December 7, 1948, Henry A. Wallace correspondence [reel 45], June 1948–March 1949—Ia45-0540, Henry A. Wallace Collection, University of Iowa.
4. McNair (November 8, 1948). United Press (November 8, 1948).
5. Correspondence from Henry A. Wallace to Alexander S. Panyushkin dated December 7, 1948, Henry A. Wallace correspondence [reel 45], June 1948–March 1949—Ia45-0545, Henry A. Wallace Collection, University of Iowa; Correspondence from Alexander S. Panyushkin to Henry A. Wallace dated December 9, 1948, Henry A. Wallace correspondence [reel 45], June 1948–March 1949—Ia45-0550, Henry A. Wallace Collection, University of Iowa.
6. New York Times (November 18, 1948). Soviet ambassador Alexander Panyushkin was supposed to speak but did not owing, supposedly, to illness. Conklin (December 14, 1948).
7. Pravda, December 15, 1948, clip in "Wallace speeches" file, AVP RF, Fond 06, op. 10, P 69, file 967, p. 26.
8. Pechatnov (2006: 553–54). Wallace wrote to Panyushkin on December 29, 1948, thanking him for the dinner and following up on his suggestion that the Soviet Union send scientists to the United States to "advance the cause of peace and friendship between our two great nations." Correspondence from Henry A. Wallace to Alexander S. Panyushkin dated December 29, 1948, Henry A. Wallace correspondence [reel 45], June 1948–March 1949—Ia45-0590, Henry A. Wallace Collection, University of Iowa. See also AVP RF, Fond 0129, op. 33, P 224, file 93, pp. 7–10.
9. Stalin's notation on Molotov's draft of a cable to Panyushkin regarding his negotiations with Wallace, January 14, 1949, RGASPI, Fond 558, op. 11, file 387, p. 108.
10. Pechatnov (2006: 554–56).

11. Correspondence from Henry A. Wallace to Arthur I. Saul dated January 14, 1949, Henry A. Wallace correspondence [reel 45], June 1948–March 1949—Ia45-0684, Henry A. Wallace Collection, University of Iowa.

12. Bazykin V.I. to Orekhov F.T., January 18, 1949, "enclosing the text and [Russian] translation of "peace petition" (written by Henry Wallace), addressed to the President and to the 81st Congress," AVP RF, Fond 192, op. 29a, P 159, file 4, pp. 32–38.

13. "The MGB to the Council of Ministers of the USSR," for com. Molotov, March 29, 1951, Special File, Top Secret, RGASPI, Fond 82, op. 2, file 1029, pp. 55–56.

14. Correspondence from Alexander S. Panyushkin to Henry A. Wallace dated March 18, 1949, Henry A. Wallace correspondence [reel 45], June 1948–March 1949—Ia45-0924, Henry A. Wallace Collection, University of Iowa.

15. TASS, April 29, 1949, RGASPI, Fond 495, op. 261, part 7, p. 98–102.

16. TASS, April 30, 1949, RGASPI, Fond 495, op. 261, part 7, p. 97.

17. Wallace, statement before the Senate Committee on Foreign Relations, May 5, 1949, in Senate Committee on Foreign Relations (1949: 418–69). White (May 6, 1949).

18. *New York Times* (September 13, 1949).

19. Kaplan (October 25, 1949).

20. Correspondence from Henry A. Wallace to Wayne T. Cottingham dated September 11, 1950, Henry A. Wallace correspondence [reel 47], August 1950–January 1951—Ia47 -0439, Henry A. Wallace Collection, University of Iowa.

21. Wallace (August 26, 1950). See also the Soviet commentary on that article: "Henry Wallace's demagogic article in the 'New Leader' weekly," TASS, August 28, 1950, New York, 9 p.m., RGASPI, Fond 495, op. 261, file 60, part 8, p. 12.

22. Correspondence from Henry A. Wallace to Julia C. Weldon dated April 2, 1948, Henry A. Wallace correspondence [reel 44], May 1947–May 1948—Ia44-0714, Henry A. Wallace Collection, University of Iowa.

23. "Wallace's Statement," October 30, 1955, TASS, October 31, 1955, from Washington, RGASPI, Fond 495, op. 261, file 60, part 8, p. 2.

24. *New York Times* (October 31, 1955).

25. Correspondence from Henry A. Wallace to Lewis C. Frank dated October 15, 1949, Henry A. Wallace correspondence [reel 46], April 1949–July 1950—Ia46-0306, Henry A. Wallace Collection, University of Iowa.

26. Committee of Information to Stalin, Molotov, Beria, Malenkov, Gromyko, Lavrentiev, Grigoryan, October 23, 1949, Alexander Vassiliev notebooks, Odd Pages [notebook], p. 34, Alexander Vassiliev Papers, Library of Congress, referring to SVR RF File 49701, Vol. 3, pp. 259, 260.

27. From the diary of V.G. Makarov, 2nd secretary at the Soviet Embassy in Washington and representative of VOKS in the USA, Record of conversation with Rev. Richard Morford, Executive Director of the National Council of American-Soviet Friendship, November 23, 1949, GA RF, Fond 5283, op. 22a, file 138, p. 240.

28. TASS, February 25, 1950, RGASPI, Fond 495, op. 261, file 60, part 8, pp. 38–42.

29. TASS, April 9, 1950, RGASPI, Fond 495, op. 261, file 60, part 8, pp. 36–37.

30. Wallace radio address, TASS, April 23, 1950, RGASPI, Fond 495, op. 261, file 60, part 8, pp. 33–35.

31. From the diary of V.G. Makarov, 2nd secretary at the Soviet Embassy in Washington and representative of VOKS in the USA, Record of conversation with Jessica Smith, June 1, 1950, GA RF, Fond 5283, op. 22a, file 204, pp. 108–9.

32. T.F. Shtykov, Soviet ambassador in Pyongyang, cipher cable to A.Ja. Vyshinsky (cc to

Stalin and six Politburo members), January 19, 1950, RGASPI, Fond 558, op. 11, file 346, pp. 65–68.

33. Acheson, speech, January 12, 1950: https://web.viu.ca/davies/H102/Acheson.speech1950.htm.

34. Halberstam (2007: 1, 47–52).

35. Filippov [Stalin] to Soviet ambassador in Peking for Zhou Enlai, July 5, 1950—RGASPI, Fond 558, op. 11, file 334, p. 79.

36. Gromyko (1988: 248–49).

37. Korea, Trygve Lie and the Progressive Party, Henry A. Wallace correspondence [reel 67], 1934–1965—Ia67-0199, Henry A. Wallace Collection, University of Iowa. "Jessica Smith report on Wallace moving in the rightwing direction," from the diary of V. Makarov, record of conversation with Jessica Smith, June 1, 1950, GA RF, Fond 5283, op. 22a, file 204, pp. 108–9. "Progressive Party and the events in Korea," from the diary of V. Makarov, record of conversation with Jessica Smith, August 9, 1950, GA RF, Fond 5283, op. 22, file 205, pp. 58–62. Hagerty (July 16, 1950).

38. *New York Times* (August 10, 1950).

39. *New York Times* (July 17, 1950).

40. *Washington Post* (July 20, 1950).

41. Hagerty (July 16, 1950).

42. See, for example, Correspondence from Carl Von der Lancken to Henry A. Wallace dated August 1, 1950, Henry A. Wallace correspondence [reel 47], August 1950–January 1951—Ia47-0003, Henry A. Wallace Collection, University of Iowa; Correspondence from George Wagman Fish to Henry A. Wallace dated July 25, 1950, Henry A. Wallace correspondence [reel 46], April 1949–July 1950—Ia46-0944, Henry A. Wallace Collection, University of Iowa; and Correspondence from A. J. Muste to Henry A. Wallace dated August 1, 1950, Henry A. Wallace correspondence [reel 47], August 1950–January 1951—Ia47-0002, Henry A. Wallace Collection, University of Iowa.

43. *New York Times* (August 7, 1950).

44. Resignation letter, Henry A. Wallace to C.B. Baldwin, in correspondence from Henry A. Wallace to Curtis D. MacDougall dated August 8, 1950, Henry A. Wallace correspondence [reel 47], August 1950–January 1951—Ia47-0075, Henry A. Wallace Collection, University of Iowa.

45. Moscow (August 9, 1950).

46. *Washington Post* (August 10, 1950).

47. Correspondence from Curtis D. MacDougall to Henry A. Wallace dated August 11, 1950, Henry A. Wallace correspondence [reel 47], August 1950–January 1951—Ia47-0147, Henry A. Wallace Collection, University of Iowa.

48. *New York Times* (August 11, 1950). See also Correspondence from Henry A. Wallace to Wayne T. Cottingham dated September 11, 1950, Henry A. Wallace correspondence [reel 47], August 1950–January 1951—Ia47-0439–Ia47-0440, Henry A. Wallace Collection, University of Iowa.

49. *Washington Post* (November 16, 1950).

50. Henry A. Wallace Open Letter to Mao Tse-Tung in Correspondence from Henry A. Wallace to Donald G. Lothrop dated September 30, 1950, Henry A. Wallace correspondence [reel 47], August 1950–January 1951—Ia47-0534–Ia47-0536, Henry A. Wallace Collection, University of Iowa. *New York Times* (September 30, 1950). Parke (November 13, 1950).

51. Wallace (January 5, 1948).

52. *New York Times* (November 13, 1950).

53. Filippov [Stalin] to Soviet ambassador in China, October 1, 1950, for immediate transmission to Mao Zedong and Chou Enlai, RGASPI, Fond 558, op. 11, file 334, pp. 97–98. RGASPI, Fond 558, op. 11, file 334, p. 150. Parke (November 13, 1950). On the same day, Soviet (secret) TASS reported on Wallace's radio interview (Columbia) about his change of mind in regard of Russia. RGASPI, Fond 495, op. 261, file 60, part 1, pp. 2–4.

54. *New York Times* (December 4, 1950).

55. *New York Times* (January 3, 1951).

56. *New Times* (November 23, 1950). *New York Times* (November 24, 1950).

57. *New York Times* (August 13, 1950).

58. Salisbury (October 4, 1950).

59. Filippov [Stalin] to Mikhail Silin, Soviet Ambassador in Prague, for passing the message orally to Klement Gottwald, August 27, 1950, Wilson Center Digital Archive, referring to a still classified file in RGASPI, Stalin Papers, Fond 558, op. 11, file 62, pp. 71–72.

60. Letter, Cde. Filippov [Stalin] for Mao Zedong, October 5, 1950, Wilson Center Digital Archive.

61. Steil (2018: 369).

62. *New York Times* (January 22, 1951).

63. Wallace, statement before the House Committee on Un-American Activities, January 26, 1950, in House Committee on Un-American Activities (1950: 1069–99), *Hearings Regarding Shipment of Atomic Material to the Soviet Union During World War II.*

64. Leslie Groves to Henry Wallace, Henry Stimson, and George Marshall, "Present Status and Future Program," August 23, 1943, roll 5, Correspondence ("Top Secret") of the Manhattan Engineer District, 1942–1946, National Archives microfilm publications, NARA. Houghton (2019: 106). House Committee on Un-American Activities (1950: 1076), *Hearings Regarding Shipment of Atomic Material to the Soviet Union During World War II.* Joint Committee on Atomic Energy (April 1951: 954), *Soviet Atomic Espionage.*

65. See, for example, *Washington Post* (October 20, 1951); Krock (October 11, 1951); Alsop (September 14, 1951); *Washington Post* (October 11, 1951); *New York Times* (September 24, 1951), "Texts of Documents Outlining Wallace's Position on China Policy"; *New York Times* (October 10, 1951); *New York Times* (October 18, 1951); and *New York Times* (September 24, 1951), "Wallace Disowns 'Soft' China Policy."

66. *New York Times* (March 18, 1952).

67. Wallace (September 7, 1952).

68. Culver and Hyde (2000: 521) provide no source for their claim.

69. Correspondence from Henry A. Wallace to Adlai E. Stevenson dated October 29, 1952, Henry A. Wallace correspondence [reel 49], September 1953–May 1954—Ia49-0130, Henry A. Wallace Collection, University of Iowa.

70. Correspondence from Henry A. Wallace to Dwight D. Eisenhower dated November 5, 1952, Henry A. Wallace correspondence [reel 49], September 1953–May 1954—Ia49-0136, Henry A. Wallace Collection, University of Iowa.

71. Correspondence from Henry A. Wallace to Cyril Clemens dated November 6, 1952, Henry A. Wallace correspondence [reel 49], September 1953–May 1954—Ia49-0138, Henry A. Wallace Collection, University of Iowa.

72. Correspondence from Henry A. Wallace to Glen H. Taylor dated April 18, 1956, Henry A.

Wallace correspondence [reel 59], December 1931–1964—Ia59-0796, Henry A. Wallace Collection, University of Iowa.

73. Correspondence from Henry A. Wallace to Dwight D. Eisenhower dated February 19, 1957, Henry A. Wallace correspondence [reel 51], April 1956–March 1958—Ia51-0666, Henry A. Wallace Collection, University of Iowa.

74. Correspondence from Henry A. Wallace to Dwight D. Eisenhower dated December 31, 1957, Henry A. Wallace correspondence [reel 51], April 1956–March 1958—Ia51-0842, Henry A. Wallace Collection, University of Iowa.

75. Correspondence from Henry A. Wallace to Dwight D. Eisenhower dated November 26, 1956, Henry A. Wallace correspondence [reel 51], April 1956–March 1958—Ia51-0520, Henry A. Wallace Collection, University of Iowa.

76. Correspondence from Henry A. Wallace to Dwight D. Eisenhower dated August 10, 1959, Henry A. Wallace correspondence [reel 52], April 1958–April 1961—Ia52-0380, Henry A. Wallace Collection, University of Iowa.

77. *Des Moines Register* (June 11, 1958). *Boston Globe* (March 28, 1960). *The State* (May 13, 1960). *Bridgeport Post* (November 26, 1962).

78. *Marshfield News-Herald* (March 29, 1961).

79. Correspondence from Henry A. Wallace to Dwight D. Eisenhower dated December 11, 1956, Henry A. Wallace correspondence [reel 51], April 1956–March 1958—Ia51-0543, Henry A. Wallace Collection, University of Iowa.

80. Culver and Hyde (2000: 522–23).

81. Folsom (October 20, 1960).

82. *New York Times* (October 6, 1960).

83. Folsom (October 27, 1960).

84. *New York Times* (November 19, 1965).

85. Phillips (October 6, 1963).

86. Culver and Hyde (2000: 523–24).

87. *New York Times* (November 19, 1965).

88. Wallace told a visiting friend in 1965 that "the policies of Truman and Byrnes"—which he associated with Vietnam—would "yet make this country bleed from every pore." (Culver and Hyde: 2000: 529).

89. *New York Times* (January 15, 1956). Harkness and Harkness (May 22, 1960).

90. *New York Times* (June 9, 1957). Culver and Hyde (2000: 527).

91. Folsom (September 5, 1962).

92. Phillips (October 6, 1963).

93. See, for example, Schwarz (April 2004).

94. Phillips (October 6, 1963).

95. See, for example, Phillips' obituary in *The New York Times*. Saxon (November 15, 1975).

96. Culver and Hyde (2000: 527–28).

97. *New York Times* (November 19, 1965).

98. Correspondence from Henry A. Wallace to Lyndon B. Johnson dated August 11, 1965, Henry A. Wallace correspondence [reel 55], August 1964–1966 and undated—Ia55-0641-Ia55-0642, Henry A. Wallace Collection, University of Iowa.

99. Wijkman (February 22, 2019: 176).

100. *New York Times* (November 19, 1965). *Washington Post* (November 19, 1965). Culver and Hyde (2000: 528–30).

101. *New York Times* (November 19, 1965).

102. Wallace himself, in a letter to President Eisenhower dated March 10, 1953, referred to the great practical agricultural importance of adhering to the "rigid discipline of modern genetics." Correspondence from Henry A. Wallace to Dwight D. Eisenhower dated March 10, 1953, Henry A. Wallace correspondence [reel 49], September 1953–May 1954—Ia49 -0430, Henry A. Wallace Collection, University of Iowa.

INDEX

ILLUSTRATION CREDITS

FIRST INSERT

7. Courtesy of Wallace Centers of Iowa archives, Des Moines, Iowa

8. Nicholas Roerich Museum archive, reference number 401271

9. Bettmann/Getty Images

10. Bettmann/Getty Images

11. Library of Congress, Prints & Photographs Division, photograph by Harris & Ewing, LC-DIG-hec-24784

12. Library of Congress, Prints & Photographs Division, photograph by Harris & Ewing, LC-DIG-hec-25720

13. Bettmann/Getty Images

14. Everett Collection Historical/Alamy Stock Photo

15. George Skadding/The LIFE Picture Collection/Shutterstock

16. Henry Wallace with Colonel Ilya P. Mazuruk, Siberia, 1944, Henry A. Wallace Collection, Special Collections, University of Iowa Libraries

17. Henry Wallace at Magadan, Siberia, 1944, Henry A. Wallace Collection, Special Collections, University of Iowa Libraries

18. Henry Wallace with mission members and Russian escorts, Russia, 1944, Henry A. Wallace Collection, Special Collections, University of Iowa Libraries

19. Henry Wallace with a group of men, Siberia, 1944, Henry A. Wallace Collection, Special Collections, University of Iowa Libraries

20. Henry Wallace with government officials, Siberia, 1944, Henry A. Wallace Collection, Special Collections, University of Iowa Libraries

21. Members of mission posed with Russian escorts at party headquarters, Seimchan, Siberia, 1944, Henry A. Wallace Collection, Special Collections, University of Iowa Libraries

22. Henry Wallace pointing at map, Siberia, 1944, Henry A. Wallace Collection, Special Collections, University of Iowa Libraries

23. Henry Wallace hoeing with Chinese man, China, 1944, Henry A. Wallace Collection, Special Collections, University of Iowa Libraries

24. Associated Press

25. Bettmann/Getty Images

26. Everett Collection Historical/Alamy Stock Photo

27. Bettmann/Getty Images

28. Bettmann/Getty Images

SECOND INSERT

1. Everett Collection Historical/Alamy Stock Photo

2. Thomas D. Mcavoy/The LIFE Picture Collection/Shutterstock

3. Associated Press

4. Courtesy of Wallace Centers of Iowa archives, Des Moines, Iowa

5. National Archives photo no. 6012389-B-027

6. Bettmann/Getty Images

7. Bettmann/Getty Images

8. Associated Press

9. George S. Mills, Jr. Papers, State Historical Society of Iowa, Des Moines

10. National Archives photo no. 306115-NWL-46-BERRYMAN-A035

11. RGASPI, Fond 558, op. 11, file 387, p. 10. Provided by Dr. Svetlana A. Chervonnaya

12. RGASPI, Fond 558, op. 11, file 387, p. 4. Provided by Dr. Svetlana A. Chervonnaya

13. Dave Mathias/*The Denver Post*/Getty Images

14. Jacob Harris/Associated Press

15. Bettmann/Getty Images

16. Irving Haberman/IH Images/Getty Images

17. Irving Haberman/IH Images/Getty Images

18. Associated Press

19. Mr. and Mrs. Henry A. Wallace casting ballots, White Plains, New York, 1948, Henry A. Wallace Collection, Special Collections, University of Iowa Libraries

20. Jerry Cooke/Corbis/Getty Images

21. Slim Aarons/Stringer/Getty Images

ABOUT THE AUTHOR

BENN STEIL is senior fellow and director of international economics at the Council on Foreign Relations. He is the author of *The Marshall Plan: Dawn of the Cold War*, winner of the New-York Historical Society's Barbara and David Zalaznick Book Prize in American History and the American Academy of Diplomacy's Douglas Dillon Award. His previous book, the prize-winning *The Battle of Bretton Woods: John Maynard Keynes, Harry Dexter White, and the Making of a New World Order*, was called "a triumph of economic and diplomatic history" by the *Financial Times*. He lives in New York with his two boys.